The Psychology of Crime is an overview of current theory and research in criminology. While its emphasis is largely psychological, it also gives considerable weight to sociological perspectives, and succeeds in integrating the two approaches neatly to discuss the scholarship on the criminal justice system and criminal behavior.

The book begins by laying out the empirical data on offenses, offenders, the police, and the courts. The definition of criminal behavior and the workings of the criminal justice system determine who is called a criminal and, in turn, who should be studied in criminology. In setting out the main findings for which theories of crime must account, Philip Feldman does not neglect the possibility that the operation of the criminal justice system may both compound the crime problem and make explanations more difficult.

The second section of this work describes and assesses the major approaches to the explanation of crime. Beginning with biological factors and proceeding through individual differences, including intelligence, personality, and mental disorder, it moves on to childhood behaviors and experiences within the home, school, and with peers, and social factors of economics, culture, and community. This section then provides a broad overview of sociological theories of crime and demonstrates the overlaps between these and several psychological approaches. The final chapter in section II gives a full account of cognitive/behavioral theories, focusing on social learning and on rational choice theory. The final section covers the range of social attempts to respond to offenses and offenders. Feldman examines the methods in current use, from probation to the death penalty, as well as the psychological and social impact of imprisonment. He reviews psychological treatments for offenders, mainly behavioral in emphasis, and discusses a range of attempts at crime deterrence. This book systematically examines the evidence for hopes that criminal behavior can be controlled and changed. Its breadth of coverage and firm base in psychology are unique in the current literature making it especially valuable as a text for undergraduate and postgraduate courses across the social sciences.

The psychology of crime

The psychology of crime

A social science textbook

Philip Feldman

University of Leeds

Published by the Press Syndicate of the University of Cambridge
The Pitt Building, Trumpington Street, Cambridge CB2 1RP
40 West 20th Street, New York, NY 10011-4211, USA
10 Stamford Road, Oakleigh, Victoria 3166, Australia

First published 1993

Printed in the United States of America

Library of Congress Cataloging-in-Publication Data

Feldman, M. Philip (Maurice Philip)
The psychology of crime : a social science textbook / Philip Feldman.
p. cm.
Includes bibliographical references and indexes.
ISBN 0-521-33120-X. – ISBN 0-521-33732-1 (pbk.)
1. Criminology. 2. Criminal psychology. I. Title.
HV6025.F393 1993
364.3–dc20 92-31968
CIP

A catalog record for this book is available from the British Library

ISBN 0-521-33120-X hardback
ISBN 0-521-33732-1 paperback

To my family

Contents

Preface

There can be no question that sociology has been "the major parent discipline of criminology for perhaps fifty years" (Hirschi and Rudisill, 1976, p. 15) and remains so today. Yet . . . "The allocation of the field of criminology to the more general area of sociology has been as much a matter of professional turf-taking as it has been a rational division of intellectual labor . . . If a boy is humiliated by his teacher, that is "social class" and admissible in criminological theory, but if he is humiliated by his father, that is child psychology and inadmissible (Bordua, 1962, p. 247). We detract nothing from the sociological pioneers of modern criminology in pointing out that some of what they did is more properly construed as psychology. (Monahan and Splane 1980, p. 18).

Criminology became a coherent body of thought in the eighteenth century when enlightened men on both sides of the Atlantic began rational analyses of the harsh and oppressive systems of justice then in being, including the common use of the death penalty for trivial offences. The nature of criminal law, the causes of crime and the treatment of criminals were all examined. A key figure in this movement was Cesara Beccaria (1738–1794) a young Italian aristocrat. His brief essay *On Crimes and Punishments* evoked immediate acclaim and controversy. The system, he asserted was savage, stupid and corrupt. It should and could be rationalized. Punishment should be prompt, public and the least possible amount proportionate to the crime. Beccaria's ideas influenced first the English and then the American legal systems. By 1861, only four capital offences remained in England: murder, treason, piracy, and setting fire to arsenals, of which only murder was more than a rarity. Forty years earlier, more than 200 offences had been punishable by death. The notion of the rational man and, hence, by implication, of the rational offender, had become very active.

The foundations of the sociological approach to criminology were laid by a number of European writers such as Quetelet (1796–1874), who began the statistical study of offences – the essential basis for any empirical research into crime and criminals. The nineteenth century also saw vigorous developments in biological and psychiatric approaches. Darwin's work on evolution led to the work of an Italian, Lombroso (1836–1909), which had much influence before falling into disrepute. In the USA, Isaac Ray (1807–1881) carried out studies in forensic psychiatry which led to separate treatments for the mentally ill offender. Shortly after the turn of the century, the development of scales of intelligence by Binet enabled studies of a possible link between crime and intelligence. Initial positive findings were followed by negative ones and, recently, by a renewed interest – a frequent sequence of events in the social sciences.

In the 1920's and 1930's modern criminology emerged as an academic discipline, dominated by sociology and particularly by the idea that crime was due to the social environment in which the individual lived. To the extent that individual personality was seen as important, the key influence was the psychoanalytical approach, originated by Sigmund Freud (1856–1939), which interpreted crime as the expression of tensions and conflicts within the individual. It was the major influence in psychological therapy, particularly in the USA and, hence, dominated rehabilitation work with offenders.

Then came the "new criminology" of the 1950's and even more of the 1960's. This had several origins. The first was an increasing skepticism about individual theories of crime causation (not only the biological/psychological approaches but also the previously central sociological emphases on social influences). The key question became why some persons and not others were labeled as criminals, shifting research attention to those employed in the criminal justice system, who were perceived as instruments of social control. The criminal law came to be seen as reflecting the interests of the ruling minority. It followed that much of the official statistics of crime were seriously biased, enabling and justifying the suppression of deviance and of deviants as defined by the ruling group – such as blacks and the poor. The growth of the American counterculture, including the use of "recreational" drugs such as marijuana was also important. The question – was this a crime if millions did it? – helped to fuel skepticism about the criminal law in general. A final factor was the growth of political protest movements, both violent and non-violent: against the Vietnam War and in favor of black civil rights. It was alleged that police power was used to suppress political dissent, which was thus criminalized, so that the criminal law was again a device to control deviance from the views of those in power.

More recently, the pendulum has swung again. There has been a return to empiricism, to careful measurement – in short to the scientific method – as opposed to assertion and polemic. The methods and findings of psychology have been drawn on to a very much greater extent than hitherto, particularly the areas of learning and human development, and biological approaches have been revived. But, much remains. The criminology of the 1960's has made a permanent contribution. Both traditions have influenced this book.

The Psychology of Crime is in three parts. The first is essentially descriptive and sets out major findings concerning the four components of the criminal justice system – offenses, offenders, the police, and the courts. It isolates a number of questions about crime and criminals which demand explanations. The second part attempts to provide them: it consists of six chapters, the first three of which deal with different aspects of the view that crime is a function of individual differences in biological predisposition, in personality, and in psychological abnormality. The next three chapters cover material on environmental influences: childhood development, broad social factors, and social learning. The final part overviews the nature and effectiveness of attempts to control crime. One chapter covers conventional penal methods, some of very long standing, both custodial and non-custodial. The next two deal, respectively, with the application of psychological therapies to offenders, particularly those with a behavioral basis, and with attempts to prevent the occurrence of crime.

Two *caveats* are in order. The first is that this book is concerned predominantly with the seven FBI Part 1 Index offenses against property and persons. The book has much less to say about occupational, organized, or political crime. This reflects the current concerns of the discipline of criminology – demonstrated by the eleven annual volumes (to 1989) of *Research in Crime and Justice*, the leading current repository of criminal justice scholarship. Second, the material covered in this book is drawn almost entirely from the English speaking world on the two sides of the Atlantic, mainly from the USA, but to a discernible extent from Britain. This reflects both the preponderance of published research and the author's lack of access to literature other than in English. That it is also true of the great majority of English language publications in criminology only emphasizes the need for much wider future coverage as well as for international research projects.

Fifteen years have passed since the publication of my first book applying psychology to the subject matter of criminology, *Criminal Behavior*, since when I have been enormously impressed and encouraged by the quality of work in the field. I have drawn on the work of many scholars, and I want to express particular admiration for that of Albert Bandura and David Farrington. Additionally, I have been very stimulated by *Crime and Human Nature*, by James Wilson and Richard Herrnstein.

This textbook is intended particularly for undergraduate and post-graduate students of psychology, but I believe that it will be relevant to sociologists and social scientists in general, trainee lawyers and policemen, and to professionals in all the disciplines concerned with the explanation and control of crime.

PART I

Description

1. Offences

> No national characteristics, no political regime, no system of law, police, justice, treatment or even terror, has rendered a country exempt from crime . . . scarcely any can claim to have checked its accelerating momentum
> (Radzinowicz and King 1977, p. 15).

This chapter, the first of four on the criminal justice system, falls into two sections: the first gives a qualitative description of the major groups of crime, from the Index offenses to political crimes, concluding with a brief historical overview; the second is quantitative, setting out the methods used to measure the total volume of crime and the results obtained – which must be treated with caution. The major emphasis throughout is on the USA, but some relevant international comparisons are made. A brief final section introduces the very difficult question of the costs of crime.

1.1. Definitions

Crime

There is no single definition of crime acceptable to all. In effect, a crime is anything forbidden or punishable by the criminal justice system. "A crime is an act that is capable of being followed by criminal proceedings, having one of the types of outcome (punishment, etc.) known to follow these proceedings" (Williams 1961, p. 21). This is circular, but it is clear-cut and is the essential starting point, whether we want to make comparisons between groups or to ask if the current criminal law should be expanded or contracted.

It has been argued (e.g., Quinney 1974) that the criminal law is imposed by the group in power, so that the law is a series of general commands backed by coercive threats. The law is then a weapon to maintain the domination and privileges of a few over the many. An extreme example of this is the slave-owning system, once common in the USA. It was not a crime if the slave owner assaulted or killed the slave; it was one if the slave resisted or absconded (and those who helped him to do either also broke the criminal law). In South Africa it was for many years a crime for a black to live in a white area. Thus, by analogy, the current laws of theft are designed to protect the property of the rich from the poor. But there are problems with this view. First, the poor are much more likely to be the victims of crimes against property and persons: they are easier targets. Second, it is widely held that people have the right to disobey laws they see as cruel and oppressive. In World War 2, many Europeans risked their lives to hide the victims of the Nazis, and for many years Russian citizens were consigned to slave labor camps for asking for free speech.

Nevertheless, there is much common ground. Both in the capitalist West and the still-communist parts of the East, practically all societies disapprove of certain behaviors, prominent among which are murder, rape and theft (Lemert 1972). Differences are found, but in the procedures for dealing with offences, and in methods of interrogation, rather than in the definition of crime (a convicted thief in some Moslem countries loses a hand; suspects are routinely tortured in many countries).

The core of criminal law is the same, but the border moves. Here we come to the so-called *victimless offences*. In addition to protecting property and persons, the criminal law has been used also to direct the behavior of private individuals in situations usually termed "moral – to do with drink, drugs, sex and gambling. In a hesitant and partial way there have been some contractions of the criminal law in these areas. Suicide, and attempted suicide, homosexual behavior between consenting adults, adultery and prostitution have all been wholly or partially removed from the criminal law, as have gambling (in some Western countries though not the USA) and abortion. All of these are examples of decriminalization. In some countries, such as The Netherlands, the use of the drug marijuana, has also been removed, in large part, from the criminal law. That `the USA seems unlikely to follow quickly is indicated by the case of Judge Douglas Ginsburg, nominated in November, 1987, to the US Supreme Court by President Reagan. Initially seen as an exemplar of legal conservatism, he admitted to using marijuana in the 1960's and his nomination was withdrawn.

As some offences are decriminalized others join the body of those proscribed – essentially as societies become more complex and government regulations increase (Radzinowicz and King 1977). The invention of the internal combustion engine led to whole new classes of offence: speeding, drunken and dangerous driving, and even failure to wear a seat belt. There are other examples: with increasing affluence, humanitarian concerns led to laws penalizing the neglect, or abuse, of children, of animals and of employees. Scientific and industrial advances resulted in laws covering fraud by credit card, marketing incompletely tested, eventually dangerous, drugs or food products and the betrayal of industrial secrets.

A crime is some act or omission in respect of which legal punishment may be inflicted. But, that is not the end of the story. The age and state of mind of the offender must also be taken into consideration. If, for example, a person is killed or injured by another, the killing or injury would not be criminal if the aggressor were too young, too deranged or too weak-minded to form the kind of intention that would render him liable to punishment.

And there is a further complication. Victims of offences which have the characteristics of robbery, rape or burglary may not wish to report their experience to the police. If these incidents do not come to light in any other way, by police activity, for example, or by the reports of witnesses, they remain without formal definition as crime. In effect, crime does not exist. A further stage in the process of crime creation is the acceptance or rejection by law-enforcement agencies of reports of crime; a sizeable proportion of reported offenses never reach the official statistics. Both types of omission are discussed in this chapter.

Public opinion plays an important part in defining the boundaries of the criminal law and in the sentencing policy of the courts. Over the past decade, crime and lawlessness have been consistently mentioned as the first, second or third issues about which the American people are most concerned (Roper Organization 1985). A cross-cultural survey by Scott and Al-Thakeb (1980) indicated that representative samples in seven Western countries and Kuwait recommended the severest penalties for violent crime, followed by drug offenses. The Kuwaitis were the most severe overall, with Americans more punitive than other Western respondents.

Within the USA, Wolfgang (1985) measured seriousness scores for a range of offences. A national sample regarded violent crimes as more serious than property offences. They also took white collar crimes and drug offences seriously. One of the highest scores (39.1) was given to a factory causing the death of 20 people by knowingly polluting a city water supply. Running a narcotics ring (33.8) was seen as more serious than skyjacking (32.7), and selling heroin for resale (20.6) was more serious than rape if the victim's injuries did not need hospitalization. There was general agreement as to specific crimes but there were exceptions: blacks and other minority groups gave lower average scores than whites, and victims gave higher scores than nonvictims. The above finding concerning white collar crime is supported by Cullen, Mathers, Clark, and Cullen (1983) in a survey carried out in Illinois.

Criminal

It is convenient, though not entirely satisfactory, to say that a criminal is simply a person who has committed a crime; the word suggests a continuing series of behaviors, though the terms "habitual", "persistent", "recidivist", and, increasingly, "high-rate", are used for the more frequent offenders. In the USA, "delinquent" and "delinquency" are used in the context of juvenile offenders (typically under 18). This book uses frequently the term "criminal behavior" to refer to all the events associated with an act legally defined as a crime.

1.2. The index crimes

The Federal Bureau of Investigation receives reports on crime statistics from law enforcement agencies covering more than 95 per cent of the total US population. (The considerable difficulties with official statistics are discussed later in this chapter.)

Prior to 1958, the Federal Bureau of Investigation listed crimes under two broad categories: Part I and Part II Crimes. The former were "major" or serious; Part II were "lesser". Since 1958, the FBI has concentrated on Part I crimes because they establish an index to measure the trend and distribution of serious crime in the USA – hence the term "Index offences". They are considered to be those likely to be reported to the police, and are further divided into Violent crime (murder and nonnegligent manslaughter, aggravated assault, forcible rape and robbery) and Property crime (burglary, larceny-theft and auto-theft). Table 1.1 sets out the definitions of Index offenses (Federal Bureau of Investigation 1976). Arson has been added as an eighth

Table 1.1. *Definitions of FBI Index crimes*

Index crimes	Definitions
Murder and nonnegligent manslaughter	Murder is defined as the wilful killing of another. The classification of this offense, as well as of other Index crimes is based solely on police investigation, as opposed to the determination of a court or other judicial body.
Aggravated assault	The unlawful attack by one person upon another for the purpose of inflicting severe bodily injury, usually accompanied by the use of a weapon or other means likely to produce death or serious bodily harm. Attempts are included, since it is not necessary that an injury result when a weapon is used which could result in serious injury if the crime were successfully completed.
Forcible rape.	The carnal knowledge of a female through the use of force or threat of force. Assaults to commit forcible rape are also included.
Robbery	The stealing or taking of anything of value from the care, custody or control of a person in his presence, by force or the threat of force. Assault to commit robbery and attempt at robbery are also included.
Burglary	The unlawful entry of a structure to commit a felony or theft.
Larceny-theft	The unlawful taking of property without the use of force, violence or fraud. Includes shoplifting, pocket-picking and purse-snatching.
Motor vehicle theft	The unlawful taking or stealing of a motor vehicle, incuding attempts.

Source: *FBI Uniform Crime Reports*. US Department of Justice, Washington, DC, 1976 (adapted from Nietzel 1979, p. 20).

Index offence, but too recently to figure in analyses of trends. Arrest information is still reported for Part II offences, which include forgery and fraud, prostitution and driving under the influence of drink, as well as drug offenses and child molestation, which the general public would certainly regard as "serious".

In the USA, Index offenses reported to the police regularly exceed ten million per year and 1 in 20 inhabitants. For reasons which will become clear later, the precise quantitative data for Index offenses, for both totals and individual offenses, are less important than broad comparisons between years, between offenses, and between the USA and other countries. The annual rate for property offenses rose sharply in the 1960's and early 1970's before stabilizing and then falling somewhat in the 1980's. The rise in annual rates for person offenses continued rather longer, until about the end of the 1970's, before stabilizing and falling slightly. The complex reasons for these shifts are discussed later in this chapter.

Arrests for Index offenses represent only about one fifth of all non-traffic arrests; one in every three such arrests is for simple public drunkenness (President's Commission 1967). Reported property crimes are ten times as frequent as reported violent crimes, but for arrests the disparity drops to about four to one, indicating the much greater chances of being arrested for violent than for property offenses (largely because the assailant is often known to the victim).

Homicide (murder and nonnegligent manslaughter)

About 20,000 cases are reported to the police annually, perhaps 2 per cent of all violent crimes. American homicide rates vary greatly between different areas of the country. The highest ones, which are found in the west south central States (Oklahoma, Texas, Arkansas and Louisiana) exceed those of the lowest group (New England) by between three and four to one. There are even more massive variations within cities. In one year, out of 489 criminal homicides in Houston, Texas, over 87 per cent occurred in four areas, all located near the center of the city (Wolfgang 1985). Males are twice as likely to be homicide victims as females, males aged 25–34 are more likely than any other age group, and blacks are at least eight times as likely as whites. Offenders and victims are frequently acquainted and often live in the same neighborhood. Connected with this is the fact that almost half of all homicides occur in the home of either the offender or the victim. When strangers are killed it is most frequently during the commission of another offence such as robbery or burglary (Barlow 1981). From American figures for 1983, Goldstein (1986) concluded that about 20 per cent of murders could be linked to another crime, while 44 per cent were associated with arguments. The ready availability of guns in America and the high level of gun ownership seem related to the fact that US homicide rates are very much higher than those of Western Europe. Over half of all American murders are committed with a firearm, mainly with a handgun. The majority of reported homicides are *cleared* (a perpetrator is apprehended or is identified as unapprehendable), the clearance rate being much higher than for any other Index crime.

Aggravated assault

While not as well researched, the findings for assault resemble those for homicide. Over the years, assault has remained at about one half of all reported violent crimes. Both victims and those arrested are disproportionately young black males who live in the inner cities. Knives are the weapon most frequently used.

Many murders and assaults take place in family settings, with the victims frequently being wives (or other cohabitees) and young children. While official data on family homicides may be reasonably accurate, they are likely to understate very considerably the true level of assaults on wives and children. Many assaulted wives fail to complain because of fear of reprisal. Young children are incapable of complaining, and neighbors hesitate to interfere. American data suggest that assaults on wives occur in one couple in 25, at an average frequency of nearly twice per year (Gardner and Gray 1982). For child assault, the true figures are at least as high (Minchin 1982).

Forcible rape

The key elements in the legal definition of rape are sexual intercourse and lack of consent. When force, or the threat of force, is also present, then an Index offence has resulted. Sentences are usually higher when bodily harm has been caused. Official data suggest the same sort of increases in the 1960's as for other violent offenses, but official data are extremely unreliable. The only certainties are that the number of rapes reported is on the increase but that this is still far less than the true figure. Population surveys provide an alternative source to police statistics. One survey of US households Hindelang and Davis (1977) suggested a figure of 315 per 100,000 (at least ten times higher than the official figure). But, even this is probably much too low an estimate. An American study by Russell (1982) involved female interviewers who were carefully trained and then matched with a random sample of interviewees for race, age, and class. Forty four per cent of the sample reported at least one rape or attempted rape. Russell considered that less than 1 per cent was reported to the police.

There is considerable under-reporting for most offences (see below) but that for rape is particularly massive, for the following reasons: fear of the assailant returning and repeating the assault; a desire not to go through further humiliation and distress (there is a good deal of information available to women as to the unpleasantness of police and medical interviews and examinations); the fear of being probed and not believed by their own families and friends; and the potential distress of a lengthy appearance in court. While the official aspects of this listing have improved in recent years (helping to account for increases in reporting rates), it remains true that rape is still kept hidden by the great majority of victims (Feldman 1987).

Both rape offenders and victims tend to be under 25, and of the same race. (Arrest and victim surveys agree that about 20 per cent of offenders are adolescents, Davis and Leitenberg 1987.) Blacks are over-represented, both as victims and as assailants. The single most common setting for the assault is a home, usually the victim's. Most rapists are unarmed, but when a weapon is carried it tends to be a knife (McDermott 1979). McDermott also concluded that most victims sustained some form of injury. The extent of injury may depend in part on the motivation for the rape (discussed in Chapter 9).

Robbery

The history of robbery goes back thousands of years, being mentioned in the earliest criminal codes. It involves the actual or threatened use of violence to deprive the victim of things of value – money, goods or services. In medieval and later times robbers became romanticized in the stories of Robin Hood and of a series of highwaymen, and many Hollywood films have depicted American robbers from Jesse James to *Bonnie and Clyde*.

Reported robberies comprise about 40 per cent of Index violent crimes. There are wide differences between robberies: in location (from the street to a bank); in method (physical force alone or possession of a weapon); in the type of weapon where one was used (gun or knife); and in the amount of monetary loss (from a few dollars to many thousands of dollars). A number of studies (e.g., Conklin 1972, Sagalyn 1971) indicate several general features of recorded robberies in America: more than one half take place in the open (in streets and parking lots, etc.); rates are highest in the larger cities and lowest in rural areas; they tend to be carried out by young males (15–25) on males, usually over

21, who are strangers to them; the robber is in possession of a weapon, but this is usually used to coerce and victims tend not to be injured.

Henderson (1986) has distinguished between two situations in which violence occurs in the course of stealing. In the first it is simply instrumental in achieving the goal of obtaining money, and offenders report a lack of emotion. The second can be described as a "burglary gone wrong": the offender has entered a home intending to steal without coming into contact with the householder, but does so, loses control and hits out; what was intended as a simple burglary may escalate to murder.

Burglary

About 30 per cent of property offenses take the form of burglary. As perhaps three million per year are reported in the USA annually and a further large number go unreported, it is a relatively common crime. Burglary is an experience which many victims find frightening, both in actuality and in prospect.

Burglaries are more likely in the poorer areas of inner cities than in wealthier ones, despite the greater rewards of the latter, because of their greater proximity to potential offenders as well as the homes concerned being typically less well defended. Offenders range from relatively unskilled, usually young, "amateurs" to skilled and experienced professionals. Research (e.g., Scarr 1973) suggests that: burglaries are more likely to involve residences than commercial establishments; most losses are of cash or items easily convertible into cash; they take place mainly when owners are away (at night in shops, etc., by day in private homes); and most involve forced entry, particularly those carried out by amateurs. Of those arrested, blacks are over-represented, but less so than for violent offenses.

Larceny-theft

This is the most frequent of all the Index crimes, accounting for nearly 60 per cent of property offenses annually. Many states treat theft under $50 as petty and therefore to be excluded from the Index offences. There is very considerable under-reporting for theft, so that the clearance rate of somewhat below 20 per cent for reported Index theft considerably overstates the chances of being caught. As we shall see in Chapter 2 probably a majority of the population has stolen at least once; the vast preponderance goes unpunished. Hence, "thieves" range from most average citizens, who can recall the occasional theft as a teenager, to skilled adult professionals who derive most or all of their income from theft. Of the many varieties of theft, shoplifting is perhaps the most widespread, particularly since the advent of the self-service shop.

Motor-vehicle theft

Because the FBI and many states include within this category taking a vehicle against its owners' wishes or knowledge for a short period (known as "joy-riding") it is impossible to know what proportion of the published figures for this offence actually refers to stealing for gain. The same problem makes equally impossible the assessment of clearance rates. But motor-vehicle thefts do demonstrate the close relationship between the total number of an item, and the ease of access to it, and the frequency with which that item is stolen (or "borrowed" as the case may be): vehicle thefts rise as the number of cars in circulation increases, until some major new barrier to theft, such as steering wheel locks, is introduced, at which point the rate falls (Clarke 1980).

1.3. Other offences

This section reviews two nonIndex crimes which cause great public concern – child molestation and drug offences – and several major categories of crime which, together, involve much greater financial costs than the Index offences combined, as well as much social damage. These are organized crime and the so-called "white collar" crimes (occupational and corporate offenses), and political offenses.

Child molestation

The term molestation implies an act of unwanted sexual intrusion, if not of actual physical aggression, against a person aged under 16. The degree of intrusion varies from fondling to a physical assault in excess of the forcefulness necessary to secure a sexual goal with an uncooperative victim. Child molestation includes sexual involvement with close family members, such as parents or siblings, when it is termed incest, and with people outside the immediate family, when it is given the medical term pedophilia. Molestations may be either heterosexual (the assailant and the victim are of opposite sexes) or homosexual (both are of the same sex). In almost all cases the adult concerned is a male.

Much less research has been carried out into incest than into pedophilia, but even in the case of the latter the bulk of work on assailants has been on convicted offenders (see Marshall and Barbaree 1989, for a review). A British study by Wilson and Cox (1983) of members of a pedophile organization found that nearly three-quarters worked with young children (*not* the same as saying that three-quarters of those so employed are pedophile!). Marshall and Christie (1981) found that 58 per cent of a sample of incarcerated child molesters had physically abused their victims in excess of the force necessary to secure sexual goals with an unco-operative victim; 25 per cent of a group of outpatient child molesters had used similar gratuitous violence (Marshall 1982).

There appear to be no separate official figures for child molestation, but it would be safe to regard them as a major underestimate even if they were available. An American survey (Finkelhor 1979) found that 19.2 per cent of women students and 8.6 per cent of males reported a sexual contact with an adult during their childhood. Their first such experience most usually took place between the ages of 8 and 12; the great majority were never mentioned to anyone by the children at the time. A comprehensive review of research by Browne and Finkelhor (1986) found clear evidence that many victims suffer both short- and long-term emotional damage.

Arrest and victim surveys indicate that at least 30 per cent of all offenders are adolescents, and 50 per cent of adult sexual offenders against children reported that their first such offense was during adolescence (Davis and Leitenberg 1987).

Drug offenses

Criminologists use the term drug to refer to any psychoactive substance (one having the capacity to alter mental states and hence to influence human activity, Barlow 1981). This definition includes alcohol, nicotine and caffeine, as well as barbiturates and tranquilizers, in addition to the substances now the focus of the criminal law (principally, marijuana, cocaine and heroin).

From 1919 to 1933, the USA banned the manufacture, supply and use of alcohol. In the years of alcohol Prohibition the law was flouted widely by the population in general, and a network of illegal manufacturers and distributors sprang up. The major beneficiaries of Prohibition may have been organized crime groups (see below). At the same time there was an undoubted fall in alcohol related problems of all kinds, but finally the arguments for decriminalization won out. There are still restrictions on the sale of alcohol to minors, but these seem to have general public support.

From 1914, similar restrictions have been in force in the USA on opium and its derivatives. Prior to that date, between 1 and 4 per cent of Americans were regular users of opiates, often in the form of patent medicines such as Mrs Winslows Soothing Syrup (Brecher 1972). For the most part they were middle-aged, middle-class white women: the group which now uses barbiturates (Goode 1972).

According to *The Economist* (1989a) Americans consume proportionately more drugs than people in other industrialized countries. At the time of writing, about 30 million were taking an illegal drug of some kind fairly regularly (about 18 million smoke marijuana, 5 to 6 million ingest cocaine; a stable, and ageing, half million are stuck with heroin or its substitutes; and the remainder are on a mixture of chemical pills and powders). Large numbers have tried drugs at least occasionally, with cocaine and its derivatives rising rapidly in popularity. However, the rate of increase in drug use may be slowing, and the hard core of addicts (those physically dependent on a drug) may not be much more than 2 million (one-quarter million on heroin, and most of the rest on cocaine). The middle classes seem to be turning away from drugs, much as they have rejected both cigarettes and alcohol. The main current problem is the person who has become addicted to cocaine, or to crack (cocaine mixed with baking soda and water and costing little more than the price of a cinema seat). Crack goes straight to the central nervous system, triggering an instant short-lived potent reaction so that the smoker seeks a rapid repetition.

Such addicts seem increasingly to be the poor and the poorly educated. The social characteristics of those calling a cocaine help-line changed markedly between 1983 and 1987: the university educated fell from 50 per cent 16 per cent and the unemployed rose from 15 per cent to 55 per cent (*The Economist* 1989a). This implies that addicts are increasingly likely to support their habit (despite the relatively low price of crack) by criminal means. Even several years ago (Moore 1983) drug users were disproportionately represented among those arrested for street crimes, viz. robbery, assault, and burglary; among heroin users, crime levels were correlated with levels of drug use. Also, as the cocaine supply outstrips the demand, gangs battle for the ''franchises'', so that in 1988 Washington had a record number of murders, more than half drug-related (*The Economist* 1989a).

A complex international network is involved in the supply of drugs such as cocaine. Peasant farmers in Columbia and other third world countries sell their crops to middlemen who pass them on to large scale operators for smuggling into the US by means ranging from backpacks to light planes, and finally into the hands of pushers, the small-time salesmen who supply users and addicts. Of all the links in the supply chain, it is the pusher who is the most visible to enforcement agencies. At the present time, the US administration is mounting a major campaign against drugs. It seems likely to have the same limited amount of directly attributable success as previous such efforts, not because of incompetence or lack of effort, but because the use of drugs (the end point of the entire enforcement enterprise) is essentially a victimless offence. (The police rarely have an aggrieved complainant so that law enforcement is extremely difficult and depends heavily on informants and undercover agents.)

American public opinion is very concerned about drugs such as marijuana and cocaine, and supportive of strong enforcement practices. There is as yet little backing for extending to drugs the kind of legalization which, overnight in 1933, removed tens of millions of alcohol users from the sanctions of the criminal law.

1.4. Other categories of crime

This section deals with another way of looking at the descriptive literature on crime, turning from individual offenses to general categories: organized crime, occupational and corporate offenses, and political crimes.

Organized crime

The general public knows the term well: it evokes a series of colorful characters, mainly, though not exclusively, of Italian origin: Al Capone and ''Legs'' Diamond in the thirties and, more recently, Vito Genovese and ''Lucky'' Luciano. A string of Hollywood films, such as *The Godfather 1* and *11*, *Prizzi's Honor* and *Married to the Mob* depict mobsters as amusing, even loveable, and certainly as vital and exciting. The ''mob'' seems as much a part of the American scene as Halloween and spring baseball training.

The general notion is of a large group, or series of groups, organized on business lines to engage in criminal activities on behalf of their members. There may be a nation-wide crime syndicate (Cressey 1969) or merely a series of local groups, having loose working relationships with each other (Ianni and Reuss-Ianni 1973). But criminologists do tend to agree on a number of key features which combine to make organized crime a phenomenon different from other forms of criminal activity. First, the organizations exist for the specific purpose of making money by whatever means are available. Because the most lucrative means are usually illegal, the bulk of the activities of organized crime groups are criminal. The major objective of these activities is to supply illegal goods and services to those who seek them. Examples include gambling, prostitution, illegal drugs (alcohol during Prohibition, cocaine today), and loan sharking (lending money at rates of interest far above those of banks, but without the constraints exercised by banks). Second, there are connections with government and politics so as to smooth and protect the operation of such activities. This involves continued attempts to corrupt the police and public officials. Third, this is a family business, or at least new recruits are of the same ethnic group as existing members, and the group is termed a "family", the same degree of loyalty being expected as in families in general. This enables the smooth hand-over of the reins of the business from one generation to the next, assisted by a set of continuing rules of conduct which are embedded in the culture of the ethnic group concerned (Ianni and Reuss-Ianni 1973) and which assist in the maintenance of secrecy.

The first organized crime groups were drawn from poor Irish immigrants in the nineteenth century. They made money by extortion from brothel owners, gambling proprietors and others who supplied illegal services, as well as providing politicians with the means of intimidating opponents. In turn this led to political power and influence for the gangs themselves – an early example of the transition to respectability, or at least semi-legality, which is one of the features of organized crime today, often through the purchase, or enforced take-over, of a legitimate business. Next came Eastern European Jews, then Italian immigrants and finally the Puerto Rican immigrants and native black Americans of the present day, with the Italians (and Sicilians) perhaps the most enduring and successful (Barlow 1981). Indeed, organized crime seems one of the key paths to the attainment of the American dream for the initially poor and powerless.

The survival of organized crime depends crucially on its ability to supply a number of products, activities and services, such as drugs, gambling and sex, which are demanded by large sections of the general public, but which are currently illegal under the criminal law. It is striking that the much the same mix of needs is supplied by Japan's flourishing organized crime gangs (*The Economist* 1990a).

A second important factor has been the adaptability of those involved. For example, how do you provide illegally earned money with an alibi and yet retain access to it? The answer is money laundering, the international end of organized crime which handles in excess of $30 billions annually – roughly the Gross National Product of Ireland. The traditional way to move a smallish sum ($1 million or less) is to hand-carry it to a Swiss bank and place it in an anonymous, numbered account, from which it can be invested (often in legal oulets) for the benefit of the organization. More recently, trading companies have been set up, whose profits go in uncheckable directions. In America, the Racketeer Influenced and Corrupt Organizations Act (RICO) provides for financial penalties equivalent to three times the sum involved in the crime concerned. In 1987, America's courts seized cash and assets worth $500 million dollars belonging to drug traffickers alone. This is, of course, only a fraction of the sum retained by organized crime groups (*The Economist* 1988b).

Occupational offenses

Some 50 years ago, Sutherland (1940) coined the term "white collar crime" to denote crimes committed by "respectable people" in the course of their jobs, essentially against the interests of consumers. Today, the single term has been replaced by two: occupational and corporate crime. Occupational crime involves criminal acts for the benefit of the individual offender, for example, against the interests of one's employer. Corporate crime consists of criminal acts committed in the course of business in which the principal benefactor is the corporation, not the individual (Chambliss 1988). Crimes by self-employed individuals, such as doctors or lawyers, against, for example, clients, do not fit precisely into either category but, because they are carried out on behalf of "the office" (whether legal or medical), it is convenient to classify them under corporate offenses. It is even more difficult to categorize crimes by politicians and public officials. For this reason, as well as for their great importance, they are discussed separately.

Occupational crimes include accepting bribes (for example, from a rival of the employer), embezzlement, and pilfering. Embezzlement means keeping for oneself goods or money with which one has been entrusted. It is listed as a separate offense by the FBI, and constitutes no more than one tenth of one per cent of annual arrests. This is likely to represent a very small fraction of actual offenses of embezzlement. Pilfering from workplaces is sometimes large and persistent, and is found in factories, post-offices, building-sites, hospitals, railways, docks, airports, and road transport – whenever materials, equipment or manufactured goods pass through people's hands and can be slipped out for use or sale (Radzinowicz and King 1977). No separate official figures of recorded or cleared pilfering are provided, but it is probable that employee theft is a much bigger source of loss than shoplifting. It was estimated at $1.3 billion in 1967 (President's Commission 1967). Today that would be closer to $20 billion in the retail field alone (losses from plants, offices and warehouses may be much larger, but are difficult to estimate). The ultimate loser is the consumer, in the form of higher prices.

Computer crime (from illegal copying of software to the use of computers to carry out a fraud) is a recent development and exemplifies the point that crime follows opportunity. Companies are wary of advertising their vulnerability; on one estimate only 20–25 percent of computer frauds are reported. Yet a survey by the American Bar Association of 283 large organizations found that 48 per cent of them admitted to having suffered from computer crime. Seventy of these quantified their losses, which ranged from $145 to $730 million (*The Economist* 1986).

Corporate crime

More than 200 years ago, Adam Smith (1723–1790, author of *Wealth of Nations*, the first masterpiece in political economy) warned against the instincts of businessmen: "People of the same trade seldom meet together, even for merriment or diversion, but the conversation ends in a conspiracy against the public or in some contrivance to raise prices." In the same article in which Adam Smith was quoted, *The Economist* (1987a, p. 17) stated ". . . millions of customers are ripped off daily by cosy cartels . . . trade barriers of every kind stand between the consumer and the cheaper goods and services he would prefer."

This was in reference to *restraint of trade*, one of the major sub-groups of corporate crime. Since 1890 it has been illegal in the USA to reduce competition and hence cause higher prices to the public. One of the most celebrated American cases involved 21 corporations and 45 senior executives in the heavy electrical equipment field. They were involved in price-fixing and bid-rigging over a decade that had cost government and the taxpayer many millions of dollars. The companies involved included General Electric and Westinghouse (Smith 1961).

The general theme of *product safety and health* is now at the center of public attention. According to Chambliss (1988), the pharmaceutical industry is probably the worst offender. He cites an investigation by Braithwaite (1984) which found that from 1972 to 1974 a majority of the US clinical investigators in the pharmaceutical industry failed to comply with such legal requirements as informing volunteers for experiments of possible dangers. Skolnick and Currie (1979) chronicled the decision of the Ford Motor Company to continue in production the Pinto, a car they knew to be unsafe. Officials estimated that the total cost of the resulting lawsuits would be markedly less than the costs of retooling the production line and fixing thè design fault. In the event, Ford paid out millions of dollars in damages, but was found not guilty of murder in a trial brought in Indiana as the result of people killed in a Pinto crash (cited by Chambliss 1988).

Advertisements are supposed to avoid statements which are untrue, or misleading. Barlow (1981) cites the *New York Times* of 1974 and 1978 as listing dozens of charges and official decisions against advertising by a range of companies.

Clinard (1968, p. 271) quotes Dr. Paul R. Hawley, director of the American College of Surgeons: "The American people would be shocked at . . . the amount of unnecessary surgery performed on patients throughout the country." A study of over 6,000 hysterectomies performed in West Coast hospitals found 13 per cent to be unjustified (Doyle 1953). Illegal practices by lawyers include misappropriation of funds entrusted to them, and securing false testimony. Trade union officials have engaged in such criminal activities as misappropriation of union funds and the use of fraudulent means to maintain control of their unions.

Insider trading is a specialized financial offence. It involves abusing privileged financial information to make money from dealing in shares or other financial instruments. The person concerned may make enormous sums (up to hundreds of millions of dollars) at the expense of other investors. In the latter part of the 1980's, regulatory authorities, such as the Securities and Exchange Commission, made strenuous efforts to provide a "level playing field" so that all investors could compete on equal terms. The number of cases prosecuted in the Southern District of New York (serving Wall Street) rose from none in 1981 to 21 in 1987 (*New York Times* 1988). Sentences involve short terms of imprisonment (served in open prisons) and/or very large fines. The latter seem more usual. For example, Drexel Burnham, Lambert, an investment bank, having pleaded guilty to six charges, was fined $650 million. Just over a year later it filed for bankruptcy, meaning that it and its 5,300 employees were no longer in business (*The Economist* 1990c).

Political offenses

This is a term with different meanings according to the part of the world one is looking at. In totalitarian states many thousands have been killed or have suffered long periods of incarceration merely for expressing opinions unnaceptable to those in power. The judicial system becomes an obedient instrument of political repression. Examples are widespread, from Soviet Russia up to the middle 1980's, to Iran under both the ayatollahs and their predecessor, the Shah. In a democracy such as the USA, those political crimes which come to light involve public officials, both elected and appointed, and concern either financial activities or the illegal pursuit of political power or of policy objectives.

Political crimes for money include accepting bribes from business men to place public contracts with them, as well the direct misappropriation of public funds. *Time* (1972) noted that in New Jersey alone 67 officials, from mayors to postmasters, had been indicted and 35 convicted over the previous 3 years. Other examples listed ranged from Miami to Albany (NY). Convictions of corrupt federal officials rose from 51 in 1974 to over 400 in 1983, probably due to more assiduous efforts to discover and prosecute wrong-doing rather than to a real increase in corruption (US Department of Justice, 1984). Many presidents have been embarrassed by the illegal activities of their associates, the most recent being President Reagan; during the first 5 years of his two terms, over 50 public officials appointed during his administration were forced to resign, many of them from very senior positions.

The two most famous examples of political crimes for power or policy objectives are the Watergate scandal and the Iran-Contra affair. The former involved a complex plot to damage the chances of the Democratic Party in the 1972 presidential election and, when fully brought to light, resulted in the first resignation of a US President. It also led to the criminal convictions of Mr Nixon's Vice-President, Attorney General, and several of his Presidential advisors.

At the heart of the Iran-Contra affair was a law, passed by Congress in the middle of the 1980's, which prohibited the USA from supplying arms to the Contra rebels against the Sandinista regime, then in control in Nicaragua. At the same time the country was very concerned about the fate of American hostages held in Lebanon by various terrorist groups sympathetic to, or controlled by Iran, then deeply embroiled in a punishing war with Iraq. A plan was hatched whereby, through a colorful collection of Saudi, Iranian-born and Israeli middle-men, American arms were supplied to Iran. The resulting income was used to buy arms which were then shipped to the Contras. The idea was that in gratitude for the arms they received the Iranians would ensure the release of the hostages – a happy ending which finally got under way towards the end of 1991, well after the end of the Iran–Iraq war, and for largely unconnected reasons. To date two of the alleged principal participants in the plan have been brought to trial: former Marine Colonel Oliver North, who received minor sentences for the minor charges eventually brought against him, more serious ones being dropped, and a former national security adviser to President Reagan, Vice Admiral John Poindexter, who was convicted in April, 1990, for his part in the attempt to cover-up the affair, rather than in the crime itself; he also received a fairly light punishment.

As a concluding comment on political, occupational and corporate offenses, it is safe to state that those which come to light are only the tip of a huge iceberg. However, we should not go to the other extreme, and assert that the average "respectable" adult, whether employed or self-employed, assembly-line worker, public official or senior executive, spends his entire working life in the pursuit of illegal self-advantage. The point is simply that criminal activities are not confined to the stereotypic American "criminal" (who will emerge from this and the next chapter as young, male, black and poorly educated). Instead, they are found in all sections of the population. The common denominator between the "white collar criminal" and the "street offender" is the illegal pursuit of personal gain; *both operate in the settings available to them*, from the street to the executive suite.

1.5. Historical trends in crime

Shifts over time

According to Radzinowicz and King (1977), early in the 19th century the levels of crime in the large cities of the industrializing nations of the West were very high. They fell in the latter part of the 19th century, rising again in the mid 20th century. Overall, and very roughly, the pattern is that of a U-shaped curve (Lane 1980).

An analysis by Gurr (1981) of the trends for violent crime indicates that a post-1960 increase in violence in most Western countries was preceded by a much longer period of decline. For example, in Britain the incidence of homicide has fallen by a factor of at least ten since the 13th century. The recent tripling in rate is small by comparison. In the USA, the long term trends have been obscured by three great surges which began about 1850, 1900 and 1960. The latter two seem largely attributable to sharply rising homicide rates among blacks.

The long term declining trend may be linked to cultural changes in Western society, particularly a growing sensitivity to violence and the increasing development of internal and external controls on aggressive behavior. Gurr (1981) lists several general factors which help account for historically temporary deviations from the long term downward trend in interpersonal violence: warfare, which tends to legitimize individual violence; the stresses of the initial phases of rapid urbanization and industrialization; sudden economic prosperity and decline; and demographic factors, particularly an increasing percentage share of young males in the population.

The rate of crimes against property surged sharply throughout the Western World between about 1960 and the late 1970's/early 1980's. Between 1960 and 1978, reported robberies more than tripled, burglaries nearly tripled and auto thefts more than tripled.

Explaining the shifts

Concerning the long term changes between 1860 and 1980, Wilson and Herrnstein (1985) make a number of suggestions:

1. The years in which the ratio of young persons (15–24) to the rest of the population was at its highest were also the years of rising crime rates (e.g., the 1960's and 1970's). Conversely, in periods of declining ratios of young persons (e.g., 1930–1955) crime rates were declining or stable. The effects of an increasing proportion of young people

include a greater burden on parents and greater competition for jobs and wages. In the 1950's, young men earned a larger relative income (compared with the national average for all males) than in the 1970's (Easterlin, 1978). The unemployment rate of the young depends on the size of the youth cohort as well as on the prevailing economic conditions.

2. The introduction of professional police forces in the latter half of the 19th century (see Chapter 3), together with a greater use of prison sentences, was associated with a subsequent fall in crime compared with the early 19th century – in effect, the costs of crime rose.

3. There has been a changing investment in "impulse control", the major components being the temperance movement and the public school movement. Up to the 1830's, a rapid increase in alcohol use led to a counteracting temperance movement over the next 100 years. Between 1829 and 1850, the consumption of alcohol per head fell from 100 gallons to 21 gallons per year. (This is somewhat speculative but plausible; Wilson and Herrnstein provide no data on the implied correlations between reduced levels of alcohol consumption and reductions in crime.) The public school movement originated among Protestant church schools and emphasized "character formation." (Again, no data for any connection with crime rates are provided by Wilson and Herrnstein.)

The 1960's were the antithesis of these moves toward increased social and self-control: sanctions against crime were reduced; as the "baby-boomers" reached adolescence, there was a shift in moral values from self-control to self-expression, with a consequent youth market and a youth culture, and to the decriminalization of public drunkenness, plus the private use of "recreational" drugs.

Wilson and Herrnstein's speculations have some intuitive appeal but, other than the evidence concerning the population share of the young (considered in more detail below), data are in short supply.

1.6. How much crime: methods

There are two main ways of answering the question. The first has been in use throughout the West for many years and today, to an increasing extent, elsewhere in the world. As indicated earlier, it involves the painstaking collation, usually by the police, of crimes reported by the public to the police, termed the official statistics. In the USA these have the special name of the Uniform Crime Reports (UCR). The second method began in the 1970's in the USA and Britain, and is now being introduced into many Western countries. It involves a regular survey of a random sample of the population at large to check whether or not they have been the victims in the recent past of a specified list of crimes. In the USA this is known as the National Crime Survey (NCS).

The Uniform Crime Reports

Wolfgang (1971) has listed the following purposes of official statistics:

1. To measure the total volume of crime and to plan counteraction.
2. To map the statistical distribution of criminal acts in the population in general, and by such indices as age, sex, class, and ethnic group.
3. To classify criminal acts by their seriousness.
4. To establish basic data for theory building and hypothesis-testing.
5. To measure the enforceability of legal norms.
6. To measure the efficiency of preventive measures and the effectiveness of treatment of different types of offender.
7. To measure the impact on crime of other social variables, such as television.
8. To measure the changes in crime rates in ethnic sub-groups.
9. To measure the extent of impairment of the freedom of citizens.
10. To compute the total current costs of law enforcement and plan future budgets.

The above is an admirable list of objectives; much of the rest of this book concerns research related to them. But their achievement depends on the statistics collected giving an accurate picture of the true facts of criminal behavior. Serious omissions or biases can lead to serious distortions, both of research efforts and findings, and of social policy.

The UCR include both Part I and Part II offenses, but omits both drug and vehicle offenses. From it is produced the *Crime Index*. This is a simple number obtained by adding together all reported incidents of each crime. Year to year fluctuations help to indicate trends in a nation's *crime rate* – that is the rate at which crimes occur in reference to population size at a given point in time, for the total population, or specified sections of it.

The National Crime Survey

This began in the USA in 1973. Interviews are held every 6 months with a carefully selected sample of 604 households throughout the country. All household members over 12 are asked their experiences concerning Index crimes. Each criminal act is counted once, in terms of the most serious act which took place in the incident (ranked by the seriousness classification used by the FBI, Steffensmeier and Harer 1987).

The UCR concerns only crimes "known to the police;" in principle, the NCS includes both reported and unreported crimes, provided that they are both recalled and reported to the interviewer. UCR crimes are against people in general *plus* business organizations, government agencies, etc. It follows that for some offences the population base is different, e.g., for burglary the NCS base is households; that for the UCR is the entire population.

Hough and Mayhew (1985), writing about the British Crime Survey, set out a number of issues which apply to the method everywhere, irrespective of country. In its favor is that it reveals much unrecorded crime, that it contradicts police statistics – for example, in England and Wales robberies increased much less quickly than police statistics suggested – and that it provides much new information on victims and on the risks and consequences of victimization. Conversely, the victim survey method can only uncover crimes which have clearly identifiable people as victims: it cannot easily count crimes against organizations (e.g., fraud and shoplifting) or "victimless" crimes (e.g., drug related offenses), or crimes by organizations. People fail to remember relevant incidents in the "recall" period, and report crimes which in fact occurred earlier. Middle class people are more prepared to define minor incidents as assaults. Sampling errors are inevitably large when a crime is relatively rare. It is unclear who defines the crimes surveyed – the law, the police, or the survey population – and it is often uncertain whether or not an incident is a crime, for example, a blow to the face in the street as compared with that on a sports field (in fact, a deliberate sports blow is now increasingly regarded as a crime).

Since 1980, the age adjustment method has been applied to both UCR and NCS data to produce true (actually, *truer*) changes in individual crime rates when different time periods are compared. Essentially, the adjustment takes into account the share of each age group in the total US population, and applies this to the crude arrest rate, etc.

The dark figure

"The recorded figures of crime are huge but the reality behind them everywhere looms far larger. The sinister word *dunkelziffer* (dark figure) was coined at the turn of the century to express this hidden reality. The dark figure of crime . . . was readily accepted . . . since it represents a very general phenomenon" (Radzinowicz and King 1977, p.42). According to these writers even murder is under-represented in the crime figures. The conventional wisdom is that murder is in a class of its own, a crime that can seldom be concealed, seldom go unpunished. Police resources are concentrated on bringing the killer to account. This is one crime, at least, where the official statistics come very close to reality. But, as they point out, the family (nearly half of all known murders are committed by "friends" or close relatives of the victim) can also be the ideal shelter for murder and its concealment. The use of poison or drugs and the faking of suicide are obvious examples. The very old and the very young are easy targets. Medical certificates may be based on misleading information; most important of all is the question mark over people who just disappear – thousands each year in modern times.

In general, the dark figure comprises two sets of omissions: reporting by the public to the police and recording by the police.

Reporting. Greenberg and Ruback (1985) set out a three-stage model of victim decision-making. First, the victim must label the event as a crime, next he must evaluate its seriousness and, finally, he must decide what to do. They assume that the victim has two main motives, a sense of injustice and a feeling of vulnerability, and that these lead to a fear of subsequent victimization. Calling the police is only one of the ways of reducing stress. He could also report to superiors, or seek the advice of friends, neighbors or family. Because of the emotional arousal due to his distress, the victim is highly responsive to social influences in deciding whether or not to report the event.

There is also a considerable rational and calculative element in his thinking. This is make clear by Skogan (1984) in a major review which draws on many years of NCS and international data. He considers that the victim's decision concerning reporting may be the most influential in the criminal justice system: he is the gatekeeper for all that follows (actually a *further* series of gates, as will become clear in the rest of Part I.) Skogan's main conclusions follow:

1. The decision to report depends on a calculation of costs and benefits. Nonreporting means both no compensation for the victim (assuming this is available) and that the criminal justice system cannot go into action.

2. If nonreported crimes were included, the clearance rate would fall sharply, implying an even lower lever of certainty of punishment than at present.
3. Differential nonreporting – which partly determines which offenders are liable to arrest and which are not – may be to some extent influenced by race, sex and age.
4. Inevitably, our knowledge of offenders is largely derived from those who are caught, thus markedly affecting theories of crime.
5. Reporting patterns influence police roles. If most attacks are by strangers on the weak, then the police are indeed protectors, but if attackers are more equal nonstrangers, their role is more complex.
6. Reports are the raw material for police planning and budget claims.
7. Nonreporting affects both resource allocation (some areas are more protected than others) and crime prevention programs (the greater the involvement of citizens in them, the more they will report and the higher the "crime figures" as a result – which might suggest the failure of the program!).
8. If the poor, minority group members and those hostile to the police, report less, then it is they who suffer most from the disadvantages of nonreporting.

Many of the above points concern police behavior and are expanded on in Chapter 3; they are included here to demonstrate the interdependence of the various elements of the criminal justice system.

Reports to the police of robberies range in frequency from 44 per cent to 63 per cent and of burglaries from 44 per cent to 68 per cent of those which victims actually recall (Skogan 1984) In only two of over twenty studies were there very large disparities between victim reports and police files. (Nevertherless, the numerical findings just listed give ample scope for variations in police response to citizen reports by both crime features and victim characteristics). According to Skogan (1984) all surveys of Western industrial democracies indicate that most citizens both have telephones and assume that the police are at least somewhat responsive to their needs. He expects reporting rates to be much lower in the less developed nations, in which citizens have to walk to report and the police are less professional.

Skogan's review found perceived *seriousness* to be the most important factor determing reporting by the victim. Most of the explainable variation was related directly to the characteristics of the incident: was the offence completed or only attempted?; was there injury or financial loss, etc.? The more serious the offense (on the Wolfgang scale – see above), the higher the reporting rate. Next came *insurance*. For example, the NCS for 1973 found that 74 per cent of burglaries from insured homes were reported, against only 44 per cent of uninsured ones.

A sense of *obligation* and *efficacy* is of some importance. Reporting confers a feeling of good citizenship, meaning an obligation both to help the community and to prevent future crime. Conversely, when the police are seen as unlikely to be effective, reporting is much less likely. Not surprisingly, *self-perceived culpability* plays an important part: those in some sense "responsible" for their own plight, for example, a person drinking at the time of the incident, are much less likely to report.

Demographic factors vary in significance. There are no important differences according to type of location: urban, suburban, or rural. In general, sex differences are small, but women, particularly black women, are consistently more likely to report than are men. The elderly (60+) are more likely to report personal incidents (51 per cent) versus 42 per cent of the under 60's. Combining age and sex sharpens the differences even more. For assaults, NCS reporting data are: teenage males (29 per cent); males in their thirties (51 per cent); females in their thirties (59 per cent).

So far as relationships are concerned, the largest differences for rape are between strangers and nonstrangers. The former are much more likely to be reported; the fear of revenge by nonstrangers seems important. *Attitudes toward the police* have very little effect – even extreme differences in attitude, for example between ethnic groups.

There is less research on reporting by *third parties* but police files make it clear that many incidents are reported by persons other than victims. In many work situations, victims are encouraged not to call the police themselves but instead to notify superiors.

Reasons for *not reporting* are reviewed by Radzinowicz and King (1977). The most frequently stated reason, given in half to two-thirds of cases, is "not worth the trouble of going to the police." Related to this is "the police wouldn't want to be bothered" (about 25 per cent of cases; respondents give more than one reason for not reporting). About one third indicate that the matter is a private one (assault by family members, theft by a child or a friend). Linked with this is the fear of revenge by the culprit or his friends (this is more true of women than of men). Personal inconvenience, e.g., losing time from work to attend court, was mentioned by 10 per cent.

Biblarz, Barnowe, and Biblarz (1984) found two major combinations of variables in the decision to report serious crimes (about 20 per cent were not reported in their study). On the one hand, reporting was related to a composite index of integration (higher socio-economic class, having a social support network, stability of residence and employment, and few personal difficulties). On the other hand, nonreporting, particularly of crime against property, was associated with low income, problems with anxiety and depression, unfriendly neighbors, plans to move residence, and a lack of nearby friends and relatives.

Rape is a special case, having an exceptionally low reporting rate, probably well below 10 per cent, as indicated earlier. Ease of conviction (e.g., a black assailant and a white victim, the use of a weapon, and a severe injury) increase the probability of a report (Lizotte 1985).

Skogan (1984) sees as the main consequence of nonreporting that the dark figure contains a disproportionate number of minor offences, i.e., the dark figure is not as bad as it first seems. Nevertheless, nonreporting is so considerable as to reduce the potential deterrent effect of the criminal justice system. He considers it unlikely that reporting can be substantially increased. Moreover, police actions, or their absence, can be very off-putting. NCS data indicate that the police do not respond in about one quarter of the cases in which they are summoned. Citizen involvement in crime prevention programs and knowledge of local government and similar issues increase the reporting rate. A massive educational program would be needed to increase reporting substantially over the present level.

Recording. Even if a crime is reported, it may not be recorded by the police. First, the complaint may be found to be without a basis, or to be a deliberate falsification. Next, the complaint may be listed under another head (e.g., theft as lost property), is dealt with by an informal warning (as in the case of a child stealing apples from an orchard) or is handled by conciliation (for example, family violence). If all possible entries were actually to be made and followed up the work would swamp the criminal justice system. Other examples of offenses in which the police are likely to be highly selective are driving too fast, getting drunk, and gambling in the wrong place.

The police may both understate crime (both volume and gravity), to show the efficiency of a police force, and overstate it, to support the need to reinforce the police, in numbers, status or equipment. Dramatic transformations in apparent criminality, including serious crime, have followed changes in methods of police recording.

> "In 1949, the FBI refused to publish any more crime reports from New York, since it did not believe the reported figures, which showed the city, twice the size of Chicago, to have many fewer robberies. New York responded by centralizing the procedure for collecting and recording complaints. This brought to light five times as many robberies, not to mention fourteen times as many burglaries, and left Chicago far behind. In 1960, Chicago also centralized its records: its robberies thereupon overtook those of New York. In 1966, New York once more tightened its controls, and so regained the lead in honestly recorded dishonesty" (Radzinowicz and King 1977, p.54).

While the UCS functions as a kind of check on the NCR, there is no parallel check on police recording. What is not recorded is lost. Implications of the dark figure: according to Radzinowicz and King (1977) these are as follows:

1. It is very difficult to ascertain the true composition and trends of criminality (unless we assume that the proportions of recorded and hidden crime stay the same; this is very unlikely).
2. It restricts and distorts our knowledge of offenders, because it is difficult to study those who are not caught. Nearly all research is on those who are caught and confined.
3. The attitudes of society to crime, to criminals and to punishment is inevitably unrealistic, being based on recorded crime. What would be these attitudes if the dark figure were known and added on?
4. The dark figure weakens deterrence. Those who get away (even in part) have no or a reduced exposure to punishment. "The calculation of chance is as applicable to the commission of crime as to many other activities"(Radzinowicz and King 1977, p.67).

Clearly we must approach the quantitative data on crime with great caution.

1.7. How much crime: results

NCS data make it clear that many criminal events are relatively trivial. Table 1.2 (NCS data from 1975 to 1984, Gottfredsen 1986) shows that

Table 1.2. *Number and per cent distribution of households touched by crime, by type of crime, 1975–1983*

	1975	1977	1979	1981	1983
Households touched by:					
Any NCS crimes (%)	32.0	31.3	31.3	30.0	27.4
Violent crime (%)	5.8	5.7	5.9	5.9	5.6
Rape (%)	0.2	0.2	0.2	0.2	0.1
Robbery (%)	1.4	1.2	1.2	1.3	1.1
Assault (%)	4.5	4.7	4.8	4.7	4.2
Personal larceny (%)	16.4	16.3	15.4	13.9	13.0
Burglary (%)	7.7	7.2	7.1	7.4	6.1
Household larceny (%)	10.2	10.2	10.8	10.2	8.9
Motor vehicle theft (%)	1.8	1.5	1.6	1.6	1.4
Household touched by crime (thousands) (*N*)	23,377	23,741	24,730	24,863	23,621
Households in United States (thousands) (*N*)	73,123	75,904	78,964	82,797	86,146

Source: Bureau of Justice Statistics, 1985 (adapted from Gottfredsen 1986, p. 255).
Note. Detail does not add to total because of overlap in households touched by various crimes.

about one third of NCS households annually report being victimized, but that only 5 or 6 per cent have a member suffering violent crime; most of those do not experience bodily injury, and of those that do, most receive no more than brief medical attention. For most victimizations there is no direct physical confrontation: violent crimes, such as assault, robbery and rape, are the least common. The most probable victim is not a person but a business. There is much repeat victimization, and some victim proneness (some organizations, geographical areas and persons are at much greater risk than others). For example, in 1970, two-thirds of all robberies took place in 32 cities with only 16 per cent of the population.

UCR and NCS data agree in indicating certain temporal correlates of crime: personal violence occurs disproportionately in the late evening and early morning; personal larceny during the daytime; violence is largely outside the home (the risks of assault and rape are greater on the street). But nonstranger assaults are mainly in the home and these are under-reported, so that nonhome assaults are over-represented in the statistics (Gottfredsen 1986).

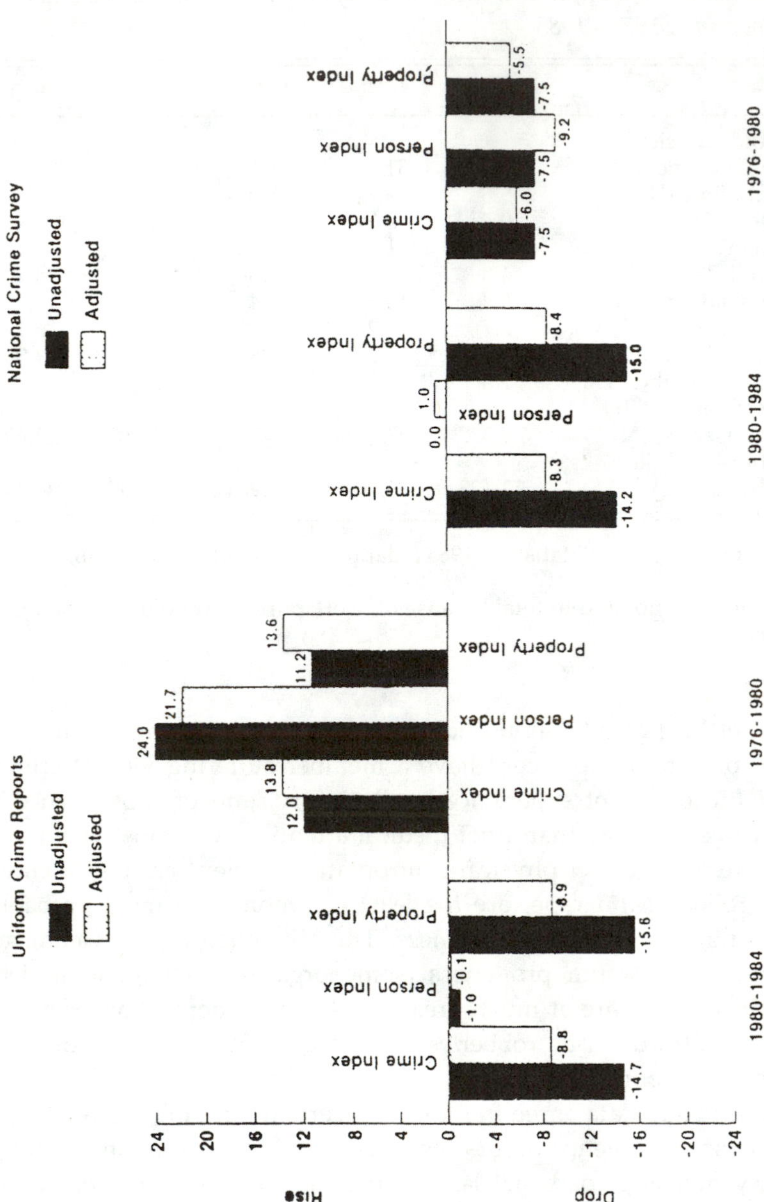

Figure 1.1. Percentage change in UCR/NCR Index crimes for 1980–1984 and 1976–1980 (from Steffensmeier and Harer, 1987, p. 37, reprinted by permission of Sage Publications, Inc.).

Steffensmeier and Harer (1987) applied the age adjustment method to UCR and NCS data for 1980 and 1984 in order to measure the change in the crime rates between the two years. Figure 1.1 shows the effect of doing so for 1976–1980 and 1980–1984 for both UCR and NCS data. In all cases, applying the adjustment reduces the amount of change. Between 1980 and 1984 there was a decline in the UCR Total Index of 9 per cent, due almost entirely to a decline in the Property Index (i.e., in crimes against property). The crude (unadjusted decline) in the UCR Property Index was 15.6 per cent, so that 43 per cent of the decline was explained by the drop in the share of young people in the population. Similarly, the NCS data show an 8 per cent drop in the Property Index, about one-third of which is accounted for by the age adjustment. In both cases, we still have to explain the portion of the fall not due to the age adjustment.

The lack of change in the Person Index for both methods may be related to the higher average age of 35 for such offenses as against 21 for property crimes, meaning that in the years under consideration the "baby-boom" generation had passed the peak age for the latter,but not yet for the former. The 15–24 age group peaked in size in the mid-1970's, (then comprising nearly 19 per cent of the total US population), held steady until 1980, and is set to decline rapidly to a projected 13 per cent in 1995 (see Figure 1.2 for the graph of US age distribution 1970–2000, Steffensmeier and Harer 1987, p. 37). They estimate that 40–50 per cent of the increase in index arrests in the 1960's was because the young, high-risk, group was growing faster than other groups in the population. The decline in property crime between 1980 and 1984 was faster (at 11 per cent) in the Mid-West and North East, which have stable and ageing populations, than in the West and South (5 per cent) where there is much in-migration. The age structure of a population must always be taken into account when estimating both crime trends and police effectiveness.

Steffensmeier and Harer (1987) point out that there was a clear drop for theft, burglary and homicide from 1980 to 1984 (though not for rape, aggravated assault, and motor vehicle theft) even after the age adjustment. They assert the need for additional explanations for the drop and consider the *cohort hypothesis*. During the years since the mid-sixties there have been major shifts in the size of youth cohorts. Other things being equal, larger cohorts mean higher crime rates than smaller ones (Easterlin 1978). In large cohorts there is a glut of young people in the labor market, with more competition for jobs and education. Those

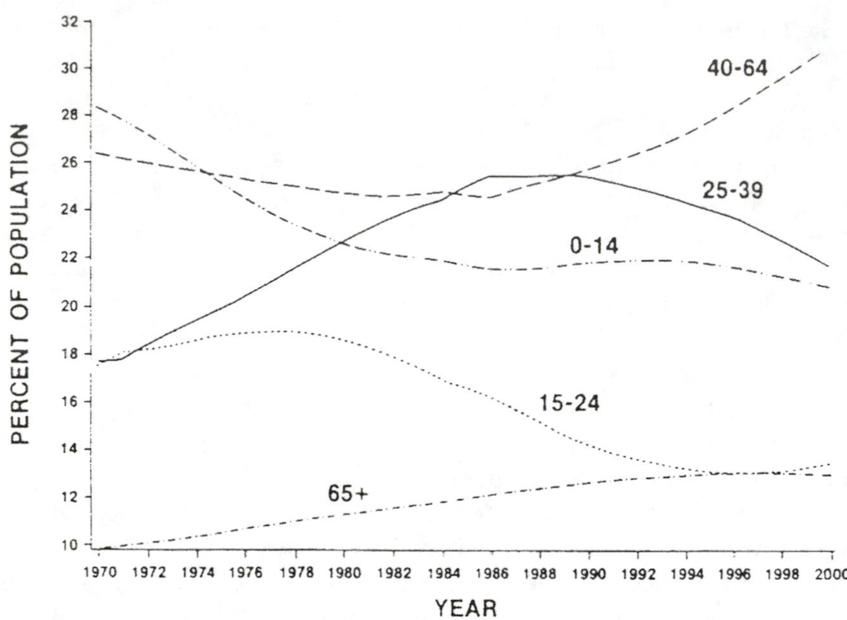

Figure 1.2. Graph of age distribution, United States 1970–2000 (from Steffensmeier and Harer, 1987, p. 27, reprinted by permission of Sage Publications, Inc.).

with a sense of failure, turn to crime. As the size of the cohort declines, so does the crime rate. But this does not explain the lack of fall in the rates for theft and motor vehicle theft – which may remain "easier" offenses than burglary (made more difficult by improved home security) and there may also have been a "displacement" (see Chapter 12 for a discussion of this term) to different, *nonIndex* crimes such as check and credit card fraud, and particularly to drug dealing.

Steffensmeier, Streifel, and Harer (1987) tested the cohort size hypothesis on UCR Part 1 arrest data for 1953 to 1984. They found large age and period effects but only a small effect of cohort size. Cohen and Land (1987), however, using data for murder and motor vehicle theft, found that the hypothesis could not be rejected, but they did have to take into account trends in the business cycle, in criminal opportunities (e.g., the number of cars in relation to the number of young males), and in the rate of imprisonment.

Figure 1.3 (Steffensmeier and Harer 1987, p. 38) shows US age distributions projected to the year 2000. It indicates that if age com-

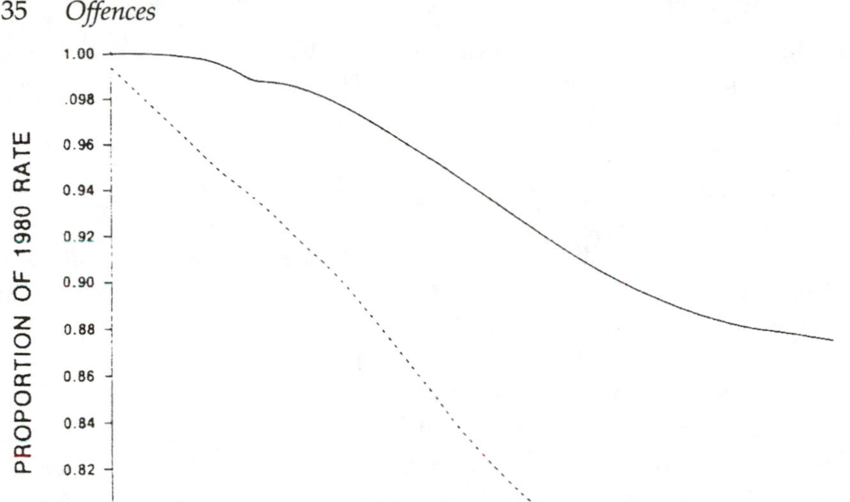

Figure 1.3. Projected age-adjustment effects for person and property crimes to year 2000 – solid line represents person; dashed line represents property (from Steffensmeier and Harer, 1987, p. 39, reprinted by permission of Sage Publications, Inc.).

position changes alone determine the crime rate, property crimes will continue to fall (as a proportion of the 1980 rate) until 1995, after which they will move upward, as the proportion of 15–24 year olds in the population slowly increases again. Person crimes will drop more slowly to 2000, but will continue to do so even beyond that year because the at-risk population for such crimes is older than for property crimes. The maximum total drop is predicted to be 13 per cent for person crimes and 20 per cent for property crimes.

A note of caution (Farrington and Dowds 1984) is in order. These researchers point out that, for hypotheses to be tested satisfactorily, police recording practices need to be standardized. The rapidly increasing computerization of police forces of the past few years means less apparent scope for not recording reported offenses, but they have resulted in vast increases in recorded crime and, hence, in tasks for the police, who then may become more selective. Much more research is needed in which crime surveys showing changes in crime are compared with police recording practices in the same area.

1.8. International comparisons

This is inevitably a difficult exercise. The definitions of crime vary somewhat between countries, as do the probabilities of a crime being reported or recorded. Less than a dozen countries (including the USA and the UK) offer anything near to full and reliable statistics. Allowing for this, the picture is clear of a steady rise in the rate of crime in the two decades to 1980 in all the advanced industrial countries, with the exceptions of Japan and Switzerland, which are discussed below. The USA maintains a clear lead, particularly for serious property crimes and for person crimes: "New York has 31 times as many armed robberies as London, Philadelphia 44 times as many criminal homicides as Vienna, Chicago more burglaries than the whole for Japan, Los Angeles more drug addiction than the whole of Western Europe" (National Advisory Commission on Criminal Justice 1973, p. 352).

Whereas the ratio of recorded property crime to personal crime is about 8 to 1 for the developed world, it is about equal for the developing nations. The *per capita* rate for property crime is about three times higher in the developed than in the developing countries; conversely, the rate for crimes against persons in the latter is twice that in the former (Wilson and Herrnstein 1985). In the developing countries, crime is now rising at a significantly faster rate than in the developed world, possibly due to the declining hold of traditional control systems such as religion (Viccica 1980), but increasing opportunities (because of increased wealth) and a growing youth population are alternative explanations. The shift from person to property crime with development is shown within a country also, for example, as one moves from the more to the less developed regions of the Soviet Union area (Shelley 1981).

Before leaving the developing nations, it should be pointed out that they are particularly vulnerable, often on a vast scale, to such offenses as smuggling, traffic in narcotics, and bribery in the exploitation of mineral rights. The economies of several countries, for example, Colombia, have become heavily dependent on growing and producing illegal drugs such as cocaine.

Special cases

Japan. Between 1962 and 1977 there were increases in the crime rate in all major western cities of between 30 per cent and 300 per cent, but in the two largest Japanese cities, Tokyo and Osaka, the rates actually declined, by 13 per cent and 37 per cent, respectively. While there was no decline in Japanese juvenile crime there was at least no increase (Martin and Conger 1980). Looking at specific years, in 1974 the USA, had four times as much UCR index crime as Japan had crime of any sort (excluding traffic offenses, Bayley 1976). The true gap may have been even higher: Wilson and Herrnstein (1985) speculate that more crime is reported in Japan than in the USA, because of a greater sense of social responsibility. In the 1970's the risk of being robbed was 208 times greater in the USA than in Japan (Bayley 1976). In 1983, the Japanese authorities became concerned at the rise in "senseless" street murders – there were 13 in the whole country in that year. In its report, the *New York Times* (1983) commented that this is what would be expected in a single bad weekend in New York City.

What is so special about Japan? First, it should be pointed out that, in contrast to other advanced countries, the Japanese youth population *declined* by 30 per cent between 1966 and 1974 (Martin and Conger 1980). Next, while Japan has fewer police officers than the USA per head of the population (*New York Times*, 1983), it has more per recorded offense (Wilson and Herrnstein 1985). (The complex relationship between police manpower levels and crime rates is discussed in Chapter 3.) In Japan, both police prestige and professionalism are high, possibly the reason for the very small annual number of complaints against the police (Vogel 1979). The informal system of social control in Japan may be both more powerful and more pervasive than in the USA. Whereas Japanese prosperity has increased consistently for several decades, with very low rates of unemployment, the USA has had intermittent recessions and persistently high levels of youth unemployment, particularly among blacks. This economic theme will be returned to in Chapter 8.

A leading newspaper summarized as follows the Japanese situation at the end of the 1980's:

> "The picture is becoming more like the West . . . The ratio of arrests to crime fell from 62 per cent in the first half of 1988 to a record low of 47 per cent in the first half of 1989. (The arrest

> ratio was then similar to West Germany's, but still twice that for the USA) . . . There are 3,200 organized crime gangs . . . with an annual income of $9.3 billion . . . some 40 per cent of the 86,500 gangsters known to the police belong to one of the three main crime syndicates (up from 22 per cent ten years ago) . . . In the first half of 1989 more crimes were committed by people aged 14–19 than by adults, the first time this has ever happened. "(*The Economist*1989c, p. 47).

Nevertheless, most Western countries will look enviously at Japan's recorded rate of crime in comparison with their own.

Switzerland. Clinard (1978) attributes the relatively low rate of crime to the highly homogeneous nature of Swiss society, in which the local community and various membership groups within it (family, school, etc.) exert strong pressures toward conformity. Mention should also be made of consistently low unemployment, great economic stability and prosperity, and the absence of social unrest.

Homicide: the USA versus the rest

Beane (1987) has presented age- and sex-adjusted data for 76 countries which indicate that the USA has higher rates than 61 of them. Almost all of the remaining 15 are Third World countries. The point is reinforced by Christofell and Kiang (1983), who demonstrated that the atypically high homicide risk in the USA begins in early childhood, and is particularly serious for males. Black males seem most at risk: between the ages of 25 and 35 homicide is the leading cause of death for blacks, and the black death rate from homicide is eight times that for whites (Hawkins 1985). In the 1960's, murders using guns were 48 times more frequent in the USA than in Britain, West Germany and Japan combined (approximately the same total population for the three taken together as for the USA alone, Walker, 1971). The importance of the availability of firearms (much greater in the USA than elsewhere) will be discussed in Chapter 9. (However, robbery plus murder seems to have been on the decline in the USA since 1981 (Cook 1985)).

The costs of crime

Phillips and Votey (1981) describe two approaches to assessing the monetary impact of crime. The first is to count the number of offenses

(UCR not NCS) and assign an average cost to each class of offense, updated by the number of offenses in each category and the dollar value for the year concerned. This was the approach of the President's Commission on Law Enforcement (1967). Thus, for 1965, the seven Index crimes resulted in losses of $1.4 billion (at 1965 prices), less than 10 per cent of the total $15 billion bill for all offenses (over 50 per cent of which was attributable to illegal goods and services like narcotics, prostitution, gambling, etc.). At 1992 prices, the current total bill is at least five or six times higher. Most Index property crimes involve small amounts of goods or money, but there is the occasional spectacular exception, like the March, 1990, theft of art treasures from Boston's Gardner Museum, estimated at $200 million, which included two Rembrandts, a Manet, a Vermeer and five paintings by Degas.

The second method combines the seriousness scale of Sellin and Wolfgang (1964) and the dollar loss to produce a measure more related to the true social cost. Nevertheless, it is the first method which dominates practical discussions.

Nietzel (1979) states that while the total cost of crime is unattainable, information about some specific cost elements might be useful. He cites data from the President's Commission (1967) which show that property offenses not in Part 1 of the Index, such as fraud and embezzlement, make much more of a financial impact than do Part 1 property crimes. A 1974 estimate for the main occupational and corporate crimes puts the economic costs at $47 billion (Chamber of Commerce of the United States 1974). At 1992 prices this would amount to at least $105 billion.

But even this figure pales against the estimated $300 billion cost by the year 2000 of the Federal bail-out of the savings and loan industry, the biggest financial debacle in the USA since the Great Depression of 1929. Hundreds of thrift institutions have failed, some due to negligence, but many because of fraud by their executives, assisted by back-room deals with corrupt politicians. The courts will be busy for years with civil and criminal cases arising from the scandal. The inevitable consequence of the huge cost to the American taxpayer will be higher taxes, and reduced social programs (*New York Times*, 1990).

The economic impact of crime includes the cost of the criminal justice system. In the mid 1960's this was more than $4 billion per year, of which the police accounted for 65 per cent, the courts and prosecution service about 10 per cent and the corrections system (prisons, etc.) about 25 per cent. The President's Commission estimated that private resources spent about $2 billion, mostly for preventive security, body-

Table 1.3. *The costs of crime*

Wounding with intent	£.p	Theft from unattended motor vehicle	£.p
1. Report by 999 call	1.88	1. Report by telephone	00.10
2. Policemen sent to scene	48.24	2. Policemen sent to scene	11.52
3. Ambulance and treatment for victim	766.08	3. Auto insurance – premium and claim (admin.)	158.00
4. Two weeks loss of earnings for victim	240.80	4. Police officer investigation	4.28
5. Criminal injuries compensation	1,011.00	5. Police officers arresting	4.28
6. Two officers arresting	5.15	6. Custody officer	6.38
7. Prisoner's meals at police station	2.28	7. Interviews and statement	8.56
8. Legal aid: remand	74.24	9. Administration	6.64
committal	295.41	10. Other	2.10
Court	1,472.60	TOTAL COST	205.52
9. Court costs	3,342.15		
10. Custody on remand (11 weeks)	1,848.00		
11. Prison sentence (11 months)	22,088.00		
12. Other	187.58		
TOTAL COST	31,380.41		

Source: Northumbria Police, UK: examples based on minimum costs adapted from *The Economist* (1988c).

guards, and private detectives. To take just one of these figures and update it: the cost of corrections in the early 1990's is about $24 billion per year.

Turning to Britain:

> "The most inefficient criminals are shoplifters. Last year [1987] they took an average of only £53 a haul . . . in contrast, thefts from vehicles typically yielded £197, house burglaries £723; and thefts from firms by employees netted £1,099 . . . Stealing £50 from a pensioner undoubtedly causes more direct suffering than taking £500 from a supermarket. A big bank stated that a loss of over £7 million from crime was not a major problem" (*The Economist* 1988b, p. 21).

The dollar rate to the pound sterling at the time was about $1.50. The police of Northumbria (a county in northern England) have produced a detailed analysis of the costs (to the State) of wounding with intent compared with theft from an unoccupied vehicle – the first exceeds the second by about 150 times (Table 1.3; source *The Economist* 1988c, p. 21).

In the early 1970's, Richmond (1972) estimated at $34,481 the cost to the American public of a person who makes his first appearance in the juvenile court at the age of 16 and is then in and out of trouble for the next 25 years. In the early 1990's this would be at least four times as high to allow for dollar inflation.

It is difficult to put an overall valuation on the loss of life or personal injury involved in violent crime (although this is done continually by the civil courts and by insurance companies for loss by accident or negligence). While the losses of goods and money can obviously be measured, other costs are less easily quantified: for example, the anguish of being a victim and the considerable inconvenience, sometimes distress, of appearing as a witness. The next chapter discusses the adverse psychological consequences suffered by the victims of crime, whether personal or property.

2. Offenders and victims

> *Paucis carior est fides quam pecunia*: Few do not set a higher value on money than on good faith. Sallust
> (Gaius Sallustis Crispus, 86–34 BC).

Chapter 1 was concerned with offenses, that is with acts. This chapter deals with actors, i.e., with offenders and their victims. The first section describes the methods used to secure information about offenders and the results obtained. The second concentrates on victims: who they are and the effects they suffer.

2.1. Offenders: methods of study

Introduction

This part outlines the strengths and weaknesses of the research instruments which provide information on offenders: UCR, NCS – both described in Chapter 1 in the context of offenses – and the self-report questionnaire, introduced for the first time. A further method of studying offenders, that of direct observation, is also set out, together with a brief discussion on the randomized experiment, widely used in applied psychology but very sparingly in criminology. All of these instruments and methods may be used on a single or on repeated occasions, sometimes over many years; both approaches are discussed. Next, the results obtained are outlined, from the prevalence and incidence of offending in the general population, through criminal careers, specialization and professionalism in crime, and solitary versus group offending, to the demographic correlates of crime (age, gender, ethnicity and social class).

In North America, the term *delinquency* traditionally includes both criminal (Index as well as nonIndex offenses) and status offenses, such as drinking alcohol below the legally allowed age. The continuing American tendency to eliminate status offenses (Farrington 1987b) should result in more comparability between Britain and North America. In both parts of the world delinquency refers to offenses by *juveniles*, defined in the UK as between 10 and 17; in most American states the minimum age for delinquency can be as low as seven, with the maximum just before the 18th birthday.

Juveniles tend to carry out their crimes in groups, raising the question of whether the individual is the most appropriate unit for analysis. Measures based on offenders will overestimate the number of offenses committed: thus, one carried out by three persons together counts as three offenses. It follows that if blacks committed the same number of offenses as whites, but more persons were involved in each offense on average, it would be concluded that offending was more prevalent among blacks. The issue of *co-offending* (Reiss 1988) is considered later in this chapter.

Official statistics

UCR arrest reports are more accurate than reports of crime, because there is no reason to under-record, but they do have some limitations (Wilson and Herrnstein 1985). First, many of those arrested are then released (for example drunks), and family members, such as husbands, may not be arrested even for a known assault on a wife. Second, only a proportion of crimes are cleared. It cannot be assumed that those cleared are a representative sample of those committed. There may be differences in clearance rates between offenses, as well as variations in police surveillance and arresting practices towards different population groups, at least for the less serious offenses.

Reports of convictions (those who have traveled the full route from crime to sentence) are even more problematic, because at *each* stage between surveillance and sentence there is a possibility of bias against particular population groups – again, more so for the less serious offenses. Chapters 3 and 4 consider these issues in detail.

Victim surveys

In addition to information about offenses, the NCS and similar surveys also ask questions about the offender. Clearly this is only possible, even in principle, where there has been contact between offender and victim, as in offences such as rape, robbery and assault; and even in those cases, the victim may get only the most fleeting impression, with much room for well-established stereotypes to determine subsequent recall.

Self-reports by offenders

A sample of the population of interest (the general population, males under 18, etc.) is presented with a list of offenses and asked to indicate whether or not they have ever carried them out. Sometimes they are also asked about the frequency, whether or not they were caught and, if so, with what result. Hood and Sparks (1970) list three important purposes of self-report studies: first, they permit an assessment of how many people have offended and how frequently; second, they abolish the notion of a typology of "offenders" and "law-abiding citizens", replacing it by a dimension of frequency of offending; and, third, they enable a comparison of "official" offenders, labeled as such by the courts, with those not so labeled, for whatever reason. Also, there is a further purpose: explanatory studies of crime, carried out solely on those who have been convicted, may deal with biased samples; the additional use of the self-report method helps to avoid this problem (Feldman 1977).

Although one of the earliest self-report studies (Wallerstein and Wyle 1947) concerned adults, the overwhelming majority have involved schoolchildren or students, thus omitting those who had "dropped out" by the age studied, who were playing truant on the day of the study, or who were in institutions for offenders, as well as the entire population past their early twenties. This problem of over-concentration on youth is not, of course, inherent in the method, but several other problems may be, so that there are still strong arguments for preferring official statistics, set out by Hindelang, Hirschi, and Weiss (1981):

1. There is much skepticism as to whether people are willing to report fully on their offenses – they lie, cheat, and steal in real life, why not in response to self-report questionnaires? Essentially, this argument relates to the reliability and validity of the method – does it produce consistent results and are those results confirmed by other methods? Hindelang et al. (1981) reviewed a series of studies which indicated an average reliability of at least 0.8, and in many cases higher. In their own self-report study, carried out in Seattle, they obtained reliabilities above 0.9, regardless of class, race and sex.

Thus, we can move on to validity – does the method measure what it claims to, the real level of offending in the population at large? This is something of a problematic exercise, because the data with which self-reports are compared are inevitably official statistics – themselves flawed, as we have seen. Other than the direct observation of criminal behavior (unavoidably severely limited in scope, see below), there is no real alternative. Both in their own and in other studies Hindelang et al. (1981) found strong links between self-reported delinquency and self-reports of official contacts (arrests, etc.), official police and court records, and unofficial sources such as data from other informants.

A major exception to these generalizations is provided by young black males, with police records, who tend to under-report on self-report scales by between 10 per cent and 33 per cent. Farrington (1987b) suggests that those with extensive official records under-report in any event – possibly they have become wary of self-incrimination – and blacks are more likely than whites to have such records. Whatever the reason, it is likely that the self-report method is significantly less valid with black males with police records than with other groups, a generalization confirmed by Lab and Allen (1984), but not by Dunford and Elliot (1984).

Farrington (1987b) points out that self-report and official methods agree much more on prevalence than on incidence. For example, in the well-known Cambridge study of young London males (see below for details) Farrington (1983a) found that the number of burglaries admitted by the sample was ten times the number for which they had been convicted.

2. Research based on official statistics is consistent with the predictions made by traditional theories of delinquency. This begs the question: traditional theories may be wrong, and official statistics the product of self-confirming prophecies. Officials, from the police to judges, may see what they expect, possibly on the basis of traditional theories. A reasonable conclusion is that we should select research samples on the basis of both official statistics and self-reports.

3. The last argument concerns the comparability of studies. This requires not only the detailed specification of the samples used but also similarity of questionnaire items – both are far from being achieved.

Examples of self-report studies. The strengths and weaknesses of the method are indicated by the following two examples.

1. Hindelang et al. (1981), carried out in Seattle. The researchers sampled official nondelinquents, delinquents with a police record only,

and delinquents with court appearances. The samples were then stratified by race, sex and median income of their section of the town (a rough measure of social class, but carried out for whites only). Respondents from each of the resulting eighteen subject pools were then randomly assigned to one of four modes of administration: anonymous questionnaire; anonymous interview, nonanonymous questionnaire, and nonanonymous interview. Consent was obtained from both the participant and his/her parent or guardian. The location rate of those targeted for the study ranged from 99 per cent for the white female upper-income nondelinquents to 51 per cent for black female court-appearance delinquents (56 per cent for their male equivalents). Next, of those located, varying percentages refused to participate, the final percentages remaining of the original target populations not exceeding 60 per cent, raising the question of how representative of their sub-groups were the eventual participants? Another doubt concerns the interviewers – no information is given as to their sex, training, supervision, and any planned matching between interviewer and participant, all found to effect the answers given in other sensitive areas of life, such as sexual behaviour (Feldman 1987).

The rates of official delinquency (whether police, or court records, or both) ranged from a low of 7 per cent (white female, upper income) to a high of 47 per cent (black males, income groups combined), reducing the doubts as to the representativeness of the participants.

The basic self-report instrument used consisted of 69 items, in 5 categories: official contacts with the criminal justice system; serious crimes not detected; general delinquencies; school offenses and offenses within the family. Test-retest and internal consistency reliabilities were as high for questionnaire as for interview administration, and there was no effect of anonymity. The reverse record checks (an officially recorded offense is compared with the participant's recall of the event) were satisfactory overall, though not for black males with court records, as indicated earlier. Finally, re-interviews with subsets of the samples, in which they were led to believe that a "lie detector" was operating, led to changes in answers of 8–9 per cent for both white and black males, mostly in the direction of more offenses being admitted, indicating no serious problem with the original results. However, Huizinga and Elliots' (1984) comment on the need for more aids to recall is relevant both to this study and to self-report work in general.

2. A British study (Belson 1975). This consisted of interviews with

1,445 London boys aged 13–16, who were drawn randomly from nearly 60,000 London homes. They were brought to the research center by car and were paid for their participation. Eighty six per cent of the target sample were located and interviewed. The questions were constructed and administered with great care but were restricted to the offense of theft – 44 types in all, varying from "I have kept something I have found" to "I have taken a car or truck."

Direct observation

All three methods described so far have serious flaws: the official statistics reflect the behavior of official agencies as well as of offenders; self-report and victim surveys are also rather biased and indirect measures of offending, and both have to be validated against official records as an external criterion. Instead:

> "Our knowledge about the nature and incidence of offending would be increased greatly if more research projects were carried out in which offenses were observed as they occurred. [Nevertheless] . . . direct systematic observation of offending is not easy to arrange . . . offenses occur with low predictability and low probability, observers may have reactive effects in deterring potential offenders . . . and may be in physical danger . . . offenders . . . try to commit offenses in such a way that they are not observed . . . [but] . . . more efforts should be made by criminologists to use this method" (Buckle and Farrington 1984, p. 63).

There are two possible approaches: participant and nonparticipant observation. Feldman (1987) gives examples of both from another area of psychological research in which direct observation is both desirable and difficult, that of human sexual behavior. Participant observation is exemplified by Humphreys (1970), who took on the role of a police lookout in a men's public bathroom, a location habitually used by those homosexuals who prefer transient encounters to long-standing relationships. He was able to trace and interview many of the participants. Not many researchers would show such dedication to duty. Much the best known example of nonparticipant observation in the field of sex research is that of Masters and Johnson (1966) who, in an 11 year period, recorded over 7,500 complete cycles of female sexual responses and over 2,500 male ejaculatory experiences.

Polsky (1967) argues strongly for the use of participant observation with offenders. This requires a lengthy period of time during which the observer becomes accepted as an observer by the career criminals of interest, learns their special language and generally blends in with the background, finally accompanying them on their criminal expeditions. Polsky's argument is well taken – what he proposes is standard in anthropology – but in practice criminologists have confined themselves mainly to interviews well after the events concerned, typically with convicted prisoners.

Nonparticipant observation seems more feasible, but only with offenses which are relatively frequent and are committed in public. One possible solution is "to provide systematic controlled opportunities for offending to members of the public" (Buckle and Farrington 1984, p. 63). Farrington (1979) discusses a number of experiments in which people were given opportunities to claim dishonestly coins which had apparently been dropped on the sidewalk. As he points out, such studies raise ethical issues, and can be carried out only with minor acts of dishonesty.

The "dropped coin" and similar studies are examples of the *randomized experiment*, discussed in detail by Farrington (1983b) in the context of criminology, and defined by him as a systematic attempt to investigate the effect of variations in one factor (the independent variable) on another (the dependent variable), for example, the effect of drug dosage on sleep. Participants are randomly assigned to groups representing different levels of the independent variable of interest, preferably by the use of a table of random numbers. In the "dropped coin" experiment, the independent variable might be the presence or absence of an onlooker (in fact an accomplice of the experimenter).

Farrington (1983b) lists a number of advantages of randomized experiments: they allow the testing of causal hypotheses (what caused what?); they have high internal validity (did a change in one variable really produce a change in another?); they eliminate selection effects (e.g., some special feature of the sample under study); any effects obtained cannot be attributed to the history or motivation of the participants or to their familiarity with the tests used. When randomization is not possible, for technical or ethical reasons, matching two groups on what are believed to be key attributes is a partial substitute, but large numbers are needed and there may be some key variable on which the groups were not matched. In practice, neither design may be possible, and the researcher has to assume that the groups are similar in every respect except the one of interest. For example, in using the coin-drop experiment to compare the honesty of police and males in general, the assumption is made that the two groups are similar for all variables thought to determine casual dishonesty; any difference found can then be attributed to membership, or not, of the police force.

Farrington (1983b) provides a useful check list of nineteen questions for the person reading a report of a randomized experiment, from "what was the hypothesis to be tested and what theory was it derived from?", to "how far can the results be generalized to other places, and samples?" He recommends preceding hypothesis-testing research by hypothesis-generating research. Very approximately, this corresponds to this author's distinction between the descriptive and the explanatory stages of scientific research. In the main, Part I of this book concentrates on the former and Part II on the latter.

For obvious practical reasons, randomized experiments are not possible with most real life crimes, but shoplifting is a naturally occurring offense which lends itself to systematic observation (the descriptive stage of research). At least four studies have been carried out to date in which random samples of shoppers were followed through stores by observers. In three of these (Astor 1971, Group 4 1972, Marks 1975) only one observer followed each shopper from entering to leaving the store. The fourth study (Buckle and Farrington 1984) used two observers watching from different directions. In all four cases the researchers believed, but could not be certain, that no shopper was aware of being observed. Hidden cameras would obviate this problem, but a large number would be needed, greatly adding to the cost of research.

Buckle and Farrington assert the possibility of testing hypotheses about shoplifting by a randomized experiment, with observed shoplifting as the dependent variable. They also argue for combining methods: studying shoplifting by both interview and observation. Such a study should involve several occasions, rather than a single one; it is likely that shoplifting, in common with many offenses, is repeated, possibly frequently, over long periods of time. There are major problems associated with such a study, desirable though it is. Not the least of these is the ethical dilemma of the researcher concerned, who would have knowledge of a large number of thefts. As a citizen, the researcher is required to inform the police; failure to do so might lead to punishment. At the time of writing there had been no reports of the research method argued for by Buckle and Farrington.

The longtitudinal study (LS)

This is the repeated measurement of the same people, or of a sample from the same population (Farrington 1979). Its main purpose is to follow the course of development and to measure the prevalence of a phenomenon at different age levels as well as the effects of particular events or experiences. In criminology, the method is used to study criminal careers (the natural history and prevalence of criminal behaviors at different ages) and to predict their start and finish and the effect of penal measures as well as the transmission of crime from one generation to the next.

Farrington (1979) discusses a number of methodological problems of LS. The first concerns the choice of method, the alternative being the cross-sectional (single occasion) study. The LS avoids the problem of whether the observed differences are due to selection effects because each participant acts as his own control. On the other hand, there is an inevitable amount of attrition – some participants die or prove untraceable despite repeated attempts to find them – and analysis is restricted to those tested at every point. Next comes the testing effect, the influence of an initial interview on the responses given on a second or subsequent occasion. This is avoided by the cross-sectional method. Also, over the sometimes lengthy periods of time involved in LS work, changes in research instruments may well occur. It is difficult to separate out any effects due to personal development from those due to different periods or eras, so that one needs more than one cohort (a group of participants with some feature in common, such as being born in the same week). A combination of the two methods seems ideal but in practice a single, cross-sectional, study is used very frequently, sometimes for preference (see Gottfredsen and Hirschi 1988 for a spirited attack on the LS method, and Blumstein, Cohen, and Farrington 1988, for an equally stout rebuttal), but more usually for reasons of cost. Another issue concerns prospective (forward looking) versus retrospective (backward looking) research. The former is more difficult, because it is much more time consuming and hence expensive, but it avoids the inevitable biases and distortions when people try to make sense of the past, sometimes the distant past.

A key question for LS research is the use of official records as opposed to self-reports. The advantages of official records is that they are often immediately and cheaply available, they cover a lengthy period, and they are usually recorded at the same time as the event.

Their main disadvantage is that they are seriously incomplete, and so may be a biased and unrepresentative sample of the true number of criminal acts. Only between 3 per cent and 15 per cent of criminal acts result in a police contact, but it is true that those convicted tend to have committed the most offenses, so that official records can be used to identify the most criminal minority, although not to estimate the true prevalence of delinquency. It will be recalled that the Seattle study (Hindelang et al. 1981) reported a serious discrepancy between official records and self-reports for black youths with convictions. In apparent contrast, in their longitudinal study of London boys, West and Farrington (1977) found that only 6 out of 101 official delinquents failed to admit court appearances and only seven out of 228 official nondelinquents claimed court appearances which were not in the records. But, this study was of white boys only; the white participants of the Seattle study had a similarly close match between official records and self-reports.

Essentially, official records exist for use by administrators and as guides to social action (changes in the law or to support the case for more resources for the police, etc.) and not for the convenience of researchers. The problems encountered by the latter include: difficulty of access to records, e.g., it may be quicker to interview; records are often destroyed after some time to save space, and there is much inconsistency in reporting by the police and the courts, as well as random human errors; and the categories used are legal, not behavioral, and conceal wide variations ("burglary" covers a range of crimes, from a multi-person armed raid on a bank, resulting in the loss of millions of dollars, to a robbery by a single assailant using minimal force and a small sum of money taken, and "no further convictions" could be due to death, emigration, hospitalization, reform, or skill at avoiding detection or conviction). For all of these reasons, interviews are needed to clarify and amplify both records and case histories. Interviewers should be properly trained, both in general interview skills and for the particular sample under study, their work should be quality controlled with checks for interviewer bias and, ideally, interviewers and respondents should be matched for ethnicity, age and sex.

In planning a longitudinal study many compromises have to be made, one of which is the size of the sample. It should be large enough to provide enough positive cases (e.g., persons with official convictions) for statistical analysis, but not so large as to exceed the resources available. Guaranteed resources are needed, ideally over a long period;

in practice, two to three years money is granted at a time. Disasters can imperil the best-planned study: many of the records in the Philadelphia study (Wolfgang, Figlio, and Sellin 1972) were lost in a fire. The Cambridge study was nearly ended by a garbled newspaper account. Stability of staffing is very important, but contracts are usually for a year at a time, and many staff seek advancement and a variety of experience. Inevitably, valuable new instruments emerge which cannot easily be incorporated. Similarly, it is difficult to add new research hypotheses along what may be a very long road (at the time of writing, the Cambridge study had reported data for 24 years). Over such a long period participants emigrate, die, change their address, or simply refuse further involvement, and in the USA the mobility of young males is particularly high.

Finally, the essential argument for longitudinal studies is that one *cannot* test and formulate theories of crime without the basic information on the natural history of offending and the progress of offenders through the criminal justice system which the LS method provides (Farrington 1979).

Farrington (1979) lists eleven large-scale LS studies, of which the Philadelphia and the Cambridge studies are particularly good examples. In the first of these, Wolfgang et al. (1972) traced the police records of all boys born in 1945 who lived in Philadelphia at least between their tenth and eighteenth birthdays. They were able to find the great majority of the cohort, 9,945 in total. All recorded acts also received a seriousness score based on the Sellin–Wolfgang index (Sellin and Wolfgang 1964). The authors accepted the desirability of self-report data but did not obtain them. Note also: this is a retrospective study, the participants were not followed forward in time and retested at intervals; there is no information on family, school, and work history, or on personality; and girls were not studied. However, the sample is a very large one, and much valuable information resulted, particularly on the links between convictions and ethnicity and social class, as well as on police and court responses to recorded crimes.

In contrast, the Cambridge study is a prospective one of a very much smaller sample, 411 boys, first recruited in 1960, when they were between eight and nine, from six junior schools in one area of London. The sample has been re-interviewed every two years since, and the latest report at the time of writing (Farrington 1988) takes them to the age of 32. A wide range of information has been collected, including police and court records, family conditions and parental behavior, school performance and behavior, work performance, and personality features. West (1982, p. 8) states, accurately and modestly of the study to which he has devoted much of his working life:

"It was an unremarkable and traditional white, British, urban, working class sample. . . . findings are likely to hold true of many similar places in southern England but they tell us nothing about delinquency in the middle classes . . . girls, or immigrant groups."

Having covered much ground on the methods of studying offenders we can now turn to the results obtained.

2.2. Offenders: results

Prevalence

This means *the number of persons committing criminal acts in a given population*. Offending is widespread, much more so than the official statistics of offenders suggest. "Both in the United States and in England . . . by the age of eighteen somewhere between 10 per cent and 20 per cent of the male population will have been convicted by a court of a criminal offence . . . Self-report studies indicate that they represent on average only a quarter of those who have actually committed these offences" (Hood and Sparks 1970, p. 47).

Scandinavian studies reveal a similar picture (Elmhorn 1965, Christie 1965), as does Belson's (1975) British study: almost all respondents admitted to "I have kept something I have found"; 70 per cent had stolen from a shop; 35 per cent from family or relatives; 25 per cent from work (inevitably a major underestimate – most of the sample were still at school); 25 per cent from a car, or truck; 17 per cent had "got into a place and stolen"; 5 per cent had taken a car or truck. This study concerned boys aged 13–16; there was plenty of time for increases in these percentages before the sample passed the peak age for theft – approximately the late 'teens.

Self-report studies of adults are, unfortunately, few and far between. A very early one was carried out by Wallerstein and Wyle (1947), who mailed a questionnaire of 49 offenses to 1,800 New York men and women. (It should be noted that the samples, both those initially targeted and those who responded, might well have been nonrandom, but the results are in line with those of younger groups.) Two-thirds of the males and 29 per cent of the females admitted at least one felony (approximately those which later became Index offences). A large scale

Table 2.1. *Observational studies of shoplifting*

Study	Description and location of shops	Percentage shoplifting (N)		
		All	Men	Women
Astor (1971)	New York department store 1	8.4 (500)	6.4 (156)	9.2 (344)
	New York department store 2	5.2 (361)	5.7 (135)	5.3 (226)
	Boston department store	4.4 (404)	2.0 (149)	5.4 (255)
	Philadelphia department store	7.8 (382)	6.0 (132)	8.8 (250)
Group 4 (1972)	UK department stores	0.8 (524)	1.9 (158)	0.3 (366)
	UK supermarkets	2.0 (494)	2.3 (131)	1.9 (363)
Marks (1975)	5 Dublin department stores	5.5 (567)	4.4 (180)	5.9 (387)
Buckle and Farrington (1984)	UK department store	1.8 (503)	2.8 (142)	1.4 (361)

American study (Clark and Hollinger 1983) found that one third of a group of employees, sampled from retail, manufacturing and service organizations, self-reported stealing company property.

Observational studies of shoppers indicate the percentage of those followed through a store who shoplifted on a single occasion. Table 2.1 combines the results of previous studies, set out by Buckle and Farrington (1984), with their own findings. The American and Irish figures are higher than the British ones, possibly because of detailed differences in research methods, or in the perceived ease of detection. It is at least possible that, had the same samples been followed for a large number of occasions, much higher figures would have been recorded, and a subsequent self-report study of a group already observed while shopping would be of great interest. In any event, the point is made once again: offending is frequent in the general population; the next question is whether this is more than intermittent and occasional for all but a minority – that is, "how delinquent are the delinquents?"

Criminal careers

There are two traditional measures of the frequency of offending by individuals: *incidence* and *crime rate*. Incidence means *the number of criminal acts per offender* and the crime rate is *the number of criminal acts in the total population of interest, divided by the size of the population*. Both are often further analyzed by age, sex, and so on. But researchers are interested in much more concerning offenders: the seriousness of the offenses carried out; the probability of arrest; changes in these and other variables over the course of many years, and in how to predict criminal activity from as early an age as possible. There are massive individual differences in offense rates (from a total absence to persistent high rates over many years).

Hence, a more recent approach is to chart criminal *careers*. This provides a crime rate for individuals, plus age of onset, the active length of the career and its age of termination, as well the time interval between offences (Farrington 1987a). (The term "career" implies also an income in money or goods, as it would for a business, professional, or any other type of working career, so that the pattern of benefits – and of costs, such as fines and imprisonment – would also be of great value; so far, researchers have not studied these to any significant extent.) It may be that the traditional approach is more suitable for the majority of the population who offend occasionally, while the criminal career approach is more applicable to the minority, whose offending is both more frequent and more serious (Farrington 1987a). For example, in the Cambridge study, 82 per cent had "broken the windows of an empty house" but only 11 per cent admitted to burglary (West and Farrington 1977).

There are major variations even in the relatively high-offending minority: a small percentage of the population is responsible for a large proportion of recorded and cleared serious crime. For example, the median (most frequently occurring number) burglary rate of all those convicted in the USA is 5.5 per year, but that of the most active 10 per cent is 230 per year; for robberies, the respective figures are 5 and 87 (Greenwood and Abrahamse 1982).

A particularly valuable self-report study by Dunford and Elliot (1984) provides a great deal of information on serious, high-rate offenders. They used just two dimensions to define the career offender – frequency of offending and persistence of a high rate over time. Thus the career offender was one who displayed a high frequency over a long period, omitting all other variables such as seriousness, age of onset, specialization, and environmental features, such as family background. (A different approach, which emphasizes these variables, is set out shortly.)

Dunford and Elliot drew on the data of the American National Youth Survey, which was carried out by annual interview between 1976 and

1980, inclusive. Seven birth cohorts, born between 1959 and 1965, and aged 11 to 17 at the outset, were studied. Seventy three per cent (1,725) of those approached agreed to participate, the rate of attrition over the 5 years being 13 per cent with little difference by age or sex. The self-report measure used consisted of 47 items – all the UCR Part 1 offences except for homicide, 60 per cent of Part 2 and a range of other UCR offenses. Age, sex and socio-economic status were also recorded. Four "delinquency types" were delineated, ranging from nondelinquent (0–3 self-reported offenses and no Part 1 offenses) to more than 12 self-reported offenses of which three or more were Part 1. Respondents were placed in one of these categories for each of the 5 years of the study. Validation was by official arrest data. The percentage of those arrested increased about sevenfold from category one to four and the mean number of arrests per person by about twenty times. Similarly large differences were found for self-reported offenses, with offense rates per 100 youths for assault varying from 0 in type 1 to 459 in type 4, and for "general delinquency" (all offenses except status and traffic) from 459 to 11,571. Type 4 offenders were disproportionately male, urban, lower-class and black.

Next, all those who figured in types 3 and 4 for two or more consecutive years were considered separately, and were further divided into serious career offenders (type 4 for two years or more) and nonserious career offenders (all the rest). The former were significantly more likely to be urban and male but ethnicity was not significant – raising the possibility that the official statistics over-represent blacks. While serious career offenders were significantly more likely to have an arrest record over a three year period than the other groups (who ranged as would be expected) *seventy five per cent of them had no arrest record, despite being involved in serious and frequent offenses*. Dunford and Elliot conclude from this that official data should not be used to select groups of "offenders" and "nonoffenders" for research studies. It is true that as the number of self-reported Index offenses rose so did the probability of arrest but, at least for the ages covered by the NYS, most serious offences went unpunished. Taking the 23 respondents with the most serious self-reported records (more than twenty Part 1 Index offenses in a three year period) 78 per cent of them had no record of a police arrest and four of the five who had a record were arrested for nonIndex offences (and even if the offender concerned is arrested at an older age, he may by then have a well-established belief in the benefits of crime).

The high quality of this study is demonstrated by the fact that about 3,000 jurisdictions were searched in order to construct individual arrest records (meaning that very few official contacts will have been missed), and all data were protected by a Privacy Certification from the Department of Justice and a Certificate of Confidentiality from the Department of Health and Human Services, the latter leading the authors to conclude that their results would not be affected by under-reporting by blacks.

Chaiken and Chaiken (1984) also focused on high rate offenders, but used only official statistics and studied imprisoned adults (2,200 inmates in California, Texas and Michigan), the most serious of whom they termed "violent predators" (VP's): those who had committed a range of Index 1 offences as well as having a history of drug dealing. Ten per cent of the VP's had committed between them over 135 robberies per year as well at least 18 assaults, 516 burglaries and over 4,000 drug deals – all many times higher than the 90th percentile of those who specialized in each category. They conclude that reducing the number of VP's on "the street" would have a marked effect on the crime rate. But doing so requires that they can first be identified and eventually predicted. As we shall see in Chapter 10, this is an extremely difficult task and, even if possible, raises serious ethical problems.

Conclusions on criminal careers (based on Petersilia 1980)

1. Less than 15 per cent of the total population (men and women combined) will be arrested for the commission of a crime, of whom 50 per cent will never be arrested for another (but there are great differences between men and women, black and white). Only about five per cent of the population will show the beginnings of a criminal career – but once three contacts with the police have been recorded, the probability of a further one is over 70 per cent.

2. Criminal careers begin early in life, usually by 14–17. The earlier they start the more likely they are to continue into adult years; however, relatively few juvenile offenders become adult criminals.

3. The average self-reported rate for those active in robbery is about 5 per year, as against 16 per year for burglary and 155 for drug sales (an indication of the appeal of the last as compared with the two former offenses).

4. The probability of arrest for an individual criminal act is no more

than 0.10 on average, but varies widely, from less than 0.01 for drug offences to about 0.20 for robbery (note the greater reward – cost odds in favor of the former). Pre-crime planning and preparation reduce the probability of an arrest by a factor of five. Those who plan their offenses do so from their teenage years.

5. Arrest, conviction and incarceration rates increase as criminal careers advance – in contrast to offence rates, which tend to decline – because surveillance of known offenders is greater and more of them become "known" with increasing age. Conviction, rather than acquittal, also becomes more likely, as does a prison compared with a non-prison sentence. As careers progress, offenders spend a diminishing amount of time "on the street" until their active criminal activity abates; prior criminal record has a powerful effect on the response of the criminal justice system.

6. Income from crime increases somewhat with age but averages only a few thousand dollars a year. However, there must be wide individual variations, with hopes kept high by the successes of others; moreover, income from crime can be added to by legitimate work, social benefits, etc.

Specialization. The question is whether offenders are "specialists" or "generalists" in their criminal behavior. Farrington, Snyder, and Finnegan (1988) analyzed the complete juvenile careers of nearly 70,000 offenders using 21 offense types. They found a small, but significant, degree of specialization, superimposed on a great deal of versatility. Specialization increased with successive referrals. The most specialized offences (status offences excluded) were burglary and motor-vehicle theft. Nearly 20 per cent of offenders were identified as specialists. These results make clear that many property offenders, particularly those with longer careers, can be regarded as specializing in a particular offence, implying the development and deployment of a set of professional-level skills.

Professionalism. It seems likely that most recorded crime, against property as well as against persons, is the work of "amateurs" who engage in street crimes as the opportunity arises, interspersed with income from other sources. But a significant proportion of property offenses, particularly those involving substantial sums, is carried out by professionals who work diligently at their specialized crimes.

A number of criminologists have followed the pioneering example of

Sutherland (1937), whose study of a self-described professional thief ("Chic Conwell") indicates the overlaps between professionalism in theft and in legitimate areas of human work. A more recent example of the genre is provided by King and Chambliss (1982).

Professionalism in crime has existed for centuries (Cressey 1971). The areas of activity today include burglary, shoplifting, robbery, confidence games, pickpocketing and auto-theft. Perhaps most important of all, it is clear that organized crime is a highly professional business. Given the huge scale and complexity of the operations involved it could hardly be otherwise.

Criminally relevant skills are developed, like any other occupational expertise, by both example and personal experience. Professionalism means thorough planning, and the careful weighing of risks and alternatives, as well as pride in one's chosen profession and adherence to the code of conduct of the profession. As indicated above, pre-crime planning and preparation reduce the probability of an arrest by a factor of five (Petersilia 1980). It is this sort of statistic, together with the greater ability of professional offenders to avoid conviction even when arrested (see below on the "fix") which supports the need for much more research on offenders who are rarely, if ever, apprehended.

As matters now stand, our information about the skills and life styles of professional criminals comes almost entirely from retrospective accounts by convicted offenders, some still in prison, some on parole. A good example is a study by Gibbs and Shelly (1982), who interviewed eleven "commercial burglars" for between two and eight hours each. All were in custody in NY State and all had been involved in the theft of money or goods, in transit or storage, worth a minimum of ten thousand dollars. The theft of money from a supermarket safe involves a crew of from two to six members. The relevant skills include opening safes with tools and explosives as well as bypassing alarm systems with simple electronic devices. Additional tools of the trade include a police-scanner radio and walkie-talkie sets for communication between the crew. These burglars looked for supermarkets with a substantial amount of cash on the premises, located in a relatively isolated area from which escape would not be difficult. By observing the market for several days and by watching the manager's deposit patterns at the local bank, they could estimate the volume of sales and the amount of cash remaining in the store on a particular day, and hence select the day which would yield the biggest haul.

A second form of commercial burglary involves the hi-jacking of trucks in transit. Trucks are attractive targets because they contain large quantities of goods which are ready for transport, and the goods are less well-protected than in a warehouse or shop. One interviewee specialized in delivery trucks transporting household appliances. From a careful study of local newspapers he ascertained which department stores were having sales and then waited two or three weeks for deliveries of sale goods to begin. In some cases the theft of a truck-load of goods involved collusion with the driver, but when there is no driver "co-operation" the burglar must know how to stop the truck and deal with the driver. The contents of the truck are transferred at a prearranged spot to a second truck; the stolen vehicle is then driven away and abandoned. The key to success is to have a buyer for the load before it is stolen. The buyer is usually a major fence who has the means to distribute the goods through legitimate retail channels. Such contacts are built up over a period of years. Some burglars move on to become fences.

These interviewees made clear how they learned their skills: "You might say, everything I've learned, I've learned in jail . . . how to break down an alarm system . . . how to wire . . . everything would be explained" (Gibbs and Shelly 1982, p. 321). Their criminal activities brought considerable financial rewards, much of which were spent rapidly on cars, drink, clothes and women, up to $50,000 a year on "life in the fast lane." But Gibbs and Shelly (1982) also state (p. 324): "one of the guiding principles of the thief is to invest part of the score."

An important aspect of professional crime is the "fix". Not only does he try to minimize the risk of the crime itself, the professional seeks to reduce the risks of conviction (and hence of confinement, and time away from his work and life-style) should he be caught. The object is to uncouple one link in the chain of law enforcement, by corrupting ("fixing") one of those who can "help," including police, lawyers and judges. According to Barlow (1981), professional fixers handle many of the legal problems faced by professional criminals. The fixer may be a local politician who, in return for a substantial sum, suggests to the judge concerned that the judge's chances of re-election would be markedly assisted by "taking care" of the case concerned (Martin 1952). A study by Inciardi (1975) of professional criminals indicated that the fix brings the desired results. Those interviewed claimed that only 6 per cent of arrests led to convictions, and of these about 40 per cent involved prison sentences of less than one year. The former figure is particularly striking; overall, about one-third of arrests lead to convictions (Forst 1983: see Chapter 4 for more detail on this point).

Co-offending

This refers to the situation in which there is more than one offender for a given criminal act. Statistics and court records do not usually distinguish between solo and co-offenders; Reiss (1988) argues that it is very important to do so. Incapacitation may have an effect on the future crime rate unless the accomplices of those concerned are deterred. If it were possible to identify those high-rate offenders who recruit many others into delinquency, or who have a substantial effect on the individual crime rates of large numbers of offenders, these "offender recruiters" could be targeted for special intervention. Reiss (1988) has collected the scattered research literature. (Most of the data are derived from the official statistics of convictions. Because co-offenders, as compared with solo operators, could be incriminated by their colleagues, with a subsequent high probability of arrest and conviction, this might inflate the proportion of "co-offender offences"). The main conclusions from Reiss' overview follow.

1. In 1982, just over a half of all robberies involved a single offender – but only a quarter of all robbery offenders acted alone, and there were equal proportions of groups of two, three, and four, or more, offenders. Knowing the mumber of co-offenders in each offence in a criminal history enables a more precise estimation of the future crimes which might be prevented by incapacitating that offender.

2. When all the incidents in a criminal career are considered, a large proportion of offenders show neither an exclusively solo nor an exclusively co-offending style. For example, of 467 Peoria juveniles apprehended for at least one burglary over a seven and a half year period, 17 per cent always worked alone, 19 per cent only with accomplices, and 63 per cent moved between the two (Peoria Crime Reduction Council 1979).

3. Self-reports of males show higher rates of lone offending than do official records of apprehension for the same offenders. Then, because major crimes against persons involve higher rates of lone offending, it is possible that adult solo offending, as compared with that of juveniles, is disproportionately concentrated on more serious offenses.

4. The modal number of offenders in a crime from the age of 12 on is two; four or more is relatively uncommon after 14–15, but the majority

have accomplices until their early 20's, after which they are more likely to act alone.

5. High rate juvenile offenders affiliate with one another in peer groups. A Swedish study (Sarnecki 1982) found that the criminally most active 6 per cent of a group of over 500 juvenile offenders (three times as many suspected crimes per member as the average for the group) all belonged to the same three gangs. Most offender pairings are of short duration, but the most criminally active offend in pairs and they preserve their particular pairings longer than do the less active. The most actively and seriously delinquent juvenile suspects were 45 times more likely to commit crimes with the same associates than the least active and serious.

6. The stability of group affiliation (most data are from the USA) is threatened by the transiency of urban populations, by incarceration and by the development of conventional life styles (marriage, regular employment, joining a training program, entering the military, etc.).

7. Juvenile co-offenders are almost always of the same sex, but this is less true for adults. Among violent multiple-offender victimizations reported to the NCS in 1982, 19 per cent involved women as offenders (7 per cent with other women only, 12 per cent with men or with both men and women). According to West German police statistics for 1982, women are more likely to work solo than men – because women are concentrated in offences such as shoplifting, in which higher proportions of offenders work alone, and because of the general absence of organized womens' gangs. Blacks are less likely than whites to work alone (60 per cent versus 72 per cent of all violent crime victimizations for 1986). Mixed-race offender pairs or groups are infrequent, indeed mixed-sex is about twice as likely as mixed-race. It follows that most accomplices are of the same race and sex.

8. Offenders tend to work alone in the cases of murder, sex offenses and the most frequent white collar offences, but with co-offenders for common thefts, robberies and burglaries (in West Germany, eight out ten of the former group are solo offenses against only two out of ten for the latter).

9. A substantial majority of both personal and household crimes are close to the residences of offenders and victims. Juvenile offenders typically select co-offenders from their own "turf." Reiss suggests that it is the territorial concentration of young males who lack the firm control of parental authority that leads them into a peer control

system which supports co-offending, and simplifies the search for accomplices.

10. There is much evidence that older brothers recruit younger ones as co-offenders, whereas older sisters seem to have the opposite effect.

Age

"Criminal behavior depends as much or more on age as on any other demographic characteristic – sex, social status, family configuration, etc." (Wilson and Herrnstein 1985, p. 126). As detailed below, crime peaks in the teenage years and then declines. Why is this so? The following conclusions are based partly on a review by Farrington (1986) of many of the quantitative issues concerning age and crime.

1. The official statistics for comparable offenses (Index, Part I) reveal similar pictures for England and Wales (1982) and for the United States (1983). In the former, the crime rate peaked at 15, in the latter, at 17, both peak ages being the last year in compulsory education in that calendar year. (To make the point further, the peak age for 1938 in England and Wales was 13 – at that time the last year in full-time education). For 1980, UCR arrest data indicate that almost 60 per cent of arrests for Index property crime were of those aged 20 or younger. For Index violent crimes the figure was 37 per cent. Correcting for the population shares at each age, 15–19 year olds had four times the average for the whole US population and, compared with 50–54 year olds, they were 16 times more likely to be arrested (Wilson and HerrnsTein 1985). These general points are illustrated graphically in Figs. 2.1 (separate arrest rates for males and females for 1982, Farrington, 1986) and 2.2 (1984 rates for burglary, robbery, and aggravated assault, Blumstein 1988). The latter indicates that the decline with age in arrests for assault is somewhat less marked than that for burglary.

2. The above figures refer to all crimes combined. Because most recorded and convicted crime concerns property, and property offenses are those which peak in the teenage years, these are also the peak years for all crime aggregated together. But there are some variations in the peak years for different types of crime. FBI figures for 1977 (Cline 1980) show the following to be the characteristic offenses of adolescence: motor vehicle thefts, larceny-theft and burglary. Those most associated with young adulthood (21–26) include assault and drug law violations.

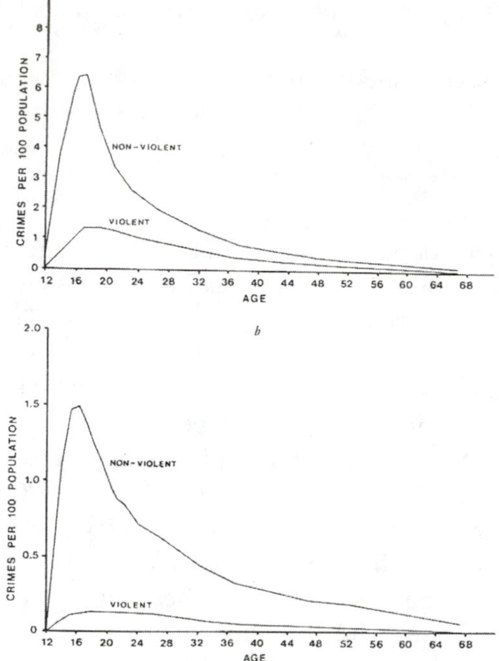

Figure 2.1. The relation between age and crime (a) for American males, and (b) for American females. The graphs in both show the rate of arrests per 100 population for Index offenses in 1982. *Source*: Federal Bureau of Investigation, 1983 (from Farrington, D.P., 1986, Age and crime, in M. Tonry, and N. Morris (Eds.), *Crime and Justice: An Annual Review of Research*, Vol. 7, p. 193. Chicago: University of Chicago Press).

3. The concentration of offending among the young has increased progressively from 1940 to 1980 (Steffensmeier 1989, on the basis of UCR data for 1940, 1960 and 1980), suggesting an increasing discontinuity in the transition from adolescence to adulthood in the past half century.

4. The cumulative prevalence of arrests for Index offenses alone – i.e., the number of people arrested for such offenses over the whole of their lives, beginning at the age of minimum responsibility – is 14 per cent for American whites, and 51 per cent for nonwhites (data for 55 large US cities, Blumstein and Graddy 1982). The bulk of those ever arrested have had this experience by the age of 30.

5. Whereas prevalence clearly declines with age from the teenage peak, this is not the case for incidence, which does not decline until after 30 plus (Blumstein and Cohen 1979, for arrest reports of serious

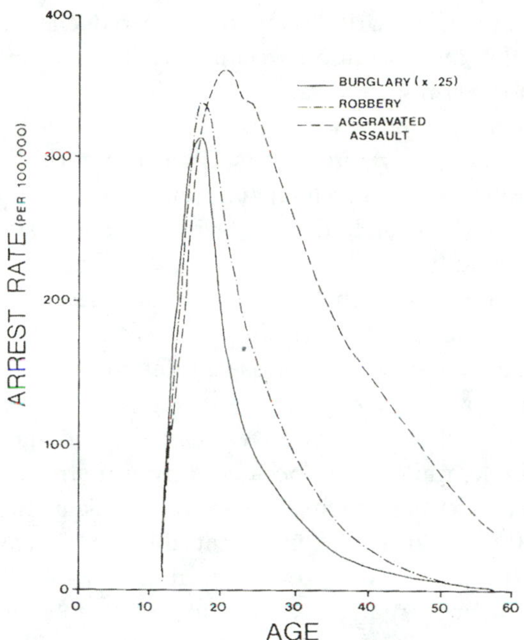

Figure 2.2. Age-specific arrest rates for burglary, robbery and aggravated assault. *Source*: Federal Bureau of Investigation, 1984 (from Blumstein, A., 1988, Prison populations: a system out of control? in M. Tonry, and N. Morris (Eds.), *Crime and Justice: An Annual Review of Research*, Vol. 7, p. 244. Chicago: University of Chicago Press).

crime; Farrington 1983a, for self-reports). This means that those who *continue* to offend – most desist – tend to do so at much the same rate from their teens until well into adulthood.

6. Those first convicted early (between 10 and 12) offend at a consistently higher rate and continue for a longer period of time than those first convicted at later ages (Farrington 1983a). West (1982) reported that, compared with early starters, those first convicted over the age of 18 were less likely to have deprived backgrounds and parents with criminal records.

7. There is less information available for the age of termination of offending than for the age of onset. Gibbens (1984) followed up 200 English boys who had served institutional sentences in their teens. After 10 years, 43 had no further reconvictions, but a further 15 years saw 14 of these reconvicted. Blumstein, Cohen, and Hsieh (1982) found that the residual career length of high-rate offenders peaked at 30–40

(that is, their criminal activities went into clear decline during these years, implying that incapacitation would have its major effect between 30 and 40 and not before (see Chapter 10).

8. Cullen, Wozniak, and Frank (1985) cite FBI statistics which indicate that the elderly constitute less than 1 per cent of the total offender population, a figure which has remained constant for many years. But it is at least possible that the criminal justice system is more lenient with the elderly – as with females (see Chapter 4), and there are some interesting data from Buckle and Farrington (1984). In their observational study of shoplifting, shoppers aged over 55 were significantly more likely to steal than those under this age (they give no information as to how age was estimated).

Why the strong relationship between age and crime? Farrington (1986) looks to biological factors (because physical strength and skills, important for many crimes such as burglary, peak in the teens) and to changes in the social environment at this time, which sees the culmination of the move away from parental control. After the age of 20, most young men marry, settle into steady jobs and leave delinquent peer groups. Wilson and Herrnstein (1985) also point to the increased numbers of legitimate sources of reward for what they term noncrime. The shifting pattern of costs and benefits with increasing age – for most offenders the costs of crime increase and the benefits decrease – is emphasized by Shover (1983), who suggests that many former high-rate and persistent offenders are eventually worn down by the increased surveillance and heavier punishments enforced by the criminal justice system.

Gender

"If men behaved like women, the Courts would be idle and the prisons empty" (Wootton 1959). This dramatic statement by one of Briain's most distinguished social scientists overstates the true situation, but the gender gap is indeed large, and any recent narrowing seems largely confined to relatively minor property offenses.

The gender gap is of long standing. Early in the 19th century Quetelet found that females accounted for less than 25 per cent of all arrests (Wilson and Herrnstein 1985). Farrington's detailed review (1979) indicates that the gap is still significant across a wide range of data sources. The following is based partially on his main conclusions.

1. US official statistics indicate that the male–female delinquency

prevalence ratio increases from 3.7 at age 13–14 to 5.2 at age 18 (FBI 1984). For juveniles aged 16, the ratio was highest for burglary (15.8), robbery (14.6), murder (10.2), and vehicle theft (8.8). It was close to the average ratio for all offences (4.6), for aggravated assault (5.6), and arson (5.2), and lowest for theft (2.7). Self-report data suggest rather lower, but still substantial, differences, both for overall ratios and for specific offenses. The National Youth Survey (Elliot, Dunford, and Huizinga 1983) found the self-reported gender ratios for overall prevalence to vary around around 2.9. The ratios were 4.2 for burglary, 2.7 for vehicle theft, and 5.5 for theft of over $50. The importance of the value of money involved in a theft for the sex ratio is shown in the Seattle self-report study in which the ratios for whites were only slightly above 1.0 for sums below $50 but increased to 9.6 for sums over $50 (Hindelang et al. 1981).

2. Sex ratios for *incidence* are rather lower than for prevalence, suggesting that once females have begun to offend they do so more like males. In the second Philadelphia cohort (Wolfgang and Tracy 1982) the gender ratio for the cumulative prevalence of delinquency was 2.3, while for incidence it was 1.8 (both from police records). Self-report data show a similar pattern (Elliot et al. 1983, National Youth Survey).

3. As indicated above, there is some tendency for women to gain on men with increasing age. For US official statistics (Farrington 1987a) the cumulative prevalence of convictions shows the highest gender ratio at 17 (5.6). Therafter, it declines steadily to 4.7 (age 21) and 3.0 (lifetime). The decline reflects the fact that over one fifth of males, as against only one tenth of females, had their first official offense before 21 – females start later and then slowly reduce the gap, although it still remains at ages 60–64 (a sex ratio of 2.3).

4. Victimization surveys confirm the overall gender gap. Women are only a small percentage of all offenders reported by victims (in 1976, 4 per cent of robberies and 5 per cent of burglaries, Nagel and Hagan 1983).

5. What of changes over time? A study by Cerncovich and Giordano (1979) of a single jurisdiction (Toledo, Ohio) from 1895 to 1975, a length of time unique in the literature, suggests that by the end of that period women were catching up with men for arrests. Smith and Visher (1980) analyzed 44 studies of varying methodological adequacy covering the period between 1946 and 1979. They found that the relative involvement of men and women was trending toward similarity for both self-

report and official data, with the rate of trend greater for the former. However, the gap was closing in minor crimes, rather than in major ones. The shift seemed to be stronger among young than among older women, implying that recent changes in the roles allowed for the sexes in many areas of life might be impinging on criminal behavior also.

Steffensmeier (1980a) carried out a detailed analysis of UCR data from 1965 to 1977 to test whether the earlier male–female gap was narrowing and, if so, for which offenses. He found that for violent and for serious crimes (excluding larceny) and white collar crimes, women were not catching up over the period studied. For larceny, fraud and forgery women made arrest "gains." Both adult and adolescent females made gains in larceny, and there were no changes in role behaviors for either older or younger women. He concludes that, in the decade and a half to 1977, sex differences in adult crime changed little. Nagel and Hagan (1983) are in general agreement. They divided offences into "masculine" ones (robbery, burglary and auto-theft) and petty property crimes. The former were still male preserves; in the latter women made some gains, but most of the "dollar threat" (the value of money or goods stolen) is still posed by men. A report by Franklin (1979) of a large retail organization in which most employees were women found that the majority of detected employee thefts were by men, and that male thefts involved larger sums. The reasons for the continued link between gender and crime are discussed in Chapter 5, and the possibility that a contribution to this may be made by a greater leniency towards women by the criminal justice system is raised in Chapter 4.

6. Thus far, male – female differences have been discussed without regard to ethnicity. Relatively few studies provide data, the earlier ones suggesting that black females were more similar to black males than white females were to their male counterparts. This is supported by the Seattle self-report study of Hindelang et al. (1981) which found that, for a range of serious offences, both property and personal, gender ratios were higher for whites than for blacks. (However, the doubts about the reliability of self-reports by black males with court records, noted earlier, suggest caution about this result.)

The descriptive profile of the "typical female offender" matches that for males: young, black, poorly educated, unemployed or in an unskilled job, unmarried and free of dependents (Wolfe, Cullen, and Cullen 1984, data from a Southern US city, 1969–1975). This takes us on to the next major demographic correlate of crime, the black–white distinction.

Ethnicity

There is no more tangled, complex and emotionally charged area in criminological research and penal practice than that of the contribution of the American black minority to crime. On the one hand, blacks are vastly over-represented in prison populations, in the official statistics of arrest and in victim reports for robbery and assault; on the other, the disparity in self-report data, while still present, is considerably less marked. For some commentators, the total pattern of evidence points to the probability of serious bias against blacks at every stage of the sequence from surveillance to sentence. Alternatively, if the disparity survives attempts to demonstrate bias, they implicate major social disadvantage as the explanation for the greater black involvement in crime; eliminate the disadvantage and you will eliminate the disparity in the crime figures.

For those who accept the reality of the black–white gap, the self-report data noted above are a serious embarrassment, to be accounted for by the unreliability of the self-report method with black respondents. The quantitative data on offending relevant to the dispute follow. Research concerning the possibility of official bias in arrest and sentencing is considered in Chapters 3 and 4, respectively, and the conditions of black life in American inner cities are discussed in Chapter 8.

1. On January 31, 1981, 46 per cent of the prisoners under state and Federal jurisdiction were black. In states such as New York, California, Texas and Florida, the 1981 incarceration rate for the black population was five times that for whites, in Michigan and Illinois it was nine to one and nationwide it was six to one (Chilton and Galvin 1983). Blacks are also over-represented in arrest figures: 26 per cent for all arrests; 34 per cent for all Index offenses, and 46 per cent for rape, robbery and assault (Federal Bureau of Investigation 1982). For 1983, the disparity was even more marked: 49 per cent of all arrests for rape, 39 per cent for aggravated assault, and 62.5 per cent for robbery; the percentages were as high or higher for those under 18 (Federal Bureau of Investigation 1983). Overall, blacks are also over-represented among arrests for property crime (by three to one) and for some white collar crimes (for fraud, forgery, counterfeiting and receiving, about one half of all

arrests, and for embezzlement, about one quarter). However, they are under-represented for tax frauds and for securities violations (Wilson and Herrnstein 1985, citing FBI data for 1981).

The Philadelphia study tells the same story: blacks offically recorded as offenders exceeded whites for both of the socio-economic levels into which the cohort was divided. The black–white disparity increased as the comparison moved from one-time offenders, through recidivists (two to four offences) to chronic offenders (more than four). It was clearest of all when the quantitative measure of seriousness was studied. For example, all 14 homicides were attributed to nonwhites, as were 38 out of the 44 rapes (Wolfgang et al. 1972). (The above figure for rape is likely to represent so minimal a proportion of the true number as to be useless as a basis for ethnic, or any other, comparisons.)

British data (e.g., Ouston 1984) support the picture of a significantly highter prevalence for blacks (definition: they or their parents were of West Indian origin), with the gap for females being higher than for males. Incidentally, for Britons of Asian origin (India, Pakistan, Bangladesh) the gap is in the opposite direction, with whites significantly exceeding Asians (Mawby, McCulloch, and Batta 1979). The same finding has been reported for California – white prevalence rates exceed Asian, in this case Japanese and Chinese (Elliot and Voss 1974).

2. To a considerable extent, black–white differences in the official statistics are in prevalence rather than in incidence. The number of crimes committed per year on the street is similar, but the proportion of blacks who commit at least one crime is much higher than the proportion of whites (Petersilia 1985, Blumstein and Graddy 1982). Similar conclusions were drawn by Wolfgang et al. (1972) for the Philadelphia survey and by Hindelang et al. (1981) for Seattle. This is an important link in the chain of evidence. It suggests that a higher proportion of blacks than whites have at least one contact with the police for offenses which *potentially* lead the offender along the track to prison, depending on a sequence of decisions made by representatives of the criminal justice system, from the police to judges.

3. Self-report data tell a rather different story to the official statistics. In the Seattle study, black–white ratios ranged between 0.8 and 1.3 for males, and 0.9 and 1.7 for females. The serious doubts of Hindelang and his colleagues as to the reliability of the self-report method with black males holding police records have already been mentioned.

Those responsible for the National Youth Survey (Elliot et al. 1983) felt much more confidence in the reliability of their data. For Index offenses black–white prevalence ratios varied between 1.0 and 1.5, and for incidence the variation was between 0.8 and 1.1. Individual Index offenses showed some variation: whites exceeded blacks for both prevalence and incidence for vehicle theft and theft over $50; blacks exceeded whites, for both comparisons, for aggravated assault, and the picture was mixed for burglary. Huizinga and Elliot (1984, p. 1.3) conclude:

> "There were few, if any, substantial and consistent differences between the delinquency involvement of different racial groups. This finding is not unique . . . it does not appear that differences in delinquent behavior can provide an explanation for observed race differentials in incarceration rates."

4. However, victim surveys do tend to support the official statistics as indicating a greater black involvement – at least in those offences in which the offender is visible. Hindelang (1978) noted that 62 per cent of those arrested for robbery were black, as were 62 per cent of those described by their victims, and Hindelang (1981) found that, for rape and assault, blacks were over-represented among arrestees compared with victim reports – but only by 10 per cent. This supports the view that self-report data *might* understate black–white differences in crime, because of under-reporting by some black official delinquents, so that genuine ethnic differences do exist. But, these could be due to the over-representation of American blacks in lower SES groups (75 per cent of the NYS black sample) and, hence, to the conditions of life among the less well-off, particularly the special nature of black poverty. Thus, compared with inner-city whites, blacks living in ghetto conditions might be both more likely to begin offending and to persist, rather than desist, because of the lesser availability to blacks of the rewards of noncrime.

Social class

Age is quite unequivocal as a way of differentiating between people (assuming an accurate birth certificate is available), and sex is also usually unarguable. Ethnicity is less certain (is a person with one black grandparent white or black?) but, in research practice, assignment to ethnic group does not seem to pose major problems. In contrast, social class is fraught with problems of definition which make it difficult to compare research reports and to interpret conflicting findings, as indicated by the following summary.

1. Both in the USA (Wolfgang et al. 1972, the Philadelphia study) and in the UK (Wadsworth 1975) there is a significant over-representation of working-class youth in the official statistics of offenders, in the former for both blacks and whites taken separately.

2. However, a review by Hindelang et al. (1981) of five American reports found only low or zero relationships between official delinquency and class – with the partial exception of the Philadelphia study in which there was a relationship at the level of area of residence but not at that of the individual. Braithwaite (1981) has argued that studies of class and crime must distinguish between subgroups within the working class (the "stable" and the "unstable") and that failure to do so explains the relative lack of reported relationships. However, Johnson (1980) was careful to separate out these two subgroups, and still found no more than a very modest correlation between self-reported offences and membership of either.

3. Indeed, the self-report literature is generally not supportive of a class–crime link (reviewed by Hindelang et al. 1981). In the Seattle study itself, a reverse record check found no differences in reporting overall according to social class, indicating the validity of the self-report measure for both classes. The results showed a small correlation with social class (measured by median income in the census tract concerned) of 0.17 at the level of the area of residence but not at the individual level (as in the Philadelphia data). There was a slight tendency for working class youth to be over-represented for vehicle theft and for the use of force in carrying out a theft, and there was a surplus of the middle class in drug offenses and check forgery. The NYS data led Elliot et al. (1983, P. 149) to conclude: "Class differences in both prevalence and incidence are found for serious offenses. For males, class differences are found in the incidence of nonserious delinquency and global delinquency."

4. It is worth remembering that, as a group, self-report studies are largely confined to teenagers. It is possible that, as suggested for blacks, lower-class youths in general may be somewhat more likely to begin offending earlier than other social classes, and considerably more likely to persist beyond the age at which most young people cease. Both trends may be particularly marked in the socially most deprived areas of cities, in which both law-abiding social models and the rewards for noncrime are sparse.

2.3. Victims

An account of the National Crime Survey was given in Chapter 1, together with the major findings on offenses which such surveys reveal. In this section, the focus is on victims, who they are and what they suffer, as well on the anticipatory fear of those who see themselves as potential victims.

Who are the victims?

An overview by Empey (1982) finds that young people are more vulnerable than their elders, males more than females, blacks more than whites, the poor more than the affluent (at least for violent crime) and city dwellers more than country people. When all these factors interact, the prototypic victim, particularly of violent crime, is a young, poor, black male, living in an urban ghetto, with the young, poor, white, male not far behind, followed closely by the young, poor, black female.

The 1984 British Crime Survey (BCS, Hough and Mayhew 1985) is in broad agreement, reporting that the least likely to be victims of violent crime are the elderly. Those most at risk were young men who spent several evenings out each week and drank heavily. Motor vehicles were the targets of one third of the property crimes covered by the BCS; those most at risk were those who left their cars on the street overnight. The average household could expect to be burgled once in 40 years, but this fell to once in 13 years for those in the inner cities. In a further analysis of BCS data, Sampson and Wooldredge (1987) confirmed that victimization rates were highest for the young, the single, and those who go out frequently at night and leave their homes empty. Burglary victimization was directly related to the proportion of single person dwellings in the community concerned, to unemployment, and to housing density.

For robbery, the highest rate American group (the young, the unemployed, low income, black, and living alone) had ten times higher than the average risk (NCS data for 1973 to 1980, Cohen, Cantor, and Kluegel 1981). Sparks (1982) states that larceny and burglary rates are highest for those at the extremes of the family income scale. The poor are vulnerable because they are the least able to protect their property and are in the closest proximity to burglars; the rich are vulnerable because they have more to be stolen. In the case of homicide, US males are twice as likely as females to be victims, with males aged 25–34 more likely than any other age–sex group and nonwhites 15 times more likely than whites (Holinger 1979).

A detailed analysis of NCS data for 1981 (Wilbanks 1985) indicates that violent crime is largely intraracial: whites choose whites as targets and are largely victimized by other whites; blacks are mainly victimized by other blacks. But black offenders are more likely to choose white victims than vice versa. Wilbanks considers that this implies different motives – black assaulters are strangers expressing hostility to whites in general; their white counterparts are largely known to their victims. Likewise, black rapists are expressing their hostility both to whites and to women; whites are expressing their anger against women only.

There is much support for the view that women suffer violence disproportionately, compared to men, at the hands of those they know well and from husbands/cohabitees especially (Worrall and Pease 1986, British Crime Survey data for 1982). Such crimes are reported significantly less often to the police than are assaults against males, irrespective of the degree of injury. Drawing on NCS data, Innes and Gressett (1982) found that the rising female labor force and changes in family structure both expose women to increased risks of victimization. The latter point relates to the rapid rise in the proportion of female-headed households. It is amplified by Sampson (1985), who draws on NCS data for 1973–5 to demonstrate that, compared with other citizens, vulnerability is greatest for females who are heads of households, living in poverty, in conditions of dense housing. Within this group, those with little knowledge of the area (presumably the most recently arrived) face additional risks.

Figures 2.3–2.5 represent personal victimization in the form of graphs (Fig. 2.3 by sex of victim, Fig. 2.4 by race, and Fig. 2.5 by age, in all cases for the same five Index crimes).

Effects on victims

The American Psychological Association Task Force on the Victims of Crime and Violence (Kahn 1984) listed the following as potential psychological consequences of victimization: depression, anxiety, paranoia, loss of control, shame, embarrassment, vulnerability, helplessness, humiliation, anger, shock, feelings of inequity, increased awareness of mortality, tension, malaise, and fear. There are also

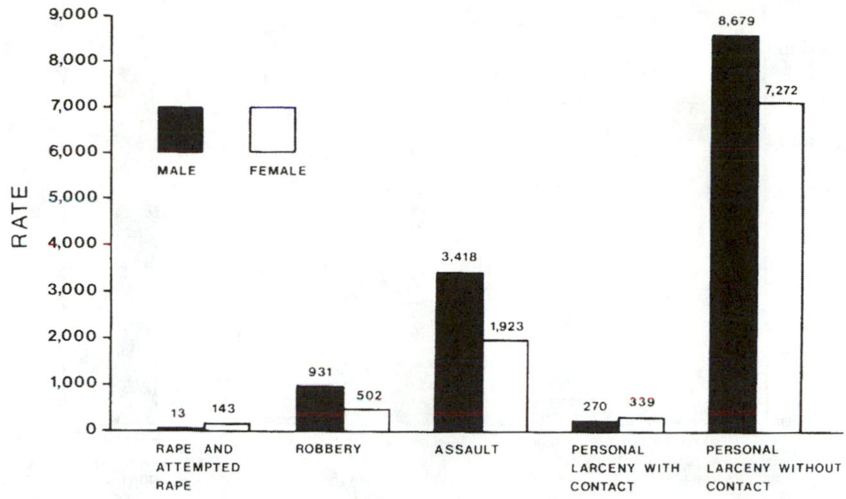

Figure 2.3. Estimated rate per 100,000 persons twelve years of age or older of personal victimization, by type of victimization and sex of victim, United States, 1982 (from Gottfredsen, M.R., 1986, Substantive contributions of victimization surveys, in M. Tonry, and N. Morris (Eds.), *Crime and Justice: An Annual Review of Research*, Vol. 7, p. 263. Chicago: University of Chicago Press).

potential interpersonal consequences: extreme mistrust of others, social isolation and difficulty in interacting with family and friends, divorce, and work difficulties. Obviously, not all of these results follow to the same extent for all victimizations and irrespective of the situation. At one extreme might be a prolonged rape involving serious injury and in the home of the victim; at the other, it might be the theft of a pocket book carelessly left in a public place and containing little of value. The worse the victim's mental health prior to the crime, the more severe the psychological impact (Biles, Braithwaite, and Braithwaite 1981).

Several hundred British burglary victims were interviewed by Maguire (1980) some weeks after the event. The response rate was 62 per cent; it is possible that the most distressed were under-represented. The most frequent male response was anger; females were more likely to recall fear or shock. Although only 4 per cent of the sample came face-to-face with the intruder, 6 per cent were described as still acutely

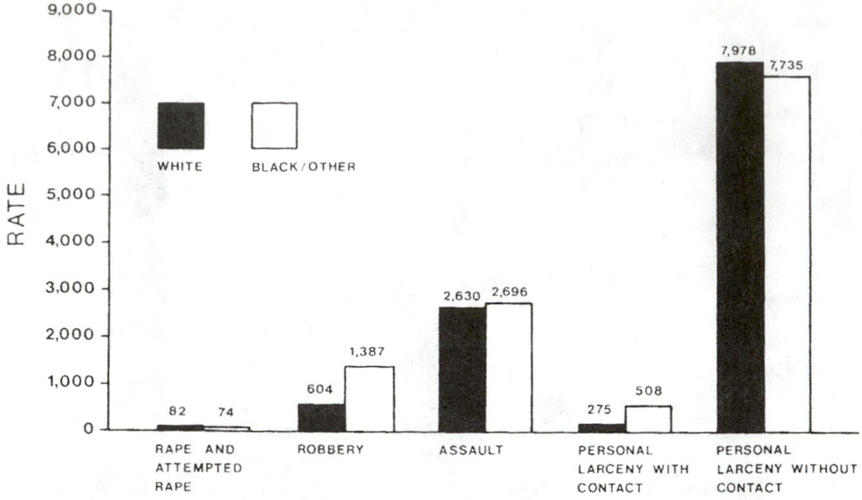

Figure 2.4. Estimated rate per 100,000 persons twelve years of age or older of personal victimization, by type of victimization and race of victim, United States, 1982 (from Gottfredsen, M.R., 1986, Substantive contributions of victimization surveys in M. Tonry, and N. Morris (Eds.), *Crime and Justice: An Annual Review of Research*, Vol. 7, p. 264. Chicago: University of Chicago Press).

distressed, most of whom were elderly working-class females. The next level of distress, "considerable impact", comprised 19 per cent and also comprised a majority of females. Overall, 65 per cent still felt some kind of an effect four to ten weeks after the burglary, and 15 per cent were still frightened to be alone in the house. Generally, the emotional impact was greater than the financial loss, and the worst effected were single, divorced or widowed women. Victims of serious crime who subsequently changed their telephone numbers were found by Wirtz and Harrell (1987) to have higher levels of psychological distress 6 months after the crime than 1 month after; those who did not change their numbers declined in reported distress over the period. Some victims suffer long term effects, and Wirtz and Harrell also found that a range of individual and community responses intended to help them had little significant effect on the recovery process.

A review by Skogan (1987) confirmed the complex relationship between victimization and subsequent fear of crime. For some victims,

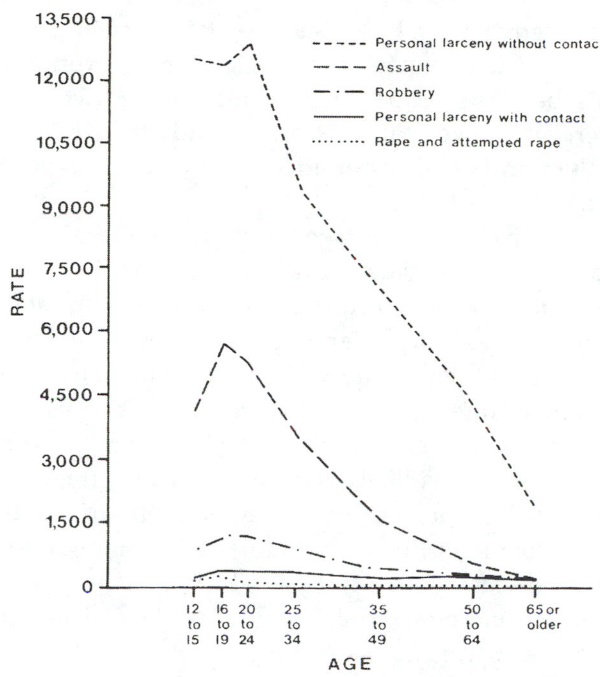

Figure 2.5. Estimated rate per 100,000 persons twelve years of age or older of personal victimization, by type of victimization and age of victim, United States, 1982 (from Gottfredsen, M.R., 1986, Substantive contributions of victimization surveys, in M. Tonry, and N. Morris (Eds.), *Crime and Justice: An Annual Review of Research*, Vol. 7, p. 265. Chicago: University of Chicago Press).

fear increased, for others the experience actually reduced it, particularly for those who had taken subsequent precautions (e.g., installed better locks, taken out insurance, went out after dark in groups, etc; the issue of "target-hardening" is discussed in Chapter 12).

For his own study, Skogan (1987) interviewed over 1,700 residents of single family dwellings, nearly all black, in seven selected high crime areas of Newark, NJ, and Houston, TX. The first interview was carried out prior to victimization, the second, one year later, when a proportion had experienced a crime. Most victims reported a decrease in distress in the months after victimization, but for some the effects persisted, or even increased. Several variables affected the response: social isolation, poverty of resources (low income, poor education) and being female and elderly were all associated with prolonged/increasing distress, as was a previous experience of victimization (prior to the study) when this had been coped with badly. Rape victims suffer particularly severe psychological distress in addition to frequent physical injury; the former is compounded by the attitudes of family, police and courts (Osborne 1982).

Should victims fight back? Ziegenhagen and Brosnan (1985) analyzed a 13-city National Crime Panel data set of 3,679 robbery incidents, and concluded that victim resistance to robbery is not often associated with serious injury, but is linked to preventing the successful execution of the crime. Thus victims can limit crime. This is in contrast to the advice these authors claim is often given by criminal justice system professionals, namely to exchange property losses in return for escaping physical injury. However, it is likely that most citizens, unless highly proficient in martial arts or themselves armed, will follow the advice of the professionals, seeing their first duty to themselves and not to crime control. Chapter 9 discusses the factors which enhance or reduce aggressive behavior, including having the capacity for retaliation, being prepared to use it, and adversary awareness of both.

The fear of crime

A number of studies agree that the fear of crime is a rational response to the possibility, or the actual experience, of victimization. A national US sample of nearly 1,500 (Baumer 1985) indicated that fear was much greater in large cities than in small towns and rural areas, and in women and the elderly than in males and the young. The 1982 British Crime Survey (Maxfield 1984) reported similar results. In this study, 60 per cent of elderly women in inner cities felt very unsafe walking alone at night. It is an apparent paradox that the group most at risk in this situation – young males – is also the least fearful The paradox is resolved by the fact that a very large proportion of those most fearful of crime avoid the situations they most fear. Indeed, 12 per cent of the population of the inner cities say they never go out at night. These are likely to be old people living alone, for whom fear of crime further reduces the quality of already impoverished lives. Were they to go out as freely as the young it seems likely that their victimization rates would be significantly in excess of those of young males: hence, the above conclusion of the rationality of fear of street crime by the inner-city elderly. By staying at home the elderly can avoid being attacked in the street. But this still leaves victimization in their own dwellings, and they report being particularly fearful of fraudulent entry by a stranger (posing as an official, or as a service person, etc., Jones, 1987). For citizens of all ages, it is the combination of a high probability of victimization and the seriousness of the anticipated crime which produces the most fear, and fear is most disabling when coping responses are not available – because coping resources are minimal or the anticipated distress is so great as seriously to hinder advance counter-measures (Warr 1987).

Crime is a source of great distress, but has also a continuing allure. Murder has always been a major theme both of serious literature (there are more than 60 murders in Shakespeare's plays) and of "light" entertainment – the crime novel has figured in the list of best sellers since its first appearance over a century ago. When Agatha Christie "killed off" her famous private detective Hercules Poirot he had front page obituaries. Criminals are romanticized, from *Bonnie and Clyde* to *The Godfather*.

The British public much admired the 1964 Great Train Robbery, in which 15 men held up the Glasgow-London mail train and escaped with $8 million – at that time a record. "As a certain newspaper guy in one of the Runyon stories puts it, many legitimate guys are much interested in the doings of tough guys and consider them very romantic." (Iddon 1954, p. 5).

3. The police

> . . . The protection of life and property, the preservation of public tranquility and the absence of crime will alone prove whether the objects for which the police were appointed have been attained. . . . [These] instructions . . . are not to be understood as containing rules of conduct applicable to every variety of circumstance that may occur in the performance of their duty; something must necessarily be left to the intelligence and discretion of individuals. . . . [Be] civil and attentive to all persons of every rank and class.
> (From the instructions given to the London Metropolitan Police, the World's first fully professional force, by their first Commissioner, C. Rowan, 1829.)

This chapter deals in the main with the topics which were at the heart of the tasks set out by Commissioner Rowan: functions; effectiveness; discretion; behavior toward the public. It also includes two topics which Rowan did not mention; the police as people, including training, stress, and misbehavior, and the place of interrogation and confessions in police work.

3.1. History

Three major police strategies, watching, walling and walking, all concerning with crime prevention, have persisted from pre-industrial times to the present day (Sherman 1983). Watching involves the surveillance of potential targets, often by volunteers; its current incarnation is Neighborhood Watch (see below). Walling, now termed "target hardening," means making the target more difficult to get at, by strengthening defences of all kinds. It is discussed in detail in Chapter 12. Walking, which today may mean patrolling in a police car, uses by far the most public finance and an increasing share of private resources, and is the most intrusive on civil liberties.

In pre-industrial societies, watching was not only a key form of social control but was also one of the few entertainments available to the bulk of the population (Sherman 1983). By the 15th century, English village society assigned watch duties to adult males in turn. They were unpaid, but the wealthy hired substitutes. By the 18th century, England had developed a full time force, paid for from taxes, but its major shortcomings led to a fresh start in 1829 and the formation of the Metropolitan Police.

For many years the police foot patrol officer walked his "beat," watching, accumulating local knowledge, and picking up gossip. This system was then replaced by the two-officer patrol car, aimed at making a rapid response, usually to a telephoned request, but with no local contacts, so that the police role shifted from crime prevention to waiting to respond to the commission of a crime.

American developments

Until well into the 19th century, American local governments had very limited powers to administer the criminal law. Enforcement was often left to the victim, and individual initiative was encouraged by the offer of rewards for the capture of badly wanted felons. Groups formed impromptu posses to chase offenders or break up disorderly crowds, and there was a combination of watchmen, constables, sheriffs, and marshals. The system was cheap and the costs fell largely on complainants or victims, who paid fees for each item of service (Lane 1980).

However, after three major riots in four years, Boston commissioned a small group of city police in 1838. New York followed in 1844 and Philadelphia in 1854. The first American detective bureau to be part of a police department was set up in 1846, and was soon copied. The London model of a uniformed police force met stiff resistance but was eventually followed. There was little opposition to the police being armed – unlike the practice in London. The first National Police Convention was held in 1874, and in the late 1890's the International Association of Chiefs of Police was formed. Since then the major American developments have been the formation of the Federal Bureau of Investigation (a national organization – police forces are still under local control), an increased emphasis on prevention and, ironically, a marked revival of private policing by businesses and affluent neighborhoods (Lane 1980). There are large differences in the selection, training and organization of police departments at the different levels (state, county, city, and local) at which they operate (Lockhart 1983). Today, there are about 25,000 police forces in the USA. This seems an extreme case of decentralization; many European countries have national police forces and, even though Britain retains the principle of local control, the trend is toward amalgamation – there are now only 43 separate police forces. In the USA, the control of the police is both local and political; in Western Europe, control varies, but is usually more remote from the political level than in America.

3.2. Police functions

The relative lack of research on police behavior and functioning has been documented by Sherman (1980). That there is no lack of potential research issues is made clear by a nearly exhaustive listing of police functions set out by Bayley (1979). Each is performed in at least one Western country; most are true of the USA.

1. Protecting life and property.
2. Enforcing the criminal law.
3. Investigating criminal offenses.
4. Patrolling public places.
5. Advising about crime prevention.
6. Conducting prosecutions.
7. Sentencing for minor offenses.
8. Maintaining order in public places.
9. Guarding persons and facilities.
10. Regulating traffic.
11. Controlling crowds.
12. Regulating and supressing vice.
13. Counselling juveniles.
14. Gathering information on social and political life.
15. Monitoring elections.
16. Conducting counter-espionage.
17. Issuing ordinances.
18. Inspecting premises.
19. Issuing permits and licences.
20. Serving summonses.
21. Supervising jails.
22. Impounding animals and lost property.
23. Advising members of the public and referring them to other agencies.

24. Caring for the incapacitated.
25. Promoting community crime prevention activities.
26. Participating in the policy councils of government.

This very wide range of tasks led Bayley (1979) to define the police as a group authorized in the name of the community to use force within the community to handle whatever needs doing.

Measures of police activity

Bayley (1979) proposes three measures.

1. Formal assignments of personnel. Most attention is attracted by patrolling, criminal investigation, traffic regulation and auxiliary administration, but police activity aimed at preventing crime has also grown greatly – special units work with high risk groups, with juveniles, with recidivists and so on.

2. Occasions for action. This includes the development of specialized units (traffic, criminal investigation, community relations, riot control, etc.). Patrol officers spend much of their time as peace officers. Differences in patrol work will depend on such factors as public confidence in the police (the greater this is, the more requests for help), police emphasis on crime prevention (the greater, the more will noncrime requests for assistance be taken seriously), and the size of the force per unit of population (the smaller this is, the more the police will concentrate on criminal investigation).

3. Outcomes. Because police action is discretionary, outcomes of actions can vary greatly, from nothing recorded to arrest and prosecution. The police can decide not to enforce the law for the following reasons: the matter is judged too trivial to tie up resources; enforcement is judged to be against the preferences of the community; enforcement might close down a useful source of information (Kadish and Kadish 1973). There is always the possibility that police discretion might shade into police bias.

Community policing

According to Skolnick and Bayley (1988), there is an increasing consensus among police chiefs from California to Singapore that the current move towards community policing (CP) is highly desirable. Merely heightening police activity in the face of rising crime seems to have relatively little effect (see below), and the associated rise in public fear necessitates both a shift towards prevention and increasing the involvement of the public. In short, the police and the community should become "co-producers of crime prevention." CP has four main elements (Skolnick and Bayley 1988):

1. Community based crime prevention. The center piece of this is the Neighborhood Watch system – groups of local citizen volunteers who work with the police mainly by watching and reporting (its effectiveness is discussed in Chapter 12). The most highly developed and long-standing version is in Japan, where local groups distribute information, sell security hardware, publish newsletters, maintain close liason with the police and occasionally patrol the streets.

2. The reorientation of patrol activities. This means the shift of a large portion of police personnel from the emergency response system to crime prevention. The most dramatic change is the redeployment of police from motor vehicles into small decentralized police posts (called *koban* in Japan, mini-stations in Detroit), where they organize Neighborhood Watch schemes, teach self-protection and advise institutions with special security needs. There is also a widespread return of foot-patrols, which deepen, extend and personalize police–public interactions.

3. Increased public accountability. CP involves not only listening sympathetically but also creating opportunities to do so as well as a shift from the "steward" model (the police chief publishes an annual report) to the "partner" model.

4. The decentralization of command. Local sub-station commanders are free to adapt to local priorities and problems, but this means that the police must be able to think on their feet and act without referring to more senior officers.

Community policing thus threatens traditional police roles, and requires new skills and perceptions. Skolnick and Bayley (1988) list potential obstacles to CP, from the culture of policing (newcomers learn from established officers to be suspicious of "outsiders" – including the general public – rather than co-operating with them), through the need to shift from the two-officer car to the single-officer (and hence more lonely) foot-patrol, to the inertia of police unions who suspect CP will reduce the size of police forces. Yet there should be benefits to the police as well as to the public, such as greater job-satisfaction, professional stature and career development.

To date, there is little hard evidence on the value of CP. Skolnick and Bayley (1988) cite a 1 year pilot project in Singapore in which, compared with control areas, CP areas saw a decline in serious crime, a rise in reports of minor crime, and an increase in an already high sense of public security. American studies seem to be handicapped by a lack of effective implementation of intended changes. Also, the image of the policeman as "thief-taker", rather than as "crime-prevention officer," dies hard with both public and police. For both, it is criminal investigation – carried out by plain-clothes detectives – where the action is.

Criminal investigation

The most comprehensive study was one carried out by the Rand Corporation at the request of The National Institute of Law Enforcement and Justice (Chaiken, Greenwood, and Petersilia 1979). It included a questionnaire survey of over 150 of the 300 law enforcement departments with over 150 full-time employees, on-site investigations of 25 of them and the detailed monitoring of the activities of individual investigators and supervisors over several days. Statistical and file data were also available. The main results were as follows:

1. Because of wide variations in definitions and practices, neither clearance nor arrest statistics for Index crimes is a suitable measure of police effectiveness. Administrative discretion plays a major part in the former, and "arrests" can be made for an "investigation" with no subsequent charge. Moreover, both reflect the activities of uniformed patrol officers and the public more than those of investigators. In fact, only 2.7 per cent of all Index crimes cleared could be attributed to the special techniques used – the sifting of forensic evidence, the methodical elimination of suspects, and the use of informers. (But those crimes which were cleared did include the most publicly visible crimes, particularly homicide and commercial burglary. For all the rest the contributions of victims, witnesses, and patrol officers are more important.) A broadly similar picture emerges from research in Britain (Hough and Heal 1982).

2. Many cases receive no more attention from an investigator than a quick reading of the initial crime incident report. However, homicide and rape invariably result in investigatory activity, and at least 60 per cent of all other serious crimes receive a minimum of one half hour of detective time. It follows that the average detective does not work on a large number of cases per month and may have a backlog of hundreds, even thousands. Most case-work time is spent in reading and review-

ing, and in locating and interviewing victims. In cases which are solved, detectives spend more time in postclearance processing than in identifying the perpetrator. About 25 per cent of detective time is spent on crimes never solved (and easily recognizable as insoluble from the start, according to the researchers).

3. Few crimes are solved by fingerprint collection and identification, but increased effort at the former is more productive than the latter. A study by Stenross (1984) suggests that fingerprints are collected after a burglary according to the level of distress of the victim – if force was involved and/or the objects stolen were of sentimental value.

4. Police interviewees justified criminal investigation because of contacts with the victim, but in most cases the police responded, filed a brief report, and then made little subsequent contact.

The Rand report recommended that the police should try to enhance public involvement, by emphasizing the part played by the public whenever a major crime is solved. Mitchell (1984) found that victims or their friends or relatives provided the police with evidence relevant to the identity of the defendant in more than half of a sample of cases he examined. The reliability of eyewitness reports is discussed in Chapter 4, and the role of bystanders in crime prevention in Chapter 12.

Hough and Heal (1982, p. 35) sum up criminal investigation research as follows:

> ". . . crimes fall into two main categories: those which are difficult to detect and those which are easy . . . even if resources were increased the detection rate would in all probability be only marginally affected . . . but . . . crimes of spectacular outrage are in most cases eventually cleared up (even if good luck plays an important part in their detection) . . . some research suggests that clearance rates improved when investigative departments were reorganized on team policing lines".

Interrogation and confession. Interrogation by the police is an integral part of criminal procedure (Inman 1981, Hilgendorf and Irvine 1981). While there are obvious social and psychological elements, there has been little systematic research (Farrington 1981).

Confessions are difficult to retract and lead to strong pressures from all sides to plead guilty, so saving the court's time and enabling the case concerned to join the list of those cleared. In Britain, 70 per cent of interrogations lead to confessions; only 4 per cent of those charged with indictable offences (roughly similar to Index cases) are given a jury trial; confessions by the majority of those charged expedite the criminal justice process.

In both Britain and the USA, confessions are part of what Inman (1981) calls the low visibility side of the system, the other elements of which, the pre-trial handling of suspects, bail, and plea bargaining, are considered in the next chapter. Inman asserts that confessions by the accused are second only to mistaken identity as causes of wrongful conviction. Hilgendorf and Irvine (1981) state that they are often retracted with the same apparent spontaneity and conviction as when they were made.

During the past 55 years a series of highly publicized political trials in communist countries have produced "confessions" of guilt by former pillars of the regime concerned. The process by which these were produced is brilliantly described by Koestler (1940).

Inman (1981) considers that, under appropriate conditions, most people can be induced to confess, whether or not they are guilty. The anxiety evoked by the procedure leads to an increased talkativeness – even when the accused is informed of his rights. "Get them to make the first admission, no matter how small: 'yes, I drink a lot'. You've immediately got them going" (British police officer, cited by Deeley 1971). Both the conditions of the interrogation and the manner of the interrogator may increase the probability of a confession. The suspect is away from familiar and supportive surroundings, often in a stark room with a special arrangement of furniture, interrogator and suspect are in close proximity, and the power and the ability of the former to take the initiative are strongly emphasized. It is useful for the interrogator to feign sympathy, to express concern for the welfare of the suspect and to deceive him as to the strength of the evidence against him. Cautions as to silence and other rights may be delivered so as to minimize their impact, particularly if the suspect is poorly educated or overwrought.

Vulnerability and persuasion are helped by displays of sympathy by one of two interrogators, the other being authoritarian in manner but subordinate to the first. Confessions, particularly if made in the absence of threats, lead the confessor to believe in their truth, a clear deduction from the theory of cognitive dissonance (Festinger 1957).

Hilgendorf and Irvine (1981) consider that all confessions involve a reliability risk, and that certain circumstances of interrogation carry that risk to the point of inadmissibility. It should therefore be in the interests of the police and courts to detect a false confession at the point at which it is made, by improving police training in interrogation (e. g., reduce directive questions and check the information given by the suspect).

As indicated, empirical research is in its infancy. Farrington (1981), who observed 76 interrogation interviews of 60 different suspects on behalf of the 1981 Royal Commission on Criminal Procedure, concluded that his work was little more than hypothesis generating. But it seems a reasonable guess that the more experienced the suspect in the "rules of the game" the less likely will be a false confession. However, it is just the beginner who needs most to be protected from a course of action which might lead him on to the track of repeated offences and increasingly severe sentencing.

3.3. Police effectiveness

Both the general public and many senior police officers believe that crime can be curbed either by increasing the severity of punishment, spending more on the police, or both. The first belief is discussed in Chapter 10 under the general heading of deterrence; the second is considered below.

Police manpower and crime

In the British context, Carr-Hill and Stern (1979) concluded: (i) areas with high levels of policing have high rates of crime; (ii) the higher the clearance rate in an area, the lower the crime rate; (iii) the more police that are allocated to an area, the lower the clearance rate. They attribute these results to an increase in police manpower leading to more crimes being recorded, allowing no conclusions to be drawn about police effectiveness from manpower research.

In line with this view, two American studies (Loftin and McDowall 1982, and Bennett and Bennett 1983) concluded that the police manpower effect was virtually nonexistent unless very large variations, well outside normal practice, are introduced. Specific variations in manpower levels are looked at below.

Conventional patrol

Studies of *foot*-patrol go back over 35 years, but the early ones were methodologically unsatisfactory. A thorough analysis in Newark, New

Jersey (Police Foundation 1981) found removing or adding patrols to have no effect on crime, whether measured by recorded rates or victim surveys. However, increased foot-patrol did lessen the fear of crime, an outcome of some significance.

A careful study of *mobile* patrol was carried out in Kansas City (Kelling 1974). Variations in patrol level had no effect on crime (again by either recorded crimes or by victim surveys); nor was the fear of crime affected (mobile patrol is inherently less visible than foot-patrol). Studies of "fast response" by mobile patrol have been similarly negative (Sherman 1983). Improvement in response time seems unlikely to produce more arrests, because most victims turn to friends or neighbors before calling the police.

Specialized patrol

Several studies indicate that specialized patrol, an aspect of deterrent policing now in widespread use under a variety of names, achieves some impact on crime but also raises a number of problems. Increasing the number of uniformed patrols in the New York subway system reduced subway crime but robbery on buses increased, suggesting displacement to easier targets (Chaiken, Lawless, and Stevenson 1974). However, other American studies have similarly indicated the effectiveness, both of "saturation" patrolling (Schnelle et al. 1977), and of "targeting" well known criminals (Pate, Bowers, and Parks 1976), in both cases without displacement.

Sampson and Cohen (1988) argue that police departments with a legalistic style generate policies of proactive (i.e., deterrent) patrol by a high traffic citation rate and frequent stops of suspicious/disorderly persons. This, in turn, may decrease the crime rate, either directly, by increasing the probability of arrest, or indirectly, through the general deterrent effect of increased social control. To test these propositions, they examined robbery rates in 171 American cities for 1980 and found that proactive policing did reduce robbery rates independently of such determinants of crime as poverty, inequality, and family disruption, the effect being greatest for adults and for black offenders.

As against this positive support for deterrent policing, problems associated with specialized patrolling include considerable expense, and a reputation for heavy-handedness in the area covered, as well as the possibility of displacement (Hough and Heal 1982).

Police strikes

The absence of a service gives an opportunity to evaluate its general impact. Some police strikes (for example, Boston in 1919 and Montreal in 1969) have resulted in widespread looting and disorder. Others, such as the 1971 strike in New York which lasted six days and involved 85 per cent of the patrol force, were not associated with a loss of order. A survey by Pfuhl (1983) of 11 US cities examined the impact of municipal police strikes on reported rates of robbery, larceny, burglary and auto-theft. He concluded that strikes had neither a systematic nor a significant effect: a victim survey would have been preferable.

Concluding comment

It seems likely that police *visibility* is as important for many citizens, particularly those most fearful of crime, women and the elderly, as police effectiveness, as measured by its actual impact on crime. Moreover, as Hough and Heal (1982, p. 46) conclude in explaining why the gains from additional deterrent policing are likely to be negligible: "Small increases [in the risks of being caught] may simply not be noticed by offenders; large increases may be achieved only at considerable cost – in terms both of finance and of disrupted community relations. Deterrent policing may have the unintended consequence of amplifying criminal behavior – by reducing the opportunities for convicted offenders for going 'straight', by fueling resentment against authority, or by confirming people's conception of themselves as law-breakers."

The evidence for such effects of police activity is discussed below, and further in Chapter 8 under the heading of labeling theory. Hough and Heal argue for: "A reallocation of responsibility for crime control from the police to the community [and] an inversion of the conventional proposition that the police need the help of the public in fighting crime. People need the help of the police in protecting themselves against crime" (Hough and Heal 1982, p. 47). As the two principal means of self-protection they suggest opportunity reduction, for example by target hardening, and emphasizing the community element of community policing. Both themes are taken up in Chapter 12.

3.4. Police discretion

Two statements by Chambliss (1969) give the flavor of work on police discretion. In the first, he claims that those persons are arrested, tried and sentenced, who can offer the fewest rewards for nonenforcement of the law and who can be processed without creating any undue strain for the organizations which comprise the legal system. The second spells out his position so as to allow an empirical test. It asserts that the "lower-class" person is (i) more likely to be scrutinized and therefore to be observed in any violation of the law; (ii) more likely to be arrested if discovered under suspicious circumstances; (iii) more likely to spend the time between arrest and trial in jail; (iv) more likely to be found guilty; and (v) if found guilty, more likely to receive a harsh punishment than his middle- or upper-class counterpart. In all cases, it can be assumed that Chambliss would intend these statements to predict a greater severity toward blacks than whites – indeed most of the research evidence concerns ethnicity rather than class. The first two propositions concern the police and are discussed below; the next three are within the discretion of prosecuting lawyers, jurors, and judges and will be taken up in the next chapter.

Surveillance

Matza (1969, p. 183) stated: "The main bias . . . follows from how and where the police look when no one has fallen under suspicion". Patrol levels and police conscientiousness may both vary; do they do so significantly and, if so, in relation to the objective characteristics of an area, such as a high rate of crime, or does any variation discovered relate to the attributes of persons known to live in the area (class, race, etc.)?

Differential patrol, as a descriptive fact, seems likely, although direct evidence is hard to come by. Gibbons and Krohn (1986, p. 92) state:" . . . police patrol and surveillance activities are differentially concentrated in minority communities." Differential police surveillance is one possible explanation of Belsons' (1975) London finding that the better-educated sons of better-off fathers were markedly less likely to be apprehended than their less well-educated and less well-off counterparts – but there is no way of testing this from his data.

Further inferential evidence comes from an analysis by Sampson (1986) of information from the 171 US cities which, in 1980, had a population of over 100,000. Sampson combined census data, such as economic and family variables, with official sanctions, such as arrest rates, to produce "demographic specific" offending rates and sanction measures. He also recorded the level of "police aggression" in each locality. Aggression was defined as the number of arrests per officer for disorderly conduct and drunken driving (on the assumption that a high level of police activity for minor offenses implied a very high level indeed for more major ones; see above for data from Sampson and Cohen (1988) on "proactive policing"). One of his findings was a significant inverse effect of police aggression on robbery rate (the greater the level of aggression, the lower the rate) which was due almost entirely to its deterrent effect on black offenders. Sampson suggests that this may stem from differential patrolling policies (higher levels in black neighborhoods than in white), but did not test this hypothesis directly.

Disposal

There are major variations in police actions following contact with a suspect, but is the variation related to legal features such as the seriousness of the offence, the strength of the already available evidence and so on, or to extra-legal features (once again, class and race)?

Wilson (1968) studied the police departments of "Eastern" and "Western" cities, both with a population of more than 300,000. The police of the former (described as modern and professional) arrested a larger proportion of those in contact with the police than did those of the latter (described as informal and fraternal). Major changes over the years, within the same police departments, in the proportion of juveniles stopped by the police and referred to the courts, have been reported by McEachern and Bauzer (1967) and Bordua (1967).

Does the undoubted variation in disposal involve bias against particular groups? In general terms, cautioning, rather than arrest, is more likely with younger suspects (Hood and Sparks 1970), females (Walker 1965), and middle-class as opposed to working-class boys (Gold 1966).

So far as ethnicity is concerned the earlier studies gave a mixed picture. Both Black and Reiss (1970) and Lundman, Sykes, and Clark (1978) portray the police "as operating in a relatively legalistic fashion, rather than in terms of prejudices and biases. The police seem to be more impressed by the nature and seriousness of offences than by any other factor" (Gibbons and Krohn 1986, p. 90). Other studies (e.g., Ferdinand and Luchterhand 1970,) reported different results, supporting the view that higher rates of referral to court of black male juveniles were not simply due to the greater seriousness of their offense. And Wolfgang et al. (1972), in their Philadelphia study, found that, whereas 13 per cent of white "one-time" offenders were arrested (as opposed to some less severe action), the figure was 30 per cent for blacks. These authors comment: "However we split and splice the material at hand, nonwhites received more severe dispositions" (Wolfgang et al. 1972, p. 220).

Landau (1981) reported that while legal variables played a major role in the decision of the London Metropolitan Police to arrest or not, some nonlegal factors, such as ethnic group membership, also had a significant effect, with blacks involved in violence and burglary being treated more harshly than whites.

Two particularly well-conducted more recent studies provide support for the assertion of police bias against blacks in arrests. Huizinga and Elliot (1987) analyzed NYS data and found no significant differences between blacks and whites either for delinquent behavior overall or for high frequency offending. Nor did blacks carry out offenses involving greater physical injury to victims or the use of weapons. What did distinguish blacks from whites was the greater chance of being arrested. For less serious offences the black/white disparity in arrest rate was 7:1; for more serious ones it was 2:1. These results indicate that blacks are at a higher risk of arrest than whites given the same apparent behavior.

A large scale observational study by Smith (1986) collected data from 60 neighborhoods served by 24 police departments in three metropolitan areas. In all, nearly 5,700 police–citizen contacts were observed on 900 patrol shifts. Arrests were significantly more likely when the complainant requested an arrest and when the suspect was black and male and acted antagonistically towards the police. Also, the police used more coercive authority towards blacks than whites (defined as the threatened, or actual, use of force by the police when the suspect was unarmed). Complicating these results were the findings that the police were less likely to file reports involving black than white victims (implying under-recording of offences by blacks) and that suspects encountered in lower-status neighborhoods ran three times the risk of arrest as compared to those met in the highest status neighborhoods, independent of type of crime, race of suspect and his demeanor. The neighborhood of a police–suspect encounter thus emerges as important, alongside the ethnicity of the suspect. The decision to arrest or not was more constant the more serious the offence.

A reasonable conclusion is that, with all other factors held constant, there are real differences between police departments, and perhaps even between individual police officers within the same department, in the extent of bias against blacks. Some officers will be found to show little or no bias, others a considerable amount. Any discrimination according to race is likely to be found more reliably for the less serious crimes.

Police–juvenile encounters

Differences in the demeanor of suspects and in the ways in which police relate to suspects have attracted most attention in attempts to explain black/white variations in the chances of being arrested, purely legal factors, such as offense seriousness, being held equal.

There are several relevant reports. None is entirely satisfactory, because none involves the direct and systematic observation of a random set of juvenile–police encounters over a sustained period of time. Nevertheless, because they all point in the same direction, their cumulative effect is to support the view that what happens in the course of police–juvenile encounters helps to explain police decision-making in general and, in particular, decisions to arrest or not.

Bordua (1967) found that Detroit police filed petitions (i.e., brought suspects to court) in 67 per cent of cases identified as showing "honest" attitudes, as against 80 per cent of those displaying "antisocial" attitudes. Sellin and Wolfgang (1964) reported that the police in Philadelphia based their dispositional decisions on both legal considerations and on nonlegal ones, such as the general appearance of the offender and his or her attitude toward the police.

The largest and still the best study was reported by Piliavin and Briar (1964) over a quarter of a century ago, based on field notes of police–juvenile encounters over a 9 month period. In the 10 per cent of cases which were serious, arrest was almost universal, and irrespective of offender attributes or behavior, but in the remainder, police decisions were influenced by extra-legal factors. On-the-spot identifications as "bad-guys" led to more severe dispositions, Youths so described were often older boys, and blacks, and those who failed to display the deference many police officers felt to be appropriate. There was a vicious circle in urban ghettoes:

> "Police harassment of 'suspicious' black youths led those youngsters to see police contacts as a routine . . . aspect of their lives. In turn they responded in a hostile or indifferent manner to the

> police who then felt little compunction about referring them to court in large numbers. The high arrest and referral rate for black youths was then taken by the police as evidence in support of the stereotype of most blacks as potential criminals" (Gibbons and Krohn 1986).

Similar results were reported by Werner et al. (1975), the key behaviors required by police of juveniles being politeness, cooperation, presenting prompt evidence of identity, and answering questions. Garrett and Short (1975) suggest that the presentation of a "cooperative" demeanor may be hindered for some youths, questioned in the presence of their peers, by a contrary requirement (modeled and reinforced by the same peers) to appear tough and hostile even at the cost of a more severe response by the police. Box (1971) asserts that middle-class persons are better at creating the impression desired by the police, and women may, on average be more socially skilled than men, so that the combination of being lower-class, male and black is the one most likely to result in the vicious circle described above by Gibbons and Krohn (1986) and by Hough and Heal (1982, p. 39) as follows:

> ". . . the slightest suspicion that the police are acting heavy-handedly or discriminating against particular groups, such as blacks, can precipitate a downward spiral of antagonism between the police and increasingly large sections of the population".

This is all very different from the 1829 injunctions of Commissioner Rowan, set out at the beginning of this chapter. But we should not be surprised: the police are human beings, with human prejudices, and tendencies to stereotypic thinking and short cuts in action, tendencies which may be reinforced by the special and largely separate world in which policemen spend their daily lives, both at work and at leisure.

3.5. The police as people

There is a scarcity of research about the psychological and social aspects of the judiciary and of attorneys, probably as important as the behavior of the police in explaining the operation of the criminal justice system. In contrast, we have some information about the police, from their personality and training, through police misbehavior, to the nature and effects of the stress of police work.

Who are the police?

In both America (Bayley and Mendelsohn 1969) and Britain (Box 1971) the police are young, with 25 per cent of uniformed police under 25 and another quarter under 30. Their parental occupations tend to be skilled manual or a little higher. There is little recruitment from professional and managerial backgrounds, and equally little from the unskilled working class, which supplies a very large proportion of Index crime convicted offenders. The police are also socially distant from the upper classes who make the laws the police are required to enforce. A large proportion finish high school only, but there is an increasing tendency in both America and Britain for "fast track" policemen to take college degrees after entry to the force. Again in both countries the police tend to the right-wing in politics. For example, Bayley and Mendelsohn (1969) found that 49 per cent of Denver police voted for Barry Goldwater, the (right-wing) Republican candidate for President in 1968, as against 24 per cent of the general population. In line with this is a further finding of Bayley and Mendelsohn concerning police attitudes. There were majorities for the propositions: "crime emanates from the disadvantaged more than from the well-to-do community" and "the involvement of racial minorities in crime is greater than for other ethnic groups." Of course, both statements might attract equal support from the general population.

A study by Fenster, Weidemann, and Locke (1973) of New York police and a sample of the general population matched for educational background found the police group to be on average less dogmatic and less neurotic, but to have higher IQ scores, implying them to be a superior subsample of the population from which they are drawn. A more recent study (Lawrence 1984) of randomly selected police samples found essentially the same results, with those personality features which were deviant from the general population to be largely adaptive to the job: the police samples were more reserved, detached, critical, conscientious, persistent, practical, down-to-earth, socially aware and self-sufficient than matched groups of "civilians". But there were wide variations within the police samples, with those who deviated most from police averages the most susceptible to the stress of police work (see below).

Police training and socialization

The process of molding civilians into policemen starts with the selection of acceptable applicants. Apart from weeding out those who test too low on a battery of examinations, a key aspect of the process is an interview by senior officers which helps to exclude those whose values and opinions would make it hard for them to "fit in" with their future colleagues (Bent 1974). Reasons for joining the police are typically mundane; applicants more often stress job security and good pay than any other factors.

Then comes the actual training. Harris (1973) went through one such course as a participant observer. During the 12 weeks of training, the recruits had nearly 90 hours on patrol work and nearly 80 on the law and on court procedures, but only 16 hours on community and race relations and police ethics – all areas crucial for the exercise of discretion. The emphasis was on actions, not on social sensitivity. Great importance was attached to defensiveness (how to avoid, or at least how to deal with, complaints from the nonpolice world, some of whose members, such as politicians, lawyers, and judges, had to be placated more than others for the sake of the police in general). And in an emergency only the police could be relied upon. This sense of separateness and depersonalization (nonpolice are to be seen as members of groups and not as individuals) was assisted by the paramilitary command structure and formality of the force. It all adds up to being professional, with a sense of belonging to a selected elite. Loyalty is to one's colleagues and superiors, rather to the general public. (In this respect there is a strong resemblance to other professions with well-established traditions, such as medicine and the law). A longitudinal study by Bennett (1984) found that the process of socialization to police norms continued during the probationary period after training.

Suspicion goes along with the defensiveness already noted. It speeds up the process of doing the job to be able to label and categorize on the basis of initial impressions rather than collecting all the facts which are available. Werthman and Piliavin (1967, p. 68) term this pragmatic induction: "Past experience leads them to conclude that more crimes are committed in the poorer sections of the town than in the wealthier areas, that Negroes are more likely to cause public disturbance than whites, and that adolescents are a greater source of trouble than other categories of the citizenry . . . [they] then focus attention on those categories of persons and places felt to have the shadiest moral characteristics."

The police may well be correct in their categorizations, but there is also a strong element of the self-fulfilling prophecy.

The police and the public

A review of a small number of items on attitudes to the police included in the NCS for 1975 (Garofolo 1977) suggests that most people gave their local force favorable ratings, with no differences found according to income. While both blacks and the young were markedly less positive than the overall average, negative ratings did not predominate even among the least favorable sub-group (only 25 per cent of the youngest black group gave the police the most negative rating possible. Moreover, no blame was attached to the police for the "crime problem."

A similarly favorable pattern was revealed by the British Crime Survey for 1984 (Hough and Mayhew 1985). But there were also certain criticisms: one fifth of victims who called the police were dissatisfied with the service they received, the main complaint being lack of action; nearly one fifth of young males complained of misconduct on the part of the police, including the use of undue force, corruption, false accusations and wrongful arrest. (The general issue of police lawbreaking is reviewed below). More recently, there has been a marked worsening of public respect for the British police (Mori Organization poll in 1989, cited in *The Economist* 1990b).

The criteria for success differ between police and public (Jones 1982); the former emphasize technical skills and efficiency, and believe that the public agrees with them. In fact, the public value most highly the quality of their personal contacts with the police and how the police present themselves. In the interests of improved police–public relations, many police departments have considered replacing the traditional uniform by a more "civilian" style of dress. A review of such changes by Mauro (1984) found no positive effects. On the contrary, the public associate uniforms with greater helpfulness, competence, better judgement and a faster response to their needs.

Given the disproportionate contribution of blacks both to arrests and to the numbers in prison, both of which may reflect bias by some white police and judges, should there be an attempt to recruit more blacks into the police force? Walker, D.B. (1983) found support for this from both black and white serving police officers as likely to improve the quality of law enforcement. (As of 1990 there were 400 black police chiefs in the US, much better than in the past, but still well below a proportionate share.)

Police misbehavior

It would be surprising, given both the pressure for results from the public and from their superiors, and the inevitable attempts by offenders to avoid punishment, if the police were the only occupation so far studied with a perfect record for good behavior. Deviations from the standards expected take two major forms: abuse of authority and corruption.

Abuse of authority. This includes both the misuse of force, at the extreme amounting to actual brutality, and falsifying evidence so as to secure convictions which would not otherwise be obtained.

In everyday practice, reasonable force means that degree of force necessary to secure a legal goal (such as arresting a suspect) without endangering innocent citizens. Going beyond this – misusing force – still involves an acceptable goal; it is the means which are in question (e.g., using strong physical restraint to arrest a suspect where no resistance has been offered) not the ends. The term brutality involves also unacceptable ends, such as using force to satisfy a personal whim or prejudice, as when a group of police officers beat up a group of Asian youths in London's Holloway Road (*The Economist* 1990b).

Britain also provides examples of framings (falsified evidence): "The Guildford Four, Irish people imprisoned [for several years] for a bombing they did not commit, after evidence had been suppressed by the police, have belatedly been released" (*The Economist* 1990b). Framing is not confined to crimes which outrage the public, such as the IRA bombing with which the Guildford Four were charged. In December, 1989, "Mr Rupert Taylor got £100,000 (in compensatory damages) after the jury decided the police had planted drugs on him" (*The Economist* 1990b). British juries may be less inclined to trust police evidence than in the past: "Last summer Mr. Frank Critchlow was acquitted on drugs charges despite the testimony of 66 policemen" (*The Economist* 1990b).

How widespread is the abuse of authority? An American study by

Reiss (1971) found about 10 per cent of police–public encounters to involve some form of what the interviewees considered police misconduct. In most cases this involved abusive language and ridicule, but about one-third were cases in which excessive force was alleged to have taken place while the suspect was in police custody, and hence in no position to constitute a threat. Such accusations are, of course, unsupported by independent witnesses, but they occur with sufficient frequency to cause concern.

Corruption. From time to time a major official enquiry documents a range of corrupt practices, particularly in connection with the receipt by the police of routine payments from the owners of gambling establishments or of those providing illegal sexual activities. The Knapp Commission, an enquiry into the New York City Police Department, established that the monthly share per man from gambling establishments ranged from $300 in midtown Manhattan to $1,500 in Harlem. Corrupt officers also collected substantial amounts from narcotics dealers (Knapp Commission Report 1972).

Roebuck and Barker (1974) have produced a useful typology of police corruption, of which we have already met the protection of illegal activities, such as gambling and drug supply, and the fix. The remainder include: the "shakedown" (the police know about a crime but do nothing about it in exchange for a bribe – this differs from the fix in that it precedes and avoids an arrest); opportunistic theft (for example from victims or arrestees); direct criminal activities (against both the persons and the property of the general public); and taking advantage of the special knowledge and opportunities available to the police.

As yet there is only the most sketchy information on the scale of such illegal activities, but there are two studies on the views of corruption held by the police themselves. In the first, 270 rookie police officers from 91 American forces were asked to estimate the amount of corruption and misconduct in their force. Estimates varied directly with the size of the department, but no force, even the smallest, was seen as totally free of misconduct (Baker 1983). This fits in with a survey by Felkenes (1984) of police officers in three departments in southern California. Thirty eight per cent felt it was not wrong to accept small gifts from the public and 52 per cent agreed with or were neutral about the idea that officers sometimes have to use unethical means to enforce the law. Yet, both practices are contrary to the Law Enforcement Code of Ethics. In line with this contradiction, 75 per cent of those sampled said they relied mostly on their own personal ethics and not on those of the profession to guide their professional actions.

Finally, the results of a study carried out in New York for the Patrolman's Benevolent Association, not long after the Knapp Report (*Sunday Times* 1974), may be seen either as reassuring evidence that the police are more law-abiding than the public, or as a disquieting indication that many are all too human. The researchers used hidden cameras to compare the behavior of ordinary citizens with that of police officers who had previously passed "integrity tests" given by the Police Department. Whereas 84 per cent of the public kept a wallet when handed it by an undercover agent posing as a member of the public, only 30 per cent of police officers did so.

Police stress

The speaker is Detective Lieutenant Christy French in Raymond Chandler's *The Little Sister*:

> "We're coppers and everybody hates our guts. . . . As if we didn't have to handle one hundred and fourteen homicides last year out of three rooms that don't have enough chairs for the whole squad to sit down on at once. We spend our lives turning over dirty underwear and sniffing rotten teeth. We go up dark stairways to get a gun punk with a skinful of hop and sometimes we don't get all the way up and our wives wait dinner that night and all the other nights. . . . And nights we do come home, we come home so goddam tired we can't eat or sleep or even read the lies the papers print about us. . . . And just about the time we drop off the phone rings and we get up and start all over again. Nothing we do is right, not ever. Not once. If we get a confession, we beat it out of the guy, they say, and some shyster calls us Gestapo in court and sneers at us when we muddle our grammar" (Chandler 1989, p. 187).

Lieutenant French is in no doubt that police work is highly stressful, perhaps uniquely so: bad working conditions; lack of essential equipment; unpleasant tasks; physical danger; disrupted family and personal life; humiliations in court, and public dislike. But is this in fact the case, using objective indices to compare the police with other occupations? The review which follows draws largely on Davidson and Veno (1980).

The term stress means physiological and/or psychological strain, usually lasting for a period of time, which threatens the ability of a person to go on coping with a given situation. The consequences of excessive stress (what is experienced as "excessive" varies widely between individuals) include a range of psychological and physical problems, as well as suicide, strained or fractured marital and social relationships, absences from work, poor job performance, high job-turnover and out-of-control drinking and drug-use. The sources of stress are termed stressors, and include both factors intrinsic to the job and those external to it. Many police stressors are shared with other occupations, a few are more or less specific to the police. It is the *combination* of stressors involved in police work which may be unique.

Stressors intrinsic to police work include the following:

1. Shift work. This is true for many occupations and in all of them it is difficult to reconcile the job with family and social life.
2. Job overload. This relates to the complexity and variety of a job. Both are features of police work which many officers find positive, rather than negative, but most would welcome less routine paperwork.
3. Job underload. Essentially, this means insufficient complexity and variety and is associated in a range of jobs with fatigue, anxiety and depression. A major source of stress in police work is likely to be the need to remain alert in an intrinsically monotonous context, such as a lengthy spell of surveillance of a residence or a suspect. While there has been much psychological research on vigilance tasks (such as watching a radar screen) there has been little on having to vary unpredictably between long periods of alert inactivity and short bursts of extreme activity (the situation in police "stake-outs").
4. Physical danger. Participation in violent incidents is often perceived by both police and the public as a major stressor, but the frequency of such participation may be associated with a higher than average tendency to suspiciousness and defensiveness. And danger may be seen by some police officers as adding a spice to the job.
5. Poor equipment. Together with the right type of manpower this seems an important stressor.
6. Attendance at court. This is experienced as stressful by many policemen, particularly when court schedules are inconvenient and the sentence passed is considered too lenient.
7. Role in the organization. There seems more conflict between different police roles for patrol officers, who have to combine

what are seen as the intrinsically different tasks of thief catching and community liaison, than for those in administrative jobs.

8. Police organization. Problems center around poor communication, particularly with superiors, the lack of clear and well-established guidelines for action, insufficient participation in decision-making and instability due to frequent personnel changes. The lack of career development is an important source of stress. (In Britain, for example, 80 per cent of the police force are in the lowest grade of constable, and the criteria for promotion are murky, *The Economist* 1990b).

Stressors in the external environment include relationships with family and the community. Police work is hard on the family, shift work makes family social life additionally difficult, and the police family itself is seen as different by its neighbors, so that social contacts tend to be with other police families.

A study by Lawrence (1984) related some of the above stressors to personality, measured by the 16PF (Cattell, Saunders, and Stice 1957). Those who deviated in their scores from the rest of a sample of 104 police officers in three Texas departments with an average of nine years in the force tended to score significantly higher on a number of stressors. Officers who were suspicious and sensitive to threat were unusually bothered by court appearances and by unfavorable judicial decisions. The most obsessional officers were particularly disturbed by faulty equipment. Physical danger was not seen as a key stressor, possibly because in most cases it could be controlled.

Comparisons with other occupations. So far as physical ailments usually considered related to stress are concerned, it seems the police are a high-risk occupation, ranking about tenth for coronary heart disease, among a large number of occupations, despite recruits having to pass stringent fitness tests and the police being on average younger than most other occupational groups. While there are few or no direct tests of mental health status, American police seem to be at a higher risk for suicide than other professions (possibly because of the ready availability of service firearms, the most frequent method of suicide), particularly taking age into account. Divorce rates also seem higher than in the general population.

Methodological problems of research into police stress include:

1. There is a lack of prospective, longitudinal studies of police and of comparable groups who entered other jobs, which would follow

them from the point of entry, and so include those who leave, possibly quite early, in response to experienced stress. Violanti (1983) carried out a cross-sectional study (all groups were measured at the same time, the assumption being that they were initially comparable) of levels of stress at four successive stages of a police career, each lasting between five and seven years. He found a significant curvilinear relationship between stress and police career stage: stress increased in the first two stages and then decreased in the next two, perhaps because police officers, by then older, were in less "front-line" positions; another possibility is that those most affected by stress left early in their police career.

2. The term "police" covers a wide range, as Malloy and Mays (1984) point out, including the following: a white officer on patrol in Harlem; a black officer on patrol in Marin County, California; a state trooper on radar duty on an interstate highway; a deputy sheriff in a sleepy Southern town; and an officer assigned as a computer programmer. Police stress research should specify the settings and tasks involved.
3. Dependent measures of stress should include direct well-established indices such as check-lists of psychological and physical problems, supplemented by face-to-face interviews and physical examinations, and psychophysiological measures during routine police activities, as well as indirect measures such as absenteeism and personnel turn-over. Drug and alcohol use should also be assessed.
4. Gender. Female police officers have additional problems to those of their male colleagues (Johnson 1991, Young 1991), possibly because of the hostility expressed towards them by the latter.
5. Personality. More studies are needed of the interaction between personality variables, stressors and responses to stress.

Overall, it seems clear that police stress is a very real problem, but probably much more so for those on the street in high-crime areas: Lieutenant French had a point.

4. The courts

> . . . In 1752, James Stewart, Aucharn, was taken before the High court of Justiciary at Inverary, charged with being an accomplice in murder. The victim was Colin Campbell of Glenure. The jury included Colin Campbell of Carwhin, Duncan Campbell of South Hall, James Campbell of Inveray, James Campbell of Rasheilly, James Campbell of Rudale, Colin Campbell of Skipness, Duncan Campbell of Glendaruel, Colin Campbell of Ederline, Neil Campbell of Duntroon, Archibald Campbell of Dale, Neil Campbell of Dunstafnage.
>
> The jurors were picked from the list by the Bench, Archibald Campbell, Duke of Argyll, in his capacity as Lord Justice General, presided. James Stewart was hanged.
>
> In his *Collection of Celebrated Criminal Trials* (1780), Hugo Arnot, advocate, allowed himself the comment:
>
> This trial . . . points out the propriety of . . . alterations in the criminal law of Scotland: first that the prisoner should . . . have the power of challenging a certain number of jurors without cause assigned.
>
> The right of peremptory challenge was brought in by Act of 1825. Yours faithfully,
>
> ANGUS STEWART
> (Letter to *The Times*, June 19, 1984)

This chapter divides court procedures into two broad areas: the trial and the sentence, in both cases focusing on descriptive and research material which is either of psychological interest in itself or continues from the two previous chapters the general question of bias in the criminal justice system against particular groups. The chapter concludes with the special case of the insanity defense.

4.1. The trial

Although relatively few cases reach the courts of those which have the potential to do so, the numbers are large in absolute terms, so that about two million Americans serve as jurors annually in 200,000 civil and criminal cases. Trial processes have captured the attention of both lay and scholarly audiences for their symbolic, not their numeric, importance. One trial can establish a legal precedent with significant effects on many future cases (Monahan and Loftus 1982).

Images of the trial

According to Miller and Boster (1977), the trial can be seen as a rational, rule-governed event, as a test of credibility, and as a conflict resolving ritual. In the first of these "images," the trial is portrayed as part of a collective search for truth dating back to Aristotle, 2,400 years ago. The task of marshalling evidence is performed by two trained and disinterested dialecticians who present it to the decision makers. But can the latter weigh correctly, laying aside their preconceptions, the information which is presented by witnesses, and can witnesses observe and report accurately? Both professional judges and lay jurors may be prejudiced: a system of challenge to the latter has been developed, as has the convention of instructing the jury to disregard inadmissible evidence, but both are of doubtful effectiveness, as we shall see below.

The second image sees the trial as a test of credibility. Judges and juries must weigh not only information and evidence but also the veracity of opposing evidential and informational sources (the way information is presented, the qualifications of witnesses and so on). Judgements as to credibility are based partially on such fixed attributes of individuals as appearance, race, and sex, and could be markedly affected by the stereotypes held by judges and juries. There is some research on attitudes to defendants; little or none on attitudes to witnesses. Witnesses when testifying could show symptoms of increased arousal, which might be understood as anxiety due to inexperience, or might be regarded as indicating that the witness is untrustworthy. Conversely, those who have acquired greater self-control might be seen as more credible – even though they are, in fact, lying.

Third, the purpose of the trial has been seen as creating a sense that justice has been done: to give the accused his "day in court," so that the open trial is worthwhile even if less efficient than, for example, video-taping trial material for later presentation to judges.

In practice, elements of all three images enter into the reality of the criminal trial. There are serious attempts at objectivity, intertwined with subjective elements – all the court room participants are subject to human emotions and human errors. The question is whether emotions and errors operate equally across defendants, or whether some are treated less equally in some systematic way.

Selective impunity

There is no question that there is ample opportunity for bias to occur during the several stages from arrest to sentence. At least 1.5 million persons are arrested for Index crimes in the USA each year, of whom about one in nine is sentenced to imprisonment (Forst 1983). Because of a widespread reluctance to keep records, relatively little is known about the subsequent disposal of juveniles arrested for such offenses, but it is clear that the vast majority is released at some stage following initial police contact (Gibbons and Krohn 1986).

Turning to adults, only about 40 out of every 100 of those arrested for Index crimes come to trial. The remaining cases are "rejected" by prosecution lawyers at an initial screening as unlikely to result in a successful prosecution. Of the surviving 40, the judge dismisses four on technical grounds and two cases are eventually dropped by the prosecution (they cannot present a defendant for whatever reason). Of the 34 remaining, 27 plead guilty, typically to a lesser charge so as to secure a lighter sentence (this is discussed below under the heading of plea bargaining), and the remaining 7 go to trial, at which two are acquitted. Of the 32 who are convicted (27 plus 5), 20 go to prison, usually for less than one year (Forst 1983).

Cases are dropped by the prosecution mainly because insufficient evidence, either physical or eyewitness, is produced by the police. The police have both to provide evidence and to persuade witnesses to appear. Forst et al. (1981) demonstrated wide variations in police performance. They assessed 10,000 police officers in seven jurisdictions in 1977–1978 and found that 12 per cent of them produced half the convictions; 22 per cent made arrests which yielded no convictions. These findings held after a range of controls was exercised, such as opportunity to make an arrest and type of crime. The high conviction rate officers were more persistent in finding witnesses and in following up an investigation. (Differences in performance are hardly surprising; they exist in all professions, but perhaps in few to such a great extent.)

The district attorney has much latitude: "The greatest discretion in the formally organized criminal justice network" (Reiss 1974). The typical DA's office has about 100 felony cases per attorney per year. In many cases, the evidence is clearly very weak and prosecutions are dropped, even if a serious crime is involved; in others, it is obviously strong (they go to trial unless the matter is very trivial). But within these obvious boundaries there is much discretion, even when written guidelines are available. There appear to be no data on the decision-making process in the area of uncertainty (Forst et al. 1981).

Howard (1974) points out that the job of the judge is getting harder as Americans turn to the courts to settle social and personal disputes once handled by the family, or the church. The proliferation of criminal offenses (which almost certainly exceeds those decriminalized) was noted in Chapter 1. The results are interminable delays (an average of 2 years in civil cases is not uncommon), and assembly-line processing in urban courts, particularly criminal courts. In the 1970's, the average workload per judge (even excluding traffic cases) was between 2,500 and 4,500 per month and the average trial time $1\frac{1}{2}$ minutes (Howard, 1974). Even a 5 per cent increase in not guilty pleas would paralyse the courts. Hence, the importance of plea bargaining and of bail, both considered below.

Bail

Schlesinger (1983) defines bail as "a sum of money posted by the defendant or his representative to secure his release from jail until the disposition of his case." Failure to appear means forfeiture of the sum, and hence it is set high enough to ensure his appearance. It is usual for judges to have much discretion both in deciding whether bail is given and in setting the amount. (The accused is brought before a judge or magistrate shortly after arrest.) Because a defendant with insufficient means might be denied bail a system of *bondsmen* has developed. They charge at least 10 per cent of the sum set for bail and can refuse a client, thus overriding a judge prepared to grant bail. Only 33 per cent of those granted bail are convicted, as against 60 per cent of those refused (Schlesinger 1983). However, this may be due, at least in part, to bail being denied to the most serious cases and to those against whom the evidence is particular strong. If an accused person remains incarcerated he is less free to prepare a defense.

Plea bargaining is more likely on the part of those denied bail and those too poor even to pay the bondsman. Denying bail is very costly –

amounting to more than $100 million annually in pre-trial custody expenses. But, Schlesinger (1983) argues, the bail system allows out the better-off, who may continue to offend while on bail (committing offences of high frequency such as drug-dealing). Over 10 per cent of those on pretrial release are rearrested while on bail (Wice 1973).

An analysis of 286 cases processed by an American court of initial appearance (Bock and Frazier 1984) showed that offense characteristics and the demeanor of the accused were both important in decisions to release on bail, and that the combination of the two was more important than either alone. A study by Ebbesen and Konecni (1975) indicated the importance of the district attorney's recommendation to the court.

Plea bargaining

A plea of guilty, but to a lesser charge than that originally pressed, is definitely rewarding to the criminal justice system: the offense joins those cleared by the police; and the overloaded court machinery proceeds more swiftly. Whether it is more rewarding to the defendant than a not guilty plea is more moot. Two studies indicate the complications. Lafree (1985) found that defendants convicted at trial received more severe sentences than those who plead guilty, controlling for case severity, for the evidence and for offender characteristics. McAllister and Bregman (1986), in a study of hypothetical legal scenarios, concluded that as the severity of the potential sentence and the probability of conviction increased, prosecutors were less willing to plea bargain, defense attorneys more willing. In general, they found a prosecutorial bias in favor of plea bargains and a defense bias toward going to trial. Bearing in mind that two out of seven trial cases result in an acquital and that defense fees are related to the total time spent on a case these results are not surprising. They suggest the importance both of legal representation for the accused and of the competence of the defence lawyer.

American evidence on plea bargaining (Newman 1956) indicates that those legally represented at all are much more likely to plead guilty to a lesser charge (in many cases thereby receiving a noncustodial sentence), as are those employing private counsel as opposed to being represented by a publicly funded defender (Oaks and Lehman 1970). It is a reasonable assumption that the better-off (a group which will include many of those connected with organized crime) are more likely to be legally represented, and if so to employ private rather than public counsel. The latter seem likely to be more competent (the contrary assumption, that the most able lawyers prefer to work for the smallest fees, seems less credible).

The jury system

Introduction. Although the right to trial by jury is the cornerstone of the American and British legal systems, comparatively little is known either about its history or its current workings. The system has always attracted both praise and scorn to a degree unparalleled by any other legal institution (Baldwin and McConville 1980). Its defenders argue that it is an independent and essential element in the proper enforcement of the criminal law, acting as a restraint on any tendency to oppress. But can juries understand legal instuctions and are they competent fact finders; is the composition of juries appropriate to the task assigned to them; are jury verdicts affected by the size of the jury (6, 12, etc.) or by rules allowing convictions on the basis of nonunanimous votes?

Strict prohibitions on research into real-life juries make it difficult to answer such questions. An attempt by Kalven and Zeisel (1966) to record the actual deliberations of jurors (with the consent of trial judge and counsel, but the jurors were not informed) was followed by many states making it a criminal offence to record jury proceedings or in any way to interfere with the jurors pre-verdict. In the UK, it is usually held that revelations about juries can amount to contempt of court. Some indirect methods of studying juries, and the results obtained, follow shortly.

The voir dire. This is the process of producing an impartial jury. Blunk and Sales (1977) have provided a useful overview. The voir dire examination (literally to see and to say) enables the trial judge to discharge his obligation to dismiss veniremen (those summoned for jury service) found unfit for trial duty. Counsel are allowed a set number of peremptory challenges when the judge refuses to act. The voir dire examination by counsel is proper so long as it tries to discover the veniremen's state of mind directly or indirectly related to the trial in question.

Counsel have available to them a number of strategies for the voir dire.

1. They can accept the first 12 veniremen without question or ceremony. A variant of this is accepting them and, histrionically, declining with a grand gesture the opportunity to question and explicitly stressing faith in the jury system in general and in these 12 jurors in particular. This approach is taken in the belief that the jury's first impression of counsel is critical in increasing their receptivity toward his arguments.
2. The voir dire can be used to the full in the belief both that indepth questioning will reveal prejudices and biases and that veniremen's first impressions of counsel are important and will be well revealed by a lengthy examination. There are obvious difficulties: it is hard to elicit prejudices; verbal reports of beliefs may lack predictive validity; counsel may investigate the wrong prejudices or veniremen may simply lie; perhaps most important, veniremen may resent questioning and so develop an unfavorable attitude to counsel. Hence:
3. An indoctrinational strategy has developed around 2, above. It involves hypothetical questions to analyze potential areas of prejudice so as to ingratiate counsel with veniremen and make them aware of, and test their reactions to, certain aspects of the case (counsel's theory of the case, acceptable defences, etc.). The questions posed are intended to influence the jury; counsel has little interest in the answers. This method is much deprecated judicially.

Methods of Studying juries. Baldwin and McConville (1980) point out that most methods are indirect and, hence, inevitably imperfect.

1. Autobiographical accounts by jurors are unavoidably partial and idiosyncratic, conveying a wide spectrum of views, from the adulatory to the appalled.
2. The publicly expressed views of legal practitioners. These are much less varied, usually being positive, but inevitably do not allow generalization.
3. The systematic collection by researchers of jurors' opinions. These suggest a general lack of understanding of legal concepts.
4. Simulated jury panels. The great advantage of this approach is that their deliberations can be recorded and analyzed and systematic variations introduced. In the usual version, a mock jury is presented with a reconstruction of a real trial, perhaps a tape of actors reading from a trial transcript. A further develop-

ment is the shadow jury, which is put into the courtroom alongside, as it were, the real one. Their subsequent deliberations are then recorded (e.g., Diamond and Zeisel 1974). While the shadow jury is much more exposed to courtroom reality than simulated juries, neither has to determine the fate of the defendant in question.

5. The performance of juries is pitted against the views of other participants in trials. This method was pioneered by Kalven and Zeisel (1966). Baldwin and McConville (1980) consider it to be "the most illuminating;" nevertherless, the judges or counsel studied "recollect in tranquillity," whereas the jurors made their decisions in the context of the actual trial.

Research on jury selection. In the USA prior to 1968, the "key man" system was often used. This meant that key members of the community recommended people for jury service. In 1968, The Jury Selection and Service Act required voting lists to be used as sources of jury pools so that the representativeness of juries improved. But the young, racial minorities and the poor are still significantly underrepresented (Hans and Vidmar 1982) and ". . . in many jurisdictions [this] is substantial and dramatic" (Van Dyke 1977, p. 24). Baldwin and McConville (1980) point out that the major causes of unrepresentativeness lie in the way juries are selected, from an "eligible" pool relying heavily on voting lists which notoriously underrepresent young blacks. This is linked to administrative discretion, usually vested in court clerks, and there is some evidence of informal discrimination at the initial selection stage, fewer women than men being called.

Courtroom challenges to jurors are extremely rare in Britain (one in the early 80's was thought to be the first for 150 years) but are very much more frequent in the USA, particularly in trials for murder (see below) and in those with political overtones. In the 1972 trial of the Berrigan brothers on conspiracy charges, a group of social scientists conducted community surveys to determine the characteristics of people favorable or opposed to the defendants and then constructed ideal juror profiles so that defense attorneys had much information on which to base their challenges. The same techniques have been used in other celebrated cases. In describing this approach. Hans and Vidmar (1982) raise doubts both as to the effectiveness and the ethicality of such work.

In the USA, about 5 per cent of jurors are removed for cause, that is by the judge, on the basis of voir dire responses. Removal by peremptory challenges (by counsel)are more frequent. In the federal courts, in felony cases, each side is given five challenges, in misdemeanors, two, Rights to challenge are used frequently, particularly by the defence – about three times more often than by the prosecution.

Most simulation studies show no effect of the sex of jurors but a few suggest women to be more defense oriented, except in the case of rape, in which they lean more toward the prosecution in their decisions (Hans and Vidmar 1982). Demographic and attitudinal data show a very limited ability to predict verdicts (Penrod 1980). Greater specificity of attitude questions (e.g., towards rape in a rape case) improves predictions. In principle, lawyers should try to assess case- specific attitudes rather than either general attitudes or demographic variables.

In fact, the evidence on attorney effectiveness in weeding out biased persons is somewhat contradictory (Hans and Vidmar 1982). They cite a study by Zeisel and Diamond (1978) as the only one providing direct information on this issue over a number of cases. The latter arranged for the challenged and rejected jurors in 12 cases to attend the trials concerned and to vote at the end of each concerning their verdict. In addition, Zeisel and Diamond interviewed the empanelled jurors at the end of the trial to get their votes on the first ballot (it is often the case that several rounds of voting are needed to reach a sufficient majority). This enabled them to reconstruct the first ballot vote of the original jurors in the absence of challenges. In two of the 12 trials the difference between the two first ballot votes was large enough to have produced a different verdict in the absence of challenges (i.e., the attorney's challenges were effective in these cases). There were great variations in attorney's abilities to eliminate biased jurors. Zeisel and Diamond concluded that, under the usual conditions of limited information about juror attitudes, most attorneys are only marginally effective most of the time in weeding out biased jurors.

A rather different approach to the effectiveness issue was taken by Jones (1987). Noting that jurors frequently distort their replies to questions during the voir dire she asked whether more accurate information was elicited by the judge or by attorneys. The attitudes of potential jurors were assessed both by questionnaire and then verbally in court. She found that attorneys were more effective than judges in eliciting candid self-disclosure from potential jurors and that participants changed their answers almost twice as often when questioned by judges as by attorneys. Jones concluded that the presence of the judge during challenges evokes a considerable pressure towards conformity among jurors to a set of perceived judicial standards. This is reduced by attorney-conducted voir dire, allowing individual biases to emerge and those holding them to be rejected.

Hans and Vidmar's (1982) overall conclusion seems sensible: jury composition is probably not very important for the normal run of criminal cases but may be for the minority of political or socially controversial trials in which juror attitudes are likely to be polarized and the right to challenge might be crucial. However, in view of the retention of the death penalty for murder in the USA, juror attitudes to the capital sentence have been of great interest, both to legal practitioners and to researchers.

A special case: death qualification. This is the process by which the courts identify and exclude from capital juries those persons whose views on the death penalty are considered incompatible with the duties of capital jurors (Fitzgerald and Ellsworth 1984). It followed from the case of *Witherspoon* versus *Illinois* heard in the US Supreme Court in 1968. The Court decided that those unwilling to impose the death penalty, on principle, regardless of the evidence, should be excluded from the jury concerned. Subsequently, in *Hovey* versus *Superior Court* (heard in the California Supreme Court in 1980), a contrasting group was identified – automatic death penalty (ADP) persons, who would always vote for the death sentence, irrespective of the facts of the case.

Fitzgerald and Ellsworth (1984) suggested that death qualified juries (those from which persons who are anti-capital punishment have been excluded under *Witherspoon)* might be biased against capital defendants. They compared the demographic characteristics and attitudes to capital punishment of a random sample of over 800 eligible jurors in Alamedo County, CA. Just over 17 per cent were "excludable", including significantly greater proportions of blacks than whites and females than males. Death qualified respondents were consistently prone to favor the point of view of the prosecution, to mistrust criminal defendants and their counsel, to take a punitive attitude to offenders, and to be more concerned with crime control than with due process.

Two further studies by this group of researchers add to the case against death qualification. Both used video-simulated murder trials and included death qualified as well as excludable participants. The first (Cowan, Thompson, and Ellsworth 1984) found that death qualified persons were significantly more likely to vote guilty, both on an initial ballot and after an hour's deliberation in 12 person juries, when these consisted solely of death qualified participants, than when they were mixed (two to four excludables took part). Mixed juries were more critical of witnesses and were better able to remember their evidence than those which were homogeneous, so that diversity may improve the vigor, the thoroughness and the accuracy of jury deliberations. And Thompson, Cowan, Ellsworth, and Harrington (1984) found death qualified jurors to be more favorable to the prosecution and to express less regret concerning erroneous convictions, but more regret about wrong acquittals, compared with excludables. Horowitz and Seguin (1986) also found death qualified jurors to give the most severe sentences. In a study of actual jurors, Moran and Comfort (1986) reported that those favorable to capital punishment tended to be white, male, married, politically conservative and authoritarian. They reported reaching their verdicts more quickly and participated more in jury discussions than their demographic and personality counterparts.

The evidence against the system of death qualification seems clear and unequivocal, but Turkington (1986) points to the decision of the US Supreme Court of April 1986, in the case of *Lockhart* versus *McCree*. By a majority of five to four the Court decided that excluding jurors opposed to the death penalty does not violate a criminal defendant's right to a fair trial. The Court made it clear that its decision was reached without regard to social science research, which suggests that death qualified jurors are more prone to convict precisely when the evidence is ambiguous. The Court based its decision instead on legal analysis, but the majority did note "several serious flaws in the social science evidence accepted by the lower courts," asserting that many studies were irrelevant and that all were simulated. In contrast, the four-person minority termed the scientific evidence "unanimous and overwhelming" (a rare state of affairs in the social sciences!). Had the Court ruled in favor of McCree (i.e., if one justice had voted for instead of against) 1,714 death row inmates, convicted by death qualified juries, could have requested new trials (Turkington 1986). The question of the death penalty for homicide is taken up in Chapter 11.

Jury size. The jury trial is an expensive method of resolving questions of guilt and responsibility (not least to jurors, who may lose considerable time and income), so it is not surprising that the great majority of cases are settled otherwise. There has also been much debate in the US both about jury size (6 versus 12; the research has been on simulated juries) and about the shift from unanimous to majority verdicts (10 out of 12). Baldwin and McConville (1980) conclude that 6 person juries can be as representative as 12, although there is no saving in court time or cost (savings to the potential jurors are not mentioned) and 12 person juries enjoy more public confidence. The evidence is that "majority rule" juries cease debate when the majority is reached, speeding up court proceedings, but once again there seems greater public confidence in the former unaminous system.

Defendant characteristics. The great bulk of research has been of the simulated type. The probability of a guilty verdict is raised by the defendant being in custody pre-trial rather than free on bail, by evidence of extenuating circumstances being offered personally by the defendant, rather than by an impartial witness, and by the defendant protesting innocence too vehemently (Monaghan and Loftus 1982). The more attractive the defendant, both in behavior (a good citizen, kind to others, etc.) and in appearance, the more he is liked; and the more he is liked the more leniently he is judged (e.g., Efran 1974, Dion 1972). A limitation has been shown by Sigall and Ostrove (1975): in a simulated situation somewhat harsher "sentences" were given to an attractive than to an unattractive swindler – this being considered an attractiveness related crime. The attractiveness–leniency relationship held strongly for burglary.

There seems no simulated work on general demeanor (e.g., answering fully and immediately, a polite and respectful yet dignified manner, etc.), yet it is likely to be the total impression, perhaps maintained for several days, which exerts its effect on the jury, rather than physical appearance alone.

Ellwork and Sales (1978) severely criticize most of the simulated jury research as indicating a marked ignorance of courtroom realities. Nevertheless, a major study by Kalven and Zeisel (1966) tends to support the importance of defendant characteristics in influencing real-life jury verdicts. They carried out a questionnaire analysis of how judges sitting alone would have decided a trial actually tried by jury, finding agreement between judge and jury in 78 per cent of nearly 4,000 cases. Of the remainder, the juries were more lenient in 19 per cent of cases, the judges in only three per cent. Both "doubt" (the need to be certain beyond reasonable doubt) and "sentiment" were major influences on the greater average leniency of juries. The latter included the following: the defendant has had a hard time recently;

an accomplice has escaped punishment; the victim was held partly to blame; the defendant had certain personal attributes (old age, widowhood), followed certain occupations (e.g., clergyman) or he made a good courtroom impression (attractiveness or repentance).

The performance of juries. This has been one of the main preoccupations of researchers into the jury system. Baldwin and McConville (1980) note that some reviewers consider juries, both real and simulated, to be very competent, deciding their verdicts solely on the evidence. But they themselves are much more cautious:

1. The considerable evidence that mock juries are markedly influenced by defendant attributes, and the possibility that this is as true of real life juries, was reviewed above.

2. "Juries are as likely to understand the meanings of the words in the judge's charge as if they were written in Chinese, Sanskrit or Choctaw" (Frank 1949). Arens, Granfield, and Sussman (1965) have also pointed to the difficulties juries have in understanding the more technical content of instructions. (A comprehensive overview by Ley, 1977, shows the problems patients have with doctor's communications.) Severance, Greene, and Loftus (1984) have reviewed the considerable evidence concerning juror difficulty in understanding judge's instructions. They developed a set of standard instructions to improve those revealed by their research as problematic, using legal as well as psychological criteria. The revised set was found to increase significantly the understanding of mock jurors, compared with a standard set, and a survey of experienced judges indicated their strong preference for the revised set.

3. A high proportion of jury acquittals is not seen as justified by other participants (judges, lawyers, etc.). Conversely, in about 6 per cent of convictions doubts are expressed by two or more of the other main participants (including the police), indicating that certain juries were too easily convinced of the defendant's guilt. (The study by Kalven and Zeisel, 1966, which contains evidence of major judge–jury divergence, was described above.) As Baldwin and McConville (1980) point out, we need to know if these questionable verdicts are evenly distributed, across both defendants and offenses, or are biased, for example, against minority groups and toward serious crimes.

4. Even when ordered to do so, jurors do not ignore evidence presented which is then ruled as inadmissible. They are affected by pre-trial publicity, and they do not give a reduced weight to witnesses

who qualify their testimony under cross-examination (Monahan and Loftus 1982).

5. It may be that juries are less able than professional judges to avoid the pitfalls of eyewitness testimony (reviewed below).

Baldwin and McConville (1980) conclude that the jury trial is an unpredictable method for discriminating between the guilty and the innocent, and that the reverence accorded the system is misplaced and excessive.

Nevertheless, research data from both the USA and Europe indicate that the "adversarial model" (prosecution, defence, judge, and jury) found in the English speaking world is seen as more fair than the "inquisitorial model" (defense lawyers are present at every interrogation, there are separate judges for the examination and the trial, and no jury) used in most European countries (Monahan and Loftus 1982). Perhaps reluctantly, Baldwin and McConville (1980) agree that alternative systems might be equally imperfect. The jury system seems set for a long lease of life.

Eyewitness testimony (ET)

Introduction. Juries are strongly influenced by the testimony of eyewitnesses, and the police and the prosecution are eager to secure such testimony – it is sometimes the only evidence available to the prosecution. Jurors respond to the expressed confidence of witnesses in what they claim to have observed.

Evidence. Following a major miscarriage of justice in England, The Devlin Committee reported in 1976 (Loftus 1981). It examined all line-ups in England and Wales in 1973 and found that 347 cases were prosecuted when the only evidence was identification by one or more eyewitnesses. Seventy four per cent of the accused were convicted.

Several experiments confirm the potential influence of eyewitness testimony. In one (Loftus 1974), participants received a description of an armed robbery resulting in two deaths. When they were given a version involving solely circumstantial evidence, only 18 per cent "convicted" the accused. A second version, involving weak evidence plus eyewitness identification, resulted in the conviction rate rising to 72 per cent. Wells, Lindsay, and Ferguson (1979) showed that witness confidence, not accuracy, determined jurors decisions to believe ET – yet confidence and accuracy were unrelated. A review of research by

Whitley and Greenberg (1986) confirmed that eyewitness confidence was an important factor in jurors perceptions of witness credibility. Further support was given by their own studies (Whitley and Greenberg 1986), which showed that the perceived expertise of a witness also varied as a function of his perceived confidence.

In criminal cases, most ET is presented by the prosecution, after which the defense may challenge. How effective is the defense in undermining the initial impression made by a confident eyewitness? In a study by Loftus (1974), an eyewitness was discredited by the defense cross-examination which showed that the witness had poor vision. But when the witness stuck to his story the percentage convicting dropped only slightly. It seems that even a destructive cross-examination raises serious doubts only when a previously confident witness actually retracts his evidence.

A review by Loftus (1981) indicates the complexities of the long sequence of events between the observed event and the appearance of the witness in court. As is usual in the psychological literature on memory, she divides the process into acquisition, retention and retrieval. In the first of these, witnesses are more accurate when: exposure time to the event is longer rather than shorter; the event is less rather than more violent; witnesses are not undergoing extreme stress or fright, they are generally free from biased expectation, are young adults rather than children, and are asked to report salient, rather than peripheral, aspects of the event. Relevant prior training helps accuracy concerning detail (e.g., clothing in a report by a fashion designer) but there is no improvement in accuracy concerning other details, such as facial appearance. Turning to retention, witnesses are better able to retain a recent than a distant event, and new information can enter between the event and ones recollection of it so as to alter that memory. Retrieval is particularly sensitive to detailed variations in courtroom procedures: witnesses produce the most complete and accurate accounts when they are first asked to recall the event in their own words and then answer specific questions; biasing words in a question (did the cars smash into each other, rather than hit each other) can contaminate witness recollection; instructions to a witness can influence the quality of recollection ("don't worry about mistakes" results in more errors than "be careful of mistakes").

Clifford (1979) adds some further important research findings concerning accuracy: it is affected by the significance of the event to a witness – if he was unaware a crime was in progress, it will be poor; it is reduced both by increased distance and by poorer visibility; an experienced observer, such as a policeman, is more accurate than an inexperienced one. The important factors for an identification parade are the elapsed time between the crime and the parade, how the parade is composed and conducted and what the witness believes his role to be – both suggestion and bias have powerful effects.

Facial recognition is a specific aspect of eyewitness identification. Cross-racial identification is usually less accurate than intra-racial: there is generally a specific difficulty in recognizing individual members of a race different from one's own. Some faces are rarely falsely recognized, some frequently; the former are those typically rated as highly unusual (Loftus 1981). There is some evidence that the public equates facial deformity/abnormality (more easily recalled than regular features) with abnormality of personality and that they hold stereotypes of a "typically criminal" appearance, possibly influencing the selection of the "one who did it" in a line-up (Bull 1979). (However, it is also true that very attractive faces are better attended to, recalled and recognized, than averagely attractive ones; the offender who "merges into the crowd" probably is the least well noticed and recalled.)

Reducing the impact of faulty testimony. The Supreme and various appelate courts have sought to reduce the likelihood of juries being influenced by unsafe testimony (Loftus 1981).

1. The right to counsel. There has been little or no psychological research on the accuracy of line-up identification with and without counsel, but the presence of counsel is likely to be beneficial to the accused, allowing some control over such variables as the similarity of nonsuspects to the suspect.

2. Cautionary jury instructions. Because judge's instructions tend to be long and tedious and are often poorly comprehended, they provide insufficient protection. A study by Katzev and Wishart (1985) illustrates this. They gave simulated juries either a standard set of judicial instructions, a statement combining these with a summary of the trial evidence, or the first two combined with a comment on eyewitness testimony. The last condition resulted in fewer pre-deliberation guilty verdicts, shorter deliberations and a reduced likelihood of reaching a guilty or a hung verdict, implying both more protection for the accused and more efficiency. A contrary finding is reported by Cutler, Dexter, and Penrod (1990) who found that judges' instructions failed to increase the skepticism of juries concerning eyewitness evidence.

3. Expert psychological testimony. Judge and jury may hear an expert witness present testimony on the topic of eyewitness accuracy, so as to help them evaluate eyewitness evidence. Some lawyers claim this invades the province of the jury (Loftus 1981), but over the years the level of agreement within a profession has emerged as a central criterion of acceptability by the judge. To evaluate this within the profession of psychology, Kassin, Ellsworth, and Smith (1989) surveyed 63 experts on ET about their courtroom experiences and opinions. At least 80 per cent agreed that data on a range of issues were accurate enough to be presented in court, including the wording of questions, line-up instructions and the accuracy–confidence correlation. The main objective of the respondents was to educate the jury, and they believed that juries are more competent with the aid of experts than without. The latter assertion is borne out by Rahaim and Brodsky (1982), who showed that both lawyers and jurors relied on innacurate, commonsense notions of ET, although lawyers were aware of the spurious correlation between accuracy and confidence. Loftus (1981) cites three studies (e.g., Loftus 1980) which indicate that exposure to an expert witness on ET reduces the impact of eyewitness testimony (the belief in accuracy is lowered, and convictions are less likely on the basis of ET alone).

Goldstein (1977) is particularly critical of eyewitness evidence, pointing out that, while in principle recognition memory is like other techniques used in law, in practice it differs in important ways: it is not a perfected skill (unlike, for example, fingerprinting); judgements by eyewitnesses are not open to either public or private scrutiny, instead the witness alone carries the facts but in a form which makes them immune to objective measurement; the stored memories change with time (most forensic data can be recorded, stored and produced for the trial, all without change). Goldstein concludes that facial recognition memory is less accurate, by several orders of magnitude, than the accepted forensic techniques. Moreover, it is impossible to know when and by whom errors will be made, and there is no hope of improvement – errors are inherent in the human observer and his defective memory system.

Nevertheless, Goldstein (1977) is not in favor of abolishing ET. Instead, he proposes that eyewitness testimony should not be admissible when it is the *only* class of evidence available in a criminal trial; indeed, no official police action should be taken on the basis of ET alone – there must be corroboration from another class of evidence.

Enhancing ET: the special case of hypnosis. Many policemen believe that eyewitness memory can be enhanced markedly by hypnosis, to the extent that a number of police departments, such as Los Angeles, have had extensive training programs (Smith 1983). Does hypnosis have the desired effect? An extensive review of controlled laboratory studies (Smith 1983, p. 387) concluded:

> [they have] "consistently failed to demonstrate any hypnotic memory improvement . . . the relevancy of these studies may be questioned because they use verbal, frequently non-meaningful stimuli, in a low arousal environment [but] several recent studies that have used more forensically relevant, arousal-provoking stimuli persist in showing no hypnotic advantage."

A review by Mickenberg (1983) makes it clear that American courts have been very cautious in admitting testimony induced by hypnosis. He argues that hypnosis is analogous to any other means of refreshing a witness memory, and that the process of "refreshment" presents a substantial possibility that the induced recollections will be innacurate, tailored to police suggestions, or even a complete fantasy. Moreover, the hyper-suggestibility that causes restored memories to be unreliable is inherent in the hypnotic process and can neither be eliminated nor controlled. Courts that have admitted hypnotically induced testimony have denied defendants the right of effective cross-examination of witnesses, and assumed too great a risk that a verdict will be based on fantasy or improper suggestion. Mickenberg concludes that a better rule is to prohibit any such hypnotically induced testimony. In fact, according to Smith (1983, p. 387, from a statement by the California Supreme Court in March, 1982, in the case of *People* versus *Shirley*, 1982):

> "It appears to be the rule in all jurisdictions in which the matter has been considered that statements made under hypnosis may not be introduced to prove the truth of the matter asserted, because the reliability of such statements is questionable."

On the other hand, Orne (1981), one of the leading authorities on hypnosis research and practice, suggests that hypnosis may be useful in a criminal investigation, when the facts are not known or are presumed, to obtain leads which may then be used to produce independent evidence, the results of which can be tested in court. Orne goes on to list the many more instances in which it is either not useful or is unsafe. He proposes minimal safeguards against the various abuses to which hypnosis might be subject: it should be conducted by a specially trained psychologist or psychiatrist with no involvement in the case either with the prosecutors or the investigators; all contacts with the hypnotized person to be taped; no-one other than the two people concerned to be present. In practice, it might well be simpler to exclude hypnotically induced testimony completely. Less dramatic methods for improving the reliability of ET, which do not require that the juries become more skeptical, include the cognitive interview (Geiselman et al. 1984) and imposing on the police a rigid set of procedures in the conduct of identification tests (Wagenaar and Loftus 1990). The former, which helps witnesses retrieve the memories of what they witnessed, seems promising.

Concluding comment. Perhaps the most striking point of all concerning ET is one made by Loftus (1981): much of what is known about the faulty memory of eyewitnesses may apply equally well to judges and juries – we know little of their ability to record, store, and retrieve accurately the mass of information with which they are presented. This is particularly important in the case of jurors, each of whom serves only once, and who are not allowed either to take notes or to have access to the records of court proceedings. As Loftus suggests, this is a major area for future research.

4.2. The sentence

Police discretion was discussed in Chapter 3, and prosecution discretion in the first part of this chapter. The judiciary also has a significant amount of discretion, so that the possibility of bias against particular groups arises once again.

Judicial discretion

Austin and Utne (1977) define discretion (fairly loosely) as the ability to take decisions and perform acts not subject to review by outside authorities. Discretionary power means that a plethora of variables – legal and extra-legal – may influence judges' and jurors' appraisals of a case and their ultimate decisions. A number of these variables, as they affect jurors, have already been discussed. Judicial decision making is influenced by inputs from all the main courtroom actors, but the judge is the central character; his influence predominates, even in a jury trial.

This is shown by the way the judge exerts a *centralized control over the flow of information*: he rules on the admissibility of evidence; oversees courtroom procedure; instructs the jury on matters of law; and may prevent the participants and even the media from discussing the case outside the courtroom. Most important of all, in the vast majority of cases, the judge sets the sentence for convicted offenders (albeit, within guidelines which are increasingly explicit).

Judicial decision makers are in a continual tension between the strict application of the letter of the law and a range of possible interpretations (Austin and Utne 1977).

> "The decisions during the trial, including the decision that ultimately defines the defendant as a convicted criminal, are made by men as social beings. . . . though the criminal trial is an exercise in fact-finding and logical deduction, it is a product of human action. Could something else be expected?" (Quinney 1970, p. 159).

The judge has to reconcile with his own general preconceptions and responses to the specific trial the divergent views and expectations of the prosecution, the defence and the community. There is ample room for divergence between apparently similar cases.

Sentencing disparity

The President's Commission (1967) collected considerable evidence on disparities between sentences and the Prison Reform Committee of the Florida Bar Association provides the following example (cited in American Friends Service Committee 1971, p. 127):

	Case 1 (harsh)	Case 2 (lenient)
County	Escambia	Dade
Age	20	18
Offense	Robbery	Robbery
Details	Robbed male of $18.52	Robbed male of $12
Weapon	Knife	0.38 revolver
Prior felony convictions	None	None
Sentence	Life	Five years credit for 50 days jail time.

An extreme example from the UK is provided by Grunhut (1956): the proportions of young people put on probation by the magistrates (nonprofessional judges advised by legally trained officials) of two adjacent towns were 12 per cent and 79 per cent, respectively.

Sources of disparity

Offence related. An overview by Forst (1983) showed the following factors to be important in determining the severity of a sentence: the seriousness of the offense; the prior record of the offender; a plea of guilty. The last usually results in a lighter sentence than a plea of not guilty followed by conviction.

Judge related. According to Forst (1983), the judge is a more important source of variation in sentencing than the offense itself. A Canadian study of full-time, professional, magistrates (Hogarth 1971) demonstrates that judges develop different philosophies concerning sentencing which influence their responses to a wide range of offenses, partly irrespective of the legally related details of the individual case. He asked a large sample to assign a sentence to 150 cases described in detail in writing. Only 7 per cent of the variation between magistrates was related to general facts about the case and the offender; 50 per cent was accounted for by their general attitudes (surveyed separately) to "justice", "deviance", and "punishment". For example, those who believed "punishment corrects" were much more likely to give an institutional sentence than a fine.

In a study of American district judges asked to make sentencing decisions on repeated occasions on simulated cases (same crimes and offenders), McFatter (1986) found that for most of the crimes detailed disparity was between occasions, rather than due to principled disagreements between judges. This means that at least a proportion of those studied gave different sentences to the same case the second time round, suggesting a poor memory, or the lack of an overriding judicial philosophy, or the influence of very temporary personal factors.

Offender related. This potential source of sentencing variation has received more research attention than the first two. Four major variables have been considered: gender, ethnicity, social class, and age.

An overview of research on *gender* has been provided by Nagel and Hagan (1983). They consider that the sex of the offender has different effects at the various stages of the criminal process, being greater at sentencing than at the preceding points. The effect is not very large, but remains after controlling for a variety of other variables. Overall, female defendants received less severe sanctions than males, particularly when they were married. Greater leniency was given to females found guilty of property, than for person, offenses (this was not so for males). These patterns were most pronounced when the offenses were less serious. Two studies which appeared after Nagel and Hagan's review (Wilbanks 1986, Johnston, Kennedy, and Shuman 1987) found the same tendency for greater leniency toward females, though again not for the most serious offences.

Whereas females fare better than males at the sentencing stage this is much less marked at the "front end" of the sequence, particularly where plea bargaining is concerned (Nagel and Hagan 1983, Figuera-McDonough 1985), possibly because fewer financial resources are available to female than to male defendants. Moreover, there has been persistent discrimination *against* women for status offences, particularly those thought to mirror immorality (sexual promiscuity is "expected" for males, hence not thought "deviant"). This general pattern has persisted from the 19th century to the present (Schlossman and Wallach 1978), though it seems now to be less marked than in the past (Krohn, Skinner, Massey, and Akers 1983).

Nagel and Hagen (1983) suggest that the greater leniency of the courts towards women for nonstatus offences persists until the basis for such preferential treatment – itself a survival of medieval "chivalry" – becomes inappropriate. Then, either because of the seriousness of the offense and/or the evidence of departure from traditional female behavior, the accused enters the category of "evil woman" and the sex disparity is no longer found. The potential influence of chivalry is noted also by Steffensmeier (1980b), but he considers it less important as an explanation of the sex disparity in sentencing than the defendant's perceived future criminality. Moreover, Steffensmeier argues that the increasing professionalism of court officials and the bureaucratization of the courts (e.g., the increased emphasis on sentencing guidelines) may be reducing the sex disparity.

The possibility of variations in sentencing according to *ethnicity* is largely discounted by Blumstein, Cohen, Martin, and Tonry (1984):

> "Factors other than racial discrimination in sentencing account for most of the disproportionate representation of blacks in US prisons . . . blacks are over-represented in prison populations primarily because of their over-representation in arrests for the more serious crime types."

Table 4.1. *Fraction of prison racial disproportionality not accounted for by different involvement in arrest*

Crime type	Fraction (%)
Homicide	2.8
Aggravated assault	5.2
Robbery	15.6
Aggregate (all crimes)	20.5
Forcible rape	26.3
Burglary	33.1
Larceny/auto theft	45.6
Drugs	48.9

Source: Blumstein (1983, p. 250)

However, Blumstein (1988) is rather more cautious, pointing out that there could be a bias due to selection effects by the prosecution which drops the less severe charges against whites; the judge is then "raceblind." There could also be "victim discounting": when the victim is black the offender, whether black or white, gets a lesser sentence than when the victim is white. The most severe sentences are handed down when the victim is white and the offender black.

Nevertheless, Blumstein (1988) estimates that 80 per cent of the black over-representation in prison is due to their greater involvement in arrest. Table 4.1 (from Blumstein 1988, p. 250) indicates, by offense group, the fraction of blacks in prison not accounted for by a greater probability of being arrested. For the last three groups, this exceeds 30 per cent. This is a not inconsiderable figure, and Chapter 3 made it clear that police arrest behavior is by no means free from ethnic bias.

An intriguing set of information is shown in Table 4.2, which details the ratios of black/white incarceration by state (from Blumstein 1988, p. 253). Most of the lowest ratios are provided by states with large black populations (Georgia, the Carolinas, Mississipi, etc.); most of the highest by states with small ones (Wisconsin, Minnesota) usually seen as liberal, implying greater judicial bias in the latter. This is the opposite of the conventional wisdom which would see the South as more biased; this point is returned to shortly. Petersilia (1983) found that, in the three states he examined (California, Michigan and Texas), judges typically imposed heavier sentences on blacks and Hispanics than on whites convicted of comparable felonies and with similar

Table 4.2. *Ratio of black/white incarceration by State (for 1984)*

State	Incarceration rates		Black/White ratio
	White males	Black males	
South Carolina	340	1,144	3.36
Georgia	292	1,183	4.05
Nevada	545	2,285	4.19
North Carolina	320	1,355	4.23
Mississipi	196	857	4.37
Tennessee	221	994	4.50
Alabama	245	1,150	4.69
West Virginia	159	753	4.74
Kentucky	174	842	4.84
Oklahoma	318	1,617	5.08
Texas	353	1,828	5.18
Arkansas	198	1,097	5.54
Florida	351	2,007	5.72
Missouri	202	1,170	5.79
Virginia	197	1,148	5.83
Louisiana	206	1,304	6.33
Indiana	227	1,473	6.49
Colorado	179	1,169	6.53
Arizona	368	2,438	6.62
New York	192	1,300	6.77
Delaware	348	2,540	7.30
Ohio	185	1,544	8.35
Washington	230	2,032	8.83
Maryland	190	1,695	8.92
Kansas	174	1,632	9.38
Michigan	147	1,441	9.80
Illinois	101	1,067	10.56
Connecticut	226	2,460	10.88
New Jersey	101	1,132	11.21
Massachussetts	114	1,416	12.42
Pennsylvania	89	1,160	13.03
D.C.	130	1,835	14.12
Wisconsin	120	1,948	16.23
Minnesota	70	1,522	21.74

Source: Blumstein (1988, p. 253).

criminal records. These minorities both received harsher minimum sentences and served more time. According to Zatz (1987), bias has become more subtle over the years, but is still systematic.

A detailed analysis by Kempf and Austin (1986) throws light on the scattered evidence and assertions set out above. They reviewed a random sample (excluding minor offenses) of nearly 3,000 cases tried in Pennsylvania in 1977. Judicial bias against blacks was found within each level of urbanization (urban, suburban and rural) with the greatest amount in suburban jurisdictions. Kempf and Austin argue that the generally disadvantaged position of many blacks makes some of their criminal actions appear as rebellious attacks by outsiders. Together with the "known" higher crime rates of blacks, this confirms the deviant character of black offending, particularly in the mainly white suburbs. To protect the existing social order in residential areas seen as desirable (because they are almost entirely white), more severe penalties are needed than against whites. In keeping with this interpretation the most severely discriminatory sentences were given in the most affluent counties, with a 96 per cent white population, a population which demands and receives a more severe judicial action. Clearly, future research into judicial discretion should break down the overall findings into such specifics as the level of affluence of the area under study and its white/black population ratio.

Fagan, Slaughter, and Hartstone (1987) urge the importance of regarding the criminal justice system as a *sequence*, whereby even relatively small biases at each stage are amplified to larger and more significant ones as one stage is succeeded by the next; the *direction* of the bias, in this case against blacks, is the same. The earliest and apparently most trivial biases (e.g., in the decision to charge a suspect with a minor felony, rather than a misdemeanor) can begin the process of building a prior record. The accumulation of arrests then results in a greater probability of referral to court following any subsequent arrest and this influences later decisions, especially judicial disposition. In their own study of a medum-sized Western town, they controlled for a range of legal factors (for example, prior record and current offence severity) so as to assess the impact on the sentencing of juveniles of such extra-legal factors as race. Fagan et al. found race to be a consistent influence on the decision to apprehend, detain, charge and punish juveniles accused of a range of offences. At times, the disparities were confined to the less serious categories of offense; at others, they were evident for all offenses. After controlling for a wide range of offender and offense characteristics, including offense severity, prior record, weapon use and age of victim, the disposition of minority offenders was consistently more punitive. No factor other than race could be identified to explain the harsher responses to minority youth.

The possibility that it is the interaction between race of offender and of victim which is linked with judicial bias, outlined above, was taken up by Walsh (1987) in the particularly explosive area of sexual assault. He found that blacks who assaulted blacks got less severe than average penalties, whereas those who assaulted whites received more severe ones. Combining the two sets of penalties masks this finding. Walsh implies that it might be found for all offences which involve black assailants and white victims, an expectation which is supported by a study by Radeley and Pierce (1986) of 1,097 homicide defendants in Florida. Both police and prosecutors routinely classified a homicide as involving "felonious circumstances," as opposed to "possible" or "absent" ones. Blacks accused of killing whites were the most likely to be "upgraded" (by prosecutors) and the least likely to be "downgraded." The process of upgrading was significantly related to the imposition of a death sentence in cases with a white victim in which no plea bargain was offered. In this study it is implied both that the judge's hands were guided by prosecutors to deal more harshly with blacks, and that those with the fewest financial resources – more usually blacks than whites – fared worst in court.

A number of studies have looked at the influence of *social class* on judicial decisions, both as a separate variable and in interaction with gender and race, with mixed results. Thomas and Dieverdes (1975) found that juveniles found guilty of serious offences were most likely to receive harsh dispositions when they were male, black, and from lower income backgrounds. For occupational offenses, Wheeler, Weisburd, and Bode (1982) found a strong *positive* relationship between socio-economic status (SES) and severity of sentence – implying that, at least for this group of offenses, greater social status was seen as conferring greater obligations. Not living up to them resulted in more severe punishment than for those less socially privileged.

McCarthy and Smith (1986) looked at several potential correlates of the judicial disposition of juveniles (race, sex, and social class), as well as examining the justice system as a sequential process, as argued for above. They found that both race and social class, particularly taken together, increase in importance as an accused juvenile moves through the system, and particularly so at the stage of sentencing. A similar sequential and multiple-correlate approach was taken by Frazier and Cochrane (1986) in an investigation of the bases of decisions to retain juveniles in custody in the pre-trial period and of the effects of having been detained on the eventual court decision. Detention was more likely for those who were older, black, charged with more serious offences, and with prior criminal records (as usual, both legal and extra-legal factors played a part). Pre-trial detainees received both more severe actions by the State Attorney and harsher judicial sentences (even after legal and social correlates were controlled). It may not be the SES of the individual but of the neighborhood in which he lives which influences police response and, hence, subsequent court disposition (Sampson 1986). Blacks tend to live in all-black neighborhoods (see Chapter 8).

As suggested in Chapter 2, SES seems a more complex variable than either gender, race, or *age*, the final potential extra-legal determinant of judicial response to be discussed. A review by Greenwood (1986) found that, with offense characteristics held constant, the courts deal more leniently with juvenile than with adult offenders. He suggests two main reasons: first, the courts put the interests of the juvenile before those of the community; second, and linked with the first, is the availability of a range of alternatives to the institutional placement of juveniles and a heavy emphasis on their use (see Chapters 10 and 11).

An overview by the National Council On Crime and Delinquency (1984) puts the relationship between juveniles and court dispositions rather differently. Whereas the total population of "at risk" youth is declining, as are juvenile arrests, detention and training school populations are actually increasing, although fewer youths are entering them, because the average length of stay is increasing. And it is quite misleading to talk about "juveniles" as if they were a homogeneous group; while the proportion of white youths in some form of detention is decreasing, the opposite is true for blacks and Hispanics. The courts may be more lenient toward white juveniles than white adults, with the tendency having become more marked recently, but this is not the case for their disposition of minority youth.

At the other end of the age scale, Cutshall and Adams (1983) found that older shoplifters are brought to trial about as frequently as are juveniles, with both being prosecuted less often than adults in the middle of the age range. Minority groups apart, there may be an "inverted U" shaped relationship between disposition and age, with relative leniency being found at both ends of the age spectrum. The sex of the offender is likely also to play a part, as is race, so that the greatest leniency will be displayed toward older white females, and the least toward black males in the middle of the age range, with legal variables held constant. Certainly, future research into variations in court dispositions must include both legal variables, such as offense seriousness and the offender's prior record, and the extra-legal variables of gender, race, and age.

4.3. The insanity defense

In ancient Rome, an offender deemed mad was treated with leniency because it was thought morally unacceptable to add another punishment to that imposed on the sufferer by the "madness" itself.

A comprehensive review of the Anglo-American approach to the insanity defense has been given by Jacobs (1971). He traces it back to a noted British jurist, Mathew Hale who, in 1736, argued that the insane should not be punished because they do not know the consequences of their actions. The notion of diminished responsibility seems to have made its first appearance at the trial in 1800 of Jonas Hadfield, who was accused of shooting at George III, then on the throne of Britain. The powerful advocacy of his counsel, that he was suffering from a delusion and so should not be punished, even though he was "not wholly insane," secured an acquittal.

The most famous and influential insanity trial is that of Daniel McNaughton, which took place in 1843. He was charged with the murder of the Secretary to the British Prime Minister of the day, Sir Robert Peel. McNaughton claimed a set of extreme and complex paranoid delusions, one of which was that he was being persecuted by Peel (his intended target). The defense argument was that he had lost "control" having been unable to resist his delusions. His acquittal led to considerable public controversy and, several years later, to the McNaughton Rules. The key points of these were: (a) every man is presumed sane until the contrary is proved; and (b) it must be clearly proved that, at the time of committing the act, the accused was labouring under such a defect of reason as not to know the nature of the act, or that he was doing wrong. The rules clearly placed on the defense the onus of showing a causal link between a "disease of the mind" and the crime concerned.

McNaughton was the dominant test of insanity in both the American and the British courts for over a century – although some jurisdictions supplemented the "knowledge of wrongfulness" test with an additional "irresistible impulse" test. In extreme cases, this allowed a jury to acquit a defendant whose act resulted from a sudden and overpowering impulse. Then, in the early 1960's, the American Law

Institute (ALI) reshaped the insanity defense, producing two main innovations. First, the McNaughton "knowledge of wrongfulness" test was modified so as to make it easier to demonstrate lack of criminal responsibility. This was achieved by (a) excusing anyone who lacked a "substantial capacity to appreciate the criminality of his conduct" and (more importantly) (b) introducing a volitional element to add to the solely cognitive emphasis of the McNaughton rules. The latter meant that a mentally ill defendant was to be excused, not only if he could not appreciate the criminality of his conduct, but also if he lacked "substantial capacity to conform his conduct to the requirements of the law." From 1962 on, these ALI tests were widely adopted in the USA, and were supported by all but the most extreme determinists and the most punitive reactionaries (Johnson 1985).

Then came the Hinckley case. In March, 1981, President Reagan was shot and seriously wounded on a street in Washington, DC, in full view of an American TV audience. There other men were also hit, one being left permanently damaged by a bullet in his brain. The prosecution had to show that Hinckley was not so impaired in mental capacity as not to be responsible for his actions. The jury decided he was not guilty on grounds of insanity, accepting the defense claim that the accused was motivated by a desire to impress a well-known movie actress whom he had admired from a distance, thus raising a "reasonable doubt" as to his sanity (Kaufman 1982). This led to a major reappraisal of the insanity defense. The pressure for change was also fuelled by the increasing evidence that the clinical process of assessing insanity was largely idiosyncratic and unvalidated (Rogers 1987). The three major professional associations concerned (the American Psychiatric Association, the American Bar Association, and the American Medical Association) all repudiated the ALI test, particularly its crucial volitional element, but offered somewhat differing alternatives, although there was much on which the three agreed, namely:

1. It is a mistake to allow either the jury or expert witnesses to speculate as to whether the defendant had free will at some particular moment in the past, and it is clear that the psychiatric profession shares to some degree the general public scepticism concerning the objectivity of scientific evidence in this field.

2. Persons found not guilty due to mental illness should not be released outright but should be subject to civil commitment to protect the safety of the public. (This means that there is a presumption of continued dangerousness on the part of such a person; see Chapter 6 for

the connection between mental disorder and crime, particularly crimes of violence, and Chapter 10 for the predictability of dangerousness.)

3. The "criminally insane" should be treated separately from the "harmlessly mentally ill."

In October, 1984, President Reagan signed the Insanity Reform Act. This narrowed the insanity defense in criminal cases to: "The defendant, as the result of severe mental disease or defect, was unable to appreciate the nature and quality or the wrongfulness of his act at the time of the offense." The defendant has to prove his insanity by clear and convincing evidence, and there are stringent civil commitment proceedings for persons found not guilty by reason of insanity. Thus, the gradual changes of the previous 25 years were substantially reversed. Both relaxation and tightening proceeded with rather little regard for the empirical evidence concerning such matters as volitional and cognitive impairment due to mental disorder, as pointed out by the American Psychological Association, which has also urged the need to base any changes on evidence rather than on assertion (Rogers 1987).

The insanity defense in practice

A few spectacular cases, which have aroused widespread public concern, from McNaughton to Hinckley, have had major effects on the rules concerning the insanity defense. But, away from the spotlight, research findings suggest that judges rubber-stamp the opinions of expert witnesses (psychiatrists and psychologists) in everyday cases. In turn, the views of the experts are strongly affected by the defendant being diagnosed as psychotic, and/or having a history of mental hospitalization (Monahan and Loftus 1982). Moreover, the question of competence to stand trial (can the defendant understand the proceedings, etc.?) is often raised as a matter of trial strategy and not as an issue in its own right. Defense counsel might use the question to test the court's receptivity to an insanity plea. The prosecution might do so to lengthen the period for which a defendant found guilty will be confined in a mental institution.

Persons charged with violent crimes are highly over-represented in findings of incompetence (Monahan and Loftus 1982). This means either that they are indeed more likely to be incompetent or that incompetence procedures are more likely to be used as legal maneuvers in cases in which long sentences are possible (typically those involving violence).

Amnesia and crime. From time to time a claim of amnesia (memory loss) following a crime is made by the accused, raising difficult medical and legal issues, reviewed by Schacter (1986). The main varieties of amnesia are organic (pathological forgetting produced by brain damage) and functional (forgetting occurs in the absence of detectable brain pathology, typically of events just before the critical precipitating incident). In the great majority of criminal cases in which amnesia is claimed, the loss of memory has a functional origin and concerns a single critical event.

Amnesia for a critical episode may imply that behavior during that period was *automatic*. In law, automatism is behavior which is executed involuntarily, and voluntary conduct is essential for criminal liability. If an accused cannot recall an alleged crime or does not even know his own identity he cannot instruct counsel properly or assist in the preparation of a defense. In practice, the courts have generally ruled that persons suffering from amnesia are competent to stand trial (Schacter 1986).

Claims of amnesia are made in a substantial portion of homicide cases (20–65 per cent in various studies). The claim is made far less frequently in nonhomicidal violence (8–10 per cent) and almost never in nonviolent crimes. Not all claims of amnesia are genuine: some defendants simulate. A claim of amnesia after a planned crime is inevitably suspicious, and if both the onset and termination of the amnesia are sudden the claim should be viewed with caution; a gradual onset and termination are more likely to be genuine. These rules of thumb indicate the overall lack of information in the field and the difficulty experts have in detecting simulated amnesia.

The use of the insanity plea. According to Monahan and Loftus (1982) the public has the impression that the insanity plea is widespread. In fact it is used in about one cent of criminal cases brought to trial and is usually *unsuccessful* in securing an acquital. The plea is more likely to be raised by those who are older, by whites, and by females than by their counterparts. Two groups are over-represented among insanity acquitees: mothers who have committed infanticide and police officers involved in off-duty killings. Monahan and Loftus (1982) speculate that juries acquit these groups because they need to idealize certain "archetypal role relationships" (mothers are always caring, the police are always law-abiding). By excluding the "insane" from the population of "normal" mothers and policemen – who continue to fit the ideal – jurors can maintain their idealized pictures.

Data from a 1980 admissions survey by the National Institute of Mental Health gave for the first time a statistical analysis of the inpatient services provided by nonFederal general and private hospitals for the *mentally disordered offender* (Steadman, Rosenstein, MacAskill, and Manderscheid, 1988). Out of over 31,000 admissions, the largest group (58 per cent) were those found incompetent to stand trial (IST), the most frequent diagnosis being alcohol or drug abuse. Next came mentally disordered prisoners (i.e., transferred from prison for inpatient psychiatric care) who comprised 32 per cent. Only 8 per cent of the total had been found not guilty by reason of insanity (NGRI), over four-fifths of whom had received a diagnosis of schizophrenia. The remaining two per cent were mentally disordered sex offenders. It is clear that the insanity defense, as the public understands it (the two smallest of the above groups) is used successfully in only a few thousand of the several million criminal trials held annually in the USA.

PART II

Explanation

5. Biological factors

> Let me have men about me that are fat; Sleek-headed men, and such as sleep o' nights. Yond' Cassius has a lean and hungry look, He thinks too much; such men are dangerous.
>
> *Julius Caesar*, Act I, Scene II

This chapter is the first of two concerning the possibility that, with all social and learning factors held constant, some individuals are more likely to become criminals than others. It considers the genetio inheritance of criminal behavior by means of data on the anatomical correlates of crime, sex differences, chromosomal anomalies, family, adoption, and twin studies.

The main purpose of research in this area is to separate out fully the influences of biological inheritance from those of the post-natal environment. As will be seen, all methods fall short of this target, essentially because the requisite degree of experimental control is rarely, if ever, obtainable. But something remains, sufficient to keep alive the possibility that biological factors play a more than trivial role in the criminal behavior of at least some offenders.

5.1. Anatomical correlates

The quotation from *Julius Caesar* which heads this chapter embodies a very old belief, which antedates Shakespeare by at least 3,500 years. It is found in Egyptian writings, in Homer's epics, in the Hippocratic and Galenic doctrines of medicine, and in the Bible. A law of medieval England stated: "If two persons fell under suspicion of crime, the uglier or more deformed was to be regarded as more probably guilty" (Ellis 1914, cited by Wilson and Herrnstein 1985, p. 71). In the present day, it is a convention of detective fiction that criminals are recognizable by such physical features as close-set, "shifty" eyes; the previous chapter made it clear that there is much popular support for these notions.

The "scientific" basis for the belief that inherited bodily and facial features are linked to a tendency to criminality was laid by Lombroso (1911), a physician who studied the inhabitants of Italian prisons in the latter part of the 19th century. At various times he included among the physical signs of criminality: heads which were too small or too large, or which had a characteristic shape; distinctive hair, eyes, nose, lips, palate and jaw; short legs, sloping shoulders and flat feet. And he related physical features to particular types of crime: sexual offenders had full lips; murderers had sloping foreheads. Lombroso's intention was to separate such individuals – who should not be held responsible for their crimes, and should not be punished but isolated – from the remainder, whose crimes were social in origin and who should be amenable to rehabilitation. His theory fell into disrepute when it became clear that many of the "criminals" had been incarcerated for severe intellectual handicap.

Thirty years later the general approach was revived by two American researchers. The first of these was Hootton (1939a,b), a physical anthropologist who carried out a large-scale study of over 10,000 convicted male criminals in ten American states and compared them with 44,000 noncriminals on several dozen physical traits. He concluded that criminals were a physically inferior section of the population, but his study was marred by serious sampling problems, particularly in the control group. A detailed theory of personality and body build, as well as a quantitative method of measuring the latter, was set out by Sheldon (1942). His main expectation concerning criminals was that they would be markedly mesomorphic (that is well-built and muscular) rather than endomorphic (a predominance of body fat) or ectomorphic (narrow and bony).

Several studies, reviewed by Rees (1973), found the predicted association between mesomorphy and crime, but most are marred by serious deficiencies of design. For example, Gibbens (1963) and Epps and Parnell (1952) compared Oxford undergraduates with institutionalized male and female delinquents, respectively. A much better study, by Glueck and Glueck (1956), matched 500 each of official offenders and controls by age, intellectual level, race and area of residence. Twice as many mesomorphs and less than half as many ectomorphs were found among the offenders. However, McCandless, Persons, and Roberts

(1972) found no association between either convicted or self-reported offending and body-build in 177 adolescent males randomly selected from 500 members of a training school, aged 15–17.

There appear to be no studies of self-reported offending and body-build in the general population. Even if an association between the two is found, it need not necessarily indicate a direct link: first, mesomorphic juveniles may be more liable to police surveillance and hence arrest, and the same stereotype may affect adolescent males themselves, so that mesomorphs may be more likely to be recruited as partners for criminal activities; second, the influence of offender social models, themselves well-built, may be greater on mesomorphs than on those less well-built, because of the greater perceived similarity between the former and the models; finally, it seems likely that the performance of the majority of Index crimes is assisted by a mesomorphic physique, and a successful outcome increases the probability of repetition. A satisfactory test of the predicted association between mesomorphic body-build (said to indicate "underlying personality") and crime would require self-report studies of types of crime in which no advantage is conferred by any particular build.

5.2. Sex differences

Biological inheritance is transmitted genetically, the genes being organized on chromosomes. There are 23 pairs in humans, 22 homologous pairs of autosomes, and the sex chromosomes: XX in females and XY in males. Certain biological functions are peculiar to each sex: only the male can produce sperm, only the female can produce eggs, bear a foetus, give birth and suckle the young. But what of the vast range of behaviors other than those to do with conception and reproduction?

It was made clear in Chapter 2 that there are substantial differences between the sexes, for both blacks and whites, in the incidence and prevalence of crime, particularly for the more serious offences, and that any diminution of the male–female gap in the past two decades is relatively small. Several researchers have challenged claims for an inevitable effect of the Women's Movement on the sex disparity in crime. Ortega and Burnett (1987) and Curran (1984) refute "the myth of the new female criminal" citing evidence that even the relatively small recent reductions in the sex gap may be due more to police and court acceptance of the myth and hence to a more severe response by them than in the past, than to a genuinely greater rise in female than in male crime.

There is no question that certain sex differences once thought immutable are crumbling throughout the Western world and are now seen to have been social, rather than biological, in origin. The performance gap between male and female athletes constantly narrows: the male Olympic swimming records of the fifties were equalled by women in the eighties. Only 75 years ago higher education for females was rare, now it is as commonplace as for males (including such former male preserves as medicine and law). And women now serve in military combat units in most Western countries, most recently in the US Army during the Gulf Crisis of 1991.

It is hardly likely that women have become better endowed physically or intellectually in the short time period of this century. It is social convention, opportunity and training which have changed, not female biology. Why then have these major shifts not yet extended, except fairly minimally, to crime? Does it indicate that criminal behavior has a stronger biological component than many others, or is it simply that where crime is concerned the differences between the sexes in social training and opportunity, which are eroding rapidly in many areas of life, are particularly resistant to change? Steffensmeier (1980a) suggests a number of reasons for the continuing disparity between the sexes for crime, all of which are relevant to the latter suggestion.

1. Even though women are entering the work-force in rapidly increasing numbers the traditional roles of wife and mother persist, with the woman responsible for home and child-care, roles which are maintained by family and school socialization and by mass media depictions. Criminal activities would simply be too risky for those with such responsibilities. In line with this assertion, Bartel (1979) found that over half the increase in female crime in the 1960's was accounted for by a decline in the average number of pre-school children per family.

2. Although more women work (giving more opportunities to daytime burglars – usually males!) they are still concentrated in the traditional female jobs – offices, services and retail sales (most women, like most men, do not enter higher education). There is no evidence that the barriers to female entry are coming down in occupations with traditionally high opportunities for crime – truck driver, warehouse worker, deliveryman, dockworker, and other trades – which allow access to goods in transit and confer both freedom and mobility. Thus, women have not increased markedly their opportunities for theft,

for drug dealing on the street, for fencing stolen goods, or to gain specialized skills conducive to criminal acts. Even when women do enter traditional male occupations they are not allowed entry to the male "buddy" networks linked with them – after-hours drinking and gambling groups associated with criminal know-how and activities.

3. The greater current job-participation of females goes along with retention of the traditional family roles already mentioned. The two together leave little time to respond to opportunities for crime, even if they are available, and the temptation to do so may even be reduced by the resulting increase in legitimate family income.

4. Women have only a limited access to illegal acts through the criminal sub-culture and the underworld. Many autobiographical and field accounts indicate that women play subordinate roles in such settings, or are even excluded completely, so that the illegal world seems even more conservative than the legal one. The former places a high premium on physical strength, toughness and "nerve", all regarded as inappropriate for "real" women.

5. Compared with men, women still drink less and approve less of violence: two aspects that reduce their involvement in many offences.

The assignment of different roles to the sexes seems to begin very early, with parents training children differentially. Barry, Bacon, and Child (1957) found a consistent tendency across many societies for parents to induce self-reliance in boys and social conformity in girls. Common observation suggests that boys and girls are bought different toys and are encouraged to play different games, as well as physical aggression being allowed for boys but discouraged for girls. Boys are less strictly supervised than girls, both as to choice of friends and the time they are required to return home at night (Farrington 1987b).

Nevertherless, some women may be changing. Grasmick, Finley, and Glaser (1984) found that, for property offences though not for offences against persons, nonworking women and those who were employed but held traditional sex-role attitudes, had lower self-reported crime rates than those who were both employed and had non-traditional attitudes. Cochrane (1971) compared male and female prisoners with previously obtained control data on nonprisoners in the valuation placed on family security. The prisoners had a more masculine value system than the controls, but this difference may have developed after prison and not before. It would be of interest if "masculine" value systems predicted to future offending in females who not yet begun to do so.

Concluding comment

It may or may not make good social sense to train physically female and male persons differently in the areas of social life relevant to criminal behavior. But, from a scientific point, it becomes extremely difficult to separate out biological and social influences on the marked and persisting sex differences in criminal behavior. Any potential differences, based on biological predisposition, which are present at birth, may well be amplified considerably by social training, the *direction* of the effect being the same. If researchers can find groups of males and females exposed to the same training experiences and current opportunities relevant to crime, but between whom true differences in the prevalence and incidence of crime are found, then a biological explanation for crime gains support. Conversely, if such differences reduce as social training becomes more similar, then the biological explanation is weakened and the environmental one strengthened. (It would be essential to look at different groups of crime separately – for example, against property and against persons – and to use self-report as well as official data.)

Finally, even if sex differences in crime rates reduce in the coming years, differences between human beings in general, irrespective of sex, will persist and may require both biological and social explanations. Whether *separate* explanations for the criminal behavior of each sex are necessary is a quite different question. The general argument of this book is that criminal behavior is not special to any single group; the same explanatory principles can be drawn on for all. In accordance with this theme, a separate explanation for female, as opposed to male, crime will not be required. Farrington (1987b) concurs, pointing out that, in general, the correlates of male and female delinquency are the same, so that theories of male delinquency can be applied readily to crime by females.

5.3. Chromosomal abnormalities

Several sex chromosome anomalies are known: the one which has aroused the greatest interest in criminology is the presence of an extra Y chromosome in males, first described in a letter to *The Lancet* in 1961 (Owen 1972). In the next few years, several reports appeared of a raised, incidence of the XYY anomaly in institutionalized male psychopaths. A biological basis for the "aggressive psychopath" (see Chapter

6 for research into psychopathy) seemed to have been discovered, with the added possibility that other chromosomal anomalies might similarly be linked with crime.

However, a detailed and comprehensive review by Owen (1972) largely demolished the supposed link between the "XYY male" and crime. His major conclusions are:

1. The median height of XYY males in institutions is markedly higher than average, but height may have been the reason for seeking karyotyping (the technique used for identifying the extra Y chromosome) in the first place.
2. The combined prevalence of XYY males in institutions is 4–5 times that *presumed* to have been the prevalence in the general population. Studies of the *actual* rate in the new-born show it to be "not very different from that found in institutions."
3. Case studies of the behavioral characteristics of XYY males range from "schizophrenia" to "serious and hard working," but the general picture is of seriously disturbed behavior, tending towards aggression. Controlled studies, using objective measures, are much less striking:

   > "The lack of any definitive finding with what psychometric data have been collected should call into question the validity of the XYY stereotype. Because of the clear selection bias operating and the high expectancies in many reports, impressionistic data should be questioned" (Owen 1972, p. 244).

4. Crimes of violence are significantly less frequent than in suitably matched control groups.

The topic was revived by Witkin et al. (1976), who looked at the tallest 15 per cent of Danish males born between 1944 and 1947. They found 12 with the XYY amomaly, of whom five (40 per cent) had a criminal record of one or more offences, as against only 9.3 per cent for XY men. But most were minor property offences rather than involving violence. Whereas the XYY men did not differ in parental SES they had lower IQ scores and educational achievements, deficits which seemed to account for half the excess of XYY men over XY males for crime. However, the 9.3 per cent crime rate for the controls seems low, to say the least, and a further review, by Theilgard (1983), reinforces the conclusions drawn by Owen (1972). With particular reference to the Witkin et al. study, Theilgard concluded that there was little support for the notion that XYY males are particularly violent or aggressive, and that behavioral differences between XYY's and controls were not significant.

Perhaps most important of all: even if the reviews by Owen and Theilgard had supported the notion of the aggressive XYY male, their numbers in the population are so small that the vast majority of offending, including crimes of violence, would still require a non-chromosomal explanation. As it is, even this small contribution to the task of explaining criminal behavior seems very doubtful: XYY man can be laid safely to rest.

5.4. Genetic inheritance

Prior to the introduction of the twin and adoption methods (see below) the typical research procedure in the study of human genetic inheritance was to find persons showing the behavior of interest, for example criminality, and then to study their families, sometimes for several generations retrospectively, to determine the frequency and distribution of the behavior concerned. Several studies exemplify both the considerable evidence apparently provided for the genetic inheritance of crime and the basic weakness of the family method.

1. Robins (1966) carried out a follow-up study of white children referred for "anti-social behavior" to a psychiatric clinic. Only 36 per cent of the sample had both parents at home. The percentages of the fathers displaying a variety of problem behaviors thought to be associated with adult criminality were as follows: excessive drinking, 32 per cent; nonsupport or neglect, 26 per cent; desertion of wife and children, 21 per cent; poor work habits, 21 per cent; physical cruelty, 20 per cent. In addition, 48 per cent of the mothers and 23 per cent of the fathers were psychologically disturbed or mentally handicapped.

2. Robins, West, and Herjanic (1975), in another long-term follow-up study, this time of black children, found that convicted parents tended to have convicted children and, as juveniles, to have had similar rates and types of offences.

3. Farrington, Gundry, and West (1975), using data from the Cambridge study of English working-class boys, also found that convicted fathers and mothers tended to have convicted children. Indeed, only 5 per cent of the families in the sample provided half the convictions.

4. Osborne and West (1979), again drawing on the Cambridge data, reported that the mere existence of a paternal criminal record, however

minor or long past, was strongly associated with the delinquency of sons.

One or more of the following major methodological problems sharply reduces the apparent support provided by each of these studies for a genetic contribution to criminal behavior:

1. The children were reared in the parent's home (even if father deserted at some point he was there for some years, and mother remained throughout childhood). It is impossible to separate out "bad genes" from either parental examples of criminal behavior or inadequate parenting, both connected with childhood delinquency (see Chapter 7 for the detailed evidence).

2. The children were exposed to neighborhood modelling influences, potentially favorable to criminal attitudes and behaviors, from both peer-offenders and young adult offenders (see Chapters 7, 8, and 9). Criminal parents tend to live in high crime areas.

3. Some labeling by the criminal justice system may have been at work – the misbehavior of a youngster may be more likely to lead to a conviction if he/she is known to come from a family with a criminal record.

For these reasons it is simply impossible to separate out genetic from environmental influences on crime using the family method; the next two methods have at least the potential to do so.

Adoption studies

Typically, this method involves tracing children who were given up for adoption, preferably very early in life, and comparing the criminal records of the children, first with those of their biological parents and then with those of their adoptive parents. (It is usual to concentrate on male adoptees and on fathers; the much lower frequency of female crime would require much larger samples and hence a lengthier and more expensive inquiry). The genetic hypothesis predicts a significantly stronger association between the criminality of adopted boys and their biological fathers than with that of their adoptive fathers: once the genes have set the track the boy remains on it, relatively irrespective of environment. The value of this method for testing the genetic hypothesis depends crucially on adoption agencies adopting the same adoption policy for the children of fathers known to be offenders and of those not known to have a criminal record: the agency should be no more likely to place the former with an adoptive father with a record than with the latter. The immediate family environments (and ideally the neighborhood also) would then be the same for the two sets of boys. The possibility that this sort of neutral adoption policy may not always be followed by adoption agencies is a major methodological problem for the adoption method and should be borne in mind when considering the relevant studies.

1. Schulsinger (1972) drew from a Danish adoption register 5,000 children adopted at an early age between 1924 and 1947, of whom 57 (termed index cases) had been diagnosed as psychopathic. He compared them with 57 controls from the same register, matched for age, sex, social class, age at adoption and "in many instances for neighborhood of rearing" (the incompleteness of this control is a failing). He found the frequency of diagnosed psychopathy among the biological relatives of index cases to be $2\frac{1}{2}$ times that of the control group – just short of an acceptable level of statistical significance. However, the concept of psychopathy is of doubtful reliability and validity, as will be seen in Chapter 6. Moreover, the diagnosing physician may well have been aware of the case histories of the relatives of the index cases, increasing the probability of the same diagnosis being applied to the child.

2. Crowe (1972). This study is more satisfactory as it deals with actual offenses, albeit officially recorded, rather than a psychiatric diagnosis. Forty one female offenders gave up for adoption 52 children who were between 15 and 45 at the time of the study. The control group was drawn from the state index of adoptions and was matched with the index cases for age, sex, race and age at adoption. Only two controls, as compared with eight index cases, had an official arrest record. Both figures seem very low: in their Philadelphia study Wolfgang et al. (1972) found a recorded contact with the police by the age of 18 in one-third of those surveyed. Admittedly, the Crowe group was not divided by sex, but even so the completeness of arrest information seems in doubt. Nevertheless, the disparity in arrest records (eight to two) remains. At least two major nonbiological reasons for this suggest themselves: a greater police surveillance of boys known to have criminal mothers; a differential adoption policy for the children of known offenders from those not so known. No information was provided on the criminal records of either set of adoptive parents.

3. Hutchings and Mednick (1975) first matched 1145 male adoptees with an equal number of nonadopted boys so as to control for factors

Table 5.1. *Rate of criminality*

	Fathers	
Adoptees	Adoptive	Biological
Criminal	22%	49%
Non-criminal	10%	31%

Source: Hutchings and Mednick (1975).

such as age and social class and then focused on two sub-groups within the adopted group: 143 boys with a criminal record and an equal number without such a record. The key comparison concerned the criminal records of the biological and adoptive fathers of the two sub-groups. The results are shown in Table 5.1. At first sight, the marked disparity in criminal records between the biological fathers of boys with and without a criminal record (49 per cent versus 31 per cent) supports the genetic view of crime. But it should be noted that the *adoptive* fathers of criminal adoptees have a rate of criminality which is more than twice that of the adoptive fathers of noncriminal adoptees (22 per cent versus 10 per cent). This can only be handled by the genetic hypothesis if we assume that the "genetically predisposed" boy leads into crime his adoptive father, whereas the nonpredisposed one does not! A more plausible explanation is that the adoption agencies concerned were not neutral in their adoption policies.

4. Mednick, Gabrielli, and Hutchings (1984). This is the largest systematic adoption study to date. It is based on all nonfamilial adoptions in Denmark between 1924 and 1947, a total of 14,427 male and female adoptees and their biological parents. For 4,000 of the male adoptees there was enough information on parents to assess the potential contribution of parental criminality. (In principle, adoptive parents are selected by Danish agencies only if they meet various criteria, including being free of criminal convictions for at least five years before the placement of the child. Nevertherless, it is clear from Table 5.2 that the adoptive parents – mothers and fathers combined – were far from free from such convictions prior to five years before adoption.

The proportion of boys with at least one conviction rises from 13.5 per cent for those who had neither adoptive nor biological criminal

Table 5.2. *Percentage of adoptive sons who have been convicted of criminal law offences*

	Are biological parents criminal?	
	Yes	No
Are adoptive parents criminal		
Yes	24.5%i	14.7%ii
No	20.0%iii	13.5%iv

Source: Mednick et al. (1984); adapted from Wilson and Herrenstein (1985, p. 96).

parents to 24.5 per cent for those with both adoptive and biological criminal parents, with the other two groups falling between. The most interesting comparison is between the sub-groups marked ii and iii. The respective percentages of 14.7 and 20.0 suggest that the criminality of the biological parents is somewhat more important than that of the adoptive parents, implying the greater importance of the genetic transmission of some criminally related factor. Next, particularly for property crimes, there was a steady rise in the percentage of boys with convictions for crime as biological parent criminality rises from zero convictions to three plus. When the biological parents had three or more property convictions they were more than twice as likely to produce a son with at least one offense than biological parents with no property convictions. Major upheavals between 1924 and 1947, including economic depression, a World War and occupation by a foreign power, had no effect on the stability of these results. Nor were they affected by the exact age of adoption (nearly 90 per cent had been placed by the age of two), by whether the biological parents offended before or after adoption, or by the adoptive parents knowledge of the biological parent's criminal records.

This is an impressive study, in both design and analysis. It gives strong support to a significant biological contribution to criminal behavior. Nevertheless, it would be reassuring to have had unequivocal evidence of a neutral policy by the adoption agencies concerned. As Trasler (1987), p.190, puts it: "This area of research is a methodological minefield because of the complex and unexplicit policies of adoption and fostering agencies."

5. Van Dusen, Mednick, and Gabrielli (1983), in a further analysis of

the Mednick et al. (1984) data, showed that the adoptive family was by no means without influence. In this case, it was family SES which was under study; in future studies it would be highly desirable to investigate in addition social and family variables of probably greater importance, such as child rearing practices.

6. Bohman, Cloninger, Sigvardsson, and Von Knorring (1982). This large Swedish study confirmed and extended the Mednick study. The results for 862 adopted males were much the same; those for 913 adopted females were, if anything, even more clear-cut, suggesting the greater contribution of genetic influences to female crime. (This result would be expected for any group with a relatively low crime-rate; the point will be returned to below.)

Twin studies

The existence of two types of twin, the identical (monozygotic, MZ) which are genetically identical and the fraternal (dizygotic, DZ) which are not, potentially enables the genetic contribution to a variable to be assessed with more accuracy than either of the two previous methods. Unfortunately, a major assumption is required when comparisons are made between the members of MZ and DZ pairs reared together. This is that the social environment is the same for the members of the two types of twin pairs. However, it cannot be assumed that parents, or anyone else, treat both types of twin in the same way or that any differences in treatment are randomly distributed, not being more marked for either type of twin pair. For this reason, the most satisfactory studies are those of twins reared apart from as near birth as possible (e.g., both twins have been adopted, but by different families). If the concordance (roughly the similarity) between the members of the MZ twin pairs reared apart is as great as between MZ twins reared together, and greater than that between DZ twins reared together, a strong genetic contribution to the behavioral variable in question is indicated (and its strength can be stated quantitatively).

Unfortunately, because of the obvious practical difficulties (MZ twins are relatively rare; separated ones even harder to find) only a small number of systematic twin studies have used this design for any area of human behavior, and none for criminal behavior. However, a strong contribution of genetic inheritance to the personality dimension of extraversion has been shown by Shields (1962) and extraversion seems to be related to offending, as will be indicated in Chapter 6. Hence, we

Table 5.3. *Twin studies of criminal behavior*

Authors		Monozygotic No. of pairs	Monozygotic Concordance (%)	Dizygotic No. of pairs	Dizygotic Concordance (%)	*P*
Lange (1929)		13	76.9	17	11.8	< 0.005
Rosanoff and co-workers (1941)		37	67.6	28	17.9	< 0.001
Kranz (1936)		31	65.6	43	53.5	N.S.
Stumpfl (1936)		18	64.5	19	36.8	N.S.
Christiansen	MM	67	35.8	114	12.3	< 0.001
(1968)	FF	14	21.4	23	4.3	
	MF			226	3.5	

Source: Feldman (1977).
M = male; F = female; N.S. = not significant.

can attach some weight to the studies set out in Table 5.3. None is completely satisfactory methodologically, the earlier studies being particularly doubtful. But, taken together, they suggest a significantly higher concordance rate for MZ than for DZ pairs – in other words they supply evidence of a probable genetic contribution to criminal behavior.

Much the most complete and satisfactory of the studies in Table 5.3 is that by Christiansen (1968). It is based on the 6,000 pairs of twins born in the Danish islands between 1880 and 1910, where both twins survived to the age of 15. Christiansen looked not only at concordance rates for convictions in general but also at rates according to severity of sentence, social class and area of birth. Concordance was lower for both MZ and DZ twins for offences dealt with by fines than for those which led to imprisonment, typically more serious in nature. He found a higher concordance for MZ than DZ pairs in middle-class subjects and those born in rural districts than for their working-class and urban counterparts. According to Christiansen, these results fit in with the higher rates of crime in the latter two groups, because higher rates increase the relative importance of environmental variables and decrease those of genetic factors. (In the same way we can expect a greater MZ – DZ gap in females than in males, indicating a greater genetic contribution to female than to male crime. Christiansen's data in Table 5.3. support this expectation.)

The positive tone of the studies in Table 5.3 is partially dampened by a twin study reported by Dalgard and Kringlen (1976). They surveyed all the male twins born in Norway between 1921 and 1930 and tried to interview (as opposed to consulting only official records, the method used by nearly all other researchers in this field) all pairs in which at least one twin had been convicted. The 31 MZ pairs had a higher concordance rate for offenses (25.8 per cent) than the 54 DZ pairs (14.9 per cent), but the difference did not reach an acceptable level of statistical significance. DZ twins, who felt emotionally close to each other, were just as similar in their conviction records as were MZ twins.

These results show the importance of establishing the details of the environments to which members of twin pairs have been exposed. Dalgard and Kringlen (1976) followed all other studies mentioned so far in using only official data on offending. Rowe (1983) collected self-report data, from both MZ and DZ pairs, but he mailed his questionnaires to potential respondents, obtaining a response rate of only 50 per cent and established zygosity (MZ or DZ) by analysis of the data returned by post. These technical shortcomings reduce the weight which can be attached to the overall finding of a significantly greater MZ than DZ concordance.

The desirability of studying twins reared apart was mentioned earlier, as was the great difficulty in doing so. Christiansen (1977) has brought together the few reported cases of separated twins in which at least one has a criminal record. The results are consistent with the genetic hypothesis, but the numbers available are too few to enable firm conclusions to be drawn.

Concluding comment

Despite the many doubts raised about unsatisfactory methodology, there is enough evidence for a biological contribution to the criminal behavior of at least some persons to justify a search for the manner in which this contribution is expressed. The most likely candidate is genetically transmitted personality variables. These are considered in the next chapter. While biological variables may predispose to criminal behaviors they then interact with environmental influences. The relative weights of hereditary and environment will vary between people; it is very unlikely that either one will be the sole influence.

6. Individual differences

> Higgins: "... Doolittle: either you're an honest man or a rogue." Doolittle: "A little bit of both, Henry, like the rest of us: a little bit of both."
>
> Bernard Shaw, *Pygmalion*, Act 5 (1912)

This chapter focuses on individual differences as explanations for crime. It deals with intelligence, personality, and mental disorder, all of long-standing interest, both as "core" areas of applied psychology, and as sources of hypotheses concerning criminal behavior.

6.1. Intelligence

Introduction

The first scientist to construct an objective test of human intelligence was Francis Galton (a cousin of Charles Darwin). However, his tests, developed between 1860 and 1880, and largely to do with sensory functioning, failed to gain acceptance. Instead, the first successful and widely adopted test was devised by a Frenchman, Alfred Binet, whose work began in the 1890's and emphasized verbal skills such as reasoning. The Binet test crossed the Atlantic and, by the end of World War I, intelligence testing was in widespread use in the USA. The main attraction of intelligence tests is that, whatever "intelligence" is, a test such as the Wechsler–Bellevue is both highly reliable and a reasonably valid predictor of educational performance. There is evidence of a strong contribution of genetic inheritance to intelligence as measured by formal tests (Shields 1973), An association between criminal behavior and intelligence test scores would thus give some support to biological views of crime causation.

Intelligence and crime

The first studies date from the early decades of this century and indicated a strong relationship between crime and low intelligence (Goddard 1921). (Research, both in these and in subsequent studies, has concentrated very largely on convicted offenders.) As testing methods improved, the initially very large disparity in favor of official nonoffenders declined until it averaged out at about 8 points of IQ (Hirschi and Hindelang 1977). Because of the high reliability of intelligence tests and the large numbers studied, this relatively small difference is of some potential importance in helping to explain the development of criminal behavior, but first certain controls have to be exercised in order to rule out alternative explanations for the results.

1. SES. Officially designated offenders are drawn largely from the less well-off, and members of lower SES groups have lower than average tested intelligence. Hence, SES has to be controlled for. When this is done, the relationship between intelligence and crime remains (demonstrated by several studies, reviewed by Hirschi and Hindelang, 1977) and further confirmed subsequently in a large scale Danish study by Moffit, Gabrielli, Mednick, and Schulsinger (1981).

2. Are the less intelligent more likely to be caught? That is, does low intelligence impair either or both the selection of crimes with lower detection rates or the performance of offenses once they have been selected? The association between intelligence and crime remains unchanged when crime is measured by self-report (West and Farrington 1977).

3. Yea-saying. It remains possible that low intelligence is associated with admitting crimes, both in police interrogation and in self-report questionnaires. In the latter case, yea-saying may be associated with difficulty in reading certain items; it is easier to admit to the content of the item than to struggle on with trying to read it. However, Quay (1987a), who mentions this hypothesis, makes it clear that as yet it remains untested.

Quay (1987a) concludes that none of these, or other possibilities, is powerful enough to explain the consistently obtained eight point difference; the difference is real and its nature and origin need to be examined.

Verbal and nonverbal intelligence. Typically, intelligence tests consist of two sub-groups of tests, one involving verbal skills, such as word knowledge, verbally coded information, and verbal reasoning, and the other nonverbal, for example, assembling objects and completing pictures. The IQ disparity between official offenders and nonoffenders is largely in the verbal sub-group, the two being very much closer for nonverbal scores. Thus, the question becomes: why is there a disparity in verbal intelligence in favor of nonoffenders? Hirschi and Hindelang (1977) argue that low verbal IQ leads to a poor school performance because verbal skills are more important in school than nonverbal ones. In turn this results in negative attitudes to school and to success through legal channels. Criminal activities then follow.

But the direction of the effect is far from established. It may be that anti-social behavior *precedes* school failure as some studies suggest (e.g., McMichael 1979) and this order of events is strongly implied by the work of Patterson and his colleagues (see Patterson 1986) on the link between inadequate parental child-rearing skills and subsequent school failure and juvenile crime, reviewed in Chapter 7. It has also been suggested that teachers respond to information about low IQ by expecting poor school performance from those they label inadequate, an expectation which is then confirmed by teacher inattention to those of low IQ (Rosenthal and Jacobson 1968). Subsequent research has failed to confirm initial support for this approach, and it is now largely discredited (Pilling and Pringle 1978).

High IQ and crime. Even the most enthusiastic supporters of a link between crime and low IQ will agree that some offenders will be found to have high IQ scores. This is very likely to be the case when we move away from street crimes to organized crime and corporate crime, both of which require considerable skills, of the kind likely to be associated with high verbal scores. Unfortunately, there appear to be no studies of intelligence within these two crime categories; as usual, research is largely confined to young offenders apprehended for street crimes.

A review by Gath (1972) indicates that juveniles with IQ's over 115 (the average of the general population is 100) are both less often caught and, if convicted, are less likely to be sent to institutions, thus avoiding their potentially criminogenic effects. The possibly "protective" effects of relatively high IQ scores are indicated also in a Danish study by Kandel et al. (1988). They showed that men at "high risk" for a career of crime (defined as having a father with a serious record of crime) were able to avoid crime (at least being officially designated as an offender) if they had a high IQ. They interpreted their results in terms of the reinforcement of law-abiding behavior through the success in the school system which is allowed by a high IQ.

Concluding comment

It seems that a low verbal IQ is one factor, of many, associated with officially designated criminal behavior (the others, as we shall see, include personality and child rearing practices). Quay (1987a), p. 114 suggests that they have joint, as well as separate, influences on crime:

> "In the early years lower IQ may make a child vulnerable to poor parenting and [may] even make poor parenting more likely. The probability of this increases if the IQ deficit is accompanied by a fussy or a difficult temperament, motor over-reactivity and poor inhibitory control. All of these combine in the early onset of troublesome behavior. The affected child is now at a double disadvantage when he enters school. He has both less intellectual ability, particularly in the verbal sphere, to cope with academic problems and he has oppositional and aggressive behavioral problems alienating to teachers and peers . . . both are likely to lead to school failure . . . which reinforces more conduct-disordered behavior. . . . All of these factors and others (e.g., deviant parental and peer models) interact to produce behavior which is legally prescribed."

6.2. Personality

No very sharp line divides intelligence from personality, but it is usual to apply the former term to cognitive aspects of individual differences in behavior, the latter to temperamental and motivational aspects, so that we shall find terms like extroversion, aggression and impulsivity, rather than verbal and nonverbal skills.

Three models of personality

The first can be dismissed quickly. In everyday speech it is usual to speak of people as being aggressive or unaggressive, stable as opposed to neurotic, as if they were permanently at one or the other extreme with no shading between. An example of this *typological* model of personality is the doctrine of four basic temperaments, choleric, sanguinic, phlegmatic and melancholic, advanced by the second century Greek physician Galen. It was abandoned in the early years of modern personality research, which began at the end of the 19th century.

Its successor was the *dimensional* model of personality, which asserts that people are not either one personality type or another but occupy points on continuous dimensions, such as extraversion and neuroticism, each position shading into the next. It is assumed that their positions are relatively constant over time and that people will respond to new situations in ways which are predictable from their standing on the dimension concerned. Questionnaires, typically self-administered, give a quantitative score for each dimension. Essentially, this approach expects behavior to be *consistent* in different situations and at different times.

In contrast, the *specificity* model of personality, first made explicit by Watson (1919), emphasizes that learning experiences and current situational stimuli interact to produce differences between people. In short, the specificity (or behavioral) model attributes individual differences in nonintellectual areas of behavior largely to external events and not to "personality." A well argued account of this approach can be found in Mischel (1968), and a more recent, and considerably modified version, in Bandura (1986). Current behavioral theorists place a much greater emphasis than earlier ones on cognitive variables, as will be seen in Chapter 9, which applies this approach to crime. Essentially, the controversy between the dimensional and specificity models in the field of crime will be settled by how *consistent* people are in their criminal behavior, irrespective of variations in their learning history and in the current situation. If there is little cross-situational and cross-temporal consistency in criminal behavior then there is no reason to expect personality measures, based on the assumption of consistency, either to correlate with criminal behavior, or to discriminate between people according to their frequency of offending.

Consistency in criminal and associated behaviors

Introduction. An important ground-clearing operation by Loeber and Schmalling (1985) involved a meta-analysis of 28 studies of child psychopathology. (A meta-analysis combines the quantitative results of a large number of research reports, and then applies various statistical analyses to the data. It is increasingly preferred to the "box-score" approach of totting up the number of published results for and against a prediction; see Bangert-Drowns, 1986, for a technical account.) Loeber and Schmalling's analysis yielded a single dimension, which they termed "overt-covert anti-social behavior." At one end of the dimension are "overt" or "confrontive" behaviors such as arguing, temper-tantrums and fighting, and at the other "covert" or "concealed" behaviors such as stealing and truancy. In the review of consistency research which follows, these two broad groups of behavior will be discussed separately. A major limitation of the studies to date is that most of them concern children, frequently young children.

Covert behaviors. The earliest report, and still the most comprehensive, is by Hartshorne and May (1928). They studied the consistency of cheating and lying by nearly 11,000 schoolchildren who were administered a large number of tasks. By systematically varying the rewards for successful performance and the apparent probability of detection for cheating or lying, the authors were able to measure the extent of consistency (measured by correlations) across tasks and variations within tasks.

Correlations tended to be low, averaging around 0.2, a result considered by both Harshorne and May (1928) and Mischel (1968) to support the specificity view. However, a reanalysis of the original data by Burton (1963) gave stronger support to the consistency position. Nevertherless, there was still much variation between the children, which related to *changes in the situation* – as predicted by the specificity position.

More recently, Nelsen, Grinder, and Mutterer (1969) found a "low to moderate" consistency in response to temptation measures by 100 sixth grade children, suggesting an intermediate level of consistency.

Overt behaviors. This area has both attracted many more studies and provided more support for the consistency position. Most of the research has been longitudinal (testing consistency over time) rather than across situations. Olweus (1979) reviewed 12 studies of aggressive behavior, measured by a variety of means, including observer ratings, peer nominations and direct observation, at intervals ranging from 6 months to 21 years. The average correlation was 0.63 which, after an appropriate technical correction, rose to 0.79, indicating very considerable consistency for aggression by young people (typically male subjects). Several more recent studies have provided somewhat lower but still significant correlations between measures of aggression across time (Feshbach and Price 1984, Huesmann, Eron, Lefkowitz, and Walder 1984, Loeber and Dishion 1984). It is of interest that Lefkowitz, Eron, Walder, and Huesmann (1977) found lower cross-temporal correlations for boys than for girls. Aggression was less frequent for the latter; as noted in the previous chapter, the rarer the behavior the more likely is a biological contribution.

The Cambridge Study (Farrington 1978) also found substantial continuity for aggression: of those rated most aggressive at 8–10 years, 59 per cent were in the most aggressive group at 12–14 (compared with 29 per cent of the remainder) and 40 per cent were so at 16–18 (compared with 27 per cent of the remainder). Data from this report enable us to move from behavioral aggression to officially designated violent crime: the boys who were severely aggressive at 8–10 were especially likely to become violent offenders (14 per cent as against 4.5 per cent), and 70 per cent of those with records of violent crime at 21 had been rated as among the most aggressive of their peers at the age of 12, in comparison with 23 per cent of those without such records.

Concluding comment. The above results all concern people under the age of 21. It is possible that studies of adults would produce a different outcome, but it does seem likely that situational and temporal consistency is moderate for covert behaviors (analogous to offenses against property), rather more substantial for overt behaviors (analogous to offenses against persons).

Personality correlates of crime

Introduction. There seems, then, some basis for expecting personality measures to correlate with criminal behavior and to discriminate between offenders and controls. Two major approaches will be considered, both of which involve the questionnaire measure of personality: multivariate inventories, in which several dimensions are measured by the same questionnaire, and univariate inventories, involving a single dimension. In both cases, people report on those areas of their own behavior represented by the questionnaire items concerned. Questionnaire scores are simply the quantitative total of items endorsed. Ideally, they should stay relatively constant over situations and time – certainly that is the underlying assumption. But the self-descriptions concerned are inevitably responsive to everyday experience. For example, prison life may well affect questionnaire responses, so that it is impossible to know, for example, if an apparent association between personality scores and crime would have been found before entry into prison unless pre-prison measures are also available, a rare occurrence.

Multivariate inventories. Early reviews found little or no support for an association between personality and criminal behavior (Metfessel and Lovell 1942, Schuessler and Cressey 1950), and the pattern has been maintained since (Hindelang 1972, Tennenbaum 1977). A subsequent overview by Arbuthnot, Gordon, and Jurkovic (1987) drew similarly negative conclusions. The principal multivariate inventories used have been the Minnesota Multivariate Personality Inventory (MMPI), the California Personality Inventory (CPI), the Jesness Inventory (JI), the Personal Opinion Survey (POS) and the Eysenck Personality Inventory (EPI). The conclusions which follow are based on Arbuthnot et al. (1987) and apply to the first four inventories listed. (The EPI is considered separately below because it is associated with a major theory of personality which makes clear-cut and testable predictions about many areas of behavior, including criminal behavior.)

1. There are numerous conceptual and methodological shortcomings (e.g., problems in sampling and in subject variability, and with the methods of interpreting profiles).

2. Such problems apart, there has been no great improvement over earlier findings of a lack of relationship between multivariate inventories and criminal behavior.

3. Nevertherless there are some indications that several of these inventories may be useful in classifying young offenders into meaningful sub-groups (see below).

Univariate personality constructs. Once again there has been a massive research effort, and once again Arbuthnot et al. (1987) are largely, though not uniformly, unimpressed. (Material on sociocognitive constructs, mainly to do with individual differences in moral reasoning, which they consider more promising, is covered in Chapter 7 in the context of child development.)

1. Time orientation. The hypothesis is that offenders are strongly bound to the present, paying little attention to the future. Arbuthnot et al. (1987) conclude that time orientation measures do not discriminate in a simple and consistent way between delinquents and nondelinquents (or between sub-groups of delinquents). Any differences found seem related to differing histories of institutionalization.

2. Impulsivity and the inability to delay gratification. These variables probably overlap conceptually with time orientation. There is some indication of a greater impulsivity of officially designated delinquents, but this may relate to a greater probability of being caught, rather than a higher probability of offending.

3. Sensation seeking. It is argued (e.g., Farley and Sewell 1976) that offenders have a greater need for stimulation than nonoffenders, due to operating at a lower than average level of physiological arousal. If there is a shortage of socially acceptable stimulating behaviors, high sensation seekers will carry out arousing criminal behaviors. However, differences between offenders and controls on questionnaire measures of sensation-seeking are modest at best.

4. Locus of control. According to Rotter (1966) people differ in the extent to which they expect outcomes to be directly consequent on their own actions. Those at one end of the dimension, who perceive life-events as largely controlled by luck, fate, or powerful others, are termed "externals," at the other end are the "internals," who see themselves as being in control. The prediction is that offenders should score nearer the external end of the locus of control dimension than nonoffenders. The results of studies are inconsistent, perhaps due to the multidimensionality of what is supposed to be a unidimensional scale. Subcultural differences, between offender and control groups, also complicate matters in some studies.

5. Self-concept. A widely offered prediction is that offenders will have a more negative self-concept (a poorer opinion of themselves) than comparable nonoffenders. Here there are some relatively consistent findings: as predicted, offenders do have a poorer self-concept (but it is still better than the view of them held by parents and teachers). This is particularly the case for middle class white youth. Unfortunately, the direction of causality is unclear – is it the delinquent label or delinquent activity which lowers self-esteem? Wells and Rankin (1983) carried out a path analysis (a method of establishing the sequence of a set of events) and found that, when prior causal factors (school grades, social rejection, etc.) were controlled, no substantial effect of offending on subsequent self-esteem remained.

6. Aggression. The univariate measures discussed so far have a simple predicted relationship with crime, for example, low self-esteem is expected to correlate with high criminality, and vice versa. In contrast, the link between questionnaire scores and crime for the most frequently used approach in the field of aggression is more com-

plex, involving an interaction between the "underlying" tendency to aggression and environmental instigation to violence. Megargee (1966) suggested two broad groups of physically aggressive persons. The first, termed *under-controlled* is chronically low in self-control and is easily provoked to aggression. The second, and much less obvious group, is chronically *over-controlled,* with rigid inhibitions against overt aggressive behavior which is not displayed until the level of anger aroused is high enough to overcome their strong inhibitions. Research to date has resulted in a mixed picture (e.g., Henderson 1982, McGurk and McGurk 1979) but, from the theoretical point of view, Megargee's theory is important in its explicit recognition of personality–environment interaction – typically lacking in the personality literature.

Finally, persons extreme on aggression are often said to display consistent *dangerousness,* a concept discussed in Chapter 10.

It is clear that, once again, the results of research on univariate inventories are equivocal at best. Future work should focus on the interaction of environmental and personality variables, and should be carried out in community, rather than institutional, settings using self-reports, as well as official designations, to produce samples of offenders.

Delinquent sub-types

According to Quay (1987b), we should take a middle course between the view that delinquents are homogeneous, and the opposite one, that they are infinitely varied. Instead, he argues for a relatively small number of sub-groups. His review of the search for them suggests that, typically, four patterns are found, set out below in terms of their major associated behaviors:

Undersocialized	Socialized	Attention-deficit	Anxiety-withdrawal
Assaultive	Bad companions	Preoccupied	Hypersensitive
Disobedient	Group stealing	Short attention span	Shy
Destructive	Loyal to delinq. friends	Daydreams	Socially withdrawn
Untrustworthy	Truants	Sluggish	Anxious
Boisterous	Stays out late	Impulsive	Sad

1. Undersocialized. This is the pattern most troublesome to society. Those who display it are the least amenable to change and have the

most pessimistic prognosis for adult adjustment of any of the four patterns.

2. Socialized (or socialized aggressive). They have good peer relations in the context of delinquent activities, such as stealing, and drug use. There is no need to ascribe psychopathology to this group, whose behavior may be an adjustive response to environmental cues – the inner-city environment abounds in opportunities for criminal acts which are reinforced by frequently successful outcomes.

3. Attention-deficit. The characteristics listed seem less obviously related to delinquency but, according to Quay (1987b), the pattern of cognitive and behavioral features is susceptible to environmental influences which lead to delinquency in the right circumstances.

4. Anxiety-withdrawal. Quay (1987b), and many others consider anxiety to be a major motivator of behavior. Acts such as auto-theft could be motivated by a felt need to escape or to avoid situations giving rise to subjectively experienced distress.

Data on the relative prevalence of the sub-groups are so far sparse (Quay 1987b), but analyses of two samples of federal institution inmates, classified by Cavior and Schmidt (1978) according to the procedures set out by Quay and Parsons (1971), produced the following results: group 1, 18 and 33 per cent: group 2, 28 and 29 per cent; group 3, 30 and 16 per cent; group 4, 28 and 22 per cent. In short, the two aggressive groups accounted for 42–62 per cent and the two non-aggressive for 38–58 per cent. The results for the latter pair are surprising, suggesting that overt aggression is often not the primary behavior problem of legally delinquent youth.

Correlates of the sub-groups. Most of the work to date has concerned comparisons between the undersocialized aggressive and the socialized sub-groups. For example, Henn, Bardwell, and Jenkins (1980) found that the latter were discharged from institutions at a younger age, were less likely to return, and had a lower probability of being convicted and incarcerated as an adult, particularly for a violent crime.

Concluding comment. We have here the beginnings of a potentially valuable approach to the problem of relating individual differences in personality to crime; research is now moving into the area of biological correlates of the sub-groups (Quay 1987b).

Personality theories and crime

This section concerns attempts to explain crime in terms of two very different theories of personality: those of Sigmund Freud, the originator of psychoanalysis, and of Hans Eysenck, one of the major proponents of the dimensional/consistency view of personality.

Psychodynamic theory. The Freudian approach to human behavior had its origins in the treatment of individual patients. In the same way, the psychoanalytical explanation of crime draws heavily on delinquents interviewed in clinics. It is basic to Freudian theory, both in general and as applied to crime, that all human behaviors are motivated, with latent meanings to all actions, meanings which remain unconscious. An understanding of behavior, delinquent or otherwise, requires the analysis of the individual, whether patient or offender.

Binder (1987) has given a brief but incisive account of Freudian theory as applied to crime, the core of which is contained in two quotations from Abrahamsen (1960, pp. 56, 74):

> "Every element that prevents children from developing in a healthy way, both physically and emotionally, tends to bring about a pattern of emotional disturbances which is always at the root of antisocial or criminal behavior. Such behavior, when found in youngsters, is called juvenile delinquency."

> "The psychopathology of the juvenile delinquent and of the emotionally disturbed nondelinquent is manifold because each youngster goes through the same psychological development, although each one experiences it differently. Both may be said to be fixated at one or more stages of their development."

Many psychoanalytical theorists see criminal acts as being undertaken in order to maintain or rectify "psychic balance." A second group argues that crime is a form of neurosis – but expressed in overt acts rather than in psychiatric symptoms. Yet others assert that crime is a substitute form of gratification for needs not satisfied in the family – the youngster then turns to the delinquent gang for acceptance and recognition. The thinking of a final group is related to the sociological concept of anomie (discussed in Chapter 8) which includes the assertion that the search for success in a success-oriented culture is most traumatic for those least equipped to compete – the passive, the compliant and the dependent. Such persons repress these attributes and go to the other extreme, that of aggressive delinquency, which both denies weakness and brings material rewards.

A study by Stott (1980) is a good example of psychoanalytical work on crime. Overall, Stott bases himself on Bowlby (1946), whose theory and research on early maternal deprivation is assessed in Chapter 7. Stott asserts two psychic needs of the growing child: self-realization (coping with reality and being valued by peers); and care and affection from an adult. Denial of either leads first to discomfort and then to anxiety which, if severe enough, triggers off delinquent behavior aimed at certain ends, all of which seek to restore emotional equilibrium. They include: a search for excitement in order to avoid anxiety; retaliation against parents; attention-seeking from parents; and seeking removal from home and compensation for inferiority by adopting a pose of bravado. In short, crime is seen as serving psychic rather than material needs.

As well as displaying the core elements of the theory, this study (of 102 youths aged 15–18 in English institutions for young offenders) exemplifies the psychoanalytical research method and its weaknesses. The theory does not lead easily to clear-cut, testable predictions, the confirmation or nonconfirmation of which then strengthens or weakens a theory. Each case was interviewed individually by Stott himself, with no checks for reliability, and there were no standardized questionnaires or other quantitative procedures. These are general failings of the psychoanalytical approach, which is further damaged by its unrelieved record of therapeutic failure, both with neurotic problems (Rachman and Wilson 1980) and with offenders (see Chapter 11).

Eysenck's theory of personality and crime (Eysenck 1977). This stems from a more comprehensive theory of personality, developed over many years (e.g., Eysenck 1967) on the basis of a range of studies, from statistical analyses of questionnaire items to laboratory measures of psychomotor skills and human psychophysiology. One of the theory's great merits is that it makes predictions which are clear-cut, testable and refutable. A brief version of Eysenck's theory of personality and crime follows; a fuller account is given in Feldman (1977, pp. 143–161).

According to Eysenck, there are three basic dimensions of personality: extraversion (E); neuroticism (N) and psychoticism (P). Scores on the three, which are measured by the Eysenck Personality Inventory

(Eysenck and Eysenck 1975), are used to make predictions in a wide range of contexts, from cigarette smoking to criminal behavior. Whereas both the E and N dimensions approximate in the general population to the classic bell-shaped distribution, scores on P tend to be J shaped, most people obtaining low scores (Eysenck and Eysenck 1968).

E actually consists of two semi-independent components, impulsiveness and sociability, but scores are usually given for E overall, rather than for the two components separately. In idealized form the high E scorer displays sociability, activity, optimism and outgoing and impulsive behavior, the low E scorer (the introvert) the opposite of all these. The physiological basis for E is said by Eysenck to be the general level of cortical arousal (lower for extraverts). Low arousal is said to be associated with the poorer learning of a range of tasks, including the acquisition of social rules by punishment, particularly during childhood. It follows that, with equal opportunities to learn social rules, extraverts will respond less well than introverts. Hence, they will perform more illegal acts, both in childhood and later on. The clear prediction is that higher E scores will be associated with higher levels of offending.

The person high on N is likely to be variable in mood, sensitive to insult and hurt, anxious, restless and rigid; once again, the opposite applies to the low N scorer. The autonomic nervous system is considered to be the physical basis for N; high N scorers are said to react strongly, with excessive fear reactions, and to painful stimuli such as those involved in the punishment learning of social rules. This interferes with efficient learning and, hence, the prediction for N: high scores will be associated with higher levels of offending.

The high P scorer is characterized by the following features: solitary (not caring for other people); troublesome (not fitting in with others); cruel; lacking in feeling (for others' troubles); and sensation-seeking. It is tempting to regard P as standing for psychopathy, rather than psychoticism. The P dimension is said to be associated with the frontal lobe of the cortex. The prediction for P follows directly from the content of the P items: the higher the P score the higher the level of offending.

As well as predictions for the individual dimensions there are also combined predictions, so that those high on all three would be expected to have the highest levels of offending, those low on all three the lowest levels. A summary of a very large number of studies follows.

1. *Convicted offenders*. The comparison has been between prisoners and groups of nonoffenders outside prison, with higher EPI scores predicted for the former. Reviews (Feldman 1977, Farrington, Biron, and LeBlanc 1982) find equivocal results for E, and some support for N and P.

A somewhat different approach was taken by McGurk and McDougall (1981) in a comparison of 100 offenders and 100 officially nondelinquent college students. Both groups contained eN (introverted and neurotic) and En (extraverted and stable) individuals, but EN and PEN persons were found only in the delinquent sample. However, in all of these studies the comparison groups are clearly inappropriate because of the different settings of the two groups (the prison experience may reduce scores for E and increase those for N and P).

2. *The general population*. In these studies, *self-reported* offending has been correlated with EPI scores, the prediction being that the correlations would be significantly positive. This was very strongly supported by Allsopp and Feldman (1975, 1976) for 11–15 year old British schoolgirls and schoolboys, respectively. In both studies those above the median for all three dimensions had the highest self-report scores, those below the median on all three the lowest. The results were more powerful for E and P than for N. A similar outcome was found by Allsopp (1975) for a very large sample of London boys. Rushton and Chrisjohn (1981) reported on eight Canadian samples, mainly of students. In all cases, there were strong relationships between self-reported offending and P and E; those with N, though still statistically significant, were less impressive.

A quotation from West and Farrington (1977, p. 158) concerning the personality features of the Cambridge Study boys chimes in with some of those of the Eysenckian dimensions. Unfortunately, they did not administer the EPI to their study population. The following is based on a range of other reports and scales.

> "Virtually every comparison suggested that the convicted delinquents were more deviant. They were less socially restrained and more hedonistic, more impulsive, more reckless and distinctly more aggressive and prone to physical violence than their nondelinquent peers. They smoked, drank and gambled more, had a faster lifestyle, . . . were more sexually promiscuous, avoided educational pursuits, . . . spent more and saved less."

Two potential alternative explanations of the results for self-reported offending and EPI scores should be noted, together with some major gaps in the underlying theory.

1. The results obtained are correlations only; whether EPI scores are *causal* for crime remains to be demonstrated. It is possible that test scores are influenced by the consequences of criminal activity, rather than causing that activity. The argument was presented above that it is inappropriate to use prison populations to test predictions from Eysenck's theory of crime and personality because test scores may reflect the effects of prison life. We should be equally cautious about the results of studies of the general population. If offending is socially rewarded in a particular setting, high-rate offenders will have increased opportunities for social mixing, resulting in an increased score for E. Repeated derogation of victims and denial of their distress, both important elements in the maintenance of criminal behavior (see Chapter 9), may increase P scores. The potential effects of criminal activity on N scores are less clear-cut. The easy avoidance of detection might reduce them, with difficult avoidance having the opposite effect. As indicated above, the results for N are indeed less powerful than for E and P.

2. It is also possible that E, N, and P are all positively associated with yea-saying, so that high scorers on the three dimensions are more likely to admit to criminal acts on self-report scales. To date, no studies have tried to control for these two factors.

3. Eysenckian theory concerns the acquisition of criminal behaviors; it is largely silent about their performance in response to instigating events and their maintenance over long periods; both are of major importance for a full explanation of criminal behavior.

4. Moreover, the theory is far from complete, even in the area of acquisition; both a background of parental affection and the use by parents of positive reinforcement for approved behavior are highly relevant in training children in social rules; Eysenckian theory emphasizes only punishment as a training method (see Chapter 7).

5. As will be made clear in Chapter 8, many social factors are important in explaining criminal behavior, including the community of residence and the state of the labor market. Such factors play no part in Eysenckian theory.

Nevertherless, the Eysenckian personality dimensions are likely to play a useful part in a comprehensive explanation of criminal behavior. Their value is enhanced by data on the inheritance of E, N and P, which make it clear that genetic factors contribute significantly to all three dimensions. The correlations for both E and N between members of MZ pairs, reared together, are as high as for MZ pairs reared apart, and both are very significantly greater than for DZ twins reared together (Shields 1962). So far as P is concerned, there are data only for twins reared together: they show a significantly higher correlation for MZ than for DZ twins (Eysenck 1977). These results are relevant to the general issue of consistency in criminally related behaviors.

Consistency revisited

Supporters of consistency and specificity both tend to assume that a certain level of consistency in a population is contributed to equally by all members of that population. An alternative approach is that *people vary in their consistency* (Alker 1972, Feldman 1977). The evidence for this goes right back to Hartshorne and May (1928), who noted that when they arranged their schoolchildren in order of consistency, some always behaved honestly, others always dishonestly, and the majority varied, according to the particular situation. Olweus (1975) reported a similar finding for aggression: over a year of observation of Norwegian schoolboys, a minority were always either "bullies" or "whipping boys"; the majority were consistently neither.

At this point, an important contribution by Fulker and Eaves (1973) is relevant. They showed that the heritability of both E and N (i.e., the genetic contribution to the two dimensions) was much greater for those scoring low or high than for the middle-scoring majority, for whom environmental influences were much more important (they did not report data for P; it is reasonable to expect a similar result). Combining the findings for variability in the consistency of behaviors analogous to crime with the Fulker and Eaves evidence on variation in heritability according to personality score yields the following possibility: for a minority of the population, criminal behavior, or its absence, is strongly under genetic influence, expressed through personality variables such as E, N, and P. Those who score highly on all three would be expected to offend across a wide range of situations, except when there is a particularly unfavorable combination of low benefits and high costs; those who score low would be expected not to offend, except in the most extreme combinations of high benefits and low costs. The majority, scoring in the middle ranges, will offend inconsistently and will be strongly under the control of the current pattern of temptations and constraints in each specific situation, as well as of the outcomes of their previous experiences. It may be, as implied earlier in this chapter, that the relative contributions of genes and environment will vary between overt and covert offenses (analogous to offenses against persons and property, respectively). There seems more consistency for the former, so that the proportion of the population for whom genetic control is more important than environmental control may be greater for person than for property offenses.

Genetic influences are only one source of behavioral consistency: others which have been strongly argued for are consistent behavioral outcomes and consistent cognitive appraisals of outcomes, irrespective of their actual consistency (Blackburn 1989). The first of these means that a consistent pattern of past reinforcements, particularly in childhood, increases the possibility of similar behaviors in the future. For example, if the first three attempts at offenses were all both very easy and highly rewarding, a fourth is extremely likely. The second possibility suggests that expectancies for a particular outcome, once they are well established, may override the objective balance of subsequent rewards and costs.

Concluding comment. It is unlikely that any single source of behavioral consistency will tell the whole story: genetically based personality variables, reinforcement history and habitual cognitions will all play a part. Variations in the current situation will then come into play. Whatever the exact mix of "consistency" and "specificity" in determing criminal behavior, this chapter and the previous one have made it clear that biological influences, operating through personality variables, cannot be ignored, particularly for a minority of the population. It is this minority, some of whom fall at one end of the crime continuum, some at the other, with whom theories of crime are most concerned.

6.3. Mental disorder

The central question is: does mental disorder change the probability of criminal actions, up or down, or is the probability the same, irrespective of mental state? The material which follows is in two parts: the first concerns psychological problems other than anti-social personality disorder (psychopathy); the second deals solely with that diagnosis.

Problems in research; general issues

Suppose it is found that the proportion in prison suffering from mental disorders exceeds significantly that which would be expected in the general population. Before we could accept this as evidence for a link between mental disorder and crime we should note several major alternative explanations for the apparent link (Feldman 1977, Chapter 7).

1. As compared with the mentally stable, mentally disordered persons may choose more difficult targets, plan an offense less carefully or carry it out less skilfully, all failings which increase the risk of detection, arrest and an appearance in the official statistics.

2. The police may arrest and charge a disturbed person more readily than others, if only with the laudable aim of ensuring that he is eventually helped.

3. Perhaps most important of all, penal institutions may increase the incidence of mental disorders among those placed in them; mental disorder is then an effect of crime, not a cause. Studies of different age-groups of offenders in institutions suggest an increasing incidence of mental disorder with increasing age of the offender group, from late teenagers (Gibbens 1963) to habitual offenders aged 30 plus (West 1963). In West's study, the sum of money involved in the offense immediately prior to the latest imprisonment was much less for those assessed as deviant in personality than for those judged normal. McClintock and Gibson (1961) found that the clearance rate fell as the sum of money stolen increased. Combining these two results suggests that mentally disordered persons both carry out smaller property crimes and are caught more often than the mentally stable. Having been caught several times they then receive institutional sentences, the cumulative effect of which is that, at best, their mental problems fail to improve, and they may even worsen.

It follows that we need self-report studies of offending by samples of the normal population, the psychological status of the samples being assessed by well-established questionnaires in standard use in community surveys of mental disorder (e.g., the Diagnostic Interview Schedule, Robins, Helzer, Croughan, and Ratcliff 1981). Instead, we have studies of mental disorder among those who have been in prison for varying lengths of time and for a varying number of occasions. In all cases, criminal acts are, by definition, officially designated.

Results of research: some general findings

The design of research in this field falls well short of what is desirable. An important review by Monahan and Steadman (1983) concluded as follows for two major groups of studies:

1. Subsequent arrest rate (after hospitalization and release). Before 1965, every study found this to be *lower* for the mentally disordered than for the general population. Every study in more recent years has found it to be substantially *higher*. The shift has been explained by Steadman, Coccozza, and Melick (1978) in terms of changes in the arrest rates of mental hospital patients *prior* to hospitalization. For example, overall, patients released from New York State mental hospitals in 1975 had subsequent arrest rates much higher than those of the general population. However, for patients with no arrest record at the time of hospitalization, subsequent arrest rates were actually lower than those of the general population. It was only patients with a history of prior arrests – particularly multiple arrests – who had above average rates of offending after discharge from hospital. Monahan and Steadman (1983) point out that this is consistent with a well-established criminological finding: persons arrested in the past are the ones most likely to be arrested in the future. It follows that mental hospitalization (and, by implication, mental disorder) does not seem to affect arrest rates independently of the effects of past criminality. The big increase in arrest rates for released mental patients after 1965 is attributable to a steady increase in the percentage of mental patients with a history of arrest prior to hospitalization – by 1978, 55 per cent of all males admitted to mental hospitals had a prior arrest record.

2. Those treated simultaneously for criminal behavior and for mental disorder. The conclusion is essentially the same as for the first group of studies: their rates of crime and of mental disorder are both about what would be expected from a knowledge of their demographic characteristics and their prior experience with the criminal justice system.

Monahan and Steadman (1983) draw the following general conclusions:

1. The correlates of crime among the mentally disordered seem to be the same as are found in other groups: gender, ethnicity, age, prior criminality, and SES.
2. The correlates of mental disorder among offenders appear to be the same as those of other populations: age, SES, and prior mental disorder.
3. Populations characterized by the correlates of both crime and mental disorder can be expected to show high rates of both – and they do.

It is important to note that these findings refer to the mentally disordered in general and to offenders in general. Two other possibilities remain. First, a particular category of crime (such as offenses against the person) may be found to have a special association with mental disorder in general or with a specific disorder. Second, a particular mental disorder may be found to have a special association with crime in general or with a specific category of crime. These two possibilities are explored in the next section of this chapter.

Violence and mental disorder

A review by Howells (1982, p. 168) concludes:

> "The studies . . . are not entirely consistent in showing a higher rate of violent offending in patients, but . . . suggest an elevated risk . . . [which] . . . is a function of a small proportion of mental patients rather than of mental illness itself . . . it has not yet been demonstrated that mental illness *per se* is significantly and causally related to violent behavior."

Howells (1982) points out that, as for crime in general, the best predictor of future violent crime by the mentally ill is past violent crime. This has been amply demonstrated for the general population by the career approach to criminal behavior research (see Chapter 2). Studies in mental illness and crime have used almost entirely a cross-sectional approach, as shown by Mulvey, Blumstein, and Cohen (1986), who argue for an extension of the career and longitudinal methodologies to the issue of mental disorder and crime.

While the bulk of the work on mental disorder and violence concerns official statistics of crime and diagnosed rather than community-surveyed mental disorder, one study (Steadman and Felson 1984) used self-reported violent behavior during the year prior to the survey to compare the relative incidence of violence among ex-mental patients, ex-offenders, and the general population. In support of research relying on official statistics, the evidence suggests that *ex-offenders* engaged in violence more frequently than the other two groups. Compared with the general population, ex-mental patients appeared to use weapons more frequently but were no more likely to injure other people.

There seems then some descriptive evidence of a link between some mental patients and violence. A number of studies point to schizophrenia, and specifically the paranoid sub-group, as being the most important contributor to this link.

Schizophrenia. This is a major form of psychosis (mental disorders which severely disrupt the everyday lives of those affected, typically in the areas of mood and thinking). Taylor and Gunn (1984) surveyed the total intake to London prisons over a four months period. Out of 2,700 prisoners, nearly 9 per cent were psychotic, of whom more than two-thirds were suffering from schizophrenia, and of men convicted of homicide 11 per cent were so diagnosed (the expected proportion in the general population is under 1 per cent). The authors point out that, since many murderers commit suicide, the figure for homicide and schizophrenia may be an underestimate. Conversely, as indicated earlier, mental disorder almost certainly increases markedly the probability of detection.

The American Secret Service makes a major attempt to reduce the risks of assassination attempts against public officials by interviewing persons seeking an audience with the President. Those thought in any sense mentally disordered are then professionally assessed. Between 1970 and 1974 over 300 "White House cases" (nearly one quarter of whom threatened a prominent public figure) received hospital treatment, the majority of whom had a diagnosis of paranoid schizophrenia (Shore 1985).

Howells (1982) concludes that those diagnosed as schizophrenic are marginally more at risk for violent offenses than are those in other mental patient categories or in the general population, but that the overwhelming majority of schizophrenic patients are never arrested for crimes of violence. (And an equally overwhelming majority of those arrested for person offenses are not schizophrenic.) The psychological features probably most involved are delusional, particularly paranoid, beliefs (Daniel McNaughton, see Chapter 4, is a famous example). However, only a minority of schizophrenic patients have such beliefs, of whom the great majority do not commit crimes of violence, so that additional factors must be sought to provide a full explanation of violent offenses by those paranoid schizophrenics who do commit them.

Depression. West (1966) noted that depression is often observed in those murderers who survive suicide attempts. The problem here is how to separate an intropunitive reaction to the offense (guilt over what happened) from a depressed mood preceding the offense. In hospital settings, those diagnosed as depressed are not more violent than other groups of mental patients or than nonmental patients (Fotrell 1980). It seems likely that the violence of *some* depressed people is engendered only in intimate relationships over a prolonged period of time. Such relationships are less likely in hospitals than in family settings.

Organic syndromes. The electroencephalogram (EEG) is a record of the electrical activity of the brain. In an early report, Hill and Pond (1952) found a higher proportion of abnormal EEG's than expected (on the basis of their incidence in the general population) among murderers labelled "irrational" and "legally insane" than among those labelled "incidental," "motivated," and "sexual." Subsequent studies (e.g., Gibbens, Pond, and Stafford-Clark 1959, Loomis 1965) have been less successful in associating EEG abnormalities with criminal behavior.

A related interest has been in the extent to which impulsive aggression is linked with epilepsy – a problem frequently associated with an abnormal EEG. Although epilepsy is more common in prisoners than in the general population (Gunn 1977), it is rarely an explanation of violent crime. For example, a large scale survey of prisoners by Gunn and Fenton (1971) found only two cases in which epilepsy appeared to have a causal relationship with an aggressive offense. When Gunn (1977) matched epileptic and nonepileptic prisoners, few differences in criminal behavior were observed. Even when epilepsy and aggression appear to be related, other explanations are possible (Gunn 1979): brain malfunction may cause both the violence and the fits; fits may lead both to social stigmatization and to subsequent reactive aggression; environmental factors could produce both fits and aggression (e.g., being battered as a child); "criminal impulsive" life styles may produce brain damage (for example, head injuries following reckless driving).

Property offenses and mental disorder

As noted earlier in this chapter, psychodynamic theory asserts that much crime is motivated not by monetary gain but by deeper causes. Particular emphasis is placed on shoplifting, said to exemplify *kleptomania*. This is defined as "a recurrent failure to resist impulses to steal objects that are not for immediate use or for their monetary value: the objects taken are either given away, returned surreptitiously, or kept and hidden" (Marshall and Barbaree 1984, p. 431).

Gibbens, Palmer, and Prince (1971) found the rate of admission to British mental hospitals between 1964 and 1969 of 1,500 female shoplifters convicted in 1959 to be three times the rate for the general population, with age and sex controlled. But it is possible, as these authors point out, that the mental disorder followed conviction and was a response to it, rather than preceding and "causing" the offense. Also, only a small proportion of shoplifters are convicted. Psychologically distressed persons are likely to shoplift less efficiently and, hence, are more likely to be caught. A later study (Gibbens 1981) of 500 convicted shoplifters found that the great majority were young people (aged 10–18) whose motives involved mainly personal profit. It seems unlikely that the concept of kleptomania will contribute much to the explanation of crime.

Antisocial personality disorder

Concepts and definitions. In earlier literature what is now called antisocial personality disorder was termed "psychopathic" or "sociopathic." Classical German psychiatry (see Schneider 1959) used "psychopath" as a generic term for personality disorder of any kind, whether it is the individual himself who is damaged or whether his behavior causes damage to others. In Anglo-American usage it came to be reserved for the latter. Cleckley (1964) was very influential in defining the key personality features of such persons. (Note that we talking, almost, of a *type* of person, an approach abandoned in personality research in general, see above.) While the reliability of the diagnosis of psychopathy is low, psychiatrists do tend to agree on the defining features of the psychopath (Gray and Hutchinson 1964, Davies and Feldman 1981). As set out by Cleckley (1964), these are said to be: 1, lack of guilt or remorse; 2, inability to profit from experience; 3, inability to delay gratification; 4, inability to form lasting emotional ties; 5, stimulus seeking; and 6, superficial charm.

The third edition of the *Diagnostic and Statistical Manual* (DSM III) (American Psychiatric Association 1981) replaces "psychopath" by "antisocial personality disorder". DSM III lists the following criteria, all of which must be present for the diagnosis of antisocial personality disorder to be made: current age at least 18; onset before the age of 15, with no intervening problem-free period of five years or more; and no evidence of mental retardation, schizophrenia, or mania. Another nine features are then listed by DSM III, at least four of which must be present. Four of the nine are related to four of the Cleckley criteria, but stimulus seeking and lack of guilt or remorse are not included. The latter omission is surprising in view of the very frequent appearance of the term in the relevant research literature (Marshall and Barbaree 1984). The DSM III nine are as follows, where the numbers in parentheses refer to the Cleckley criterion considered by Marshall and Barbaree (1984) to be essentially the same: inability to sustain consistent employment; inability to function as an effective parent; failure to accept social norms evidenced by persistent criminal behavior (2); irritability and aggressiveness; impulsivity (3); inability to maintain enduring sexual/affectional relationships (4); disregard for the truth, including "conning" others for profit (6); and recklessness.

Problems with research

Marshall and Barbaree (1984) consider the DSM III criteria to be an improvement over the Cleckley list, both because of the use of such behavioral features as employment and parenting and the "satisfactorily high" inter-rater reliabilities (i.e., psychiatrists not only agree what antisocial personality disorder means, but agree when they see it).

However, two critical comments are in order. First, all nine criteria are open to disagreement (for example: what does "consistent" employment mean?; how "irritable and aggressive" does one have to be to qualify?; and, particularly important, how "persistent" does criminal behavior need to be, and is it to be measured by official statistics, by self-report or by other methods? Second, while one of the inter-rater reliabilities mentioned in DSM III is reasonably high (0.87, Spitzer and Fleiss 1974) the other (0.65, Spitzer, Forman, and Nee 1979) indicates a significant degree of disagreement – not surprising in view of the definitional difficulties indicated above.

There is evidence from studies of mentally disordered violent offenders that, rather than a single "type" or category of antisocial personality disorder, there are four sub-groups (Blackburn 1986, 1989). The four are termed by Blackburn: primary psychopaths (impulsive, aggressive, hostile, extroverted); secondary psychopaths (impulsive, hostile, socially anxious and withdrawn), and two others (conforming, and inhibited) which represent different forms of over-controlled aggression (see above for a discussion of this concept).

Howells and Hollin (1989) point out that the same four sub-groups are to be found in the offender population generally, rather than only among violent prisoners, whether in prisons or hospitals (Widom 1978a, Henderson 1982). However, there are marked differences, both in personality and in behavior, between the sub-groups. For example, whereas primary psychopaths are low in anxiety and high in extroversion, the secondary sub-group is introverted and high in anxiety. And Blackburn (1984) found 52 per cent of primary psychopaths, but only 8 per cent of the inhibited group, to have a history of repeated violent acts. From all of this, it is clearly desirable for explanatory research to be carried out on separate sub-groups within the overall grouping of antisocial personality disorder. But this has not been the case: the great majority of research reports concern undifferentiated "psychopaths," and use a wide range of selection criteria (Hare and Cox 1978), making it very difficult to compare results.

A further problem is that, with occasional exceptions, research has been carried out on persons in institutions, whether prisons or hospitals for mentally abnormal offenders. Some studies select their "psychopath" group from the total population of prisoners in the institution, so that all have an equal chance of appearing in the "psychopath" and "nonpsychopath" groups. In other studies, the psychopath group comprises those previously diagnosed by a psychiatrist, using criteria of inadequate reliability. Perhaps the most telling criticism of the near exclusive use of institutional populations comes from Robins (1966), cited by Hare (1970, p. 115), one of the major researchers in this field: "Only a small proportion of the psychopathic population is actually referred to psychiatrists." We might add that an unknown proportion is at any one time outside prison and that many never come into any kind of contact with the legal system. As Hare himself points out: "Research with the more socially successful psychopaths is badly needed . . . there are real difficulties in obtaining suitable subjects" (Hare 1976, cited by Widom 1978b, p. 71).

In an attempt to overcome this problem, Widom (1978b) placed advertisements in a Boston "counter-culture" newspaper for people who were "charming, aggressive, carefree . . . impulsively irresponsible but good at handling people and at looking after number one" (Widom 1978b, p. 72). Of the 73 people who responded 28 finally participated in the study (23 males amd five females). Their occupations ranged from radio program director to bartender. The great majority met Robins' (1966) criteria for "sociopathy" which overlap with the DSM III list. All but three were drug users and most were multiple users. Unfortunately, no data were collected on self-reported offending. Nevertheless, Widom's report shows that research into antisocial personality disorder can move outside institutions.

To sum up: we need studies on noninstitutional populations, differentiated into sub-groups by methods which have a high degree of reliability. In contrast, the research to date, which is reviewed below, has been carried out on institutional groups, usually not differentiated into sub-groups, and selected by a variety of methods, some of low reliability. In reviewing the research, the older term "psychopath" will be used rather than "antisocial personality disorder" because that is the one employed in the great majority of research reports.

Research results

A large number of studies have compared psychopaths with others on laboratory measures of avoidance learning. This interest stems from one of the major defining features of the diagnosis – the apparent failure to learn from experience, particularly the experience of punishment. According to a number of researchers (e.g., Hare 1970) this is due to an *inability* to learn to avoid aversive stimuli (i.e., punishment) despite ample opportunities to do so. In turn, the failure to avoid punishment is said to be caused by a low level of cortical arousal, leading to a pathological need for stimulation (Quay 1965). Thus, there are two sets of relevant studies: physiological responses and avoidance learning.

Physiological responses. The general prediction is that psychopaths will have lower resting levels of cortical arousal and will be less responsive to external stimuli on a number of physiological measures, typically skin conductance and EEG, both thought to indicate arousal. A detailed review of the literature by Siddle and Trasler (1981) concludes that, compared with other groups, in some studies (but by no means all) psychopaths have diminished levels of resting skin conductance, or of spontaneous fluctuation in skin conductance, or diminished reactivity/habituation to stimuli. In a further review, Trasler (1987) was very cautious, concluding that skin conductance measures depend on the exact conditions of the experimental situation and that, until more precise techniques are developed, the question of consistent differences in conductance between psychopaths and others cannot be resolved.

Syndulko (1978, p. 154) concludes a review of EEG studies: "Data from the few available studies do not support the notion of simple differences in cortical arousal levels between sociopaths and controls." Syndulko (1978, p. 149) also comments: "While a subset of subjects labelled sociopaths do show an excessive incidence of EEG abnormalities . . . the sociological, clinical and psychological characterisics of this sub-set are not known."

The physiological studies mentioned so far all involved persons diagnosed as psychopaths during adulthood, and are open to the general criticisms of research on psychopathy listed earlier. But we have also two prospective studies of people in the community who were followed up some years later to compare their original EEG records with subsequent offending. Petersen et al. (1982) measured the waking and sleeping EEG's of nearly 600 Swedish children before the age of 15. Twelve years later about 10 per cent had at least one officially recorded offense. Offenders had more slow brain wave rhythms of the type associated with low arousal, especially if their offending began early. And Mednick, Volavka, Gabrielli, and Itil (1981) found a significant relationship between EEG records collected in 1972 and criminal records acquired by 1978, particularly between theft and the pattern indicating low cortical arousal. While these two reports are interesting, neither mentions the diagnostic status of those with both early low arousal, as indicated by their EEG patterns, and subsequent criminal convictions. It may be that a higher proportion of this sub-group approximated to the criteria for antisocial personality disorder than of those with normal EEG patterns, but this potential link must await further studies.

As for stimulus seeking, questionnaire measures show psychopaths as unusually high on measures of sensation seeking, but so are recreational sky-divers (Blackburn 1978).

Avoidance learning. The specific prediction here is that psychopaths will be poorer than controls at learning avoidance responses to painful stimuli such as electric shocks. Support has come from a series of studies (see, for example, a review by Trasler, 1973) with a minority of contradictory evidence. However, several alternative explanations should be noted. First, psychopaths may be selectively unresponsive to electric shock as an aversive stimulus (most studies of avoidance learning use shock rather than alternatives such as loud tones (Marshall and Barbaree 1984). Second, psychopaths show normal responses to shock if they are rewarded for doing so (e.g., by receiving cigarettes or money, Hare and Thorvaldson, 1970). Third, the likelihood of punishment seems important; psychopaths perform as well as controls when the probability is high, less well when it less certain (Siegall 1978). Marshall and Barbaree (1984, p. 425) conclude: "Thus, psychopaths are responsive to punishment but only when it is relevant to them and they believe it is likely to occur. Psychopaths do not appear to have a constitutionally defective response system to punishment."

There is another set of results which is contrary to the basic assertion of failure to learn from the experience of punishment. Gibbens, Pond, and Stafford-Clark (1959) compared diagnosed psychopaths with a sample of other offenders for frequency of future offending and found it to be the same. Both Walker and McCabe (1973) and Black (1977) found only weak differences in reconviction rates between psychopaths and other discharged mentally disordered offenders. Much the best predictor of future offending in both studies was the frequency of past offending – the usual finding, as has been noted earlier.

Interpersonal behavior

According to Eysenck (1977, p. 55): "The psychopath presents the riddle of delinquency in a particularly pure form, and if we could solve this riddle in relation to the psychopath, we might have a very powerful weapon to use on the problem of delinquency in general." Certainly, the concepts of psychopathy and antisocial personality disorder, with their implications of a lack of feeling for others, particularly for their distress, remind us that criminal behaviors involve victims as well as offenders, damage to the former as well as benefits to the latter.

Unfortunately, there have been relatively few studies of behavior toward others, comparing psychopaths and controls. Sutker (1970) reported that sociopaths showed higher skin conductance responses than controls to a stimulus paired with shock to another person. She interpreted this result as indicating that sociopaths are at least as sensitive to social cues as others. However, it is not simply social awareness which is at issue, but responsiveness to others, particularly to their distress, a topic which has not attracted research attention.

Widom (1976) found that, in a Prisoner's Dilemma game, primary psychopaths functioned as well as controls (male nurses), cooperating well over a period of time; secondary psychopaths performed less responsively towards their partners. It should be noted that of the 22 pairs which played the game, none involved a psychopath and a control as partners; it is the behavior of psychopaths towards the non- or at least less-psychopathic majority which is of interest. This aspect underlies work by Howells (1983), which is based on the proposition that diagnosed psychopaths tend to make attributions of negative intent to other people – that is, they habitually perceive others as sources of negative, rather than positive, reinforcement. Rather than wait to test this expectation they "get in the first blow." Support for this approach was obtained by Howells (1983), using a special measure of cognitive evaluations, and in a descriptive study by Rime, Bonvy, and Rouillon (1978), who reported that those diagnosed as psychopaths had an "over-intrusive social presentation." Compared with others, they leaned forward more and looked more at a partner in conversation, while smiling less. These behaviors produced a "spontaneous attitude of retreat" in others – who withdrew from the interaction – thus confirming the belief of the psychopath participants that others are hostile.

Concluding comment

Despite many conceptual and methodological inadequacies, some progress has been made in delineating the behaviors associated with the diagnostic category of antisocial personality disorder (formerly psychopathy) and in separating out the possible sub-groups of the category. But, research has failed to demonstrate clear differences between diagnosed psychopaths and others which are relevant to the defining criteria. Although neither avoidance learning nor physiological findings can be ignored entirely, studies of the interpersonal behaviors of the sub-groups, preferably using noninstitutional participants, may be of much greater potential value for explanations of crime and particularly of attitudes and behaviors towards victims.

7. Childhood development

> Train up a child in the way he should go and when he is old he will not depart from it.
>
> *Proverbs*, xxii, 6

7.1. Introduction

This is the first of three chapters which examine the importance of social influences and experiences for the explanation of criminal behavior. It focuses on childhood and adolescence, and proceeds from an account of research on moral development, through parental child-training and the importance of family experiences for early and subsequent offending, before moving outside the family to schools, peer groups and the impact of the media, particularly television, on children and adolescents. The overall emphasis in research on childhood and crime has been on failures to acquire socially acceptable behaviors and on the reasons for failure, which are seen to lie in dysfunctional families, specifically in inadequate parenting, both in itself and in interaction with influences outside the home, and with individual differences between children.

7.2. Moral development

There are two major descriptive systems of moral development, those of Piaget, and of Kohlberg. The former is more of historical importance; the latter provides the major focus for current research on moral development. Both are rather sparse on the detail of the socialization process, emphasizing instead that, providing the right broad conditions are available, moral development will occur almost inevitably. Also, both systems explicitly assume the unfolding of a sequence of changes which are roughly correlated with age as the individual matures, changes which are largely independent of specific learning experiences but arise from the inherent structure of human cognitive functioning. It has been asserted, without supporting evidence, that systems of moral development have a biological basis: "A large number of biological mechanisms undoubtedly conspire to provide the precondition for moral conduct" (Hogan 1973, p. 218).

Piaget's theory

This theory (Piaget 1932) forms part of a series of monumental researches into cognitive development in general over a period of half a century. He argues that there are three principal stages in cognitive development. During the first, from age two to age seven and termed the pre-operational stage, actions are internalized as thoughts, and tend to precede thought. Events are perceived in absolute, not relative terms. This is pre-eminently the stage of *ego-centrism,* during which others are perceived to revolve round the self. The second stage, from age seven to adolescence, is termed the stage of *concrete operations*. During this stage the child is capable of operational thinking (making comparisons between events and relating them to each other). In the third, which begins with adolescence, the child is able to carry out formal *cognitive operations,* such as comparing future relationships and events.

Relating this general structure to moral development, Piaget characterizes the first stage as one in which the rules are given by powerful others, the second in which children perceive that they can invent and modify rules, and the third in which they perceive the primacy of abstract rules over the particular situation. There will tend to be a time lag, according to Piaget's approach, "practical morality" (behavior) preceding "theoretical morality" (the attitudinal component). This fits in very well with the general view of contemporary behavior theorists such as Bandura (1986).

Kohlberg's theory

This theory (set out in detail by Kohlberg 1964) is more complex than Piaget's. It postulates six stages, in three blocks of two stages each. Like Piaget's stages, each is age-related, though Kohlberg tends not to specify the age involved, being more concerned with emphasizing the sequential ordering of the stages. Stages five and six may be combined into one, as in Arbuthnot, Gordon, and Jurkovich (1987) p. 159, paraphrased below.

A. The pre-moral period.

Stage 1. Moral behavior is based on concrete rules (breaking laws results in punishment).

Stage 2. Each person seeks the maximum return to himself, largely irrespective of the return to the other (breaking laws results in a loss to oneself).

B. The period of conventional conformity to rules.

Stage 3. Persons conform and adjust to others (breaking laws will make people think badly of you).

Stage 4. There is a respect for and a duty to those in command, such as social and religious authorities, and a need to avoid their censure (breaking laws engenders disrespect for the law and can lead to social instability).

C. The morality of self-accepted principles (the period of autonomy).

Stage 5. The full development of universal principles of ethics and justice, which may transcend those of the existing legal systems (breaking laws is generally unacceptable since they are made with common agreement; but they may be broken if they violate fundamental human rights, for example an "illegal military order" to shoot civilians so as to "teach a lesson").

An overview of the two systems. There are several major common features of Piaget's and Kohlberg's systems (Aronfreed 1968).

1. There is a sequence of age-correlated changes, summarized as follows: (a) The judged severity of a transgression is first related to the amount of visible damage, and later shifts to the intention of the transgressor. (b) The younger child sees justice as given. The older relates the severity of a transgression to its consequences for others. For the younger child the scale of punishment is a function of the severity of the offense, whereas the older takes into account attempts at restitution. (c) Finally, there is a transition from the rules being seen as fixed and unchangeable to being relative to persons and situations, and mutually changeable.

2. In general, the younger child takes into account only what is good or bad for the actor. The older child makes a gradual shift from social conformity, through the need to take the welfare of others into account, to the highest stage of intrinsic right and wrong.

Research on moral development

Two major areas will be reviewed: the first concerns the stages of development themselves and the second concerns differences between delinquents and others in moral knowledge (related to the stage of moral development attained).

The sequence of moral development. Snarey (1985) examined 45 cross-cultural studies of Kohlberg's system and found much support for the full range of stages, and thus for the general applicability of the system. (He notes also some bias in the system in favor of complex urban societies and middle class populations.) However, an earlier review of relevant research (Feldman 1977, pp. 36–37) indicated several specific shortcomings which apply to both systems:

1. The stages may be successive, but movement through them depends on *learning*, and the direction of development can be reversed by appropriate learning experiences.
2. The rate of movement through the stages is similarly dependent on specific learning experiences.
3. Neither system specifies how the hypothesized structures of conscience are acquired. Any satisfactory theory of socialization must spell out how social training experiences modify attitudes and behaviors and the consequences of different kinds of experience. A detailed example of such a theory is provided by Aronfreed (1968, summarized by Feldman 1977, pp. 41–50).

Individual differences in moral reasoning. A review by Arbuthnot et al. (1987) of studies comparing official delinquents and controls drew the following conclusions:

1. There are clear differences in moral attitudes toward the acceptability of various offenses.
2. As expected from 1, most studies show delinquents to have attained lower stages of moral development than nondelinquents.
3. One study which failed to do so (Jurkovic and Prentice 1977) nevertheless found a sub-group assessed as psychopathic to be at stages 1 and 2, whereas other delinquents and nondelinquents approached stage 3. Similar findings have been obtained for the undersocialized aggressive sub-group described in the previous chapter.

4. Nevertheless, as Arbuthnot et al. (1987) point out, many delinquents are found at the higher stages of moral development. There is as yet no information on any differences between them and the larger number of delinquents found at the lower stages.

5. There are consequences for moral development level of different child-management practices. These are discussed in the next section of this chapter.

Finally, there are three important gaps in this field – as in so many areas of criminology. The first is the absence of longitudinal studies which track changes in moral development stages over time. It is quite possible that functioning at the lower stages of moral development may be a *consequence* and not a *cause* of delinquent behavior. The second is that all studies to date appear to be of officially designated offenders; they should be supplemented by groups selected by self-report. Third, there is a dearth of studies of adults as opposed to juveniles.

7.3. Training children

Introduction

Parenting is a learned skill like any other; "instinct" is not enough. The current emphasis is on techniques and resources, and in general on the current family situation in which parents and children interact. The concern of an earlier generation of researchers with parental personality as affecting behavior towards children is now less marked though still present. There is an increasing interest in the direction of effect being two-way: as well as parents influencing their offspring, children influence the way their parents behave towards them.

Techniques of training and dimensions of care

Hoffman and Saltzstein (1967) distinguished three broad training techniques for responding to proscribed behaviors by children (including behaviors analogous to delinquency, such as lying, and temper-tantrums).

1. Power assertion. The use of physical punishment and/or the deprivation of material objects or privileges, or the threat of punishment or deprivation.

2. Love withdrawal. The parent more or less openly withdraws affection, for example, by ignoring the child, or threatens to do so.

3. Induction. The parent develops empathic and sympathetic responses in the child by referring to the consequences of the child's action for the parent ("you've upset me," etc.).

The first method is associated with the development of an external orientation, based on the fear of external detection and punishment. The latter two, and particularly induction, lead to an internal orientation characterized by the self-control of behavior, independently of external sanctions (Aronfreed 1968). Compared with punishment, induction provides the child with cognitive and emotional resources both to examine and correct transgressive reactions and to avoid them in the future.

In their own study, Hoffman and Saltzstein (1967) found that the highest level of moral development (in terms of Kohlberg's stages) in a sample of middle class children was associated with the induction technique, the next with love withdrawal and the lowest wtih power assertion. In their working class sample the use of induction was infrequent and the relationships between technique and moral development less clear-cut. An overview of more recent studies by Arbuthnot et al. (1987) indicated broadly similar results to those of Hoffman and Saltzstein with middle-class children. Homes which emphasized power assertion and love withdrawal rather than induction resulted in children with lower levels of moral development than those in which parents encouraged participation and joint problem-solving. Hoffman (1975) found in a sample of middle-class parents that mothers tended to use induction techniques more often with girls than with boys, and that the former displayed more consideration for others, boys focusing more on achievement.

A rather different theoretical approach has been taken by Hogan, Johnson, and Emler (1978). They emphasized two major dimensions: warm versus cold, and permissive versus restrictive. Each of the four possible combinations of extreme positions will produce distinctive patterns of behavior, as follows:

1. Warm-restrictive parents: children will value adult approval, readily internalize rules and keep them.
2. Warm-permissive parents: children will be self-confident and socially out-going, but will frequently ignore or bend rules.
3. Cold-restrictive parents: children will be anxious and sullen but compliant; anger will be turned in on themselves.

4. Cold-permissive parents: children will be hostile and defy rules, with a high probability of delinquency.

These dimensions have some intuitive appeal, but are couched in rather general terms. However, they should be borne in mind in the section of this chapter which concerns families and crime.

Family interaction patterns

In the studies considered above, both moral development and parental technique were assessed indirectly; the former by questionnaire, the latter by interview. In contrast, a major program of research, by Patterson and his associates at the University of Oregon, involves the direct observation of parent–child interactions as well as the measurement of children's overt behaviors, in the home and elsewhere, by both observation and by parent and teacher ratings. They record repeated sequences of interaction in the family home using standardized, clearly described and hence replicable methods of observation. The account of their work which follows below and in the next section draws heavily on Snyder and Patterson (1987). A key point is that if chronic offending is found to be associated with certain family interaction patterns in the childhood of those concerned, this has implications for crime prevention – parents currently engaging in incorrect patterns may be trained in more appropriate methods. Work on this aspect of the Oregon program is reviewed in Chapter 11.

Snyder and Patterson (1987) organize their data round four major themes: discipline; positive parenting; monitoring; conflict and problem-solving. The consequences for delinquency of their inadequate or inappropriate use are set out below in the section headed Families and crime.

Discipline. Effective methods involve the accurate definition and labeling of certain behavior as excessive or antisocial, the consistent tracking of those types of behavior over time, and the use of effective (though not harsh) methods to inhibit them.

Positive parenting. This refers to parent–child interactions which foster interpersonal, academic and work skills, and encourage the development of socially acceptable behaviors. It involves the accurate labeling and tracking of the desired behaviors and giving positive reinforcement for performance. Parental interest in the child, the communication of that interest, and shared activities supply parental models of skilled behavior, and mean that parents and children give each other positive reinforcement.

Monitoring. This refers to the extent to which parents are aware of their childrens friendships, their free-time activities and their physical whereabouts when outside the home. Effective monitoring means setting clear rules about when the child should come home, persons and places that are approved or proscribed, as well as parental awareness of school attendance and performance, and TV and movie viewing. It implies also occasional checks on whether the rules are being kept, and disciplinary action when they are not. As children get older they spend a decreasing amount of time with their parents, so that monitoring plays a more central role as the age associated with early offending (8–10) is reached.

Problem solving and conflict. All families experience constant minor irritants and problems in their daily lives, such as arguments between family members or with people outside the family. Many also have to deal with major crises such as unemployment or divorce. Whether the problem is major or minor, a successful solution requires that families acquire and use adequate problem-solving skills and coping strategies. The failure to do so may facilitate antisocial behaviors in several ways. For example, unresolved problems distract parents from applying their parenting skills effectively. Ineffective problem-solving may lead to overt aggression as a short-cut to a solution; "success" in the conflict may then make this the preferred pattern of behavior in future disagreements as well as serving as an unsuitable model for children.

Deficient family interaction patterns

Patterson (1986) sets out four key hypotheses, produced by several decades of work by the Oregon group:

1. Disrupted family management skills lead to antisocial behavior by the children of disrupted families, first in the home and then elsewhere, including school.

2. Noncompliant and coercive features of the behavior of such children increase both the risk of rejection by "normal" peers and academic failure.

3. Such behaviors in the home lead first to parental rejection and then to low self-esteem.

4. The combination of academic failure, rejection by peers and low self-esteem leads to academic drop-out and a high risk for offending.

The basic idea underlying their research program is the key role of child rearing practices in determining both pro- and antisocial child behaviors. If parents fail to teach a reasonable level of routine compliance by their children the result is a series of coercive exchanges between parent and child. These are then displayed in school also, so that most social encounters are battles. If parents fail to punish effectively minor coercive behaviors, these lead to repeated and coercive interactions and then to habitual aggression. Each family member "trains" the others to become aggressive in behavior.

These researchers have analyzed large numbers of family interaction sequences which show groups of apparently trivial behaviors (noncompliance, whining, teasing, yelling, disapproval) as the learning bases for aggressive behaviors, the end-point of many sequences being physical attack. In some families there may be dozens of daily sequences of attack and counter-attack leading to positive outcomes for the more aggressive participant. Children who thus learn that either aggression or counter-aggression are successful proceed from a high rate of coercive behavior (whining, yelling, temper-tantrums) to the final use of physical aggression (Patterson 1986).

The parents of such children threaten, nag, scold and bluster, but do not follow through on their threats until, at irregular intervals, they explode and physically assault the child. In two studies overviewed by Patterson (1986), about 40 per cent of the antisocial behavior (aggression, temper-tantrums, minor stealing, etc.) in pre-adolescent boys was accounted for by inept parental behavior.

Patterson (1980) reported the mean rates of aversive behaviors per minute to be 0.73 for 2–4 year olds, 0.42 for 5–6 year olds and 0.21 for 8 year olds. These were the figures for normal children. The rates of aversive behavior for 8 year olds referred for treatment as behavior problems were virtually identical with those for normal 2–4 year olds.

The fathers of children referred to Patterson and his colleagues for stealing were the least likely of several comparison groups to punish aversive behavior by their children (Patterson 1980). Even when they did so there was a significant increase in deviant behavior, including stealing. The reason for this is said to be an inadequate pairing of parental threats and appropriate back-up punishments. Instead the parents yell, scold, threaten and occasionally physically assault the child. Patterson considers that more effective parents are more likely to follow the threats and scoldings with punishments such as the withdrawal of privileges.

Risk factors for deficient interaction patterns. Patterson (1986) lists the four as follows.

1. Families suffering from social disadvantage (lower SES with poor occupational skills). However, correlations are only of the order of 0.30, meaning that it is far from inevitable that the poorly-off make poor parents.

2. Relatively unskilled parents. It is striking that poor parenting skills seem to be inter-generational. The deficient skills of grandparents are correlated with the antisocial behavior of both their children and their grandchildren (Elder, Liker, and Cross, 1983).

3. A child with a "difficult" temperament. Some children are simply more difficult to raise than others, everything else being equal. (The relevant background material is covered below.) There is much evidence for a link between a difficult temperament and subsequent antisocial behavior (Sameroff and Seifer 1983). This is particularly the case when the parents are unskilled in child management.

4. Major stressors in daily life. Parental attempts at effective child management are disrupted by financial problems, medical conditions, and substance abuse. Divorce is a special stressor which leads to one parent having to cope alone. The same problem affects families which have only one parent from the outset (particularly common among black Americans – see Chapter 8). A study by Baldwin and Skinner (1989) confirmed the applicability to single-mother families of the general Patterson model originally developed with two-parent families.

Resources. As well as the level of skills available to them, "resources" include the amount of time parents have for child-training as well the number of parents present.

A home in which there is only one parent will have fewer relevant resources (information, time, and money) to fight through the legal process from arrest to sentence, leading to an increased possibility of a more severe disposition and, hence, of a further offense (see Chapter 4). A single parent has to carry out all the chores alone; there is simply less time for child-training. As a result, the child may spend more time outside the home exposed to potentially criminogenic peer-group influences. The "fault" is not necessarily a deficit in parental skills, but in the learning experiences the child has outside the home. The same argument applies to families in which there is marital strain: parents distracted by their own problems have less time to train children consistently, and may even welcome relief from the company of the child. And in all families under strain the temptation might be to use those techniques of training which are less time-consuming in the short-term but are less effective over a longer period (power assertion, rather than induction).

Constitutional factors and child management

In an important review, Bell (1968) discusses the long-held assumption that the child is a *tabula rasa* ready for the imprint of social training by the parent. In fact children differ from birth in several features which influence parental behavior toward them. Bell makes particular mention of person orientation. Babies high on this will be more responsive to parents, and thus induce higher levels of care (and perhaps the use of induction, rather than power techniques).

It follows that some children will be "easier" than others to train. Thomas, Chess, and Birch (1968) were able to classify children soon after birth into those who were "easy" (regular in body functions and in sleep habits), and "difficult" (withdrawn, intense, irregular in habits, crying readily and frequently), with many babies falling between the two extremes. Independently of parental handling, the easy children adapted to almost any child-rearing style, the difficult ones required exceptional patience and skill. Freedman (1974) showed that these differences are constitutional in origin: identical twins were significantly more similar than fraternals for social awareness and smiling. Subsequently, Thomas and Chess (1984) found that the difficult children were four times as likely than the easy ones to be referred for psychiatric help in later years.

Concluding comment

Overall there is good evidence that there is a sequence of events from poor parenting skills to antisocial behavior in boys (all research to date has been on boys). The next section extends the story from antisocial behavior to legally designated delinquency. There are various modifying variables such as parental resources and constitutional factors in children, but the general implication is that if all parents were highly skilled in child-management there would be a dramatic drop in crime by their offspring.

7.4. Families and crime

Family interaction patterns and delinquency

Before reviewing the links between delinquency and the major parenting themes delineated by Snyder and Patterson (1987) two longitudinal studies, one American and one British, give the flavor of work in this field.

The American study (McCord 1979) extended over nearly 40 years in all. It began in 1939 when 235 boys, thought to be at risk of later delinquency, were visited in their homes by counsellors as part of the Cambridge-Somerville Youth Study, one of the first large-scale attempts to prevent delinquency by psychological therapy. (The therapeutic aspect of this work is discussed in Chapter 11.) In 1957, coders rated the 1939 descriptions of "home atmosphere" (parental relationships and child rearing methods) and between 1975 and 1978 the original group were traced and the court records of Massachusetts examined. Six out of seven home atmosphere variables were positively related to subsequent (officially designated) crime, "father absence" being the only exception. With SES controlled, the two most important predictors were maternal affection (for the boy) and parental supervision; where these were low, delinquency was high, and vice versa.

The British study (Wilson 1980) was over a much shorter time span, but points the same way, and used self-reports as well as official statistics. Parental supervision, assessed before the age of 10, was much more important than either social handicap or a parental record of delinquency in predicting the delinquency rate of over 200 British boys by the age of 17, but all three predictors were statistically significant. However, when the prediction was to self-reported offending, only parental supervision remained significant.

In these two reports, both of which figure in Snyder and Patterson's (1987) review of family interaction patterns and antisocial behavior and delinquency, supervision is related to "monitoring" (defined above). The review (13 studies in all) includes cross-sectional, as well as the technically more satisfactory, longitudinal studies and a variety of measures of antisocial behavior, from temper-tantrums to officially designated property and person crimes.

Monitoring. This is the most important of the four interaction themes, as indicated by the percentage of the variance in antisocial behavior accounted for (1–46 per cent). Parental monitoring is significantly related to the variety and frequency of delinquent behaviors, and increases in importance during adolescence. Because monitoring helps to minimize adolescents' contacts with delinquency-promoting circumstances, activities and peers, it is difficult to separate out the direct from the indirect effects of monitoring.

Discipline. When this is described as lax, neglectful, erratic, inconsistent, overly harsh or punitive, it is found to be predictive of adolescent delinquency and aggression, for both self-reported and official delinquency and for person as well as property crimes. "The disciplinary practices [of the parents] of recidivists are worse than those of one-time offenders which, in turn, are worse than those of nonoffenders" (Snyder and Patterson 1987, p. 220). It should be noted that the strength of the relationships obtained range from 1 per cent to 40 per cent of the variance in child antisocial behavior. Two somewhat different disciplinary styles have been found associated with antisocial behavior: "lax," and what Patterson and Snyder term "enmeshed" (harsh but inconsistent, so that the child is sometimes punished, sometimes not, in an unpredictable manner; the importance of the *schedule of reinforcement* for antisocial behavior is discussed in Chapter 9).

Positive parenting. Parental coldness and rejection, minimal involvement with the child and a lack of shared leisure time are all predictive of delinquent behavior, both self-reported and official. But once again the range of the variance accounted for is great – from 1 per cent to 28 per cent. And, as Snyder and Patterson point out, the relationship between positive parenting and child behavior is inevitably reciprocal: antisocial children encourage parental rejection, so that the longitudinal research method is to be preferred. (It is much more difficult to establish the direction of the relationship by the cross-sectional method.)

Problem solving and conflict. This is the least powerful of the four themes – the variance accounted for ranges from 1 per cent to 18 per cent.

"However, it appears that those families whose members are highly irritable and have inadequate problem-solving and coping skills to deal with stress are more likely to produce or already have a delinquent child" (Snyder and Patterson 1987, p. 229). Once again, we must note the last point, having a delinquent child may both increase irritability and cause problems for which existing skills are inadequate. In the longitudinal studies cited by Snyder and Patterson the amount of variance acounted for by problem-solving exceeds the extremely modest level of 4 per cent only in one study (Elder et al. 1983) in which the dependent measures were "temper-tantrums" and "difficult child;" both are a long way from either official or self-reported offending.

Snyder and Patterson (1987) point out a number of deficiencies in the research to date: studies of inner-city groups have so far been the exception rather than the rule; the direction of effect is reciprocal, not one-way from parents to children; it may be that genetic rather than environmental effects are important – both inadequate parental practices and child antisocial behaviors could be due to shared genetic predispositions. (Also, overall, the proportions of the variance accounted for are consistently higher for cross-sectional than for longitudinal studies.) Nevertheless, the data reviewed, together with the more extensive overviews covered below (Loeber and Stouthammer-Loeber 1986, 1987) indicate the general value of the family interaction approach as part of a wider perspective on childhood and crime.

Broken homes

Current work on the effects on children of being reared in a home broken by death or divorce (usually the latter) is linked to earlier theory and research by the notion of *attachment*. This is defined by Ainsworth, Blehar, Walters, and Wall (1978, p. 302) as: "The affectional bond or tie that an infant forms between himself and his mother figure – a bond that tends to be enduring and independent of specific situations." The belief of many child psychologists is that the development of the bond is not inevitable, and that its absence has important psychological and behavioral consequences, one of which may be antisocial behavior.

The general thesis of a link between inadequate attachment and delinquency has its origin in work on *maternal deprivation* by a British psychiatrist, John Bowlby, who in turn was strongly influenced by the Freudian approach to personality development discussed in Chapter 6. Bowlby's views are set out in the following quotations. The first asserts the link between the child's need for maternal affection and the development of mental health; the second relates deprivation of affection to the development of criminal or psychopathic behaviors:

> "Essential for mental health is that a child should experience a warm, intimate, and continuous relationship with his mother (or permanent mother substitute) in which both find satisfaction and enjoyment".

(Maternal deprivation is defined as " . . . a state of affairs in which a child does not have this relationship;" Bowlby and Salter-Ainsworth, 1965, pp.13–14.)

> "Maternal separateness and parental rejection are believed together to account for a majority of the more intractable cases [of delinquency]" (Bowlby, 1949, p. 37).

In short, it is argued that the emotionally deprived child becomes the criminal who offends without remorse for his victim. The affectionless character follows from events in the first three or four years of life: a lack of opportunities to become attached to a mother-figure; periods of separation from the mother of three to six months; shifts from one mother-figure to another. All three types of experience are asserted as causal of criminal behavior, separately or in combination (Bowlby and Salter-Ainsworth 1965, p. 54).

Evidence. Bowlby himself contributed two empirical studies (Bowlby 1946, Bowlby, Ainsworth, Boston, and Rosenbluth 1956). The first gave strong support to the general theory, the second very limited support, but both were so deficient methodologically as to be without value as tests of the theory linking emotional deprivation with delinquency (Morgan 1975.)

Subsequent attempts, up to the early 1970's, to test the hypothesized link gave a mixed picture, but a key point is that negative findings tended to come from the better designed studies (reviewed by Feldman, 1977, pp. 39–41). A selection of more recent studies follows:

1. Wadsworth (1975). The British National Sample regularly follows up 5380 children born in one week in March, 1946. Those raised in families broken by divorce or desertion were more likely to become officially delinquent than those raised in intact families.

2. Hamparian, Schuster, Dinitz, and Conrad (1978). A study of all juveniles born in Franklin County, Ohio, between 1956 and 1960 found that those with at least one arrest for a violent offense were less likely than the average juvenile in the area to live in two-parent homes.

3. Elliot, Knowles, and Canter (1981). An analysis of NYS data found both the incidence and prevalence of self-reported delinquency to be higher among youths living with one biological parent than with both.

However, the Cambridge-Somerville Youth Study found that boys from broken homes were no more likely than to offend than those from intact ones (McCord 1979). And a review of 18 studies of female-headed families (Herzog and Sudia 1973) found that seven reported more delinquency in father-absent homes, four reported less, and seven gave a mixed picture. A study by Kellam, Adams, Brown, and Ensminger (1982) indicates a further complication. More than 1,000 children growing up in the predominantly black Woodlawn section of Chicago were followed up for more than 10 years. By 1982, self-report data indicated that those boys who had been in mother-only families at six to seven were more delinquent at 16–17 than those who had lived with two parents in those early years. But temperament was also important and interacted with family setting. Boys from "low-risk" families (both parents present in the early years) who were unaggressive were the least likely to become delinquent; the most likely were aggressive boys from mother-only families. Boys who were aggressive at an early age were likely to become delinquent irrespective of family type. (They may have been exposed to inadequate family interactions of the kind described above, or were biologically predisposed to aggression, or some combination of the two.)

Wilson and Herrnstein (1985) suggest a number of reasons for the contradictory findings of studies on broken homes, the most important of which is the lack of agreement as to the meaning of the term "broken home." It is not enough to define this as the absence of one parent, typically the mother. Studies tend to lump together families which have been single-parent from the birth of the first child with those which have shifted from two parents to one. If there has been a break, researchers should distinguish between several possible types. There may be different consequences of death and divorce and, if the latter, whether the divorce was contested or agreed and the extent of access to the child(ren) of the parent not granted custody. The separation may have been sudden or protracted and marked by repeated returns and departures. And the pre-divorce relationship may have been more distressing than the actual rupture.

Until studies select and define their groups much more precisely, employing agreed criteria for a "broken home" (and preferably use the prospective, longitudinal approach and self-reported as well as official data), the lack of agreement will continue.

Abusive homes

There is no doubt about the widespread occurrence of physical violence against children by their parents, as indicated in Chapter 1. But the definitional and methodological problems found in the work on broken homes are even more marked in research on child physical abuse and its possible consequences for criminal behavior by abused children. One of the most widely accepted generalizations among clinicians is that those who were abused as children abuse their own children, and that both generations are over-represented in statistics of violent crime. But is it in fact the case that "violence begets violence"? A comprehensive review by Widom (1989) makes the following major points:

1. Many studies involve case histories of doubtful statistical usefulness.
2. The empirical evidence showing that abuse leads to abuse is fairly sparse and most is methodologically problematic: there is an over-dependence on self-reported and retrospective data and on inadequate documentation of childhood abuse or neglect as well as an infrequent use of control groups.
3. Existing studies do suggest a higher likelihood of abuse by parents if the parents were themselves abused as children. But many adults who abuse were not abused in their own childhood.
4. Among the abused the majority become neither delinquent nor violent offenders. Also, most delinquents were not abused as children.
5. It may be that neglected children show higher levels of subsequent violent behavior than abused children, but it is difficult to separate out the two influences.
6. The path from early abuse/neglect to adult violence is very complex. Other life stresses are likely to have an important impact. The age at which abuse/neglect occurs, the characteristics of the perpetrator(s) and of the child and the child's perception of events may all be important.
7. Research is needed on factors which protect children against the consequences of abuse or against being abused in circumstances in which it might be expected but fails to occur.

Finally, Trickett and Kuczynski (1986) found that abusive parents used physical punishment, regardless of the type of child misbehavior, as compared with control parents who were more likely to match their response to the misbehavior. This suggests a basic lack of skill in child management, which might be responsive to training.

7.5. Childhood variables and crime

Introduction

This section draws heavily on two major reviews by Loeber and Stouthammer-Loeber (1986, 1987) of the association between a wide range of childhood factors and later delinquency. These reviews differ from Snyder and Patterson (1987) discussed above. The latter concerns only those family interaction patterns identified by the Patterson group. In contrast, the reports by Loeber and Stouthammer-Loeber include many scores of studies and cover a much wider range of factors (although inevitably blurring the fine detail of parent–child interactions). Most of the studies reviewed in their 1986 report are retrospective, meaning that the comparison was made when the subjects had already been identified as delinquent; only a small proportion is prospective. Their 1987 review focused exclusively on the latter type of study, but even of these, most involved only a small number of repeated assessments, making it difficult to reconstruct changes over the years of childhood and adolescence. Moreover, few of the studies reviewed used direct observations of behavior (whether parent–child interactions, aggression, and so on); most involved some form of rating or questionnaire measure. But, these massive surveys are inevitably a mixed bag. Some studies are methodologically satisfactory, most have major shortcomings. Authors of surveys have to make do with the material at hand, and their conclusions (as in this case, see below) are inevitably cautious. Nevertheless, taking the two reviews together, they represent the best current distillation of the material in this field and deserve to be read in full.

Results

1. The best predictors of later juvenile delinquency are early conduct problems: aggression, stealing (unofficial reports by parents and teachers), truancy, lying, and drug use. They are not only predictive, many years later, of delinquency in general, but especially of serious delinquency, and in some instances of recidivism.

2. Children are at high risk for later delinquency and aggressiveness if they do not "outgrow" aggressive behavior by early adolescence. A majority of later violent delinquents appear to have been highly aggressive as children; similarly, early theft predicted later theft and burglary, and early drug use was associated with later drug use.

3. Juvenile arrest or conviction is a predictor of adult arrest or conviction but the *seriousness* of a juvenile offense seems to be a better predictor of continued serious offending in adulthood.

Thus, the best predictors of later delinquency were serious early delinquency or analogous behavior. The remaining predictors, though in some cases substantial, were all less powerful.

4. The next best set of predictors was individual family variables. Of the specifically child rearing variables, poor supervision and parental rejection of the child were the strongest; lack of discipline and lack of involvement were somewhat less powerful. Parental criminality and aggressiveness and marital discord were moderately strong predictors. Parental absence, parent health, and SES were all weaker predictors. The most powerful of all in this category were multiple family handicaps.

5. There was some prediction from poor school performance to later delinquency, but the evidence suggests that the effect is influenced by accompanying conduct problems. On the basis of these and other handicaps, a majority of eventual chronic offenders can be recognized in the primary school years. (A more detailed review of the potential link between school and delinquency is given below.)

Methodological issues, and limitations on the results

1. In retrospective studies (the majority), the measurements are not independent because the outcome (i.e., delinquency) is known.

2. In prospective, longitudinal studies, selective attrition is a problem, and groups at the highest risk for later offending usually have the highest attrition rate. (This is a particularly severe problem in a highly mobile society like the USA).

3. The number of studies per predictor variable is small, so that generalization to other populations is hazardous.

4. Some studies concern special groups already designated as deviant, in which the predictive power of early precursors of delinquency tends to be higher than in (the much more numerous) normal populations.

5. There is a lack of studies on the prediction of self-reported delinquency.

6. There are few studies of black or other minority populations. (This is a particularly important gap in the literature.)

7. Prediction is not the same as causation. (Nearly all parents find it hard to train "difficult" children, and very few studies control for this factor.)

8. A high proportion of those thought to be at risk do not become chronic offenders (the false positives, typically about 60 per cent of the "at risk" group). This sort of over-prediction could lead to the inclusion of the wrong children in training programs. The prediction of false negatives – those predicted not to be delinquent but who do become offenders – is much less of a problem, averaging about five per cent.

Implications

1. The various family handicaps can interlock:

(a) Deviant parental values may be followed by family conflict because parents overlook trivial conduct problems, seeing them as age-appropriate. The children then move to more serious antisocial behavior, at which point the spouses are pitted against each other in mutual blame and undermining.

(b) Family conflict may be followed by neglect. Problematic behavior by a child persists for a long period, resulting in parental dislike for the child, and a lack of persistence in effective discipline.

(c) Family disruption may be followed by neglect or conflict. For example, after chronic discord, parents are more coercive, or are so absorbed in their problems that they exercise less, or less effective, supervision.

2. There may be cumulative effects of family handicaps:

(a) Multiple family handicaps increase the risk of later delinquency.

(b) Families at risk of producing delinquent children are those that have to cope with a temperamentally difficult child, especially one who is overactive, impulsive, or with a short attention-span; those who have limited resources to cope with such a child are even more at risk. Limited resources include poor child-rearing skills, disruptions that tend to interfere with the deployment of these skills, such as marital discord, loss of a partner, social isolation, or lack of social support from outside the nuclear family, and poor parental physical or mental health. All of these can be aggravated by economic handicap and by large family size. These implications echo Patterson's (1986) conclusions (see above).

3. Changes over time in children's conduct problems.

(a) Normative improvements in early problems. Most children outgrow behavior typical of toddlers and pre-schoolers, such as whining, temper-tantrums, and seeking too much attention.

(b) Conversely, there may be a progression to more serious and more varied problems. Such children fail to outgrow early problems. Instead, they expand their repertoire of problems and progress to illegal acts.

(c) Some children who develop new problems in late childhood or early adolescence then desist, especially in late adolescence.

4. Changes over time in parental practices.

(a) Parents often have their own schedule for acknowledging a child's independence, and may lag well behind their children's schedule. Parents also differ in the speed with which they adopt more age-appropriate, child-rearing practices.

(b) Sometimes parents are immobilized in their existing methods as a result of long-standing and major struggles, particularly with chidren who were difficult to rear from the start. They may hope, even, that the child will leave home.

(c) Sometimes an unfavorable change in family circumstances leads to conduct problems. For example, new marital discord by the age of 14 is associated with increased aggressiveness in boys not previously aggressive (Farrington 1978).

(d) Conversely, there is evidence that when risk factors are reduced child behavior problems are also reduced, for example in children separated from a parent because of family discord or deviant parental behavior (Rutter 1981).

Vulnerability and survival

The results presented so far for childhood and family factors and crime make it clear that many children are highly vulnerable to later delinquency. Chapter 10 will discuss attempts to combine such predictive factors into a single index which might then be used to select children for a preventive treatment program. Quite apart from planned interventions, it is clear from the large number of false positives in all predictive studies (see above) that many children who are highly vulnerable to later delinquency nevertheless avoid crime. It is possible that some have merely escaped detection, and might still be convicted with a longer period of follow-up. Nevertheless, some follow-up periods are very long indeed (for example the Cambridge study has now tracked the original group of eight year olds to the age of 32) and the factors associated with "survival," though diverse and fragmentary to date, make some sense.

Farrington (1988) found that those who remained unconvicted at 32, despite having features at eight or nine identified as predictive of later offending, tended to have few or no friends at the age of eight, no siblings with behavior problems, unconvicted parents, and low daring. At 32, many were still socially isolated, but the majority were leading relatively successful lives (good relationships with wives and children, good accommodation and a history of continuous employment).

Werner and Smith (1982) followed for over two decades all the children born in 1955 on Kauai, one of the Hawaiian islands. Most of the six hundred they tracked lived in low-income families. As expected, a majority of those who had experienced four or more stressful events by the age of two had developed serious learning or behavioral problems including delinquency by the age of 18. But some surmounted all the obstacles. These "invincibles" had certain favorable features which combined to increase their mothers responsiveness to them: they were cuddly, active and affectionate as infants with few health problems, as well as having a high IQ. In addition, they were typically first-born, allowing close and mutually rewarding contact between mother and child.

Finally, Stumphauzer and colleagues have pointed out that some young men avoid crime, even when living in very high crime areas which provide many highly visible models of repeated and often successful offending. They analyzed the relevant "trouble avoiding behaviors" in the *barrios* of Los Angeles. These included knowing how to interact with both gang members and the police so as to avoid conflict with either, and having a repertoire of rewarding alternative behaviors to crime, including car-repairing and other skills. Older brothers, with trouble-avoiding behaviors already in their repertoire, modelled them to younger brothers who, in turn, kept out of trouble (Stumphauzer, Aiken, and Veloz 1977).

7.6. Schools

Delinquency and school performance

"A long series of studies – from 1936 to the present – have found negative associations between school performance (grades, educational tests, or liking for school) and delinquency" (Gottfredsen 1981). While this is the case for officially designated delinquency, and in both black and white samples, the relationship is less strong with self-reported delinquency, particularly for black males (Hindelang et al. 1981). Nevertheless, the link between poor school performance and delinquency seems sufficiently strong at the descriptive level to require explanation. Three major candidates are listed by Wilson and Herrnstein (1985): predispositions (IQ, temperament and home discipline); schools as intervening variables (predispositions exacerbated by the school experience); and the school experience alone. Before surveying the relevant research we should remember that schools are in business to teach; they are not set up to answer research questions, however valuable to teachers the answers may be. As a result, it is very difficult to separate out predisposing factors either from each other or from the school experience itself.

Predispositions. Those who favor this explanation assert the following:

(a) Low IQ, particularly low verbal IQ, leads to difficulties with school work and eventually to drop-out from school. In addition, a low verbal IQ may lead to a poor understanding of the consequences of one's actions, a limited ability to delay gratification, and poor verbal communication.

(b) Those who are temperamentally impulsive, extroverted and aggressive find school boring, confusing and unrewarding. It is more exciting, first to truant and then to drop-out.

(c) Children subject at home to inconsistent disciplinary practices enter school without having acquired a strong connection between actions and consequences, and so find it relatively harder to respond to teachers, the new sources of authority, than those consistently disciplined by their parents. The same effect follows from a failure to form strong bonds of affection with one or both parents.

A number of studies provide relevant findings. Dishion, Loeber, Stouthammer-Loeber, and Patterson (1984) reported that, although a range of academic, interpersonal and job-related deficits correlated with both official and self-reported offending, academic-skill deficits (presumably related to verbal IQ) did so most strongly. Powers and Witmer (1951) found that the most delinquent of the Cambridge-Somerville boys both had lower average IQ's than the remainder and were more likely to be described by teachers as troublemakers, aggressive and impulsive. West (1982) also reported that boys rated as troublesome by primary school teachers became delinquent in secondary school. Spivack, Marcus and Swift (1986) found a positive relationship between school misconduct through grade 3 and police contacts during adolescence. They identified an early high-risk pattern in both males and females among inner-city blacks: a child who was both initially disruptive and subsequently failed to modify his/her own behavior to fit in with others was likely to be in conflict with authority early in life and to continue the opposition into adolescence.

Schools as intervening variables. This hypothesis predicts an interaction between child attributes and teacher response, and is the essence of the "Pygmalion effect" reported by Rosenthal and Jacobsen (1968), who claimed that large IQ changes came about due to teacher expectations. However, by 1971, of nine attempted replications none was found to have had more than a very small effect (Eliashoff and Snow 1971). Research has failed to demonstrate also that children placed in low ability tracks commit more offenses than those placed in other tracks (Wiatrowski, Griswold, and Roberts 1981). Moreover, Rutter and Giller (1984) found an association between low IQ and antisocial behavior *before* school age, undercutting the notion that low aptitude children become frustrated by teacher rejection once in school, and hence turn to offending.

The school experience. Do different "kinds" of school have different rates of delinquency, irrespective of individual differences between their pupils, such as IQ, and personality? Rutter, Maughan, Mortimore, and Ouston (1979) surveyed all the 10 year olds in one part of London and followed them until the age of 14. The sample was working-class with a mean IQ below the national average. Twenty five per cent of all fathers had been convicted, of whom one-third had been in prison. The boys attended 12 schools in all. The school attended made a significant difference to delinquency rates, which varied very widely between the schools. The key factors which distinguished the schools from each other were the "intellectual balance" of the pupils (the higher the proportion of the most able the better), and the "ethos" (a teaching style which emphasized the value of school work, rewarded good performance and used firm but fair disciplinary procedures). Both were associated with lower delinquency rates.

A very large American study (Coleman, Hoffer, and Kilgore 1982) of 60,000 students in 1,000 public, private and parochial high schools found the two latter types of school much less likely than the former to have serious problems of fighting, vandalism, truancy, drug abuse, and verbal abuse of teachers. The effects were still significant, though less powerful, when measurable skills and traits were controlled for.

It is worth pointing out that in the case of both studies *parents* as well as schools may differ. Parents with the approach to discipline found in "high ethos" and in parochial and private schools may send their children to such schools; the schools thus receive groups of boys amenable to the style offered by the school. Farrington (1972) found that boys who behaved badly in primary school were much more likely to be sent to a secondary school with a high delinquency rate, and vice versa.

The same was the case for truancy, an important precursor of delinquency: those with high rates of truancy went on to have high rates of delinquency, and every significant result obtained with delinquents – in terms of family and personal attributes – was found also with high rate truants (Farrington 1980). It followed that the differences in the secondary schools in their truancy and delinquency rates were due primarily to their differing intakes. (This has echoes of differential adoption placements according to the prior history of the biological parent, see Chapter 5). A fairer test of the third hypothesis would result if there was a true random assignment of boys to schools offering clearly different "management styles." There appear to be no such studies as yet.

The community context

A very different approach is taken by Toby (1983), who argues that a school has a high crime rate because it is located in a high crime community. In such communities there is less parental supervision and less teacher support for parents (and vice versa) than in their low crime counterparts. Teachers no longer have the absolute authority they once had and, in addition, have to cope with increased racial and ethnic tensions as minority groups have moved into inner-city areas. Toby gives a vivid description of schools which mirror the communities in which they are located: many students arrive an hour or more late; others come on time but wander round the school for the rest of the day; students who are hostile to learning undermine those who are keen; teachers become discouraged, reduce their efforts and leave (the departure of some is hastened by assaults by students); their replacements are unlikely to be of the highest calibre. And so the downward spiral continues.

Viewed from this perspective, schools cannot be understood except in the context of their communities, a concept which is a major focus of the next chapter. Toby reminds us that children live in a social setting, the most important representatives of which, so far as they are concerned, are their peers.

7.7. Peers

Introduction

The bulk of research on peers and delinquency concerns adolescents – young people between 12 and 18 – pre-adolescents seem almost entirely ignored. Yet it is obvious that children mix with each other and, hence, might influence each other from quite an early age, certainly from at least 7 or 8. It is clear from, for example, the Cambridge Study (West and Farrington 1977) that, for many boys, offending begins at the age of 8 and that the earlier it begins the more likely it is to continue. We need longitudinal studies of samples of young children which will track the complex interactions of attitudes to offending, friendship patterns, family and school background and self-reported offending over the period from early in the primary school to the end of the school years. Those studies we have are usually cross-sectional and deal with adolescents (and mainly with boys). The brief review which follows focuses on friendship groups, rather on than gangs: the latter are dealt with more fully in Chapter 8 in the context of some traditional sociological explanations of crime.

Peers and crime

It was made clear in Chapter 2 that a good deal of offending by young people takes the from of co-offending – offences which are carried out by two or more persons rather than by a lone individual. With increasing age there is an increasing tendency for offenders to operate alone, except for offences which require greater numbers for a successful outcome. There is good evidence that juvenile offenders associate with other offenders. For example, studies reviewed by

Hindelang et al. (1981) found much support for an association between a positive response to the question "have any of your friends been picked up?" and self-reported offending. In their own study they found generally high correlations (0.45–0.88) between this question and both self-reported and official delinquency for all four ethnic/sex groups. To some extent the apparent link with delinquent peers may be exaggerated by police reactions: Morash (1984) found that those who broke the law with peers were the most likely to have an arrest record, independently of both the frequency and the severity of offending. Despite this result, a significant association between the delinquency of a person's friends and the person's own offending is found often enough to justify further enquiry.

What is the direction of the expected effect (is crime followed by friendship with other offenders or vice versa?)? And what is it about youth *groups* which apparently causes an increase in crime? On the latter question, Wilson and Herrnstein (1985) suggest that peer groups supply their members with attitudes conducive to crime: (a) by enabling males to prove their manhood (one of the core needs of the lower-class culture) by participation in crime; (b) by teaching ways of achieving middle-class goals of material affluence, legal access to which is blocked by poor educational performance.

Data are scarce on both questions, and Hirschi (1969) casts doubt on a direct causal link between peer groups and crime. As usual, most of the boys in his sample who admitted delinquent acts also had delinquent friends. But Hirschi concluded that both were due to the breakdown of social controls expected to inhibit crime, such as a strong attachment to home and school. The more delinquent the boy the less value he attached to the opinions of his friends. The latter finding has been supported by Cartwright, Howard, and Reuterman (1970) and by Verlade (1978); both reported that the most delinquent boys drift in and out of peer groups. (This suggests that many of them might be in the delinquent sub-group termed undersocialized aggressive, discussed in Chapter 6, members of which are both heavily delinquent and have poor peer relationships; in contrast, the socialized aggressive sub-group gets on well with its peers.) Moreover, we need to know the time course of the relationship between peers and crime – peer groups may be more important in launching a criminal career than in maintaining it. A valuable study would be one which assigned young offenders to the sub-groups delineated by Quay (1987b) and then tracked for both delinquency and friendships for several years.

Explanations. Assuming that there is some kind of peer group effect, Wilson and Herrnstein (1985) suggest a number of possible determinants:

1. The kind of criminal behavior. Breaking and entering, drug and alcohol abuse, and vandalism are often carried out in groups; stealing small sums, selling drugs and robbery are more likely to be solitary offenses.

2. The kind of youth. Richards, Berk, and Forster (1979) suggest that peer influences are greatest for youths from upper-middle class backgrounds for whom the shared "fun" of law-breaking is more important than the proceeds, if any, of crime.

3. The kind of group. An organized gang – with a name, an emblem, ritualized initiation ceremonies and a specific "turf" to defend – provides a much more powerful set of social reinforcers for members than does a casual group of friends who meet for the occasional beer.

It is important to add that observational learning (people learn through the observed experiences of others as well through their own direct experiences) is likely to play a key role in all peer group influences relevant to delinquent behavior. This very important aspect of learning is covered in Chapter 9.

Morash (1986) found that gender had a major effect on the type of peer group to which an adolescent belongs. Girls tend to join the less delinquent groups and he sees this as a salient factor in accounting for their lower levels of delinquency. But what leads to the original selection of a "less delinquent group?" Morash (1986) speculates that the current slow drift toward an increase in minor female delinquency means that peer groups containing models of female delinquency are available increasingly to girls, but that the process will be a very lengthy one.

Family variables are also likely to interact with peer group influences. Patterson and Dishion (1985) found that poor parental monitoring, and low levels of academic skills, as well as deviant peers, combined to produce increased levels of delinquent behavior by seventh to tenth grade male adolescents. These authors urge the need for a replication of their study using the longitudinal method. This would enable the relationship of the above variables to be tracked through time. They point out that an even more stringent test of the independent variables (and one rarely found in the criminological literature) would be to manipulate one or more of them, for example by giving remedial training to a random sample of parents deficient in monitoring skills.

The prediction would be of a reduced delinquent involvement by their sons, as compared with those of equally deficient parents not given special training, all other factors remaining constant.

This prediction is in line with a report by Steinberg (1986). He found that those boys in grades 5–9 who were relatively removed from adult supervision were more susceptible to peer pressure to engage in antisocial activity than their colleagues who were under close supervision. Boys who went straight home after school, even though they were alone rather than with their parents (who were still at work), were less susceptible than those who went to a friend's house. In turn, the latter were less responsive to pressure than those who described themselves as "hanging-out." Those who had been raised "authoritatively," and those whose whereabouts were known to their parents were also less susceptible.

Concluding comment. The last two studies are examples of the fine-grained and multivariate approach to research demanded by this very complex topic. As we move forward through the age range, the potential number of variables which might account for a relationship with crime, apparently found for any one of them, grows. It thus becomes increasingly essential to control for alternative explanations. The longitudinal method, followed by a manipulative study, as advocated by Patterson and Dishion (1985), is the approach of choice. As matters stand at present, we have a possible link between peer influences and crime and a number of plausible explanations as to why this might occur.

7.8. The media and crime

A section on the media and crime is included in this chapter rather than in any other because the weight of research interest has been on the potential influence of the media (in practice this means television) on children and adolescents, rather than on adults. It is a truism that TV viewing has consumed many thousands of hours by the time the age of 18 is reached, much of which involved programs depicting crime, particularly violent crime: the question is, does this matter in terms of increasing the crime rate?

Assertions

Many social scientists hold strong opinions, typically unfavorable, about the influence of television. For example, Bandura (1973, p. 271):

. . . There is no longer any justification for equivocating about whether children or adults learn techniques of aggression from televised models. People who watch television for any length of time will learn a number of tactics of violence and murder. Television is a superb tutor. It teaches how to aggress and by the way it portrays the functional value of aggressive behavior.''

A more conservative set of conclusions, reached a little earlier by Singer (1971), anticipated much of the subsequent research as well as the current consensus, as follows:

1. It is true that there is much aggression displayed on the media but the present evidence is unclear as to how much of a direct impact there is on actual violent actions.
2. Specific persons may be affected, not necessarily frequent television viewers, but those who lack their own imaginative life.
3. A high level of observed, justified aggression may lower inhibitions against overt aggression.
4. Televised violence is less influential if it is stereotyped and far removed from the real life of the viewer, an example being TV westerns.
5. The research to date has not yet duplicated the actual conditions of individuals viewing TV in their own home surroundings.

Research findings

Wilson and Herrnstein (1985) point out that almost all research on television and crime has focused on violence and, within that issue, on whether TV enhances or replaces the satisfaction of acting violently. The first could be due to disinhibition or to modeling, or both, and the second is typically attributed to catharsis (the release of emotion through watching the emotions of others).

There are three main research methods: natural variation, laboratory experiments, and field studies in the real world.

Natural variation. This is much the easiest of the three, involving no manipulation and requiring only the logging of events as they occur. But it allows only correlations to be established rather than causal links, so that the results obtained could have been due to other, unmeasured, factors. There are two major sub-groups: the short-term effects of single, heavily televised, spectacular events and the long-term effects of various levels of exposure, typically to televised violence.

(a) In the two months after the suicide of Marilyn Monroe in 1962 there were 300 more suicides than would have been expected during this period (Phillips, 1974; in fact a very small increase in percentage terms). Also, just after newspaper and TV accounts of major heavy-weight fights the number of reported homicides is up by one eighth (Phillips 1983). The increase peaks three days after the fight and is greatest for the most publicized ones. (The increase in homicides is directly contrary to the predictions of the catharsis theory of aggression, which would have expected a decrease.)

(b) But it is the long-term effects of continued exposure to televised violence which most concern social critics such as Bandura, quoted above.

The Rip Van Winkle Study was started in 1960 by Eron and colleagues. They examined the TV viewing habits and the behavior of 875 third grade children in a semirural area of upstate New York. The children were assigned an aggressiveness score on the basis of peer nominations. IQ scores were also available, as were estimates of family discord (obtained from interviews with parents). The child's three favorite programs were listed by his/her mother and their content subsequently classified as violent or nonviolent. Ten years later, both aggressiveness and viewing habits were again measured and in the same ways; additional data gathered at this time included MMPI scores, self-reported aggression and police records. After a further 10 years, when the participants were nearly thirty, they were reinterviewed and the overall results analysed The main findings of the study (Huesman, Eron, Lefkowitz, and Walder 1984a) were as follows:

1. Early signs of aggression, particularly in males were predictive of later aggression (the general finding set out in Chapter 6).
2. The children who were the most aggressive watched the most TV.
3. Those with a lower IQ were more likely to be aggressive.
4. Viewing TV violence at an early age not only correlated with later aggression but actually helped to cause it, independently of IQ, father's occupation, parental discord, and even of the amount of TV watched.

These findings held only for boys (Lefkowitz et al. 1977). There are three further limitations: (a) the study did not measure TV watching directly but used information provided by mothers as to their children's preferences; (b) the statistical technique used was such that the results were potentially spurious (Rogosa 1980); (c) both the amount of viewing at 8 and subsequent levels of aggression may have been due to some underlying common factor such as biological predisposition, parental training method, early companions, or some combination of these (Feldman 1977).

Two further longitudinal studies (Huesman, Lagerspetz, and Eron 1984b, Milavsky, Stipp, Kessler, and Rubens 1982) came to opposite conclusions: the former supported the results of the Rip Van Winkle Study; the latter did not. And we should note some further contradictory results. Singer and Singer (1983) followed four groups of preschool children for 4 years. Logs of home TV viewing were sampled for 2 week periods several times a year and the spontaneous play and aggressive actions of the children were recorded by observers who were blind to the home-viewing scores. Singer and Singer found that heavy viewing of aggressive action shows was linked to overt aggression and was not explained by habitual patterns of family aggression. However, both parental emphasis on discipline by force (power assertion, see earlier in this chapter) and fewer hours of sleep for the child contributed independently to aggression by these children. In contrast is a study by Messner (1986) with a much older age-group. Contrary to his own expectations, he found that aggregate levels of exposure to TV (all types of material) were *inversely* related to rates of violent crime.

Laboratory experiments. In real life, aggression aroused by an experience such as watching a particularly violent movie might dissipate rapidly in the press of everyday activities. Laboratory conditions allow the immediate effects of such an experience to be recorded rather precisely. Walters and colleagues found that both working-class men and middle-class students administered longer and more severe "shocks" when allowed the opportunity to do so after viewing violent scenes from movies (Walters, Thomas, and Acker 1962, Walters and Thomas 1963). Additionally, Dunand, Berkowitz, and Leyens (1984) had males watch movies with either an aggressive or a neutral content, either alone, or with a passive spectator, or with a fellow viewer who reacted actively to the content of the movie. The combination of an aggressive content movie and an active partner elicited the most post-movie aggression. This situation is relatively close to the one in which violence on the field during a sports contest is followed closely by off-field violence between fans.

Naturalistic settings. Laboratory studies of TV and violence have been criticized (e.g., Leyens, Camino, Parke, and Berkowitz 1975) because in real life people are exposed to violent stimuli repeatedly, though perhaps intermittently, rather than via a single laboratory exposure. (For example, the sports fan has experienced many incidents of on-field violence and has built up a set of attitudes and behavior concerning the rival supporters). Moreover, typically, the effects of movies have been tested immediately post-exposure and in the same context, rather than over time and in a real life setting.

Leyens et al. (1975) tried to overcome these problems in a study carried out in a Belgian private institution for boys with behavior problems. The boys, who lived in four cottages, were re-assigned on the basis of careful observation to two pairs, each of two cottages. In each pair, one cottage had a relatively high level of aggression by its occupants, one a relatively low level. Every evening for a week violent films were shown to one cottage of each pair, neutral films to the other. Observations of behavior were carried out during the viewing week and again in the post-movie week. Compared with the pre-movie week, there was a sharp increase in physical aggression in both high and low aggression cottages immediately after exposure to violent films. This was in spite of the presence of the observers. The aggression persisted in the originally high aggression cottage in the post-movie week. Conversely (and unexpectedly), aggression declined in the two cottages exposed to neutral films, an effect which persisted in the post-movie week. The explanation may have been a modeling effect by the heroes of the "neutral" films – in fact they were "good, naive and altruistic" (Leyens et al. 1975, p. 357). These results were confirmed by a subsequent study in the USA by the same research group (Parke et al. 1977).

Concluding comment

Wilson and Herrnstein (1985) suggest that at best there may be a significant correlation between TV viewing and aggression for aggressive children with low IQ's who spend more time watching than the average, particularly material which is both simple and violent. But this is far from establishing causation, even for such children. Freedman

(1986) concurs, pointing out that while the laboratory experiments (reviewed by Friedrich-Cofer and Huston 1986) give some support to the causal hypothesis, neither the longitudinal nor the field studies does so – and they are much more important as critical tests of the hypothesis. In this light, Freedman's earlier conclusion (1984) seems reasonable: "[the overall results] account for only a trivial proportion of individual differences in aggression."

However, Berkowitz (1984) draws a potentially important distinction between "trivial" and "small." He agrees that the probability of overt aggression following televised violence is low, but even if it is as low as one in 100,000, this could well mean 100 more violent acts with an audience of 10 million – and American audiences are often much bigger than this. Berkowitz's point is well taken, but it is almost certainly unrealistic to argue for censorship on such grounds – the viewing of millions would have to be restricted because of the possible social damage caused by a few score persons. (On the other hand, for very many years, the Hays Code resulted in restrictions on the content of American movies, in the name of family purity, which today seem quite ludicrous.)

So the argument will continue. Before leaving it, we have a reminder, from Dietz, Hazelwood, and Harry (1986), that television is not the only entertainment medium which might instigate aggression and other criminal activity by the minority referred to above. Their paper concerns detective magazines, referred to by the authors as "pornography for the sexual sadist." A content analysis of contemporary detective magazines revealed covers which juxtapose erotic images with images of violence, bondage and domination. The articles themselves provide lurid descriptions of murder, rape and torture. The magazines publish advertisements for weapons, and for burglary and car-theft tools. With the aid of case histories, the authors illustate how these magazines might facilitate the development of highly deviant sexual fantasies. It may be that socially isolated individuals with a strong tendency to ruminate about deviant fantasies, and in some cases to act on them, make particular use of the magazines described by Dietz et al. (1986), but there seems no information on this crucial point.

8. Social and economic theories and factors

> Its the same the whole world over,
> Its the poor wot gets the blame,
> Its the rich wot gets the pleasure,
> Ain't it all a blooming shame.
> 1914–18 War song. Anonymous

8.1. Introduction

This part of the book is essentially concerned with psychological explanations of crime, but a review of sociological approaches is also necessary and is attempted in this chapter. Inevitably, it will be non-specialist, but adds an important dimension to the view of crime usually taken by psychologists, one which is largely confined to learning experiences and their cognitive consequences, and to individual differences in predisposition to criminal behavior. Instead, sociological approaches tend to emphasize external influences which affect large numbers of people. They deal with the broad brush of economic, cultural and social influences rather than the fine grain of individual behavioral experiences.

The chapter falls into two sections. The first covers a number of sociological theories of crime, from the "main-stream" strain and control theories to the more "radical" social labeling and Marxist approaches. The theory of differential association, which emphasizes learning and cognition, links up with the next chapter which gives a contemporary psychological account of these variables as they apply to the explanation of crime.

The second section focuses on some important current areas of social and economic research into crime, emphasizing empirical findings rather than theoretical issues. It begins with cultural and community influences, including daily life in black American settings, and moves on to the general economic approach to crime, as well as the specific impact of unemployment and of income inequality.

8.2. Sociological theories of crime

Strain theories

A number of theorists have tried to explain one of the major facts of officially designated criminal behavior – that it appears to be heavily concentrated in the lower social groups.

Merton and anomie. Several sociological theorists base themselves on the concept of "anomie," originally described by Durkheim in the 19th century (a fairly recent edition appeared in 1970). For example, Merton (1969) conceives of anomie (cited by Box, 1971, p. 105) as:

> . . . "a disjunction between the cultural goal of success and the opportunity structure by which this goal might be achieved. Since the lower strata were discriminated against in educational and occupational market places, this was the group least likely to realize the American dream . . . No wonder that from these strata so many pursued deviant activities; only such activities offered an available route to success."

In short, legitimate desires which cannot be satisfied by socially acceptable behavior "force" lower class persons into delinquency.

Cohen and adolescent status problems. According to Cohen (1955), many working class children experience status problems because of their lack of success in meeting middle-class standards of successful school performance. The consequent frustration and anxiety is dealt with by a "reaction formation" whereby middle-class values and norms (previously accepted) are now rejected. Instead, working class adolescents display a contempt toward property, expressed by destructive acts, rather than by theft.

Several criticisms may be made of this theory. First, it applies, explicitly, only to acts of destruction against property, and ignores the whole range of offenses against property and persons. Second, it assumes, without supporting evidence, that working-class children almost invariably accept middle-class values (a problem with the strain theories in general), at least initially. Finally, the theory is further limited by concerning only those working-class adolescents who both accept middle-class values and fail in school.

Cloward and Ohlin (1960) and the role of alienation. This theory differs from Cohen's and is an improvement on it in several ways. First, it equates criminal behavior not with destructive but with acquisitive behavior. Second, it avoids the difficulties of the reaction formation concept, substituting "the withdrawal of approval from middle-class norms." However, it retains Cohen's notion that middle-class norms are initially accepted but later rejected when they fail to lead to educational success, as well as his emphasis on the juvenile gang as providing psychological support. A study by Gordon, Short, Cartwright, and Strotbeck (1963) is of some help here. They found that adolescents in general, both offenders and nonoffenders, do accept middle-class *pre*scriptions of the desirable goals of life. However, the extent of acceptance of middle-class *pro*scriptive norms (behaviors that are not allowed in order to reach agreed goals) declines as the social level goes down.

Problems with strain theories. These include:

1. School performance. As indicated in Chapter 7, a number of studies support the view that poor school performance is correlated with juvenile offending. But this is different from the assertion either that poor performance causes offending or that offending is a substitute for an original goal of academic success reasonably held on the basis of superior academic ability.

A study by Hargreaves (1967) exemplifies the difficulty of demonstrating a causal link between "strain" and school performance. He found the percentage in each stream of a British secondary school who admitted to recent involvement in theft to be as follows: A stream, 7 per cent; B, 43 per cent; C, 73 per cent; C, 64 per cent. (The reduction from C to D does not not fit in with the general theory; moreover, the disparity between the A stream and the rest is much greater than Belson's findings – see Chapter 2 – would lead one to expect from a British sample.) Hargreaves also found that upper stream boys had similar values to those of their (middle-class) teachers; those in the lower stream did not. In the upper streams, high status among peers was positively associated with academic record; in the lower streams the most popular boys were the most anti-school and anti-authority. Hargreaves argues that the behavior of each group of boys is a response to the educational aspirations held for them by their teachers – high for the upper streams and low for the lower streams – and that this situation exemplifies the consequences for behavior of the social labeling process (see below). However, the evidence set out in chapters 6 and 7 makes it clear that the "Pygmalion" theory is now thoroughly discredited. Moreover, Hargreaves omitted a number of key steps, including a measure of social attitudes to school and authority on entering the school and again after educational assessment and teacher feedback to pupils. A causal relationship, supportive of the theory, would have been suggested by the following sequence: some high ability boys had initially the same values as their teachers; high expectations were held out by teachers for their success; instead there was actual educational failure; this was followed by a change in values away from those held by teachers, and an increase in offending. In short, the strain theory is best tested by a longitudinal approach rather than the cross-sectional approach adopted by Hargreaves.

Moreover, there is a readily available alternative explanation for Hargreave's findings which anticipates the social learning approach taken up in the next chapter. As each boy enters the school he joins an existing social learning situation. The apparently brighter boys are placed in the A stream, the older members of which have relatively low levels of offending. The duller ones are placed in the lower streams, the older members of which have relatively higher levels and are thus more likely to provide social models of offending. In other words, boys may acquire directly a variety of behaviors, including criminal behaviors, by observing those of their peers with whom they associate most frequently, rather than indirectly in response to the label assigned them by teachers. This suggests that any boy, whether bright or dull, placed with boys with an existing high level of criminal activity will be more likely to learn criminal attitudes and behaviors than if he were placed with boys with a low level of criminal activity. The importance of the school setting as a predictor of criminal behavior was shown in Chapter 7; it is reasonable to suppose that the same applies to the setting provided by streams within a school.

2. Access to opportunities. Palmore and Hammond (1964) followed the records of youngsters involved in a welfare program in Greater New Haven, Connecticut, between the ages of 6 and 19, by which time 34 per cent had become known to the police or the juvenile courts. They argue that the Cloward and Ohlin theory implies that deviance should be particularly frequent among youths cut-off from

legitimate opportunities and who live in circumstances in which illegal opportunities are numerous. the results agreed: delinquency was most common among black youngsters who were school failures, living in situations of high family and neighborhood deprivation. Delinquency rates were much lower among white youths who were school successes and from stable families, living in neighborhoods relatively free from criminal influences. (But this is exactly what would be expected by a social learning approach; there is no need to postulate vague concepts like alienation.)

3. Status frustration. Reiss and Rhodes (1963), in an attempt to measure strain in terms of status deprivation, asked a large number of boys in the Nashville Metropolitan area if their peers had better clothes and lived in better houses. They found that the majority of those who were delinquent did not experience status frustration. Moreover, they found that it was the working class youths in areas largely populated by other lower-class persons who were most likely to engage in delinquency and not those living in mixed areas, who would have been predicted by strain theory to experience the greatest amount of status frustration and hence to be the most delinquent.

In addition, strain theories cannot explain middle-class crime, they ignore the question as to why crime is most frequent among unattached young males (apparently the least in need of conventional material rewards), and neglect individual differences in crime rates which suggest personality and family variables as important explanatory factors.

Gibbons and Krohn (1986) conclude that the overall evidence on strain theory is that delinquency is not the result of a disparity between aspirations and outcomes but of a lack of commitment to conventional society, leading in turn to the low aspirations of those who have become delinquent. This is the general position of control theory, considered shortly.

The sub-cultural approach and the adolescent gang

The central assertion made is that members of a sub-culture in which offending is frequent become offenders simply by conforming to the prevailing social norms (Mays 1963). Thus, juvenile delinquency is not a deviant adaptation to "strain " but a conforming response to the majority. For example, Miller (1958) argued that delinquency is a product of long-established, durable, traditions of lower-class life, rather than the result of responses to conflicts with middle-class values. Lower-class culture is most strikingly embodied in "the other America" of rural migrants, particularly blacks, living in urban ghettoes and of relatively recent immigrants, frequently illegal, such as the Chicanos from Central America (but not by the economically much more successful Asian immigrants). Such persons, who are at the bottom of the social pyramid, form a more or less permanent "underclass." Later in this chapter are details of black American life in such inner-city settings.

The male adolescent peer group on the streets is both the training ground and the milieu in which lower-class males seek a sense of maleness, status and belonging. According to Gibbons and Krohn (1986), the broad themes (the key concerns) of this group are: "trouble" (keep out of contact with the police and other social agencies); "toughness" (bravery and daring); "smartness" or "street smarts" (living by one's wits and by hustling); and "excitement" (weekend activities which are at the opposite pole from much of the routine monotony of everyday life).

In their extreme form, gangs offer their members very powerful rewards and control a great deal of their lives. For example, the Chicano gangs of Los Angeles influence a larger fraction of neighborhood boys and for a longer period of their lives, than do other local gangs, being deeply involved in the use and marketing of drugs (Moore 1978). Gangs may also provide great continuity over time in the lives of their members. Jacobs (1977) described three black gangs (the Blackstone Rangers, the Devils Disciples and the Conservative Vice Lords) and one Chicano gang (the Latin Kings), all based in Chicago. In time, they came to organize half the prisoners in Stateville, a large Illinois prison. They also controlled their members when they were back on the streets. Chapter 2 described Swedish evidence that high-rate juvenile offenders associate with each other within peer groups, the most criminally active preserving their pairings much longer than the less active (Sarnecki 1982). A study of Los Angeles teenagers (Klein and Crawford 1967) found that official delinquency rates were higher in those sections of the gang between whom there was the greatest amount of social contact.

But many gangs consist of much looser and more transient associations of teenagers, as Hood and Sparks (1970, p. 86) point out: "In the last ten years . . . research has challenged basic assumptions . . . of the concept of the highly organized gang . . . as a criminally oriented subculture . . . with internal solidarity and group loyalty within gangs."

It seems reasonable that criminal activities form only part of the *raison d'être* of even the most highly organized gangs. Nevertheless, the very fact that simple friendship and social support are important rewards of the membership of social groups in general, including adolescent gangs, makes them potentially powerful settings for the acquisition of criminal attitudes and behaviors by young males, particularly those who spend most of their time on the streets, rather than in study or in other adult-approved activities.

Control theory

In contrast to the first two approaches, control theory seeks to explain the occurrence of juvenile crime in all social classes. As set out by Hirschi (1969), it pays some attention to the positive learning of criminal behaviors but concentrates mainly on learning *not* to offend. It starts with the question: "Why don't we all break the law?," and answers that the law is kept only when special circumstances exist, in which the appropriate social training in being law-abiding can occur. The success of social training is considered by Hirschi to depend on *attachments*, *commitments*, and *beliefs*, and there is no need for special motivational concepts such as strain.

Attachments mean the emotional intensity of one human being's involvement with another. They become low when a representative of the social order, such as a teacher, rejects an adolescent by assigning him to a lower stream. In his turn the boy, who feels insulted, rejects the teacher, the source of the insult, and the values for which he stands. Commitment refers to the rational element in the social bond. Individuals do not persist in a line of activity unless there is some return. This is similar to an analysis of behavior in reward – cost terms: the greater the overall gain from any particular behavior, the more likely it is to be carried out; the greater the overall loss, the less likely. Individuals make subjective evaluations of the elements in the reward – cost matrix. (In fact, Hirschi largely leaves out the reward side, concentrating mainly on the losses which follow arrest and conviction.) Finally, beliefs refer to the extent of acceptance of law-abiding norms.

A connected theory is that of norm-containment (Reckless 1962), which has a double aspect: the ability of groups to transmit norms effectively and to hold their members within bounds, and the retention of norms by the individual as an inner control over behavior. Two constraints on deviant behavior are postulated, external and internal. External controls are those exerted by the police and other agents of the legal system; internal controls are those within the individual, his total set of attitudes against carrying out deviant behaviors. Both reduce the probability of such actions. Individuals who can be classified as strong – strong (in both internal and external containment) will have a very low probability of committing crimes, whereas those who are classified as weak – weak will have a very high probability.

In short, a person offends because his ties to the conventional order either have not been formed strongly or have broken down. Control theory represents in part a nonpsychological way of talking about childhood training in social-rule keeping which was discussed in detail in Chapter 7. In addition, there is a considerable emphasis on rewards and costs in the performance and maintenance of criminal behaviors. But it has little to say about the initial acquisition of such behaviors. Nor does control theory have any place for individual differences such as personality and intelligence – a common omission from sociological theories.

Control theory has led to a large number of empirical studies (see Gibbons and Krohn, 1986, for an overview). For example, Hindelang (1973) found that juveniles on poor terms with their parents were more likely to have carried out delinquent acts, and involvement with school (indicated by grade-point averages, school aspirations, and time spent on homework) was inversely related to delinquency (the more involvement, the less delinquency). And Hindelang (1973) also found that those juveniles who believed in the legitimacy of conventional rules were less likely to commit delinquent acts.

The problem with such studies, as Agnew (1985) points out, is that, although there has been much support for control theory predictions, virtually all tests of them have been cross-sectional, and not longitudinal, in nature. This is, as always, a serious problem, because delinquency may be the cause and not the result of a failure of social control, and the direction of an effect cannot be established by cross-sectional work. Agnew (1985) carried out a longitudinal test of Hirschi's theory using data from a national sample of delinquent boys. He found that social control variables explained only 1–2 per cent of the variation in future delinquency, and suggests that cross-sectional studies have exaggerated the importance of control theory.

A further damaging criticism comes from Patterson, DeBarsyshe, and Ramsey (1989). They refer to the general finding (see Chapter 7) that the parents of antisocial children employ harsh and inconsistent discipline, with little positive parenting and poor monitoring and supervision. Two interpretations of these results are possible. The first is provided by control theory, which sees them as evidence for disrupted parent – child bonding (attachments). The result is a failure to identify with parental values concerning social conformity and, hence, a child lacking in internal controls. Several large-scale surveys have produced evidence consistent with this hypothesis. For example, youths with negative attitudes to school work and authority tend to be more antisocial (Hirschi 1969, Elliot, Huizinga, and Ageton 1985). But many of the correlations are very small, and it is difficult to disentangle the direction of effect, as pointed out above. In contrast, a social-interactional perspective (Patterson 1986, see Chapter 7) uses the longitudinal approach to demonstrate that it is failures in training by family members which lead to antisocial behavior, which *then* results in weaker parent – child attachments. Conversely, improvements in parental discipline and monitoring due to special training for parents lead to reductions in antisocial behavior (see Chapter 11) and, by implication, to stronger attachments.

The scientific status of control theory is thus fairly weak, but some observations by Chaiken and Chaiken (1983), set in a wider social perspective than that of parents and children, suggest the continued potential usefulness of the general notion of social control. They point out that all societies see the period between puberty and taking on adult responsibilities as troublesome, to be filled with rituals and ceremonies or special forms of time-consuming training – academic, occupational or sporting – until the demands of marriage and work take over. Those societies which fail to channel adolescent energies effectively have usually had high rates of deviance among the unmarried and among marginally employed young males (Bales 1962). Moreover, this interim period is lengthening progressively as puberty begins earlier in each successive generation. The period of stay in school is also extending, delaying entry into the labor force, so that the (criminogenic) adolescent period is almost twice as long as in the past. This could explain why offending begins earlier than several decades ago (Shannon 1980) with adolescents progressing sooner to more serious crimes (Wolfgang and Tracey 1982).

Chaiken and Chaiken (1983) go on to argue that a gradual breakdown in control helps to explain why the increase in crime was greater in the 1960's and 1970's than the size of the baby boom would have predicted (see Chapter 1). This may have led to a self perpetuating spiral: teenage groups commit more flagrant crimes; the community concerned disintegrates; the resulting loss of social control means more opportunities for criminal behavior, and hence more crime occurs (Lewis and Maxfield 1980). But such speculations, while appealing, require careful empirical testing, so far largely lacking, and a much simpler explanation for the excess of the increase in crime over the rise in the age group is readily available. This is the surge in criminal opportunities provided by a period of rapidly rising living standards, to which Chaiken and Chaiken (1983) also refer, a theme which will be expanded upon in the next chapter.

Social labeling theory

Lemert (1951) argued for transferring attention from criminal behavior to the reactions it elicited. There are acts to which reactions are *possible*, a pool from which those who operate the criminal justice system may select certain people to be labeled as criminals. (In the same way, those who operate the mental health system are empowered to select certain behaviors as embodying mental illness.) It follows that the aim of any "explanation" of criminal behaviors should be to uncover the processes by which labels are given and accepted. The focus thus shifts from those who receive labels to the activities of those given the power to label. Thus, the central theme of labeling theory is that deviant behavior arises from attempts at control; it is a response to activity on the part of those officially designated as "labelers" and "controllers".

Social labeling theory has influenced psychological research into abnormal behavior. For example, Ullmann and Krasner (1969) placed heavy emphasis on labeling concepts in their explanatory theory of schizophrenia. They began with two general axioms: any behavior, even the most bizarre, may be learned; persons frequently take on the roles they have been assigned by others. They cite studies which indicate that patients convey the impressions the physician seeks; it is only bizarre responses which are reinforced, nonbizarre ones are ignored, and so are extinguished. Officially designated labeling agents, psychiatrists and psychologists, are thus responsible for the maintenance, if not the initial appearance, of schizophrenic symptoms. Ullmann and Krasner somewhat overstate their case (for example, there is ample evidence of an important genetic contribution to schizophrenia, Rosenthal 1971). Nevertheless, a well-known study of simulated mental illness by Rosenhan (1973) provides powerful evidence for the paradoxical contribution of the social apparatus, ostensibly set up to treat the problem, to its maintenance and enhancement, if not to its origin. And Freedman and Doob (1968) furnish some evidence for the assertion that people led to believe that they are "deviant" behave differently from others given feedback that they are "normal." (Against this should be set the lack of research support for the supposed "Pygmalion" effect in schools – see Chapters 6 and 7.)

In the criminological context, Welford (1975) distinguishes three key hypotheses of labeling theory:

1. No act is intrinsically criminal. This is fairly persuasive in the case of victimless offenses, but it was noted in Chapter 1 that property and personal offenses are proscribed in most, if not all, cultures and times. Either this is not a key hypothesis or the theory suffers a damaging blow.

2. The sequence of events from surveillance to the type and severity of sentence received is a function of offender rather than offense characteristics. The evidence concerning this was considered at length in Chapters 3 and 4. It was concluded that there was some support for the view that some police officers and some sentencing agents are biased against some social groups, particularly black, working-class, males. The effect is a cumulative increase in the probability of moving from one stage of the sequence to another and finally of receiving a more severe sentence, as compared with other social groups, following the same offense. Moreover, severity of disposition is related to an increased probability of reoffending (see Chapters 3 and 4). Thus, attempts at control may have a counter-productive effect: instead of diminishing offending, there may be an overall *enhancement*. This is the core of the labeling approach. The evidence cannot be ignored, but it should also be recalled that as offenses become more serious the bias against certain groups declines, as does, by implication, the value of the labeling approach.

The label applied by control agents may become known to others in society. Their reactions to the labeled individual may help to maintain his deviant behavior, possibly even to enhance it, by reducing the possibility of alternative behaviors. A number of studies support this assertion. For example, Christiansen (1969) studied the recidivism rates of World War II Danish collaborators sent to prison, following the end of the war, for a minimum of two years. The rate was markedly lower for those who subsequently returned to South Jutland, an area of strong Nazi sympathies, than for those returning to other areas where such sympathies were less marked. This result may be interpreted as indicating that post-prison social rejection was less severe for the South Jutland group than the rest, so that they were less likely to turn to other crimes. (Such studies would be improved by the inclusion of direct measures of social acceptance/rejection).

There is some evidence of a correlation between recidivism and unemployment (see below), but the relationship could be due either to those with a worse record being less likely to seek employment, or to fail to obtain it despite persistent attempts, or to both. A study which controlled for the variable of employment-seeking was carried out by Schwartz and Skolnick (1964). They found that the potential employers of unskilled workers, when presented with the files of imaginary applicants, were markedly less likely to offer employment when the file mentioned a police record than when it did not. Even when an acquittal, confirmed by an exonerating letter, followed a recorded charge, the probability of an offer of employment was reduced compared with a file free of any police involvement.

3. Labeling is a process that eventually produces identification with a deviant image and sub-culture. (That is, the labeled individual finally applies to himself the label originally applied by the agents of social control and taken up by significant others such as employers). It is asserted that the deviant's self-concept changes to bring his total set of attitudes into line with his deviant behaviors. The self-label is seen as serving a positive purpose: by identifying with a subculture, the deviant is able to maintain a favorable self-image – a purpose assisted by the process of "rejecting the rejectors" (Schrag 1971). It should be noted that the hypothesis of self-labeling as deviant seems not to have been tested empirically. Until it has been we can draw no conclusions about it.

Overall, the labeling approach makes a useful contribution to explaining the development and maintenance, of criminal behavior, if not to its initial occurrence. The reactions of those who operate the criminal justice system must be included in the total pattern of the consequences of criminal behaviors. But why does labeling occur? One explanation is provided by the Marxist perspective, the most radical of all sociological theories of crime; an alternative view comes form experimental psychology.

The Marxist (radical-conflict) theory of crime

Essentially, this follows on from the version of strain theory which asserts that young working-class males offend because they are denied legitimate means of access to the goal of affluence held out as desirable in capitalist society. A further stage is to ask: why are these groups denied access, and what is the role played by social control agents in the process?

Attempts at answers have come from sociologists working within a Marxist frame of reference (e.g., Quinney 1974). In general terms, they assert the following: the capitalist system is the central cause which generates, and must therefore control, excess labor; this control is exerted by means of the criminal justice system which defines certain behaviors as crimes, and thus generates both crime and criminals.

A more detailed argument, specifically applying to juveniles, has been set out by Greenberg (1977). He asserts that the disproportionate involvement of juveniles in major crimes is the product of the historically changing position of youth in industrial societies. They are subjected to three major pressures: exclusion from the world of work (by a long period of compulsory education) deprives them of the opportunities to finance the intensive leisure activities emphasized by current teenage norms; stigmatizing school experiences directed particularly at low-status unemployed males provoke them into hostile and aggressive responses; the fear of failure to achieve male status positions, common among juveniles in later adolescence, leads to violent, but status attaining, patterns on their part. Greenberg sees no remedy in sight with the continuing growth of hi-tech industry (requiring high qualifications) and of services (mainly staffed by females) at the expense of the old smoke-stack industries which provided employment for large numbers of unskilled young males.

Colvin and Pauly (1983) applied Marxist theory to parent – child relationships by arguing that the kind of inadequate parenting revealed by Patterson's studies (1986) arises from the power relationships to which most lower-class workers are subjected. Because these are coercive, they reduce their capacity, in their role of parents, to deal with children in anything but a repressive way, hindering the development of affectionate bonds between parents and children. As a result, children are less interested in activities important to parents such as school, so that social bonds are weakened and delinquency becomes a likely outcome.

A critique of the Marxist approach. As part of one of the major intellectual positions of this century, the application of Marxist theory to crime can produce apparently powerful arguments, but both theoretical and empirical analyses have revealed crucial shortcomings:

1. The assertion that Marxist societies achieve a higher level of human life than their capitalist rivals was finally exploded at the end of the 1980's when the peoples of Eastern Europe crushingly rejected Marxist-based systems in favor of market-led economies.

2. In the specific case of crime, advanced capitalist countries have not been shown to have higher delinquency rates than countries with other economic systems. (Crime figures from the Soviet Union were notoriously unreliable.) Some capitalist societies, such as Japan and Switzerland, have low rates of delinquent behavior.

3. Lack of parental skill seems much more related to a lack of training in parenting than to the "brutalizing" effects of life in a capitalist economy. When unskilled parents receive special training, their skills improve, as do parent – child relationships, and antisocial behaviors by children diminish (see Chapter 11).

4. Is it true that in capitalist societies the criminal law reflects the influence of the dominant (capitalist) class? As Sparks (1980) points out, it is clear that in 19th century England it did so, for example, through the laws on poaching, but what has this to do with contemporary capitalism? And it is also true that, in this century, the machinery of the criminal justice system has been used on behalf of employers – well exemplified by the history of American labor relations – but these large scale efforts to break strikes, for example, are responses to organized threats to the industrial order, not to individual acts of deviance.

5. Lower-class respondents to surveys are no more likely than their middle-class counterparts to subscribe to the famous dictum "property is theft." In fact, on scales of crime-seriousness, they give higher scores to crimes against property than do middle-class respondents (Sparks, Genn, and Dodd 1982). It is quite clear that both classes want to hang on to their property, and also to protect their persons against assault, so there seems no class basis to the two central areas of the criminal law.

6. Marxist theory sees the prison system as removing part of the oversupply of labor from the market, with the threat of prison deterring a large number of crimes. As the demand for labor increases, parole is given more easily, and vice versa. Over the whole of a nationally-

drawn sample, Galster and Scaturo (1985) found that the relationships between unemployment and new commitments to prison by the courts, as well as with conditional releases from prison, were both opposite to the predictions of Marxist theory. Moreover, the strength of these relationships did not vary consistently over the business cycle, as the theory would have predicted.

Overall, as Sparks (1980) concludes, the Marxist theory of crime is of marginal importance, both as a general explanation of crime and as a specific explanation of the reliable finding of a bias in some parts of the criminal justice system against young, black, lower-class males, particularly for less serious offenses.

A psychological explanation of labeling behavior. Feldman (1977) drew on experimental psychology for an alternative approach which has two aspects. The first, discussed in Chapter 3, is that the "cooperativeness" and general social skills of middle-class offenders increase the chances of a caution as opposed to a formal charge and a court appearance. The second explanation, related to the first, is that *once* the stereotype exists that the middle-class (and whites) are more law-abiding, it will determine patterns of police surveillance as well as the other steps in the sequence set out in earlier chapters.

There may well be an intended positive side to the bias of the police and the courts, the assumption being that the personal circumstances of certain offenders (such as inadequate parents in the case of juveniles) are less capable of preventing reoffending than are those of others. It would be preferable for the members of the criminal justice system not to set up their own sociological guidelines. In fact, people in general, including many police and sentencing agents, tend to view the world through stereotyping blinkers, the purpose of which is to simplify the conduct of everyday life. Mischel (1968) has argued persuasively that trait views of personality – which go beyond the evidence concerning behavioral consistency (see Chapter 6) – can be explained in terms of the general human tendency to think in categories, rather than in subtle specifics.

Much earlier, Bartlett (1932) showed how human perception and memory dealt with evidence not easily assimilated into existing categories by the processes of "labeling" and "sharpening" (ignoring inconsistencies and heightening congruities). How much easier to carry out both processes *in advance*, by constructing a stereotype of the "typical" offender, which then influences the pattern of surveillance and arrest. In that their professional behavior is partially determined by categoric and stereotypic modes of thinking, many police and sentencing agents are simply demonstrating that they are responsive to the same psychological processes as are other human beings.

Thus, the labeling approach, buttressed by experimental psychology, helps to account for the excess of young, working-class and black males in the official statistics of offenders. But it is silent about the explanation of crimes by other social groups (such as older persons and whites in general, and middle-class males and females). The final sociological approach to be considered tries to account for crime in all groups, as well as (by implication) for the relatively greater contribution by certain groups which still survives even when we move beyond the official statistics.

Differential association theory

First propounded over 50 years by Sutherland (1937), this sets out to explain how criminal behavior develops and in what circumstances. Its central emphasis is on learning, as the following nine statements (taken from Sutherland and Cressey, 1970), which contain the core of the theory, make clear.

1. Criminal behavior is learned.
2. Criminal behavior is learned in interaction with other persons in a process of communication.
3. The principal part of the learning of criminal behavior occurs within intimate personal groups.
4. When criminal behavior is learned, the learning includes (a) techniques of committing the crime (sometimes complex, sometimes simple), and (b) the specific direction of motives, drives, rationalizations and attitudes.
5. The specific direction of motives and drives is learned from definitions of the legal codes as favorable or unfavorable.
6. A person becomes criminal because of an excess of definitions favorable to violation of the law over definitions unfavorable to violation of the law.
7. Differential association may vary in frequency, duration, priority and intensity.
8. The process of learning criminal behavior by association with criminal and anti-criminal patterns involves all of the mechanisms that are involved in any other learning.

9. While criminal behavior is an expression of general needs and values, it is not explained by them, since noncriminal behavior is an expression of the same needs and values.

It should be noted that statements 1 and 8, in particular, clearly emphasize learning as the central explanatory principle of criminal behavior, rather than the surrounding social conditions, biologically based predispositions, unconscious motives, or any other alternative causal view. In this sense it was a remarkable anticipation of later thinking. But, inevitably, Sutherland's theory consists of a set of assertions, largely unanchored in empirical findings, and imprecise in its language. It was formulated much more briefly by DeFleur and Quinney (1966, p. 4) as follows:

> "Overt criminal behavior has as its necessary and sufficient conditions a set of criminal motivations, attitudes and techniques, the learning of which takes place when there is exposure to criminal norms in excess of exposure to corresponding anticriminal norms during symbolic intercation in primary groups."

Burgess and Akers (1966) have translated the first eight of the above statements into the language of the operant approach to learning. But there is no need to restate Sutherland's inevitably naive conceptualizations in the language of contemporary psychology. Doing so is an interesting intellectual exercise, but it is much simpler to apply learning and other principles at the core of experimental psychology directly to the observed phenomena of criminal behavior. This is the main task of the next chapter, which is concerned not only with the process of acquiring criminal attitudes and behaviors, but also with their performance and long-term maintenance, both of which were neglected in Sutherland's formulations.

8.3. Cultural influences

Chapter 1 set out a number of speculative attempts to explain differences in crime rates between time periods and countries, in terms of very broad social changes within the same country and of cultural differences between countries. This section continues the discussion, as it affects the developing world, on differences between American generations and on the continuing puzzle of relatively low Japanese crime rates.

Developing countries

As nations advance economically there is a relative shift in importance from person to property crime as well as an overall increase in crime rates. Why should this be so? Wilson and Herrnstein (1985) advance as the most popular explanation: changes in social life with progressive population shifts from rural villages, through small towns, to the sprawling cities which are now a feature of many Third World countries. This leads to an increase both in property ownership and hence in the number of criminal opportunities, and in the anonymity of ownership (people are more likely to steal from transient strangers than from long established neighbors). At the same time, there is said to be a reduction in social control with the decline of the extended family (close and distant relatives all living in close proximity), and the rise of the nuclear family (parents and children only living together, with no relatives nearby). In its most fragmented form, the "family" consists of a single parent (typically the mother) and one or more children. The strikingly high frequency of single-parent families among black Americans is discussed below.

Welford (1974) argues that the increase in affluence is the key underlying factor, with rises in crime rates accompanying increases in GNP (gross national product). As GNP increases so do criminal opportunities, but a complicating factor, discussed in the economic section of this chapter, is the extent to which the rising affluence is widely distributed, or is confined to a relatively small section of the population.

Back to Japan

Although by the end of the 1980's Japan was becoming more like a number of European countries in terms of crime rates, the gap was still marked, and was very great indeed in comparision with the USA. Wilson and Herrnstein (1985) point to a number of cultural factors which, taken together, result in much higher clearance rates for serious crimes than in the USA (60 per cent versus 20 per cent in the early 1970's, Vogel, 1979). They suggest that reporting rates are also markedly higher, again due to the same factors. These fall in two groups, to do, respectively, with differences between the American and Japanese criminal justice systems and with the background cultures. The former include markedly less emphasis on the accused's right to silence (a key feature of the American system), and a greater proportion of confessions which combine to produce a higher probability of conviction, following a charge, in Japan than in America. The implication is that this, in turn, has a marked deterrent effect on potential offenders.

So far as the background culture is concerned, Wilson and Herrnstein point to the ethnic and cultural homogeneity of the Japanese population (the opposite of the American "melting pot," the fact that Japanese towns preserve the close social contacts of village life thus reducing anonymity, the strong emphasis on group solidarity and achievement (and hence on not shaming the group by antisocial behavior), and a concern with social obligations, as opposed to civil and other rights.

Moving away from the cultural to the psychological, Japanese average IQ scores are consistently higher than those of the USA (110 versus 100, Lynn and Dziobon, 1980) implying a smaller proportion of the population in the lower IQ ranges associated with increased crime rates (see Chapter 6).

But other factors also have to be taken into account. As suggested in Chapter 1, there are major economic differences between the two countries: whereas Japan has had very low rates of unemployment for several decades, American rates have been consistently much higher and especially so among minority youth; there seems much greater continuity of employment – at least in the large companies "jobs for life" is a well-known Japanese feature; training for skilled work appears much more in evidence in Japan, again particularly in the major organizations.

So the argument will continue, all the more so as Japan is not only catching up with America economically, but might even be drawing ahead.

American society

Two major studies demonstrate a progressive increase in the incidence of crime among American adolescents. Males born in Racine, Wisconsin, in 1949 were more likely to be charged with theft, assault and burglary by the age of 17 than those born seven years earlier (Shannon 1978) and Philadelphia boys born in 1958 had rates for burglary, homicide and robbery which were, respectively, two, three, and five times higher than those born in 1945 (Wolfgang and Tracy 1982). It should be noted that in both cases the difference between the generations was in incidence, prevalence rates being the same (about one third of the age group in each case). This means that the later-born generation was no more likely to begin offending but, once having begun, offended at a higher rate, implying that they experienced greater opportunities and rewards, a lower probability of detection, less severe punishments, or some combination of these factors.

Wilson and Herrnstein (1985) prefer a more personality-based explanation, suggesting that those growing up in the 1960's were more "present-oriented" (less able to delay gratification) than the earlier generation. In support of this they cite data from Davids and Falkoff (1975) which suggested an increase in the present orientation of delinquent adolescents surveyed in 1974, compared with a group tested in 1959. However, Davids and Falkoff gave no repeat data for non-offenders and none on the number of offences commited by their two cohorts, so that their results are of limited relevance. Information for student populations comes from Aidala and Greenblatt (1986), who compared the moral evaluations of a number of activities furnished by 1983 students with those of earlier cohorts (1929, 1939, 1949, and 1959). Unfortunately, there are no data for years between 1960 and 1982 – argued by Wilson and Herrenstein among others as the period of moral decline – and their data were confined to college students. For this population, at least, disapproval ratings of most of the behavior examined changed little between 1929 and 1983 (stealing, cheating, accepting bribes, endangering others, having an extramarital affair). Much the largest shift was in the noncriminal area of attitudes to premarital sexual experience, with the decline in condemnation greatest among female students.

Despite the lack of solid evidence for a generational shift in present orientation, Wilson and Herrnstein (1985, p. 418) state: ". . . there are many possible explanations for why young offenders are more present oriented today," thus converting a testable assertion for which at present there is little evidence into a reliable finding which requires explanation. However, doing so enables them to consider two possibilities, which are of interest in themselves as potential explanations for the undoubted generational shift in the incidence of crime, noted above.

1. Compared with earlier generations, low-birth-weight (subsequently learning-disabled) children have a higher survival rate. It is possible that they are harder to train in socially approved behavior and, hence, more likely to become offenders. Data on these points are

scarce but, in a large scale British survey (Douglas 1960) of premature birth (associated with a greater incidence of minor brain damage than full-term births), there were significant correlations between premature birth and "bad behavior" as rated by teachers, but only in working-not middle-class children. It may be that the parents of the latter had sufficient skills and resources to cope with difficult-to-rear children, whereas those of the former did not. In any event, we are dealing here with a possible interaction between improved perinatal care, resulting in more children surviving birth, and the known fact that certain children (possibly including those with minor brain damage) are more difficult to rear than others, with the former more likely to become offenders, and not with a 1960's outbreak of "present orientation."

2. Family training was less firm and consistent for the "high-crime" generation than for earlier cohorts (by implication, providing immediate gratification, rather than training in delaying rewards). Wilson and Herrnstein mention only one study. Waters and Crandall (1964) compared three groups of socially similar mothers, raising children in 1940, 1950 and 1960. They reported a consistent decline in maternal coerciveness between the three cohorts but, as detailed in Chapter 7, methods emphasizing coercion are the *least* effective in promoting moral development, and in any event the authors gave no data on the delinquency levels of the three cohorts. Nevertherless, Wilson and Herrnstein take their argument further, linking the data on a declining use of coerciveness with a generational shift in the kind of advice offered by popular magazines on child-rearing (Wolfenstein 1955), from an emphasis on "character development" (1890–1910) to a concern with "personality development" (1920–1930). This hardly helps their general case: the 1920–1930 babies were teenagers in the 1930s and 1940's – years of relatively *low* crime rates.

More in line with Wilson and Herrnstein's general approach that it is the overall moral climate which helps explain variations in crime rates is a report by Stark, Doyle, and Kent (1980), which found an overall correlation of −0.36 between church membership and officially recorded crime rates. The correlations were higher for property crime (−0.45) than for violence (−0.20). Unfortunately, they provide no data on self-reported offending. Moreover, theirs was a cross-sectional study; a longitudinal approach would have controlled for the possibility that as people begin offending they drop out of church, rather than their preferred conclusion – that church membership largely prevents offending.

A comment on cultural hypotheses and studies

It may be that future research will overcome the massive conceptual and methodological difficulties involved in this area. At present, despite the undoubted appeal of its grand scale and plausible assertions, "culture" as an explanatory variable does not take us very far toward a social explanation of crime.

8.4. Community

Reiss (1986) sets out two main reasons for the value of community studies in explaining crime:

1. Most social investigations tend to concentrate on the individual – both offender and victim – and fail to collect information relevant to community variations in crime rates. However, it has been known since the early 19th century that within the same town there are areas of high, as opposed to low, crime. These were mapped for Chicago by Shaw and McKay (1931), who showed that the high crime areas persisted despite large and rapid turnovers of populations, implying that in some way the crime rate was influenced by the neighborhood itself.

2. The usual procedures for selecting samples to be studied do not yield a random sample of individuals from an identifiable community. Instead we need a longitudinal study, with repeated observations, at the community level, enabling the study of the community, as well as that of individuals. The community is then one of the major units for observation, and the impact of demographic changes can be assessed.

Community crime rates

"Communities, like individuals, can have careers in crime" (Reiss 1986, p. 2). In pursuit of this dictum Schuerman and Kobrin (1986) focused on a number of high crime rate communities in Los Angeles County, comparing their crime rates in 1950, 1960 and 1970. They found these neighborhoods to be in three stages of development:

1. Emerging. Relatively new high crime areas, they were largely free from crime in 1950, had moderate to high rates in 1960 and high rates by 1970.

2. Transitional. They had moderately high rates in 1950 and continued to show an upward movement in the next two decades.

3. Enduring. High crime areas for the full 20 year period.

The main demographic changes associated with increasing crime were a rise in residential mobility and an increase in broken families and in single persons (unmarried, divorced, etc.). Land use changes included shifts from owner to renter occupation and from single to multiple dwelling units – overall, a slow process of abandonment, both by settled families and by well-established businesses. The most striking socio-economic change was a reduction in the unit share of semi- and unskilled job holders (the "respectable poor") in favor of "discouraged" workers no longer seeking employment, plus a consistent 20 year rise in the proportion of dwellings deemed overcrowded. Transitional and enduring neighborhoods showed a consistent (and high) minority population; in emerging areas this was on the increase over the 20 years, both for the share of the black population overall and for non-white female labor force participation (suggesting an increasing proportion of black single mothers).

The first signal of more crime to come is an increase in multiple dwellings and in renter occupied housing, then a rising proportion of minority ethnic groups, single-parent families and unattached individuals. Next, there is a change in SES variables and, finally, subcultural changes. It is the speed of change and not just the fact of change which predicts the rate at which crime rates will rise. The first decade sees a fairly slow change in land use, the second a much more rapid shift in SES and subcultural variables.

Schuerman and Kobrin (1986) suggest that while it might be possible to rehabilitate emerging areas – by decelerating, preferably reversing, demographic and SES changes – type three areas are probably "lost territories."

Crime rates and gentrification

The implication of Schuerman and Kobrin's last point is that a seemingly inevitable drift into a high crime area might be prevented by the deliberate encouragement of gentrification (middle-class persons move into previously poorly off areas and improve thereby a whole range of social indices). McDonald (1986) points out that the emergence of gentrification in the 1970's surprised most observers, because it appeared to contradict the general trend of urban decline. The middle classes were suddenly and unexpectedly moving into neighborhoods where the crime rate was notoriously high. There are contradictory hypotheses concerning the effects of gentrification on the crime rate: (a) the newcomers offer more lucrative targets – hence crime should increase; and (b) middle-income people commit less crime than do those on lower incomes – the displacement of the latter by the former should reduce crime.

McDonald (1986) collected time-series data from 14 gentrified neighborhoods in Boston, New York and San Francisco. The neighborhoods resembled each other in architecture and in locational amenities and in attracting young, middle-class, professionals without families. An analysis of the crime rates between 1970 and 1984 indicated tentatively that gentrification leads an eventual reduction in crimes against the person but has no significant effect on rates of property crime. Moreover, the relief from the long term trends of urban decline may be only temporary in gentrified neighborhoods. While crime rates fall somewhat they remain fairly high, eventually wearing down the newcomers, so that they finally move out and the district resumes its former character. (Presumably, this reversal depends on the extent of gentrification: whether it affected just a few streets or a majority of the neighborhood).

Future research on the consequences of gentrification for crime rates should study who is being displaced by whom: on the one hand if those displaced are elderly and their replacements are families with teenage children the result might actually be an increase in crime; on the other hand if the newcomers are couples without children and those replaced are single mothers with teenage children the effect should be a sharp reduction in crime.

Neighborhood decline and the fear of crime

Sampson (1986) sees the critical triggering events which shift an area from relative stability into major demographic and economic decline as disinvestment (business people take their businesses elsewhere) plus demolition and demagoguery (the area gets a bad name), as well as regional, even national, economic trends which are out of the hands of local decision makers.

Once the cycle of decline begins, feedback processes increase the level of fear, and other problems add to those of crime, including physical deterioration, social disorder and group conflict over the "control" of the neighborhood turf. The fear of crime undermines the capacity of a community to deal with such problems. People withdraw into their own immediate homes, no longer being involved in the wider community, so weakening informal social controls and organized community life. The result is a deterioration of local business conditions, further disorder and crime – a vicious cycle which feeds on itself.

A critical factor in decline is "white flight" from the cities. The massive suburbanization since the late 1940's may be the most important consequential effect of increased crime in the USA. Urban areas are now divided into "chocolate cities" and "vanilla suburbs," leading to a massive inner-city disinvestment and a huge outward shift in the location of jobs.

Sampson (1986) argues that, partly as the result of an increased fear of crime in the inner cities, American society is faced with a concentration in these areas of long-term unemployed persons who are heavy consumers of public services and are outside the main stream of economic development. The process of flight is not confined to whites: it is joined by younger and more affluent blacks. He concludes that, while gentrification might produce a modest reversal of this trend, there is no good evidence that the pace of gentrification is faster than that of urban decline.

Community, social problems and lifestyle

There may be considerable differences in a range of social indices between apparently similar neighborhoods. Rutter (1978) compared samples of working-class families from Inner London and the Isle-Of-Wight (IOW, an island off the Southern coast of England). The economic circumstances of the two communities were much the same but the London 10 year-olds had twice the frequency of behavior problems of their IOW counterparts. And the London families had much higher levels of stress, particularly marital discord and broken homes, which were particularly severe on women. Those with low income, little schooling and low social mobility were strongly constrained by their neighborhood boundaries, within which was played out the whole pattern of everyday life, both rewards and punishments. The lifestyle of the immediate area was therefore much more important than for middle-class persons, who move easily between their own and other neighborhoods.

Suttles (1986) has given a good description of this type of restricted lifestyle, the keypoint of which is "provincialism," meaning that residents are preoccupied with those differences between people – age, sex, ethnicity, territoriality (whose turf?), and reputation, all useful in predicting who is a threat to safety – and not with occupational or educational attainments, which are distant, low-probability reinforcements. Given that there is no escape from living in the neighborhood, how can the inherent dangers best be anticipated and hence avoided?

In such an area, young men carry weapons not for status but for safety. But why is street life seemingly so much more threatening than half a century ago? In such earlier descriptions of poor inner-city areas as that by Whyte (1943) there was indeed crime – but not random street violence – organized politics was strong and there was attachment to the community, and stable families. More recently, the more law-abiding have moved out, depriving current young people of local models of respectable behavior.

8.5. Ethnicity

Introduction

"Victimization surveys and victim's descriptions to the police of those who "got away" paint a similar picture . . . the volume of crime is strongly correlated with the size of the black population . . . trends and conditions in the community exercise a disproportionate impact on the overall crime rate" (Skogan 1979).

According to Fox (1978), crime rates can be predicted quite accurately, using only the percentages of the population which are non-white and aged 14–21 and the consumer price index. His use of these indices produced predicted crime figures for 1972 per 100,000 of the population which were remarkably close to the actual outcome.

In a very oversimplified sense, both Skogan and Fox seem to be saying: the more blacks, particularly young blacks, the more crime. The detailed data set out in Chapter 2 suggest a rather less dramatic but still fairly clear-cut black/white difference in crime rates, particularly for crimes of violence. Why should this be so?

Before turning to possible answers to this question, we should note a key point. To a significant extent black/white differences in crime are in *prevalence*, rather than in *incidence* (Petersilia 1983). The actual numbers of crimes committed annually by blacks and whites on the streets are quite similar. The key difference is in the proportions of the two groups involved in *some* crime – significantly more blacks than whites commit at least one offense (confirmed by Blumstein and Graddy, 1982). This is a very important point, suggesting that while blacks are more likely to carry out casual crime, whites are more likely to be high-rate offenders.

Explanations

Constitutional factors. These are reviewed by Wilson and Herrnstein (1985) and cover both personality and intelligence. (By placing them under the heading of constitutional factors, Wilson and Herrnstein assume that both have a largely constitutional basis, whereas a partial one would be more correct in general, and the frequently large sociocultural differences between whites and blacks, see below, mean great care has to be taken in ascribing to genes rather than to experience any personality or intelligence differences which are found between ethnic groups.)

Elion and Megargee (1975) found that blacks in federal prison had higher psychopathic deviate scores than either prison whites or black college students. The explanation may have been a differential effect of prison on blacks and whites. To check this we need personality data on black and white samples from early in their criminal careers. Osborne (1980) studied 123 school-age black twin pairs, 82 per cent of whom were identicals, and found no significant genetic component for scores on two personality tests. Even if he had, it would have meant only that the personality scores of blacks, like those of whites, have a partly genetic basis. (There is strong evidence for a genetic contribution to the scores of white samples on other personality tests, such as the EPI – see Chapter 5.)

The evidence for a broad association between crime and low IQ scores, particularly low verbal IQ, was set out in Chapter 5. The general finding of significantly lower black than white average verbal IQ's (e.g., Osborne and McGurk 1982) means that there are proportionately more low IQ blacks available for delinquency than low IQ whites (Wolfgang, Figlio, and Sellin, 1972). Yet, as Wilson and Herrnstein (1985) point out, constitutional factors cannot be the whole story: for example, homicide rates among blacks nearly doubled from the early 1960's to 1973, much more quickly than among whites (Rose 1981). Only 10 per cent of the rise was attributable to the relatively greater youthfulness of the black population. Wilson and Herrnstein conclude that we must look at nongenetic factors to provide the bulk of the explanation of black/white differences in the prevalence of crime.

The sub-culture of violence. This refers to specific social settings within the broader American culture in which violence is regarded as a more or less normal response to a range of instigating events which would not lead to a violent response in other settings. "The significance of a jostle, a slightly derogatory remark, or the appearance of a person in the hands of another are stimuli differentially perceived and interpreted . . . Quick resort to physical combat appears to be a cultural expectation, especially for lower socio-economic class males of both races" (Wolfgang 1958, p. 188).

While Wolfgang was careful not to give an ethnic basis to the subculture of violence, specifically attributing it to class, rather than to race, many authors apply the term solely to the lower- class black culture. Hawkins (1983) argues that in doing so they ignore, or at least de-emphasize, a range of historical, structural, situational and economic factors which might better explain the undoubted high rate of homicide by blacks. Moreover, the reaction of the law is seldom examined (i.e., the more severe response of police and courts to blacks than to whites). Hawkins suggests an alternative theory which emphasizes the historical devaluing of black life (first by whites, but then accepted by blacks themselves) as well as the more punitive response of the criminal justice system to prehomicide behavior by blacks, and the direct effects of economic deprivation. Shoemaker and Williams (1987) also consider factors other than ethnicity to be of overriding importance. They compared blacks, Hispanics and native Americans for the use of blows and of firearms. Demographic (the proportion of young males in the population concerned) and area of residence variables were more powerful explanatory factors in the tolerance and use of violence than was ethnic background. They concluded that the influence of ethnicity on violence was minor and indirect.

A somewhat different approach was taken by Silberman (1978) who, while accepting the subculture of violence thesis, seeks to explain greater black violence in terms of the black experience in America. He argues that, unlike any other immigrant group, American blacks were subject to slavery *in America*. For many years they hid their anger at this under a mask of docility. Once it no longer had to be concealed their anger was expressed and the black crime rate rose, particularly when middle-class blacks left the ghetto, removing social models of law-abiding behavior. However, the evidence for his argument is thin. Harris and Lewis (1974) found that black prison inmates were less likely than their white counterparts to identify themselves as part of the "criminal class."

Moreover, most blacks suffer from racism, but only a minority become high rate offenders. Anderson (1978) found that among black bar regulars the talk is not of hatred of whites but of admiration for successful black criminals (where success means a high income). And Wilson and Herrnstein (1985) cite Bureau of Census reports which indicate that black suicide levels have been persistently lower than those of whites. If there had been a shift from bottled-up anger to its overt expression, there should have been a fall in black levels of suicide in a relatively downward direction, paralleling an increase in violent crime. Finally, it should be recalled that most black violence is directed against other blacks and not against whites. All told, the sub-culture of violence theory does not fare very well.

Net advantage. As Wilson and Herrnstein (1985) argue, the undeniably bleak economic context of black life cannot be the whole story. In the 1960's, out of all the city's districts, San Francisco's Chinatown had the lowest average income, the highest unemployment rate, the highest proportion of families under $4,000 annual income, the lowest educational attainment, the highest TB rate and the highest proportion of sub-standard housing (Tagaki and Platt 1978). Yet, in 1965, only three persons of Chinese ancestry were sent to prison in the whole of California. Similar findings have been reported for the San Francisco Japanese community, though for an earlier period (Beach 1932). It follows that social isolation and poverty are not inevitably associated with crime among racially distinct groups. Differences are found even when the comparison is between native American and West Indian origin blacks living in the same inner-city areas: in the 1930's native blacks were heavily over-represented among the inmates of New York State prisons; immigrant blacks were equally heavily under-represented (Reid 1939).

In all such comparisons we must remember that black Americans are not immigrants; they have lived in America longer than most American sub-groups. Many recent immigrants have a major stake in being law abiding and hard working. They may still succeed in the economic struggle; many ghetto blacks know that they have failed comprehensively. Moreover, as described in Chapter 1, there is heavy participation of several immigrant groups in organized crime (much less frequently convicted than the street crimes which are more typical for young blacks).

Inadequate socialization. Do black families, particularly single parents, socialize their children less well than their white equivalents and, if so, why? In 1978, more than one-half of all blacks under 18 were living in mother-only families, of which half were below the poverty line (Spanier 1980). Shinn (1978) reviewed 14 studies of the effect of father-absence on school achievement in which black groups were included. It was detrimental in only six, and in the largest of these, involving 26,000 participants, the effects were only minor. A more direct approach was taken by Kellam et al. (1982). They found that black children from mother-only families were more likely to be judged by their teachers as maladaptive than other groups. And by high school the mother-only group was more likely to self-report delinquent acts than their fellows.

Black life in America

Attempts to explain black/white differences in crime in terms of social and economic factors need to be underpinned by a detailed comparison of black and white communities in contemporary America. Hacker (1987) summarized descriptive data from a wide range of sources to give a remarkable picture of the social and economic deprivation experienced by a substantial portion of black Americans. It involves a *combination* of impoverished inner-city social settings, inadequate resources (both human and material) for effective socialization, and drastic social segregation, and an absence of models of legally achieved material success.

1. More than 60 per cent of black infants are born out of wedlock. Almost as many black families are headed by women. A majority of black children live with their mothers (in father-absent households). All of these figures are three to five times those for white Americans and *three times* those for blacks of only one generation earlier. There was little change from emancipation to the 1950's so that, for more than 80 years, most black households had been headed by two parents. (This means that the changes of the past 40 years, including the "feminization of poverty" cannot have been due to the "plantation legacy".)

Since the black population is disproportionately poor, all of these black/white differences, with their implication of a sharply reduced capacity for effective child-training during the past three decades, may relate to class and not to ethnicity as such, but the black poor are not only deprived, they are also *segregated*, of which more below.

2. There are massive black/white differences in youthful sexual activity, pregnancies and births, even when education and income are controlled: 75 per cent of black females begin sexual activity before 18 as compared to 50 per cent of whites. And there is also a difference in the use of contraception (significantly less among sexually active black girls than their white counterparts). As a result 40 per cent of black girls have become pregnant by the age of 18, as against 20 per cent of whites. This 2:1 disparity becomes 4:1 for births to unmarried girls aged 15–19. By 18, one in every four unmarried black women is a mother, and this increases to 40 per cent by the early 20's. Almost all unmarried black (and white) mothers aged 15–19 keep and raise their babies. The outcome of all this is that over half of all black women who have had families have never been married. The relative proportion for white women is only one seventh.

3. The fastest growing group is the three-generation household (a mother, often teenaged, with one or more children, sharing a small, crowded apartment with her own mother, a grandparent in her thirties). The extended family, which provides a wider base of support, is less evident than in the past. Between 1970 and 1987 black multi-generational households increased threefold. Most of these young mothers dropped out of school to bear and care for their babies. Fathers, often equally young, drop by from time to time.

4. All of the above applies to over one half of young black women, half of whom in turn had no wish for early and unmarried motherhood. Hacker points to the behavior of young black men as a key factor. Only 39 per cent of black men aged 25–34 are married and live with their wives as compared with 62 per cent of whites. (And at least 20 per cent of this age group is missed by census takers, implying a lack of settled jobs, even settled addresses. Of those black men the census reaches, less than half have full-time jobs.)

5. In 1986, approximately the same number of white and black single mothers were below the poverty line (about 1.3 million in each case). But blacks form only 12 per cent of the population. And there are differences between the two impoverished groups: whereas of the white mothers, 46 per cent had only one child, 71 per cent of the blacks

had two or more. And twice as many white as black mothers received support payments (from fathers).

6. Overall, white and black poverty groups seem two distinct populations. More than two-thirds of families among the black poor are headed by women, as against one third of whites. And lower-income whites are more likely than not to be elderly couples and to live in nonmetropolitan areas.

7. In 1954, over 75 per cent of black men had full-time jobs. By 1986, this was true of only 40 per cent. Many jobs formerly held by black men are now the province of black women. More black women are employed than are black men, and more finish school – they hold two thirds of all the professional-level jobs occupied by blacks (the comparable figure among whites is 48 per cent). If black women can avoid early motherhood, they are much more likely than black men to finish high school with the literacy and good diction employers expect.

For black males raised in segregated neighborhoods, as many are, prowess in the streets counts for more than anything else, and there is a disdain for jobs that pay only "chump change." They see themselves as native-born Americans: parking cars and washing-up in restaurants are thought suitable for immigrant Hispanics and Asians – not for blacks.

8. The respective graphs for family income (in 1986) differ markedly: black families form a pyramid with a majority receiving under $20,000; that for whites is more like a Greek cross, with families on $35,000 outnumbering those on less than $20,000. Although only 10 per cent of white families had less than $10,000 per year, this was true for 30 per cent of blacks. Moreover, this poorest group tended to consist of single mothers among blacks, but elderly couples among whites.

9. The majority of blacks still live in all black neighborhoods as opposed to integrated ones (over 90 per cent in Chicago, 75 per cent in New York). Even the newest minority groups are less segregated. In one poll only 12 per cent of blacks preferred segregation, as against 86 per cent whose preference was for a more equal mix. In response to black entry into a formerly all white area, whites stay and new ones even enter as long as the black population is below 8 per cent of the total. But when it reaches 20 per cent, at least one quarter of the whites leave and no new ones enter. This phenomenon of white flight leaves the neighborhood all black or nearly so. Equally important is the departure of better-off blacks to new locations. Those left behind lack role models of steady employment and family stability.

Teenage parenthood is most pronounced in segregated settings, in which schools, housing and acquaintances are almost entirely within one's own race.

Hacker (1987, p. 33) concludes his review as follows:

> "Being black and poor is a very different condition from being white and poor . . . white youths across the country from inner Boston to rural Arkansas commit crimes, drop out of school and become parents in their teens . . . in most cases, however, those who do so are not typical of their areas or neighborhoods, which tend to be solidly working-class . . . few white districts . . . are predominantly poor in the way so many black sectors are . . . It is social and cultural isolation – a climate whites never really know – which more than any other single force encourages the early siring and bearing of children without thought for the future."

Finally, two more recent reports illustrate further the severe social deprivations of many black Americans. In 1950, Detroit had a population of nearly 2 million, of whom 15 per cent (about 300,000, were black. By 1990, it had fallen to a little over 1 million, with a black proportion of over 70 per cent (over 700,000). This means a drop in the white population of Detroit from 1, 700,000 to less than 300,000 in only 40 years. There has been a massive flight from the city of Detroit to its independently governed suburbs, first by the white middle classes and then by black professionals. While Detroit's population has fallen, its murder rate has increased tenfold, from six murders a year per 100,000 people to about 60 per 100,000 in 1990. (*The Economist* 1990e).

The homicide theme is taken up in a report from the National Center for Health Statistics. For the first time this century, the life expectancy of American blacks declined in two successive years, 1985 and 1986. This seems due, in part, to a much steeper rise in the black homicide rate, compared with that for whites – 15 per cent versus 5 per cent. Overall, 1 in 20 black men may now expect to die by homicide (*The Washington Post* 1988). Between the ages of 25 and 35 homicide is the leading cause of death for blacks, and the black death rate from homicide is eight times that for whites (Hawkins 1985).

Of course, there is a rising black middle class: in 1986, over 8 per cent of blacks had a family income exceeding $50,000 (versus 22 per cent of whites). By 1990 there were nearly 400 black mayors (including Mayor Dinkins of New York, as well as over 40 black generals, one of whom, General Colin Powell, is currently the Chairman of the Joint

Chiefs of Staff, having previously been National Security Advisor. But a large black under-class is being left well behind, seemingly locked-in to a perpetual cycle of deprivation. Clearly, any attempt to account for black/white differences in crime rates must seek to control for the massive social and economic differences between most whites and most blacks.

8.6. Economic factors

Introduction

The economic approach to the explanation of crime is based on an essentially *rational* view of human behavior. Broadly speaking it has two forms. In its more restricted form, it suggests that criminal behavior will occur when a person feels in some way materially *deprived*, whether by poverty or by unemployment and whether in absolute or in relative terms, compared with others in his society. The implication of this form is that when society has rid itself of poverty, unemployment and major inequalities of income, crime will diminish sharply.

A more general version (and the one favored by many professional economists) is that crime is possible in all social groups, up to and including the most wealthy, and not only among those temporarily or permanently deprived. In this view, crime is a function of a perceived opportunity for personal gain (whether material or nonmaterial) and the balance of rewards and costs (including detection and punishment) concerning that opportunity.

Neither version of the economic approach has much to say about either the initial process of becoming an offender (for example the impact of childhood experiences and of social settings) or about the possibility of consistent individual differences in the probability of acquiring and performing criminal behaviors when objective opportunities, rewards and costs are all equal.

The economic approach to crime

The following is based on Ehrlich (1979) and on Phillips and Votey (1981). The basic assumptions of the economic model are:

1. Maximizing behavior. Crime is committed under conditions of uncertainty regarding potential sanctions and rewards. Offenders are

assumed to behave as if they seek to maximize their *expected utilities*. This means that all potential offenders, even the perpetrators of "crimes of passion," respond on the whole to costs and gains, prices and rewards, in much the same way, although not necessarily to the same extent, as the individuals who pursue legitimate or socially approved activities. That is, the offender is a member of the human race who, like participants in legitimate endeavors, will try to maximize his well-being.

2. Unbiased expectations. Because criminal decisions are made under conditions of uncertainty, maximizing behavior involves assessing the probability of "success." This is inevitably *subjective* to the offender, whereas the risk measures used in empirical research are based on *objective* observations. The economic approach assumes (implicitly) that they are identical, or at least systematically related.

3. Stable preferences. The distribution of individual preferences for crime is to a significant degree stable across different communities, over reasonable periods of time. (This means that people are more or less the same, and what varies is opportunity, incentive and so on).

This potentially very powerful approach to the explanation of crime is taken up in the next chapter, in which it is set in the context of psychological research and theory on both the "rational offender" and on subjective factors which mean that rationality is often only partial – in crime as in other areas of human behavior. The remainder of this chapter concerns the more restricted version of the economic approach.

General prosperity

Thomas (1925) correlated the British business cycle (the fluctuations in several economic indices) for the years 1854–1913 with a variety of social indices including crime statistics, and found that burglary showed a strong tendency to increase in the lean years, with theft behaving in the same way, though less strongly. However, as Walker (1965, p. 91) points out, "[such observations] . . . have been overshadowed by the more spectacular long-term trends of both economic conditions and crime, in which a steep and steady rise in the standard of living of practically all social classes in Western Europe and the Americas has been accompanied by a steep and steady rise in the rates of crime, including property crime." He argues that affluence increases both the awareness of material possessions (through the communications media) and the opportunity to acquire them illegally (for example, theft from unattended vehicles increases as vehicle ownership increases).

Poverty

Many years ago, Burt (1923) was unimpressed with poverty as a causal factor (cited by Feldman, 1977, p. 192):

> "Since of the total inhabitants of London no more than 30 per cent belong to the lowest social strata . . . the amount of delinquency coming from those lower social strata is, beyond question, disproportionate; nevertheless, in the higher and more prosperous ranks its frequency is still unexpectedly large . . . poverty can hardly be the sole . . . cause . . . if the majority of delinquents are needy, the majority of the needy do not become delinquent."

Self-report data were unavailable to Burt; had they been then he might have been even less impressed with poverty as a causal factor. Nevetherless, his conclusion was probably too sweeping and certainly too simple: the current emphasis is on *relative* deprivation (the individual's own situation compared with other people who are available for comparison; their number is vastly increased by the electronic media). Two areas of research embody this emphasis on relativity: the link between crime and unemployment and that between crime and income inequality.

Crime and unemployment

Early studies (reviewed by Wootton, 1959) indicated that the level of unemployment among offenders depended partially on the general level of unemployment. While offenders were more frequently out of a job than controls, this may have been because they were less employable (i.e., less skilled) and, hence, the first to go when times were hard, or because they were less likely to seek work, or because, having lost a job, a new one was harder to find by someone with a criminal record. Wootton also found that offenders changed their jobs about twice as often as controls. This may have been because they were more impulsive, or less suitable for the jobs they took up, or because they were dismissed when their criminal record was discovered by an employer.

In any event, other early studies show that those with previous convictions seem more likely to offend during periods of unemployment than at other times. Morris (1951) found that over 72 per cent of 270 "confirmed recidivists" were unemployed the last time they recommenced their criminal activities. This would be expected by a behavioral view: a well-learned response (offending) will be performed for an expected reinforcer when an alternative response (paid employment) is either unavailable or requires more effort to obtain than a criminally attainable goal. Once a behavior has been acquired it *may* be performed; from this point of view unemployment is best seen as a potential instigator for the performance of already acquired criminal behavior. But will unemployment increase the likelihood of a first offense, all other sources of influence (biological and environmental) being held constant?

A reward–cost approach to this question suggests a differing effect according to the probability of re-employment in general and the relationship between re-employment and detection. When the probability of a particular individual being re-employed is very low and detection is irrelevant to those chances, unemployment will probably be an important positive instigator to crime, both initial and continuing. Conversely, when unemployment is perceived as temporary and re-employment would be made less likely by detection, the individual concerned may be even more law-abiding than when he is employed. Clearly, the blanket term "unemployment" must be analysed in terms of the probability of re-employment for the particular individual at the particular time and place. Unfortunately, neither the earlier research, discussed above, nor the more recent studies, has been designed with such considerations in mind; the unemployed are seen as a homogeneous group.

A review by Freeman (1983) sets out the major methods of study of unemployment and crime, together with the resulting research findings to that date:

1. Time-series analysis. The crime rate is compared with the level of unemployment and related market indicators over time. This has problems in that many variables tend to move together at the same time (known as collinearity), making it difficult to pick out the independent effects of each. The results of this approach suggest a connection between increases in crime and in the rate of unemployment – but the effects are too modest to explain the continual upward trend of crime during the 60's and 70's (when unemployment was sometimes up and sometimes down). It seems that if the unemploy-

ment rate is halved (as during the early 1980's) the crime rate falls by about 5 per cent. Carr-Hill and Stern (1983) throw doubt on even this modest conclusion. They studied data from England and Wales for 1970–1981 and concluded that there was no significant association between the increase in recorded crime and increases in unemployment.

2. Cross-sectional analyses across geographical areas. These are free from the problem of collinarity as well as from other pitfalls of the time-series method, but areas may differ in unmeasured ways, and migration may blur inter-area differences. The majority of cross-sectional analyses do show the predicted link, but there are stronger correlations with the nonlabor market variable of criminal sanctions.

3. Comparisons of offenders and nonoffenders. The direction of any effect obtained remains in doubt. While offenders do have poorer work records, this could be because both crime and unemployment are caused by some third factor, such as "personality." Potential offenders may actually choose unemployment as a better preparation for crime. Moreover, they may be only very loosely affected by the overall level of unemployment – they are at the back of the queue so that, even if unemployment is low, they are still left out. There can be no inference from general employment conditions to the experiences of particular social groups.

4. Longitudinal studies. The advantages of this method have been argued throughout this book. In this context, as in many others, it is important to follow a group of people for many years, preferably from well before they enter the labor market. Farrington et al. (1986) looked at the official crime figures between the ages of 14 and $18\frac{1}{2}$ for the Cambridge study population, according to whether the person concerned was at school, in full-time employment, or unemployed. The figures were higher during periods of unemployment than during periods of employment for the same youths. This was particularly true for offenses involving material gain, for the younger age group (15–16) and for youths with lower status jobs.

A study by McGahey (1986) of employment and crime patterns among "high-risk" youth in Brooklyn, NY was longitudinal but retrospective. It used self-reported labor-market information, official criminal histories, an ethnographic analysis (intensive life-history interviews with smaller sections of the overall samples), and comparisons of white, black and Hispanic neighborhoods. During the summer of 1979, arrestees were interviewed within a few hours of arrest and prior to arraignment. The main findings were:

1. Persistent unemployment among adult residents limited the development of stable households and of youth employment opportunities.

2. The resulting lack of social controls contributed to the persistence of crime in some poor urban neighborhoods.

3. Property crime, drug sales, and other illegal activities provided an income to youths in neighborhoods where legitimate employment opportunities were scarce or provided only low wages and sporadic hours.

4. Public policy on crime control has concentrated on providing delinquents with vocational training but the results are not encouraging. The reasons for this include: training has little significant effect on marketable skills, particularly at times of high unemployment; the programs are only another erratic source of low income, augmenting and alternating with irregular and ill-paying jobs, transfer (welfare) payments and crime; and participants in projects enter them when they are already well-established in the habit of offending. (See Chapter 11 for a review of psychologically based employment projects for young offenders.)

5. The lifestyle of the neighborhood to which young offenders return from training projects seems particularly important. An improvement in an individual's income is often seen as a temporary windfall, to be shared with friends and neighbors, and not as a permanent feature to be reserved for one's own use. The income from employment projects is spent rapidly on consumption for friends, peers and families, vanishing into the larger pool of community poverty.

Nevertherless, advertisements for low-skill, modestly paid jobs in big cities attract large numbers of applicants (Clark and Summers 1982) so that high unemployment is mainly due to the lack of jobs. But it is also true that young men in many inner-city areas do not value success achieved through legitimate employment. For such men "being able to make it" while avoiding the "work game" is a strong, pervasive and consistent goal (Hippler 1974). Sub-cultures like this persist, model and shape new youngsters, and may be more powerful for many young men than the job opportunities introduced by outsiders (see Chapter 9 for a discussion of the differential effectiveness of competing social models).

Like Freeman (1983), Wilson and Herrnstein (1985) found no clear empirical support for a *causal* link between unemployment and crime in either direction, as opposed to correlations between the two. And the studies they reviewed tended not to control for other factors known to affect the crime rate, such as changes in the age composition of the population and differences between American states in the probability of punishment for offenses. Both unemployment and the crime rate may be measured inaccurately and these inaccuracies vary from place-to-place. Moreover, the definition of unemployment varies, as do the age groups under study and the crime involved. Finally, and of particular importance, crime and noncrime are not mutually exclusive choices; people can choose *both* (i.e., offending, both in and out of work, depending on opportunity – which may even be greater in the work-place).

At present, until better research is carried out, the most plausible conclusion is that unemployment and crime are both "caused" by some common, underlying variable, such as low verbal IQ (among a number of others), which makes it both hard to get a job and to learn the social rules against crime. This hypothesis requires a prospective study, such as that by Bachman, O'Malley, and Johnston (1978) which began in 1966. Their Youth in Transition study chose boys at random from all entering high school that year in a particular area and followed them for eight years as they went through high school (or dropped out), and then as they found jobs, joined the unemployed and/or committed crimes. They concluded that "the child is father to the man" – with the differences between the 20 year olds the same as those found in grade 10. Indeed, occupational attainments, occupational status and self-reported offenses were predictable from measures in the first year of high school. Controlling for IQ and family SES, high school drop-outs were twice as likely to be unemployed as those completing high school and very significantly more likely to be self-reported offenders, at least as teenagers. These authors conclude: "Delinquency differences are linked to educational and occupational circumstances [at age 20] and are largely a reflection of long-standing patterns which preceded the post-high-school experiences we have been examining" (Bachman et al. 1978, p. 184).

A similar conclusion was drawn by West and Farrington (1977) from their Cambridge Study boys. Those who by their early 20's were either official or self-reported offenders were much more likely than non-offenders (by both methods) to have unstable job records with frequent job changes and periods of unemployment. Of those with an unstable employment history, half were known to the police and four fifths reported themselves as being highly aggressive. Scarcely any lost a job because of a previous conviction. Most behavior problems were apparent early in life, well before they entered the labor market. No attempt was made to measure how much crime could be attributed to employment experiences (including unemployment), but they concluded that the delinquent section of their sample had not only done badly at school but also had low motivation, indifferent attitudes to work and aggressive antisocial attitudes to situations arising at work. They drank and smoked heavily and, even if they earned well, saved little and got into debt.

Wilson and Herrnstein (1985) conclude that while these longitudinal studies do not disprove a causal link between unemployment and crime they suggest that long-standing individual differences are associated with and precede both crime and unemployment. Moreover, they summarize other studies as showing that IQ scores, personality, and family background variables and educational attainment explain most of the success and failure encountered by people in labor markets in general.

Finally, a general comment by Phillips and Votey (1981) on the economic trends of the 80's and 90's is of value. They suggest that the current pattern is one of an increasing number of women seeking jobs and competing for them with young males who are less attractive to employers (briefly, they are less reliable) and hence will be squeezed out of the labor market, as a result turning to crime, so that young males will continue to increase their already dominant share of serious felony offenses (see Chapter 2). This implies a strengthening future link between crime and unemployment. In practice, the situation is not quite so clear cut. There are indeed increasing numbers of women in the job market, but many are in new jobs such as supermarket checkouts and micro-chip assembly. Nevertherless, a fundamental fact of social life in the USA seems to be a high rate of youth unemployment, particularly among blacks.

Income inequality

Proponents of income inequality as a major factor in crime assert that it is not the absolute amount of poverty which is important but the variation in income between the extremes of rich and poor. The greater this is, the more the resentment on the part of the poor, a resentment expressed in increased rates of crime compared with countries in which the gap is less. It would be expected that the same prediction could be made within a country: the regions with the greatest income inequality would have the highest rates of crime. The bulk of the studies have concerned crimes against persons rather than against property.

Homicide. One of the earlier reports was by Braithwaite and Braithwaite (1980). They found very significant correlations between income inequality and homicide rates for 31 countries which had contributed to international crime statistics for most of the years 1955–1974. Avison and Loring (1986) compared homicide rates for 32 nations: both income inequality and ethnic heterogeneity (the amount of variation in a country's racial mix) were significantly related to differences between countries in homicide rates. There was also an interaction between the two, so that the highest rates of crime were in those countries in which there were high levels of both. Lester (1987) confirmed the income inequality–homicide link for a sample of 23 countries (a mixture of developed and third world nations).

Messner and Tardiff (1986) moved from cross-national comparisons to the situation within a single country, the USA. In fact, they studied 26 neighborhoods of Manhattan, New York. Their main hypothesis was that a high degree of inequality within a neighborhood leads to high rates of relative (that is, perceived) deprivation and then to high rates of homicide. They found only weak support either for the prediction or for an association between homicide rates and racial heterogeneity. Rather, it was certain neighborhood characteristics which emerged as significant predictors of homicide rates: the relative proportion below the poverty line and the percentage of the neighborhood's inhabitants who were divorced or separated. In all neighborhoods, homicide rates tended to be highest in areas of extreme poverty.

The importance of the proportion of young people in a population as well as of income inequality was demonstrated by Krahn, Hartnagel, and Gartrell (1986) (this is the usual link between age and crime – see Chapter 2). They found also that the effects of income inequality on homicide are stronger in more democratic nations, explaining this as being due to a greater public awareness of the existence of inequality in such countries.

Violence. Blau and Blau (1982) found a strong association between inequality in family income and rates of violent crime in general in the 125 largest American metropolitan areas, an association which persisted after controlling for region, ethnicity, city size and absolute level of poverty.

Rape. Smith and Bennett (1985) analyzed 1980 data for 88 US metropolitan areas with extremely high or low rates of rape. Poverty, but not income inequality, contributed to differences between these communities. Moreover, other demographic factors, most notably the percentage of divorced and separated persons in a community, were more important predictors (repeating the findings reported by Messner and Tardiff, 1986, for homicide; see also Chapter 2 on the characteristics of victims of crime, including rape).

Property crime. At first sight, an obvious effect of income inequality should be a rise in property crime, but Blau and Blau (1982) found no such association. However, the situation may be more complicated than expected: greater inequality means both more wealthy persons who, presumably, protect themselves better than the average, and more very poor ones, many of whom will be elderly or will, in some other way, lack the resources to carry out crimes against well-defended properties and persons.

The chronic problem of low income among blacks. Two studies focus on income inequality between blacks and whites. Joe (1987) hypothesized that at least part of the reason why minority youth are over-represented in the criminal statistics is that they see few prospects for future economic success. In comparison with whites, blacks are over three times more likely to be poor, their median income is only half, their net worth (total assets minus liabilities) is only one-twelfth, and blacks are twice as likely to be jobless as white men. Joe argues that, without radical changes, black youths are likely to remain outside the mainstream economy, and hence the picture of major income inequality will remain.

In a similar vein, Duster (1987) points to the massive loss over many years of jobs in the manufacturing sector of the economy. These were the major entry portal into work for unskilled teenagers, among whom blacks were and are heavily over-represented. The prospects for blacks can only worsen as the trend from manufacturing to service jobs continues. And automation is eliminating jobs in both sectors of the economy as the remaining unskilled jobs move to low-wage overseas economies. Today, service jobs seek high qualifications and experience

– hence there is a strong demand for well-qualified older women to return to work after bearing children. Teenagers have increasing difficulty in going straight from school into work, and this is particularly true for young blacks (among black American males aged 16–19 the rate of unemployment is now 50 per cent, versus 20 per cent for their white counterparts). A brief training is not enough. The result is the apparently *permanent* underclass described earlier.

This is an appropriate point to end this chapter: perhaps the most important of all the social factors discussed in it as potentially related to Index crimes is the combination of being young, male, poor – and black and segregated.

9. The cognitive-behavioral approach

> The depradator who has escaped punishment due to his offense is constantly present; an encouraging example of success to all his class.
>
> (Chadwick, 1829)

9.1. Introduction

The previous chapter covered a range of social and economic factors and sociological theories concerned with the period after childhood and potentially relevant to the explanation of criminal behavior. Much of this material emphasized two key explanatory factors: (a) the *social setting* outside the home, in which adolescents and adults spend large parts of their waking lives; and (b) the performance of criminal behavior is largely *rational*. This chapter will make considerable use of these two factors in applying to the task of explaining crime some of the central areas of experimental psychology: learning, and cognitive and social psychology. In doing so, it draws on theory and research set out in Feldman (1977) as well a good deal of work published since then, as this general approach, termed the *social learning theory* (SLT) of crime, gathers momentum.

In setting out this theory, the author wishes to acknowledge his intellectual debt to Albert Bandura. During the past three decades, Bandura has produced a series of major theoretical analyses of human behavior which are based on the methods and findings of experimental psychology. Over the years, he has broadened his earlier emphasis on learning to give greater weight to the importance of social and cognitive factors. The term social learning theory is his, and I have built on his application of the theory to aggression (Bandura, 1973) to deal with crimes against the person, followed by an extension to crimes against property.

The rationality of much criminal behavior was given a largely theoretical treatment in Feldman (1977). Since then several researchers, most notably Clarke and Cornish (e.g., Clarke and Cornish 1985) have taken the approach much further, and have drawn on considerable empirical research as well as setting out models of the development of the *rational criminal* (Cornish and Clarke 1986), embodied in their *rational choice theory* (RCT) of crime.

This chapter consists of four main sections: the first sets out a general framework for the explanation of criminal behavior within the the context of social learning theory, drawing on the experimental psychology of learning, cognition and social behavior. The next two apply the framework, respectively, to crimes against property and to crimes against persons. Section three concludes with a detailed illustration of social learning theory applied to the person crime of rape. Section four gives an outline of rational choice theory, together with an application of the theory to the property crime of burglary, and concludes with an appraisal of these two cognitive – behavioral approaches, followed by a speculative account of their application to occupational, organized and political crime.

Sections 1–3 of the chapter use a standard sequence of *acquisition* (the process of becoming an offender), *performance* (the situational variables which determine whether or not an offense, once acquired, will be carried out), and *maintenance* (the long term sequence of outcomes of criminal and alternative behaviors which determine the continuation of a criminal career). The sequence used in section 4 by rational choice theory is similar in content, though the terminology is different, and a fourth stage is added, that of *desistance*. The explanatory elements drawn on by social learning theory vary in content but remain the same in form. For example, the social setting in which people spend their days is of crucial importance, whether it is a street gang or Wall Street. The key psychological processes involved (for example observational learning and the cognitive control of behavior) are also the same, irrespective of the individuals concerned. Similarly, the key elements of rationality and choice of rational choice theory remain the same, irrespective of the crime to which they are applied.

The emphasis in this chapter on post-childhood events in no way negates the major importance as *precursors* of criminal behavior of individual differences (partly biologically based), of childhood experiences, and of background social and economic factors, covered in Chapters 5–8. All these precursors set the stage for the behavioral events and their cognitive consequences which are discussed below.

9.2. Social learning theory of crime: a general framework

Some general principles.

"... people are neither driven by inner forces nor automatically shaped and controlled by external stimuli. Rather, human functioning is explained in a model of triadic reciprocality in which behavior, cognitive and other personal factors, and environmental events all operate as interacting determinants of each other." (Bandura 1986, p. 18).

Bandura (1986, p. 22) agrees that "genetic factors affect behavioral potentialities. Both experiential and physiological factors interact, often in intricate ways, to determine behavior." An explicit emphasis on bio-social interaction is central to this book. Behavior is not to be explained by either component alone but by the two acting in combination.

Capabilities

Within the above perspective, Bandura defines the nature of persons in terms of a number of *basic capabilities*, set out briefly below.

1. Symbolizing capability. The human capacity to use symbols (both verbal and nonverbal) provides a very powerful means by which people alter and adapt to their environment, as well as enabling them to transform experiences, even transient ones, into internal models that serve as guides for future action. Symbols help people to give continuity and meaning to their experiences, as well as conferring the ability to test possible solutions in advance of action, and to ... "discard or retain them on the basis of estimated outcomes before plunging into action" (Bandura 1986, p. 18).

Bandura anticipates the criticism that the foregoing necessarily implies that behavior is always fully rational:

> "Rationality depends on reasoning skills, which are not always well developed or used effectively ... people make faulty judgements when they base their inferences on inadequate information or fail to consider the full consequences of different choices ... [and] ... they often mis-sample and misread events in ways that give rise to erroneous conceptions ... Thought can thus be a source of human failing and distress as well as of human accomplishment" (Bandura 1986, p. 19).

This is a key point which should be borne in mind in the frequent references to the relative rationality of criminal behavior in later sections.

2. Forethought capability. Bandura asserts that behavior is not simply reactive to the immediate environment. Instead, because most behavior is purposive, it is regulated by forethought. People both anticipate probable consequences and set themselves goals. Of course, future events cannot, in themselves, determine behavior, but their cognitive representations can help to do so. As Bandura puts it: "Cognized futures thus become temporarily antecedent to actions" (Bandura 1986, p. 19). This is as true of the "street level" offender thinking of his next mugging as of the international statesman redrawing the map of a region.

3. Vicarious capability. Whereas learning by direct, personal, experience has been given priority in psychological theories, almost all the phenomena of direct experience are also found to occur vicariously, by observing other people's experience and its consequences for them. There is an obvious application to criminal behavior of the following: "The more costly and hazardous the possible mistakes, the heavier must be the reliance on observational learning from competent exemplars" (Bandura 1986, p. 20). As noted in Chapter 7, Bandura places great emphasis on the media, particularly television, as crucial sources of the observational learning of crimes against the person. While the present author has raised strong doubts about this degree of emphasis (there are plenty of more immediate sources for learning about aggression – in the home, the school and the street), Bandura's general point of the importance of observational learning is very well taken.

4. Self-regulatory capability. Much of human behavior is motivated and controlled by internal standards and by self-evaluations of one's own actions. In the criminal context, this may mean getting satisfaction from a theft requiring a particularly high level of skill. "Professional pride" is unlikely to be confined to socially respectable activities.

5. Self-reflecting capability. Bandura (1986, p. 21) makes two key points here: "By reflecting on their varied experiences and on what they know . . . [people] . . . can derive knowledge about themselves and the world around them." While such activities usually reflect experience accurately, "They can also produce faulty thought patterns through reciprocal causation. Forceful actions arising from erroneous beliefs often create social effects that confirm the misbeliefs."

An example of the latter point was given in Chapter 6 in the context of attempts to explain psychopathic behavior as arising out of mistaken attributions of negative intent on the part of others (Howells 1983).

Acquisition

Four areas of basic research concern the social influence of other people and, hence, help to explain the process whereby a person becomes an offender, having been previously law abiding. All four take place within social settings. The account which follows is given in more detail in Feldman (1977, Chapter 3).

Observational learning. People acquire behaviors through their own direct experiences (behavior-contingent learning) and by observing the experiences of others. Thus, observational learning (OL) is concerned with behaviors which are acquired without any direct reinforcement to the learner. Instead he observes the behavioral experiences, including their consequences, of another person, termed a model.

Bandura (1973) points out a number of reasons for the major importance of OL, including avoiding costly mistakes (of obvious relevance to criminal behavior) and speeding up the pace of learning. The effects of OL are the same as those of behavior-contingent learning: the acquisition of new patterns of behavior, the strengthening or weakening of previously learned inhibitions and the facilitation (in performance) of previously learned responses. Moreover, OL facilitates the suppression of behaviors previously displayed by the observer.

Observational learning enables the acquisition not only of overt responses but also of covert emotional and cognitive responses. The fidelity of both types of response to an observed outcome is assisted by the observer consciously verbalizing to himself what he sees or hears. Also, modeling effects are increased by raising the level of physiological arousal of the observer to an optimal level, beyond which the efficiency of learning declines. Very broadly, the more complex the response to be learned the lower the optimal level, so that to copy a skilled form of crime requires a relaxed alertness for maximum success; imitating the behavior of a mob is made more likely by a much higher level of arousal.

Attitude formation and change. The most widely accepted of the many attempts to define the term attitude have emphasized its evaluative component. Attitudes are thus favorable or unfavorable beliefs about an act or event, object or person. They represent both potential behaviors and the evaluation of previously carried out behaviors.

A preliminary verbal communication, aimed at changing an existing attitude, may increase the probability of a person performing a particular act; once performed and positively reinforced it will be repeated, a likelihood strengthened by the cognitive representation and rehearsal of the act. In the context of shoplifting, the sequence of events would run as follows: a person whose existing attitude is relatively unfavorable to shoplifting, is confronted by a persuasive message to the effect that (a) detection is unlikely, and (b) most people like us (e.g., teenagers) shoplift. Depending on several characteristics of the message (see below), the previous attitude may change to one favorable to shoplifting. Given a suitable opportunity, and the required skills (which also can be acquired from others, possibly the person giving the message), the shoplifting act will be performed, probably successfully in view of the very low rate of detection of shoplifting. It will then be reflected on and probably repeated, with a cumulative strengthening of the now favorable attitude toward shoplifting for each subsequent successful offense. Conversely, if the first attempt at shoplifting fails (anything from detection and punishment, to a very small return and a good deal of anxiety), repetition is much less likely, and the attitude is likely to return to the original one – which may be held even more strongly than before the attempt at attitude change.

The variables which determine the amount of change of a currently held attitude in the direction of a spoken or written communication have been thoroughly reviewed by McGuire (1969), who divides the matrix of communication into five components: the source, the message, the channel, the receiver and the destination. A brief summary follows of Feldman's (1977) application of McGuire's scheme to the criminological context.

Communications from a person already offending in favor of criminal activity will be most effective in changing the attitude of the recipient in the direction of criminal activity when the offender is successful, likeable, socially powerful and can administer and withhold social reinforcements such as attention, approval and friendship which are valued by the recipient, and when the two are in frequent contact. It is important that agreeable information is presented first, that the message is delivered in a pleasant context, and face-to-face. Acceptance is also more likely if the receiver has had a recent experience of failure in some important area of his life, is encouraged to engage in cognitive rehearsal ("sleep on it"), and has well-developed habits of doing so. The message is even more effective if the person delivering it also supplies weak and easily countered arguments against criminal activity ("yes, you might be caught, but the odds in your favor are at least 20 to 1, and only mugs get caught"). This is termed immunization against persuasion (McGuire 1969).

Social situations. It is convenient to divide these into two-person and group influences.

1. Two-person situations. The effectiveness of a person A as a dispenser of social reinforcement is largely related to the degree of positive or negative attraction he has for person B (Berscheid and Walster 1969). Suppose that A, a current offender, is trying to communicate to B, who is currently law-abiding, attitudes favorable to offending. B has few friends, admires A greatly and seeks his friendship. If giving B his friendship is made contingent by A on an overtly expressed change of attitude by B, his influence attempt is likely to be successful, first in changing the attitudes expressed verbally by B and, eventually, in bringing about a change in B's overt behavior. Conversely, if B has many friends, does not admire A, or value his friendship highly or seek his support in some other way, the influence attempt is much less likely to be successful. The rewardingness of one person for another is contributed to also by his status and by his power over objective resources such as money and occupational advancement, as well as over less tangible assets such as friendship.

2. Group influences. Membership of groups provides many opportunities both for observational learning from social models and for developing an awareness in group members of the rewardingness of models and, hence, the extent to which it will be advantageous to emulate them. In addition, persons who contribute to the cohesiveness of a group by conforming to the norms of the majority will be rewarded, those who do not will be punished, for example by exclusion from the group. One of those norms may be to behave illegally, such as joining in price-fixing by a group of dealers, or stealing from the work-situation. The "odd man out" will be unpopular in both instances. Groups exact a price for the social support and friendship they provide.

Thus, there are general pressures toward conformity which will influence new members of, for example, a professional group in which illegal practices are common. Such practices will be modeled more effectively by leading members than by less senior ones. Validation by group leaders markedly increases the acceptability of apparently illegal behaviors; the greater the power of the leader, the greater the effect. Examples include President Nixon in the run-up to Watergate and in its aftermath, and senior figures of Wall Street firms eventually convicted of financial crimes.

As a general rule (to which there are exceptions, Myers and Lamm, 1976), groups accept higher levels of risk than those taken by individuals prior to discussion by the group. Whatever the explanation for this "risky shift" phenomenon, it is of considerable criminological relevance. For example, an individual seems more likely to decide on a criminal act in the context of a group. If the act is rewarded he may then repeat it on his own. An important source of an increase in risk-taking by groups is that there is a mutually reinforced tendency to avoid information which is likely to increase anxiety, such as the consequences of an offense being detected.

Social settings. The importance for the acquisition of criminal behaviors of the setting within which individuals, whether children or adults, spend their time, has been stressed throughout this book. All four of the social influence processes discussed above take place in social settings. Quite simply, some settings are more criminogenic than others. This is true of families, teenage and adult friendship groups, and of work settings, from the board room to the assembly line. While most parents try to train their children in socially acceptable behaviors, many of them fail, despite good intentions, because they lack the appropriate skills or resources or because their child is unusually difficult to train. And some parents will themselves carry out successful crimes which become known to their children. In other instances, children will hear conversations between their parents about the admired criminal acts of other adults. There is also evidence (Wootton 1959) that the presence of one offender in a family is associated with the increased probability of another.

Unlike the case of parents, there is no particular onus on peer groups to train socially acceptable behaviors before, during, or after adolescence; some will do so, but others will model criminal behaviors to their members, often repeatedly, and over long periods of time. Evidence comes from Belson's (1975) British study: he found that the onset of offending was strongly related to associating with boys already stealing. Knight and West (1975) reported the importance of exposure to social models in the development of persistent offending by the Cambridge Study boys.

There is considerable specificity in the crimes modeled in different social settings. Spergel (1964) asked children living in three areas of an American industrial city: "What is the occupation of an adult in your neighborhood you would most like to have ten years from now?" In "Racketville," the most affluent of the three areas, two-fifths of the inhabitants being Italian-American, 80 per cent of the children named "some aspect of syndicated crime." In "Slum Town," two-thirds of the inhabitants of which were Puerto Rican and a quarter black, most of the children talked about "defending the turf" (joining a fighting gang), fighting being the major activity of the local gangs. Finally, in "Haulberg," where the main crime was car theft, that was indeed the activity most frequently mentioned.

Clinard (1952) gives an example from a different level of the social scale. He describes how businessmen learned black market practices during World War II by association with existing black market operators.

The importance of models carrying out illegal behaviors in a particular social setting is at least as great for offenses against persons as against property. The use of violence as a means of resolving personal disputes (in fact, of course, illegal) varies from country to country, region to region, and by neighborhood within a single city. For example, nearly 90 per cent of all cases of murder in Houston, Texas, were found to occur in a small number of areas in the city center (Clinard 1968). Amir (1972) emphasizes a particular sub-culture as supplying a social learning setting for rape. In general, the material on high crime communities in Chapter 8 amply supports the importance of social settings for the acquisition of criminal behaviors.

Overt behaviors. The social influences described above come together when a person who has acquired attitudes favorable to an offense actually carries it out for the first time. If this has a positively reinforced outcome, another increment is added to the previously induced attitude change. In turn, the further strengthened change of attitude (now strongly favorable towards the offense concerned) increases the probability of the crime being repeated when the next opportunity occurs (or is made to occur), and so on, in a sequence of action and reaction between attitude and behavior in both directions.

Performance

We have reached the point at which an individual has criminal behavior in his repertoire. Will he perform the act at least once more? The question resolves itself into: what are the major factors which determine whether a criminal act is performed? They include the *opportunity* for performance, the *incentives* for doing so, and the individual's *subjective appraisal* of *situational variables* relevant to the possible crime, including the *target*, the *risks* attached to it and the *legitimate alternatives* for reaching the same goal. The performance phase concerns single instances of a criminal act; long sequences of crime are considered in the next section under the heading of maintenance.

In addition, we have to consider a set of factors, termed *criminogenics*, which may tip the balance toward committing a crime, as opposed to crime-avoidance. All of these key variables are set out below, as they concern crime in general, and again in later sections, if appropriate, as they relate to crimes against property and against persons, first as broad categories and then in the context of specific examples of these categories.

Opportunity. Several authors have argued for the overriding importance of the sheer volume of criminal opportunities available to potential offenders. This is true in both developed and developing countries (Toby 1979). For example, Chaiken and Chaiken (1983) point to the rapid recent increases in the production and purchase of lightweight consumer durables – such as TV and VCR sets – which mean many more potential targets. A second factor is easier access to such opportunities as more people spend vacations away from home, and the increasing proportion of households in which both partners work. In short, there are more targets and fewer "guardians." Very large numbers of people congregated together provide increased opportunities for street crime – examples come from mass demonstrations, street carnivals, and sports contests.

The importance of the general level of opportunity applies also to crimes of violence, according to Cook (1986), although his example comes from the reverse direction. He notes the diminution in violent crime in Massachusetts since the 1975 implementation of the Bartley – Fox gun law in that state (the illicit use of firearms was made punishable by a one year mandatory prison term). Landes (1979) has documented the fall in aircraft hi-jackings which followed the introduction of much tighter screening procedures for passengers and baggage.

Incentives. Behaviors are carried out, or avoided, in large part because of their anticipated consequences, also termed incentives. Bandura (1986) lists the following incentives as motivating the full range of human behaviors. They apply equally to criminal behavior.

1. Primary incentives. These include food, drink, and sex. All three are influenced by external factors as well as by internal bodily factors: for example people are prompted to eat by the sight of appetizing food as well as by actual hunger, and the stimuli which evoke sexual arousal differ between cultures.

2. Sensory incentives. "Many human activities are regulated by the sensory feedback they provide . . . novelty and change generally increase, and repetitiveness reduces, the effectiveness of discrete sensory events . . . [but] in many situations, seeking a change in stimulation might reflect the push of boredom, rather than the pull of novelty" (Bandura 1986, p. 233). The relevance of sensory incentives is likely to be greater early in a criminal career than later, when financial returns become more salient (Petersilia, Greenwood, and Lavin, 1978) and for person as opposed to property crimes.

3. Monetary incentives, . . . "money can purchase most anything people desire – commodities, properties, human services . . . privileges . . . social influence" (Bandura 1986, p. 235). Hence the great attraction of property crimes, which offer the prospect of money or of goods which can be exchanged for money, or which enable the offender to use his own money for other purposes.

4. Social incentives. The importance of social rewards for the acquisition of criminal attitudes and behaviors was discussed earlier. They are likely to influence the performance phase also: "It is difficult to conceive of a society . . . completely unmoved by the respect, approval and reproof of others" (Bandura 1986, p. 235). The same will apply to the prospect of success or failure in crime. In the case of an individual whose social contacts are largely with professional criminals, status is directly enhanced by a successful and undetected crime of significant size.

5. Status/power incentives. "Most groups are structured in terms of status and power relations. Social power provides a measure of control over the resources and the behavior of others . . . jurisdiction over the group's life, . . . social recognition, . . . and [they] are better able to

further their personal interests and desires" (Bandura 1986, p. 238). Of course, an improvement in social status may also follow from a major financial gain from crime. Because this is more likely to accrue from a series of crimes than from a single one, it is discussed in the section on maintenance.

6. Self-evaluative incentives. The incentives listed above all come from external sources. In addition, through a successfully carried out crime, people obtain information as to the level of their performance, contributing to their internal sense of professional pride.

Other variables. The rest of this section sets out the factors which lead a potential offender to take a particular criminal opportunity out of several, or to reject all of those currently available. The list is deliberately inclusive, so as to cover both property and person crimes. Not all of the following variables will influence the performance of every instance of every type of crime, and those which do operate will do so to varying extents. This will become more clear in the separate sections on the main categories of crime, and in the specific examples of crime within the main categories.

1. The target. Cook (1986) lists several features of a target by which potential offenders are influenced. These are: *propinquity* (the less time needed to search for an acceptable target the better); *pay-off* (targets offering higher returns are more attractive than the opposite); *vulnerability* (potential targets willing and able to defend themselves and/or their possessions are less attractive than those with weaker defensive means and intentions); *access to law enforcement* (it is very important to minimize both the probability and the severity of punishment – see below – so that the more attractive criminal opportunities are provided by those who are the least likely to complain to the police). Cook points out that there is also a compensation mechanism – the most attractive targets tend to be aware of their appeal to offenders and seek to protect themselves. In turn, potential offenders are likely to take into account the greater difficulty of such targets and either seek less well defended ones, prepare themselves more thoroughly, or avoid them completely.

Targets vary widely in difficulty, from the shelves of poorly protected supermarkets, to a bank vault protected by a series of massive barriers. It follows that shoplifting is commonplace, raids on well-defended banks a relative rarity. As well as variations in ease of access and of entry, the difficulty heading also includes differences between targets in the ease of rapid escape from them to relative safety. Motor vehicles assist here but only if there is a clear exit road.

2. The risk involved. The probability of intervention by the police, other security personnel, or bystanders are all part of risk assessment by a potential offender. The higher the perceived chances of detection and the more severe the expected punishment following conviction, the less likely will a criminal opportunity be responded to. (This very general statement is amplified considerably in the next chapter in a discussion of deterrence.) Professional criminals will try to minimize both – see the material on the "fix" in Chapter 2. And, in any event, the more professional and well organized the offender the lower the chances of detection. As discussed in Chapters 1 and 2, the probability of detection varies between both offenses and offenders. Quite apart from relatively low clearance rates, other than for homicide, many offenses go unreported or unrecorded, all facts which are known to many high-rate offenders. Some may even underestimate the true risks of detection, low as they are. The converse is probably true for many low-rate offenders and for nonoffenders.

Punishments for a detected and convicted offense include both legal and social aspects. As indicated above, the legal component of punishment seems less important than the likelihood of detection, particularly for offenders who have experienced previous sentences and regard punishment as a professional risk, to be taken into account as one of the factors in the decision matrix, but not as an overriding negative argument. However, with increasing age and more severe sentences in prospect as a criminal record worsens, those with little recent success and much failure may regard the prospect of a further long prison term as a good reason to reject all but the safest opportunities.

As Bandura (1986) points out, there will be wide individual variations in the estimation of legal sanctions, with those who rarely or never offend overestimating the risks. Social sanctions are very heavy for such persons, exerting a powerful restraining effect, so that a small fine for a minor offense might imperil a potentially successful career and/or one's social life. This implies law-abiding behavior even when the objective risks are known to be low. (However, this is much more true at the acquisition stage; once criminal behavior is well established in a person's repertoire, social sanctions will exert a less powerful restraint.)

3. Skills and resources. Special skills are needed to perform many

property crimes, from great financial expertise in the case of stock exchange offenses, to technical knowledge concerning safe-breaking. Crimes of violence seem more likely when the potential offender is skilled in methods of physical attack. The availability of special tools and equipment is also important for many crimes, the more so, the more complex they are.

4. Opportunity to attain the same objective by legal means. Bandura (1986) argues that deterrence is most effective when the offender concerned has legal means of access to the rewards he seeks. But this is likely to be true more at the acquisition than at the performance stage. Once people have begun offending they seem able to combine legal and illegal sources of income. This applies both to black ghetto dwellers who move back and forth between unskilled jobs, welfare payments, and crime, and to certain Wall Street operators, who supplement large salaries with massive returns from financial crimes. In general, this variable may be more relevant for the performance of property than of person crimes, but there will be circumstances in which it will influence the performance of the latter also: for example, a person may assault another in order to exact revenge for some hurt for which legal redress is available, but which is expected to be very time-consuming and grossly inadequate, even nonexistent (for example, many victims of crime "take the law into their own hands").

The above general variables all suggest an essentially *rational* appraisal of a criminal opportunity. When incentives are high, the target is easy, the risks are low and the relevant resources are available, an opportunity for a particular criminal act will be responded to by a person who has the act in his behavioral repertoire. The converse is also true: when the opposite levels of these variables are present, the opportunity will not be taken. Intermediate combinations of levels (for example, a high incentive and considerable available resources, but a difficult target and a high level of risk) will result in less predictable decisions, in which the balance between a criminal act and crime-avoidance may be shifted toward the former by other influences, particularly those which follow.

Criminogenic factors. This is the term for substances, such as alcohol and drugs, or objects, such as firearms, the ingestion of which in the case of the former, the possession of which in the case of the latter, may increase the probability of a criminal act being performed by a person who has it already in his repertoire, when a more rational appraisal might result in the rejection of the opportunity. This heading also includes the short-term level of physiological arousal of a potential offender.

Moore (1983) and Wilson and Herrnstein (1985) have assembled evidence for the view that drugs, alcohol and guns potentiate crime in general, both property and personal. The latter distinguish between the indirect effect on crime of drugs such as heroin and cocaine (it is the need to obtain money to buy the drug which increases crime) and the direct effect of alcohol (as the level of alcohol in the blood-stream rises, crime seems more likely, particularly violent crime).

1. Drugs. Drug abusers figure disproportionately among those arrested for street crimes such as robbery, assault and burglary. The level of criminal activity (whether measured by arrests or by self-report) is higher for daily heroin users than for the rest of the population, and among heroin users levels of crime relate systematically to increases and decreases in heroin use.

However, only a proportion of all heroin users are "junkies" (those who use heroin at least daily), so that there is much variation in the "need" to steal to obtain it, and even for junkies there are ways of obtaining drugs without theft. Moreover, most studies of junkies (e.g., Kaplan 1983) show that they begin offending before becoming addicted, and many of those in treatment continue to commit crimes when they are no longer drug-dependent. These findings suggest that drugs are more relevant to an explanation of crime for the performance phase than for acquisition and maintenance. So far as performance is concerned, the key point seems to be whether or not the addict is on a "run" (that is using his drug at a high level, compared with intermediate periods of relative abstinence). The difference in crime levels is about five or six to one between the two states and applies to a wide range of street offences. When the addict needs money for drugs he needs it fast, there is no time to plan, either the crime or the getaway, so that less of the relevant information is sought and appraised and more risks are taken than a strictly rational approach would indicate.

2. Alcohol. Moore (1983) points out that, while there is no clear physiological link between alcohol and aggression (a major role being played by cultural expectations), alcohol does act as a disinhibitor, so giving a license to act aggressively, for example in spouse-abuse. It also increases the helplessness of potential victims as well as reducing the skill of offenders both in planning their crimes and in carrying them

out, so that they are more likely to choose innapropriate ones and to be caught, particularly for ill-judged property crimes. Cohen, Dearneley, and Hansel (1956) demonstrated that the effect of relatively small amounts of alcohol on highly experienced and skilled British bus drivers was to make them more optimistic about their ability to drive their buses between gaps of varying sizes, while impairing their performance. In short, both judgement and performance deteriorated. In the criminal context, this suggests that alcohol makes potential offenders more optimistic about the risks involved and less able to deal with them. As a result, more offenses will be committed and the rate of detection and of punishment is also likely to increase. For crime, as for other skilled performances, sobriety pays.

3. Guns. Guns are more dangerous than other weapons: the death of a victim of robbery or assault is more likely if the assailant uses a gun than if any other weapon is involved (Cook 1983). (It is true that the victim is less likely to be *injured* in gun-use crimes than in others because the victim is more likely to comply, but not all assailants are cool enough to use only the threat of force, so that gun availability sharply increases the chances of death in the course of a violent crime – or as the result of a domestic quarrel.)

Cook (1983) points to the ready availability to the US public of firearms, particularly of handguns, the typical type of gun used in violent crime. In the late 1970's there were between 100 and 140 million firearms in private possession. By 1990 the number had reached about 180 million. In both cases, about one-third were handguns (*The Economist* 1990f). The total volume of handgun import and manufacture for the 1970's exceeded the total volume for the preceding six decades combined. There has been a proportional shift toward handguns: in 1959 only one quarter of all households owning weapons had at least one handgun; by 1978 this proportion had grown to one half.

4. Arousal level. The more complex a skill, the more its performance is impaired as the short-term level of arousal increases. This very general statement has a good deal of experimental support (Feldman 1964). As Easterbrook (1959) puts it, "the number of cues utilized in any situation tends to become smaller with increases in emotion." It follows that as the level of arousal increases beyond an optimum, criminal decision-making is less and less rational, increasing the chances of failure – exactly as in other human activities. This is likely to be true of both property and of personal crimes. In the former, an

above optimal level of arousal seems likely to "short-circuit" a considered analysis of the relevant factors; in the latter, an opponent may be attacked when prudence would dictate otherwise.

Maintenance

The previous section dealt with the appraisal by a potential offender of a single criminal opportunity. This section concerns the effect of the outcomes of a series of offenses in maintaining or diminishing such behavior over a lengthy period of time.

External reinforcement. In general, behaviors, including criminal behaviors, are strongly controlled by their consequences, both those experienced by the offender himself and those experienced by observed, and significant, others. Positive outcomes of crime (rewards markedly outweigh costs) will tend to maintain criminal behaviors, negative outcomes (costs outweigh rewards) will tend to diminish them. (Positive outcomes are essentially those listed above under the heading of incentives).

As well as being separately important, financial and status incentives may also be linked over time, perhaps a considerable period of time. Illegally acquired wealth may be invested in a legitimate business enterprise, the consequent success of which is a source of social status and power for the parents and also gains access for their children to valued social opportunities, including marriage to less wealthy but socially more prestigious families. The current wealth and status of a number of American families had their origins in the illegal activities of earlier family members during the Prohibition years.

If all crimes were reported and cleared we could expect a very rapid diminution in the crime rate. Instead, the opposite is true, as we have seen in Chapters 1 and 2. Many crimes are not reported, of which some are not recorded, and clearance rates for most offenses are rather low, even for those which are pursued with vigor by the police. Moreover, these low rates probably overstate the negative side of the long-term reward/cost balance. The offender may be detected and punished but he may consider this an acceptable outcome if the punishment is not too severe and he has had some reward: in property crimes detection may well be some time later, and by then his proceeds may well have been either enjoyed or salted away; in person crimes, whatever positive return was intended has been attained once the attack has been completed successfully.

The situation is further complicated by the *schedule* on which positive reinforcements have been received. It is well known that reinforcements received on an intermittent schedule are strongly resistant to extinction. It is the central reason for people playing fruit machines for long periods of time – their attempts to win are kept going by the occasional, unpredictable, success. This general rule can be expected to apply to criminal behaviors also. For example, if a person shoplifts twice, both successfully, and repeats the offenses a further four times, all four resulting in failure, it is highly likely that he will then desist. However, given the fact that this is an offense in which the odds are heavily on the side of the offender, it is much more likely that even if he is caught four times that these will be distributed randomly over a very large number of offenses with positive outcomes. The result will be an intermittent schedule of reinforcement of the type most calculated to maintain offending behavior (the technical term is variable-interval, variable-ratio) exactly as in the case of the fruit machine addict, only more so. The odds in favor of many offenders are such that *once* the first offense has been carried out successfully, the behavior is more likely to be maintained than to cease.

A criminal behavior ceases either when there has been a lengthy series of negatively reinforced outcomes (e.g., the punishment is such as to weigh heavily on the cost side of the balance) or when the person concerned changes his subjective appraisal of the odds involved (perhaps because of increasing age and physical decline). Alternative, legal, sources of money, property, or of the satisfaction obtained from physically damaging an opponent are also important. Unless these are readily available, even occasional positive reinforcements will maintain criminal behaviors, except in the face of very severe punishment – and severe levels are unlikely to be experienced early in a career. Most early offenders can expect to proceed up a hierarchy from mild to serious penal outcomes. By the time a severe level is reached the behavior concerned may be very well maintained, on a schedule highly resistant to extinction, and particularly so if alternative legal behaviors are not readily available. Finally, as indicated above, positive reinforcements for crimes, obtained by significant social models, will help to maintain criminal behaviors by observers whose own experienced schedule of reinforcement might otherwise tend toward extinction of the behavior. Once again, this will be most true when alternative legitimate behaviors are unavailable (or significantly more difficult, or markedly less likely to produce the desired results).

Cognitive consequences and distortions. Cognitive activity takes place over time. Some persons spend more time in thought than others, but with the exception of a few fictional Rambos no-one is totally involved in action, with no intervals for reflection. Moreover, the fact of cognitive activity means that considerable distortions of objective reality may occur. It is central to much of social psychology that people try to maintain cognitive consistency between their attitudes and their actions, and that they experience a subjective sense of discomfort when there is inconsistency. It is easier to resolve this by changing one's cognitions than one's behavior (Berkowitz 1969).

Bandura (1986) has listed the mechanisms through which the internal control of behavior is *selectively* activated or disengaged. The selectivity is aimed at avoiding the subjective discomfort caused by a discrepancy between an action and a previously held belief or attitude, for example, a first or early criminal offense carried out by someone who sees himself as generally law-abiding.

1. Moral justification. This operates on the nature of the behavior itself. "What is culpable can be made honorable through cognitive restructuring . . . reprehensible conduct is made personally and socially acceptable by portraying it in the service of moral ends" (Bandura 1986, p. 376). As an example, Bandura points to military training: people who have been taught to deplore killing as immoral can be transformed rapidly into skilled combatants. In the criminological context moral justification is likely to be associated with political crimes.

2. Euphemistic labelling. "Actions can take on very different appearances depending on what they are called. Euphemistic language thus provides a convenient device for masking reprehensible activities" (Bandura 1986, p. 378). Thus, mercenaries speak of "fulfilling a contract" when they mean murder, and the nuclear power industry terms a disastrous explosion an "energetic disassembly". Euphemistic labeling will be found very widely in both political and corporate crime.

3. Advantageous comparison. A bad act can be made to seem trifling, even benevolent, by contrasting it with something manifestly worse. Stalin justified the destruction of countless Russian smallholders in the 1930's by pointing to the eventual triumph of socialism for which it would pave the way. Many other acts of physical agression

and much property destruction, particularly in the context of political crimes, exemplify this mechanism.

4. Displacement of responsibility. This operates by obscuring the relationship between actions and the effects they cause. Nazi death camp commandants and their staffs felt little personal responsibility for their enormous crimes; they were simply carrying out orders. There are many examples of offenses, often in the political context, for which those responsible made a similar claim, but shortly after World War II the Nuremberg Accords declared that people could not shelter behind this excuse: they had to take personal responsibility for their illegal actions.

5. Disregard or distortion of consequences. "When people choose to pursue activities harmful to others for personal gain . . . they avoid facing the harm they cause or minimize it . . . especially . . . when they act alone and cannot easily escape responsibility" (Bandura 1986, p. 381). Offenses against persons and property inevitably involve victims in pain and suffering or at least personal loss: examples of cognitive distortion will be given below.

6. Dehumanization. The more victims are seen as fellow human beings the harder it is to avoid sympathy for their distress. If, instead, they can be dehumanized – by being given a derogatory label such as "nigger" or "whitey" – they are no longer viewed as people with feelings and can more easily be damaged. Both property and person crimes provide many examples of dehumanization by offenders.

7. Attribution of blame. Offenders seek to exonerate themselves by attributing the blame for their actions to the victim. The most obvious example is that of rape – a claim that in the past was frequently accepted by the courts. It will be found also in other person crimes and to some extent in property crimes.

These mechanisms are not applied with equal intensity and frequency to everyone, but much more to victims or potential victims: friends and family remain for the most part the objects of tender concern. Nor do they immediately transform a person responsive to the distress of others into one able to damage them without apparent remorse. Rather, there is a gradual disinhibition of concern for victims over time, and as an offending career proceeds it is likely that the mechanisms listed above operate *in advance* of the offense, making them easier to operate and increasing the likelihood of the offense occurring (Feldman 1977).

Some persons, for example, those high on the Eysenckian personality dimension of psychopathy (see Chapter 6), may find this easier than others right from the beginning of an offending career. And other individual differences are also likely. Feldman and McCulloch (1971) suggested that variations between clients in response to various forms of behavior therapy could be accounted for in part by learned or innate individual differences in the cognitive rehearsal, outside the treatment situation, of the events which occurred in treatment. Effective rehearsal supplements and strengthens effective learning (Bandura and Jeffrey 1973, Meichenbaum and Goodman 1971). In general, more obsessional and more introverted people may rehearse more frequently and intensely. This notion may be particularly relevant to the task of explaining particularly violent crimes such as some sexual offenses and sadistic murders.

There may also be individual differences in the content of what is rehearsed, with some persons more attentive to pleasant information, others to unpleasant information (Merbaum and Kazaoka 1967). If so, this will help to explain why some people persist in crime, despite repeated lack of success, while others desist following only occasional punishment: the former may filter out failure and rehearse only their successes; the latter may do the opposite. It is tempting to identify these two sets of persons as, respectively, highly extroverted and highly introverted.

9.3. Crimes against property

Acquisition

Attitude change. Initially unfavorable attitudes to offences against property may be modified prior to an offense by persuasive communications, as indicated above. After the offense, the attitude change is strengthened the more the act is positively rewarded. (The extreme case of reward would be the external reinforcement of a high financial return plus the internal reinforcement of the skill deployed in leaving no trace of being involved in a difficult crime.)

The more successful the outcome the more rapid and resistant to relapse will be the switch from a previous habit of avoiding property crimes, acquired through early socialization, to a set of attitudes favorable to such acts. Of course, in real life, there will be a constant flow of vicarious and actual experiences relating to the continued avoidance of some property crimes while carrying out others, resulting in the development of a range of attitudes and behaviors, each specific to a particular class of criminal opportunity (shoplifting, stealing from unoccupied vehicles, breaking into a home, etc.). These will vary from situations in which the individual would virtually never transgress, to those in which he would do so very frequently.

Observational learning. The greater the opportunity for the observational learning of property crimes the more likely it is that they will be acquired. This is true both for repeated opportunities for such learning, whether in the street or in an occupational setting, and for the more occasional but highly spectacular event reported in the media.

Modeling effects are dependent on the power, the status, the interpersonal attraction and the ethnic group membership of the model concerned. Modeled behavior which is judged by the observer to be markedly inappropriate to the model will have a much less imitative effect than behavior judged relatively appropriate (Dubanoski 1967). Hence, a black boy of high status among his peers, and known to have carried out a successful theft, will be a much more effective model for black boys from the same community than a middle-class white female, similarly observed. In the same way, if the chairman of a finance house demonstrates an illegal financial manipulation to his colleagues, this will have a much more powerful effect than the same behavior carried out by a junior employee.

Direct reinforcement. Through repeated rewarding experiences, stimuli associated with successful property offenses (for example, chain stores with few staff, open car doors, etc.) will become cues for future theft behaviors. Cues which signal the need for caution will also be learned, as will those which indicate that it is safe to act. Environmental stimuli thus acquire discriminative control over property offenses such as shoplifting. Over time, positively reinforced responses are retained in one's repertoire and negatively reinforced ones are dropped from it, the process being speeded up both by social settings which provide initial opportunities for observational learning and by cognitive rehearsal. The greater the former, and the stronger the habit of the latter, the faster will the process take place.

Social settings. There is a progression in social settings from one highly unlikely to result in the acquisition of property offenses as part of one's behavioral repertoire, to one highly likely to produce such a result. The former extreme is experienced by a child growing up in a low crime community, as part of a family no members of which have property offenses in their repertoire, headed by parents who have the child rearing skills discussed in Chapter 7 and adequate resources for deploying them with a child who is easy to rear. The child attends a school which includes few or no models of property offending and does so right through adolescence, by which time he has acquired many skills relevant to worldly success by legitimate means, and is esposed repeatedly to models of such success. As the result of all this he has strongly held beliefs that property crime is wrong and he has never carried out such behavior.

The other extreme is represented by a child whose family includes several professional property offenders, living in a community in which other such families are common, so that most social models the child encounters are successful property offenders. Samuel (1981) reports that the life histories of property offenders indicates that their criminal involvement is often initiated by relatives, friends and acquaintances; their drift into crime is unremarkable, even natural. There is no need too invoke social influence mechanisms such as attitude change to explain the development of criminal attitudes and behaviors relevant to property crime by such persons, their development is almost inevitable, as is the acquisition of relevant skills in shoplifting, auto theft, and so on.

Between these two extremes there are many detailed variations. For example, somewhat nearer to the low-probability end is a child growing-up in a family similar to that of the first example but which lives in a high crime area. The child has learned from his parents not to steal but when exposed to neighborhood models of such behavior may change first his initial unfavorable attitudes and then actually carry out a property offense. Whether or not this sequence occurs will depend on which persuasive communications and social models he is exposed to and on his own intellectual and personality endowments.

The acquisition of property offense behaviors occurs after, as well as during, adolesence. Many occupations provide relevant persuasive communications, social models and criminal opportunities, from that of longshoreman, through the restaurant trade, to the financial world.

Performance

The performance of an offense against property, the opportunity for which has arisen, or has been created, is likely to be influenced by the following factors.

Incentive. Property incentives include most of those listed above. Monetary incentives are the most obvious. They include cash, which can be spent immediately, on both primary reinforcers such as food and sex and on consumer goods, or after the slight delay involved in fencing stolen goods for money. For more far-sighted property offenders there will also be the long-term incentive of a major acquisition such as a home and its contents. Social incentives include an enhanced status among offenders for a successful, major property crime, and access to a wider range of friendships among them.

Self-evaluation is also important as an incentive; a skilled performance is as satisfying to a thief as to a legitimate craftsman or professional. Sensory incentives (such as "fun" or "excitement") seem likely to be relevant only early on in an offending career.

Risk. In general, property offenses have low clearance rates, as indicated in Chapter 1. Once offenders have built up some experience of this (both their own and by observation) they are likely to find that this is true for themselves also, so that the risk of detection attached to any particular opportunity is fairly slight. They will also find, again by experience and observation, that punishments are relatively mild, at least early in a career. The deterrent value of punishment is further reduced because the proceeds of a property offense can be retained and enjoyed when the punishment is over. This is likely to be an important decision-making factor both for those who habitually deny anxiety and for offenders in general whenever the prospective return is perceived as large.

Target. Winchester and Jackson (1982) found that the most important factors determining victimization by burglary, apart from the apparent rewards, were whether the house was occupied and the siting of the building which either facilitated or restricted access: houses standing in their own grounds were more likely to be burglarized than those in the middle of a row. Likewise, Waller and Okihiro (1978) found that apartment blocks protected by a doorman had very low levels of burglary. Walsh (1978) reported that shoplifters are more likely to select as targets self-service stores from which it is easier to steal than from small shops. (How easy is demonstrated by a large survey of American chain stores: shoplifting as a percentage of sales rose as high as $7\frac{1}{2}$ per cent for fashion accessories, with an overall average of over 2 per cent; department stores are hit significantly harder than the rest, *The Economist* 1991).

Skills and resources. Offenders will match themselves to a potential target in terms of the resources required for a successful crime. Weaver and Carroll (1985) recruited self-described expert and novice shoplifters by means of a newspaper ad followed up by a telephone sift. The final pool of 17 experts claimed a median of 100 shoplifting acts overall and at least 10 in the past year; the 17 novices reported zero acts. The interviewees (aged 18–62, with no difference between the two groups) then walked through retail stores with instructions to think aloud concerning criminal opportunities. Half of each group received an additional instruction to form an intention to steal during the shopping trip. The verbal protocols indicated that the experts were much more efficient and "strategic" in their shoplifting considerations, selecting appropriate items by size (larger items were less attractive because they were more difficult to conceal) and working out ways to overcome obstacles such as store personnel and security devices. In contrast, the novices were deterred by almost any difficulty. The selection level for "expertness" seems rather low in this study; 10 thefts in the last year smacks more of an experienced amateur than a professional thief. Nevertheless, the point is made; the more expert the shoplifter, the more rational he/she is in appraising and overcoming obstacles (or in aborting the operation completely – see Walsh, 1978, for another study of experienced shoplifters).

Shoplifting is a crime requiring comparatively little in the way of special resources. In contrast, a large scale bank-robbery may need, as well as detailed advanced planning, technical skills and equipment for a rapid break-in as well as a reliable get-away car and driver. Sophisticated financial and computer crimes demand very special expertise.

Opportunity for legitimate gain. This is complex. McCandless, Persons, and Roberts (1972), studying a institutional sample of American adolescent boys, found a significant relationship between self-reported offending and perceived legitimate opportunity ("Is it hard to find a good paying, honest job in your area?"), but only for white inmates, the trend for blacks being in the same direction but short of statistical significance. As we have seen, many well-established offenders combine legal and illegal sources of income, but a beginner will probably be less tempted by a criminal opportunity when he already has a legitimate source of income than will the former.

If potential property offenders were fully rational it would be only the variables of the incentive, the target the risk, the skills and resources, and the opportunity for legitimate gain which would determine their decision to respond to a criminal opportunity, or to reject it, with a resulting clearance rate will below even current figures. However, many offenders will be either relatively deficient in the ability to process such information efficiently or lack full access to the relevant information, seriously reducing full rationality. This means that either inappropriate targets are selected or the crime is inadequately planned or executed.

In addition, several other variables may influence the potential offender's decision, mainly in the direction of reducing the rationality of the choice and, hence, limiting the chances of success.

The concurrent presence of an offending model or models. If one member of a teenage pair of friends is shoplifting the other might be more likely to do so than if he were alone. This is suggested by a number of laboratory studies by Blake and associates which demonstrated the relevance of models in increasing or decreasing the probability of a transgression (e.g., Blake 1958). They found a marked interaction between the presence of a model and the level of incentive. For example, under extreme temptation, participants disregarded both a nontransgressing model and external surveillance. The status of the model is also important; high status models are more successful in inducing imitation, even in the face of external surveillance, than are low-status ones, particularly when incentives are high (Lippit, Polansky, and Rosen 1952). It may be the awareness of this effect which leads judges to hand out stiff sentences, intended to be exemplary, to senior businessmen convicted of financial crimes, or to pop stars found guilty or drug possession.

Reduced self-esteem. A number of reports, for example Aronson and Mettee (1968), suggest that temporarily lowering the self-esteem of students by giving them derogatory feedback from a personality test increases the incidence of dishonest behavior on a subsequent task. The converse was also found. This suggests that poor performance on a task considered important by the person concerned (as opposed to what is thought important by a teacher, for example) may make that person more receptive to an opportunity for a crime.

The victim. To some extent this is covered by the target variable: the easier the target the more likely will be a property offense, all other factors being held constant. But there may also be an additional element: the judged "wrongness" of a target. Using hypothetical situations, the author found that both institutional adolescent offenders and secondary schoolboys considered themselves significantly less likely to retain a purse dropped by a pensioner than one dropped a businessman and less likely to steal from a friend than from a stranger (unpublished data). In line with the latter finding, Kiesler, and Pallack (1967) found that a commitment to future interaction increased attempts to influence a fellow worker on a laboratory task to behave correctly, implying, though somewhat indirectly, that transgressions are reduced by an expectation that one would have to face the victim again.

Psychopathology. Moore (1984) reported a clinical study of 300 people in the age range 16–73 who had appeared in court for shoplifting. He found that financial benefit and not psychological "compensation" was the major motivation in over two-thirds of cases, so that most shoplifting in this sample was ". . . premeditated, purposeful, habitual and conscious, goal directed behavior." (Similar research, with much the same result, was reviewed in Chapter 6.)

It is possible that a small proportion of shoplifting accusations is associated with "absent-mindedness" while shopping by people who combine ill-health, and extreme preoccupation with their own thoughts with what the authors term "unwise supermarket practices" (Reason and Lucas 1984), but it is clear that the vast majority of shoplifting acts are explained by financial incentives.

Criminogenic factors

1. Drugs Substances such as cocaine and heroin have an indirect effect on property crime, as indicated earlier. Those on a run may require immediate cash, which can be obtained only by crime. The urgency of the need is likely to reduce sharply the rational appraisal of opportunities, so that a less than fully appropriate one is selected.

2. Alcohol. The same lack of exact appraisal is likely to be associated with the ingestion of more than a small amount of alcohol. This has the important effect of impairing the judgement of even skilled performers, so that the wrong target is selected and their performance is impaired – a double hazard. This will be even more true of beginning property offenders.

3. Guns. While the possession of a gun will improve the ability of a skilled and experienced robber to overcome resistance without having to inflict physical damage, in the hands of an inexperienced user – or one affected by alcohol or a drug - it might lead to selecting a too well-defended target, and hence to either total failure, or a serious person crime, which is pursued vigorously by the police.

4. Arousal. This is of particular relevance to person crimes, but a too-high level of arousal will influence the selection and outcome of property crimes also. As indicated earlier, the more complex the decision, or the more difficult the task, the lower the optimal level of arousal. Someone who is habitually emotionally labile, and hence easily excited by relatively minor events, will frequently be incapable of full rationality. Major emotional upsets which impair the judgement and performance of most people will do so for offenders also. Considerable experience helps people to perform effectively despite exposure to highly arousing events, but it must often be the case that such events cannot be predicated fully and hence guarded against, and may hinder the performance of even the best planned crime.

Maintenance

External reinforcement. Clearance rates tend to fall as the size of property crimes increases (McClintock and Gibson 1961). This suggests that the bigger prizes are sought and won by the more competent offenders. It is clear that both the personal experience of a successful outcome and the observed successful experience of others are widespread.

Even if a crime leads to an eventual punishment the outcome may not be entirely negative, depending both on the actual return (money, property, social status, etc.) and on when the returns are received. Clearly, a $100,000 haul which is retained will help to mitigate the pains of a prison sentence; the latter will be experienced as much more negative if no money was retained from the offense.

The powerful influence of frequent rewards in maintaining criminal behavior is illustrated by an interview with Danny, aged 20, who claimed 700 burglaries in a 5 year period, interspersed with two short stretches in a juvenile penal institution and one in prison (Beattie 1982). Danny was "recruited" at the age of 15 by a 16 year old friend, his first burglary being a huge success – easy access, and a significant sum of money spent quickly and enjoyably. (This is reminiscent of the beginners luck of many compulsive gamblers, Dickerson 1984). Danny quickly acquired the relevant skills and moved from general burglaries to a specialized interest in porcelain figures, taken from jewellers, which had a ready market with collectors. He claimed never to have been caught on the job, only through information supplied by police informers, and went on: "In ten years time I'll either be doing a ten-year stretch or living it up. I'm not going to change my life-style . . . burglary is the only real skill I've got."

Cognitive consequences and distortions. In the context of offenses against property this means making statements to oneself which derogate the victim ("he's a mug anyway," an example of dehumanization), deny the extent of his distress ("he's covered by insurance" – this is distortion of consequences because he may not be insured and victims suffer in nonmonetary ways), or assert that the responsibility for any damage is really the victim's ("he should have been more careful with his money," an example of attribution of blame).

For example, Danny (Beattie 1982) didn't spare much regret for his victims: "Why should I, the people I burgle can afford it, and jewellers are all bent and bump up insurance claims. Another thing, I never burgle poor people or old people." (It could be said that the greater ease of such targets is more than offset by the poorer returns available.)

9.4. Offences against persons

Introduction

There is a very large literature on aggression, the experimental analog of offenses against persons. Much of what follows in this section is drawn from that literature; the analogy seems a reasonably close one.

Bandura (1973, p. 8) defined aggression as follows:
"Injurious and destructive behavior that is socially defined as aggressive on the basis of a variety of factors, some of which reside in the evaluator rather than the preformer."

This needs expanding and spelling out, as follows:

1. Aggressive acts (that is, offenses against the person) both damage victims and have consequences for the aggressor, both positive and negative.

2. Social judgements of what constitutes aggression/a violent offence are very important because they influence reporting by an onlooker or a complaint by a victim. They depend on the following: the intensity of the aggressor's behavior; the level of the display of pain or injury by the recipient and the actual severity of the injury; the intentions attributed to the aggressor and his relationship to the recipient (until fairly recently male spouses and parents had a relatively free hand with female partners and children, respectively: the terms battered wives and children date only to the 1960's); the characteristics of the performer – sex, age, social class and so on are also taken into account as are the relative capabilities of those concerned (the difference between a "fair" fight and an unfair one).

Finally, the social observer himself is important, his attributes and beliefs influencing his judgement of an observed act. For example, Blumenthal, Kahn, and Andrews (1971) reported that most of their respondents labeled student demonstrations (against the Vietnam War) as violent behavior, but did not consider it violent when the police struck the demonstrators; a small minority held the reverse of these views. To some extent then, violence, like beauty, is in the eye of the beholder. There is a vast difference between the social evaluation of a premeditated attack on a helpless child and that of an assault on the football field in the heat of the game. For the most part, though, there is widespread agreement as to most instances of interpersonal violence, at least within one culture and one time-span (for example, the USA in the last decade of this century).

Acquisition

Exactly as in the case of offenses against property, initially unfavorable attitudes toward violent behavior may be changed by persuasive communications, and by social interactions with other people, ranging in number from one person to a crowd. (Some people hold attitudes favorable to aggressive acts from an early age which translate readily into overt behaviors, requiring no preliminary modification. This will be particularly the case for children reared by parents with inadequate skills, resources, or both, as detailed in Chapter 7.)

Social settings. Many people grow up in social contexts in which interpersonal violence is an everyday occurrence, so that they will both use it themselves and accept its use by others, partially irrespective of their own childhood experiences. The level of violence varies between countries, regions and cities within countries and even between different neighborhoods. It also varies across time. Until a few centuries ago murder was accepted in nearly all of Europe and in all classes as a method of solving interpersonal conflict (Clinard 1968). In the present day Middle East it is expected that the father and brothers of a Moslem girl deflowered before marriage will wreak physical vengeance on the person responsible for this assault on family honor.

People then either learn aggressive attitudes and behaviors from the start, or after an earlier period of opposition to them. (Of course many individuals remain opposed to the use of aggression, except for unusual situations, and there are societies in which physical aggression is totally rejected in any circumstances, for example, the Amish communities of Pennsylvania.)

The learning processes by which aggressive attitudes and behaviors are acquired are the same as for offenses against property: direct and observational learning, with the important addition of *classical conditioning.* A number of animal studies have shown that previously neutral stimuli can acquire aggression-eliciting properties if they are paird with stimuli previously associated with the elicitation of aggression, for example, pain (Vernon and Ulrich 1966) and brain stimulation (Delgado 1963). Human studies have shown that symbolic and vicarious experiences are also effective: Insko and Oakes (1966) paired neutral with negative words and demonstrated that the former then evoked hostile responses. Berkowitz (1974) has emphasized the importance of associative learning for the acquisition of aggressive responses. There may be two stages in the process whereby cues become eliciting stimuli for aggressive responses: (a) an aggressive attitude is classically conditioned; (b) such attitudes prompt aggression, either following modeling or by direct stimulation of the potential aggressor in appropriate circumstances (Berkowitz 1972).

Direct learning. Aggressive behaviors are performed in response to external or internal stimuli (an opponent with whom one is in conflict; an internal state of anger arousal). Once performed, such an act will have a consequence varying from complete success in achieving the performers objective (the intended victim is killed or injured, or acknowledges the superiority of the assailant, etc.) to complete failure (the attacker is injured, the intended victim is not and the attacker is arrested and punished). The nearer the outcome is to the former the more likely it is to be repeated when a subsequent opportunity arises; the nearer it is to the latter the less likely is repetition, depending on the exact outcome, the nature of the opponent on that occasion (a less powerful one might be more easily overcome in the future) and the availability of alternatives for achieving the same objective.

Observational learning. Modeling leads to new patterns of aggressive behaviors, the strengthening of previously learned inhibitions against aggression and the facilitation of previously learned aggressive responses. There is evidence of the retention of even briefly modeled aggressive responses over a period of six months (Hicks 1965), implying the importance of rehearsal processes, as well as that of external reinforcement. Responsiveness to an aggressive model is increased by prior arousal, indicating the energizing properties of emotional arousal (Nelson, Gelfand, and Hartmann 1969). General tactics, as well as specific responses may be modeled, particularly following exposure to several models (Bandura 1973).

What determines which model will be copied when both aggressive and nonaggressive models are available? The relevant variables include the extent of exposure to the two, their relative power and status, the outcome of the aggressive or nonnagressive responses previously made by the observer in comparable situations and – a point little mentioned by modeling theorists – the physical attributes of the observer concerned. If the person is so weak that no appropriate target is available, even a consistent and sole exposure to aggressive models will not lead to overt physical aggression by physically poorly endowed observers. (This is the importance of gun availability; as noted above, the possession of a gun and a rudimentary knowledge of how to use it transforms all but the most frail persons into equally damaging adversaries.)

Modeling effects may be rather subtle. Bandura and Walters (1959) reported that some of the parents they observed verbally modeled aggressive behavior toward people outside the immediate family and positively reinforced verbal reports of its occurrence, while modeling nonaggressive behavior within the family. The sub-cultural transmission of aggression by modeling is widespread, changing even previously peaceable persons into aggressors, as in the case of military service (Bandura 1973).

The potential importance of television for the modeling of aggressive attitudes and behaviors was discussed in Chapter 7. It was concluded that it was likely to play only a relatively small part for the bulk of the population. Nevertherless, there seem specific instances in which the media depiction of crimes of violence has influenced the imitation of successful tactics by observers. A single-case example concerns a French Army deserter who took five hostages before finally surrendering to the police after the authorities had paid him a ransom of $1 million. He stated that his technique was modeled on that used the previous week by men who took hostages in a Paris bank (*The Grardian* 1975). Holden (1986) developed a mathematical model of what he termed "contagion," and applied it to aircraft hi-jacks in the USA between 1968 and 1972. He found that successful hi-jacks generated additional attempts of the same type. Conversely, unsuccessful attempts had no such effect.

Performance

Many of the conclusions set out below are based on laboratory studies, using special experimental arrangements in which either the capacity to inflict injury on an opponent (typically by inflicting "electric shocks") or the "distress" of the opponent, or both, are simulated. Nevetheless, because these data both cohere with each other and fit in with findings from field studies of aggression and of legally defined violent offenses, they form a systematic framework, as for the performance of property offenses.

What determines whether or not an aggressive response will be performed in response to an opportunity for such an action once it has become part of a person's behavioral repertoire? Once again, the general approach taken here is to emphasize the importance of the balance of rewards and costs as perceived by the potential performer. This appraisal may be significantly less rational and more influenced by short-or long-term emotional factors than is the case with offenses against property, as we shall see.

The incentive. With the exception of robbery, in which violence, whether threatened or actual, is essentially carried out in order to acquire money or goods, monetary incentives seem much less critical for person than for property crimes. Primary incentives, particularly sexual ones, will be important in the case of rape, though often combined with power incentives; a detailed analysis of rape is given below.

The pursuit of both social approval (many social settings applaud physical prowess, with a consequent increase in rewarding social interactions and in the range of friendship choices for those who display it, even in a criminal context) and of status and power are important incentives for person crimes. The aim is to achieve additional status and power and to retain existing levels of both: "In aggressive gangs, where status and social power are tied to fighting prowess, members fight challengers within their own group and from rival gangs. Threats to status provoke quick, aggressive counteraction in efforts to preserve the existing power relations." (Bandura 1986, p. 238).

Sensory incentives (e.g., novelty and excitement) seem important in explaining both "senseless" property violence and "random" physical attacks on strangers. Nevertheless, in both cases it is likely to be the more vulnerable targets which are selected (see below). Finally, self-evaluation incentives will play a part in the instigation of person offenses, for example, the opportunity to carry out an effective physical attack using well-practised skills or weapons, the result of which can be reflected on with pride.

The target. In the case of person crimes, several features of the adversaries need to be considered separately.

1. Sex of aggressor and victim. A large-scale review by Eagly and Steffen (1986) concluded that the highest levels of aggression are displayed by men toward men and the lowest by men toward women, although it is striking that these differences are greater in laboratory than in the much more important field settings (many rapes result in serious physical damage to the female victim). Men and women tend to think differently about aggression, with women more guilty and anxious about the consequences of aggression, more vigilant about the harm that aggression causes its victims, and more concerned about the danger that aggression might bring to themselves.

2. Capacity for retaliation. Dengerink and Levendusky (1972) found that laboratory subjects reduced their level of overt aggression when their opponent was known to have the ability to inflict a more massive

retaliation than they themselves had available. Even if the opponent failed to use this capacity, its threat was sufficient.

3. Perceived intent of the opponent. Both Epstein and Taylor (1967) and Greenwell and Dengerink (1973) reported that the level of aggression used by laboratory subjects was a function more of an opponent's perceived intention to aggress than the actual level of aggression he used. Conbining this finding with the previous one, it seems that aggression is most sharply reduced in the face of an opponent who has not only a massive retaliatory capacity but is perceived as being ready to use it. Interviews with muggers showed that victims are chosen who are unlikely to resist, while yielding a satisfactory return (Lejeune 1977).

Difficulty. A series of British studies of vandalism (property damage) in public places, reviewed by Mayhew and Clarke (1982), demonstrated the importance of the difficulty variable in attacks against physical objects, as well as against persons. For example, seat damage to one-man operated buses was over 20 times greater for the upper as for the lower deck. Even when the upper deck alone was considered, damage to the back seat was seven times greater than to the front seat. In both cases it is relative proximity to the bus operator which seems crucial.

Risks. Whereas a fully rational appraisal of an opportunity for attack might often caution avoidance, the opportunity is nevertheless often taken because of the overriding pressure of the instigating events such as emotional arousal, leading to an inevitably higher risk of detection and punishment than for property crime.

A close degree of proximity to the victim is usually necessary in order to inflict physical injury (and rape is of course impossible without it). This means that the victim may be able to recall critical details of the assailant for subsequent complaint and court hearing. Bystanders may also provide eye-witness testimony, as may the neighbors of victims. Merry (1981) interviewed seven young men living in an American inner-city housing project who claimed responsibility for many robberies. She described them as being very pragmatic, carefully weighing the risks involved – of being observed, of the police being called, and of losing their escape route. A key factor in their selection of targets was that the young men knew their neighborhood intimately, particularly the residents and their likely reactions to either witnessing a robbery or being the victim. One street was "good," meaning that its inhabitants were never on the look-out. Another was "poor," for the opposite reason. Some people were known to shout but not to call the police, others to call, but not to shout (so that robberies in their proximity were particularly to be avoided).

Typically, person offenses receive more severe punishments than do property offenses: capital punishments are confined to the former, and most life and very long sentences are associated with violent offenses. Indeed, if a property offense also involves violence the resulting penalty is typically much more severe than for theft alone. While rape is similarly subject to relatively harsh sentences, it is a special case within the overall field of violent offenses: not only is the reporting rate for rape very low, so is the clearance rate for those rapes which are reported – because strangers are so frequently involved. It follows that the number of attempted rapes will probably remain high despite increased sentences and fewer acquitals in recent years.

Skills and resources. Perceived risks interact with the assailant's own skills and resources and those thought to be possesed by the intended victim. What would be a highly risky assault for person A on C might be seen as straightforward by B because of his significantly greater prowess with fists or weapons. The availability of lethal weapons is also important, hence the importance of guns, which require relatively little skill to operate at close quarters, and transform the power relationship between adversaries – enabling a physically weak person easily to overcome a physically much stronger opponent.

Alternative, legal, routes. Both murder and assault frequently arise from personal disputes between individuals well known to each other. In other cases the arguments which are terminated by a physical attack occur between strangers. Rapes often involve anger directed at a specific female, or against the victim as an exemplar of other females against whom the assailant feels resentment. In all these instances, the argument or resentment might have been resolved or satisfied by nonviolent means, such as discussion and compromise, either directly between the parties, or by resort to the Law as an impartial arbiter. Alternatively, one or both parties might have turned to other ways of damaging their opponent, for example by spreading false stories about him, whether verbally or in writing. Whether or not such alternatives are taken depend on their availability, as perceived by both parties, and on their successful use in earlier conflicts, compared with an effective resort to physical violence. People who have already learned to use violence, both by modeling and by direct reinforcement, will use it again, often even when alternatives are theoretically available, depending on the perceived power of the opponent and his intention to use his power, and the level of emotional arousal of the combatants.

The presence of a model already performing aggressively. Bandura (1973) drew the following conclusions:

1. The effects of modeled aggression, in descending order of importance, depend on the rewards which follow if the observer matches his response to that of the model, the personal attributes of the model and the personal attributes of the observer.

2. Observers perceive rewards as being greatest for imitating models whom they perceive as intelligent, competent, powerful and of high status. Such attributes are considered by observers to generalize widely over situations.

Prior emotional arousal. A number of studies reviewed by Feldman (1977, Chapter 3) support the conclusion that high levels of aroused anger reduce the importance of a model in increasing the probability of an aggressive response. Similarly, a powerful modeling situation will effectively incite aggression even in an individual low in anger arousal. Thus, both prior anger arousal and modeling facilitate overt aggression; each will do so alone if present at a sufficiently high level. When the level of one variable is relatively low the additional presence of the other markedly enhances the probability of an aggressive response; when both are high such a response is extremely likely.

The availability of a weapon exerts more powerful instigating effects when a potential assailant is emotionally aroused than when he is relatively quiescent (Berkowitz 1974). He suggests that in such states of high arousal aggressive behavior is a more "impulsive and involuntary response" than when the individual is less aroused – when attacks are better designed to produce planned benefits and to avoid detection. A high proportion of 65 British assaults studied by Berkowitz (1978) were triggered by anger which arose during the course of an argument, the main aim of the assailant being to hurt the opponent. Because high levels of emotional arousal distort judgement, particularly in complex situations, criminal organizations much prefer "stone killers," who kill without emotion, as opposed to "animals," who kill almost at random (Teresa 1973).

The reasonably consistent links between income inequality and violent crimes, set out in Chapter 8, fit in at this point. Income inequality seems likely to be an important source of anger arousal, particularly when people become aware of their relative poverty, due to a rapid increase in the ownership of televisions or the sudden openness of a newly democratic, formerly totalitarian, country.

Prior aversive experiences: physical. Pain and physical assaults are likely to enhance aggression by the recipient, but the prior learning of appropriate responses is a major prerequisite, even in animals (Powell and Creer 1969). Bandura (1973) suggests that pain facilitates, but does not inevitably provoke, aggression, the probability of which is increased by direct confrontation with an opponent in a confined space, lack of opportunity for flight, and significant experience of fighting. Indirect pain, such as the threat of long-term aversive consequences which are much worse than the current level of aversive stimuli, may also provoke aggression, but may equally lead to a self-deluding denial of the likelihood of future threat – as witness the appeasement policies of the European democracies prior to World War II.

In an early laboratory study, Baron and Bell (1975) looked at the apparent relationship between "long hot summers" and outbursts of collective violence, such as racial conflicts in American cities. They found that although uncomfortably hot conditions facilitated aggression by nonangry persons, they had the opposite effect on previously angered individuals. A review by Anderson (1989) concluded that, whereas laboratory studies have continued to produce inconsistent results, the much more relevant field researches show a clear link between heat and aggression. Anderson suggests as the most promising explanatory model one based on attribution theory: people mis-attribute to another person the responsibility for the discomfort which is actually due to the increased heat.

Recent research has indicated the considerable importance for violent behavior of "thermal stress" (high humidity, plus high temperature – long hot summers in overcrowded settings). Data for 10,000 assaults in Dallas in 1980 and 1981 showed a marked and continuous increase in assaults of all kinds as heat stress rose (Harries and Stadler 1988). A review by Michael and Zumpe (1986) of 27,000 reports of wife battering indicated a statistically significant annual rhythm, with the maxima in summer and a close relationship of the rhythms to detailed changes in temperature in a range of locations. A similar finding was reported by Michael and Zumpe (1983) for rape.

Prior aversive experiences: verbal. Threats and insults serve as another set of instigating stimuli for aggressive responses, Toch (1969) studied prisoners with a history of violent behavior and found that the major factors precipitating such acts were insults concerning their manliness and general "reputation." He found also that those policemen who were most prone to use violence in the course of their duties used strong, as opposed to mild, verbal threats early in a confrontation with a suspect, often passing quickly to the only remaining step in the hierachy of aggressive behaviors – overt violence – possibly because severe threats aroused more hostility in the suspect than would have been provoked by mild ones.

Withdrawal of reinforcers. There is general agreement among behavior theorists that withdrawing or sharply reducing well-established reinforcers is subjectively experienced as aversive. The most frequently described responses to such an experience are depression and aggression. The response adopted depends partly on the outcome of previous experiences of such circumstances, and the presence in the person's repertoire of an overt aggressive response as an alternative to withdrawing into a depression. In animals, and by implication in humans, attack reactions may be precipitated both by withdrawal of reinforcers and by shifting to a more effortful schedule (more output is required for the same return, Hutchinson, Azrin, and Hunt, 1968). Overcrowding has also been associated with aggression. It may be that it is the contrast between a previous level of crowding and a harsher one which is aversive; the topic is dealt with in detail in Chapter 10, in the context of prison conditions.

Frustration. When behavior aimed at a goal is blocked, the result may be an increase in efforts to achieve it, perhaps by an aggressive response, or a sharp decrease, depending on the success or failure of past attempts, either by oneself or by appropriate social models, to overcome obstacles, as well as the relative degree of deprivation suffered. If matters have been going well, a check to the flow of rewards may be much more aversive, because of the sharpness of the contrast, than a frustration which is only one of many experienced over a prolonged period. A further important determinant will be the comparison between oneself and others judged to be similar in their circumstances. Bandura summed up as follows: "Frustration is likely to provoke aggression in individuals who have learned to behave aggressively and for whom aggression has a functional value" (Bandura 1973, p. 174).

Punishment. The intended effect of punishment is to inhibit an undesired behavior, such as aggression, but it may also have the unintended and opposite effect of instigating aggression. First, aggressive tactics may be modeled to the person being punished, for example, by parents to children. As detailed in Chapter 7, the Patterson group, found that parental reliance on punitive modes of control promotes coercive behavior in their children, which then evolves into a physically aggressive style of behavior. This conduct alienates the aggressors from most of their peers so that they move towards an antisocial peer group.

Second, while low levels of aggression may be inhibited by punishment, even without the provision of alternative responses, higher levels are much less likely to be inhibited, particularly when the aggression has not yet found its intended mark – at which stage punishment may even lead to an increase in subsequent aggression.

Third, reducing the risk of anticipated punishment to a potential aggressor is likely to instigate aggression. The *perceived* risk of punishment for an aggressive act is reduced in a number of ways: if the act can be carried out anonymously this is likely to reduce the probability of detection; group aggression diffuses responsibility for the act between many (as in mob violence); the condoning of an aggressive act by a recognized holder of authority (for example, the political superiors of the aggressor) even if other powerful bodies, such as the courts, remain condemnatory; finally, avoiding the visible marks of aggression, as in the use of rubber implements which leave no mark on the victim.

Guns. Two criminogenic factors are of importance: guns and alcohol. (The relevance of drugs is indirect – people assault or kill in order to retain or to acquire the profits of drug-dealing; there seems litle evidence that cocaine, heroin and so on, in themselves, potentiate aggressive behavior.)

Intercity and interregion differences in gun involvement are related quite closely to differences in patterns of gun ownership between cities and regions (Cook 1983). The cities with the lowest rate of firearm ownership (those in New England and the Atlantic region) are also those with the lowest gun involvement in violent crime. Conversely, the cities with the highest rates of ownership (those in the South, South Central and Mountain regions) have the highest rates of gun involvement).

The possession of a firearm both makes the potential offender feel more secure from retaliation and increases the potential damage to a victim. A large proportion of violent attacks in America are by people using guns. The presence of a gun in an assault or robbery increases the probability of a wounding becoming a homicide. More than 60 per cent of American homicides are committed with firearms (Cook 1983). Cook makes a number of other important points: guns are usually superior to other weapons readily available for use in violent crime-even in the hands of weak and unskilled assailants they kill quickly, from a distance and relatively impersonally; guns are particularly valuable against relatively invulnerable targets – hence gun availability facilitates commercial robbery and lethal assaults on people otherwise able to defend themselves against attack.

The value of a gun in a violent crime is linked to the vulnerability of the victim. If he or she is unarmed, alone, small, frail, or impaired by alcohol, vulnerability is high, irrespective of the weapon available to the assailant, and the probability of success (for example, in a robbery) is only slightly affected by the type of weapon employed (or none). But a gun is more or less essential for success in robbing a bank or in murdering a policeman. It follows that the more vulnerable the target, the less likely is a gun to be used. When a violent offender has the time and the ability to plan ahead he is more likely to equip himself adequately – where "adequacy" is directly proportional to vulnerability. But it is also true that the mere availability of a weapon increases the likelihood that it will be used, particularly by the inexperienced and those easily aroused emotionally.

A national sample of American victims, surveyed by Skogan (1978), found that in reported noncommercial robberies only 8 per cent of victims resisted when a gun was involved, compared with 15 per cent when other weapons were involved. While he found very little relationship between robbery success rates and weapon type for personal robbery, there was a very strong one for commercial burglary, in which success rates were 94 per cent for gun use, 65 per cent for knives and 48 per cent for other weapons. The probability of gun use for commercial targets increased with the number of employees: 44 per cent for one employee, 68 per cent for two. Cook (1983) comments that these results could have two explanations: robbers attacking lucrative and hence well-defended targets carry guns to increase their chances of success; those who happen to have guns are more likely to go for lucrative and well-defended targets.

Cook (1983) points out that the decision to kill is easier and safer to implement with a gun than with other commonly available weapons. The availability of a gun may often be crucial in escalating into a homicide that might have remained a minor injury with no weapons available or a wounding if only a knife were to hand. In 1977, 68 per cent of male homicide victims were shot, versus 51 per cent of female victims, suggesting that many male victims could have been overcome only with the use of a gun. This is supported by the finding that, in 1977, whereas 97 per cent of women who killed their spouses did so with the use of a gun, this was the case for 78 per cent of men. Once again, the retaliatory power of the opponent and his expected readiness to use it is important.

Some gun-murderers are convicted of a murder which is their first and only violent act. What could have been a lesser violent offense was turned into murder, perhaps by the lethality of the weapon to hand. Clarke and Mayhew (1988) draw an interesting analogy between suicide levels as a function of easy access to a method of self-destruction at times of great distress and gun availability at critical moments in interpersonal disputes. They note that between 1963 and 1975 the mean number of suicides in England and Wales declined, unexpectedly, by over one third, at a time when suicides continued to increase in most other European countries. They attribute this to the progressive removal of carbon monoxide (CO) from the public gas supply. In 1963, suicide by CO accounted for more than 40 per cent of all suicides. By 1975, it had been all but eliminated. Few of those denied access to gas appeared to have attempted suicide by other means. Clarke and Mayhew (1988) conclude that blocking a standard opportunity, even for a strongly motivated act such as suicide, need not inevitably mean displacement to other means of achieving the same end. The implication is that a good deal of homicide is due to the availability of a gun to a potential assailant at the time of a major interpersonal dispute or in the course of a robbery; had a gun not been available, either a lesser injury or no injury would have resulted.

Alcohol. It is often assumed that alcohol enhances aggressive behavior and hence is positively associated with violent offenses. This is supported by self-reports by alcoholics, by clinical observations (both reviewed by Mello, 1972) and by data drawn from the official statistics of crime. Wolfgang (1958) found that alcohol had been used by the assailant, the victim, or both, in two-thirds of 588 Philadelphia homicides. And US Bureau of Justice Statistics for 1983 (cited by Wilson and Herrnstein, 1985) indicate that, nationally, prison inmates were three times as likely as males of the same age not in prison to say that they drank two or more ounces of alcohol a day. But both results may be explained, at least in part, by the probability that alcohol may increase the chances of being caught; self-report studies of random population samples are preferable.

Moreover, laboratory studies suggest complex relationships between alcohol levels, expectations concerning the likely effects of alcohol on one's behavior and personality variables. Taylor and Gammon (1975) found that whereas a high does of alcohol increased aggression, a low one reduced it. No group was included which received a drink they believed to be alcohol. Such a placebo group was included in a study by Lang, Goechner, Adesso, and Marlatt (1975). They reported that male social drinkers, led to believe they had drunk alcohol, were significantly more aggressive than those who thought they had consumed a nonalcoholic drink, regardless of the actual alcohol content of the beverage administered. The authors concluded that it is the *expectation* of alcohol which facilitates aggressive behavior, and that this is particularly true for persons who find it difficult to overcome inhibitions against an increase in anger arousal, resulting in an increase in overt aggression. However, it may be that in real-life situations a high level of alcohol will increase aggressive responding irrespective of what the individual has been led to believe. Moreover, the outcomes of previous responses to the particular instigating stimulus concerned will be of great relevance. Alcohol may potentiate an *existing* aggressive response; it may be less likely to lead to the performance of such a response unless it is already in the repertoire of the person concerned. This is supported by Boyatzis (1974), who found that men who were aggressive at "parties," following the consumption of alcohol, were more likely to have had a history of getting into fights than men who were not.

The last finding suggests the importance of personality variables, a possibility supported by Renson, Adams, and Tinklenberg (1978), who found that heavy drinkers who are hostile, unstable, or "rebellious" were those most likely to engage in violent behavior. O'Leary, Donovan, Freeman, and Chaney (1976) reported that "aggressive drinkers" were more likely than others to have an external locus of control. Such drinkers attribute responsibility for things going wrong to others, including traffic accidents and episodes of violence. Donovan and Marlatt (1982) found that those who had the most drunk-driving accidents (three times higher than the lowest of five groups into which the total sample was divided) were rated highest on hostility, irritability, resentment, and sensation-seeking; the latter group were highest on depression and moodiness.

Maintenance

In general, the long-term course of aggressive acts is strongly governed by the exact outcomes of such acts, both positive and negative. These may be more age-linked than are crimes against property, the relevant skills and attributes for which may decline more slowly than is the case with person offenses, in which physical strength and speed play a major role. As thieves get older they can change their specialty to financial offenses or to receiving stolen goods, both essentially sedentary occupations; there is no similarly less physically demanding alternative for person offenses.

That murder may be repeated many times in the absence of detection and punishment is attested to both by the relatively rare cases of multiple murders by lone individuals and the much more frequent instances of mass murder in the name of political ideologies, for example during World War 2 (Hausner 1967).

External reinforcement. Aggressive actions are often followed by outcomes satisfying to the aggressor. These may be material (money, goods, etc.) or, if not directly material, are nevertheless tangible, such as social status or social approval. An advance in status is a more powerful reward than social approval, both in actuality and in anticipation (Martin et al. 1968), because both the gain in status and the prospect of its loss, have the more far reaching effects, particularly when there are many competitors. Social approval, though less effective than a gain in status, is nevertheless effective in maintaining aggression, whether received directly, or by aggressive models, and in field as well as in laboratory settings (Bandura 1973). In certain settings, such as Germany between 1933 and 1945, aggression toward special groups received unusually sizeable official rewards, particularly of social status and social approval, vastly increasing the number of those carrying out assaults and murders (Hausner 1967).

The level of modeled aggression is directly proportional to the ratio of rewards to punishments received by the model (Rosenkrans and Hartup 1967). The same is true of direct aggression by the aggressor himself. Aggressive behavior, like most behavior, is relatively easy to extinguish when there is a sudden and prolonged shift from a high level of positive reinforcement to a zero level. But, it is likely that most person offenders experience instead long-term intermittent schedules, so that desistance is a long time coming. Moreover, aggressive responses maintained by intermittent schedules generalize well to new situations. This suggests that assaulters may rather easily shift to robbery and vice versa.

Because the expression of injury by a victim may inhibit continued physical attack, verbal aggression may be substituted, provided that it achieves the same ends. Displays of suffering by the victim may have either reinforcing or inhibiting effects, depending on their level and the extent to which they serve as evidence of successful aggression. The further removed is the victim from the aggressor, the more his distress can be discounted and the less its inhibiting effect (Milgram 1974). But, overt evidence of victim distress will be well tolerated, both by experienced aggressors and by those anticipating particularly substantial rewards. In general, the greater the costs of aggression (both victim distress and retaliatory punishment) the greater must be the rewards in order to more than counterbalance the costs. Overt victim distress reduces aggression when the level of aggression displayed is relatively low (as in laboratory settings) but is likely to do so much less when aggression is high (as in person offenses). Moreover, the more physiologically aroused the aggressor, the less able will he be to discriminate victim pain from victim anger. Typically, the effect of the latter would be to enhance aggression, unless it signalled an impending and effective retaliation – when the aggressor might resort to flight.

Self-reinforcement and cognitive distortions. As well as being socially or materially positively reinforced for violence, people also reinforce themselves for accomplishing a self-appointed aggressive task, and do so across a considerable period of time and for many successive acts of violence. It is likely that some people acquire during adolescence self-reinforcement systems in which frequent aggressive behavior is a source of great self-esteem (Bandura and Walters 1959). Hausner (1967) gives a graphic description of Eichmann (one of the main agents of the Nazi "Final Solution" for European Jewry) as exemplifying a self-reward system in which the destruction of this particular out-group was a great source of pride.

Self-arousal helps to maintain anger and, in turn, aggressive behavior, and self-arousal is itself maintained by thoughts of the intended target (Bandura 1973). Thus there is both an anticipation of a future act of violence and an internal review of a completed one. Initially, it will be helpful for persons whose violent acts are discrepant with previously held attitudes unfavorable to violence to use mechanisms of cognitive distortion. For example, aggressors may deny the severity of a victim's pain (disregard/distortion of consequences), persuade themselves that he is unworthy of pity (dehumanization) or assign to him/her the responsibility for the violent incident ("she was asking for it", "he should have let me have what I wanted;" both are examples of the misattribution of blame).

Eventually, the need for cognitive distortions after the event will be avoided by the habitual anticipatory justification of an intended aggressive act, often by stereotyping the intended victim as a member of a group toward whom aggression is normal, even desirable. The process is assisted by replacing an evocatively unpleasant term such as "murder" by the euphemism "termination," thereby providing a continuing cognitive framework for violent behavior.

A specific person offense: a social learning theory view of rape

Acquisition. Sanday (1981) reviewed information on 156 societies studied by anthropologists and divided them into rape-free societies, rape-prone societies, and the rest, concerning which there was insufficent information. He classified 47 per cent as rape-free and 18 per cent as rape-prone. In the former, there was a high degree of sexual equality, a high value placed on females and on "feminine" qualities and relatively low levels of interpersonal violence. In contrast, the latter were marked by high degrees of male–female antagonism, male dominance over women (for example, the control of their property) and high levels of interpersonal violence in general. Without assigning Western society in general to the rape-prone category, it seems reasonable to suppose that some Western social settings, at least, model and reinforce the latter set of attitudes toward women, so that those who grow up in them are more likely than other males to acquire attitudes and behaviors favorable to rape.

Allied to this is a very strong assertion by the feminist movement that rape is essentially not sexual, but is, in fact, aggression directed against women, a view supported by the widespread use of violence over and above what is "necessary" to coerce the rape victim – for example, many serious injuries are inflicted after the sexual act has been completed (Groth 1979). Two types of aggressive rape have been described: the instrumental (carried out to obtain some kind of environmental reinforcer, such as the recognition of the rapist's masculinity and power) and the angry (in which the rape is triggered by an unpleasant event leading to anger, the reinforcement obtained by the assailant being the pain suffered by the victim). Frequent prior aversive events include arguments, domestic problems, jealousy and rejection. The source of the aversive event may be the victim herself or someone else entirely. Groth (1979) estimated that 40 per cent of his sample of 500 rapists were of the anger type.

Background attitudes held by many males are also important. In a study by Burt (1980), participants were asked to judge a number of aspects of rape and their resultant attitudes were then correlated with various features of the participants. The results showed a statement such as "the woman was getting back at the man" (by claiming she had been raped) to be part of a general set of "rape-supportive" attitudes which involve sexual relationships being seen in adversarial terms, and violence in the context of sexual intercourse perceived as normal. Indeed, many rapists, at least of those who are apprehended and convicted, have a marked history of violence in general: over 50 per cent of a large sample of rapists reported by Christie, Marshall, and Lanthier (1979) had previous convictions for nonsexual assault, most of them serious enough to have attracted prison sentences. And another 30 per cent had been convicted for nonviolent offenses. This fits in with the conclusion drawn by Gebhard, Gagnon, Pomeroy, and Christenson (1965, p. 205):

> "The majority of sexual aggressors against (female) adults may be succinctly described as criminally inclined men who take what they want, whether money, material or women, and their sex offenses are by-products of this general criminality."

Are convicted rapists extreme in holding violent attitudes toward women? A number of studies indicate this to be the case, and show also that men who hold extreme sex stereotypes are more arousable by aggressive pornography than are nonrapist controls (e.g., Check and Malamuth 1983). Bandura (1986) concludes that considerable exposure to violent erotica increases both the general acceptability of violence toward women and of the specific rape myth that women desire sexual assault. Moreover, males exposed to modeled sexual assault behave more aggressively toward women than if exposed to modeled non-aggressive sexual intimacy. Thus, a generally violent social training is directed also toward sexual behavior.

For many persons, particularly those who are socially unskilled with females (true of a large proportion of convicted rapists, Christie et al. 1979) exposure to pornography lays the ground for fantasies which can be cognitively rehearsed with great frequency, and hence achieve considerable control over overt behavior. The wide availability of video players and of tapes of pornographic movies, including depictions of the most violent forms of rape, provides repeated opportunities for private viewing and rehearsal, often accompanied by self-masturbation, as well as a constant flow of new material. This repeated sequence of events powerfully associates sexual arousal and relief with fantasies of sexual violence.

The phase of acquisition then, emphasizes together with the importance of exposure to social models in certain social settings (young men who have already raped), the opportunity to learn markedly anti-female stereotypes, an exposure to erotic pornography which depicts rape scenes, a low level of heterosexual social skills, and a prior history of interpersonal violence. The more of these predisposing factors are present, together with a belief in the low probability of detection (objectively correct), the more it is likely that an opportunity for rape will be responded to, probably during adolescence (Groth, Longo, and McFadin 1982).

Performance. Once the first rape has been performed successfully and is therefore in the repertoire of the young man concerned, the act is likely to be repeated. The situational factors which increase the probability of performing a rape are those for violent acts in general, together with a sexual component in the case of some rapists. Briefly, these are as follows.

1. Opportunity (access to an available victim).
2. Incentive (there are likely to be sexual, as well as status/power, self-evaluative, and sometimes social, incentives).
3. Target (the less well-defended the more likely is a rape and,

typically, women are easier targets for rape then are men as targets for assault because, on average, they have a lower capacity for fighting back).

4. The perceived risk (this is probably low; it is likely that many rapists are well aware that a large majority of rape victims do not report their experience to the police, see Chapter 2).

5. The possibility of legal access to the desired goal. In principle, this is easy in the permissive West if the goal is largely sexual, but in practice many rapists lack even rudimentary social skills, and there is no legal means of expressing anger by causing physical injury to females.

6. The presence of a model or models (of obvious importance for group rape).

7. Emotional arousal, particularly anger. A number of prior events are potential sources of anger arousal directed against females, including aversive physical and verbal experiences, the withdrawal of valued reinforcers, frustration and punishment.

Specific environmental stimuli will also become triggers for rape by a particular individual, due to their association, through classical conditioning, with previous acts of rape, for example a particular type of victim and setting (e.g., a student living alone, with the act occurring after dark).

Maintenance. The long term maintenance of rape behavior is assisted by self-reinforcement (the satisfaction of either aggressive or sexual motivations or both), by the repeated cognitive rehearsal of the entire sequence of events, including the victim's distress, accompanied by masturbation (particularly important for the more solitary individual) and by the very low probability of detection and punishment (Groth et al. 1982). It follows that a well-established rapist ceases his activities only when he is detected and punished on several successive occasions (almost certainly true of only a small minority of rapists) or when advancing years markedly reduce his ability to coerce physically an intended victim. It follows that rape careers seem likely to be lengthy.

Finally, it should be noted that the above theory inevitably draws heavily on convicted rapists. While we now have careful studies of self-reported rape victims, comparable research on self-reported, but undetected, rapists is largely lacking.

9.5. Rational choice theory

Introduction

Cook (1980) focuses on the potential offender as someone who operates *rationally*. He asserts that potential criminals weigh the possible consequences of their actions, both positive and negative, and take advantage of a criminal opportunity only if it is in their interest to do so. In setting out this assertion, Cook looks back to Jeremy Bentham (1748–1832) and to one of his basic propositions: "The profit of the crime is the force which urges a man to delinquency. The pain of the punishment is the force employed to restrain him from it. If the first of these forces is the greater, the crime will be committed; if the second, the crime will not be committed" (quoted by Zimring and Hawkins, 1973, p. 75). Cook accepts that people will respond differently to equivalent criminal opportunities because they differ: in their willingness to take risks; in their "preference for honesty;" in their evaluation of "profit" from a crime – most of all in crimes in which the pay-off is something other than money (rape, vandalism, etc.); and in their objective circumstances (income, the value they place on their time, their skills in successfully committing crimes and in evading capture, their reputations in the community). Both profit and pain are evaluated differently by different persons, but it is true for people in general that changes in either the probability or in the average severity of pain will cause some people to change their minds and, hence, their behavior. Small changes in either probability or severity will affect only those close to the "point of indifference."

The theory in outline

This rapidly developing approach has been elaborated by Clarke and Cornish into the *rational choice theory* of crime (RCT), which makes several assumptions, set out by Cornish and Clarke (1987):

1. Offenders seek to benefit themselves by criminal behaviors.
2. Doing so involves making decisions and choices, however rudimentary these might be.
3. The decision-making process is constrained by the time available (many criminal) opportunities have a limited life-span), by the availability of relevant information (frequently this will be incomplete) and

by the offender's own cognitive abilities (related, presumably, to verbal IQ). It follows that rationality will be limited, rather than complete.

4. Both the decision-making process and the factors taken into account by offenders vary greatly at different stages of decision-making and between different crimes (and presumably also between different offenders within crimes; there are marked differences in success-rates, as noted in Chapter 2, with planning ahead being a key feature of the more successful offenders).

Cornish and Clarke (1987) argue the need to be (a) crime-specific when analyzing criminal choices and (b) to treat decisions as relating to varying stages of the involvement of an offender in a particular crime. Thus, they distinguish between initial involvement, the event, continuation, and desistance (the first three are fairly similar to this author's terms, acquisition, performance, and maintenance). The general sequence of involvement should be analyzed separately from factors such as target selection which are related to the crime itself. (Essentially, this group of factors all concern the performance phase of involvement.)

The rational choice perspective asserts that specific crimes are chosen by offenders and are committed for specific reasons. We need to understand the factors which are taken into account by offenders when they perform a rudimentary cost–benefit analysis of a range of factors, including the incentive, or anticipated pay-off, the risk involved, and the skills needed, all in relation to their goals, motives, experience, abilities, expertise, and preferences. All of these variations combine to make criminal opportunities differentially attractive to particular individuals and groups. They are termed by Cornish and Clarke (1987) their *choice structuring properties*.

The following is a list of choice structuring properties for crimes involving cash (i.e., money rather than goods, from bank robbery to computer fraud, Cornish and Clarke 1987).

1. Availability (number of targets, accessibility).
2. Awareness of method (i.e., technical know-how).
3. Likely cash yield per crime.
4. Expertise needed.
5. Planning necessary.
6. Resources required.
7. Solo versus assistance required.
8. Time required to commit.
9. Cool nerves required.

10. Risk of apprehension.
11. Severity of punishment (if caught).
12. Instrumental violence required.
13. Confrontation with victim.
14. Identifiable victim.
15. Social cachet [in the criminal world] (safebreaking versus mugging).
16. Fencing accessories (getting rid of any goods stolen, together with the main target, money).
17. Moral evaluation.

The above were derived by Cornish and Clarke (1987) on an *a priori* basis. Detailed research might result in their modification, and they are certainly not all taken into account by every offender.

Clarke and Cornish (1985) base RCT very explicitly on economic models of criminal decision making [which] "effectively demystify and routinize criminal activity. Crime is assumed . . . to involve rational calculation and . . . as an economic transaction or as a question of occupational choice" (Clarke and Cornish 1985, p. 156). Economic models of crime are not confined to those motivated by financial gain, but are extended also to crimes of violence.

Another source of RCT is to be found in information-processing models and strategies in relation to real-life decision-making (Kahneman, Slovic, and Twersky 1982), which are then applied to criminal decision-making (e.g., Carroll 1982).

Research findings

The most important evidence concerning the rational choice theory of crime comes from recent research into specific offenses carried out by professional property offenders, and is exemplified below. But, the scene was set by several earlier researchers, who presented respondents with hypothetical criminal situations to ascertain both the extent to which they could combine information concerning rewards and costs, and which are the more important of such variables. In a series of studies, Rettig and colleagues (e.g., Rettig 1966, Rettig and Turroff 1967) gave students a hypothetical criminal opportunity in which several potential determinants of a decision to steal were systematically and simultaneously varied. The greatest effect was exerted by the amount of punishment involved – this exceeded both the probability of detection and the incentive present.

Feldman (unpublished data, described in detail in Feldman, 1977) adapted Rettig's approach to younger and academically much less able populations of adolescent institutional offenders and to school pupils matched for age and intelligence. The detailed results make clear the importance of the exact combination of rewards and costs to a decision whether or not to offend – in this case breaking in to a house. Throughout, the level of cost involved exerted a more powerful effect when rewards were high than when they were low. For both groups of respondents the order of importance of rewards and costs was the same: within rewards, the level of monetary incentive was followed by the degree of boredom experienced by the potential offender and then the certainty of the house containing money; the most important cost (deterrent) was the presence of a policeman on a nearby beat, followed by the level of punishment if caught, the certainty of detection and the difficulty of breaking into the house. The vast majority of "yes" answers from both groups were "rational" – boys rarely answered yes to a low temptation pairing (low reward, high cost) unless they also did so to the medium and high temptation versions of the same pair of determinants. The fact that this degree of rationality was displayed by boys most of whom were below the average level of intelligence supports the rational choice theory of crime. However, only two variables were presented at a time, one a temptation and one a deterrent, making the task cognitively more simple, but also much less like the real world in which several veriables have to be considered simultaneously, often under time pressure. Two other early simulation studies (Piliavin, Hardyck, and Vadum 1969, Piliavin, Vadum, and Hardyck 1969) also gave some support to the rational choice approach to crime.

More recent studies of subjectively perceived costs and benefits (e.g., Bridges and Stone 1986) have shown the importance of prior experience of punishment and the nature of that experience for the perceived risks of being caught for a subsequent offense. Such results indicate the importance for decision making of the individual's previous criminal history (rewards as well as costs) in addition to the current situational factors – exactly as would be expected by a broadly behavioral view of criminal behavior. The more information available on both, the more accurately can one predict an individual's response to a particular criminal opportunity (Cimler and Beach 1981).

A specific property offense: burglary

Clarke and Cornish (1985) have provided a detailed illustration of RCT, applied to residential burglary, specifically in a middle-class suburb. They point out that the offenders involved are generally older and more experienced than those operating in housing projects, but less sophisticated than those specializing in much wealthier residences.

Initial involvement: this is shown in Fig. 9.1. Boxes 1–3 refer, very briefly, to background, cognitive, and learning factors (covered in detail in Chapters 5–8 and the first two sections of this chapter). Next, the budding burglar (who has probably already carried out more minor offenses) passes through a series of decision points, of which two, boxes 7 and 8, are considered by Clarke and Cornish to be of particular importance. ". . . box 7 is the individual's recognition of his 'readiness' to commit this particular offense to satisfy certain of his needs for money, goods or excitement . . . [he] has decided that under the right circumstances he would commit this offense" (Clarke and Cornish 1985, p. 167).

"The second decision (box 8) . . . is precipitated by some chance event . . . the . . . need for money . . . drinking with associates who suggest committing a burglary . . . he may perceive an easy opportunity . . . during the course of his routine activities" (Clarke and Cornish 1985, p. 167).

Next comes a consideration of the variables associated with the criminal *event*. These are set out in Fig. 9.2, and concern successive yes/no decisions (this area and that house within the area). Both decisions emphasize the relatively greater ease of access and escape and the greater affluence of the final choice. Clarke and Cornish point out that this is an idealized model and that full rationality may often not be attainable: ". . . the decision process may be telescoped, planning may be rudimentary, and there be may last minute (and perhaps ill-judged) changes of mind . . . alcohol may cloud judgement" (Clarke and Cornish 1985, p. 170).

In many cases, burglars commit hundreds of offenses over a period of years. This process of *continuance* is shown in Fig. 9.3, which focuses on a number of important consequences of a long-term criminal career. Such consequences will include criminal convictions as well as "skin of the teeth" escapes from capture. Convictions only accelerate the move away from the straight world, ". . . as opportunities to obtain legitimate

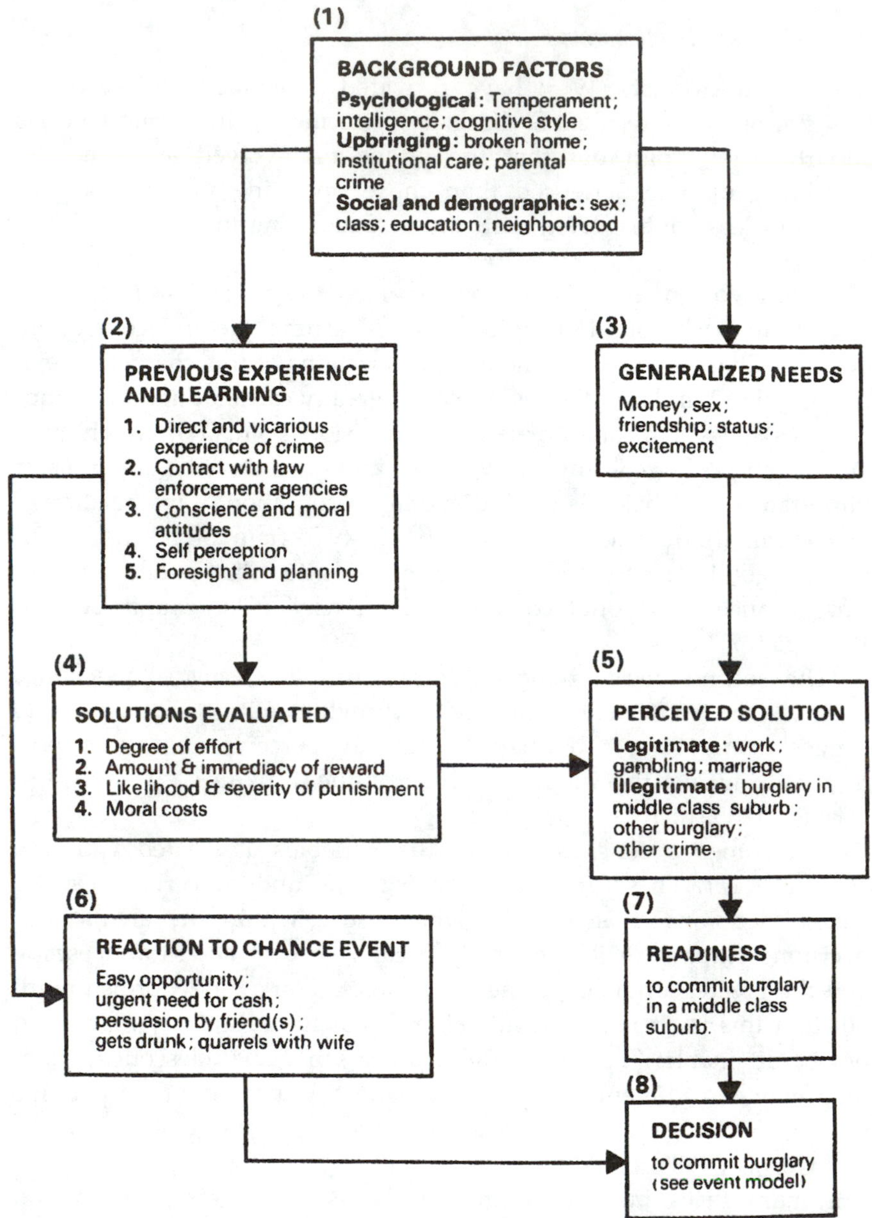

Figure 9.1. Initial involvement model: burglary in a middle class suburb (from Clarke, R.V., and Cornish, D.B., 1985, Modelling offender's decisions: a framework for research and policy, in M. Tonry, and N. Morris (Eds.), *Crime and Justice: An Annual Review of Research*, Vol. 7, p. 168. Chicago: University of Chicago Press).

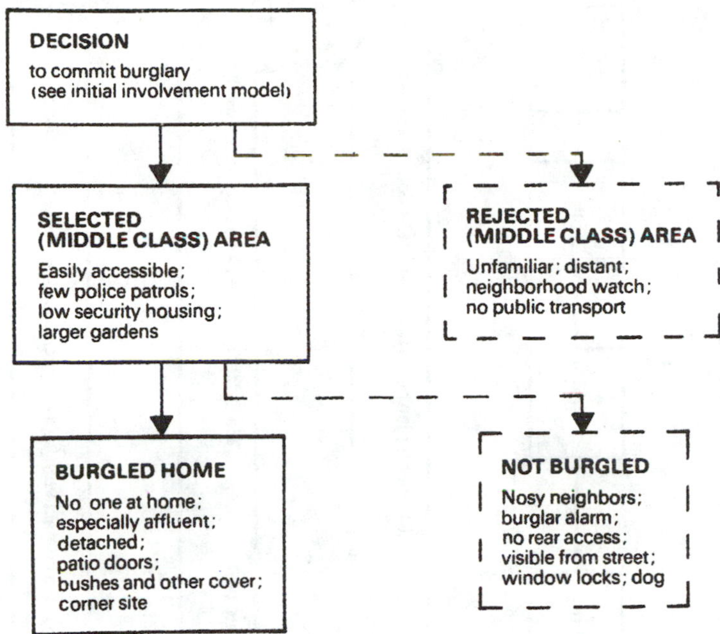

Figure 9.2. Event model: burglary in a middle class suburb (from Clarke, R.V., and Cornish, D.B., 1985, Modelling offender's decisions: a framework for research and policy, in M. Tonry, and N. Morris (Eds.), *Crime and Justice: An Annual Review of Research*, Vol. 7, p. 169. Chicago: University of Chicago Press).

work decrease and as ties to family and relations are weakened" (Clarke and Cornish 1985, p. 172).

The final stage is that of *desistance* (Fig. 9.4). Clarke and Cornish point that there is less information about this stage than the others, but the sequence set out rings true (the move to less strenuous forms of crime, to noncrime, or to some mixture of the two, is likely to start before middle-age).

Clarke and Cornish have provided us with a well worked-out model of the rational decision approach to residential burglary. Their work is supplemented and illustrated by a report by Walsh (1980), based on interviews with 45 men in British prisons who had been convicted of burglary. Their ideal target was a business firm rather than a private house (more to be stolen) and, while half used information, the other half burgled on impulse (presumably, the latter were more likely to be caught and hence were more available for interview). There was much

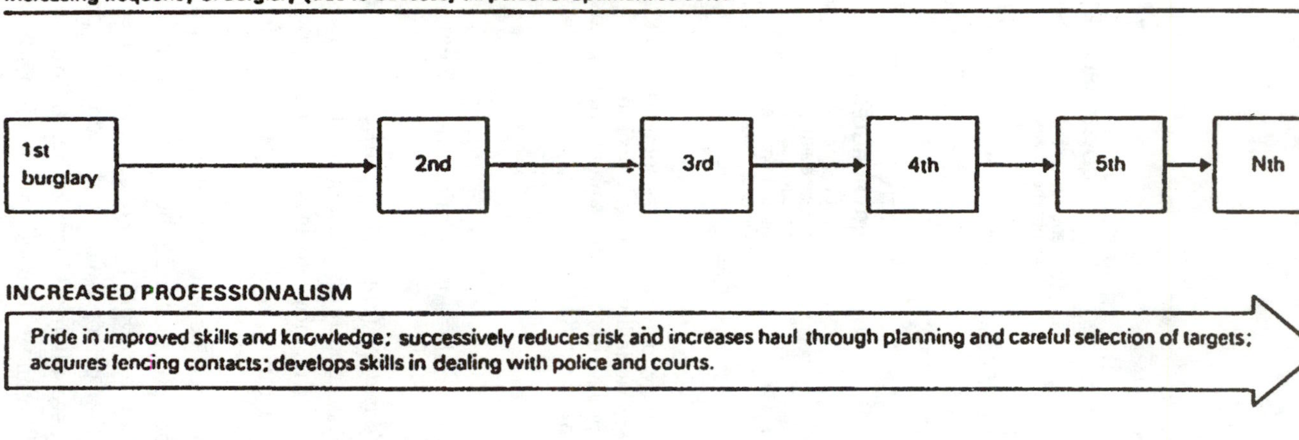

Figure 9.3. Continuing involvement model: burglary in a middle class suburb (from Clarke, R.V., and Cornish, D.B., 1985, Modelling offender's decisions: a framework for research and policy, in M. Tonry and N. Morris (Eds.), *Crime and Justice: An Annual Review of Research*, Vol. 7, p. 171. Chicago: University of Chicago Press).

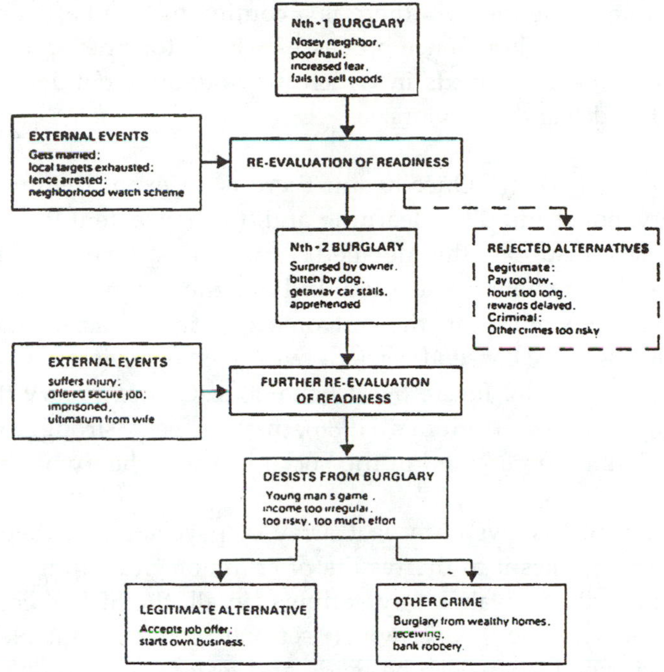

Figure 9.4. Desistance model: burglary in a middle class suburb (from Clarke, R.V., and Cornish, D.B., 1985, Modelling offender's decisions: a framework for research and policy, in M. Tonry and N. Morris (Eds.), *Crime and Justice: An Annual Review of Research*, Vol. 7, p. 172. Chicago: University of Chicago Press).

fear concerning being interrupted during a burglary, with the consequent possibility of violence and, hence, of a more severe sentence if arrested. They found it easier to justify to themselves a business than a household target (particularly if the latter were "ordinary"), adding to their preference for the former. They saw themselves as desisting with increasing age (the risks of capture increased, sentences stiffened and the risk/return balance generally less favorable).

9.6. Cognitive-behavioral approaches: appraisal

Social learning theory

Is it social? The detailed descriptions in the first three sections of this chapter make it abundantly clear that social factors play a major explanatory role in the theory – there is a continuing emphasis on social settings and on social influence processes which, together, provide the intimate, day-to-day contexts in which previous nonoffenders acquire criminal attitudes and behaviors.

Does it focus on learning? Once again, there is an explicit emphasis on both observational and direct learning and, to some extent, on classical conditioning to supply the detailed experiences whereby criminal attitudes and behaviors are learned and are then either strengthened or inhibited, depending on the outcome of criminal acts. Outcomes include the cognitive consequences of overt past behaviors, as well the cognitive precursors of future overt behaviors. Contemporary theories of learning, such as Bandura's (1986), have a very strong cognitive component, fully represented in the social learning theory of crime.

Is it a theory? SLT draws on a vast array of psychological theory and research, and applies it to the results of criminological studies both in field and in analogous laboratory settings. In all, the SLT of crime is a conventional scientific theory, which sets out general principles from which specific deductions can be made and tested.

Is it useful? This means, does it cover fully the sequence of events which comprise a complete criminal career, from initial attitude shift to final retirement?

1. Acquistion. There is a very explicit separation of the process of becoming an offender from that of the continued performance of criminal acts. The acquisition phase of SLT consists of a detailed account of how a previous nonoffender becomes an offender. The links between the biological, family and social precursors of criminal behavior and the social learning processes, set out in the first three sections of this chapter, need to be worked out more fully. (Briefly, given the same social learning experiences, some children are more likely to become offenders than others, the greater push for these is provided by some or all of biologically based personality factors, inadequate parental skills and resources and a continued exposure to high crime social settings.) These major precursors provide the basis on which detailed social learning experiences then translate a significant probability of becoming an offender into actual criminal attitudes and behaviors.

2. Performance. SLT is strong on general principles (opportunity, incentive, target, risks, skills and resources, and legal alternatives). It

also gives a very full account of the importance of criminogenic factors, and of the various sources of anger arousal, both highly relevant to the performance of person crimes, so that it provides, for example, a clearly articulated account of the performance of rape. Equally detailed applications to the performance of property crimes need to be worked out; the general principles supply the raw materials for doing so.

3. Maintenance. SLT draws on well established learning principles (e.g., external reinforcements and reinforcement schedules) to account for the long term continuance of a criminal career and on cognitive psychology for the cognitive consequences and distortions which further maintain criminal behaviors. But there is little or nothing on the social and professional consequences, set out very explicitly by RCT (see Fig. 9.3).

4. Desistance. SLT virtually fails to mention the last stage of a criminal career, that of retirement. Although it is possible to draw implications from the material set out under maintenance in the first three sections of this chapter, there is none of the explicit detail supplied by RCT (see Fig. 9.4).

In general, SLT needs to provide separate accounts of "desisters" and "persisters" (see Chapter 2) – those who cease offending relatively quickly as opposed to those who continue for many years. And there needs also to be a more explicit distinction between those who begin early (pre-teens) and those who begin later, sometimes much later.

Finally, it is valuable that SLT recognizes the part in maintaining offending played by the greater reaction of the criminal justice system to some persons more than others (the contribution of labeling theory). But this needs to be incorporated explicitly within SLT.

Rational choice theory

Is it rational? One of the principal objections which has been made to rational choice theory relates to its core: are there limits to rational calculation? Cook (1980) agrees that many offenders do not operate rationally, particularly if they are young and/or intoxicated (see above under criminogenics), are in a state of high emotional arousal, or are psychologically disturbed. These exceptions encompass a high proportion of the perpetrators of some types of crime, and Cook suggests that for such individuals and temporary states it is more accurate to speak of "limited" rather than "full" rationality.

Bandura (1986) agrees that a model of limited, rather than complete, rationality gives a better fit to the facts of criminal behavior, particularly for crimes of violence, and situations in which the cognitive control of behavior has been weakened by alcohol, a drug, or a temporary emotional state. "In general, people consider a few, rather than all, aspects of a crime-related situation and are more influenced by prospective pay-offs than by potential punishments if detected. Thus, criminal judgements are not all that different from the way people generally go about making decisions – they single out and overweigh a few factors and engage in only a partial examination of other options. They tend to reflect more on benefits than on punishments", Bandura (1986, p. 277). A second problem concerns the implication that in making their decisions potential offenders have full information about the probability of detection and the level of punishment if detected. Once again, it is the perceived risks and not the actual ones which are critical – subjective appraisal, not objective reality. Of course, some offenders are more professional than others. "Professionalism" means more and more accurate information; this applies both to Stock Exchange investors and to offenders.

There is also an overriding problem in all human decision making; most people seem to use a few habitual "rules of thumb" to achieve rapid and, hopefully, effective decision-making, rather than the detailed and systematic appraisal of all relevant information, implied by the term "rational." As Clarke and Cornish (1985, p. 160) point out (referring to the basic work of Kahneman et al. (1982), "some of these judgemental heuristics . . . can lead to error . . . too much attention may be paid to information that is readily available or recently presented . . . inductive rules may be formulated too quickly on the basis of unrepresentative data."

What is meant by choice? Cornish and Clarke (1986, p. 2) are very clear that "individuals choose to become initially involved in particular forms of crime, to continue, and to desist." Elsewhere they refer to "the reaction during the last decade [within academic psychology] against the environmental determinism of radical behaviorism and to an increasing recognition of the important role played by cognitive processes. This can be seen in the development of more sophisticated 'social learning theories' . . ." (Clarke and Cornish 1985, p. 158). The implication of the reference to individuals choosing to become involved, etc., is that they could *equally well* choose *not* to become involved. But this seems very unlikely. Without reverting to an extreme determinist position, it is reasonable to assume that a person who has a biologically based predisposition to personality features favorable to the acquistion of criminal behaviors, parents with an extreme lack of skills and resources for child training, and a prolonged exposure to a high crime social setting, is highly likely to become an offender.

Conversely, someone with the opposite biological predisposition, reared by parents with high skills and resources and who has grown up in a low crime area, is most unlikely to become an offender. To say that the first has chosen an offending career (and could equally well have chosen a different path) is to distort the meaning of the term "choice." As each precursor and each learning experience piles up successively, there is an increasing inevitability about the path to being a career offender. The fact that some high-risk youngsters do not become offenders (see Chapter 7) must also be accounted for. Both SLT and RCT need to address themselves to this issue; the answer is likely to be much more complex than that they simply "chose" not to.

If, on the other hand, the term "choice" in RCT refers to offenders selecting the most rational of the options relèvant to a criminal opportunity, then it is a useful remainder of the way many offenders proceed, much of the time.

Is it a theory? Clarke and Cornish (1985, p. 163) disclaim any such aspiration: "The models [involvement, event, etc., see above] are not theories in themselves but rather the blueprints for theory . . . Our models are concerned not just with the decision to commit a particular crime, but also with decisions relating to criminal 'readiness' or involvement in crime . . . They are schematic representations of the key decision points in criminal behavior and of the various social, psychological and environmental factors bearing on the decisions reached. . . . our aim is only to provide models that are at present 'good enough' to accommodate existing knowledge and to guide research and policy initiatives." But, although it is desirable to avoid a premature crystallization of theory it is equally important for an explanatory approach to seek generalizability, rather than being specific to each offense – even each sub-category of offense (e.g., burglary in a middle-class suburb).

Is it useful? How well do the phases cover the full sequence of events involved in becoming an remaining an offenders?

1. Initial involvement. First, there is almost nothing concerning psychological, familial and sociodemographic precursors (listed briefly

in box 1 of Fig. 9.1). They are said to be "less directly criminogenic [than the approach of 'traditional criminology'] . . . instead they have an orienting function – exposing people to particular problems and particular opportunities and leading them to perceive and evaluate them in particular (criminal) ways . . . the contribution of background factors to the final decision to commit a crime would be much moderated by situational and transitory influences" (Clarke and Cornish 1985, p. 167). While there is no inevitability about a certain combination of personality, child training and social precursors leading a person into criminal behavior, there is a sharply raised probability which the term "orienting function" hardly conveys. Moreover, they go on to say that for "certain sorts of crime (e.g., computer fraud) . . . background might be of much less relevance than his immediate situation" (Clarke and Cornish 1985, p. 167). This is very likely for social and familial factors (if only because children from poorly resourced inner-city families are unlikely to find themselves in highly skilled and responsible jobs with access to computer networks). But those who are in such jobs and who take the opportunity for fraud may well have a particular combination of personality features (for example, high E and high P in the Eysenckian system, see Chapter 6) as well as exposure to social models of illegal behavior within their job setting, which combine to shift their attitudes in favor of fraud, followed by an opportunity to carry out the act in a context in which detection and puishment seem unlikely.

Moreover, RCT has little to say about the acquisition of criminal attitudes and behaviors, set out in detail by SLT in this Chapter, beyond the briefest possible listing (box 2, of Fig. 9.1). While Clarke and Cornish explicitly acknowledge the importance of accounting for the initial involvement in criminal behavior, as well as of continued involvement, they provide no detail concerning the former. While it is a good idea to focus on specific choice points (boxes 7 and 8 of Fig. 9.1), one must also look at the rest of the very considerable iceberg, and not be mesmerized by its tip. People do not just "choose" to commit their first major offense such as burglary: a set of precursors and a lengthy learning history both underlie the decision. Finally, the consequences of that first burglary need to be spelled out: a highly rewarding experience is much more likely to be repeated than one which ends in total failure.

2. The event model. Having got their burglar to his first offense, Clarke and Cornish are good on the detailed situational features which

lead to the choice of a specific target house for a burglary attempt. However, they should discuss also the importance of appropriate skills and resources relevant to the potential target (one burglar may possess the skills needed to neutralize a sophisticated alarm system guarding an especially affluent house, another may not; and much more is needed on criminogenic factors than "alcohol may cloud the judgement" (Clarke and Cornish 1985, p. 170).

While the notion of choice structuring properties for a broad class of offenses such as those involving cash is useful, some categorization also seems indicated, to allow for generalizability, for example, the SLT listing of incentive, target, risks, and skills and resources.

3. The continuing involvement model. This is very good on the increased professionalism, and on the changes in life styles and values and in peer groups which serve to strengthen involvement with criminal values and behaviors, all of which are largely absent from SLT, as noted above. But, there is nothing on the roles of financial returns and of costs such as detection and punishment, or on the reinforcement schedule on which these outcomes are received – once again, the long term learning history of an offender should not be ignored. Nor is there any mention of cognitive reinforcements and distortions, a particularly odd omission from an approach which stresses the importance of cognitive factors.

4. The desistance model. Despite their modest disclaimer on the paucity of information concerning this final phase of RCT (Clarke and Cornish 1985, p. 172), it is reasonably detailed and is very persuasive. (The entire phase is almost entirely omitted from SLT – a major weakness as noted above.) As always, it would be desirable to extract some general principles, allowing generalizability, from the detail of the desistance model (for example, the more the successful performance of a specialist crime is dependent on physical attributes the sooner will desistance from it occur, followed by either total retirement from crime or displacement to a more sedentary offense.

An overview of SLT and RCT

Both theories draw on contemporary experimental psychology, though with somewhat different emphases. Both agree on the need to separate the process of becoming an offender from the performance of subsequent offenses and continuing over a long period or of desisting. SLT is much stronger on the first of these, RCT on the last, and both have strengths and weaknesses in the two middle phases. A combination of strengths is indicated.

SLT sets up a general framework for criminal behavior, works it out in some detail as it applies to the major categories of crime, and then seeks to apply it to specific offenses. RCT avoids a general framework, other than a temporal sequence of models, and goes very quickly to sub-types of specific offenses. Again, it would be desirable to combine these strengths – both to improve general and specific explanations of crime and to account for the different career tracks of "innocents," "desisters," and "persisters."

The inclusion in SLT of criminogenic factors, of personality variables, and of the influence of the level of arousal suggests that SLT will be much stronger than RCT on person offenses. Conversely, the greater possibility of a potential offender planning for a known reward for property offenses suggests that RCT might be stronger for these, at least for the event (performance) stage. Once again, future theoretical developments aimed at merging the approaches should capitalize on these differing emphases.

In short, it is definitely not a question of having to choose between these two examples of the cognitive–behavioral approach to the explanation of crime: rather it is one of combining their strengths and discarding their weaknesses.

Research issues. Cornish and Clarke (1986) and Clarke and Cornish (1985) provide useful discussions of appropriate research methods to facilitate further advances. Research methods to date have involved mainly retrospective interviews, which are open to considerable distortions. Moreover, they have concentrated on convicted and incarcerated offenders. As far as possible, there should be a shift to other methods, including observation (participant if this is practicable), and experimental studies of criminal decision-making and "process-tracing," either on the site of the actual criminal event or by using video films to trigger recall. To increase representativeness, there should be increased attempts to include non- or rarely-convicted offenders in research programs.

Perhaps most important of all, we need a longitudinal study of an unselected population (cf, the Cambridge Study, but preferably including both middle-class males, and females of all classes) which would track through time the sequence of attitude and behavior changes as people enter a criminal career and either continue on it or desist, as a function of familial and social influences, specific criminal opportunities, personal decisions and the positive and negative social, material and legal consequences of those decisions. Such a study should give due weight to relatively consistent individual differences in personality, to criminogentic factors and to short and long term levels of arousal.

9.6. Concluding comment

It is clearly possible to apply cognitive–behavioral approaches not only to Index and other specific property and person offenses but also to other broad categories of crime, as follows:

1. Occupational offenses. Typically, there will be a combination of visible models of offending (what to do and how to do it), high financial incentives (and long term social incentives, consequent on financial advancement), low risks, easy targets, considerable skills and constant opportunities. We can expect fairly high levels of occurrence, and probably a long run of success before detection and punishment (which in many cases will never happen). All of this will be particularly true of financial frauds and related offenses.

2. Organized crime. The main business of criminal organizations is to supply services/goods which are illegal but which users demand. Hence there are many *willing* "targets," implying a steady market, low risks, and high and reliable returns, and the development of relevant skills and resources – the objectives of all businesses.

3. Political crimes. For crimes by elected or appointed officials we have again a combination of visible models, opportunities for the acquisition of criminal behaviors, and early success, due to easy targets, low risks, good access and relevant skills. Hence, we can expect a widespread occurrence of political offenses except where there is a very strong culture of crime-avoidance among officials and/or very strong and rigorously enforced controls against their occurrence.

For crimes by a state against its own citizens, or against other states, the former are very likely if there are no strong democratic controls, together with well-established traditions of the rule of law and freedom of the press. The latter become probable when a potential aggressor state is strong and prepared to use its strength, the threatened state is weak and potentially protective states do not respond to early warning signs of an impending attack. The obvious current example of the latter is the take-over of Kuwait by Iraq in August, 1990.

PART III

Control

10. The penal system

> In all his years in camps and prisons Ivan Denisovich had lost the habit of concerning himself about the next day, or the next year, or about feeding his family. The authorities did all his thinking for him.
>
> Alexander Solzhenitsyn,
> *One Day in the Life of Ivan Denisovich*, p. 40 (1970)

The third part of this book takes up the story of the criminal justice system where it was left at the end of the first part, by turning to the consequences of court decisions, both for the offender and for society. This chapter reviews punishments, handed down and regulated by the courts. All involve some element of deprivation, whether of life, liberty, or possessions, although sometimes there is an additional intention to rehabilitate the offender. Responses to offenders which wholly, or largely, involve some form of therapy or training (most often for juveniles but sometimes for adults) are discussed in the next chapter.

The topics covered in this chapter are: the main methods of punishment, their history and efficacy, both corrective and deterrent, and some current alternatives; special issues concerning the punishment system (the death penalty, incapacitation and prison populations); the social and psychological effects of prison life; and the reliability and validity of prediction techniques applied to future offenders and to dangerousness.

10.1. Methods of punishment

Most current methods have a long history; even reparation, one of the fastest growing alternatives, can be traced back to the Babylonian Code of Hammurabi, set out in 2270 BC (Binder 1987). The review of penal methods which follows is based largely on Caldwell (1965).

Capital punishment

In the past, the penalty of death on a person convicted of a crime (not always what would now be considered serious) has included hanging, boiling in oil, crucifixion, beheading, smothering, and many other ways of forcibly ending life. Today, only electrocution, asphyxiation (by gas), hanging, shooting and beheading are in use, the first two in the USA.

Intended as a relatively painless alternative to hanging, electrocution was first used at Auburn State Prison in NY State in 1890. Asphyxiation, which involves exposure to a poison gas in an airtight chamber, and may be the quickest method of death, has been in use in the USA for the past few decades. In other parts of the world, hanging, which requires great skill on the part of the hangman, is the most widely used method.

Capital punishment has now been abolished in almost all Western countries. Its use in the USA, on the decline for several decades, has revived since the mid-1970's. Because of the considerable controversy about capital punishment in the USA, specifically American material will be discussed later in this chapter.

Corporal punishment

In medieval and early modern times the most frequently used punishment for noncapital crimes involved some form of physical pain. The methods used have included flogging, branding, mutilation, and confinement in the stocks (a timber frame with holes for the feet). Flogging is the only one to have survived in the West, usually being administered by whips or rods. Its use is now in steep decline.

Transportation

Removing a criminal from his home, to a place so far away as to make return almost impossible, was a favorite method of punishment of Russian rulers from the tsars to President Brezhnev. Among Western countries it was used mainly by Britain which, in the late 18th century, transported criminals as slaves to the American colonies. With American Independence this was no longer possible. An even more remote alternative was provided by Australia, then termed New Holland, a newly acquired part of the British Empire. The story is told graphically by Hughes (1987).

From 1788, and for the next 80 years, 121,000 convicts were transported from Britain to several of the developing settlements of Australia. Eight out of ten were thieves. The purpose was to rid Britain of it's criminal class. By that time England had developed a legal code which conferred strong rights on its citizens (for example, the presumption of innocence until proven guilty beyond reasonable doubt) and convictions were difficult to obtain. It followed that those who were convicted received severe sentences, including capital punishment for trivial offences. But to keep down the number of executions many sentences were commuted to long terms of imprisonment, so that the prisons were full to overflowing. Hence, transportation was favored, which also served to supply manpower to a remote corner of the Empire. The aims of the policy included rehabilitation and, despite great cruelties, large numbers of those transported eventually worked themselves into secure jobs and properties and became the ancestors of many modern Australians.

Imprisonment

Deprivation of liberty by incarceration in a prison was not used to any great extent in Britain before the middle of the 16th century and in Central Europe not before the early 17th century, except for political offenders and those awaiting execution. By the early 19th century prison had largely displaced capital and corporal punishment for serious crimes.

The first "house of correction" was St. Bridget's Well in London, set up in 1552 for offenders to work under strict discipline. Other jails followed but, despite the transportation of large numbers, they rapidly became rife with disease. Their inmates were regarded as the property of the warders, and were notoriously exploited. The resulting agitation for reform led to developments such as solitary confinement (to enable the criminal to reflect on his errors without distraction), supervised work (in practice sometimes the treadmill) and large purpose-built prisons, some still in use.

American prisons were at first similar to those in Britain, but by the late 18th century a penal reform movement, mainly based in Philadelphia, led to prisons, exemplified by Auburn, which emphasized dimly lit interior cells, a program of daily work, and a detailed system of often petty rules. From 1825 separate institutions were developed for juveniles – there were 65 by 1900 – which emphasized reform and education, rather than punishment, at least in intention.

In the first quarter of the 20th century it was seen as important to keep prisoners employed, both to prevent trouble and to reduce costs, so that there was a return to the emphasis on industrial work of a century earlier. But, prison industries declined due to the exploitation of inmate labor and to union opposition in a time of high unemployment. From about 1935, developments have included the provision of smaller, more flexible, facilities, with an attempt to classify inmates and place them accordingly. But the typical state prison is still a walled fortress of stone and steel, housing from several hundred to several thousand inmates. Prisons range from maximum security establishments, where the overriding aim is to prevent escape, to open institutions, sometimes (inaccurately) dubbed "country clubs" which tend to house white collar offenders. In most prisons, often crowded living quarters are occupied for 16 hours a day, or more, there is much idle time, a rigid discipline, and a monotonous daily schedule. The perennial and worsening problem of prison populations, which expand faster than new prisons are built, is discussed below.

Prisons for women. Until the 1980's, women's institutions and their inmates received relatively little attention in the literature on prisons (Rafter 1986).

In the first stage of the development of women's institutions (1790–1870) female penal units ouwardly resembled those of males – but in some instances women received inferior care (less access to services, such as health, education and religion) and were subject to worse overcrowding. The second stage (1870–1935) saw strenuous, often successful, attempts to establish a new type of prison – the women's reformatory – in which women could receive care more appropriate to their "feminine" nature. But this involved institutionalizing the differential treatment of men and women (the latter were trained to occupy "womanly" positions as wives, mothers and educators of children). This emphasis has continued in the third stage (1935–present) with the addition of occupational skills traditionally associated with women (arts and crafts, cosmetology and office work).

Training centers for juveniles. In contrast to adult prisons, most institutions for juveniles are relatively small, housing a few hundred inmates or less. Incarceration rates vary widely between states (from 41.3 per 100,000 total population in Wyoming to 2.1 in New York State, (Vinter, Downs, and Hall 1975) implying major differences in sentencing policy.

According to Gibbons and Krohn (1986) the overriding concern of juvenile institutions is to prevent escapes and large scale disturbances. For this purpose, while similar to adult institutions in intention, they cannot use the same range or extent of coercive techniques. Instead, most focus largely on the stratagems which form only a part of the control system in prisons for adults – the staff enters into tacit "peace-keeping" bargains with inmate leaders.

A vivid overall impression of institutions for juveniles, as he saw them over 40 years ago, has been supplied by Deutsch (1949). He listed "ten deadly sins" as being true of most of them. These included: monotony (e.g., an unvarying diet); the mass handling of inmates without regard to individual needs; perennially limited budgets; isolation; complacency (on the part of those in charge); excessive physical and mental punishment; enforced idleness. A more recent survey of 42 juvenile institutions in 16 states (Vinter, Newcomb, and Kish 1976) found little substantial change. While institution staff agreed that in principle "treatment" should have the highest priority, research findings indicated an excessive use of restrictive measures and controls even in day centers. Particularly in the large institutions there was a "critical mass" of tougher, recidivist offenders who reinforced each others negative views of the "system" and set the tone for the entire establishment.

Fines

In the modern sense of a punishment imposed by a court, fines were not used in Britain until the 16th century. In the USA, they are now the most frequent penalty employed by the criminal justice system. They may be a supplement to prison or a substitute for it. The amount to be paid by the person found guilty is at the discretion of the judge, but within fixed limits. Caldwell (1965) lists the arguments in favor of fines compared with other possible punishments:

1. The system is economical, costing little to administer and requiring no expenditure on the maintenance of the prisoner.
2. It is a source of revenue for the state, county or city, without interfering with the offender's source of income or his/her ability to provide for dependants.

3. There is no stigmatization or disruption of family life.
4. The offender is not exposed to the criminalizing influences of prison life and the prison population is kept down.
5. The method is flexible – it can be adjusted both to the offense and the financial means of the offender.
6. By threatening an individuals finances, fines serve as an effective deterrent, both to further offenses by the offender and to offenses by the rest of the population.
7. The income from fines can be drawn on to compensate victims.
8. Fines can be used to punish legal entities such as corporations, which cannot be imprisoned (although their executives can be).

The arguments against are fewer:

1. The amount of the fine is usually adjusted to the offense, regardless of the financial circumstances of the offender.
2. The fine is frequently paid by relatives or friends and not by the person himself.
3. The method is often used routinely – to punish habitual offenders such as alcoholics, drug addicts and prostitutes – with no reforming intention or effect.
4. The amount exacted is often too small to offset the economic gain of crime, so that repeat property offenders and drug dealers write them off as business expenses.

Probation

This refers to the sentence of an offender being suspended while he is permitted to remain in the community, subject to the control of the court and under the supervision and guidance of a probation officer (from the Latin *probare* = to prove). It is different from a suspended sentence, in which the court releases the offender into the community without supervision but with the knowledge that if he re-offends he will be committed to an institution.

The system was first introduced into the USA in 1878 in the state of Massachusetts and spread gradually so that, by 1915, 33 states had some form of adult probation. By 1917 only Wyoming had no provision for juvenile probation. Today, between one quarter and one half of all offenders convicted in the state and federal courts are placed on probation or receive a suspended sentence, with wide variations between jurisdictions.

Caldwell (1965) lists the following advantages of probation:

1. The offender remains in the community; this assists his ultimate adjustment to a law-abiding life.
2. He can support himself and his family, as well as making reparation to the victim, should this be required by the court.
3. He is not exposed to potentially criminalizing and stigmatizing prison experiences and prison populations are kept down.
4. The offender is not left alone in his attempt to adjust to the community but has the support of a probation officer.
5. The costs of probation to the public are much less than those of prison.

The arguments against (Caldwell 1965) are:

1. Probation "pampers" the offender, and thus has no deterrent effect (against this, if he is convicted while on probation he is sent to prison).
2. The offender is still at liberty and hence free to reoffend.
3. In practice, the shortage of trained personnel combines with heavy case-loads to reduce the influence of probation officers to little more than zero (but the same may be true equally of the much more expensive prison system).

The next section considers the most important question of all concerning any system, whether intended principally to punish or to rehabilitate: using criteria which are as objective as possible, how well do the components of the penal system perform in practice?

10.2. Outcomes

Introduction

The evaluation of a sentence has to take into account a number of factors, including its intended effect. For the most part, this is either corrective or deterrent. In the first case, the sentence is intended to influence the offender concerned so that he will cease offending. Deterrent effects are intended both for the offender himself and for those who have not yet begun to offend. By implication, corrective effects might include an element of training; deterrent effects tend to emphasize punishment. In practice, corrective and deterrent effects overlap considerably because the test of efficacy of a particular sentence – the rate of conviction, or reconviction – is the same. However, there are two major differences which justify separate consideration of the two effects. First, the corrective effect is often tested by setting up special experiments (e.g., type A regime versus type B). Second, by definition, whereas studies of the corrective effect are confined to convicted offenders, deterrent effects include also those who have not yet offended.

An element which sometimes influences the decisions made by sentencing agents is that of *retribution*. This is the view that the offender should suffer as he has caused others to suffer. Retribution underlies some of the arguments for the death penalty. Also, an offender deemed "incorrigible" may be imprisoned for many years for largely preventive reasons with little hope of personal reformation, but with the possibility of deterring other habitual offenders. The topic of *incapacitation*, as it is increasingly termed, is discussed below.

The range of available sentences should be evaluated in terms of efficacy, efficiency and social acceptability. The test of efficacy is well established, that of efficiency is used increasingly, and social acceptance (or rejection, for example of "cruel and unusual punishments") may be of overriding importance, particularly in Western countries. Both corrective and deterrent effects can be evaluated, potentially at least, in terms of objective and quantitative measures such as rates of first offences or of reconvictions and of financial costs, for example, those of administering the system in question. (Costs are complicated by the need to take into account those suffered by victims, both in material and in subjective terms.) A sentence framed with retribution in mind would need to be evaluated, partially at least, in terms of the subjective satisfaction of members of the society concerned, an outcome which has not been studied.

Corrective efficacy

Walker (1971) has discussed the problems associated with the measurement of corrective efficacy, problems which are shared with estimations of the efficacy of psychological and other nonpenal methods of correction, covered in Chapter 11.

1. It is essential to define what is being "corrected" – is it overt lawbreaking, or is it some other, less tangible, variable such as "immoral attitudes?" What is being corrected inevitably relates to the choice of outcome measure used: reoffending, job performance, moral attitudes, and so on.

2. There are problems in using the criterion of subsequent convictions: (a) Should we confine ourselves to the offense for which the

sentence was received, or is it a fair test of treatment to include all types of further offenses. Hence the question – what is the intended range of generalization of the corrective method concerned? (b) Are all subsequent offences known, reported, recorded and detected? The well-known deficiences of official statistics make it highly desirable to collect self-report data on offending. In practice, this happens very rarely in studies of either corrective or deterrent efficacy.

If the official statistics are both incomplete and biased, so are the results of corrective efficacy studies. It is more accurate to term the success rate the *known* conviction rate. Provided that the post-corrective response of the criminal justice system is the same at each stage, and offenders have been *randomly* assigned to different forms of correction, then we can talk with reasonable confidence about the relative efficacy of two or more methods of correction. Unfortunately, the first of these is rarely, if ever, found in studies of either correction or treatment and, while the second is increasingly the case in treatment research, it is usually absent from studies of corrective efficacy.

3. The length of the follow-up period should always be stated. There are a number of general rules as to length: (a) The more first offenders (strictly, first convicted) in the sample, the longer should be the follow-up. (b) The more recidivists in the sample, the shorter the follow-up may be. These rules essentially refer to the fact that first offenders tend to be younger than recidivists and, hence, have a longer "career" ahead of them. A cumulative analysis of the trend over time will show the point at which the differences between the groups being compared become statistically significant.

4. The "spontaneous" recovery rate should be known (those who do not reoffend despite not being exposed to any formal method of correction). One method of estimation is to follow-up people who have both offended and have self-reported their offending but have not been officially detected and convicted. This has not been done in criminology, but is now a regular feature in the study of psychological problems, in which a frequent finding is that an untreated group recovers to the same extent as one treated by some form of therapy (see Rachman and Wilson 1980).

The foregoing is a listing of what is desirable in analyses of corrective efficacy. In practice, as Gibbons and Krohn (1986) point out (in the context of juvenile crime, but their remarks apply equally to the adult field), correctional agencies frequently fail to keep even the most routine form of statistical record. This is partly due to lack of resources, but also because they have a stake in *not* knowing about their impact. If the lack of effect were to become known even their limited resources might be further cut.

In the treatment of psychological problems it is common to have a category of "partly recovered" as well as one of "completely recovered." In the same way, Murray and Cox (1979) argue for the use of a "suppression effect" (a partial reduction in the rate of offending by a person following a corrective intervention) instead of the less realistic target of a complete cessation of misconduct. We might go even further and assess the seriousness of each subsequent offense, on a standard scale (e.g., Sellin and Wolfgang 1964). Clearly, there is a deal of difference between two offenders, both with two recorded offenses during follow-up, where for one these are minor property crimes, for the other the two offenses involve armed robbery.

Despite the inadequacy of most current research into corrective efficacy, a number of tentative conclusions may be drawn about variables relevant to the official reconviction rate:

1. The fewer the previous convictions, the lower the subsequent reconviction rate. The converse, of course, follows. For example, Walker, Farrington, and Tucker (1981) analyzed one sixth of those convicted in the Metropolitan Police District (London) in January, 1971, and then followed them up six years later. Reconviction rates varied as a function of previous convictions, from 21 per cent for none, through 47 and 66 per cent (one and two–four respectively) to 88 per cent (five or more previous convictions).

2. The older the offender during follow-up, the lower the reconviction rate. At first sight this might suggest that punishment, for example incarceration, succeeds eventually, a second "dose" proving more effective than a single one, particularly as the second institution has to cope with those with whom the first has already failed, apparently a more difficult group than those new to confinement. But there are at least two other explanations. First, as people get older they may cease offending not because of the impact of the penal system but because greater earning power has increased their legitimate access to goods, their need to provide for a family, or both. Second, we do not know that they have ceased offending, merely that they have not been reconvicted. It is possible that they have learned skills which enable them to evade detection/conviction more readily and/or have learned which offenses combine the best returns with the least risk of detection.

3. Females have a significantly lower reconviction rate than males, when the sexes are matched for age and penal history.

4. Reconviction rates vary by offense. An extreme example is provided by child molestation. The apparent reconviction rate is very low, with rates as low as 5 per cent being found for the typical follow-up period of three years. But, Soothill, Way, and Gibbons (1980) found that "serious failure" rose to 15 per cent when the follow-up was extended to seven years. Moreover, as Davis and Leitenberg (1987, p. 424) point out "a once convicted offender may . . . repeat an offence many times with many victims without getting convicted again." The lower the detection rate, the lower the reconviction rate, so that for offenses with very low detection rates, such as drug dealing and child molestation, reconviction rates are very questionable measures of corrective or treatment efficacy.

It follows that studies of corrective efficacy should, at the minimum, control for sex, age, previous criminal career, type of offense and the length and number of occasions previously in confinement. Alternatively, offenders should be assigned randomly to the corrective methods being appraised. In the latter case the number in each of the groups under test should be sufficiently large to ensure that all relevant variables are likely to be present equally in all groups.

Methods of punishment: conclusions. Despite the many problems with the data on corrective efficacy, a number of tentative conclusions were drawn by Hood and Sparks (1970). For the most part they have stood the test of the years since then and are set out below, together with some more recent assertions and findings.

1. For many offenders a period of probation is likely to be as effective in preventing reoffending as an institutional sentence. Glaser (1983) reminds us that most offenders are supervised in the community (the proportion is three to one compared with those sent to prison). His review of research evidence concludes that probation for new offenders helps to prevent criminalization whereas, for more habitual offenders, an appreciable period of confinement is more effective in preventing recidivism. If the latter are to be supervised in the community, very close control is necessary, such as random drug tests for ex-addicts (McGlothian, Anglin, and Wilson 1977). However, for "low-risk" offenders (typically those at an early stage in offending, or with good job prospects and/or in stable marriages), a marked reduction in frequency of contact with probation officers does not increase the failure rate. The same emphasis on the need for more intensive surveillance of many offenders sentenced to probation emerged from a Rand study of

probationers in California (Petersilia, Turner, Kahan, and Peterson 1985). This group suggested a form of punishment intermediate between prison and probation which would incorporate intensive surveillance, restitution and substantial community service. Alternatives and supplements to conventional penal methods are discussed in the last section of this chapter.

2. Fines are more effective than either probation or imprisonment for first offenders and even for most recidivists of all age groups. However, giving a noncustodial sentence might raise the current crime rate. (While offenders are in prison they are removed from criminal opportunities.)

3. Longer prison sentences do not reduce the reconviction rate compared with shorter ones. As the average length of a prison term increases so does the pressure on accommodation. This is part of the issue of prison populations, discussed below.

Several researchers have argued for the minimum possible level of intervention, particularly with first offenders. For example, Wolfgang et al. (1972) concluded from their Philadelphia study that first-time offenders were more likely to reoffend if they had been arrested than cautioned. Similarly, Klein (1974) found that juvenile first offenders were less likely to be rearrested in police departments with a "high diversion" policy (not taking juvenile offenders to court) than in those with the contrasting "low diversion" policy. In a subsequent study, Klein, Teichman, Lincoln, and Labin (1977) found that the further a juvenile had been processed within the criminal justice system, the greater the chance for rearrest: juveniles who had been counseled and released were rearrested 25 per cent less often than those who had been cautioned. (Juveniles were randomly assigned to treatment groups.)

However, there is much controversy around the issue of "minimum response" to first offenders. For example, McCord (1980) interprets the literature as follows: "Those who have been released without official processing for their arrests are more likely to commit subsequent crimes, to commit Index crimes and to commit crimes against persons.

The apparent lack of *demonstrated* and *unequivocal* success of any conventional penal method (as indicated, a reduction or cessation of criminal behavior may have occurred in response to social circumstances, such as marriage and a steady job, rather than to punishment) has led to the search for other methods, some derived from clinical psychology, which are considered in the next chapter. Of course, it remains possible that the apparent lack of overall success may mask two opposing effects: some offenders may be deterred from reoffending; others may be more likely to reoffend following punishment. Combining those improved with those worsened masks the opposite effects. If this is so, the next step is to match persons with probable response, by some form of prediction method. The very limited progress made towards this end is discussed in the last section of this chapter.

A psychological critique of current methods of punishment. Essentially, behavior is changed by a combination of positive and negative reinforcements. Within the penal system, positive reinforcements include attempts to train offenders in noncriminal ways of earning money and an emphasis on sport, to instil a general respect for social rules. But, positive reinforcement for approved behaviors tends not to be applied in any systematic way, and the penal system places much more emphasis on negative reinforcement, meaning the withdrawal of a positive reinforcer. Examples include the loss of money involved in fines and imprisonment (confinement means potential earnings are reduced) and the deprivation of access to valued social reinforcers (friends and family, heterosexual activities, etc.). Within the custodial institution, there may be further negative reinforcement – such as loss of privileges for banned behaviors. There is little or no attempt to associate systematically, alternative, socially approved, behaviors with the reduction of criminal behaviors.

But even the most psychologically sophisticated treatment plan will be seriously handicapped by two problems which are outside the control of both "punishers" and "treaters." First, even if offenders are apprehended, negative consequences are rarely contingent in time with the performance of a crime. (An example of an immediate negative consequence is the application of the "Denver boot" to an illegally parked car; this sort of outcome is experienced by Index offenders only when they are caught in the act and find this unpleasant – perhaps because of the social stigma attached.) More usually there is a considerable delay before sentence. Second, the most obvious point must be kept in mind always: only apprehended offenses are available for negative reinforcement, and most crimes go unpunished. For most offenders, as indicated in the previous chapter, their criminal career is an unpredictable sequence of mainly positive, with some negative, reinforcements, leading to the probable maintenance of the criminal behavior. All of this means that there are unavoidable major limitations to improvements in the corrective efficacy of the penal system.

Deterrent efficacy

In Chapter 9 I discussed the notion that a good deal of crime involves a more or less rational analysis of the balance of rewards and costs related to a criminal opportunity. The study of deterrent efficacy focuses on the cost side – the penal system as it is experienced and perceived by offenders and potential offenders.

As is the case with corrective efficacy, deterrent efficacy is much more frequently tested by inferences from the official statistics of offending than by specially set-up experiments. In both cases, certain assumptions have to be made (Walker 1971).

1. The statistics of crime are collated and listed in a uniform way over the period of interest – usually substantial.
2. During this period the penalty for a given offence is *changed*.
3. The change is publicized and a check is made of potential offenders' knowledge of the change. In practice, this is rarely attempted, let alone attained.
4. The probability of being detected for the offense should be known to potential offenders, or at least the level of their knowledge should be measured.
5. During the period of time in question no other social change has occurred, such as an increase or decrease in the opportunity for carrying out the offense, or in the level of police surveillance, which could be responsible for any change observed in the level of offending.

In the real world, such a degree of experimental control is probably unattainable, so that the "other changes" should be measured, and their effect controlled for by appropriate statistical techniques.

Once again, as in the case of work on corrective efficacy, the above requirements are rarely, if ever, attained in practice. For example, there is much public ignorance of the true risks of detection, and many potential or actual offenders may find it difficult to connect risks with crimes, perhaps because of low intelligence. Moreover, factors such as population density, employment levels, age composition, all important in affecting the level of crime, are rarely taken into account in assessing the deterrent effect of a change in the criminal law.

Research into deterrence. Cook (1980) has reviewed a number of studies of deterrent effects which tried to assess the impact of a change in the law or in police activity. The latter was discussed in Chapter 3. Most of the former group concern non-Index offenses, such as driving under the influence of alcohol, but one study (Landes 1979) did concern the serious offence of aircraft hi-jacking, so is worth mentioning. Landes found that the introduction of mandatory screening of passengers and their baggage in 1973 increased the probability of apprehension of intending hi-jackers over the next three years, compared with earlier years, and significantly decreased the level of attempted hi-jackings over what would have been expected without these changes. Increases in the length of incarceration following conviction were also said to have played a part.

A large scale prospective study of deterrence by Piliavin, Thornton, Gartner, and Matsueda (1986) collected data between 1975 and 1979 as part of a job creation program for persons with severe and chronic employment problems: adult offenders with a history of incarceration; adults known to be drug users, and adolescents between 17 and 20 who had dropped out of school. Five thousand persons from these three groups were randomly assigned to experimental or control conditions, the former being provided with jobs for up to 18 months. About two thirds completed three interviews about contacts with the criminal justice system, at the beginning and in the middle and at the end of the program. Most saw weekly, even daily, opportunities for illegal income at a level they believed significantly exceeded the minimum wage attainable from a legitimate job, and 20–30 per cent admitted infractions of the law during the research period. The authors found much more support for the "opportunity and reward components" of a rational choice model of crime (i.e., for the benefits side) than for the risk component (the cost side). They concluded that serious and high risk offenders are not deterred by the perceived probability of detection and punishment. They speculate that such individuals may alter their behavior only in response to major shifts in their perceptions of the risk of sanctions, in part because, whereas rewards are immediate, costs are more distant, and are easier to discount.

This raises the question of the *celerity* (speed) of punishment, as compared with *certainty* and *severity*. Howe and Brandau (1980) found that speed was of moderate importance in affecting hypothetical decisions about crime, and less important than either severity or certainty. But, there are probably major differences between persons and offenses. In practice, given the long queues for court time, rapid punishment is attainable only for offenses of strict liability, punishable on the spot, such as those to do with driving.

The conflict between certainty and severity of punishment usually relates to variations in length of imprisonment, rather than other sanctions, and most studies are of drunken-driving. Increasing the certainty of punishment does seems to have an impact, especially if it is well publicized and reinforced by special police efforts. But drunken-driving is an offence with a relatively small reward, and the alternative of not drinking before driving is easily attainable. In contrast, property offenses may be highly rewarding, and legal alternatives which afford the same returns difficult to find.

So far as the length of a prison sentence (i.e., its severity) is concerned, Lewis (1986) reviewed 15 studies, most of which were consistent with the hypothesis that longer sentences deter most types of crime. But, there are a number of problems with these studies: many of the basic data contain important errors of measurement; there is much confounding of the deterrence and incapacitation effects (between what people do after prison and the fact that offending is not possible until they emerge); and there were technical difficulties in separating out the supply of crimes, available to be commited, from other variables.

The size of any deterrent effect of severity is far from uniform across population groups. In his analysis of 171 US cities, Sampson (1986) found that cities with a high risk of prison for robbery had a disproportionately low robbery rate, regardless of both the demographic features of their populations and other known determinants of crime such as poverty and income inequality. However, further analysis indicated that the deterrent effect of prison held only for juveniles (both black and white), whereas adults (again both black and white) seemed unaffected. Sampson speculates that this is because juveniles are more responsive to variations in sanctions; in contrast, adult robbers are more aware of the actual rarity of prison incarceration. (Moreover, the juvenile group includes those who would desist eventually, partially irrespective of the known level of sanctions, as they settle into adult life; most adult robbers are, by definition, "persisters.") The importance of separate analyses of deterrent effects for serious and high-risk offenders was noted above in the discussion of the study by Piliavin et al. (1986).

A central problem in trying to assess the impact of deterrent variables on crime rates is the *direction* of any effect. For example, do crime rates respond to arrests, or do the police respond to changes in the rates? A study of homicide, robbery and burglary (Decker and Kohfeld 1985) found that increases in arrests tend to *follow* increases in reported crime, so that we shall need to re-examine studies which argue that offenders' perceptions of arrest rates are an indication of deterrent effects. In the real world, it may be that there is a continual reciprocal interaction between changes in the law and in police actions and changes in the responses of offenders and potential offenders.

In conclusion, we need more studies like that by Piliavin et al. (1986) of a group of offenders followed forward over a period of time with periodic reassessments, both of behavior and of perceptions. We shall need also a careful analysis of potentially relevant individual differences. For example, some persons may find it easier than others to suppress the perceived costs of crime while enhancing the perceived benefits. In line with this, Tittle (1980) found among average adults that those who believe the risks of punishment to be low were more likely to say they would commit a crime than those who believed the risks to be high.

10.3. Alternative methods of punishment

The approaches considered below are often termed "experimental," although they are rarely tested by the random assigment of participants to the method under study or to a comparison group. More usually, "experiment" means "let's try it out and see what happens."

Reparation and restitution

In both America and Britain, offenders may be sentenced to a fixed number of hours of work on projects such as helping the handicapped, repairing churches, and clearing canals. Reparation is to the community at large and not to the particular victim.

Restitution means that by an order of the court the offender is required to restore stolen property to the rightful owner or to pay a sum of money in compensation, or both. Colson (1988) argues that restitution removes the profit from crime, even the most lucrative, because it can be set as high as the court wishes (e.g., the spectacular $750 million levied on the former Wall Street firm of Drexel, Burnham and Lambert (*The Economist* 1990c). Victims of crime can go to the civil court to obtain redress, but this can be very expensive and the offender may be insolvent, either genuinely or by design. The offender's earnings can be attached to pay the sum required, but this requires a higher level of earnings than many offenders are capable of without further criminal activity.

Despite such problems, the method is growing in popularity in the USA. A survey by Evans and Koederitz (1983) of 14 states showed that more than half of the juvenile court judges and probation officers contacted believed it to be an effective deterrent. Schneider (1986) reported the results of experiments in four widely separated communities. In all four, youths were randomly assigned to restitution or to traditional dispositions, and followed-up for two to three years. They concluded that, overall, restitution might have a small effect on recidivism, but that not all programs would achieve even this, due to differences in program management and community circumstances.

So far as the cost to the offender is concerned, restitution may be the same as a fine – provided that the court is free to set this so as to match the sum involved in the offense. The difference is that it is the victim who is compensated and not the state. It might be that there is a significant effect on some offenders in giving recompense to the actual victim and not to an impersonal court official, but research on this point seems lacking. Many might argue that replacing fines by restitution to victims retains the expenses of the trial while losing a significant source of income to the criminal justice system. No such criticism can be levelled at replacing probation by either reparation or restitution.

Electronic tagging

This refers to a device worn by a newly convicted offender or parolee which transmits information as to his whereabouts 24 hours a day to a central unit. According to Gable (1986), tagging could both reduce the costs of correction (by allowing early release, even replacing imprisonment completely) and improve offender rehabilitation (again, early release, or remaining at liberty helps to preserve previously acquired job-related and social skills). The protection of the public is also improved because the offender is aware that his movements are so precisely monitored that any deviation from approved locations will be known immediately, so that crime is made difficult, if not impossible.

Other than figures on costs (in 1986, about one half those of imprisonment, with the current gap probably more in favor of tagging as technical advances reduce the expense), there seem no data on efficacy and there are evident ethical problems (foreseen by Cohen, 1977). Moreover, there is no clear provision for generalizing post "release" the behaviors involved in resisting criminal opportunities.

Half-way houses and work-release

Both approaches are intended to reduce criminalization and to prepare incarcerated offenders for life back in the world outside prison.

The half-way house is a community-based hostel which provides some training in job and social skills and a sheltered contact with the outside world, so permitting a gradual rather than a sudden readjustment after discharge from prison. A Canadian survey by Grygier, Nease, and Anderson (1970) suggested little difference in the rate of recidivism between the half-way house and the parole system, and that the former was inevitably more expensive. Glaser (1983), reviewing American experience, is somewhat more optimistic, citing evidence that, where actuarial tables are used to predict placement, the results are better than parole alone. He considers half-way houses to be most successful in reducing recidivism with young, career offenders, provided that they are given a good deal of counseling in the acquisition and retention of jobs, as well as close supervision.

Work-release differs from the half-way house approach in that the offender continues to reside in prison while being employed in the outside community. This provides a custodial alternative to probation and parole and reduces the cost to the prison system (typically, prisons use a portion of the resulting earnings to cover room and board). Almost all states have enacted work-release programs (Knox and Humphrey 1981). (These authors point out that only a minority of prisoners are in prerelease programs of any kind.) An analysis of a 10 per cent random sample of prisoners released from North Carolina found that the decision to assign to work-release depended most on good behavior over a lengthy period, on marital status (having a good home to go back to), on age (older offenders are considered better risks) and on the most immediate offense being relatively nonserious (Knox and Humphrey 1981). Glaser's general conclusions on effectiveness apply equally to work-release programs as to half-way houses.

10.4. The death penalty

Only one of America's Nato allies, Turkey, still uses capital punishment regularly, although in two more countries the penalty remains on their statute books. In 1976, the Supreme Court re-established that the death penalty was constitutional and, as of March, 1990, 36 American states had the death penalty for murder, the great majority of whom had convicted murderers waiting on "death row." Those states with no death penalty were mainly in the North-Eastern segment of the country, and included New York and Massachusetts. In the three previous years, 127 executions had taken place in nine states, with Texas (33), Florida (21) and Louisiana (18) leading the way. Very much larger numbers were awaiting execution, about 2,400 in all, nearly 20 times the number executed in the past 3 years. Texas, Florida, and California (which had executed no-one in the three years to March 1990), all had more than 250 on death row, some for many years while a series of appeals is made and considered (*The Economist* 1990d).

Some key issues

Does the death penalty deter murder? Why is the USA virtually alone in the West in retaining it? Does the death penalty discriminate against black Americans in the way in which it is imposed?

The deterrent effect of the death penalty. A review by Sellin (1967) of the 20th century literature concluded that the death penalty had no effect on the homicide rate. However, Ehrlich (1977), using a statistically more sophisticated approach and cross-sectional data, argued that there was a substantial deterrent effect of capital punishment and, in a subsequent paper (Ehrlich 1979), produced a major critique of Sellin's methodology. In turn, Ehrlich's own techniques have been heavily criticized. A very detailed analysis by Friedman (1979) pointed out that Ehrlich omitted a number of important variables from his analysis, all of which influence the murder rate, including the average length of prison sentence for murder, the number of handguns in the general population, and the degree of income inequality. Friedman concluded that Ehrlich's study depended on a "myriad of assumptions," many of them convenient to the conclusion of a deterrent effect of the death penalty.

Bandura (1986, p. 332) argues: "The issue is not whether the threat of punishment by death can deter homicide but whether the death penalty deters homicide more effectively than imprisonment." He interprets (p. 332) the current evidence as follows:

> "Abolition of the death penalty does not lead to a differential rise in crimes no longer punishable by execution as compared with those that are. Reinstatement of the death penalty does not have a discernible effect on the rate of capital crimes. Nor does the incidence of capital crimes differ consistently before and after publicized executions. Neither police nor inmates and their keepers are any safer in States that have retained the death penalty than in those that have abolished it."

However, he concludes, cautiously, given the impossibility of a controlled experiment in which convicted murderers would be sentenced randomly to death and then to imprisonment in successive time periods, that there can be no definitive resolution of the argument. But, the gravity and irreversibility of execution (it is far from unknown for innocent persons to be executed) mean that the onus is on the proponents of the death sentence to demonstrate its superior deterrent effect. This they have failed to do, often falling back instead on more emotional arguments.

American public opinion. The death of Gary Gillman before a firing squad in 1977 marked the end of a ten year period in the USA without an execution. There were eight executions between January, 1977 and September, 1983. All were male, the youngest was 24, all but one were white, the crimes were particularly unpleasant, guilt in all cases was near to certainty, and several had asked for death. Jolly and Sagarin (1984) argue that these first eight had the characteristics "designed" to mute public protest against the death sentence, and they assert that if executions were to be resumed on a large scale the pattern could not be maintained.

In fact, there seemed no special need to convince public opinion as to the desirability of the death penalty (and no evidence of any plan to do so). Support for the death penalty has been high in America for many years, falling below 50 per cent only in 1966 and reaching 80 per cent in the late 1980's (*The Economist* 1990d). The proportion in favor drops somewhat when respondents are offered the alternative of a life imprisonment that genuinely means for life. A survey in Seattle (Warr and Stafford 1984) found that respondents were most likely to choose retribution as the primary purpose of punishment by execution.

Support for retribution increased dramatically with age and declined as educational attainment rose.

Surveys show similar results in other countries. According to *The Economist* (1990d, p. 45), the difference is that "American politicians are more likely to follow public opinion on this question, not to try to change it." In support of this assertion, they cite the 1990 election campaigns in which candidates were "indulging in ghoulish rivalry in support of execution" (*The Economist* 1990d, p. 345). One candidate put out a commercial in which he strode triumphantly past photographs of the people who had been executed while he was governor in 1983–1987; another (Mr. Mattox) adopted the slogan: "Jim Mattox. There are no endorsements for him on death row." The evidence seems to favor such politician support for the death penalty. For example, Michael Dukakis lost much ground in the 1988 presidential campaign when voters equated his opposition to the death penalty with being "soft on crime." There seems no good explanation as to why politicians in other Western countries do not suffer electorally for their opposition to the death penalty – other than that there are few who express themselves in favor.

Who is executed? In the USA, convicted murderers are more likely to be executed if they are poor, live in the South, and have killed a white person (whether they themselves are black or white). About one-half of those on death row are members of racial minorities, mainly blacks, whereas only one quarter of their victims are black (*The Economist* 1990d). A study of 14 juveniles condemned to death in four US states (Lewis, Pincus, Bard, and Richardson 1988) found that nine had major neurological impairments, 12 had been brutally physically abused by relatives and seven had suffered psychotic disorders prior to incarceration. None of these and other grounds for mitigation had been recognized at the time of trial or sentencing.

Concluding comment. Given that the great majority of those sentenced to death are not executed, and there is a consequent build-up of numbers on death row, Cheetwood (1985) foresees that many states will enact "life without release" statutes, with a consequent major impact on the numbers and composition of those in institutions. So the debate continues, with death penalty supporters arguing that it is unfair on taxpayers to expect them to finance a convict's imprisonment for life. Will America have a change of heart, or will it continue to differ from the rest of the developed countries of the world?

10.5. Incapacitation

The man in the street is apt to assert, in response to a particularly unpleasant offence: "lock 'em up and throw away the key." Cohen (1983) has contributed a thorough review of the arguments concerning very long prison sentences for career offenders.

Introduction

In the 1980's, support increased in the USA for the incarceration of high risk offenders. Prison capacity has not kept pace and, in 1981, 31 states were under court orders to reduce prison overcrowding and 37 were in litigation about some form of prison conditions. Cohen considered that for fiscal and policy reasons prison capacity is unlikely to increase rapidly. While the main impact of the baby boom population on capacity will be over by the early 1990's, the problem of making the best use of prison resources will remain, leading to the question of which prisoners (if any) are to be incarcerated for long periods.

The literature on criminal careers provides a context for Cohen's discussion. The basic assumption behind incapacitation is that the higher an individual's crime rate and the longer his career, the more crimes will be averted through his incapacitation. It follows that the effectiveness of incapacitation depends on the ability of the criminal justice system to identify and incarcerate the appropriate offenders. Three more key assumptions underlie the argument for incapacitation: all offenders are vulnerable to arrest and incarceration (the evidence supports this); the crimes of offenders taken off the streets are not replaced by those of other offenders (unlikely, according to Cohen, except for retail drug trafficking, but replacement seems probable also for the suppliers of other illegal but very lucrative goods and services, such as sex and gambling); periods of incarceration do not change the expected length of a criminal career (i.e., rehabilitative and criminogenic effects cancel out, the weight of evidence supports this). Thus, there are no major *a priori* grounds against incapacitation. What remains is the detailed examination of the empirical evidence.

There are two types of incapacitation: collective and selective. Collective incapacitation means that individuals are sentenced solely on the basis of their current offence and perhaps their prior record, with no variation on any other grounds. Selectivity means tailoring the sentence to the particular offender, according to predictions concerning his future criminal activities, so that there will be much individual variation.

Collective incapacitation

According to Cohen (1983), a mandatory five year prison term after any felony conviction would reduce serious crime by about 15 per cent; a policy of a five year term after repeated convictions would reduce it by about 5 per cent. However, as repeaters become known to the police they have more chances of arrest than beginners, so that these figures probably overstate the benefits of the above strategies. There is a further limitation to the arguments for collective incapacitation: in Washington, DC, about three-quarters of the adults arrested for Index offenses in 1973 had either no prior arrests or no prior convictions, so that only one quarter of Index crimes could have been prevented by imposing prison terms, of any length, on convicted offenders.

The impact of collective incapacitation on prison populations is likely to be substantial. Cohen estimates an increase of from three to five times in those imprisoned for "target" offences, and about one half for the total prison population. (Inevitably, longer sentences mean a larger population, which increases inexorably until the first of those sentenced under incapacitatory policies are released.)

Selective incapacitation

Substantially higher incapacitation benefits are possible when offenders vary in their rates of offending and there is a systematic policy of incapacitating high-rate offenders. However, such offenders are best identified retrospectively, so that an incapacitation policy based on the identification of future high-risk offenders must involve a very high level of error. But, picking them out early is essential for the success of selective incapacitation. This leads to serious ethical and empirical problems.

Ethical issues. A selective incapacitation policy means imprisoning for a long term to prevent crimes which would not then be committed. Both liability to imprisonment and its length would be determined by *predicted* offences, violating the widely accepted principle that punishment is for *past* criminal behavior. Several of those predictor variables which might turn out to both reliable and valid are likely to be objectionable morally or politically (e.g., age, race, and sex).

Empirical problems. In point of fact (as we shall see in more detail below and later in this chapter, when discussing prospective studies), efforts to predict future offending have not yet been very successful. The usual finding is of a high rate of false positives (predicted to offend, but not doing so, typical of attempts to predict relatively rare events) with false negatives (predicted, inaccurately, to be law-abiding) very much less frequent. Both are troubling: the former would receive long sentences, the latter short, or no sentences. It is fair to point out, as Cohen does, that the comparison should be with existing practices rather than with some, so far unattained, level of perfection. However, why shift from the present system before something markedly better is available, given the serious ethical objections noted above?

One widely cited empirical study (Greenwood and Abrahamse 1982) suggests only a slight comparative advantage at best of a scale they developed. On behalf of the National Institute of Justice they surveyed a sample of 2,170 inmates of prisons in California, Michigan and Texas, largely by self-reports of armed robberies and burglaries in their nonprison time during the two years prior to their current incarceration. On this basis the sample were divided into low, medium, and high rate offenders, and seven variables (including prior convictions and incarcerations, drug use, and employment history) were found to predict offense rate to some extent. Greenwood and Abrahamse (1982) concluded that, if long prison terms were to be given to predicted high rate offenders and average terms to the rest, armed robbery could be reduced by 20 per cent, with no increase in the size of the population incarcerated for armed robbery.

Cohen (1983) points out several serious shortcomings of this study and of the resulting Greenwood scale for predicting future offending.

1. Even if the scale is successful in distinguishing retrospectively between high-rate offenders and the rest, its *prospective* accuracy depends on past behavior being maintained – and this is less and less true the further into the future one seeks to predict.

2. The scale has not been validated, either internally (on another section of the original sample of inmates) or externally (on a completely different sample). Until these studies are done we have no estimate of the shrinkage in predictive power which is inevitable when validation is attempted.

3. Even before this takes place, the predictive accuracy of the scale is not very impressive. While reasonably good for the predicted "low rates" (76 per cent correct), it is clearly unsatisfactory with the predicted

"high rates" (55 per cent of whom would have been false positives, but would nevertheless have received long prison sentences). The Greenwood scale thus turns out to be only marginally better overall than current sentencing decisions.

Cohen concludes that if the scale is to be used for the differential sentencing of individuals it must be improved markedly so as to conform with justice, equity and due process.

An alternative strategy. Cohen (1983) advocates an *aggregate* approach. This would focus on selected target *offenses* and rely only on the type of crime the accused is charged with and his prior record, thus avoiding ethical objections. Incapacitatory policies should concentrate on those aged 33–43 who are in the middle of well-established criminal careers and with undeniable prior records. Cohen estimates that prison terms of only two years could avert between one-quarter and one-third of the remaining careers of burglars and robbers (typically a further six to eight years of activity), leading to a decrease of 8 per cent in robberies, 3 per cent in murders and 2 per cent in auto thefts. However, the prison population would increase by 7 per cent.

The same inescapable effect of an increase in prison populations from even a modest reduction in crimes such as robbery, due to selective incapacitation, has been found by Visher (1987) in an analysis of sentencing practices over the preceding two decades. He also points to the difficulty of identifying high-rate offenders with the information currently available. Farrington (1986) is rather more sanguine, basing himself on the possibility of predicting *future* high-rate offenders before the age of 13. The children so identified would receive social help rather than punishment.

10.6. Prison populations

The problem of rising numbers

A major review by Blumstein (1988) begins by pointing out that federal and state prison populations grew steadily between 1972 and 1988 after remaining steady for the first three-quarters of the 20th century – during which incarceration rates were strikingly stable. He suggests that this stability was due partly to the existence of safety valves, the most important of which was release on parole, plus much administrative discretion over such matters as assignment to half-way houses. But, parole has been under intensive assault for the past 15 years and has even been eliminated in a number of states, with no alternative method to ensure that prison numbers are kept down.

As at the end of 1986, there were nearly 550,000 inmates of state and federal prisons, and about 220,000 in local jails, awaiting trial or serving short sentences, of whom the majority were males between 18 and 30. By April, 1989, these numbers had risen to 660,000 and 340,000 respectively (*The Economist* 1989b). Black males in their twenties had much the highest rates of imprisonment – about 25 times the rate for the population as a whole. About 8 per cent of this group is in prison at any given time, and for those living in the inner cities the rate is even higher.

> ". . . on any given day more than five per cent of black males in their twenties in the USA are in state prison. Over a lifetime, 15 per cent of all black males . . . can be expected to serve some time in an adult prison. By comparison, fewer than 0.5 per cent of white males in their twenties are in prison on any one day, and only 2–3 per cent will be imprisoned during their lifetime" (Petersilia and Turner 1987, p. 151).

Blumstein (1988) points out that, while in 1988 the white black population ratio was 6.35 for the 20–24 age group, for the 10–15 age group, it was down to 5.27, implying over the succeeding decade an increase in the proportional share of blacks in the prison population.

In 1970, the incarceration rate was 96 per 100,000 of the US population; by 1986 this had risen to 227 per 100,000. International comparisons are presented in Table 10.1, which indicates major variations

Table 10.1. *Incarceration rates for eight countries*

Country	Population (millions)	Prisoners	Prisoners per 100,000 population	Rank
Australia	15.1	9,698	64	6
Hong Kong	5.2	5,339	102	3
Singapore	2.4	2,775	114	2
New Zealand	3.1	2,635	84	5
England/Wales	55.9	49,471	89	4
Finland	4.8	1,094	23	7
Sweden	8.3	1,344	16	8
United States	226.5	438,830	194	1

Source: Blumstein (1988, p. 234).

between countries per 100,000 of the population, from 16 in Sweden to 227 in the USA. Blumstein argues that this disparity must be related to the pattern of serious crime in various countries, Table 10.2 shows the ratio of prisoners per reported robbery and murder for eight countries, several of which have higher rates than the USA.

Nevertheless, it remains true that American prison populations are higher than ever, with a rapid rise both in costs (at the end of the 1980's it cost about $20,000 dollars a year to keep a man in prison and about $50,000 a year to build a new cell, *The Economist*, 1989b) and in overcrowding (e.g., in California, in June 1989, the prisons were operating at 175 per cent of capacity, *New York Times*, 1989). Many other states were in a similar plight, so that at the beginning of 1987 nine state prison systems were run by special administrations appointed by federal judges and 28 more were subject to court orders to improve conditions (*The Economist* 1987b).

Reasons for the rise

Blumstein (1988) lists them, as follows:

1. The politicization of prison policy. By the 1970's the earlier powers of parole boards to release early (and hence to control prison populations flexibly) had been eliminated or reduced. In addition, the aim of rehabilitation had largely lost its credibility, because of the apparent finding that "nothing works" (see the next chapter for a more considered view). Instead, conservatives demanded less leniency, while liberals wanted determinate sentences, so as to reduce arbitrary

Table 10.2. *Prisoners related to serious crimes in eight countries*

Country	Prisoners per murder	Rank	Prisoners per robbery	Rank
Australia	23.4	5	1.01	4
Hong Kong	55.6	3	0.45	7
Singapore	56.2	2	2.0	3
New Zealand	34.6	4	8.1	1
England/Wales	66.8	1	2.2	2
Finland	4.2	7	0.56	6
Sweden	3.3	8	0.42	8
United States	22.7	6	0.88	5

Source: Blumstein (1988, p. 236).

sentencing, and particularly the bias against minority groups indicated in Chapter 4. The overall effect has been that sentences have lengthened for many offences, and particularly for drug related charges.

2. The change in age composition. The above shifts in opinion coincided with the "coming-of-crime-age" of the baby-boomers, and the consequent rise in crime rates detailed in Chapters 1 and 2, so that there were both more offenders and a more severe sentencing policy.

What to do about the problem

According to Blumstein (1988) the alternatives are as follows:

1. Do nothing. In time the baby boomers will pass through the peak age for crime. In the interim the costs of the cycle of overcrowding – reduced control by staff, inmate riots, and political fall-out – are less than those of building the massive increases needed in accommodation, which at some future stage might even be redundant.

2. Provide more accommodation. This traditional response is unattractive when funds are tight. There is much controversy about where to put new facilities and the process of opening a new prison can take many years. Alternatives to new building by the State include taking over mental hospital buildings vacated by a major move to deinstitutionalize the mentally ill and handing the problem over to the private sector. But, the former is now being reconsidered as homeless discharged patients build up in the streets, and the latter is fraught with political and ethical problems (Borna 1986).

3. Selective incapacitation. This was discussed earlier and the conclusion was that while some modest reduction in serious crime might result, the price would be an *increase* in the prison population, not a decrease.

4. A direct reduction in the prison population. This has two aspects. The first ("front door") means diverting those convicted to alternative sentences such as probation, as well as the less traditional methods which were considered above. The second (the "back door") means shorter sentences for those who do go to prison. It is based on the notion that the severity of a sentence is less of a deterrent than its certainty, discussed earlier in this chapter. There is also a need to avoid "wasted" prison time – career offenders "retire" from crime at the rate of 10–20 per cent per year, a rate which is unaffected by the length of imprisonment, so that long sentences for relatively elderly offenders

achieve nothing extra in the way of reducing crime and take up needed accommodation (Blumstein et al. 1982).

Shortening sentences for prisoners in general is essentially the approach in several European countries. For example, The Netherlands managed to keep its prison population almost constant for the period 1840–1980 despite a fivefold increase in the general population. Although there was an increase from 29 per 100,000 in 1983 to 36 per 100,000 in 1987, this was still almost the lowest in Europe. It was achieved (despite having fewer policemen per head than most countries) by giving much shorter sentences than is usual in the USA. The result is that a much smaller proportion of the Dutch population is in prison and there is a relatively inexpensive prison system, both as compared with the USA (*The Economist* 1988a).

Fitzmaurice and Pease (1982) argue that, in order to reduce prison populations per 100,000 to those of The Netherlands, sentence length has to be reduced, rather than more people diverted from prison (the back door rather than the front). For example, in Britain, diverting convicted offenders sentenced to six months in prison or less (those usually considered for noncustodial alternatives) would reduce the number of prison sentences by 50%, but the total prison population by only 10 per cent. It is more efficient and effective to reduce all sentences by 10 per cent.

5. Population-sensitive strategies. This means linking sentencing guidelines to prison capacity. The Minnesota Sentencing Guidelines Commission uses feedback about prison capacity so that if one guideline sentence is increased, for example for robbery, another, perhaps for theft, has to be decreased. Moreover, when the prison population is over-capacity for 30 days the Governor can reduce the minimum sentence for each prisoner by up to 90 days. Altschuler (1991) is critical both of commissions and guidelines as substituting crime tariffs for a consideration of situational and offender characteristics. The use of commissions is given a limited degree of approval by Tonry (1991).

Finally, as Blumstein (1983) argues, the state must project demographic trends many years ahead. Together with an analysis of trends in specific crime rates, by sex, age, etc., this will provide information on the size of the prison population for up to twenty years ahead, allowing rational decisions to be taken about proposals with unavoidably long lead-times, such as building new facilities.

10.7. The prison: setting and problems

More than most social institutions, the prison is an enclosed world with its own structure and problems. While there is no shortage of assertion and of qualitative description, controlled observation and experiments aimed at providing quantitative information are much less in evidence.

The setting

Goffman (1968) sees prisons as examples of "total institutions," others being mental hospitals and prisoner-of-war camps. Such institutions are self-contained and largely or totally isolated from the rest of society. All activities of the inmates are carried out to an imposed schedule, under an imposed set of rules, in a single place and under a single authority, as part of an overall plan designed to fulfil the aims of the institution. In principle, these may be to rehabilitate the inmates but, in practice, they become subordinated to, and are taken over by, the requirement that the institution be run in a manner most convenient to those in charge.

Prisoners, in contrast to mental hospital patients, are far from passive. The prison is both a formal organization, set up and administered as a part of the criminal justice system, and an informal social system with a well defined code of behavior, policed by the prisoners themselves, which provides a setting for learning new skills and attitudes favorable to crime and for strengthening existing ones. The process of learning the rules set by the staff is termed *prisonization* (Clemmer 1940). A second process, *criminalization* (Erickson 1964, p. 15), refers to the impact of prisoners on each other:

"Such institutions gather . . . people into tightly segregated groups, give them an opportunity to teach each other the skills and attitudes of a deviant career, and often provoke them into employing these skills by reinforcing their sense of alienation from the rest of society."

The two processes are probably interrelated aspects of the broad training effects of prison life, rather than separate influences.

The relationship between length of stay in prison and acceptance of the norms of behavior set by the prison staff tends to be U-shaped: higher early in the sentence and before release than in the middle

(Wheeler 1961). This holds true for some groups of prisoners more than for others (Garabedian 1963), and implies that prisoners are most hostile to staff-set norms in the middle of their sentences. It is also possible that some prisoners become more law-abiding, either through enforced association with particularly unpleasant fellow prisoners or the remedial effect of some prison officers. There seems to be no longitudinal study which has followed a group of prisoners through the period from entry to discharge, to test the above notions.

However, there is some indirect evidence that adaptation to the prisoner community and its norms increases the probability of re-offending after discharge. Bondesen (1969) found that knowledge of prison slang was positively correlated with reoffending in the five years following discharge from a training school for females. Thomas (1973), in an even more indirect study, found that the more letters and visits a prisoner had from friends and relatives, the more optimistic he was about "staying out of trouble."

Violence in prisons

Individual violent incidents are endemic to prisons, that is, they are part of everyday life. In contrast, prison riots and hostage-taking are relatively rare events (Davies 1982), although in the period 1950–1955 they occurred in American prisons and reformatories at the rate of approximately two per month. In April, 1990, a major riot wrecked Strangeways Prison in Manchester, England. The last of the rioters surrendered only after 20 days of defiance. But, for most inmates their experience of prison violence will come from relatively small-scale but frequent and unpleasant encounters between individuals.

In a two year period in Birmingham Prison, England (approximately 1,000 inmates) studied by Davies (1980), the disciplinary reports submitted by guards recorded over 200 violent incidents, of which about two-thirds were fights between inmates and one-third assaults by inmates on prison officers. The "dark figure" was also considerable: over the same period injury reports made out by a doctor after an injury or suspected injury to a prisoner numbered over 500, implying that many assaults on prisoners (whether by guards or by fellow prisoners) were never recorded by guards. Indeed, the two wings of the prison with the most fights had the fewest recorded infractions of discipline, indicating considerable under-reporting. American levels of prison violence seem even higher: Fuller, Orsagh, and Raber (1977) reported that nearly 80 per cent of prisoners in South Carolina were assaulted every year.

Crowding

Mullen and Smith (1982) point out that the recommended standard of the US Department of Justice is 60 square feet of floor space per inmate. In fact, in 1978, 46 per cent of inmates were housed in less space than this per person. In some states the proportion rose to two-thirds. Since then, as prison populations have expanded faster than additional space has become available, the problem has worsened.

Prisoner density levels beyond those recommended are positively correlated with increases in: disciplinary infractions; mortality rates of prisoners aged over 45; rates of psychiatric commitments and suicides of all ages; complaints of physical illness; and recidivism (Smith 1982). But, Smith also pointed out the difficulties and inconsistencies of research based mainly on inadequate institutional records.

Gaes and McGuire (1985), who studied nearly 20 federal prisons over a 33 months period, found crowding to be the best predictor of prison violence after controlling for a large number of other variables. However, the importance of the ethnic attitudes of prisoners for the crowding–violence link was shown by Leger (1988), who reported that racial antagonism appeared to have much more impact on inmate behavior than either the actual or perceived levels of crowding. Bonta (1986) reviewed evidence of the importance of such correlates of crowding as noise, temperature, and obtrusive surveillance, all liable to increase as space becomes more restricted.

So far as recidivism is concerned, Farrington and Nuttall (1980) found a strong negative relationship between crowding and recidivism (the worse the crowding, the more reoffending after prison) in an analysis of data from 19 English prisons. However, Farrington and Nuttall (1980) agree that these results may not be generalizable to the USA because of differences in the numbers of cells planned for multi-occupancy (rare in Britain, but not in the USA).

Gaes (1985) points to a number of issues which need to be tackled in future research into crowding: most research to date has been on smaller institutions – the adverse effects of crowding may be greater in the larger ones; there is a need for longitudinal studies which will follow up inmates from the point of entry and relate the objective and subjective aspects of crowding to a range of potential effects; social comparison processes (Festinger 1954) may be very important in the perception of crowding (people compare their own circumstances with those of people to whom they are physically close: when most are in single bunks those in double bunks feel worse off, even if the former are overcrowded by most standards). Finally, Gaes suggests that crowding may be more important as a moderator variable than as a direct predictor in its own right. That is, crowding exacerbates an already stressful environment, rather than being itself an independent stressor, except at very high levels. In line with this argument is the finding that it is only in extreme crowding (e.g., 16 square feet per person), that fights break out over normally trivial matters such as left-over food (Smith 1982).

The pains of imprisonment

This is the title of a book edited by Johnson and Toch (1982) which gathers together a great deal of the available descriptive information, from the experiences of special groups of prisoners, to suggestions for mitigating the pains.

In his foreword to the book, Dunn (1982) points out that correctional practices are accountable to certain fundamental principles, the most important of which is the Eighth Amendment proscription of "cruel and unusual punishment" and its evolving criteria of whether the punishment in question is (a) so barbarous as to shock the conscience, (b) grossly disproportionate to the offense, and (c) an unneccessary and wanton infliction of pain. "Cruel and unusual" is interpreted by the courts to mean both physically harmful conditions and the occurrence of serious consequences for mental health.

Johnson and Toch (1982) remind us that the Supreme Court intends prisons to be uncomfortable: "To the extent that (prison) conditions are restrictive and even harsh, they are part of the penalty that criminal offenders must pay for their offences against society . . ." The Constitution does not mandate comfortable prisons, and prisons . . . which house persons convicted of serious crimes cannot be free of discomfort" (Supreme Court 1981).

What is an appropriate level of discomfort? While few would countenance a rat-infested dungeon most would deem too soft "white-collar prisons with tennis courts." Johnson and Toch (1982) go on to argue that, whereas in the past prison administrators saw themselves as being in the punishment business, today their main purposes are to *store* prisoners – by providing food, housing, clothing and basic amenities. As constraints such as crowding become worse, ameliorating them becomes another aim.

The main early work on the pains of imprisonment is by Sykes (1966). He pointed to five basic deprivations: liberty, goods and services, heterosexual relations, autonomy, and personal security. Also, special groups face special problems as described below. In general, those who survive best do so by becoming tougher and more pugnacious; the rest are more susceptible to stresses and have even less control over their own lives than when they entered prison.

Special groups. Prison is as heterogeneous as the world outside.

1. Those in solitary confinement. Suedfeld, Ramirez,Deaton, and Baker-Brown (1982) draw inferences potentially relevant to prison from the autobiographical accounts of political prisoners and prisoners-of-war, as well as from research into isolation and sensory reduction carried out in special settings such as flotation chambers. But, all of these are very different from the regulated, formalized and relatively limited procedures for solitary confinement (SC) in modern American penitentiaries. There are also differences in the people concerned and in their prior experiences. Political prisoners are often from intellectual and economic elites with a high commitment to a cause. POW's include many well-educated and stable career officers. Volunteers for laboratory studies of isolation are typically well-adjusted students.

In contrast, prisoners are often poor and poorly educated and from minority groups, and are usually in SC for major infractions of prison rules. Suedfeld and colleagues own study is one of the few to gather data both pre and post solitary confinement (which lasted from 5 days to 42 months in 5 prisons in Canada and the USA). This is essential if the specific effects of SC are to be assessed. No consistent differences were found between SC and the rest of the prison experience. There was some tendency to negative moods, such as anxiety, depression and hostility, as the number of SC experiences increased, but most prisoners seemed to adjust in a few days.

Those on death row are in a very special form of SC. Johnson (1982) interviewed 35 of the 37 men then awaiting execution in Alabama. Major themes which emerged included powerlessness – the inability to stop abuse or violence by guards or to maintain contact with other prisoners or families. Not surprisingly "death anxiety" was also very evident, particularly for those who were white, younger, single, had no prior convictions for violence and were without previous prison experience.

2. Lifers and other long term prisoners. In contrast to other Western countries, long sentences are frequent in America. For example, in 1974, 50 per cent of those in state facilities had been sentenced to 10 years or more Flanagan 1980).

Flanagan (1982) notes that quantitative research (e.g., Bukstel and Kilmann 1980, see below) has found no effects of confinement peculiar to this group, but believes that they will come to light if the right measures are used. He predicts that key problem areas will include the loss/attenuation of outside relationships, the fear of losing control over their lives and the lack of structure and order in the prison environment.

3. The mentally disturbed. According to Gibbs (1982), 24–64 per cent of prisoners have a prior history of psychiatric disturbance. Many would once have been the responsibility of the mental hospitals before the move to deinstitutionalize the mentally ill (see Chapter 6). A random sample of 708 women admitted to Holloway Prison, London, was screened for psychiatric disorder (Turner and Tofler 1986). Of these, 195 had a history of self-injury and 125 had past episodes of mental illness. In addition, 99 depended on opiates and 89 took mood-enhancing drugs regularly. The numbers are sufficiently large to indicate the need for improved psychiatric facilities in prisons. Certainly, it seems safe to assert that prison life is hardly likely to improve the mental health status of those with a past history of mental disorder.

4. Women in prison. There is at least one major pain of prison life peculiar to women: those who gave birth shortly before admission, or who are separated from older children, experience great anxiety and guilt, centering around such question as "will my children know me" and "will they get adequate care?" (Fox 1982).

5. Adolescent prisoners. Bartollas (1982) gives an impressionistic account of the psychological problems faced by boys and girls in training schools, problems which are most severe for first admissions and those who are not street-wise. Difficulties start on entry when newcomers are sized up by peers and must tread a fine line between being strong enough not to be exploited but not so strong as to be a threat. This experience is a familiar one to anyone entering any new situation, but the next one, that of being homosexually assaulted, even gang raped, is not.

Newcomers also take on one of a number of social roles, from aggressive through to passive, the role adopted being determined by ethnicity, street sophistication, orimes before entry, and personality. Whites and those with a record of less serious crime tend to take more passive roles.

Reforms have removed previous practices such as drab institutional clothing and the checking of incoming mail for contraband. But some humiliations remain, including strip searches on return to the campus and running through showers. There is much emotional deprivation – both sexual and nonsexual – the most distress being experienced by those who are sexually victimized (see below), particularly if this becomes known in the adolescent's home community.

6. Ethnicity. According to L. Carroll (1982) most white prisoners find it harder to stand up to prison life than do blacks and other ethnic minorities (who are increasingly in the majority in prisons). Whites are three to four times more likely than blacks to be in protective custody (i.e., from other prisoners), which means spending up to 23 hours a day in one's cell. A study in South Carolina (Fuller et al. 1977) found that intraracial assaults were frequent, with 80 per cent involving black aggressors and white victims, as did two-thirds of sexual assaults.

In many prisons, staff are almost entirely white (although black recruitment is now improving) and white staff see black prisoners as more threatening than whites, subjecting them to closer surveillance and searches and placing them more frequently on disciplinary reports (Bowker 1982).

Victimizers and victims. Sykes (1966) reported that three-quarters of the prisoners he studied played predatory social roles: 10 per cent used violence (the "toughs" or "gorillas"); 30 per cent manipulated others (the "merchants") and 35 per cent occupied both roles. Bowker (1982) considered that this remained true nearly two decades later but that both security practices and prisoner norms hide the evidence of exploitation from public knowledge.

Victimization takes physical, psychological and economic forms (Bowker 1982). Physical violence includes assault, homosexual rape, even occasional homicide, and is assisted by inadequate staff supervision, architectural designs featuring many blank areas, the availability of deadly weapons, and housing the violence-prone with the relatively defenseless. Successful assaults reduce the likelihood of future attacks by others as well bringing economic gain – money, goods, cigarettes –

and social benefits such as access to willing sexual partners and membership in higher status prison groups.

Rape, which includes all forms of enforced sexual acts, is not unknown in women's prisons, but is much more common in male institutions. Rape victims tend to be white, small, young, middle-class (at least not ghetto residents) and disproportionately convicted of child molestation or minor property crimes. Cotton and Groth (1982) point out that the trauma experienced by a male inmate victim of rape may be even more severe than that experienced by a female victim in the outside world: he has to go on living in the same institution as his attacker. They regard as very conservative the results of a survey by Lockwood (1980) which indicated that 28 per cent of the inmate population in two New York correctional institutions had been sexually victimized (from harassment to actual rape).

Bowker (1982) considers psychological victimization to be more common and to take rather subtle forms. Victims are deprived of goods or give sexual favors by being fed rumors about outside relatives or friends. Thus preoccupied, they leave cell doors unopened, or move carelessly through the institution.

Economic victimization includes loan sharking, gambling frauds, fixed and high prices, theft and robbery, and protection rackets as well as fraud (e.g., marijuana that is actually half tobacco).

Quantitative research. A review of 90 studies of the effects of imprisonment on performance, personality and attitudinal variables (Bukstel and Kilmann 1980) produced much more meager results than the qualitative material reviewed so far, as types of institutions and periods of imprisonment varied so widely. Their major conclusions follow:

1. Individuals differ widely in their responses to prolonged confinement: some deteriorate in psychological functioning, others actually improve, particularly "inadequate, passive, and dependent" inmates, and many are unchanged, so that they could not conclude unequivocally that confinement was harmful to most individuals.

2. Those who experience some type of acute psychotic episode in prison are likely to function at a lower level of efficiency, even following psychiatric intervention. (This is probably true for the population in general, but may be more so for prisoners.)

3. Punitive and custodially oriented institutions seem to have more negative effects than those with a more rehabilitative orientation.

Accounts of prisoner experiences in actual prisons were discussed above. While they concern real life events they lack experimental rigor. In contrast is a well-known study by Haney, Banks, and Zimbardo (1973), which set up a simulated prison in the cellars of the Psychology Department of Stanford University for an intended period of two weeks. From 75 undergraduate volunteers, 24, all white and middle class, were selected as being the most stable and mature and were then randomly assigned to serve as either guards or prisoners.

To increase realism the "prisoners" were arrested at their homes by genuine policemen, who informed them of their rights and then fingerprinted, searched, stripped and photographed them. They were placed in their cells, and given work assignments. Each of three cells was occupied by three prisoners for 24 hours each day. The prisoners were clothed only in a smock (no underclothing) and a nylon cap. Guards were issued with uniforms and batons and were told to maintain order, but without the use of force.

The experiment was stopped after six days because of the growing distress of the prisoners. During this period all guards arrived for work on time; some worked overtime without extra pay. The behavior of the guards varied from "tough but fair" to "cruel." Analysis of videotape records showed that most of the behaviors of guards towards prisoners were negative, including threats, physical aggression and insults. Ninety per cent of the conversation of both prisoners and guards (recorded on audiotape) consisted of prison topics, with mainly negative self-statements by both groups.

The authors major conclusions were that the setting transformed "rather easily, ordinary American students into cruel guards and passive, self-deprecating prisoners," and that the effects observed would appear even more dramatically in real-life prisons.

Can these results be generalized to actual penal institutions, or are they, as Banuazizi and Mohavedi (1975) claim, interpretable as the subject's response to the demand characteristics of the situation? That is, did they realize what was required of them, and then supply it, acting out their stereotypic images of guards and, to a lesser extent, of prisoners? To test this explanation they gave questionnaires to their own students, together with a description of the situation. Most participants correctly interpreted the aims of the experiment and predicted the guards' behaviors. In addition, Feldman (1977) pointed to several features which distinguish the simulated prison from real-life institutions: there was no inmate culture to provide the study prisoners with social support and they had no prior experience of such situations; real prison guards are trained, operate within an explicit set of rules and are accountable to their seniors; while there is much boredom in real prisons, some planned activities are provided and although prison uniform is far from smart, neither is it as bizarre as that worn in the simulation study.

Nevertheless, something remains. We need studies of real prisons which use the full apparatus of observation and recording of continuing behaviors deployed in the Haney et al. (1973) study, from self-reports of mood to video and audio tapes. In contrast, the reports we have, while ringing true, fall woefully short of the level of technical excellence achieved in the simulated prison.

Easing the pain: self-help. In general, the conclusion from the quantitative studies is that the measures used have not detected widespread psychological deterioration due to imprisonment. It may be that quantitative observations and detailed self-report, and the longitudinal method, rather than questionnaires used on cross-sections of prisoners, would produce a picture closer to the descriptions set out earlier. It is possible that the pains are real enough, but are experienced fully only by a proportion of prisoners, perhaps a minority. (Whites lacking in both street skills and physical "presence" and serving their first term in a penal institution seem the most vulnerable.) Cohen and Taylor's (1972) suggestion that many prisoners actively resist the damaging effects of prison life, so mitigating their deleterious effects, is supported by a number of reports.

Bartolas (1982) considers the most popular method of coping in institutions for juveniles to be minor conformity so as to gain more food and privileges. A smaller group "stay cool" simply "doing time" and conforming neither to staff nor peer pressures. Next comes rebellion – confronting staff in every possible way – then withdrawal, meaning running away or even suicide (usually whites who have occupied victIm roles). The least popular coping method is to adopt genuinely pro-social attitudes and prepare for a future of crime-avoidance.

Staff bias apart, for white and black prisoners, both adult and juvenile, the situation in prison largely reverses that found outside: blacks are in the superior position, and their sense of relative security is helped further by nationalist (i.e., African-American) solidarity and the continuity in prison of well-established street gangs (see Chapter 8). Thus, blacks are more resilient than whites in coping with prison, with much lower levels of psychological distress and suicide attempts (e.g., Jones 1976).

In their study of long-stay British prisoners, Cohen and Taylor (1972) found much emphasis on hobbies, such as body-building, and on "campaigning" (one prisoner wrote 545 letters to the press in 10 years, all of which had to be smuggled out). And a sense of control (as opposed to being controlled) was found by Layton-McKenzie, Goodstein, and Blovin (1987) to be related to inmate adjustment to prison life and routines.

Easing the pain: staff actions. According to Conrad (1982), four of Sykes' (1966) five deprivations are now less severe – prisoners are less isolated, poor, celibate, and restricted in initiative. But in other ways prison life is worse, particularly a sharp increase in violence, and Sykes' two essentials for a "decent prison" remain true: safety (sufficient staff and strict enforcement of rules); and lawful industriousness (the opportunity for a full day's work at a job worth doing and paid accordingly). Within the general rubric of safety, Hagel-Seymour (1982) argues that the elderly and the handicapped are sub-groups which need special "sanctuaries" (the majority of prisoners are young and vigorous).

The history and execution of a design for a model prison by Morris (1975) are reviewed by Levinson (1982). Morris emphasized a graduated release plan and a humane and secure environment. His design was put into effect at Butner Federal Prison (N. Carolina). Levinson concluded that while there was no reduction in the number or severity of disciplinary reports there were no escapes or killings and few severe assaults. A small unit set up within Barlinnie Prison in Glasgow, Scotland, houses prisoners with a particularly severe history of violence in other prisons. Several reports (e.g., Cooke 1989) have indicated a very marked reduction of violent incidents in response to a regime which emphasizes prisoner involvement in decision-making and a specially trained staff.

Bowker (1982) lists the following as the most promising methods of staff-side intervention: minor structural modifications so as to reduce the area of the prison not constantly on view to staff members; classifying inmates by victimization potential and removing the weak from the strong; breaking up large prisons into smaller and more manageable units; and reducing the length of sentences.

Let the last word be with the Dutch (The Netherlands has remained largely true to a long standing emphasis on rehabilitation as opposed to punishment): "We try to keep people whole, no worse at least than when they arrive." (J. Poelman, Deputy Governor at Schlutterswei Prison, Alkmaar, Holland (cited by *The Economist*, 1988a).

10.8. Prediction

It is often argued that if future offenders could be picked out at an early age there would be no need to expose them to the possibly damaging effects of the penal system, because it should be possible to "correct" them, as it were, in advance. Evidence concerning this is considered below, together with research on one other major purpose for which prediction techniques have been used, that of "dangerousness" or repeated violent behavior. There are major ethical questions surrounding the use of prediction techniques which will also be discussed.

A technical note

In all cases a full assessment of the accuracy of the prediction technique under test requires both that no attempt at intervention is made (events should be allowed to take their natural course) and that police surveillance is no greater than it otherwise would have been. These apparently modest rules are breached far more often than they are observed.

The accuracy of a technique always has to be compared with a *base-rate*. For example, if 70 per cent of a group of offenders is found to be reconvicted, by chance alone *any* predictor will be correct in 70 per cent of cases if the prediction is always "he will be reconvicted." To be of value, a particular technique has to be correct significantly more often than seven times out of ten. And "significance" here should mean a substantive (is it such as to make a practical difference to the operation of the criminal justice system?) and not merely statistical, significance. The higher the known reconviction rate, the more difficult it is for a technique to be significantly more accurate than chance alone. We have to consider two types of incorrect prediction: false positives and false negatives, both defined earlier in this chapter. It is usual that a number of variables predict more accurately than any one of them alone, so that they are combined by an appropriate statistical technique to form a joint predictor.

Predicting future offenders

The best known early attempt was carried out over several decades by Sheldon and Eleanor Glueck. In their 1964 paper they overviewed their work to date, citing three major predictive factors available at ages 5 and 6: family cohesiveness; supervision by the mother; and discipline by the mother. They claimed that 96.4 per cent of the children they identified in 1952 as being of low delinquency potential had not become offenders. In contrast, 85 per cent of those identified as high in delinquency potential had subsequently offended. However, Michael and Coltharp (1962) reported that the predictive scale developed by the Glueck's failed to discriminate accurately using a different sample, and Voss (1963) challenged the applicability of the scale to a population consisting largely of medium-risk children. Rose (1967) reviewed a large number of prediction methods, including that of the Gluecks. He found that all of them predicted least well in the most numerous medium-risk range and also pointed out that children identified as being at "high risk" are likely to be of lower SES and, hence, under greater police surveillance. Conversely, "low-risk" children tend to be of higher SES and less under surveillance. Thus, offending by the former is more likely to be detected. It is, of course, detection and not offending, which typically is used as the test of a prediction method. Apparent confirmation that a prediction technique is relatively successful both with the better-off and with poorer children may be no more than a self-confirming prophecy.

The poossibility of predicting future offenders was revived in the 1980's. Blumstein, Farrington, and Moitra (1985) studied delinquency careers over lengthy periods, using data from the Cambridge and Philadelphia studies, as well as from two other well-conducted longitudinal studies of young males (Shannon 1981) and Polk et al. (1981). In all cases, they were able to separate out three separate sub-groups: innocents (those never involved with law enforcement agencies; desisters (a relatively low probability of a long-term criminal career), and persisters (a relatively high probability).

Blumstein et al. (1985) found that seven variables identified the persisters in the Cambridge Study population: a first conviction between the ages of 10 and 13; an older sibling first convicted by the age of 13; having been rated "troublesome" by teachers between the ages of 8 and 10; poor school attainment by age 10; psychomotor clumsiness; a low verbal IQ between the ages of 8 and 10; and a social handicap such as a low family income. A simple statistical technique developed by Burgess (1928) was applied whereby the presence of a variable led to a score of 1; its absence to one of 0, giving a maximum possible score of seven.

Fifteen out of 23 "chronic" offenders (defined as 6 or more convictions) had a score of 4 or more, as compared with 22 of 109 "nonchronics" (between 1 and 5 convictions) and 18 out of 265 with no convictions, all by the age of 25. These results seem impressive, particularly as they concern predictors which are all available at 13 or earlier. But, further analysis shows that out of 55 boys with a score of four or more (15+22+18) *only 15* became chronic offenders, and the rest are false positives. Of the remaining 40, 22 desisted early and 18 remained "innocent" so that the majority did *not* turn out to be chronics as predicted. Farrington (1987a) acknowledges that much additional data would be needed to reach more acceptable levels of predictive accuracy, and suggests such early available information as parental child-rearing methods and having parents and friends with criminal records.

An example of the use of family information for predicting offending is provided by Loeber, Dishion, and Patterson (1984). They based their "multiple gating procedure" on both the need for economy of cost, and a combination of the best known predictors concerning conduct problems noted by parents and teachers and information on child-rearing practices. At the first gate, teachers rated seventh and tenth grade boys to produce a high-risk group which formed the basis for the next gate – a series of five telephone calls to the mothers of the group concerning their child's behavior problems in the past 24 hours, together with her knowledge of the boy's whereabouts and information about the family. This produced a smaller at-risk group which was then followed up by means of court records over the next three years. A further report (Loeber and Dishion 1988) noted that the procedure correctly identified 80 per cent of multiple offenders (those with 3 or more police contacts) and that their multiple-gating procedure was 58 per cent less expensive than a single-stage screening procedure. However, 67 per cent of those thought to be at risk did not incur a police record (the usual high proportion for false positives).

The results of these two studies sound an important note of caution. For example, suppose that on the basis of the Blumstein et al. (1985) study, we set up a training group for future "chronic" offenders on the basis of a prediction score of four or more at 13. Mixing the many false positives, who would inevitably result, with true positives might actually worsen the chances of the former of keeping out of prison in adult life (and training programs have a generally poor record of success in any event, see Chapter 11 for evidence on both points).

Finally, it should be noted that there is a considerable time-lag between the collection of prospective data, for example, those from the Cambridge Study and the events to which they are designed to predict, such as a persisting criminal career. Nevertheless, this is to be preferred to retrospective data, exemplified by those collected by the Gluecks as well as by the authors of two more recent studies: Clarke (1975) and Chaiken and Chaiken (1984).

Ethical arguments. At some future point the accuracy of predictive procedures for future offenders may improve to a level at which practical implementation becomes an important issue. Silber (1974) has set out both positive and negative arguments for this from the point of view of civil rights.

In favor of detecting the "delinquency prone" in advance:

1. It enables informal, civil, nonadversary proceedings to replace the formal, adversary nature of a criminal trial.
2. It substitutes an indefinite sentence, during which treatment is given, for a definite sentence without treatment.
3. Treatment would emphasize forming positive and supportive human relationships, and thus provide valuable social training as well as avoiding future damage to the potential offender. (As indicated above, this is doubtful.)

The arguments against are also set out by Silber (1974):

1. Infomal civil proceedings jeopardize a person's legal rights to counsel, to time to prepare a defense, to a specified judgement, and so on.
2. Civil commitment for an indefinite period is a judgement against the person, not against the act, and is a step towards a totalitarian society.
3. Once a person is committed for "treatment," normal civil liberties tend to be lost.

Walker (1971) adds a further argument against identifying future offenders: predictions may become self-confirming prophecies, for example, through increased police surveillance of "bad risks" (and decreased or absent surveillance of "good risks").

To a considerable extent the powerful objections to treating predicted offenders are mitigated by programs aimed at predisposing factors, rather than at individuals. An example is the family training approach of the Patterson and Alexander groups, introduced in Chapter 7, in which the intended benefit is to the family and its members as well to society in general. Chapter 11 discusses the efficacy of family-training methods in preventing future offending by those growing up in "at risk" families.

Predicting dangerousness

While terms like "chronic," "predatory," and "high rate" typically refer to a mixture of property and personal offences, "dangerousness" means, unequivocally, the latter. As defined by the (British) Butler Committee (DHSS and Home Office, 1975, para 4.10) dangerousness is: "the propensity to cause serious physical injury or lasting psychological harm." The critical question concerns the term "propensity:" can we, in fact, predict which individuals are likely to carry out repeated acts of violence? Even if we can do so with a high degree of accuracy, does society have the right to restrain the *potentially* dangerous?

Monahan (1984) points out that the first generation of research on the prediction of violent behavior (conducted in the early 1970's) seemed to show that psychologists and psychiatrists were vastly overrated as predictors of violence. There was a high frequency of false positive errors, inherent in the prediction of any infrequent event, and a smaller proportion of false negatives. The former leads to the wrongful detention of many in facilities for the mentally abnormal offender, the latter to great public concern when a person released as "no longer dangerous" carries out a further violent act or acts causing serious injury or death. The proponents of more and of less involuntary commitment responded differently to the findings. The former urged even greater caution in discharge policy. The response of the latter is exemplified by the conclusion of the American Civil Liberties Union: "It now seems beyond dispute that mental health professionals have *no* expertise in predicting future dangerous behavior either to self or others. In fact, predictions of dangerous behavior are wrong about 95 per cent of the time" (Ennis and Emery 1978, cited by Monahan 1984, p. 10).

Monahan suggests that both responses were overreactions and that "second-generation" thinking is more modest in both directions: "Little is known about how accurately violent behavior can be predicted in many circumstances, but it may be possible to predict it accurately enough to be useful in some policy decisions" (Monahan 1984, p. 11).

But we still need to know how to separate the policy decisions in which prediction is "accurate enough" from those in which it is not. An example of research which might in time reduce the dilemmas of decision-makers concerning the discharge, or continued confinement, of those with a serious past record of violence, is provided by Laws (1982). He describes the assessment by the penile plethysmograph of very violent sex offenders and concludes that erection measures may be an accurate predictor of the future risk of violent behavior in specifiable circumstances. Continued high sexual arousal in response to deviant stimuli (e.g., tape recordings of sadistic behaviors) which evoke no such arousal in nonviolent sex offenders or nonoffender controls means that detention should continue, as should attempts at treatment.

Ethical issues. Monahan (1984, p. 15) gives strong support to attempts by psychologists and psychiatrists to improve the accuracy of prediction of dangerousness:

> "We are talking of murder, rape robbery, assault, and other forms of violent behavior . . . when we lend professional assistance, however marginal, to improve society's control over those who will murder, rape, rob, and assault – provided that we do not let the nature of that assistance be overstated or distorted – we have nothing for which to apologize."

Morris and Miller (1985) take matters a step further by setting out some firm principles for the prediction of dangerousness under the criminal law:

1. "Punishment should not be imposed, nor a term of punishment extended, by virtue of a prediction of dangerousness, beyond that which would be justified as deserved" (p. 35).

2. "Providing that the previous limitation is respected, predictions of dangerousness may properly influence sentencing decisions and other decisions within the criminal law"(p. 36).

3. "The base expectancy rate [b.e.r.] of violence for a criminal predicted as dangerous must be shown by reliable evidence to be substantially higher than the b.e.r. of another criminal with a closely similar criminal record, but not predicted as unusually dangerous, before the greater dangerousness of the former may be relied upon to intensify or extend his punishment" (p. 37).

At first sight these are very stringent requirements – depending on the meaning of "substantially higher." Morris and Miller (1985) go on to agree that the prediction of future dangerousness of institutionalized offenders is accurate in only about one-third of cases and that the figure of one-third is a group average, so that the proportion of false positives will be very large. Nevertheless, they conclude by asserting very strongly the need for caution, even if this infringes every sharply on the liberties of many who could be freed. They give the analogy of an unexploded bomb, which is always treated as if it would explode. In the same way, the person assessed as dangerous should be treated as if he would do further violence if given the opportunity.

Walker (1983) agrees that it is wrong to go to the other extreme and *release* all three persons at risk of further major violence simply because it is difficult to predict which one of the three is the true positive. Instead he sets out five rules, to help us decide when to detain for the protection of others for longer than normal periods and when not to do so, which are more systematic and specific than those put forward by Morris and Miller (1985):

1. What sort of criminal harm should be covered? Virtually all property offenses as well as temporary harm (such as the use of an imitation or unloaded weapon) should be excluded; lasting psychological harm and disabling or disfiguring physical injury are included.

2. There should be good reason to believe that the actions covered by rule 1 were not isolated and "out of character," but had occurred on two or more occasions, separated by substantial periods of time.

3. Has there been a major change in the circumstances which gave the offender his incentive and his means of attack? For example, is the enemy concerned now dead or is the offender now so infirm as to be unlikely to repeat his behavior?

4. Is there are any less dramatic means of protecting others than detention, which seems reasonably likely to be as effective? Strict supervision might offer such a possibility (particularly when electronic-tagging is available), so might excluding the person from certain jobs such as those involving responsibility for children (in the case of child assaulters). The problem in both examples is that of enforcement over a large country such as the USA.

5. If a person is to be detained solely for the safety of others his detention should be made as tolerable as possible, indeed its conditions should be no worse, other than the deprivation of liberty, "than those which a law-abiding wage-earner would enjoy outside" (Walker

1983, p. 32). Walker agrees that this is an idealistic standard to set, but is firm on the principle.

10.9. Concluding comment

This chapter, above all, has made it clear how difficult it is to keep scientific issues separate from those of public policy and social morality. They intertwine with particular force in such topics as the death penalty and the prediction of future offending and of dangerousness. It is neither possible nor desirable for the scientist to stay aloof from such controversies, and he will inevitably have his own moral/ideological standpoint – which means that the more controversial the issue, the more rigorous should be his professional approach. Criminological research is more fraught with difficulties than, for example, the laboratory study of perceptual illusions; it demands even more scientific skill, not the other way around, as is too often the case in practice.

11. The treatment of offenders

> "I've been in the soup pretty often . . . Someone always turns up and says, 'I can't see a . . . man down and out. Let me put you back on your feet again'. I should think", said Grimes, I've been put back on my feet more often than any living man."
>
> Evelyn Waugh, *Decline and Fall*, p. 30, 1928

11.1. Introduction

In both North America and Britain, official policy toward rehabilitating (or "treating") offenders, particularly those under 18, rather than punishing or merely containing them, has swung back and forth in the past 25 years. The custodial or punitive approach, which dominated until the middle 60's, was succeeded by a more treatment-oriented model, and after about a decade or so, by a return to the original emphasis, under the impact of rising crime figures and a sense that the therapeutic approach had largely failed. At the same time there has been a continued move towards deinstitutionalization, particularly for juveniles, and an attempt to treat offenders in the community, rather than in settings remote from the real world. The combined effect of these trends has been that the major treatment projects belong to the 60's and 70's rather than the 80's, together with a continuing shift from large scale programs in institutions to less ambitious efforts in community settings.

Two other trends can be discerned within the published literature on the treatment of offenders: a sharp decline in broadly psychodynamic approaches and a concomitant increase in behavioral emphases; and parallel with this a distinct improvement in the methodological quality of the reported research – although there is still a long way to go before the level of the clinical treatment literature is reached. Finally, the overwhelming majority of treatment programs have concerned juvenile offenders or pre-offenders. Work with adults has concentrated mainly on sex-offenders.

This chapter covers the results of psychodynamic, behavioral and other attempts to prevent the development of offending in those thought to be at risk, and to intervene with those who have already established a court record. It begins with an account of major reviews of the outcome literature, before surveying individual methods and results. A final section discusses policy issues in the implementation of treatment programs and in research into their efficacy.

11.2. General reviews

In considering the question of whether anything works in reducing repeated offending, Martinson (1974) answered "nothing." Subsequent reviews have not been as nihilistic, but none has achieved more than mild optimism.

Blackburn (1980) surveyed 18 journals, yielding 40 reports of psychological programs with offenders, published between 1973 and 1978, which met minimal criteria of a clear description of procedures and presentation of results in quantitative form. The majority concerned behavioral methods, a considerable change from the mainly psychodynamic emphasis of earlier decades (see Logan 1972). About half the reports concerned behaviors directly relevant to the needs of the institution (hygiene, chores, etc.), one-third skills relevant to the program participants (academic, vocational, social, and so on), one-quarter covert processes such as subjective feelings and attitudes, and only three made direct attempts to change the illegal behaviors which had resulted in convictions. No more than half of the reports quantified the effect of the treatment concerned on reoffending, of which only five noted a statistically significant improvement for the treated group over an untreated control group. Nevertheless, Blackburn (1980) concludes that his survey provides modest encouragement to psychologists working with offenders.

A much larger survey by Garrett (1985) is bleaker in its conclusion. She carried out a meta-analysis of 111 studies, in both institutional and community settings, reported in the literature between 1960 and 1983, which concerned convicted offenders under 21 and used some form of controlled procedure. In all, 13,000 participants were involved, mainly in behavioral or psychodynamic programs, although 15 per cent of reports concerned "life skills," such as "wilderness programs." Garrett divided the 111 studies into those which were "more rigorous" (60 per cent) versus those which were "less rigorous" (40 per cent), and found that the size of treatment effects varied with rigor, being greater for the latter. In the more rigorous segment there was no statistically significant difference in outcome (reoffending during the follow-up period) between treated and untreated clients over all treatments combined. However, behavior therapy was very slightly superior to psychodynamic therapy. For both academic skills and institutional adjustment, behavior therapy was markedly superior, as were life skills programs.

Another meta-analysis, by Gottschalk, Davidson, Gensheimer, and Mayer (1987), concentrated solely on community based interventions, between 1967 and 1983, and concerned 163 reports of 90 studies, involving 11,000 participants. Once again there was, at best, only a small overall effect of treatment as compared with no treatment, and the authors note that they did not separate the reports according to rigor. However, they make two important points which will be returned to in the last section of this chapter: most of the treatments were of short duration, both in intensity and in length, so that they may simply not have been powerful enough to achieve their intended effects; there was doubt as to whether many were implemented in the manner intended by their designers.

11.3. Methods: psychotherapeutic and allied approaches

These include many variations, from simple reassurance to a full-scale Freudian psychoanalysis, lasting several hundred hours (rarely reported in the criminological context) in which therapists have sought shorter methods which would still embody the major therapeutic principles of psychoanalysis; see Chapter 6 for an account of these. The best known of the other schools of psychotherapy is that of Carl Rogers, termed *client-centered* therapy. The therapist seeks to be active but non-directive (unlike the psychodynamic approach), and the aim is to allow the client to resolve his own problems by the use of the "healthy" part of his personality.

Prevention

The most ambitious attempt is still the earliest reported, the Cambridge-Somerville Youth Study, carried out between 1937 and 1945 (Teuber and Powers 1953). Several hundred pre-adolescent boys, judged likely to become offenders, were matched in pairs and randomly assigned either to counselors free to adopt a psychoanalytic or a Rogerian approach, or to a no-treatment control group. The treatment lasted between two and eight years (weekly sessions). At follow-up in 1948 the groups were virtually identical on several indices of offending. Even more striking is the result of a 30 year follow-up of the study participants (McCord 1978). In 1975 and 1976, 90 per cent were contacted and assessed by court records and questionnaires, the return rate being approximately the same for the treatment and comparison groups. No differences were found between the groups, or between the two versions of psychotherapy, for criminal records, whether as adults or juveniles, or for serious or for minor crimes. McCord concluded that the program had no preventive effect on crime, and there were some unexpected and negative side effects: compared with the control group, treatment group members had more alcohol-related problems, more serious mental illnesses, more stress-related diseases and even died younger. In addition, the treated group were more likely to have low-prestige occupations providing less job-satisfaction.

A subsequent study by Denno and McClelland (1986) comes to the same conclusion: psychotherapy has no preventive effect on crime. They carried out a longitudinal evaluation of the Philadelphia Youth Services Centers counseling programme for youngsters thought to be on the edge of offending. Using self-reported offenses as the outcome criterion (a rarity in this field), they found no long-term difference between experimental and control groups in either delinquent or prosocial (positive) behaviors.

Intervention: institutions

Logan (1972) reviewed more than 100 outcome studies of the treatment of convicted young offenders, most involving some form of psychotherapy, and were conducted in institutional settings. He evaluated their scientific acceptability against 10 criteria, including repeatability of method, and the use of appropriate comparison groups and of conventional outcome criteria such as reconviction rates. Not one study met all 10 criteria. Since then several reviews of studies evaluating various forms of psychotherapy in institutional settings have concluded that there is no evidence for its effectiveness (e.g., Feldman 1977, Romig 1978, Quay 1987c). These reviews make two additional important points which will be expanded on below in a discussion of problems affecting all types of treatment of offenders: there are few volunteers for therapy among inmates, and staff behavior is often problematic, reinforcing inappropriate behavior by inmates and focusing on non-therapeutic tasks, so that much can go wrong between a plan and its execution.

Psychotherapy has not been used as much in the treatment of adult offenders, but a number of in-patient psychiatric units have been set up in Britain, the best known of which is Grendon Underwood, established in the late 1960's as a full-scale psychiatric prison. Prisoners are transferred to it from other prisons and are not admitted directly from the courts. It has as many staff as inmates (about 150 of each) and is organized as a "therapeutic community," the emphasis being on staff–prisoner and prisoner–prisoner relationships. All inmates meet daily in groups, each of which has a therapist. The prisoners' rooms are well heated and adequately furnished, with views over the countryside (Parker 1970).

After a two year follow up, Gunn, Robertson, Dell, and Way (1978) found a reconviction rate of 70 per cent among a sample of about 100 men who had been treated in Grendon, compared with 62 per cent of a random sample of British prisoners. However, the authors reject this comparison group as inappropriate, because the Grendon inmates had been selected for treatment, and wished to receive it. They assert that the objective of Grendon is treatment for psychological problems, not the reduction of recidivism, and that interview and MMPI data attest to the success of the former. They agree that if the aim is to assess the efficacy of Grendon in reducing reconviction then random allocation to Grendon and a control regime is the method of choice, but that this is impossible on both practical and ethical grounds. There is general agreement (e.g., Smith 1984) that both Grendon and another therapeutically oriented British unit, Barlinnie, have much lower rates of violence than similar prisons with more custodial emphases, but this is also a separate issue from that of reconviction rates.

Intervention: nonresidential settings

Once again, the results of psychotherapy are no better than those of control conditions. Extensive casework with 970 inner-city convicted young offenders as part of the Chicago Youth Development Project, compared with 570 who received no treatment, resulted in no differences in either reconviction rates, or in unemployment (Gold and Mattick 1974). Adams and Vetter (1981) used a commendably long follow-up of 10 years and found reconviction rates to be higher in a group of young offenders treated by psychodrama (in effect "acting-out" antisocial impulses) than in an untreated comparison group.

Concluding comment

It should be no surprise that psychodynamically oriented treatments of offenders have a uniform record of failure in both institutional and community settings and with both pre- and convicted offenders. There is clear evidence in controlled trials, (reviewed by Rachman and Wilson, 1980) of the lack of success of the psychotherapies with individuals who have sought help voluntarily for a range of neurotic and personality problems. We should not expect a better performance with offenders.

11.4. Methods: the behavior therapies

Introduction

The psychology of learning has been the major source of the behavior therapy approach (also termed behavior modification) to the treatment of psychological problems, but other areas of experimental psychology, particularly cognitive and social psychology, are making increasing contributions. The aim is to modify the current, behavioral problems of the individual, couple or group. A conservative view of the relatively short history of the behavior therapies (the major developments started only in the 1950s) is that their therapeutic efficacy is encouraging, particularly for phobias, anxiety problems, obsessions and sexual difficulties. An excellent high-level overview of the approach is provided by Bellack, Hersen, and Kazdin (1982).

Prevention

"Scared straight." This is a very dramatic and highly publicized approach which, though not formally behavioral, is appropriately placed here because it can be considered as an intended instance of negative modeling.

In September, 1976, the Lifers Group at New Jersey Rahway State Prison had a rap session with a group of juveniles which evolved into a program of "group intimidation more akin to shock therapy" (Homant and Osowski 1982). In April, 1978, a Los Angeles TV station filmed the documentary "Scared Straight," which was shown throughout the United States and won Emmy and Oscar awards for best documentary film. According to Homant and Osowski (1982), by that year there had been at least 28 imitation programs in the United States and Canada, with some claiming up to 90 per cent rates of success, but that careful studies were rare. In their own research in Michigan, they randomly assigned to "treatment" and control groups boys who had been referred by the juvenile courts and had individually agreed to participate. At six months follow-up, those in the JOLT (Juvenile Offenders Learn the Truth) group exposed to a confrontation session ("if you don't change you'll be in this hole permanently") were compared for police arrests with a control group: 31 per cent of the JOLT group and 29 per cent of the controls had been arrested. An even worse result was reported by Finkenaur (1982), who found that juveniles "scared straight" were more likely than controls to commit subsequent and more serious offenses.

Achievement Place. The next set of preventive approaches is less dramatic but much more carefully based. The Achievement Place program of Phillips (1968) and his associates has resulted in copies of their method in many parts of the USA. Essentially, boys between 12 and 14 who have been convicted for minor offenses and are regarded by the county court as being at risk of carrying out more serious ones, live in small groups, "as in a family" with a pair of experienced "house parents." The boys undergo a complex program based on token economy principles (Ayllon and Azrin 1968). This is a system of reinforcers, typically poker chips, applicable to nearly all behaviors, which can be distributed or removed readily in response to desired or undesired behaviors, and has been used in a very wide range of settings. There is also partial self-government, and much attention is given to skills and achievements relevant to the outside world.

Achievement Place has substantial benefits in terms of educational and social skills (Braukmann, Fixsen, Phillips, and Wolf 1975, Weinrott, Jones, and Howard 1982), but what of legally related indices? An early report was optimistic. Two years after release, the reconviction rate of a group of Achievement Place boys was only 19 per cent as against over

50 per cent of those placed on probation or committed to a conventional institution (Fixsen et al. 1972). But, as the authors point out, the boys were not randomly assigned to treatments, so that the result may have been due either to a "population effect" or to a "treatment effect" Three subsequent, large scale, studies agree in their conclusion: what is now termed the TFM (teaching family model) is not superior to comparison group home programs for recorded offenses during follow-up periods of up to three years (Jones 1978, Kirigin, Braukman, Attwater, and Wolf 1982, Weinrott et al. 1982). The last named report also considered the TFM model to be expensive relative to alternative programs, a point of great importance to those who fund facilities for offenders.

Family-based programs. According to Patterson (1986, see Chapter 7) the problems of social behavior which lead eventually to delinquency first arise in the ways parents and children interact with each other. The clear implication is a need to train many parents in effective child-management skills before their children reach the age at which they are at risk of becoming offenders. Essentially this is an example of the triadic approach advocated by Tharp and Wetzel (1969) for work in the natural environment. (The behavior therapist trains and monitors professionals or parents who then work directly with the offender or pre-offender.)

O'Dell (1974) set out the advantages of behavior modification programs with families as follows:

1. Programs can be carried out by previously unskilled nonprofessionals.
2. Many people can be trained at any one time, and relatively short training periods suffice, although Alexander, Barton, Schiavo, and Parsons (1976) tend to contradict this.
3. A minimum of professional staff is required (hence costs are relatively low).
4. Many parents like the behavioral treatment model because it does not assume "sick" behavior.
5. Many childhood problems consist of well-defined acts appropriate to a behavioral approach.

However, in a very influential book on behavioral work in the natural environment, Tharp and Wetzel (1969) suggest caution, pointing out that many parents raise objections. These include a belief that rewarding children for desired behavior is bribery, as they should be intrinsically "good." Some parents prefer punishment to positive rewards on the basis of "spare the rod, spoil the child." Others want to treat all family members equally, and see differential reinforcement as discriminatory. Still others become so angry with their children that they are unable to maintain the self-control necessary for behavior modification techniques. Finally, carrying out a systematic program requires a harmonious relationship between the partners, exactly as in other areas of behavior modification in which family relationships are the focus of treatment (e.g., McGovern, Stewart, and LoPiccolo 1975).

Both sets of arguments are well illustrated by reports of work in this area, the two most active and influential research groups being those led by Patterson and Alexander. For examples of their treatment programs and results, see, respectively, Patterson and Fleischman (1979), Patterson, Chamberlain, and Reid (1982), Alexander and Parsons (1973), Alexander et al. (1976), and Klein, Alexander, Parsons (1977). Detailed reviews are provided by Gordon and Arbuthnot (1987) and by Kazdin (1987).

The Patterson group has focused on parent training programs in general; Alexander and colleagues have in addition emphasized the relationship between therapists and client families – the "nonspecific" factors which have often been neglected in behavior therapy work.

The main findings of these two groups are as follows:

1. The patterns of interactions in families with delinquent children differ from comparison families (see Chapter 7 for more details).

2. Short-term behavioral interventions with the former families result in significant changes in family interaction patterns when compared with untreated controls.

3. These changes are related to reduced rates of recidivism for status offenses, for follow-up periods of up to 18 months. Results for criminal offenses are more variable, but Marlowe, Reid, Patterson, and Weinrott (1986) reported that, even if the Patterson method was not associated with a better outcome at follow-up than a conventional community treatment, it was significantly less expensive (presumably because there was less professional involvement). Moreover, improved family interactions were associated with a lowered frequency of offenses, giving support to the basic thesis.

4. In behaviorally treated families, but not in controls, siblings of delinquent adolescents have significantly lower delinquency rates at three years follow-up. This suggests that the parents concerned had applied their newly acquired skills to the development of appropriate

behaviors in those sibs, thereby preempting antisocial behaviors by them.

5. The better the relationship skills of the therapists the lower the drop-out rate for families in behavioral treatment and the lower the recidivism rate for status offenses.

6. Parent-management training (PMT) makes major demands on parents – they must master educational materials, make systematic observations and respond appropriately to their children over long periods of time. At least one highly co-operative parent is needed, but may not be available. Indeed, according to McCauley (1982), PMT works best in modifying the behavior of children in stable middle-class fanilies. In contrast, Patterson, Cobb, and Ray (1973) comment that mothers raising families alone and in extreme poverty have great difficulty in learning and applying PMT. I suggested in Chapter 7 that the total available resources of families, both psychological and economic, are crucial in determining the direction of child development. A practical contribution to this problem has been made by Fleischman (1979). He found that giving parents "salaries" (one dollar per day) both reduced drop-out and increased compliance with treatment tasks by low-income single-parent families.

7. Berg, Hullin, and McGuire (1979) found that, when parents of truanting children were required to attend court for any subsequent truancy, both truancy and criminal offenses were reduced, compared with a group supervised by probation officers and social workers, with no extra effort being required of the parents. This suggests that, even without PMT, if a child's misdemeanors result in some penalty for the parents they will put more effort into child management. A study which looked at the effect on offending of a combination of PMT and various forms of penalty imposed on parents for child misdemeanors would be of interest.

Intervention: institutions

Token economy based programs began to be applied in residential institutions for adult offenders in the mid-1960s against an increasing background of pessimism concerning conventional (i.e., not formally psychological) programs. By 1980, some variant of the token economy was in operation in nearly all states in the USA (Burchard and Lane 1982). Initial enthusiasm was great because criminal behaviors, like behaviors in general, seemed to be acquired in the offenders past and present environment. Hence, with an appropriate use of learning principles, socially approved behaviors could be enhanced and criminal behaviors diminished. The institutional setting, because it is physically self-contained, was thought particularly appropriate for the learning approach. Contingencies could be precisely manipulated and, given careful management of the transition, there seemed good reason to expect considerable generalization of the results of treatment from the institution to the enviroment to which the prisoner would return.

The reality was very different from initial expectations. Several of the token economies were applied in a particularly unsatisfactory manner, the most notorious example being the START program at Springfield, Missouri, which relied heavily on negative reinforcement to shape inmate compliance. Amid much legal and professional criticism this was closed after two years (see Nietzel, 1979, for a full description). In all, Nietzel reviewed six prison-based token economies and concluded that there were no meaningful outcome data associated with any of them.

What went wrong? Burchard and Lane (1982) make some key points, including resistance to change by existing prison staff, inconsistent application of the behavioral techniques used, and failure to plan properly for generalization to the natural environment. It should be noted that well-conducted token economies (reviewed by Ayllon and Milan, 1979) do improve behaviors within institutions, such as general rule-keeping and interpersonal aggression. These are not minor gains, but the crucial target must remain criminal behavior after release, on which Ayllon and Milan (1979) present no evidence.

Intervention: community-based programs

The severe difficulties of working in institutions, and the poor post-discharge results obtained have led to a major shift in emphasis in behavioral work to community-based programs, some residential, some not. In the latter, the young offender or potential offender, continues to live in his/her own home. Some programs involve professionals, but increasingly professionals work through key figures in the natural environment, usually parents.

A residential program. Ostapiuk (1982) has described in detail the SHAPE program based in an inner-city area of Birmingham, in the UK Midlands. SHAPE is a multi-stage *voluntary* behavioral program for adjudicated offenders aged, 18–24, who have identifiable social, behavioral and occupational deficits and are considered by the referring agencies (mainly probation officers) to be at risk of reoffending. The first stage, in which the participants live as a group, identifies and remedies deficits in social and work-related skills. In the second (two-person living-units renovated by the participants themselves), the gains of the first are practiced and maintained, and community contacts are increased, particularly with employers. The third stage (single-person apartments) completes the return to the community and includes a wide range of survival skills from self-care to finding and holding down a job and appropriate interactions with the police.

The first reported set of results (Ostapiuk 1982) concerned 93 young men referred between 1977 and 1979. Eighty per cent were accepted by the program staff (only those dependent on drugs or with a history of serious violent offenses were refused), but half of those accepted were put off by the spartan physical conditions of the program and others received a custodial sentence while waiting to join. Data are available on the resulting 36 participants (mean length of prior custodial experience two and a half years) who completed the program in an average stay of six months. After a follow-up of 6–18 months, only 22 per cent were reconvicted, an encouraging result, achieved at low cost: but a controlled trial is now indicated.

A temporary change of environment. The open spaces of North America encourage adventure programs in which a group of young people spends several days or weeks in strenuous physical activity, led by specialists in outdoor survival techniques, doing everything from shooting rapids by canoe to trekking with a wagon train along the old cowboy trails. By 1980 there had been more than 100 "adaptive wilderness" programs in North America (Winterdyk and Roesch 1982). They evaluated one such program and found no difference in recidivism (there were 30 participants in each of the experimental and control groups) over a six months follow-up. Institutions for juveniles have long emphasized strenuous team sports, but there is no reason to suppose that skills in either baseball or canoeing are incompatible with criminal behaviors.

Foster homes. An important current trend is to place young offenders with foster parents rather than in an institution. The foster parents are provided with some training in behavioral methods and are paid at a level markedly higher than the cost to them of looking after the child. Nevertheless, the costs per child are about half those of institutions and, because only one or two children are placed per family, the problems of criminalization and of group opposition to staff norms are avoided. In addition, the children have the opportunity to learn relevant social skills in real, as opposed to artificial, environments. An example is the Vermont Foster Parent training program (Burchard and Lane 1982). Unfortunately, despite the appeal of this approach, outcome data are still lacking.

School based programs. These are based on the assumption, not always made explicit, that educational progress can be expected to reduce initial offending or reoffending. The main tests of this assertion have been in the USA (see Filipczak, Archer, Neale, and Twinett, 1979, for a review). A particularly well-assessed example of a school based program is PREP (Preparation through Responsive Educational Programs) involving over 500 pupils in the Maryland school system. Students were recommended to the program because of failing school grades, truancy and police contacts. Training was first provided for teachers in special methods of teaching social and educational skills; the teachers then taught the pupils. An overview by Burchard and Lane (1982) of the PREP and other programs indicates that the treated groups showed moderate short-term academic gains over appropriate comparison groups, but that the gap had disappeared after a four year follow-up. Even more important, no statistically significant differences were found in nonacademic areas, including delinquency, whether these were measured by parental report, self-report, or court records. It is clear that junior school programs focusing on educational skills are ineffective in reducing initial or continued offending.

Probation programs. Training probation officers in behavioral principles began some years ago (Burkhart, Behles, and Stumphauzer (1976). How effective is such training in reducing recidivism? A large-scale study had been reported by Jesness (1975). Ninety probation officers received 40 hours of classroom training in behavioral principles, with a particular emphasis on *contingency contracting* (in simple terms, "if you'll do X for me, or stop doing Y, I'll do Z for you"). An average of 22 hours consultation time was supplied by students supervised by the therapists in charge of the study. The probation officers worked with over 400 male offenders, average age 16, nearly 80 per cent of whom had been guilty of criminal rather than status offenses. After six months follow-up no significant differences were found between the offense rates of boys who had been given contingency contracting and those who had not. Nor was there any difference between the first half of the treated group and a group of controls, similar in number, dealt with by probation officers who had not been behaviorally trained.

It is worth noting that probationers for whom their officers had an above average "positive regard" had a significantly lower recidivism rate than those held in a below average positive regard. However, these better-liked boys may well have had better recidivism records even without intervention. No data are provide by Jesness (1975) on this point.

In discussing this and other probation studies, Burchard and Lane (1982) concluded that positive regard is a necessary ingredient in contingency contracting. As just indicated, this is an uncertain conclusion from the Jesness study itself, but it seems reasonable in the context of other evidence – many clinical studies suggest that if the therapist has a positive regard for the client and this is reciprocated, drop-out is reduced and outcome is improved (Feldman 1976). Burchard and Lane's next conclusion is that, given higher regard, contingency contracting seems to facilitate the achievement of behavioral targets in a range of contexts, both clinical and criminological, but whether or not higher regard, all other factors remaining equal, might reduce recidivism, remains to be seen. Their final conclusion undermines their earlier more optimistic ones: most probation officers fail to learn behavior modification skills in conventional classroom instruction and, of those who do, most do not maintain their skills in the field unless supported by supervisors.

Employment related programs. The complex relationship between unemployment and crime was discussed in Chapter 8. A number of American studies have tested directly the general proposition that those in work are less likely to reoffend, by giving job-training to convicted offenders and then following them up to measure job-retention and recidivism.

1. Shore and Massimo (1979). Twenty male school drop-outs aged 15–17 with "a long history of antisocial behavior" (no other data were specified as to their criminal records) took part voluntarily and were randomly assigned to the program or to an untreated control group. Job placement was based on the boys' own interests and goals; support

and training concerning interpersonal problems, remedial education and job skills all continued during employment. Over a 15 year follow-up period, 90 per cent of the controls but only 30 per cent of the treated group were arrested at least once for a nontraffic violation, and 60 per cent of the controls but only 10 per cent of the experimentals served at least one prison term. In the work area, 40 per cent of the controls but 70 per cent of the experimentals were in "successful and prolonged employment." Other social follow-up data also distinguished between the two groups: 80 per cent of both groups were married but, whereas 70 per cent of the married controls subsequently divorced, this was true of only 25 per cent of the experimentals. This suggests that job-training and support assisted a successful marriage, both helped job-retention and the combination of success in job and marriage helped crime-avoidance (more precisely arrest avoidance; self-report data were not collected, a fault with all of this set of studies). Because the numbers in each group were small, matching for prior criminal history would have been preferable to random assignment. The fact that the groups did not differ on age, IQ, or social status indices suggests that the randomization was effective – but it is a great pity that larger numbers were not involved.

2. The Kentfields Rehabilitation Project (Davidson and Robinson 1975) is also marred by flaws in design and data collection. One hundred and seventeen male "chronic" delinquents took part: 95 in the experimental group; only 22 served as controls. The averages for the two groups combined were: age, 16; probation time, $2\frac{1}{2}$ years; three known offenses per year while on probation prior to the study, including theft, autotheft and burglary. The program, which lasted for only nine weeks, involved six hours a day on work projects and education. After an 18 months follow-up, only 17 per cent of the experimental group were in penal institutions as against 53 per cent of the controls. The authors concluded that had there been no program and the experimentals who stayed out of institutions had entered them in the same ratio as the controls, the total cost of care would have been $712,000. The Kentfield Project cost only $30,000. Moreover, at the end of follow-up, 35 per cent of the experimentals were employed and 25 per cent were in some form of education.

The intervention personnel were young graduates who had no special training in any of the professions relevant to the care of offenders, and local administrators liked the project to the extent of retaining it after the research period finished. On the negative side, there are no details on the pre-project arrest rates for the two groups – it is possible that the superior outcome of the experimental group was due largely, even wholly, to a better prior record.

3. Mills and Walter (1979). This study involved 53 young people (both males and females) with an average of 3.85 previous convictions, including a significant number of serious ones. Local employers were first recruited and given information on broad behavioral principles and contingency contracts were drawn up between the youths and the researchers. Next, the participants (experimental group = 30, control group = 23) were trained in pre-employment behaviors such as interview skills and regular work routines. Job placements followed, with support for the experimental group being faded out gradually. One year after the program finished, only 10 per cent of the experimentals, but 70 per cent of the controls had experienced further arrests, and 52 per cent of the controls were in institutions. Furthermore, while all the experimentals obtained at least one job (average tenure $3\frac{1}{2}$ months) and one-third still had one at follow-up, the figures for the controls were: 39 per cent obtained jobs, for an average tenure of 2.7 weeks. Once again, there was a major flaw in design: assignment to group was nonrandom and the groups were not matched for sex or for prior job experience.

4. Good, Pirog-Good, and Sickles (1986) found that employability (enhanced by skills-training and counseling in how to obtain and hold a job) was directly related to future criminal activity after training. A police record reduced the chances of a job: by 7 per cent for one court appearance and by 41 per cent for five. Those rejected from one job in the past 90 days were significantly more likely to find work than those who had not been rejected. Ethnicity was also important: whites were 50 per cent more likely to be employed than nonwhites.

Although carried out with youths living in their own homes, these four American reports have much in common with the British SHAPE program (see earlier) in some of the elements involved – a step-by-step approach to job preparation and training, and the involvement of local employers. Despite shortcomings in design, they provide some support for the usefulness of employment-based programs with young offenders and for Glaser's assertion (1979): "To combat youth crime is largely futile unless an effort is also made to provide legitimate employment." Should this effort fail, as it well might in the short-term, Rauma and Berk (1987) suggest that recidivism can be reduced by providing unemployment compensation available immediately after release from confinement. They cite a California program which did so during the 1970's and early 1980's. A 5 year follow-up indicated that recidivism was consistently lower than for a group not given compensation. Finally, two cautionary notes: first, there is no necessary incompatibility between having a job and offending – indeed, the whole range of occupational offenses depend on having a job; second, the continuing diminution in the supply of unskilled jobs (see Chapter 8) makes it more essential than ever that training for offenders in employment-based programs be for relatively high-level skills.

Non-family community programs. Fo and O'Donnell (1974) describe a "buddy system" whereby boys receive the friendship of adults in their own community in return for the performance of approved pro-social behaviors (a form of of contingency contracting). When Fo and O'Donnell compared convicted offenses by 264 boys randomly allocated to a buddy with those of 178 boys randomly allocated to serve as controls, the results were mixed. Whereas those with a previous record of offenses improved through participation in the buddy system, those with no prior record did worse. The authors suggest that participation in the program may have led to social contacts between offenders and previous nonoffenders, so that the latter learned criminal behaviors to which they were not previously exposed. Clearly, the exact numerical mix between youngsters of differing previous offense histories must be carefully planned. The selection of the buddy model is also of great importance. A subsequent follow-up study (O'Donnell, Lydgate, and Fo 1979) confirmed and amplified these results.

The importance of other offenders in counteracting the influences on some program participants of staff members and buddies (who may well be perceived by participant youths as akin to staff members) is discussed in the last section of this chapter as one of the key obstacles to program effectiveness.

Social contact with buddies is not the only potential reinforcer for pro-social behavior. Pierce and Risley (1974) suggestd a modified "time-out" approach to the director of a community center in a deprived black area. The games room of the center was affected constantly by fights, broken equipment and littered floors. The director set up a system of explicit rules and, for each violation, the games room was closed ten minutes earlier, resulting in the undesired behaviors decreasing rapidly.

On a much larger scale and using positive rather than negative reinforcement, O'Donnell, Chambers, and Ling (1973) set up an athletics program for which any boy from an economically poor community was eligible. The opportunity to play football and other games was offered as a reward for academic work and progress. During the four years of the project not one of the 200 participants had an official arrest record. Although no comparison group was set up without access to sports, the complete absence of arrests is much better than could have been expected in almost any random sample of disadvantaged youth. However, it is possible that the fact that the parents of the boys had to apply for their son's participation may have resulted in a group from concerned homes providing a good degree of social control which supplemented that provided by the project. And there are no data on the pre-program arrest record of the boys. Nevertheless, the opportunity to play sports (and, even more important, to be coached by experts) seems likely to be a very potent reinforcer for pro-social behavior by young people, and the converse – the prospect of losing the opportunity to do so – may be a very effective cue to avoid proscribed behaviors.

Such programs are replicable on a potentially very large scale indeed. For over 20 years the British juvenile courts have able been to "sentence to treatment" young offenders. That is, they are required to spend a period of time in a community based "intermediate treatment" (IT) program, typically an amalgam of education and leisure activites but with little planning or monitoring from entry to discharge. Preston (1982) described a study of one IT center in which, having gained the cooperation of existing staff, she re-designed on behavioral lines both pre- and post-assessment procedures and the intervention program itself. Contracts were drawn up between staff members and program participants (boys and girls, aged 15–16, the British school leaving age is 16) who continued to live in their own homes and attended the center daily. Nearly 90 per cent of participants had both criminal histories and a lengthy record of truancy. The contracts specified short and long term-goals in the areas of education, work and social skills and self-management (e.g., time-keeping and personal hygiene). Points were earned for achieving targets and were exchanged daily for special activities such as ice-skating, swimming and snooker (not dissimilar to pool). The overall program lasted eight months.

Preston and Carnegie (1989) compared the behaviorally managed group (n = 24) with a group which had attended the center in the year prior to the introduction of the behavioral program (n = 26), in both cases after a follow-up of one year. The former was twice as likely to be employed as the latter (50 per cent versus 23 per cent), and only about half as likely to have been reconvicted (33 per cent versus 58 per cent). Pre-program offense records were the same for the two groups. As usual, self-reports of offenses would have been desirable, but this is one of the better studies in the literature, from the points of view both of research methodology and the skill (technical and social) with which the behavioral program was designed and executed.

Social skills training. This is based on the twin assumptions that deficiencies in social interaction skills are associated with offending and that remedying them would reduce recidivism by those trained, even in the absence of any other treatment. Social skills programs typically involve such behaviors as giving and accepting social feedback, the timing and length of contributions to conversations and eye contact, and distance apart during social exchanges. A comprehensive review by Spence (1982) draws the following conclusions concerning the methodology and efficacy of social skills programs for young offenders).

1. Many studies involve single-case designs, mainly restricted to very specific responses at the micro-skill level, with assessments limited to their immediate effects in the training setting itself rather than the extent of generalization to other settings.

2. Group design studies use varied criteria for subject selection, with comparison groups often inadequate.

3. Few studies index the effect of social skills training on offending by self-report as well by official statistics.

4. There is clear evidence that short-term improvements are produced in micro-level responses within the training settings.

5. So far as the generalization of these, as well as the training of more complex skills are concerned, results are much less clear cut. In general, there has been a failure to test whether future offending has been affected.

6. Most important of all, work is needed on which adolescents would benefit from social skills programs, and which are the most important target behaviors.

In general, we still await a clear demonstration of a causal link between social skill deficits and the development of criminal behaviors. But, there are two specific areas where social skills training might contribute to a diminution in the crime figures. The first concerns crime avoidance: Aiken, Stumphauzer, and Veloz (1977) showed that knowing how to resist peer pressures helped adolescents in the Los Angeles inner-city avoid criminal involvements (see Chapter 7). Second, there is evidence, discussed in Chapter 3, that both the appearance of a suspect and his general demeanor contribute to the decision to arrest or to caution a juvenile (Piliavin and Briar 1964). Werner et al. (1975) found that juveniles can be trained to display behaviors acceptable to the police. A report by Gross, Brigham, Hopper, and Bologna (1980) claims fewer arrests after a one year follow-up for boys trained in how to talk to policemen than for an untrained control group.

Behavioral treatments for offense-related behaviors

A review by Emory and Marholin (1977) concludes that less than 4 per cent of reports of behavior modification with offenders had anything which could be described as criminal activity (theft, etc.) as a target behavior. Blackburn (1980) made the same point, as indicated earlier.

Emory and Marholin (1977) identify three possible strategies for the direct modification of criminal behaviors, each of which has severe problems. The first is to decrease them by negative reinforcement. There are three difficulties here: criminal behaviors are of low frequency, are difficult to observe, and occur in conditions over which the behavior modifier has very little control; even if these difficulties can be overcome, programs based on negative reinforcement all too easily become abused, is witness the START program discussed earlier. The second option is to change completely the environment of the offender. Since transportation ended (see Chapter 10), doing so has involved only a temporary placement in an institution. While this removes the offender from potential targets of crime for the duration of his confinement, he returns eventually to the environment in which offenses may occur, possibly even more likely to carry them out. The third possible strategy, and the most frequently used, is to strengthen behaviors which are incompatible with delinquency. The problem here is the term "incompatible." Most of the behaviors intended to fall under this head, such as educational, job or social skills, are in fact quite *compatible* with criminal behavior. Truly incompatible behaviors, such as refusing to take part in a crime or paying for goods in a shop rather than stealing them, have rarely been the targets of behavioral programs. The few published reports, almost all to do with stealing, usually from shops, are reviewed below, as are behavior modification programs with sex offenders, an important exception to the general rule of a lack of behavioral work directly concerning the problem which led to arrest and conviction.

There are two single-case reports of adult shoplifting, both of which involved covert sensitization (Cautela 1967). Essentially, the client visualizes himself in the store, stealing, being caught and then sent to prison. Gauthier and Pellegrin (1982) used a careful single-case design with a woman with 11 previous convictions for shoplifting, which she engaged in several times per week. Having been trained in the method she practised it on her own 10 times per day for five weeks and then whenever she felt tempted subsequently. At the final follow-up, 14 months later, she had reported stealing only once, when briefly out of the country. There were no officially recorded charges or convictions during the follow-up period. Another single-case report (Glover 1985) used a similar method and had a similar result.

Henderson (1983) reports using a range of behavioral techniques to alter clients' responses to stimuli which were previously "signals for stealing." A two-year follow-up of 27 children referred to child psychological services for stealing (no information is provided on offense records) resulted in a recidivism rate of 20 per cent for the behaviorally treated group compared with 60 per cent for those who received "other treatments" and 70 per cent for an untreated group. As Henderson himself points out, there was no random allocation to behavioral or comparison groups and he carried out all treatments and did most of the follow-ups. Nevertheless, other than sex offenses, this seems the only example in the literature of direct behavioral intervention in the offense related behaviors of a sizeable group.

Behavioral work with sex offenders is carried out in several countries including the USA, Canada, and Britain. After an early concentration on aversion therapy alone (typically pairing mild electric shock to the calf muscle with images which trigger the deviant act) current programs embody a broad spectrum of techniques. These include: understanding the effects on the victim of the assailant's actions and accepting responsibility for the offense, as well as insight into its motives and antecedents; counseling on the offenders own victimization experiences if any; basic sex education; elimination of deviant fantasies (aversive training is still used for this section of treatment) and reconditioning more appropriate ones (typically by paired masturbation); the cognitive restructuring of beliefs about the offense (whether rape or child molestation); learning to recognize and manage more effectively the detailed sequence of events which typically leads to the offense; social skills training, for example in anger management (Davis and Leitenberg 1987, Marshall and Barbaree 1989). It will be seen that there is a serious attempt to build treatment programs on the basis of the research findings concerning sex offenders described in Chapter 9, focusing on cognitive, social and behavioral components.

The setting in which treatment takes place is very important: earlier attempts to treat incarcerated offenders have been largely replaced either by out-patient treatment after release (Marshall and Barbaree, 1989, in Canada), or by starting the program shortly before disharge from prison and continuing it in the community together with probation officer supervision (Perkins, 1982, in Britain). A majority of the 1,000-plus sex offenders treated annually in Florida are treated entirely in the community, sometimes on a walk-in basis (Moore, Zusman, and Root 1985). In general, there is an emphasis on offenders volunteering for help; the separation of punishment, administered by the penal system, from treatment administered by psychologists after release, means that help-seeking is likely to be genuine and not coerced.

The problem of low reporting of sex offenses means that true recidivism rates are very hard to establish (Furby and Weinrott 1989) leading to overestimations of success rates in both treated and comparison groups. However, a number of reports of comprehensive treatment programs have now appeared (e.g., Perkins 1982, Marshall and Barbaree 1989) and suggest some cause for cautious optimism, although we do not yet have a fully satisfactory controlled trial. Marshall and Barbaree point out that the least responsive patients include rapists, a numerically very large group.

11.5. General issues

This chapter has mentioned a number of issues, concerning ethics and treatment, which cut across the specific methods discussed. In the section which follows these are brought together and expanded. The first set is essentially ethical, or concerns professional practise, whereas the second has to do with problems of program implementation.

Ethical/professional problems

The targets of change and the criteria for change. Psychotherapeutic and behavioral programs alike have concentrated largely on the problems experienced by the offender rather than on those caused by the offender to others. Psychotherapists tend to assume that the offender steals or assaults because of some inner distress; their targets for change include enhancing "ego-strength" or increasing insight. Behavior therapists make much the same assumption of some personal deficit in the offender. It follows that if their skills (educational, social or occupational) could be improved they would not "need" to offend. The rare exceptions to this general conclusion are provided mainly by work with sex offenders.

This indirect approach is in sharp contrast to the way behavior therapists work in the clinical field, where the emphasis is on the problem behavior itself, for example a fear of crowded places, rather on some correlate or supposed "underlying cause." The client is helped by means of a program of graduated exposure to the situations in question; success is measured by the client's mastery of them.

So far as the criteria for successful change are concerned, the agents of the criminal justice system (the police and the judiciary) and the politicians and civil servants who formulate penal policy regard reconviction rates (ideally, reoffending) as the crucial, indeed the sole, measure of program success. In contrast, psychologists, whether psychodynamic or behavioral, seem to give at least equal weight to other indices, whether skills or ego-strength. But, these targets cut little ice with the other professionals involved: however much a convicted offender improves his skills or advances on measures of maturity, these will be regarded by them as much less important than a demonstrated reduction in further offending.

The aims of therapists and clients. Whereas it is relatively commonplace for behavior therapists to ask clinical clients what they would like to achieve, such a question is rare in the case of "offender clients." This is the heart of the matter. It is questionable if many convicted offenders share the aims of those in charge of them, other than a common desire (for example, in the prison context) for a quiet and well-run institution with neither side causing difficulties for the other.

The question of common aims occurs with particular force in the context of psychologically based programs for offenders. In the clinical field, clients are treated for problems from which they often lose much and benefit little (although the possibility of secondary gain and hence of poor motivation is always relevant); hence, improvement is typically welcomed by clients when it is achieved. The success rate of behavioral treatment with such problems as fears and anxieties is generally high. It is somewhat lower with problems of "excessive appetite" (Orford 1982), such as weight control, problem drinking, and smoking, all of which confer short-term benefits but cause long-term damage. The outcome figures (measured in this case by reconviction) seem least good for criminal behaviors, characteristic of which is that the major loss is to the victim and not to the offender, who loses only if he is caught and convicted. Otherwise, so far as he is concerned, he benefits both in the short and the long term. Offenders may well be eager to fill gaps in their repertoire of educational and other skills, but why should many of them want help in changing behaviors related to criminal acts? Rather than seeking to cease criminal behaviors they may be eager merely to avoid detection and conviction.

The role of the psychologist in the criminal justice system. The above argument does not mean that it is undesirable to improve the occupational and other skills of offenders. But, if the aims of the criminal justice system are to be achieved, such improvements are only part of a comprehensive program of intervention which should also include a full analysis of the setting events and reinforcers for the performance of criminal behaviors by the offender concerned and the design of appropriate alternative behaviors and reinforcers.

When a psychologist works with a voluntary clinical client he is unequivocally the agent of the client and they can agree relatively readily on targets and methods (within certain legal and professional constraints, see Feldman and Peay, 1982). The client is the "victim" and, hence, the clear-cut focus of help, because it is his or her distress which is to be relieved. This is in sharp contrast to the criminological field in which offender and victim are two different persons. (Unless you take the view that offenders behave as they do because crime is their only available avenue to the socially approved goal of material success, albeit not by socially approved means; see Chapter 8 for an exposition of this view, which argues that offenders are responding to their own distress, in the only way left to them.)

An initial request for help typically comes from the criminal justice system and not from the client, although the latter may respond voluntarily to the offer of a change program if this is made known to him. Hence, the psychologist working in the criminal justice system is much more often the agent of the system than of the client, and it is the system which defines the goal of treatment – a reduction in future offending.

What should be the response of a psychologist to a direct request from the management of a penal institution to apply his professional skills so as to achieve this goal by a program of intervention focused primarily on criminal behaviors and not on various skill-deficits (although these may be addressed also if considered relevant)? The Task Force on the Role of Psychology in the Criminal Justice System (American Psychiatric Association 1978) produced 10 recommendations regarding the ethical practice of psychology in the system. Recommendation 10 states: "Psychologists should be strongly encouraged to offer treatment services to offenders who request them" (American Psychiatric Association 1978, p. 1110). It is clear from the discussion which follows the recommendation that "treatment" means remedying a range of deficits – much the same as those reviewed in this chapter. No mention is made of treatment aimed directly at criminal behaviors themselves, but it is reasonable to assume that the injunction "offer treatment services to those who *request* them" would apply to these treatments also. This is similar to the author's view (Feldman 1989, p. 19):

> ". . . behavioral programs with offenders or pre-offenders should be confined to those clients who have had a genuine opportunity to consider all information relevant to the methods and targets on offer, and have made a noncoerced decision to join the program (i.e., doing so does not result in a lighter, a different, or no sentence). Participation, as in the clinical setting, must be by consenting volunteers in pursuit of targets they perceive as beneficial [to themselves]."

Of course, the State must retain the quite separate right of punishment following a properly conducted trial. This is again close to the view of The Task Force, which supported the desirability, "of justly punishing people for what they have done in the past" (American Psychiatric Association 1978, p. 1110).

Working out exactly how to achieve fully informed genuine consent would itself require considerable effort, but is fundamental if progress is to be made that is both ethical and effective. It would not be surprising if offenders who volunteer were found to be those with the relatively least successful criminal careers (low personal/social returns from crime, frequent arrests and punishments) to whom nonoffending alternatives would be more attractive, both materially and socially, than to relatively successful offenders. Moreover, it would be preferable to carry out treatment programs either after the completion of a custodial sentence, or so as to overlap with discharge, as in the case of several of those described in this chapter (a noncustodial sentence makes program implementation easier, but this should not be a criterion of sentencing policy).

The rights of the offender. The approach argued for above requires that offenders/prisoners have the same rights as citizens in general concerning psychological treatment. Unfortunately, that this is far from the case is made clear by a review by Veneziano (1986) of the few American examinations of the legal status of prisoners concerning treatment. He found that the more serious and intrusive a treatment in its impact on an individual the more likely is a court to uphold procedures to obtain informed consent, thus recognizing the autonomy of the inmate. But, where treatment is thought unlikely to be actually damaging, the consent of the inmate is seen to be unnecessary. The rights of society to make some form of coercive demand on him has been upheld over the prisoner's decision to withold consent. Moreover, prisoners do not, in general, have a right to *receive* treatment, regardless of the fact that they might not be able to refuse it. And Veneziano (1986) makes clear the very great difficulty in providing for informed consent in an utterly coercive environment.

Program implementation

Alternative models of treatment. This review of treatments for offenders has been concerned throughout with what Kazdin (1987) terms the conventional model of treatment and research. By this he means a specific intervention, applied to a clinically identified group for a limited period, together with an evaluation after the treatment is terminated. Kazdin's analysis was in the context of antisocial behavior (a.s.b.) in children, but applies equally well to all types of offenses and to all groups of offenders. He lists several alternative models of treatment, as follows:

1. High strength intervention. An increased intensity of treatment (a greater amount per unit of time) might result in an improved outcome. But, there are practical limits to what consumers (clients, their parents in the case of children, and those paying for the program) will accept.

The idea of protracted and intensive treatment is not as familiar and certainly not as well accepted as is that of protracted punishment for criminal acts, and may well lead to increased client attrition. Moreover, a high strength intervention is inevitably costly. However, the question of cost-effectiveness always arises and, if a stronger intervention scores here, it is to be preferred over a weaker one.

2. Amenability to treatment. There has been little interest so far in selecting those most likely to respond to a treatment. Kazdin argues for applying a treatment to those most likely to benefit from it, evaluating it by a controlled trial and, if successful, extending it to the "less amenable." (Amenability in antisocial behavior is inversely related to an early onset of a.s.b. and to a diversity of such activities across a range of settings, as well as to such factors as having sibs and fathers with a criminal history – much the same as the predictive factors for crime discussed in Chapters 7 and 10). Moreover, amenability may be correlated with good academic performance and thus, in turn, with a high IQ (see Chapter 6).

3. Broad based intervention. There have been several attempts to provide broad based treatments, an early example being the Cambridge-Somerville Study (Powers and Witmer 1951) described earlier in this Chapter, which offered those in the experimental group, psychiatric and medical attention, academic tutoring, community programs and family counseling, in addition to the individual counseling which was its central purpose. But Kazdin (1987) argues that such extras have been unsystematic essentially, being provided "as needed." Instead, the many possible components of help should be received on the basis of explicit decision rules to determine who gets what, when, and why. Moreover, and again missing until now, the components need to be described clearly enough to prevent duplication in treatment. Observing these rules will help us know what accounted for any change, if any, which took place, allowing more cost-effective future programs.

4. A chronic-disease model. Kazdin (1987) suggests that conduct disorder (and by implication, criminal behavior) is analogous to diabetes mellitus. This is a disorder of carbohydrate metabolism which results from an inadequate production or utilization of insulin and needs lifelong care, management and treatment. In the same way, conduct disorder could be seen as a chronic condition, "needing intervention, continued monitoring and evaluation over the course of one's life" (Kazdin 1987, p. 200). He goes on to argue that conduct disorder has a broad impact, both in childhood and in adult life, and across different

behavioral settings. Treatment "failure" may point not to "nothing works" but to the need for continuous treatment and monitoring.

The evidence presented in earlier chapters makes it clear that many who offend in childhood and adolescence cease to do so by the time they become young adults, frequently without formal treatment or even punishment; and those offenders who continue their careers into adulthood typically cease offending by 35–40. There is no similar pattern in the case of diabetes, which is indeed a lifelong condition. Nevertheless, it is useful to think of criminal behavior as likely to recur over a long period, so that a single "treatment" may be insufficient. In any event there is general agreement on the need for very long follow-up periods, during which further "booster" treatments may be required. This is certainly the case in the treatment of some sexual problems (Feldman 1987). Of course, such additional treatments complicate the task of assessing the effectiveness of a program, and the final specification of a treatment program for routine use may need to include a recommendation for lengthy monitoring, and for periodic "boosters," as needed.

The integrity of treatment. When an engineer designs a bridge or an architect plans a building it is usual for the plan or design to be carried out exactly as intended; if there any changes along the way these would be deliberate and explicit. No such assumption can be made in the case of programs of psychological treatment; the literature is replete with examples of major departures from what Sechrest and Rosenblatt (1987) term program integrity. These take several forms:

1. Length. The program ends prematurely, before its intended final date, reducing the potential benefit.

2. Intensity. The amount of treatment per unit of time (e.g., hours of contact time with program staff) may be critical for success; a sub-optimal level may sharply reduce effectiveness.

3. Nonco-operation by staff. The best-designed program may founder on lack of co-operation by those in daily contact with the offender. Laws (1974) has described some of the difficulties he found in establishing and operating a token economy program in an American maximum security hospital. Nonco-operation was made more possible by the retention by existing staff of overall administrative control, patient selection and staff selection.

4. Counter-control by clients. Several studies have shown that institutional groups of offenders not only value different behaviors from

those approved of by the staff, but are more consistent in reinforcing such behaviors by their own members than are the staff in reinforcing staff-approved behaviors or even examples of staff performance (e.g., Buehler, Patterson, and Furniss, 1961). This highlights the importance of staff not only having objectives in common, but also pursuing them systematically. The achievement of common objectives between staff and clients is even more difficult.

Enhancing program integrity. Sechrest and Rosenblatt (1987) make a number of suggestions:

1. The treatment plan. This is more likely to be delivered with integrity if it is both sound and clear than if it is vague and poorly described – when failure is almost inevitable. There must be clear specifications of target behaviors, the methods to be used to select program participants, the frequency, length and circumstances of the intervention, the total package of services to be delivered, including the intended time course of the intervention, the identity of the staff to be involved, and any required previous experience and additional training. The more complex and difficult the plan, the more difficult it will be to administer, the more resistance can be expected from staff and the more will program integrity suffer.

2. The supervisory plan. A program can fail for want of adequate supervision. A satisfactory plan is one which ensures that delivery conforms to the blueprint and provides for the monitoring of staff training and of staff activities of all kinds, as well as their detailed adherence to the treatment plan.

3. The assessment plan. During and after the program there has to be an assessment of the integrity and effectiveness of the intervention. Did the sessions take place as intended (both timing and content)? Did program participants attend as planned? These points concern the documentation of service delivery. Staff commitment must also be assessed; a half-hearted staff can wreck the best-designed program.

4. Design issues. Program assessment must provide relevant information both to project "insiders" (program staff), who may be most interested in the evaluation of the process of treatment (what did we get right and where did we go wrong?) and to "outsiders" (funding bodies, policy makers, etc.) who are most interested in indices of success, such as reconviction rates.

Participants should be randomly assigned to treatment and no-treatment groups. But, this may be criticized as witholding something potentially valuable from those who might benefit. One answer is to offer the comparison group a treatment believed in by a substantial body of opinion (even in the absence of hard evidence), such as psychotherapy. Another is to remind objectors that efficacy is in doubt until the results are in and that the history of treatments for offenders teaches us that failure is far more likely than success – so nothing of undoubted value is being witheld. (In a very thorough survey, Lundman and Scarpitti, 1978, found much evidence of the suppression of treatment failures by delinquency researchers. It follows that cries of "nothing works" would have been even more strident had all results been reported.) In any event, it is important to deal with this issue at the outset.

Finally, the evidence of self-report offending, which shows rather smaller differences due to sex and ethnicity than do the official statistics, means that treatment researchers should use a variety of client groups. Doing so would also indicate the range of application of the method under study.

Concluding comment

By now it should be clear that the potential degree of success of even the best planned and executed program for offenders is relatively limited. Many offenders will refuse participation if allowed to do so; others will participate but will sabotage the program in various ways; many of those who are genuine volunteers will show only temporary shifts in criminal behavior, and others will not show even this degree of change.

Nevertherless, a total pessimism concerning the "crime problem" would not be appropriate. First, some programs, with some offenders, do seem promising. Second, a good deal of improvement is possible given adherence to the recommendations listed above. Third, even without exposure to planned procedures, many offenders reduce or cease criminal activities as they get older, marry or acquire steady jobs. Fourth, there is increasing evidence that to a large extent crime is a function of situational opportunity and of reinforcement by material and other rewards for successful performance (see Chapter 9). Reduce opportunity, and hence positive reinforcement, and criminal behaviors are less likely to be acquired and performed. The next chapter is concerned with this relatively recent approach: crime prevention.

12. Crime prevention

> It should be understood at the outset that the principal object to be attained is the Prevention of Crime.
>
> . . . The security of person and property, the preservation of the public tranquillity and all the other objects of a police establishment will thus be better effected, than by detection and punishment of the offender after he has succeeded in committing the crime.
>
> From General Instruction Book by C. Rowan, First Metropolitan Police Commissioner, 1829

Following Commisioner Rowan, the final chapter of this section of the book surveys attempts to prevent offending, but moves beyond the limited context of police action to various forms of social management. These range from the role of bystanders, residents and citizens in general, to target hardening and the potential role of the media.

12.1. The police

Very broadly, two changes in police action have been urged. The first, which was considered in Chapter 3, involves enhanced police activity in high crime areas or in the targeting of well known offenders. It has had mixed results and is costly. The second relates to the way the police handle juveniles suspected of minor offenses, or apprehended during their commission, and implies a *lighter* touch than is used at present.

Police – juvenile encounters

The previous chapter mentioned programs for training juveniles in managing their side of the police–juvenile encounter. It is probably more practicable to train the police to respond to juveniles so as to divert them, whenever possible, from the track which culminates in an institutional sentence. Toch (1969) found that those policemen who were most likely to use violence in the course of their duties used strong as opposed to mild verbal threats very early in the course of a confrontation with a suspect. This increases the likelihood of a similar response by the latter, and then a further escalation, followed by an arrest, irrespective of whether or not the person carried out the offense of which he was suspected. Goldstein, Monti, Sardino, and Green (1977) report a training course for police officers in handling aggressive suspects. As against this, there is a strong suggestion that many officers find pursuit and arrest more satisfying than low-key prevention tactics (Stumphauzer et al. 1977).

Another possible change in police policy comes from the Philadelphia Study. Wolfgang et al. (1972) found that black first-time offenders were more than twice as likely to be arrested as their white counterparts. Next, they traced the impact of a disposition for a particular offense on the probability of subsequent offenses. This showed a greater probability of a second offense if the first one had led to arrest rather than to a less severe disposition, such as a caution. In sum: "two factors – seriousness of the offense and severe disposition – are associated with a substantial portion of recidivism" (Wolfgang et al. 1972, p. 237). The suggestion is that if nonwhite lower SES boys growing up in Philadelphia had been dealt with, early in their offending career, as leniently as were their white counterparts, the proportion proceeding along the track to a long-term criminal career might have been reduced appreciably. In contrast, Klein (1986) suggests that self-labeling as a delinquent is associated with continuing a delinquent career and that the groups most likely to self-label, once arrested and charged, are those at the opposite extreme from lower SES black males – higher SES white females. He suggests, therefore, a mild disposition for the latter. Perhaps it would be sensible to argue for the mildest possible disposition for *all* first-, perhaps even second-time, offenders, allowed by the seriousness of the charge.

12.2. Surveillance

Semi-formal groups

As indicated in Chapter 3, considerably greater surveillance of high-risk areas might be effective in reducing crime, but implies a very heavy financial cost if it is to be carried out by the police themselves. Hence, volunteer alternatives are being tried, which include both the more spectacular Guardian Angels and the low-key Neighborhood Watch Scheme.

The former are unarmed, but distinctively dressed, young men and women who patrol roads and subways in the USA and Canada. According to a review by Pennell, Curtis, and Henderson (1986), Guardian Angel groups may have some limited effect on property crimes but little or none on violent offenses. However, these authors suggest that if minority youths (particularly blacks) could be recruited to serve as role models, the long term effects of Guardian Angels might be enhanced. Moreover, there is evidence that some sections of the public feel safer through the occasional presence of Guardian Angels members. Because the fear of crime experienced by potential victims, particularly the elderly, is an important cost of crime (see Chapter 2), measures to lessen fear are worthwhile. Balkin and Houlden (1983) indicate that fear is reduced by an increased presence of uniformed employees in a neighborhood, particularly when they have some kind of official status, and argue that increasing their numbers beyond the requirements of strict efficiency may be justified. When the uniforms are worn by volunteers this argument has particular force.

Neighborhood Watch schemes have proliferated in the English speaking world. Uncontrolled studies suggested that a reduction in crime is achieved in the neighborhoods concerned (e.g., Fowler, McCalla, and Mangione 1979, Perry 1984) but that controlled research into effectiveness was needed. A detailed review by Skogan (1980) drew the following conclusions:

1. Voluntary participation cannot easily be initiated or sustained in areas of high crime. The Watch schemes are disproportionately concentrated in the socially homogeneous, better-off areas of cities, the residents of which are more likely to know of the opportunities to participate and to participate when they have the opportunity.

2. Voluntary organizations with nothing to do other than combat crime tend to disappear, implying that survival depends on the schemes suppling other social and personal needs.

3. Those involved seek different sorts of support from official agencies according to the type of neighborhood. In the highest crime areas they push for major changes in social and economic policies, and access to outside resources to bring these about. In contrast, in better-off areas, preservationist groups battle against those social changes they see

as increasing their local crime rate (essentially, their interest is in maintaining property values).

4. Crime prevention by volunteers depends crucially on co-operation with the local police, but this is very difficult in poor and/or minority communities, in which relations with the police are often strained.

5. The more a Watch scheme is related to the structure of a community the more successful it is – but such specificity is difficult to transfer.

6. The demographic correlates of active involvement are income, property ownership, education, and length of residence in the community. In the suburbs, there are ample numbers of high income, well educated and long standing property owners; in the inner-cities such people are scarce and becoming scarcer. It follows that, in the former, voluntary enthusiasm is sufficient to maintain an adequate level of activism; in the latter, much public support is necessary.

Lavrakas and Lewis (1980) amplify the last point by arguing that public resources would be better invested in maintaining the active involvement of a hard core of members. In addition, social service programs are needed to help the elderly improve their sense of security.

The general public (bystander intervention)

This area of research attracted a great deal of activity after the murder of Kitty Genovese in New York in 1964, when those who heard her cries for help or watched the attack on her from the safety of their apartments failed to help, or even to telephone the police.

Unfortunately, for the practical purposes of crime prevention, these studies do not take us very far. In an earlier review (Feldman 1977, Chapter 4) the author drew the following conclusions from the (mainly simulated) research arrangements which had been used.

1. In general the acquisition, performance and maintenance of helping behaviors, of which bystander intervention to frustrate a crime is an example, are responsive to the same social and cognitive variables as behaviors in general.

2. Helping is increased by the manifest distress of the victim, the presence of a helping model, and the similarity of the victim to the bystander.

3. Restraints against helping include potential loss to the helper (whether physical or financial), his lack of self-perceived competence,

and the assumption that others are both available and willing to help (the diffusion of responsibility hypothesis).

In addition, the author suggested that an onlooker is more likely to report a crime if the report is anonymous, police protection is assured, and he or she is not required to appear in court. Sheleff and Schichor (1980) support and amplify these speculations. Writing from legal experience, they argue that bystanders are less willing to intervene the more they are aware of what will happen if they are called as witnesses in court, namely the loss of their time and hence their money, the stress, possibly amounting to humiliation, of the cross-examination, and the possibility of subsequent violence by the accused. They suggest also that the court is a "total institution" in which the convenience of judges and lawyers is the first consideration, that of witnesses the last, and cite evidence that witnesses frequently find the experience annoying and frustrating, and the tasks of recall and presentation very difficult.

They conclude that such experiences could easily become well known and so deter potential witnesses from getting involved. Indeed, a simulation study (Fedler and Pryor 1984) found that the most frequent reason for nonreporting was a desire to avoid subsequent "hassles" (involvement with the police and the courts).

Who is reported? Fedler and Pryor (1984) found that a small, well dressed, person observed shoplifting is more likely to be reported, if witnessed by a bystander, than a large poorly dressed one (the former "doesn't need it;" the latter "could do me harm"). Mawby (1985) suggests that victims seen as more vulnerable, and individuals as opposed to corporations (corner shops rather than supermarkets), are more likely to be helped, as are neighbors rather than strangers. Other things being equal (such as the potential costs of reporting), the more serious the crime observed the more likely it is to be reported, but when the meaning of an event is unclear, onlookers will tend to categorize it as less serious than it is in fact (Himmelfarb 1981).

Who reports? A simulation study of shoplifting by Gelfand, Hartmann, Walder, and Page (1973) suggested that males, the middle-aged, and those raised in rural settings were more likely to report a witnessed crime. Since then there have many such studies, although most have been in noncriminological contexts. A meta-analysis by Steblay (1987) of 65 studies found a significant amount of support for the hypothesis that "country people are more helpful than city people." The over 60's were much more likely to "report" in the study by Fedler and Pryor (1984) than any other age group. Possible explanations for this include the elderly being more public-spirited – and having more time on their hands.

To return from simulation studies to the real world of offenses, there is good evidence that many crimes are witnessed, and that witness evidence is related to the clearance rate. Both findings help to explain the persisting interest in this area of research. A national survey in The Netherlands by Steinmetz (1985) found that in 1982 no fewer than 36 per cent of those interviewed had witnessed at least one of 13 types of crime, including threatening or violent behavior (14 per cent) and shoplifting (12 per cent). Some kind of intervention (usually warning the police) was claimed by just over one-quarter of those who had witnessed an offense. Intervention was related to the personal costs of the particular involvement (warning the police was much easier and hence more frequent than a direct confrontation with the offender).

Mawby (1985) reviewed witness involvement in recorded crime in the Northern English town of Sheffield in 1971. He found that 82 per cent of reported crimes were reported by the victim as against only 7 per cent by witnesses. However, whereas only 33 per cent of the former were cleared, this was true for 57 per cent of the latter, many of which were serious.

It seems that if witnesses to crime are willing and able to observe carefully, to report immediately to the police, and to give evidence in court, the clearance rate may well rise, if only moderately. However, increasing the probability of these actions would require a massive effort in public persuasion; such campaigns in the area of crime are in their infancy, at best.

Who, if anyone, goes beyond witnessing with a view to reporting, and actually intervenes in an attempt to prevent the crime, perhaps even attempts to apprehend the perpetrator? Houston (1980) interviewed 32 people who had intervened directly in dangerous types of crime (muggings, armed robbery, bank hold-ups) in the past 10 years and compared them with "noninterveners." The interveners were more likely to have been a victim of crime or to know victims personally. They were also taller, heavier, and better trained in first-aid and life-saving (though there was no difference in physical combat skills) and were more likely to describe themselves as physically strong, aggressive, emotional and principled. This fits in with a report by London (1970) of those who risked their own lives to help others escape death at the hands of the Nazis in World War II Europe. Moriarty (1975) reported that prior preparation was also relevant – those who had been asked to do so previously were more likely to intervene to prevent a theft.

12.3. Self-protection

Unfortunately, it is impossible for victims to ensure that their particular bystander has the right combination of personality, skills and preparation. The main onus is on the potential victim to protect himself by anticipating victimization in advance and to avoid it by appropriate pre-emptive action.

By citizens

Lavrakas and Lewis (1980) analyzed data from four American communities and concluded that the self-protection methods used by citizens fall in two clusters: one concerned with avoidance, the second with access control (often termed target-hardening, see below). Avoidance behaviors involve people restricting their actions in certain contexts which they would perform in safer ones. Examples include: not going out at night, going out by day only when accompanied; at all times driving rather than walking; avoiding certain areas completely even when in a vehicle; when walking keeping clear of certain types of stranger, and carrying limited amounts of cash on one's person. Access control included locking doors and windows, and installing extra devices such as burglar alarms.

Those surveyed did not mention surveillance, whether formal, of the Neighborhood Watch type, or of the informal sort allowed by certain types of environmental arrangements (see below). But, there was much active self-protection. In one of the communities surveyed, Portland, OR, between one-quarter and one-half of those interviewed carried a gun or some other weapon for protection. Riger, Gordon, and Labailly (1982) found that American women, surveyed separately, also used avoidance tactics and access control. The use of the former was predicted by level of fear, perceived physical competence, ethnicity and education. Neither report provides information on the effectiveness of these two clusters of techniques in protecting against victimization. (To do so would require a longitudinal combination of these studies and a survey of victimization.)

By employers

A number of reports make suggestions, some tested empirically, as to how store owners, and employers in general, might reduce theft, whether by employees or by shoppers. McNees et al. (1976) measured shoplifting from a department store by checking 25 key items each day. Next, anti-shoplifting signs were introduced ("this store is protected by . . ."); the result was a considerable decrease in stealing. McClaughlin (1976) takes a somewhat different tack, suggesting that stores should reward shoppers and employees for reporting shoplifting, and that prices should be raised or lowered according to the level of shoplifting, thereby making reporting by shoppers more likely.

In a large scale self-report study of employees in a different section of industry, Hollinger and Clark (1983) found that males admitted higher levels of theft from work than females, and that certainty of detection and severity of punishment were both associated with reduced theft, but much less so for younger males than for other groups. This implies that an employer able to choose from a large pool of applicants should select older married employees and, if employing younger people, should prefer females to males (other factors being equal, such as skill and experience). Such a personnel policy, combined with high levels of apparent certainty of detection (highly visible closed-circuit TV systems) and of known severity of punishment ("all thieves will be prosecuted") should sharply reduce employee theft, according to Hollinger and Clark (1983).

Brown and Pardue (1985) describe the introduction of a personnel selection inventory as a component of the hiring procedures of a chain of South Eastern retail drugstores. Over a three year period, there was a significant reduction in losses, amounting to more than $1 million. But, there are also potential problems in such approaches, for example, illegal discrimination in hiring, and a potentially unpleasant work atmosphere leading to increased absenteeism and staff-turnover.

An insurance-based approach to employers, to improve self-protection against robbery and burglary, is urged by Litton (1982), an executive of an insurance company. He argues that the cost of insurance premiums can be a powerful means of persuading employers to take effective crime prevention measures, such as the use of high quality safes and intruder alarms, and the employment of professional carriers for valuables, as well as adequate initial vetting of new staff. Clients could also be encouraged by their insurers to insist that their architects incorporate crime-prevention devices at the design and planning stage of new buildings. Insurance discounts could be given for all such measures. Both parties would then benefit (fewer losses and fewer claims).

Employee activities

The risks for certain crimes are particularly high in such settings as shops and apartment blocks (theft) and in buses, underground shelters and parks (vandalism). Clarke (1983) argues that employees in such settings can have a major preventive role, and cites a great deal of evidence that offenders select targets where employee surveillance is low, avoiding those where it is high (see Chapter 9 for a discussion of the "rational offender"). Walsh (1978) found that shoplifters are more likely to operate in self-service stores with relatively fewer employees than in establishments in which employees are there to serve customers and hence are highly visible. Similarly, Waller and Okihiro (1978) reported that apartment blocks given protection by doormen had very low rates of burglary. British studies show that rates of vandalism are lower where some visible employee oversight is available, for example, on buses with conductors and on estates with resident caretakers (Mayhew and Clarke, 1982).

12.4. Hardening the target

The approaches to crime prevention discussed so far have involved some form of human activity. Another method is to develop a physical device which makes an offense more difficult, so reducing the probability of success and hence repetition. This is the most "obvious" of all crime prevention approaches; yet it might be the most effective. For example, Clarke (1980) noted that the British Post office had virtually eliminated theft from public call boxes by fitting steel coin containers, and that the West Germans have reduced car thefts dramatically by requiring steering locks on all vehicles. There are a number of other possibilities: cars with centrally activated locking systems; magnetized punched cards instead of keys, and goods marked with uniquely identified and indelible codes (Clarke 1983).

A study by Giswold (1984) indicates what can be achieved by the careful planning and execution of a target-hardening campaign. It took place in a business area of Portland, OR, with a high crime rate, and involved a simultaneous major improvement in street lighting and a campaign to persuade businesmen to improve security. The combined effects of these actions led to a very substantial reduction in the level of commercial burglaries in the area concerned, which was maintained over a two-year period and was not found in the rest of the city. Nor was the decline due to a reduction in business activity, or to a fall in the age-group at a high risk for crime, both factors being carefully controlled.

12.5. Environmental design

This approach originated in a book by Jacobs (1961) in which she gave the first outline of what later was termed defensible space theory. To reduce crime, Jacobs suggested: (a) buildings should be oriented towards the street so as to encourage natural surveillance (by residents and passers-by); (b) public and private domains should be clearly distinguished so that the former could be protected by paid employees; (c) outdoor space should be placed in proximity to intensively used areas, again to encourage surveillance and hence reduce vandalism.

Jacob's recommendations were based on personal observation and anecdotes. Some years later, Newman (1973) elaborated her ideas into "defensible space theory." This suggested that physical design could increase territorial attitudes and behaviors (i.e., appropriate design enhances surveillance) and hence reduce crime. Newman did provide some data but, in fact, the rate of robberies in his study was more closely related to the percentage of families on welfare in a particular housing project than to physical aspects of the buildings concerned.

According to Taylor, Gottfredsen, and Brower (1980), Newman's subsequent work did find consistent but modest links between design features, particularly surveillance opportunities, and crime, but often failed to control the relevant social variables or to specify the territorial cognitions and behaviors supposed to mediate the impact of design (which relevant behaviors are made possible by which designs?). They proposed a revised model which stressed "signs of defense" (symbolic or real barriers, erected against outsiders, which deter unwanted access), "signs of appropriation" (territorial markers that a space is being used and cared for), and the recruitment and maintenance of homogeneous social networks. The last point is a key aspect of their revised model. It asserts that cultural homogeneity increases territorial control, as do local social ties. Thus, social networks of those with much in common help the sense of "it's ours and must be looked after," and this applies to both public and private spaces.

Rubenstein, Murray, Motoyama, and Rouse (1980) found that that while changes in the physical environment can reduce crime the effects are not consistent. Moreover, beyond straightforward target-hardening, the links between such changes and crime rates remain obscure, and the behavior changes predicted by notions such as social cohesion have consistently failed to appear. However, a review by Murray (1983) noted some progress: changes in defensible space do tend to reduce the fear of crime, but only if accompanied by better policing and improved police–community relations; crime itself is not reduced. Fowler and Mangione (1982) found that fear held steady over a three year period in the "Asylum Hill" project while rising markedly in the rest of the town. Actual crime went up throughout the town, including Asylum Hill. As noted earlier, reducing fear is important, but may be accomplished by simple physical measures, such as improved street lighting, and if the reduction in fear is unrealistic it may reduce desirable precautions such as various forms of self-protection.

As for informal social networks, the link with crime control is very complex. Merry (1981) found that those who intervened (by reporting strangers to the police and so on) were a well-defined group, highly committed to the neighborhood in terms of length of residence, involvement in social networks, and time spent in daily interaction with other residents. Moreover, even such people failed to intervene if the "space" involved was that of another social/ethnic group, if they thought that the police would arrive too late, or that the intruder would retaliate against them – in fact all the reasons for nonreporting/nonintervening given in Chapter 2 and earlier in this chapter. And establishing homogeneous, long-standing groups is inevitably difficult: by definition, it takes a long time, and a deliberate attempt to create culturally homogeneous housing schemes might violate anti-discrimination laws.

O'Donnell (1980) has built, in a rather different way, on the general notion that strong social networks might increase surveillance and hence reduce crime. Crime rates are high in transient neighborhoods where people are less likely to know each other, leading to reduced natural surveillance of everyday activities,, including criminally related ones. O'Donnell and Lydgate (1980) found zoning regulations and land use to be related to crime rates, which were high in areas of high concentration of alcohol and entertainment businesses, and suggested zoning changes which dispersed such businesses more widely. (The average suburbanite, ever mindful of property values, might not welcome this suggestion.)

Yet another approach is to "remove crime from the environment" (Clarke 1983) in various ways. Examples include paying wages by cheque and not cash, reducing cheque frauds by requiring proof of identity, and cutting down the robbery of bus drivers by the use of automated flat-fare collection.

12.6. Crime prevention: problems and issues

Displacement

When one opportunity for crime is blocked, an offender has available several alternative types of displacement (Gabor 1978):

1. Geographical (trying to commit it in a different place).
2. Temporal (changing the time of the offense).
3. *Modus operandi* (a change of tactics).
4. Target (changing the objective).
5. Form (changing the type of crime).

According to Clarke (1983) none of this is inevitable. To assert that it is implies that "crime will out" due to a "disposition" to commit offenses. Clarke disagrees, arguing that whether or not displacement occurs depends on shifts in opportunities, particularly for marginal, casual, offenders (of whom there are large numbers). Clarke agrees that skilled professional criminals are likely to displace, as Gabor (1978) suggests, except when prevention measures are exceptionally tough and wide ranging (and hence expensive and inconvenient to those taking them). But a reduction in opportunity might well divert an early-career offender from criminal activities. Between "casuals" and "professionals" there is a gray area of semiprofessionals for whom the occurrence of displacement depends on finding at least one relatively easy option on the above list.

Media campaigns and other forms of persuasion

A common feature of the prevention approaches described in this chapter is that existing attitudes and habits have to change before any policy change can be introduced to bring about the intended reduction in crime. Some sort of persuasion campaign is therefore implied, whether aimed at potential witnesses, or at employers, employees, residents, automobile owners, and so on. While we have ample information as to how to design and execute such campaigns (McGuire 1980), and substantial experience of their use in health promotion, with mixed but often positive results (Matarazzo 1980), they are at a very early stage in the field of crime prevention. (There are special problems not found in health care. Any material benefit would of course be to the victim; the helper may gain in self-esteem or in the esteem of others, but may also suffer losses, both physical and otherwise. It is not surprising that a study by Bickman (1975) of a mass media campaign aimed at encouraging bystander intervention in crimes found that it had very little effect.

So far as campaigns to improve security are concerned, business men may be more responsive than householders. A study of victim households by Winchester and Jackson (1982) found that only 40 per cent of those interviewed intended to improve on their existing (low) level of security. But, as Litton (1982) indicates, higher premiums, or even the refusal of cover for noncompliance, compared with discounts for approved measures, may help to persuade householders as well as business people. Existing social networks can help or hinder media campaigns considerably – health campaign experience may be useful here (Matarrazo 1980).

Other difficulties

These have been listed by Clarke (1983) together with appropriate counter-arguments.

1. The pervasive attitude that "nothing works, so why bother?" This is easily countered: the existing evidence on crime prevention is genuinely encouraging for certain approaches at least, and further research and practical trials are justified.

2. Crime prevention reduces arguments for social reform by "papering over the cracks." But, as crime is only one of the undesirable consequences of social deprivation, reducing it leaves pressure on the others undiminished.

3. Only those who can afford protection will buy it, the rest will remain vulnerable. There is an argument for some form of "social subsidy" to encourage relatively small investments in security by those too poor to pay the full expenses of enhanced security, or even to cover the whole cost. Moreover, surveillance by social networks carries no

financial costs to their members, and may even bring returns through enhanced social contacts.

4. Security precautions can be unattractive, leading to "fortress like" buildings. Presumably they can also be attractive, or at least neutral.

5. Finally, Clarke mentions the nagging sense that "people should be morally better and not want to offend." In setting out the steps relevant to an effective persuasion campaign, McGuire (1980) included the need to analyze the value systems of those involved, whether as agents or targets, and suggests way of doing so.

12.7. Concluding comment

Crime is not going to disappear, and juveniles will continue to be recruited into the ranks of offenders, though mostly on a casual and temporary basis. The best we can hope for from programs with potential or actual offenders is a modest reduction in the flow. Crime prevention programs, particularly those based on self-interest, seem more hopeful, at least in deterring casual or unskilled young offenders from beginning offender careers. Such programs will depend ultimately for their success on the broader social context in which they are carried out. If this encourages job training and a supply of jobs for those who have been trained, crime prevention programs will achieve their maximum possible effect.

PART IV

Summary

13. Summary

This final chapter both summarizes key points in each of the preceding 12 chapters and makes a number of speculations about future developments.

13.1. Description (Section I)

Offenses (Chapter 1)

A criminal act is a legally defined behavior which may lead to punishment if it is detected and convicted. The boundaries of the criminal law change continually but the core remains, so that there is much cross-cultural consistency concerning "true crimes" (those against persons and property) and much disagreement on victimless offenses (to do with drink, drugs, sex, and gambling). The criminal law does not apply to those below an internationally varying "age of responsiblity," or to those adjudged too mentally ill to form a criminal intention, so that we must always take into account the age and state of mind of the accused.

Many crimes are not reported to the police; of those which are reported many are not recorded.

This book is concerned mainly with Index crimes, also called Part I crimes, which have two sub-groups. The violent offences are murder, manslaughter, aggravated assault, forcible rape, and robbery; property offenses are burglary, larceny-theft and auto-theft. In the USA, Index offences reported to the police regularly exceed ten million per year, 90 per cent of which are crimes against property.

Within reported and recorded violent crimes, homicides form about 2 per cent, rape a further small percentage, (but under-reporting is massive) robbery about 40 per cent and aggravated assault about 50 per cent. Larceny-theft contributes about 60 per cent and burglary about 30 per cent of Index property crimes, with auto-theft making up the rest. Child molestation and drug related offenses are outside the Index, but both cause great public concern and are far more frequent than the official figures would suggest. Organized crimes and occupational and corporate crime involve much greater financial costs than Index crimes, and political crimes may undermine the basic fabric of a society.

The fall in the crime figures during the latter part of the 19th century may be linked to the introduction of a professional police force and was succeeded by a subsequent long term rise in crime.

The official figures for the number of crimes reported to and recorded by the police are enshrined in the USA in the Uniform Crime Rate. Regular surveys of population samples are taken in several countries to record the experiences of potential victims (known in the USA as the National Crime Survey). Both have strengths and weaknesses; taken together they help to fill in the dark figure (crimes lost to view through failures to report or record). The consequences of a very large dark figure include the possibility that research into explanation may focus on the wrong questions.

Even when all the necessary cautions have been exercised there is much international variation in the crime figures between advanced industrial countries: the USA is easily highest for violent crime, particularly murder; Japan and Switzerland have relatively low crime rates.

The financial costs of Index crime in the USA are several score billions of dollars annually, including all types of crime, as well as the costs of the criminal justice system – but those of organized and corporate crime are likely to be much higher. The costs to victims include nonfinancial elements such as physical injury and psychological distress; the latter is a severe cost to potential victims.

Offenders (Chapter 2)

At each stage between surveillance and sentence there is a possibility of bias against particular groups, so that arrest records are problematic as a basis for theories about offenders. This is even more true of victim surveys, because in many offenses there is no or insuffcent contact between offender and victim. Hence use is made of offender self-report studies of the general population, which are reasonably reliable and valid (although their validity is measured against official statistics of offenders, themselves in doubt), except for young black males with police records. The major examples of self-report studies described (from both the USA and the UK) exemplify both the results of the method and the considerable gaps remaining – nearly all studies are of young males, with little on adults and not much on females. More difficult to carry out, but potentially valuable, are direct observations of offenders in action. All of those reported to date are of the non-participatory type.

Probably the most powerful research method is the longitudinal study (LS), illustrated by the Philadelphia (USA) and Cambridge (UK) studies. The LS method involves following the same group of persons over a long period of time, preferably from preoffending, recording along the way a large number of variables likely to be antecedents of, or associated with, offending, and then indexing offending and its consequences as completely as possible from a range of vantage points. Over the closing decade of this century and into the first of the next a stream of data can be expected from the largest, best designed and most comprehensive LS to date. Based at Yale University and headed by Professor Al Reiss, this will measure the impact on later offending of an extensive series of biological, social and psychological variables, from the pre-birth environment on.

Both self-report and observational studies indicate the high probability of offending by the general population, on at least one occasion, typically during the teenage years. But most people either desist early or remain very low-frequency offenders at most, and the majority of offences are carried out by a minority of the population. Within this minority, most are carried out by a smaller minority still, termed career offenders, who begin offending younger than the rest. The chances of an arrest for most offences are less than 10 per cent on average and are several times further reduced by pre-crime planning and preparation. There is a wide range across offenders, from occasional amateurs to skilled professionals who seek to maximize returns and minimize risks, as do professionals in general.

Many offenses are carried out by at least two persons, known as co-offenders. This is often omitted from official records, and is a potential source of confusion. Partners in crime are typically of the same sex and, particularly if young, are drawn from the same local friendship group.

Offending is strongly linked with both age and sex, less so with social class. The frequently asserted ethnic link is particularly complicated. The concentration of crime among the young has continued to increase over the past 50 years. The peak age for property offences is around 16–17 and for person crimes in the middle twenties. Those who continue to offend continue at much same rate until the age of 30–40, when most of the remainder then desist. The decline with increasing age suggests the influence of marriage and of steady jobs – the absence of both types of control helps to perpetuate criminal careers.

The very wide disparity between males and females for offenses is somewhat less marked for the less serious ones but remains significant.

Blacks are heavily over-represented in the figures for both arrests and incarcerations and across offences except for some types of financial crime. However, black white differences are more in prevalence than in incidence (more carry out at least one offence, no more are high-frequency offenders) and more in official figures than in self-reports. This suggests that the over-representation of blacks in prison is at least partially linked to bias in the criminal justice system against some blacks, particularly those of lower SES.

The most vulnerable potential victims are the young, the male, the black and the poor, because they are most on the street, or out at night, or by day, from their homes, which are less well protected than those of the more affluent. The elderly are least likely to be victimized (because they stay at home) but are the most fearful being the least able to defend themselves. Within violent offenses women suffer more than men at the hands of nonstrangers (spouses, ect.). The psychological effects of crime on victims are most severe for elderly females living alone, and include long-term depression and paranoia.

The police (Chapter 3)

Police functions are manifold and there are major shifts of fashion in police activity, particularly in relation to crime prevention, with a current return to community policing, and a related emphasis on citizen support, for example by Neighborhood Watch. Criminal investigation successes depend much more on the contributions of the public than on traditional detection techniques – hence the importance the police attach to securing confessions by those charged. Unfortunatily, these seem frequently unsafe as a basis for convictions, because of the combination of psychological pressures exerted by police interrogation.

Studies of police effectiveness are unclear as to whether or not deterrent styles of policing reduce crime or, if they do, whether the increased cost can be justified. Costs include local resentment at heavy handed methods, as well as financial ones.

The police have considerable discretion in both surveillance and in the choice of action following arrest. There is much assertion of bias in both, and some evidence for such assertions, particularly concerning poorly-off black males. Such biases seem least likely in the most professionally run police departments, and in cases in which both victim and alleged offender are black, and most likely where the former is white and the latter black. Police–juvenile encounters are most likely to escalate beyond the specific suspected crime when both sides lack the appropriate skills in managing the encounter.

Police behaviors in the course of their work relate to selection criteria for entry (which seem to favor entrants from upwardly mobile working-class backgrounds with illiberal social attitudes, which may subsequently strengthen due to the relative social isolation of police families from nonpolice contacts), to the training received and to the importance attached to loyalty to the force, rather than to abstract conceptions of justice and equity. Police misbehaviour includes both abuse of authority and corruption. While there are many individual and well-publicized examples of both, large-scale and careful studies remain rare, and public attitudes to the police continue to be reasonably favorable, possibly because of public awareness of the difficulties and stresses associated with the job, particularly at street level. Research suggests a range of stressors, of which the most obvious, physical danger, may not be the most severe. Police social isolation stresses families as well as officers, and stresses on officers may be more marked for female than for male.

The courts (Chapter 4)

While most criminal cases do not reach the courts, several hundred thousand do so annually in the USA. There is ample opportunity for bias to occur at each of the stages which follow police disposal and which are at the discretion of prosecuting lawyers, judges and juries. There evidence for bias on the part of at least some of those concerned, from requests for bail, through to the severity of the term imposed when a conviction leads to a prison sentence. Bias seems particularly likely on the part of juries, as does inability to bring an appropriate degree of skepticism to the evidence of eyewitnesses and to confessions following interrogation. Strict injunctions on research into real life juries have produced a range of inevitably less satisfactory research substitutes, but the case for bias seems reasonably well founded. There is also evidence that previously held social attitudes influence the willingness to convict. This is particularly important when a conviction for murder would be followed by death. The widespread practice of excluding those opposed in principle to the death penalty means that jurors who remain are all in favor of its use; such "death qualified" jurors lean more toward the prosecution than the defense, the facts of the case being equal. Also, juries seem likely to give harsher sentences to groups such as young black males.

Whereas lay people place strong weight on the evidence of an eyewitness, especially when the evidence is asserted with great confidence, such testimony is frequently marred, both by the inevitable difficulty of accurate observation of rapid events by untrained observers and by the long period between the crime and the trial. Methods designed to improve the reliability of such evidence – for example, hypnosis – seem seriously flawed, but the "cognitive interview" may have some promise.

Judicial decision-makers may be less biased than jurors, attending more frequently to the facts of the case, rather than to the attributes of the accused and the forensic skill of the lawyers. Sentencing rules obtrude on them with increasing strictness. Nevertheless, there is evidence of judicial bias in sentencing: in favor of women, at least for less serious offences, and against blacks, particularly in affluent areas with small black populations. Both race and social class increase in importance as an accused juvenile moves through the justice system, especially at sentencing; the combination of being poor and black seems even more deleterious for mature adults.

A final comment on Section I

The first four chapters support the conclusion that certain social groups are more likely than others to proceed along the track which begins with surveillance and ends in imprisonment. The final composition of a prison population is a function both of offending and being detected *and* of the bias in the behaviors of at least a section of those working in the criminal justice system. Initial disparities in offending between groups are amplified significantly, the amplification increasing the disparity at each stage in the sequence.

There is a clear implication for theories set up to explain crime:

they should be tested on the population in general, with offending behavior designated by self-report or by direct observation, as well as on offenders, including successful ones, and not only on the those who have been caught and incarcerated. The latter form the study populations for most of the research reports covered in the survey of criminological explanations which form the second part of the book. A number of longitudinal studies avoid this problem; it is not an exaggeration to assert that such studies offer the best future direction for criminology.

13.2. Explanation (Section II)

Biological factors (Chapter 5)

The belief that physical features such as facial appearance and body build predict to behavior, including criminal behavior, has a very long history. Over the past century, research interest has revived periodically but with little or no success to date.

Sex differences in crime are undoubted; that they relate to biologically based sex differences seems less likely than their link with sex differences in social training, social expectations and criminal opportunities. Despite some recent signs of narrowing, the differences look set to persist.

We need to look more directly at possible biological sources of individual differences in criminal behavior by studying differences in genetic inheritance. The possibility of a link with chromosomal abnormalities, particularly the possession of the XXY anomaly by some males, excited much initial attention in the 1960's; more recent work has found no substantial evidence.

Instead, attention has focused on the possibility of a general connection between inherited genes and crime; the research requirement is to separate, as far as possible, the influences of the post-natal social environment from those of the individual's biological inheritance. Three methods have been used: family, adoption, and twin. Family studies produced apparently impressive evidence for the inheritance of criminal behavior (which recurred over two or more generations), but failed completely to separate out social from biological factors. This fault is potentially avoided by adoption, which often occurs early in life. Once again, this research approach produces good though not unequivocal support for a significant contribution to crime of genetic inheritance. However, too little is known of the policy of adoption agencies to be sure that children are randomly assigned to families, irrespective of the known criminal histories of adoptive parents. The twin method benefits from the existence of two distinct types of twin, fraternal and identical, but to be completely satisfactory requires that such pairs are separated early and then reared apart in well recorded environments, before being compared for later criminal behavior. All studies to date fall well short of these criteria, although the data obtained are such as to suggest that the quest for the totally satisfactory twin study is well worth pursuing.

Individual differences (Chapter 6)

If there is a biological contribution to criminal behavior it is likely to operate through individual differences in intelligence, personality, and mental disorder, all of long-standing as explanations of criminal behavior, and all of which are known to have a significant genetic component.

Early studies of a link between intelligence (as measured by formal tests) and crime suggested that it was a strong one; the connection persists in more recent ones (though less powerfully), and has survived attempts at explanation by social class and differential vulnerability to detection. It seems possible that a low *verbal* IQ interacts with other variables, such as poor parenting and certain personality features, to produce school failure, school-conduct disorder, and extra-school criminal behaviors. Nevertheless, it is obvious that many offenders, particularly those who remain undetected for highly skilled offenses, have well above average IQ's.

For personality differences to contribute usefully to the explanation of crime, we need first to establish a significant degree of consistency in criminal behaviors: the evidence is for only moderate consistency across situations and time for person crimes, with more substantial levels for property crime. Such consistencies may be found more for the minority of persons at the extremes of personality dimensions than for the majority who score in the middle ranges. Despite very extensive studies, little support has been found for the hypothesized correlations between most personality variables and crime, whether measured by multivariate inventories or by single variables.

Psychodynamic studies have also yielded little of value. However, two areas of research are more promising: the division of offenders into delinquent sub-types may have both prognostic and explanatory implications, and the Eysenckian theory of personality and crime yields readily testable predictions which, while poorly supported in incarcerated populations of offenders, are consistently well supported by self-report studies in the general population and by descriptive information from the Cambridge Study. While a number of alternative explanations remain possible, these results demand further replication. It is likely that there are important interactions between relatively consistent personality features and the situational factors emphasized by the behavioral approach to crime.

The idea that mental disorder has a special connection with crime, particularly violent crime, is an old one. It is also a difficult question to answer in a clear cut way, because of the considerable methodological difficulties in the way of separating out cause and effect (for example does mental disorder cause crime or does the prison experience cause, or at least exacerbate, pre-existing mental disorder?). Little, if any, work has used self-reports of both offenses and disorder – the desirable design. Within these limitations, there seems no special link between crime and mental disorder in general. With respect to specific disorders, only the paranoid sub-group of the schizophrenias seems clearly connected to crime, specifically violent crime; and even within this segment most sufferers are not violent, and most violence is not committed by those so diagnosed.

The diagnosis of antisocial personality disorder (formerly psychopathy) has long been thought, almost by definition, to indicate a special link with crime. But, there are major conceptual and methological inadequacies with the existing body of research. While some progress has been made in both areas, clear differences between diagnosed persons and appropriate controls, relevant to the defining criteria, remain to be demonstrated. The relative absence of research into the seemingly key area of interpersonal behavior is surprising.

Childhood development (Chapter 7)

The level of moral development achieved by the individual is thought to indicate potential criminal behavior. Research in the traditions of Piaget and Kohlberg shows some support for this expectation, but we still lack longitudinal studies of moral development related to self-reported crime by adults, as opposed to cross-sectional research into offically designated juvenile offenders.

The link between methods of parental training and offending is becoming clarified by the major studies of Patterson and associates, which use direct observation of parent–child interaction sequences to measure the links between parental skills, such as discipline and monitoring, and long term child behaviors, including criminal behaviors. This group finds that initally home-based failures in socialization are subsequently expressed first in school misdemeanors and then in extra-school criminal acts. Risk factors for such sequences include social disadvantage, relatively unskilled parents, inadequate resources (both human and economic), and a child difficult to socialize from birth on.

In contrast to these relatively consistent results, several decades of theory and research on broken homes have yielded contradictory findings, partially due to a lack of agreement on the meaning of the term. Work on abusive homes suggests a very complex pathway from early abuse or neglect to adult violence, but emphasizes again the importance of child-management skills.

So far as childhood behaviors are concerned, the best predictors of later juvenile delinquency are early aggression, stealing (from home and/or school), truancy, lying, and drug use; this constellation supports the general finding that past behavior is the best predictor of future behavior in the same area. But, there are major methodological limitations on such results, including the relative lack of longitudinal studies and of work on minority populations. Family handicaps are both cumulative and interlocking, but some children seem to survive major difficulties in their early lives to escape later involvement in crime. (Conversely, many children from "good" homes nevertheless become consistent offenders.) Both results challenge explanation.

While there seems an association between school and delinquency, it is likely that many children are set on the track to subsequent crime before they enter school, so that schools may mirror both the community in which they are based and the homes from their children have come. Already delinquent peers may be rather more important as sources of criminal behavior, particularly in conjunction with such family variables as poor discipline and monitoring.

Several decades of large-scale studies into possible links between television viewing and crime, particularly violence, have not produced clear results. If anything, the claims made for such links seem more modest and restricted in the nineties than in the sixties. It may be that extended exposure to depictions of extreme sexual violence plays a part in the bizarre crimes of a few socially isolated individuals, so that future research should concentrate on such persons rather than on the viewing habits of the vast majority.

Social and economic theories and factors (Chapter 8)

Strain theories of crime stem from Durkheim's concept of anomie – the gap between what society holds out as the desirable goal of material achievement and the built-in lack of opportunity to achieve this for most of the less well-off. They are inevitably partial, dealing as they do with officially designated crime in working class groups. A number of major predictions are either not supported by the data or, if supported, can more easily be accommodated within social learning theory.

In contrast, sub-cultural theories deny the notion of strain: offending is simply the result of conformity to a local high-offending community, particularly to the local adolescent gang. But, even where this is the case, it is readily handled within social learning theory. Once again, middle-class crime is omitted.

Control theory does concern crime in all classes, but focuses on learning not to offend. It sees this as due to failures to form attachments between potential young offenders and parents and teachers – the transmitters of social norms such as the undesirability of offending. Longitudinal studies such as Patterson's show that weak attachments are preceded by poor parental discipline and monitoring; once again a sociological theory is readily subsumed within psychological research and theory.

All three of the above sociological approaches neglect the possibility of individual differences in predisposition to offending.

There is ample evidence for a partial bias by the criminal justice system against certain social groups and in favor of others, which amplifies any initial differences in offending between those groups. The search for such bias stems from the sociological theory of social labeling which directs attention to the activities of those empowered to operate the criminal justice system, including selecting those who may be labeled as criminals. There is also much psychological evidence for labeling in the context of mental illness. It is clear that labeling occurs and helps to account for the development and maintenance of criminal behavior, if not for its initial occurrence. But there is more controversy as to why it occurs. The most radical explanation, the Marxist theory of crime, fails on a number of counts, and is now of only marginal importance both in accounting for crime in general and for bias in the criminal justice system. A psychological approach to the latter points to the common human tendency to seek and achieve consistency by simplifying evidence.

In common with most sociological theories, the labeling approach deals only with crime by underprivileged groups, so is inevitably partial. Like control theory, differential association theory deals with crime by all persons. Its fundamental assertion is that crime is learned by association with existing offenders. It anticipated social learning theory by over a quarter of a century. However, the latter provides a much more detailed framework which both suggests research and accommodates research findings, so that differential association theory is now of historical interest only.

Wider cultural factors may be associated with differences in crime rates between countries and between different sections of the same country. For example, as the developing nations progress economically their patterns of crime move toward those of the developed world, in step with parallel shifts in social organization. But, the case of Japan continues to puzzle criminologists. While the gap between Japanese and American crime rates is narrowing it remains large; speculative explanations include cultural and ethnic uniformity, greater social and family control, and consistently low rates of unemployment.

Another speculation explains the increase in crime by American adolescents in the past two decades as due to a generational shift in "present" orientation which, in turn, is said to be due to a declining use of coerciveness by parents.

We are on much more solid ground when we look at community as an explanation for variations in crime rates. High and low crime areas persist over decades, despite population turnovers and even attempts at gentrification, so that communities, like individuals, have "careers in crime." There is also a process of neighborhood decline in which the economic flight to the suburbs of whites and of upwardly mobile blacks seems particularly important in decreasing informal social controls and organized community life among those who remain and in producing neighborhoods dominated by the fear of crime.

Several researchers accept the general assertion of a link between crime and ethnicity, and seek explanations in constitutional factors or in sub-cultural influences peculiar to black American life, so far with little solid support. Others, while agreeing that black Americans are on average economically underprivileged compared with whites, assert that this cannot be the whole story, pointing to lower levels of crime in other minority groups (typically consisting of recent immigrants). But relatively few blacks are newcomers; most stem from ancestors who came to America before most whites. The difference is that for the whole of that time they have been subject to official or unofficial (since the 1960's) discrimination. It is this institutionalized segregation which maintains a large section of America's blacks in communities marked by widespread social and economic deprivation. Quite simply, the inner-city black population has much more than its share of poor, young, single, low-income mothers with too limited resources, both financial and psychological, for effective child management and, hence, for instilling crime avoidance. At the same time it has few models of success through legitimate means and many models of the rewards of crime. But there is more still: there are plenty of poor whites but they are not socially and culturally isolated from their fellow Americans as are millions of the black poor. It has been said, without much exaggeration, that parts of America are little different from the Third World. From time to time, as in Los Angeles in the Spring of 1992, a spark sets off the powder keg of simmering discontent.

There are two versions of an economic emphasis in explanations of crime: the first implicates poverty, whether absolute or relative, as a major cause of crime; the second, which is more general, asserts the universal urge for material gain, irrespective of the current level of personal affluence, and focuses on criminal behavior as one route to such advancement. The latter has links with the psychologically based social learning theory of crime.

One version of a general stress on poverty as a key contributor to crime implicates relative, rather than absolute, status, both in unemployment and in income. Careful analyses demonstrate the great complexity of any link between unemployment and crime, both because the direction of the linkage may be either way, and because a third factor, for example, an individual difference variable, such as "personality," may underlie both, making it hard to learn and observe social rules and also to get and retain a job. It is likely that psychological variables will interact with such major current trends as a continuing shift from manual jobs in manufacturing, typically the preserve of males, toward nonmanual service jobs, mainly filled by women. The result is a persisting, probably growing, high rate of unemployment among young unskilled males, particularly black males.

The evidence for a link between income inequality and violent crime is more consistent between countries than between different sections of the same country. Once again, a review of the predicted linkage leads to the critical importance among social factors of being young, male, black – and poor, unskilled and segregated.

The cognitive-behavioral approach (Chapter 9)

There are two versions: Social learning theory (SLT) which stems directly from several decades of theory and research by Albert Bandura, and rational choice theory (RCT), set out more recently by Clarke and Cornish, but which can be traced as least as far back as the 18th century English philosopher Jeremy Bentham.

This book's application of SLT to the two major divisions of crime emphasizes post-childhood events, but sees them as building on the sequence of individual differences (partly biologically based), childhood experiences, and social and economic factors, including the response to offenders of the criminal justice system. The theory gives weight both to behavior and to cognitive representations and transformations of behavior.

The sequence of explanatory factors is SLT is acquisition (how criminal behaviors are acquired, performance, and maintenance (their repetition over long periods of time). The initial phase points to the importance of the social context in which persons grow up or work for providing opportunities for social influence toward criminal attitudes and away from relatively law abiding ones. In explaining this transition, much use is made of such powerful social influence variables as persuasive communications within two person and larger groups, and the control exerted by group norms. The hypothesized sequence of attitude change is relevant much more to persons previously holding law abiding attitudes; those exposed only to social models favoring crime will hold pro-crime attitudes from the outset. Once such attitudes are established, persons learn actual criminal behaviors first by observational learning (directly or by hearsay) and then by response-contingent learning (the criminal act is performed). If the performance is rewarded, there is a further strengthening of the pro-crime attitude, and an increased likelihood that the act will be repeated. This leads to phase two, that of performance. Once a particular criminal act is in a person's repertoire, the situational variables which affect the probability that it will be performed are:

1. Opportunity. The more targets, such as parked automobiles, the more auto break-ins and thefts.

2. Incentive (the anticipated return). These include primary incen-

tives, such as food and sex, sensory (fun and excitement), monetary, social interaction and gains in status or power.

3. The target. Other things being equal, a criminal act is more likely against targets of lesser difficulty, greater propinquity to the potential offender, and with lesser access to the law.

4. Risk. This refers to the probability of intervention by the police and of conviction if arrested, and to the possible level of punishment.

5. Skills and resources. These range from financial expertise in the case of fraud to the physical strength and skill needed for a successful assault.

6. Legal access to the same return. Offenders may be restrained by the knowledge that they could acquire a particular goal legally, but this seems the least important of the situational factors relevant to performance.

Several "criminogenic" factors may be influential:

1. Being a habitual drug user. This seems to potentiate crime only when the person is on a "run" and requires instant and large sums of money to maintain a current high level of drug intake.

2. Alcohol. This is again less clearly related than at first sight. Beyond a minimum level, alcohol impairs both judgement and execution: offences are less carefully selected and less well carried out; persons may then be somewhat more likely to offend, particularly against persons, but much more likely to be caught.

3. Gun ownership. The more widepread this is, the greater the use of guns in crime; the possession of a weapon both increases the offenders sense of impunity and the potential damage to the victim.

4. Arousal level. The more complex a task, the lower the desirable level of arousal for optimal performance. Beyond this point, target selection is less rational and performance worse – just as in the case of alcohol. Persons chronically inclined to rapid increases in arousal seem likely to offend less rationally than those of a more stable temperament.

Several additional performance variables are relevant to crimes against persons.

1. The sex of the aggressor and of the intended victim (male attacks on females are more likely than the reverse).

2. The intended victim's capacity for retaliation and intent to retaliate, both as perceived by the potential assailant.

3. The presence of an aggressive model.

4. The potential assailant has had prior aversive experiences (physical and or verbal).

5. The prior withdrawal of well-established reinforcers (for example the sudden loss of a job).

6. Frustration. Violence occurs in response to a major obstacle in the path of a previously attainable goal, and also when the person has learned that violence is an effective way of removing frustration.

7. Punishment. This may have the unintended effect of instigating aggression by the person receiving the punishment.

The third phase is maintenance. Like behavior in general, criminal behavior is maintained by its consequences. There are two broad groups of reinforcers: internal and external. The former include both money and status. Because clearance rates are low for most offenses (the true rate is even lower due to deficiencies in both reporting and recording) and punishment is often delayed or relatively mild, positive returns considerably outweigh negative ones for many offenders. Moreover, offenders are typically on schedules of partial reinforcement, the schedule most likely to maintain a behavior, including criminal behavior, over a long period of time.

Internal reinforcers include both the search for consistency between attitudes and behaviors and the cognitive distortions which help persons avoid the subjective discomfort resulting from an action (such as a crime) at variance with ones self-perception as a "good" person. They range from euphemistic labeling (as when a murder is termed a "contract") to attribution of blame (a rape victim was "asking for it"). Offenders will vary in their resort to distortions; early career ones will use them more than those late in a career, and personality differences may also play a part.

An example of the SLT approach is supplied by rape. The acquisition phase includes exposure to social models in one's own social setting (young men who have already raped), the opportunity to learn markedly anti-female stereotypes, the use of erotic pornography which depicts rape scenes, a low level of heterosexual social skills, and a prior history of interpersonal violence. The more of these factors are present the more likely is the first rape. Once this has occurred, the key situational variables for further rapes include opportunity (access to an available victim), a range of incentives other than monetary ones, a poorly defended target and a low perceived risk, as well as prior emotional arousal due to prior aversive experiences, withdrawal of reinforcers, and frustration. Very specific environmental stimuli will also become triggers for rape, such as a particular victim and setting. Long-term maintenance is assisted by self-reinforcement, particularly the cognitive rehearsal of the entire sequence of events.

Rational choice theory has a similar explanatory sequence (though the phases are termed initial involvement, the criminal event, and continuance, respectively), but also provides for the cessation of a criminal career, termed desistance. While it emphasizes the rationality of criminal decision making, RCT also points to limitations on rationality due to the incomplete availability of relevant information and the limitations of the offender's own cognitive abilities. Clarke and Cornish list the choice-structuring properties of a criminal opportunity, which overlap with those listed above under performance variables. Overall, the theory is based both on economic models of criminal decision making and on psychological studies of information processing. Much research, on both real and hypothetical criminal behavior, underpins rational choice theory, and Clarke and Cornish provide detailed applications to specific crimes, for example to burglary.

An appraisal of these two versions of the cognitive-behavioral approach suggests that SLT is particularly strong on the biological and other precursors of crime and on the acquisition and performance phases but omits desistance. Conversely, RCT has little or no detail on precursors or on the acquisition of criminal attitudes and behaviors, but is very good on the detailed situational features which lead to the choice of a particular target, as well as on the importance of increased professionalism and changes in lifestyle for the maintenance of a criminal career. But it is silent on the long-term learning history of the offender and on the use of cognitive processes, over and above decision taking itself. However, the account of desistance is an important strength.

The theories have much in common, but some different strengths and weaknesses. A combination of the latter would largely eliminate the former. Even as they stand, both are readily applicable to a range of specific offenses and broad categories of crime including occupational and political offenses and organized crime.

A final comment on Section II

Genetically based predispositions, mediated by personality variables, childhood experiences, particularly of inadequate or inappropriate parental training methods, exposure to high-crime communities, and possibly the experience of relative poverty, combine in varying proportions for different persons to set the scene for the acquisition of criminal attitudes and behaviors by well-established social learning processes. Next, a number of key situational variables, from opportunity through gun possession, interact to determine whether or not a particular crime will be performed by someone who now has the crime in his behavioral repertoire. The maintenance of the behavior will be determined by the long-term pattern of rewards and costs associated with that crime and will be assisted by cognitive processes which help the offender to distort his perceptions of himself, his behavior and his victims. Increasing age, and an associated shift in the relative rewards of crime and noncrime results in most offenders finally desisting. The bias against certain social groups of some elements within the criminal justice system discussed in Section A, is used by labeling theory to account for at least part of the over-representation of certain groups in prison populations. It may best be accounted for by the general tendency of many human beings to simplify their social perceptions, even if this leads to a distortion of reality.

13.3. Control (Section III)

The penal system (Chapter 10)

Most of the main methods of punishment now in use, from the death penalty to reparation, have a long history. While all have both eloquent proponents and detractors, empirical studies of efficacy, whether corrective or deterrent, are in much shorter supply, partly because of the difficulty of such studies, but also because the penal system operates on precedent and argument, rather than on empirical evidence.

Nevertheless, some conclusions on corrective efficacy can be drawn, including lower reconviction rates for females, and for fewer previous convictions. It seems that while probation is as effective as a period in prison in preventing reoffending, fines are superior to both.

Research into deterrent efficacy is similarly difficult, but an emphasis on costs and benefits, as perceived by potential offenders (the heart of the cognitive-behavioral approaches) seems likely to be useful.

Whether or not to use the death penalty for murder is a critical issue in the USA, though not in other advanced industrial countries, where it has been abandoned. In contrast, it is in increasing use in the USA. There is no agreement as to the deterrent effect of the death penalty, but one aspect makes it unique among penalties: once carried out it is irreversible. It is clear that American public opinion is largely in favor of the death penalty, and many politicians running for office demonstrate that they are tough on crime by opposing abolition. The continuing situation in most states (in the early 1990's about one-third did not have the death penalty) is one of large numbers on death row, with a much smaller proportion actually executed.

The concept of incapacitation – the use of very long sentences to take an offender off the streets and hence away from criminal opportunities – is similarly controversial. However, the evidence is more clear-cut. This is that even selective incapacitation (long sentences for high-rate offenders) results in only a modest reduction in crime, but a sharp increase in the prison population.

An alternative is to identify high-rate offenders in advance (before the age of 13) on the basis of a range of predictive factors. But at present the number of resulting false positives would both penalize such persons unjustly and expose them to criminogenic influences by participation in the same program as those corrctly identified as being at risk. Also, there are major ethical objections to such advance detection of "delinquency proneness," essentially to do with the loss of normal civil rights. The arguments for and against prediction occur with particular force in the context of the prediction of dangerousness, concerning which there are special difficulties – but which psychologists and psychiatrists continue to attempt.

Prison populations in the USA rise steadily, due both to changes in age composition and to tighter sentencing guidelines set by commissions, leading in many states to a more severe sentencing policy. The issue is critical for criminal justice policy, and hence for both the size and the composition of the prison population, Recipes for coping with the size problem range from doing nothing, through providing more accommodation, to shorter sentences (essentially the European, though not the British, approach).

The prison experience is inevitably unpleasant for most inmates, involving a range of major deprivations, which are partly alleviated by the informal social structure of prisoner life. But the problem of overcrowding affects all prisoners, and for many there are the ever-present threats of violence and victimization. Crowding (defined as space per inmate below a recommended minimum) has been correlated with a range of negative consequences including increased recidivism, but the relationship seems complex, so that crowding may best be seen as an extra hazard in an already stressful environment. Everyday violence appears endemic in most prisons, compared with widely publicized, but relatively occasional, riots.

The nature of the prison experience varies between groups, from those on death row, typically in solitary confinement and constantly uncertain as to their fate, over which they have no control, to black inmates, who are subject to a harsher regime by the largely white prison staff, but are less likely to be victimized by other prisoners than are their white counterparts, particularly those whites who are middle-class and/or physically frail. Victimization takes several forms, including physical, psychological, and economic.

While there is no lack of anecdotal accounts of the pains of imprisonment, replicable, quantitative, results are much harder to come by – possibly because of the very wide range of responses to a very varied set of experiences. Research has to be much more specific in both respects.

One way of overcoming the problem is to study simulated prisons. A particularly spectacular example of this approach produced equally spectacular results, but also excited much criticism; future research would be best conducted in real prisons but using the sophisticated methods of the simulated prison study.

Suggestions for easing the pains of prison life range from self-help by prisoners to staff actions, including the total redesign of prison structures and the involvement of prisoners in decision-making.

The treatment of offenders (Chapter 11)

While the current position concerning therapy-based approaches to offenders is not quite as bleak as a well known earlier conclusion, that "nothing works," several major reviews have found only small overall effects of treatment compared with no treatment in preventing reconvictions (typically of young offenders). A more detailed set of conclusions follows.

1. Methods based on psychodynamic principles are ineffective either in preventing initial offending or in reducing reoffending, and may even be contra-indicated – it is possible that they produce worse outcomes than doing nothing at all. These conclusions hold for both residential and nonresidential settings.

2. The majority of current programs involve a behaviorally based method. When used in institutions, such methods seem very effective in enhancing both maintenance behaviors relevant to the needs of the

institution and educational skills useful to clients. Neither achievement has much effect on subsequent reoffending. The severe shortcomings of institutions as settings for treatment programs, as well as their much greater cost, means that in general programs are best conducted in community settings. Nevertheless, there is certain to be a continued use of institutional placements for some juveniles, if only because all else has failed, or because for certain offenses public opinion demands incarceration.

3. Teaching family programs (e.g., Achievement Place) have not lived up to their earlier promise of being more effective than appropriate comparisons in preventing reconviction, and may also be more expensive.

4. Family-based interventions seem promising in preventing the occurrence of offending, but only for minor offenses, and if the families are intact, and have a reasonable income, and there is much emphasis on such therapist skills as communication.

5. For older adolescents and nonintact families, short term contingeny contracting focusing on employment-related skills seems promising in reducing recidivism, but more stringent research controls need to be exercised. If a previous offender has both a job and a stable marriage, the combination seems a relatively powerful barrier against futher offenses.

6. There is no support for school based programs, certainly as far as reducing recidivism is concerned and even for achieving improvements in educational skills.

7. Programs involving probation officers have presented great difficulties and hold little promise.

8. Programs involving a temporary shift of environment, such as adventure experiences, seem unhelpful in reducing recidivism, and the "scared straight" approach is clearly no more than a passing gimmick.

9. With the possible exception of improving social performance in police–juvenile encounters, social skills training bears no obvious relation to the behaviors involved in crime-avoidance.

10. Other than for sex offenses, studies directly concerned with offence-related behaviors are virtually nonexistent, but seem worthwhile pursuing, if only because they flow logically from the cognitive-behavioral model of crime, and the model has been relatively successful in the treatment of clinical problems.

11. However, there are very severe difficulties in generalizing from the clinic to offenders. Major problems for the treatment of offenders

include the targets of and the criteria for change, the probably different aims of therapists and "clients," counter control by clients and noncooperation by staff, all of which must be tackled before realistic and potentially effective programs can be constructed.

12. To improve outcome a number of possibilities are available, including intervening at high strength and across broad areas of behavior with the program delivered as planned, as well as regarding criminal behavior as a chronic problem, perhaps needing continuous intervention for a number of years.

13. In addition, it would be wise to confine intervention programs to clients who have had a genuine opportunity to consider all information relevant to the methods and targets on offer and hence have made a noncoerced decision to join the program (i.e., doing so does not result in a lighter, a different, or no sentence). The State must retain the separate right of punishment following a properly conducted trial.

14. Finally, many offenders desist even without formal intervention, possibly due to a combination of relatively poor returns from crime, increasing age, and the relatively greater attractiveness of alternatives to crime.

Crime prevention (Chapter 12)

1. Training and rewarding police officers for relatively low-key methods of handling police–juvenile encounters and for cautioning rather than arresting for minor offenses seems likely to divert some potential young offenders.

2. Bystander intervention, while welcome when it occurs, is unlikely to contribute more substantially to crime prevention than at present, even if massive media campaigns are conducted. Most bystanders will continue to find that the balance of rewards and costs favours nonintervention.

3. A more formal citizen surveillance scheme, Neighborhood Watch, seems well worth pursuing, providing ways can be found to combat drop-out, loss of initial enthusiasm and the possibility of displacement into neighboring, "unwatched" districts.

4. Informal self-protection. In contrast to bystander-intervention this concerns self-defense by prospective victims. Many people have already adopted sensible defensive tactics; relatively limited media campaigns might increase their number and hence reduce the number of potential easy targets.

5. Employer self-protection. Once again, self-interest and the fact that increases in security can be obtained at no great cost and may even reduce insurance premiums, should encourage both efforts and progress.

6. Employee activities. This area is again promising, with clear evidence of a reduced risk of crime due to the mere presence of employees. If "presence" becomes more planned and systematic, even greater effects should be obtained.

7. Hardening the target. Improvements in the design and hence performance of physical devices such as steering locks have shown clear benefits, and further technical advances should result in more gains.

8. Crime prevention by environmental design. The original inflated claims for "defensible space" have been succeeded by the recognition that physical arrangements which strengthen local networks make crime prevention more likely. The same may be true of larger-scale urban planning.

9. A number of important issues remain. The general concept of displacement provides an important way of organizing research into situational crime prevention. Displacement seems much more likely for skilled professionals than for casual offenders. Media campaigns aimed at crime prevention are still in their infancy, and much might be learned from the experience gained in large scale health-promotion campaigns. Additionally, a number of public concerns, largely to do with the desirability and possibility of effective crime prevention, need to be taken seriously in planning large scale policy initiatives.

A final comment on Section III

Current penal methods seem largely, possibly entirely, ineffective in reducing the extent of criminal behavior, and may even increase it through exposure to the criminogenic setting of prison. To date, psychologically based treatments for offenders do not hold out much more promise; crime prevention seems much the best prospect, but crime is not to be seen as some form of disease, to be eliminated one day by a major advance in knowledge. The best expectation is for a limited degree of reduction in the recruitment of future offenders.

References

Abrahamsen, D.
1960 *The Psychology of Crime*. New York: Columbia University Press.

Adams, R., and Vetter, H.J.
1981 Social structure and psychodrama outcome: A ten-year follow-up. *Journal of Offender Counseling Services and Rehabilitation* 6:111–9.

Agnew, R.
1985 Social control theory and delinquency. *Criminology* 23:47–61.

Aidala, A.A., and Greenblat, C.S.
1986 Changes in moral judgments among student populations, 1929–1983. *Youth and Society* 17:221–35.

Aiken, T.W., Stumphauzer, J.S., and Veloz, E.V.
1977 Behavioral analysis of nondelinquent brothers in a high juvenile crime community. *Behavioral Disorders* 2:212–22.

Ainsworth, M.P.S., Blehar, M.C., Walters, E., and Wall, S.
1978 *Patterns of Attachment*. Hillsdale, NJ: Lawrence Erlbaum.

Alexander, B.B., Barton, C., Schiavo, R.S., and Parsons, B.V.
1976 Systems-behavioural interventions with families of delinquents: Therapist characteristics, family behavior, and outcome. *Journal of Clinical and Consulting Psychology* 44:656–64.

Alexander, J.F., and Parsons, B.V.
1973 Short-term behavioral interventions with delinquent families: Impact on family process and recidivism. *Journal of Abnormal Psychology* 81:219–25.

Alker, H.A.
1972 Is personality situationally specific or intra-psychically consistent? *Journal of Personality* 40:1–16.

Allsopp, J.F.
1975 Investigation into the applicability of Eysenck's theory of criminality to the antisocial behavior of schoolchildren. Unpublished Ph.D. dissertation, University of London.

Allsop, J.F., and Feldman, M.P.
1975 Extraversion, neuroticism and psychotism and anti-social behavior in schoolgirls. *Social Behavior and Personality* 2:104–95.
1976 Item analyses of questionnaire measures of personality and anti-social behavior in school. *British Journal of Criminology* 16:337–51.

Altschuler, A.W.
1991 The failure of sentencing commissions. *New Law Journal* 141:829–30.

American Friends Service Committee
1971 *Struggle for Justice*. New York: Hill & Wang.

American Psychiatric Association
1981 *Diagnostic and Statistical Manual of Mental Disorders*, 3rd Edition (DSM III). Washington, DC: American Psychiatric Association.

American Psychological Association (APA)
1978 Report of the task force on the role of psychology in the criminal justice system. *American Psychologist* 33:1099–113.

Amir, M.
1972 *Patterns in Forcible Rape*. Chicago: University of Chicago Press.

Anderson, C.A.
1989 Temperature and aggression: Ubiquitous effects of heat on recurrence of human violence. *Psychological Bulletin* 106:74–96.

Anderson, E.
1978 *A Place on the Corner*. Chicago: University of Chicago Press.

Arbuthnot, J., Gordon, D.A., and Jurkovic, G.J.
1987 Personality. In H.C. Quay (Ed.), *Handbook of Juvenile Delinquency*, pp. 139–83. New York: Wiley.

Arens, R., Granfield, D.D., and Susman, J.
1965 Jurors, jury charges and insanity. *Catholic University of America Law Review* 14:1–29.

Aronfreed, J.
1968 *Conduct and Conscience*. New York: Academic Press.

Aronson, E., and Mettee, D.R.
1968 Dishonest behavior as a function of differential levels of individual self-esteem. *Journal of Personality and Social Psychology* 9:121–7.

Astor, S.D.
1971 Shoplifting survey. *Security World* 8:34–5.

Austin, W., and Utne, M.K.
1977 Sentencing discretion and justice in judicial decision-making. In B.D. Sales (Ed.), *Psychology in the Legal Process*, pp. 163–196. New York: Spectrum.

Avison, W.R., and Loring, P.L.
1986 Population diversity and cross-national homicide: The effects of inequality and heterogeneity. *Criminology* 24:733–49.

Ayllon, T., and Azrin, N.H.
1968 *The Token Economy*. New York: Appleton Century.

Ayllon, T., and Milan, M.A.
1979 *Correctional Rehabilitation and Management: A Psychological Approach*. New York: Wiley.

Bachman, J.G., O'Malley, P.M., and Johnston, J.
1978 *Adolescence and Adulthood: Changes and Stability in the Lives of Young Men*. Vol. 6 of *Youth in Transition*. Ann Arbor, MI: University of Michigan Institute for Social Research.

Baker, T.
1983 Rookie police officers' perceptions of police occupational deviance. *Police Studies* 6:30–8.

Baldwin, D.V., and Skinner, M.L.
1989 Structural model for anti-social behavior: generalization to single-mother families. *Development Psychology* 25:45–50.

Baldwin, J., and McConville, M.C.
1980 Criminal juries. In M. Tonry, and N. Morris (Eds.), *Crime and Justice: An Annual Review of Research*, Vol. 2, pp. 269–320. Chicago: University of Chicago Press.

Bales, R.
1962 Attitudes towards drinking in the Irish culture. In D. Pittman, and C.R. Snyder (Eds.), *Society, Culture and Drinking Patterns*. New York: Wiley.

Balkin, S., and Houlden, P.
1983 Reducing fear of crime through occupational presence. *Criminal Justice and Behavior* 10:13–33.

Bandura, A.
1973 *Aggression: A Social Learning Analysis*. New York: Prentice-Hall.
1977 *Social Learning Theory*. Englewood Cliffs, NJ: Prentice-Hall.
1986 *Social Foundations of Thought and Action*. Englewood Cliffs, NJ: Prentice-Hall.

Bandura, A., and Jeffery, R.W.
1973 Role of symbolic coding and rehearsal processes in observational learning. *Journal of Personality and Social Psychology* 26:122–31

Bandura, A., and Walters, R.H.
1959 *Adolescent Aggression*. New York: Ronald Press.

Bangert-Drowns, R.L.
1986 Review of developments in meta-analytic method. *Psychological Bulletin* 99:388–99.

Banuazizi, A., and Mohavedi, S.
1975 Interpersonal dynamics in a simulated prison: A methodological analysis. *American Psychologist* 30:152–60.

Barlow, H.D.
1981 *Introducing Criminology*, 2nd Edition. Boston: Little, Brown.

Baron, R.A., and Bell, P.A.
1975 Aggression and heat: mediating effects of prior provocations and exposure to an aggressive model. *Journal of Personality and Social Psychology* 31:825–32.

Barry, H., III, Bacon, M., and Child, I.L.
1957 A cross-cultural survey of some sex differences in socialization. *Journal of Abnormal and Social Psychology* 55:327–33.

Bartel, A.P.
1979 Women and crime: an economic analysis. In S.L. Messinger, and E. Bitner (Eds.), *Criminal Review Yearbook*, Vol. 1, pp. 88–110. Beverly Hills, CA: Sage.

Bartlett, F.C.
1932 *Remembering*. Cambridge: Cambridge University Press.

Bartollas, C.
1982 Survival problems of adolescent prisoners. In R. Johnson, and H. Toch (Eds.), *The Pains of Imprisonment*, pp. 165–79. Beverley Hills, CA: Sage.

Baumer, T.L.
1985 Testing a general model of fear of crime: data from a national sample. *Journal of Research in Crime and Delinquency* 22:234–55.

Bayley, D.H.
1979 Police functions, structure and control in Western Europe and

North America: comparative and historical studies. In N. Morris, and M. Tonry (Eds.), *Crime and Justice: An Annual Review of Research*, Vol. 1, pp. 109–44. Chicago: University of Chicago Press.

Bayley, D.H., and Mendelsohn, H.
1969 *Minorities and the Police*. New York: Free Press.

Beach, W.G.
1932 Oriental crime in California. *Stanford University Publications in History, Economics, and Political Science* 3:404–97.

Beane, G.D.
1987 Cross-national comparison of homicidal age/sex-adjusted rates using the 1980 US homicide experience as a standard. *Journal of Quantitative Criminology* 3:215–27.

Beattie, G.C.
1984 Meet the burglar. *The Guardian*, Oct. 20.

Bell, R.Q.
1968 A reinterpretation of the direction of effects in studies of socialization. *Psychological Review* 75:81–96.

Bellack, A.S., Hersen, M., and Kazdin, A.E. (Eds.)
1982 *International Handbook of Behavior Modification and Theory*. New York: Plenum Press.

Belson, W.
1975 *Juvenile Theft. The Causal Factors*. New York: Harper and Row.

Bennett, R.R.
1984 Becoming blue: a longitudinal study of police recruit occupational socialization. *Journal of Police Science and Administration* 12:47–58.

Bennett, R.R., and Bennett, S.B.
1983 Police personnel levels and the incidence of crime: a cross-national investigation. *Criminal Justice Review* 8:32–9.

Bent, A.E.
1974 *The Politics of Law Enforcement*. Lexington, MA: D. C. Heath.

Berg, I., Hullin, R., and McGuire, R.
1979 A randomly controlled trial of two court procedures in truancy. In D.P. Farrington, K. Hawkins, and S.M. Lloyd-Bostock (Eds.), *Psychology, Law, and Legal Processes*, (pp. 143–51). London: Macmillan.

Berkowitz, L.
1969 Social motivation. In G. Lindzey, and E. Aronson (Eds.), *The Handbook of Social Psychology*, 2nd Edition, Vol. 3, pp. 50–135. Reading, MA: Addison-Wesley.
1972 Words and symbols as stimuli to aggressive responses. In J.F. Knutson (Ed.), *Control of Aggression: Implications from Basic Research*. Chicago: Aldine-Atherton.
1974 Some determinants of impulsive aggression: Role of mediated associations with reinforcement for aggression. *Psychological Review* 81:165–76.
1978 Is criminal violence normative behavior? Hostile and instrumental aggression in violent incidents. *Journal of Research in Crime and Delinquency* 15:148–61.
1984 Some effects of thoughts on anti- and prosocial influences of

media events: a cognitive neoassociative analysis. *Psychological Bulletin* 95:410–27.

1989 Frustration-aggression hypothesis: examination and reformulations. *Psychological Bulletin* 106:59–73.

Berscheid, E., and Walster, E.

1969 *Interpersonal Attraction*. Reading, MA: Addison-Wesley.

Biblarz, A., Barnowe, J.T., and Biblarz, D.N.

1984 To tell or not to tell: differences between victims who report crimes and victims who do not. *Victimology: An International Journal* 9:153–8.

Bickman, L.

1975 Bystander interventions in a crime: The effect of a mass media campaign. *Journal of Applied Social Psychology* 5:292–302.

Biles, D., Braithwaite, J., and Braithwaite, V.

1981 The mental health of victims of crime. *International Journal of Offender Therapy and Comparative Criminology* 2:130–3.

Binder, R.

1987 A historical and theoretical introduction. In H.C. Quay (Ed.), *Handbook of Juvenile Delinquency*, pp. 1–32. New York: Wiley.

Black, D.A.

1977 A 5-year follow-up study of male patients discharged from Broadmoor. Paper read to the Annual Conference of the British Psychological Society, Exeter, April.

Black, D.S., and Reiss, A J.

1970 Police control of juveniles. *American Sociological Review* 35:63–77.

Blackburn, R.

1978 Psychopathy, arousal, and the need for stimulation. In R.D. Hare, and D. Schalling (Eds.), *Psychopathic Behavior. Approaches to Research*, pp. 157–64. Chichester: Wiley.

1980 Still not working? A look at recent outcomes in offender rehabilation. Paper read to the Scottish Branch of the British Psychological Society Conference on Deviance, University of Stirling, February.

1984 The person and dangerousness. In D.J. Muller, D.E. Blackman, and A.J. Chapman (Eds.), *Psychology and Law*, pp. 102–11. Chichester: Wiley.

1986 Patterns of personality deviation among violent offenders: replication and extension of an empirical taxonomy. *British Journal of Criminology* 26:254–269.

1989 Psychopathy and personality disorder in relation to violence. In K. Howells, and C.R. Hollins (Eds.), *Clinical Approaches to Violence*, pp. 61–88. Chichester: Wiley.

Blake, R.R.

1958 The other person in the situation. In R. Tagiuri, and L. Petrullo (Eds.), *Person Perception and Interpersonal Behavior*, pp. 229–42. Stanford: Stanford University Press.

Blau, J.R., and Blau, P.M.

1982 The cost of inequality: metropolitan structure and violent crime. *American Sociological Review* 47:114–29.

Blumenthal, M.D., Kahn, R.L., and Andrews, F.M.

1971 Attitudes towards violence. *Proceedings of the 79th Annual*

Convention of the American Psychological Association. Washington, DC: American Psychological Association.

Blumstein, A.
1983 Prisons, population, capacity, and alternatives. In J.Q. Wilson (Ed.), *Crime and Public Policy*, pp. 229–50. San Francisco: ICS Press.
1988 Prison populations: a system out of control? In M. Tonry, and N. Morris (Eds.), *Crime and Justice: An Annual Review of* Research, Vol. 7, pp. 231–66. Chicago: University of Chicago Press.

Blumstein, A., and Cohen, J.
1979 Estimation of individual crime rates from arrest records. *Canadian Journal of Criminology* 70:501–85.

Blumstein, A., Cohen, J., and Farrington, D.P.
1988 Criminal career research: its value for criminology. *Criminology* 26:1–35.

Blumstein, A., Cohen, J., and Hsieh, P.
1982 The duration of adult criminal careers. Final report to the National Institute of Justice. Pittsburgh: Urban Systems Institute, Carnegie-Mellon University.

Blumstein, A., Cohen, J., and Martin, S., and Tonry, M. (Eds.)
1984 *Research on Sentencing. The Search for Reform*. Washington, DC: National Academy Press.

Blumstein, A., Farrington, D.P., and Moitra, S.
1985 Delinquency careers: Innocents, desisters, and persisters. In M. Tonry, and N. Morris (Eds.), *Crime and Justice: An Annual Review of Research*, Vol. 6, pp. 187–220. Chicago: University of Chicago Press.

Blumstein, A., and Graddy, E.
1982 Prevalence and recidivism in index arrests: a feedback model. *Law and Society Review* 16:265–90.

Blunk, R.A., and Sales, B.D.
1977 Persuasion during the voir dire. In B.D. Sales (Ed.), *Psychology in the Legal Process*, pp. 31–58. New York: Spectrum.

Bock, E.W., and Frazier, C.E.
1984 The combined effect of offense and demeanor on bond decisions: basis of official typifications. *Journal of Social Psychology* 123:231–44.

Bohman, M., Cloninger, C.R., Sigvardsson, S., and Von Knorring, A.L.
1982 Predispositions to petty criminality in Swedish adoptees. I: Genetic and environmental heterogeneity. *Archives of General Psychiatry* 39:1233–41.

Bondesen, V.
1969 Argot knowledge as an indicator of criminal socialization. *Scandinavian Studies in Criminology* 2:73–105.

Bonta, J.
1986 Prison crowding: searching for the functional correlates. *American Psychologist* 41:99–101.

Bordua, D.J.
1962 Some comments on theories of group delinquency. *Sociological Review* 33:245–60.
1967 Recent trends: deviant behavior and social controls. *Annals of the American Academy of Political Science* 359:149–63.

Borna, S.
1986 Free enterprise goes to prison. *British Journal of Criminology* 26:321–34.

Bowker, L.H.
1982 Victimizers and victims in American correctional institutions. In R. Johnson, and H. Toch (Eds.), *The Pains of Imprisonment*, pp. 63–76. Beverly Hills, CA: Sage.

Bowlby, J.
1946 *Forty-four Juvenile Thieves*. London: Baillière, Tindall and Cox.
1949 *Why Delinquency?* London: National Association for Mental Health.

Bowlby, J., Ainsworth, M., Boston, M., and Rosenbluth, D.
1956 The effects of mother–child separation: a follow-up study. *British Journal of Medical Psychology* 29:211–44.

Bowlby, J., and Salter-Ainsworth, M.D.
1965 *Child Care and the Growth of Love*. London: Penguin Books.

Box, S.
1971 *Deviance, Reality and Society*. London: Holt, Rhinehart and Winston.

Boyatzis, R.E.
1974 The effect of alcohol consumption on the aggressive behavior of men. *Quarterly Journal of Studies in Alcohol* 35:959–72.

Braithwaite, J.
1981 The myth of social class and criminality reconsidered. *American Sociological Review* 46:36–57.
1984 *Corporate crime in the Pharmaceutical Industry*. London: Routledge and Kegan Paul.

Braithwaite, J., and Braithwaite, V.
1980 Effect of income inequality and social democracy on homicide. *British Journal of Criminology* 20:45–53.

Braukmann, C.J., Fixsen, D.L., Phillips, E.L., and Wolf, M.M.
1975 Behavioral approaches to treatment in crime and delinquency. *Criminology* 13:299–331.

Brecher, E.M.
1972 *Licit and Illicit Drugs*. Boston: Little, Brown.

Bridges, G.S., and Stone, J.A.
1986 Effects of criminal punishment on perceived threat of punishment: towards an understanding of specific deterrence. *Journal of Research in Crime and Delinquency* 23:207–239.

Brown, T.S., and Pardue, J.
1985 Effectiveness of personnel selection inventory in reducing drug store theft. *Psychological Reports* 56:875–81.

Browne, A., and Finkelhor, D.
1986 The impact of child sexual abuse: a review of the research. *Psychological Bulletin* 99:66–77.

Buckle, A., and Farrington, D.P.
1984 An observational study of shoplifting. *British Journal of Criminology* 24:63–73.

Buehler, R.E., Patterson, G.R., and Furniss, J.N.
1961 The reinforcement of behavior in institutional settings. *Behavior Research and Therapy* 4:157–67.

Bukstel, L.H., and Kilmann, P.R.
1980 Psychological effects of imprisonment on confined individuals. *Psychological Bulletin* 88:469–93.

Bull, R.
1979 The influence of stereotypes on person identification. In D.P. Farrington, K. Hawkins, and S.M. Lloyd-Bostock (Eds.), *Psychology, Law and Legal Processes*, pp. 184–94. London: Macmillan.

Burchard, J.D., and Lane, T.W.
1982 Crime and delinquency. In A.S. Bellack, M. Hersen, and A.E. Kazdin (Eds.), *International Handbook of Behavior Modification and Therapy*, pp. 613–52. New York: Plenum Press.

Burgess, E.W.
1928 Factors determining success or failure on parole. In A.J. Bruce, A.J. Harno, E.W. Burgess, and J. Lamdesco (Eds.), *The Workings of the Indeterminate Sentence Law and the Parole System in Illinois*. Springfield, IL: Illinois State Board of Parole.

Burgess, R.C., and Akers, R.L.
1966 A differential association-reinforcement theory of criminal behavior. *Social Problems* 14:128–47.

Burkhardt, B.R., Behles, M.W., and Stumphauzer, J.S.
1976 Training juvenile probation officers in behavior modification: knowledge, attitude change, or behavioral competence? *Behavior Therapy* 7:47–53.

Burt, C.
1923 *The Young delinquent*. London: University of London Press.

Burt, M.R.
1980 Cultural myths and support for rape. *Journal of Personality and Social Psychology* 38:217–30.

Burton, R.V.
1963 Generality of honesty reconsidered. *Psychological Review* 70:481–99.

Caldwell, R.G.
1965 *Criminology*, 2nd Edition. New York: Ronald Press.

Carr-Hill, R., and Stern, N.
1979 *Crime, The Police and Criminal Statistics*. London: Academic Press.
1983 Crime and the dole queue. *Police* 15:28–32.

Carroll, J.
1982 Committing a crime: the offender's decision. In V.J. Konecni, and E.B. Ebbesen (Eds.), *The Criminal Justice System. A Social-Psychological Analysis*. Oxford: Freeman.

Carroll, L.
1982 Race, ethnicity, and the social order of the prison. In R. Johnson, and H.Toch (Eds.), *The Pains of Imprisonment*, pp. 181–203.

Cartwright, D.C., Howard, K.I., and Reuterman, N.A.
1970 Multivariate analysis of gang delinquency. *Multivariate Behavioral Research* 5:303–23.

Cattell, R.B., Saunders, D.R., and Stice, G.
1957 *Handbook for the Sixteen Factor Questionnaire*. Champaign, IL: Institute for Personality and Ability Testing.

Cautela, J.R.
1967 Covert sensitization. *Psychological Reports* 20:459–68.
Cavior, H.E., and Schmidt, A.A.
1978 Test of the effectiveness of a differential treatment strategy at the Robert F. Kennedy Center. *Criminal Justice and Behavior* 5:131–9.
Cerncovich, J.A., and Giordano, P.C.
1979 A comparative analysis of male and female delinquency. *Sociological Quarterly* 20:131–45.
Chadwick, E.
1829 Preventive police. *London Review* 1:301–2.
Chaiken, C., and Chaiken, J.
1983 Crime rates and the active criminal. In J.Q. Wilson (Ed.), *Crime and Public Policy*, pp. 11–30. San Francisco: ICS.
Chaiken, J.M., Greenwood, P.W., and Petersilia, J.
1979 The criminal investigation process: a summary report. In S.L. Messinger, and E. Bittner (Eds.), *Criminology Yearbook*, Vol. 1. pp. 711–42. Beverleg Hills, CA: Sage.
Chaiken, J.M., Lawless, M.W., and Stevenson, K.
1974 Impact of police activity on crime: robberies on New York City subway systems. Report No R-1424, NYC. Santa Monica, CA: Rand Corporation.
Chaiken, M.R., and Chaiken, J.M.
1984 Offender types and public policy. *Crime and Delinquency* 30:195–226.
Chambers of Commerce of the United States
1974 *A Handbook of White Collar Crime*. Washington, DC: National District Attorney's Association.
Chambliss, W.J.
1969 *Crime and The Legal Process*. New York: McGraw-Hill.
1988 *Exploring Criminology*. New York: Macmillan.
Chandler, R.
1989 *The Little Sister*. London: The Folio Society (original publication, New York: Houghton Mifflin, 1949).
Check, J.V.P., and Malamuth, N.M.
1983 Sex role stereotyping and reactions to depictions of stranger versus acquaintance rape. *Journal of Personality and Social Psychology* 45:344–76.
Cheetwood, D.
1985 Capital punishment and corrections: is there an impending crisis? *Crime and Delinquency* 31:461–79.
Chilton, R., and Galvin, J.
1983 Race, crime and criminal justice. *Crime and Delinquency* 31:3–14.
Christiansen, K.O.
1968 Threshold of tolerance in various population groups illustrated by results from Danish criminological twin study. In A.V.S. de Rueck, and R. Porter (Eds.), *The Mentally Abnormal Offender*, pp. 107–20. Boston: Little, Brown.
Christiansen, K.O.
1969 Recidivism among collaborators. In M.E. Wolfgang (Ed.), *Crime and Culture Essays in Honor of Thorstein Sellin*, pp. 258–83. New York: Wiley.

1977 A review of studies of criminality among twins. In S.A. Mednick, and K.O. Christiansen (Eds.), *Biosocial Bases of Criminal Behavior*. New York: Wiley.

Christie, M.M., Marshall, W.L., and Lanthier, R.D.
1979 A descriptive study of incarcerated rapists and pedophiles. *Report to the Solicitor General of Canada*, Ottawa.

Christie, N.
1965 A study of self-reported crime. *Scandinavian Studies in Criminology* 1:86–116.

Christofell, K.K., and Kiang, L.
1983 Homicide death rates in childhood in 23 developed countries: US rates atypically high. *Child Abuse and Neglect* 7:339–45.

Cimler, E., and Beach, L.R.
1981 Factors involved in juveniles decisions about crime. *Criminal Justice and Behavior* 8:275–86.

Clark, J.P., and Hollinger, R.
1983 Theft by employees in work situations: executive summary. Washington, DC: National Institute of Justice, US Department of Justice.

Clark, K.B., and Summers, L.H.
1982 The dynamics of youth unemployment. In R.B. Freeman, and D.A. Wise (Eds.), *The Youth Labor Market Problem*. Its Nature, Causes, and Consequences. Chicago: Chicago University Press.

Clarke, R.V.
1980 Situational crime prevention – theory and practise. *British Journal of Criminology* 20:136–47.
1983 Situational crime prevention: its theoretical basis and practical scope. In M. Tonry, and N. Morris (Eds.), *Crime and Justice: An Annual Review of Research*, Vol. 4, pp. 255–56. Chicago: University of Chicago Press.

Clarke, R.V., and Cornish, D.B.
1985 Modelling offender's decisions: a framework for research and policy. In M. Tonry, and N. Morris (Eds.), *Crime and Justice: An Annual Review of Research*, Vol. 7, pp. 147–85. Chicago: University of Chicago Press.

Clarke, R.V., and Mayhew, P.
1988 The British gas suicide story and its criminological implications. In M. Tonry, and N. Morris (Eds.), *Crime and Justice: An Annual Review of Research*, Vol. 10, pp. 79–116. Chicago: University of Chicago Press.

Clarke, S.H.
1975 Some implications for North Carolina of recent research in juvenile delinquency. *Journal of Research in Crime and Delinquency* 12:51–60.

Cleckley, H.
1964 *The Mask of Sanity*, 4th Edition. St. Louis, MO: Mosby.

Clemmer, D.
1940 *The Prison Community*. Boston: Christopher.

Clifford, B.
1979 Eyewitness testimony: The bridging of a credibility gap. In D.P.

Farrington, K. Hawkins, and S.M. Lloyd-Bostock (Eds.), *Psychology, Law and Legal Processes*, pp. 167–83. London: Macmillan.

Clinard, M.B.
1952 *The Black Market*. New York: Holt, Rhinehart, and Winston.
1968 *The Sociology of Deviant Behavior*. New York: Holt, Rhinehart, and Winston.
1978 *Countries with Little Crime: The Case of Switzerland*. New York: Holt, Rhinehart, and Winston.

Cline, H.F.
1980 Criminal behavior over the life-span. In S. Kagan and D.G. Brim (Eds.), *Constancy and Change in Human Development*. Cambridge, MA: Harvard University Press.

Cloward, R.A., and Ohlin, R.E.
1960 *Delinquency and Opportunity*. New York: Free Press.

Cochrane, R.
1971 The structure of value systems in male and female prisoners. *British Journal of Criminology* 11:73–9.

Cohen, A.K.
1955 *Delinquent Boys: The Culture of The Gang*. Glencoe, IL: The Free Press.

Cohen, J.
1983 Incapacitation as a strategy for crime control: possibilities and pitfalls. In M. Tonry, and N. Morris (Eds.), *Crime and Justice: An Annual Review of Research*, Vol. 5, pp. 1–84.

Cohen, J., Dearneley, E.J., and Hansel, C.E.M.
1956 Risk and hazard. *Operational Research Quarterly* 7:67–82.

Cohen, L.E., Cantor, D., and Kluegel, J.
1981 Robbery victimization in the United States. *Social Science Quarterly* 66:444–57.

Cohen, L.E., and Land K.C.
1987 Age structure and crime: symmetry versus asymmetry and the projection of crime rates through the 1990's. *American Sociological Review* 52:170–83.

Cohen, S.
1977 Prisons and the future of control systems: from concentration to dispersal. In M. Fitzgerald (Ed.), *Prisoners in Revolt*, pp. 22–41. London: Routledge and Kegan Paul.

Cohen, S., and Taylor, L.
1972 *Psychological Survival*. London: Penguin.

Coleman, J.S., Hoffer, T., and Kilgore, S.
1982 *High School Achievement: Public, Catholic and Private Schools Compared*. New York: Basic Books.

Colson, C.
1988 Crime and restitution. The alternative to lock-them-up liberalism. *D C Policy Review* 43:14–8.

Colvin, M., and Pauly, J.
1983 A critique of criminology: towards an integrated structural-Marxist theory of delinquency production. *Sociology* 89:513–51.

Conklin, J.
1972 *Robbery and The Criminal Justice System*. Philadelphia: Lippincott.

Conrad, J.P.
1982 What do the undeserving deserve? In R. Johnson, and H. Toch (Eds.), *The Pains of Imprisonment*, pp. 313–30.

Cook, P.J.
1980 Research in criminal deterrence: laying the groundwork for the second decade. In N. Morris, and M. Tonry (Eds.), *Crime and Justice: An Annual Review of Research*, Vol. 2, pp. 211–68. Chicago: University of Chicago Press.
1983 The influence of gun availability on violent crime patterns. In M. Tonry, and M. Morris (Eds.), *Crime and Justice: An Annual Review of Research*, Vol. 4, pp. 49–90. Chicago: University of Chicago Press.
1985 Is robbery becoming more violent? An analysis of robbery murder trends since 1968. *Journal of Criminal Law and Criminology* 76:480–9.
1986 The demand and supply of criminal opportunities. In M. Tonry, and N. Morris (Eds.), *Crime and Justice: An Annual Review of Research*, Vol. 7, pp. 1–28. Chicago: University of Chicago Press.

Cooke, D.J.
1989 Containing violent prisoners: an analysis of the Barlinnie Special Unit. *British Journal of Criminology* 29:129–43.

Cornish, D.B., and Clarke, R.V.
1986 Introduction. In D.B. Cornish, and R.V. Clarke (Eds.), *The Reasoning Criminal: Rational Choice Perspectives on Offending*, pp. 1–24. New York: Springer-Verlag.
1987 Understanding crime displacement: The application of rational choice theory. *Criminology* 25:933–47.

Cotton, D.J., and Groth, A.N.
1982 Inmate rape: prevention and intervention. *Journal of Prison and Jail Health* 2:45–57.

Cowan, C.L., Thompson, W.C., and Ellsworth, P.C.
1984 The effects of death qualification on juror's predisposition to convict and on the quality of deliberation. *Law and Human Behavior* 8:53–79.

Cressey, D.R.
1969 *Theft of The Nation. The Structure and Operations of Organized Crime in America*. New York: Harper and Row.
1971 Delinquent and criminal structures. In R.K. Merton, and R. Nisbett (Eds.), *Contemporary Social Problems*, 3rd Edition, pp. 147–85. New York: Harcourt, Brace, Jovanovich.

Crowe, R.R.
1972 The adopted offspring of women criminal offenders: a study of their arrest records. *Archives of General Psychiatry* 27:600–3.

Cullen, F.T., Mathers, R.A., Clark, G.A., and Cullen, J.B.
1983 Public support for punishing white-collar crime: blaming the victim revisited? *Journal of Criminal Justice* 11:481–93.

Cullen, F.T., Wozniak, J.F., and Frank, J.
1985 The rise of the elderly offender. Will a "new" criminal be invented? *Crime and Social Justice* 23:151–65.
Curran, D.J.
1984 The myth of the "new" female delinquent. *Crime and Delinquency* 30:386–99.
Cutler, B.L., Dexter, H.R., and Penrod, S.D.
1990 Nonadversarial methods for sensitizing jurors to eyewitness evidence. *Journal of Applied Psychology*, 20:1197–207.
Cutshall, C.R., and Adams, K.
1983 Responding to older offenders: age selectivity in the processing of shoplifters. *Criminal Justice Review* 8:1–8.
DHSS and Home Office
1975 *Report of the Committee on Mentally Abnormal Offenders.* Cmnd. 6244. London: HMSO.
Dalgard, O.S., and Kringlen, E.
1976 A Norwegian twin study of criminality. *British Journal of Criminology* 16:213–32.
Davids, A., and Falkoff, B.B.
1975 Juvenile delinquents then and now: comparison of findings from 1959 and 1974. *Journal of Abnormal Psychology* 84:161–4.
Davidson, M.J., and Veno, A.
1980 Stress and the policeman. In C.L. Cooper, and J. Marshall (Eds.), *White Collar and Professional Stress*, pp. 131–66. Chichester: Wiley.
Davidson, W.S., and Robinson, M.J.
1975 Community psychology and behavior modification: a community-based program for the prevention of delinquency. *Journal of Corrective Psychiatry and Behavior Therapy* 21:1–12.
Davies, A.
1980 Assaults by prisoners in Winson Green Prison: July, 1977 to June, 1979. Internal Home Office Prison Department document.
Davies, W.
1982 Violence in prisons. In M.P. Feldman (Ed.), *Developments in the Study of Criminal Behavior*, Vol. 2, *Violence*, pp. 131–62. Chichester: Wiley.
Davies, W., and Feldman, M.P.
1981 The diagnosis of psychopathy by forensic specialists. *British Journal of Psychiatry* 138:329–31.
Davis, G.E., and Leitenberg, H.
1987 Adolescent sex offenders. *Psychological Bulletin* 101:417–27.
Decker, S.H., and Kohfeld, C.W.
1985 Crimes, crime rates, arrests and arrest ratios: implications for deterrence theory. *Criminology* 23:437–50.
Deeley, P.
1971 *Beyond Breaking Point: A Study of Techniques of Interrogation.* London: A. Barker
DeFleur, M.L., and Quinney, R.
1966 A reformulation of Sutherland's Differential Association Theory and a strategy for empirical verification. *Journal of Research in Crime and Delinquency* 3:1–22.

Delgado, J.M.
1963 Social-rank and radio-stimulated aggression in monkeys. *Journal of Nervous and Mental Diseases* 144:383–90.

Dengerink, H.A., and Levendusky, P.G.
1972 Effects of massive retaliation and balance of power on aggression. *Journal of Experimental Research in Personality* 6:230–6.

Denno, D.W., and McClelland, R.C.
1986 Longitudinal evaluation of a delinquency prevention program by self-report. *Journal of Offender Counselling, Services and Rehabilitation* 10:59–82.

Deutsch, A.
1949 A journalist's impression of state training schools. *Focus* 28: 33–40.

Diamond, S., and Zeisel, H.
1974 A courtroom experiment on juror selection and decision making. *Personality and Social Psychology Bulletin* 1:276–7.

Dickerson, M.G.
1984 *Compulsive Gamblers*. London: Longman.

Dietz, P.E., Hazelwood, R.R., and Harry, B.
1986 Detective magazines: pornography for the sexual sadist. *Journal of Forensic Sciences* 31:197–211.

Dion, K.
1972 Physical attractiveness and evaluation of children's transgressions. *Journal of Personality and Social Psychology* 24:207–13.

Dishion, T.J., Loeber, R., Stouthammer-Loeber, M., and Patterson, G.R.
1984 Social deficit and male adolescent delinquency. *Journal of Abnormal Child Psychology* 12:37–54.

Donovan, G.M., and Marlatt, G.A.
1982 Personality sub-types among driving-while-intoxicated offenders: relationship to drinking behavior and driving risk. *Journal of Consulting and Clinical Psychology* 50:241–9.

Douglas, J.W.B.
1960 "Premature" children at primary schools. *British Medical Journal* i:1008–13.

Doyle, J.C.
1953 Unnecessary hysterectomies. *Journal of the American Medical Association* 151:360–5.

Dubanoski, R.A.
1967 Imitation as a function of role appropriateness of behavior and response consequences to the model. Unpublished manuscript, University of Iowa.

Dunand, M., Berkowitz, L., and Leyens, J.P.
1984 Audience effects when viewing aggressive movies. *British Journal of Social Psychology* 23:69–76.

Dunford, F.W., and Elliot, D.S.
1984 Identifying career offenders using self-reported data. *Journal of Research in Crime and Delinquency* 21:57–86.

Dunn, C.S.
1982 Foreword. In R. Johnson, and H. Toch (Eds.), *The Pains of Imprisonment*, pp. 9–11. Beverly Hills, CA: Sage.

Durkheim, E.
1970 *Suicide*. London: Routledge and Kegan Paul (first published in French, 1897).
Duster, T.
1987 Crime, youth unemployment and the black urban underclass. *Crime and Delinquency* 33:300–16.
Eagly, A.H., and Steffen, V.J.
1986 Gender and aggressive behavior: a meta-analytic review of the social-psychological literature. *Psychological Bulletin* 100:309–30.
Easterbrook, J.A.
1959 The effect of emotion on cue utilization and the organization of behavior. *Psychological Bulletin* 66:183–201.
Easterlin, R.A.
1978 What will 1984 be like? Socioeconomic implications of recent twists in age structure. *Demography* 15:397–471.
Ebbesen, E.B., and Konecni, V.J.
1975 Decision making and information integration in the courts: the setting of bail. *Journal of Personality and Social Psychology* 32:805–21.
The Economist
1986 The law plods after computer crime. September 20, p. 73.
1987a Of crooks and cartels. February 14, pp. 17–8.
1987b Prisons: bed and board, no vacancies. March 21, pp. 47–8.
1988a Europe's least awful prisons. February 6, pp. 17–8.
1988b Cleaning up dirty laundering. August 20, pp. 63–4.
1988c The costs of crime. December 10, p. 21.
1989a Does this war make sense? January 21, p. 50.
1989b Prisons: there must be a better way. April 21, pp. 47–8.
1989c In the land of the rising gun. August 20, p. 47.
1990a Honorable mob. January 27, pp. 21–6.
1990b An old force on a new beat. February 10, p. 22.
1990c Drexel Burnham in the junkyard. February 17, p. 97.
1990d The politics of death. March 24, pp. 45–6.
1990e Toronto and Detroit. May 19, pp. 21–4.
1990f Crime in America. December 22, pp. 53–6.
1991 Shoplifting in America. January 19, p. 79.
Efran, M.G.
1974 The effect of physical appearance on the judgement of guilt, interpersonal attraction, and severity of recommended punishment in a simulated jury task. *Journal of Research in Personality* 8:45–54.
Ehrlich, I.
1977 Capital punishment and deterrence: some further thoughts and additional evidence. *Journal of Political Economics* 88:741–88.
Ehrlich, R.
1979 The economic approach to crime: a preliminary assessment. In S.L. Messinger, and E. Bittner (Eds.), *Criminology Review Year Book*, Vol. 1, pp. 25–60. Beverly Hills, CA: Sage.
Eliashoff, J.D., and Snow, R.E.
1971 *Pygmalion Reconsidered*. Worthington, OH: Charles A. Jones.

Elder, G.H., Liker, J.K., and Cross, C.E.
1983 Parent-child behavior in the Great Depression: life course and intergenerational influences. In P. Baltes, and O. Brim (Eds.), *Life Span Development and Behavior*, Vol. 6, pp. 307–22. New York: Academic Press.

Elion, V.H., and Megargee, E.J.
1975 Validity of the MMPI Pd scale among black males. *Journal of Consulting and Clinical Psychology* 43:166–72.

Ellis, H.
1914 *The Criminal*. London: Scott.

Elliot, D.S., Dunford, F.W., and Huizinga, D.
1983 *The Identification and Prediction of Career Offenders Utilizing Self-reported and Official Data*. Boulder, CO: Behavioral Research Institute.

Elliot, D.S., Huizinga, D., and Ageton, S.S.
1985 *Explaining Delinquency and Drug Use*. Beverly Hills, CA: Sage.

Elliot, D.S., Knowles, B.A., and Canter, R.J.
1981 The epidemiology of delinquent behavior and drug use among American adolescents. *National Youth Survey Project No. 14*. Boulder, CO: Behavioral Research Institute.

Elliot, D.S., and Voss, H.L.
1974 *Delinquency and Dropout*. Lexington, MA: Heath.

Ellwork, A., and Sales, B.D.
1978 Psychological research on the jury and trial processes. In C. Petty, W. Curran, and L. McGarry (Eds.), *Modern Legal Medicine and Forensic Science*. Philadelphia: F.A. Davis.

Elmhorn, K.
1965 Study in self-reported delinquency among school-children in Stockholm. *Scandinavian Studies in Criminology* 1:117–46.

Emory, R.E., and Marholin, D.
1977 An applied behavior analysis of delinquency: the irrelevance of irrelevant behavior. *American Psychologist* 32:860–73.

Empey, L.T.
1982 *American Delinquency*. Homewood, IL: Dorsey.

Ennis, B., and Emery, R.
1978 *The Rights of Mental Patients*. New York: Avon.

Epps, P., and Parnell, R.W.
1952 Physique and temperament of women delinquents compared with women undergraduates. *British Journal of Medical Psychology* 1:249–55.

Epstein, S., and Taylor, S.P.
1967 Instigation to aggression as a function of degree of defeat and perceived aggressive intent of the opponent. *Journal of Personality* 35:265–89.

Erickson, K.T.
1964 Notes on the sociology of deviance. In H.S. Beiber (Ed.), *The Other Side: Perspectives on Deviance*, pp. 9–21. New York: Free Press.

Evans, R.C., and Koederitz, G.D.
1983 The requirement of restitution for juvenile offenders: An alternative disposition. *Journal of Offender Counselling, Services and Rehabilitation* 7:1–20.

Eysenck, H.J.
1967 *The Biological Basis of Personality*. Springfield, IL: C.C. Thomas.
1977 *Crime and Personality*, 3rd Edition. London: Granada.

Eysenck, H.J., and Eysenck, S.B.G.
1968 A factorial study of psychoticism as a dimension of personality. *Multivariate Behavioral Research*, 15–31 (special issue).

Eysenck, S.B.G. and Eysenck, H.J.
1975 *Manual of the Eysenck Personality Inventory*. San Diego, CA: Educational and Testing Service.

Fagan, J., Slaughter, E., and Hartstone, E.
1987 Blind justice? The impact of race on the juvenile process. *Crime and Delinquency* 33:224–58.

Farley, F.H., and Sewell, T.
1976 Test of an arousal theory of delinquency. *Criminal Justice and Behavior* 3:315–20.

Farrington, D.P.
1972 Delinquency begins at home. *New Society* 21:495–7.
1978 The family backgrounds of aggressive youth. In L.A. Hersov and M. Berger (Eds.), *Aggression and Anti-social Behavior in Childhood and Adolescence*, pp. 73–93. Oxford: Pergamon Press.
1979 Longitudinal research on crime and delinquency. In N. Morris, and M. Tonry (Eds.), *Crime and Justice: An Annual Review of Research*, Vol. 1, pp. 289–348. Chicago: University of Chicago Press.
1980 Truancy, delinquency, the home and the school. In L.A. Hersov, and I. Berg (Eds.), *Out of School*, pp. 49–63. London: Wiley.
1981 Psychology and police interrogation. *British Journal of Law and Society* 8:1–7.
1983a Offending from 10 to 25 years of age. In K.T. Van Dusen, and S.A. Mednick (Eds.), *Prospective Studies of Crime and Delinquency*. Boston: Kluwer-Nijhoff.
1983b Randomized experiments on crime and justice. In M. Tonry, and N. Morris (Eds.), *Crime and Justice: An Annual Review of Research*, Vol. 4, pp. 257–308. Chicago: University of Chicago Press.
1986 Age and crime. In M. Tonry, and N. Morris (Eds.), *Crime and Justice: An Annual Review of Research*, Vol. 7, pp. 189–250. Chicago: University of Chicago Press.
1987a Predicting individual crime rates. In M. Tonry, and N. Morris (Eds.), *Crime and Justice: An Annual Review of Research*, Vol. 9, pp. 53–102. Chicago: University of Chicago Press.
1987b Epidemiology. In H.C. Quay (Ed.), *Handbook of Juvenile Delinquency*, pp. 33–61. New York: Wiley.
1988 Are there any successful men from criminogenic backgrounds? *Psychiatry* 5:116–30.

Farrington,D.P., Biron,L., and LeBlanc, M.
1982 Personality and delinquency in London and Montreal. In J. Gunn, and D.P. Farrington (Eds.), *Abnormal Offenders, Delinquency and the Criminal Justice System*, pp. 153–201. New York: Wiley.

Farrington, D.P., and Dowds, E.A.
1984 Why does crime decrease? *Justice of the Peace* 148, 506–9.
Farrington, D.P., Gallagher,B., Morley, L., St. Ledger, R.J., and West, D.J.
1986 Unemployment, school-leaving and crime. *British Journal of Criminology* 26:335–56.
Farrington, D.P., Gundry, G., and West, D.J.
1975 The familial transmission of criminality. *Medicine, Science and the Law* 15: 177–86.
Farrington, D.P., and Nuttall, C.P.
1980 Prison size, overcrowding, prison violence and recidivism. *Journal of Criminal Justice* 8:221–331.
Farrington, D.P., Snyder, H.N., and Finnegan, T.A.
1988 Specialization in criminal careers. *Criminology* 26:461–87.
Federal Bureau of Investigation (various years).
Uniform Crime Reports. Washington, DC: US Government Printing Office.
Fedler, F., and Pryor, B.
1984 An equity explanation of bystanders reactions to shoplifting. *Psychological Reports* 54:746.
Feldman, M.P.
1964 Motivation and task performance: a review of the literature. In H.J. Eysenck (Ed.), *Experiments in Motivation*, pp. 12–31. Oxford: Pergamon Press.
1976 Social psychology and behavior therapy. In M.P. Feldman, and A. Broadhurst (Eds.), *The Experimental Bases of the Behavior Therapies*, pp. 227–68. London: Wiley.
1977 *Criminal Behavior*. London: Wiley.
1987 *Sex and Sexuality*. London: Longman.
1989 Applying psychology to the reduction of juvenile offending and offenses: methods and results. In C. Hollin, and K. Howells (Eds.), *Clinical Approaches to Working with Offenders*, pp. 3–32. Leicester: British Psychological Society.
Feldman, M.P., and McCulloch, M.J.
1971 *Homosexual Behavior: Therapy and Assessment*. Oxford: Pergamon Press.
Feldman, M.P., and Peay, M.J.
1982 Ethical and legal issues. In A.S. Bellack, M. Hersen, and A.E. Kazdin (Eds.), *International Handbook of Behavior Therapy and Behavior Modification*, pp. 231–62. New York: Plenum Press.
Felkenes, G.T.
1984 Attitudes of police officers towards their professional ethics. *Journal of Criminal Justice* 12:211–20.
Fenster, C.A., Wiedemann, C.F., and Locke, B.
1973 Police personality, social science folklore and psychological measurement. In B.D. Sales (Ed.), *Psychology in the Legal Process*, pp. 89–110. New York: Spectrum.
Ferdinand, T.N., and Luchterhand, E.G.
1970 Inner-city youths, the police, the juvenile court and justice. *Social Problems* 17:510–27.
Feshbach, S., and Price, J.
1984 The development of cognitive competencies and the control of aggression. *Aggressive Behavior* 10:185–200.

Festinger, L.
1954 A theory of social comparison processes. *Human Relations* 7:117–40.
1957 *A Theory of Cognitive Dissonance*. Stanford, CA: Stanford University Press.
Figuera-McDonough, J.
1985 Gender differences in informal processing: a look at charge bargaining and sentence reduction in Washington, DC. *Journal of Research in Crime and Delinquency* 22:101–33.
Filipczak, J., Archer, M.B., Neale, M.S., and Twinett, R.A.
1979 Issues in multivariate assessment of a large scale behavioral program. *Journal of Applied Behavioral Analysis* 12:593–613.
Finkelhor, D.
1979 *Sexually Victimized Children*. New York: Free Press.
Finkenaur, J.O.
1982 *Scared Straight! and The Panacea Phenomenon*. Englewood Cliffs, NJ: Prentice-Hall.
Fitzgerald, R., and Ellsworth, P.C.
1984 Due process versus crime control. Death qualification and jury attitudes. *Law and Human Behavior* 8:31–51.
Fitzmaurice, C., and Pease, K.
1982 Prison sentences and prison populations in Western Europe. Paper read to Psychology and Law Conference, Swansea, UK.
Fixsen, D.L., Phillips, E., Harper, D.S., Mesigh, J., Timbers, G.D., and Wolf, M.M.
1972 The teaching family model of group home treatment. Paper read to American Psychology Association Annual Convention, Honolulu, Hawaii, USA.
Flanagan, T.J.
1980 the pains of long-term imprisonment: a comparison of British and American perspectives. *British Journal of Criminology* 20:148–56.
1982 Lifers and long-termers: doing big time. In R.A. Johnson, and A. Toch (Eds.), *The Pains of Imprisonment*, pp. 115–28. Beverly Hills, CA: Sage.
Fleischman, M.J.
1979 Using parenting salaries to control attrition and cooperation in therapy. *Behavior Therapy* 10:11–116.
Fo, W.S., and O'Donnell, C.R.
1974 The buddy systen: relationship and contingency conditions in a community intervention program for youth with non-professionals as behavior change agents. *Journal of Consulting and Clinical Psychology* 42:163–9.
Forst, B.
1983 Prosecution and sectencing. In J.Q. Wilson (Ed.), *Crime and Public Policy*, pp. 165–82. San Francisco: ICS Press.
Forst, B, Leahy, F., Shirhall, J., Tyson, H., Wish, E., and Bartolomeo, J.
1981 Arrest convictablity as a measure of public performance. Washington, DC: INSLAW.
Fotrell, E.
1980 A study of violent behavior among patients in psychiatric hospitals. *British Journal of Psychiatry* 136:216–21.

Fowler, F.J. Jr., McCalla, M.E., and Mangione, T.W.
1979 *Reducing Residential Crime and Fear: The Hartford Neighborhood Crime Prevention Program*. Washington, DC: US Department of Justice.
Fowler, F.J., Jr., and Mangione, T.W.
1982 *Neighborhood Crime, Fear and Social Control: A Second Look at the Hartford Program*. Washington, DC: US Department of Justice.
Fox, J.A.
1978 *Forecasting Crime*. Lexington, MA: Lexington Books.
Fox, J.G.
1982 Women in prisons: a case study in the social reality of stress. In R. Johnson, and H. Toch (Eds.), *The Pains of Imprisonment*, pp. 205–20. Beverly Hills, CA: Sage.
Franklin, A.
1979 Criminality in the workplace: a comparison of male and female offenders. In F. Adler, and R. Simon (Eds.), *The Criminology of Deviant Women*. Boston: Houghton Mifflin.
Frank, J.
1949 *Courts on Trial*. Princeton, NJ: Princeton University Press.
Frazier, C.E., and Cochrane, J.C.
1986 Detention of juveniles: its effects on subsequent juvenile court processing decisions. *Youth and Society* 17:286–305.
Freedman, D.G.
1974 *Human Infancy: An Evolutionary Perspective*. New York: Wiley.
Freedman J.L.
1984 Effect of television violence on aggressiveness. *Psychological Bulletin* 96:227–46.
1986 Television violence and aggression. *Psychological Bulletin* 100:372–8.
Freedman, J.L., and Doob, A.N.
1968 *Deviancy: The Psychology of Being Different*. New York: Academic Press.
Freeman, R.B.
1983 Crime and unemployment. In J.Q. Wilson (Ed.), *Crime and Public Policy*. San Francisco: ICS.
Friedman, L.S.
1979 The use of multiple regression analysis to test for a deterrent effect on capital punishment: prospects and problems. In S.L. Messinger, and E. Bittner (Eds.), *Criminology Review Year Book*, Vol. 1, pp. 61–87. Beverly Hills, CA: Sage.
Friedrich-Cofer, L., and Huston, A.C.
1986 Television violence and aggression: the debate continues. *Psychological Bulletin* 100:364–71.
Fulker, D.W., and Eaves, L.J.
1973 The interaction of genotype and environment in two personality traits. Unpublished manuscript, University of Birmingham, UK.
Fuller, D., Orsagh, T., and Raber, D.
1977 Violence and victimization within the North Carolina prison system. Paper read to the Academy of Criminal Justice Sciences.
Furby, L., and Weinrott, M.R.
1989 Sex offender recidivism: a review. *Psychological Bulletin* 105: 3–30.

Gable, R.K.
1986 Application of personal telemonitoring to current problems in corrections. *Journal of Criminal Justice* 14: 167–76.
Gabor, T.
1978 Crime displacement: the literature and strategies for its investigation. *Crime and Justice* 6:100–7.
Gaes, G.G.
1985 The effects of overcrowding in prisons. In M. Tonry, and N. Morris (Eds.), *Crime and Justice: An Annual Review of Research*, Vol. 6, pp. 95–146. Chicago: University of Chicago Press.
Gaes, G.G., and McGuire, W.J.
1985 Prison violence: the contribution of crowding versus other determinants of prison assault rates. *Journal of Research in Crime and Delinquency* 22:41–65.
Galster, G.G., and Scaturo, L.A.
1985 The US criminal justice system: unemployment and the severity of punishment. *Journal of Research in Crime and Delinquency* 22: 163–89.
Garabedian, P.G.
1963 Social rules and the processes of socialization in the prison. *Social Problems* 11:139–46.
Gardner, J., and Gray, M.
1982 Violence towards children. In M.P. Feldman (Ed.), *Developments in The Study of Criminal Behavior*, Vol. 2, pp. 1–42. London: Wiley.
Garofolo, J.
1977 The police and public opinion: an analysis of victimization and attitude data from 13 American cities. Washington, DC: US Department of Justice.
Garrett, C.J.
1985 Effects of residential treatment on adjudicated delinquents: a meta-analysis. *Journal of Research in Crime and Delinquency* 22:287–308.
Garrett, M., and Short, J.F., Jr.
1975 Social class and delinquency: prediction and outcomes of police-juvenile encounters. *Social Problems* 22:368–82.
Gath, D.
1972 High intelligence and delinquency – a review. *British Journal of Criminology* 12:174–81.
Gauthier, J., and Pellegrin, D.
1982 Management of compulsive shoplifting through sensitization. *Journal of Behavior Therapy and Experimental Psychiatry* 13:73–5.
Gebhard, P.H., Gagnon, W.H., Pomeroy, W.B., and Christenson, C.V.
1965 *Sex Offenders: An Analysis of Types*. New York: Harper and Row.
Geiselman, R.E., Fisher, R.P., Firstenberg, I., Hutton, L.A., Avetissian, I.V., and Prosk, A.L.
1984 Enhancement of eyewitness memory: an empirical evaluation of the cognitive interview. *Journal of Police Science and Administration* 12:74–80.
Gelfand, D.M., Hartmann, D.P., Walder, P., and Page, B.
1973 Who reports shoplifters: a field-experimental study. *Journal of Personality and Social Psychology* 25:276–83.

Gibbens, T.C.N.
1963 *Psychiatric Studies of Borstal Lads*. Oxford: Oxford University Press.
1981 Shoplifting. *British Journal of Psychiatry* 138:346–7.
1984 Borstal boys after 25 years. *British Journal of Criminology* 24:49–62.
Gibbens, T.C.N., Palmer, C., and Prince, J.
1971 Mental health aspects of shoplifting. *British Medical Journal* 3:612–5.
Gibbens, T.C.N., Pond, D., and Stafford-Clark, D.
1959 A follow-up study of criminal psychopaths. *Journal of Mental Science* 105:108–15.
Gibbens, D.C., and Krohn, M.D.
1986 *Delinquent Behavior*, 4th Edition. Englewood Cliffs, NJ: Prentice-Hall.
Gibbs, J.J.
1982 The first cut is the deepest: psychological breakdown and survival in the detention setting. In R. Johnson, and H. Toch (Eds.), *The Pains of Imprisonment*, pp. 97–114. Beverly Hills, CA: Sage.
Gibbs, J.J., and Shelly, P.L.
1982 Life in the fast lane: a retrospective view by commercial thieves. *Journal of Research of Crime and Delinquency* 19:299–316.
Giswold, D.B.
1984 Crime prevention and commercial burglary: a time-series analysis. *Journal of Criminal Justice* 12:493–501.
Glaser, D.
1979 Economic and sociocultural variables affecting youth unemployment, delinquency, and crime. *Youth and Society* 11:53–82.
1983 Supervising offenders outside of prison. In J.Q. Wilson (Ed.), *Crime and Public Policy*, pp. 207–27. San Francisco: ICS Press.
1987 Classification for risk. In M. Tonry, and N. Morris (Eds.), *Crime and Justice: An Annual Review of Research*, Vol. 9, pp. 249–72. Chicago: University of Chicago Press.
Glover, J.H.
1985 A case of kleptomania treated by covert sensitization. *British Journal of Clinical Psychology* 24:213–14.
Glueck, S., and Glueck, E.T.
1956 *Physique and Delinquency*. New York: Harper.
1964 Potential delinquents can be identified. What next? *British Journal of Criminology* 4:215–28.
Goddard, H.H.
1921 *Juvenile Delinquency*. New York: Dodd, Mead.
Goffman, E.
1968 *Asylums*. London: Penguin.
Gold, M.
1966 Undetected delinquent behavior. *Journal of Research in Crime and Delinquency* 3:27–46.
Gold, M., and Mattick, H.W.
1974 *Experiment in The Streets: The Chicago Youth Development Project*. Springfield. VA: National Technical Information Service.

Goldstein, A.G.
1977 The fallibility of the eyewitness: psychological evidence. In B.D. Sales (Ed.), *Psychology in The Legal Process*, pp. 223–48. New York: Spectrum.
Goldstein, A.P., Monti, P.J., Sardino, T.J., and Green, D.J.
1977 *Police Crisis Intervention*. Kalamazoo, MI: Behavordelia.
Goldstein, J.H.
1986 *Aggression and Crimes of Violence*, 2nd Edition. Oxford: Oxford University Press.
Good, D.H., Pirog-Good, M., and Sickles, R.C.
1986 An analysis of youth crime and employment patterns. *Journal of Quantitative Criminology* 2:219–36.
Goode, E.
1972 *Drugs in American Society*. New York: Knopf.
Gordon, A., and Arbuthnot, J.
1987 Individual, group and family interventions. In H.L. Quay (Ed.), *Handbook of Juvenile Delinquency*, pp. 290–324. New York: Wiley.
Gordon, R., Short, J., Cartwright, D., and Strotbeck, F.
1963 Values and group delinquency: a study of street corner groups. *American Journal of Sociology* 69:109–28.
Gottfredsen, G.D.
1981 Schooling and delinquency. In S.E. Martin, L.B. Sechrest, and R. Redner (Eds.), *New Directions in The Rehabilitation of Criminal Offenders*. Washington, DC: Academic Press.
Gottfredsen, M.R.
1986 Substantive contributions of victimization surveys. In M. Tonry, and N. Morris (Eds.), *Crime and Justice: An Annual Review of Research*, Vol. 7, pp. 251–88. Chicago: University of Chicago Press.
Gottfredsen, M.R., and Hirschi, T.
1988 Science, public policy and the career paradigm. *Criminology* 26:37–55.
Gottschalk, R., Davidson, W.S., II, Gensheimer, L.K., and Mayer, J.P.
1987 Community-based interventions. In H.C. Quay (Ed.), *Handbook of Juvenile Delinquency*, pp. 266–89. New York: Wiley.
Grasmick, H.G., Finley, M.J., and Glaser, D.C.
1984 Labor force participation, sex-role attitude and female crime. *Social Science Quarterly* 65:703–18.
Gray, K.C., and Hutchinson, H.C.
1964 The psychopathic personality: a survey of Canadian psychiatrists opinion. *Canadian Psychiatric Association Journal* 9:452–61.
Greenberg, D.F.
1977 Delinquency and the age structure of society. *Contemporary Crises* 1:189–224.
Greenberg, M.S., and Ruback, R.B.
1985 A model of crime victim decision making. *Victimology: An International Journal* 10:600–16.
Greenwell, J., and Dengerink, H.A.
1973 The role of perceived versus actual attack in human, physical aggression. *Journal of Personality and Social Psychology* 26:66–71.
Greenwood, P.W.
1986 Differences in criminal behavior and court responses among

juvenile and young adult defendants. In M. Tonry, and N. Morris (Eds.), *Crime and Justice: An Annual Review of Research*, Vol. 7, pp. 151–87. Chicago: University of Chicago Press.

Greenwood, P.W., and Abrahamse, A.
1982 *Selective incapacitation*. R – 2815 – NIJ. Santa Monica, CA: Rand.

Gross, A.M., Brigham, T.A., Hopper, C., and Bologna, N.C.
1980 Self-management and social skills training: a study with pre-delinquent and delinquent youths. *Criminal Justice and Behavior* 7:161–84.

Groth, A.N.
1979 *Men who Rape*. New York: Plenum.

Groth, A.N., Longo, R.E., and McFadin, J.B.
1982 Undetected recidivism among rapists and child molesters. *Crime and Delinquency* 28:450–8.

Group 4
1972 Are Britons 4 times more honest than Yankees? Paper submitted to the Home Office Working Party on internal shop security.

Grunhut, M.
1956 *Juvenile Offenders Before the Courts*. Oxford: Clarendon Press.

Grygier, T., Nease, B., and Anderson, C.S.
1970 An exploratory study of half-way houses. *Crime and Delinquency* 16:280–91.

Gunn, J.
1977 *Epileptics in Prison*. London: Academic Press.
1979 Forensic psychiatry. In K. Granville-Grossman (Ed.), *Recent Advances in Clinical Psychiatry*, pp. 271–95. Edinburgh: Churchill, Livingstone.

Gunn, J., and Fenton, G.
1971 Epilepsy, automatism and crime. *The Lancet* i:1173–6.

Gunn, J., Robertson, G., Dell, S., and Way, C.
1978 *Psychiatric Aspects of Imprisonment*. London: Academic Press.

Gurr, T.R.
1981 Historical trends in violent crime: A critical review of the evidence. In M. Tonry, and N. Morris (Eds.), *Crime and Justice: An Annual Review of Research*, Vol. 3, pp. 295–353. Chicago: University of Chicago Press.

Hacker, A.C.
1987 American apartheid. *The New York Review* December 3, pp. 26–33.

Hagel-Seymour, J.
1982 Environmental sanctuaries for susceptible prisoners. In R. Johnson, and H. Toch (Eds.), *The Pains of Imprisonment*, pp. 267–84. Beverly Hills. CA: Sage.

Hamparian, D.M., Schuster, R., Dinitz, S., and Conrad, J.P.
1978 *The Violent Few*. Lexington, MA: Lexington/D.C. Heath.

Haney, C., Banks, C., and Zimbardo, P.B.
1973 Interpersonal dynamics in a simulated prison: *International Journal of Criminology and Penology* 1:1–36.

Hans, V.P., and Vidmar, N.
1982 Jury selection. In N.L. Kerr, and R.M. Bray (Eds.), *The Psychology of the Courtroom*. New York: Academic Press.

Hare, R.D.
1970 *Psychopathy: Theory and Research*. New York: Wiley.
1976 Psychopathy. In P. Venables, and M. Christie (Eds.), *Research in Psychophysiology*. New York: Wiley.

Hare, R.D., and Cox, D.N.
1978 Clinical and empirical conceptions of psychopathy and the selection of subjects for research. In R.D. Hare, and D. Schalling (Eds.), *Psychopathic Behavior: Approaches to Research*, pp. 1–22. Chichester: Wiley.

Hare, R.D., and Thorvaldsen, S.
1970 Psychopathy and response to electrical stimulation. *Journal of Abnormal Psychology* 76:370–4.

Hargreaves, D.H.
1967 *Social Relations in a Secondary School*. London: Routledge and Kegan Paul.

Harries, K.D., and Stadler, S.J.
1988 Heat and violence: New findings from Dallas field data, 1980–1981. *Journal of Applied Social Psychology* 18:129–38.

Harrris, A.R., and Lewis, M.
1974 Race and criminal deviance: a study of youthful offenders. Paper read to the Annual Conference of the American Sociological Association.

Harris, R.W.
1973 *The Police Academy: An Inside View*. New York: Wiley.

Hartshorne, H., and May, M.A.
1928 *Studies in Deceit*. New York: MacMillon.

Hausner, G.
1967 *Justice in Jerusalem*. London: Nelson.

Hawkins, D.F.
1983 Black and white homicide differentials: alternatives to an inadequate theory. *Criminal Justice and Behavior* 10:407–40.

Hawkins, D.F.
1985 Black homicide: the adequacy of existing research for devising prevention strategies. *Crime and Delinquency* 31:83–103.

Henderson, J.Q.
1983 Follow-up of stealing behavior in 27 youths after a variety of treatment programs. *Journal of Behavior Therapy and Experimental Psychiatry* 14:331–7.

Henderson, M.
1982 An empirical classification of convicted violent offenders. *British Journal of Criminology* 22:1–20.
1986 An empirical typology of violent incidents reported by prison inmates with convictions for violence. *Aggressive Behavior* 12:21–32.

Henn, F.A., Bardwell, R., and Jenkins, R.L.
1980 Juvenile delinquents revisited. *Archives of General Psychiatry* 37:1160–3.

Herzog, E., and Sudia, C.E.
1973 Children in fatherless families. In B.M. Caldwell, and H.N. Riccutti (Eds.), *Review of Child Development Research*, Vol. 3, pp. 141–232. Chicago: University of Chicago Press.

Hicks, D.J.
1965 Imitation and retention of film-mediated aggressive peers and adult models. *Journal of Personality and Social Psychology* 2:97–100.

Hilgendorf, E.L., and Irvine, B.
1981 A decision-making model of confessions. In S.M. Lloyd-Bostock (Ed.), *Psychology in Legal Contexts*, pp. 67–84. London: Macmillon

Hill, D., and Pond, D.A.
1952 Reflections on 100 capital cases submitted to electroencephalography. *Journal of Mental Science* 98:23–43.

Himmelfarb, J.
1981 Bystander intervention into crime: a study based on naturally-occurring episodes. *Social Psychology Quarterly* 44:14–23.

Hindelang, M.J.
1972 The relationship of self-reported delinquency to scales of the CPI and the MMPI. *Journal of Criminal Law, Criminology and Police Science* 63:73–83.
1973 Causes of delinquency: a partial replication and extension. *Social Problems* 20:471–87.
1978 Race and involvement in common law personal crimes. *American Sociological Review* 43:93–109.
1981 Variations in sex-race-age-specific incidence rates of offending. *American Sociological Review* 46:461–74.

Hindelang, M.J., and Davis, B.J.
1977 Forcible rape in the United States: a statistical profile. In D. Chappell, R. Geis, and D. Geis (Eds.), *Forcible Rape: The Crime, The Victim and The Offender*. New York: Columbia University Press.

Hindelang, M.J., Hirschi, T., and Weis, J.G.
1981 *Measuring Delinquency*. Beverly Hills, CA: Sage.

Hippler, A.E.
1974 *Hunter's Point: A Black Ghetto*. New York: Basic Books.

Hirschi, T.
1969 *Causes of Delinquency*. Berkeley, CA: California University Press.

Hirschi, T., and Rudisill, D.
1976 The great American search: causes of crime 1876–1976. *Annals of the American Academy of Political and Social Science*, 423:14–22.

Hirschi, T., and Hindelang, M.J.
1977 Intelligence and delinquency: a revisionist view. *American Sociological Review* 42:571–87.

Hoffman, M.L.
1975 Sex differences in moral internalization and values. *Journal of Personality and Social Psychology* 32:720–9.

Hoffman, M.L., and Saltzstein, H.D.
1967 Parent discipline and the child's moral development. *Journal of Personality and Social Psychology* 5:45–57.

Hogan, R.
1973 Moral conduct and moral character: a psychological perspective. *Psychological Bulletin* 79:217–32.

Hogan, R., Johnson, J.A., and Emler, N.P.
1978 A socioanalytic theory of moral development. *New Directions for Child Development* 2:1–18.
Hogarth, J.
1971 *Sentencing as a Human Process*. Toronto: Tornoto University Press.
Holden, R.T.
1986 The contagiousness of aircraft hijacking. *American Journal of Sociology* 91:874–904.
Holinger, C.P.
1979 Violent deaths among the young: recent trends in suicide, homicide and accidents. *American Journal of Psychiatry* 136:1144–7.
Hollinger, R.C., and Clark, J.P.
1983 Deterrence in the workplace: perceived certainty, perceived severity and employee theft. *Social Forces* 62:398–418.
Homant, R.J., and Osowski, G.
1982 The politics of juvenile awareness programs. A case study of Jolt. *Criminal Justice and Behavior* 9:55–68.
Hood, R., and Sparks, R.J.
1970 *Key Issues in Criminology*. London: Weidenfeld and Nicholson.
Hootton, E.A.
1939a *Crime and The Man*. Cambridge, MA: Harvard University Press.
1939b *The American Criminal: An Anthropological Study*. Cambridge, MA: Harvard University Press.
Houston, T.C.
1980 Reporting and nonreporting of observed crimes: moral judgement of the act and actor. *Journal of Applied Social Psychology* 10:56–70.
Horowitz, I.A., and Seguin, D.G.
1986 The effects of bifurcation and death qualification on assignment of penalty in capital crimes. *Journal of Applied Social Psychology* 16:165–85.
Hough, M., and Heal, K.
1982 Police strategies of crime control. In M.P. Feldman (Ed.), *Developments in The Study of Criminal Behavior*, Vol. 1, pp. 27–50. Chichester: Wiley.
Hough, M., and Mayhew, P.
1985 Taking account of crime; key findings from the 1984 British Crime Survey. London: HMSO.
Howard, J.W. Jr.
1974 Law enforcement in an urban society. *American Psychologist* 29:223–32.
Howe, E.J., and Brandau, C.J.
1988 Additive effects of certainty, severity and celerity of punishment on judgements of crime deterrence scale value. *Journal of Applied Social Psychology* 18:796–812.
Howells, K.
1982 Mental disorder and violent behavior. In M.P. Feldman (Ed.), *Developments in The Study of Criminal Behavior*, Vol. 2, pp. 163–200. Chichester: Wiley.
1983 Social construing and violent behavior in mentally abnormal offenders. In J. Hinton (Ed.), *Dangerousness: Problems of*

Assessment and Prediction, pp. 114–29. London: Allen and Unwin.

Howells, K., and Hollin, C.R.
1989 An introduction to concepts, models and techniques. In K. Howells, and C.R. Hollin (Eds.), *Clinical Approaches to Violence*, pp. 3–22. Chichester: Wiley.

Huesmann, L.R., Eron, L.D., Lefkowitz, M.M., and Walder, L.O.
1984a The stability of aggression over time and generations. *Developmental Psychology* 20:1120–34.

Huesmann, L.R., Lagerspetz, K., and Eron, L.D.
1984b Intervening variables in the TV violence-aggression relation: evidence from two countries. *Developmental Psychology* 20:746–55.

Hughes, R.
1987 *The Fatal Shore*. New York: Knopf.

Huizinga, D., and Elliot, D.S.
1984 *Self-reported Measures of Delinquency and Crime: Methodological Issues and Comparative Findings*. Boulder, CO: Behavioral Research Institute.
1987 Juvenile offenders: prevalence, offender incidence, and arrest rates by race. *Crime and Delinquency* 33:206–23.

Humphreys, L.
1970 *Tearoom Trade: Impersonal Sex in Public Places*. Chicago: Aldine.

Hutchings, B., and Mednick, S.
1975 Registered criminality in the adoptive and biological parents of registered male adoptees. In R. Fieve, H. Brill, and D. Rosenthal (Eds.), *Genetics*. Baltimore: Johns Hopkins University Press.

Hutchinson, R.R., Azrin, N.H., and Hunt, G.M.
1968 Attack produced by intermittent reinforcement of a concurrent operant response. *Journal of the Experimental Analysis of Behavior* 11:489–95.

Ianni, F.A.J., and Reuss-Ianni, E.
1973 *A Family Business: Kinship and Control in Organized Crime*. New York: Russell Sage Foundation.

Iddon, D.
1954 Introduction to *Runyon on Broadway*, pp. 1–13. London: Constable.

Inciardi, J.A.C.
1975 *Careers in Crime*. Chicago: Rand, McNally.

Inman, M.
1981 Police interrogations and confessions. In S.M. Lloyd-Bostock (Ed.), *Psychology in Legal Contexts*, pp. 45–66. London: Macmillon.

Innes, C., and Gressett, L.
1982 *Patterns in the Criminal Victimization of Women, 1978–1978*. Ann Arbor, MI: Inter-University Consortium for Political and Social Research.

Insko, C.A., and Oakes, W.F.
1966 Awareness and the "conditioning" of attitudes. *Journal of Personality and Social Psychology* 4:487–96.

Jacobs, F.G.
1971 *Criminal Responsibility*. London: Weidenfeld and Nicholson.

Jacobs, J.
1961 *The Death and Life of Great American Cities*. New York: Vintage.
Jacobs, J.B.
1977 *Stateville: The Penitentiary in Mass Society*. Chicago: University of Chicago Press.
Jesness, C.F.
1975 *The Cooperative Behavior Demonstration Project*. Sacramento, CA: California Youth Authority.
Joe, T.
1987 Economic inequality: the picture in black and white. *Crime and Delinquency* 33:287–99.
Johnson, L.B.
1991 Job stress among police officers: gender comparisions. *Police Studies* 14:12–6.
Johnson, P.E.
1985 The turnabout in the insanity defense. In M. Tonry and N. Morris (Eds.), *Crime and Justice: An Annual Review of Research*, Vol. 6, pp. 221–36. Chicago: University of Chicago Press.
Johnson, R.
1982 Life under sentence of death. In R. Johnson, and H. Toch (Eds.), *The Pains of Imprisonment*, pp. 129–45. Beverly Hills, CA: Sage.
Johnson, R., and Toch, H.
1982 Introduction. In R. Johnson and H. Toch (Eds.), *The Pains of Imprisonment*, pp. 13–21. Beverly Hills, CA: Sage
Johnson, R.E.
1980 Social class and delinquent behavior – a new test. *Criminology* 18:86–93.
Johnston, J.B., Kennedy, T.D., and Shuman, I.G.
1987 Gender differences in the sentencing of felony offenders. *Federal Probation* 51:49–55.
Jolly, R.W., Jr., and Sagarin, E.
1984 The first eight after Furman: who was executed with the return of the death penalty? *Crime and Delinquency* 30:610–23.
Jones, D.A.
1976 *The Health Risks of Imprisonment*. Lexington, MA: D.C. Heath.
Jones, R.R.
1978 First findings from the national evaluation of the teaching family model. Paper read to the meeting of the National Teaching Family Association, Boys Town, Nebraska, October 25.
Jones, S.E.
1987 Judge versus attorney conducted voir dire. An empirical investigation of juror candor. *Law and Human Behavior* 11:131–46.
Jones, S.J.
1982 Police-public relationship – fact or fiction? Paper read to Psychology and Law Conference, Swansea, July.
Jurkovic, G., and Prentice, N.
1977 Relations of moral and cognitive development to dimensions of juvenile delinquency. *Journal of Abnormal Psychology* 86:414–25.
Kadish, M.R., and Kadish, S.H.
1973 *Discretion to Disobey*. Palo Alto, CA: Stanford University Press.
Kahn, A. (Ed.)
1984 *Victims of Violence: Final Report of APA Task Force on The Victims of*

Crime and Violence. Washington, DC: American Psychological Association.

Kahneman, D., Slovic, P., and Twersky, A.
1982 *Judgement under Uncertainty: Heuristics and Biases*. New York: Cambridge University Press.

Kalven, H., Jr., and Zeisel, H.
1966 *The American Jury*. Boston: Little, Brown.

Kandel, E., Mednick, S.A., Kirkegaard, D., Sorensen, L., Hutchings, B., Knopf, J., Rosenberg, R., and Schulsinger, F.
1988 IQ as a protective factor for subjects at high risk for antisocial behavior. *Journal of Consulting and Clinical Psychology* 56: 244–6.

Kaplan, J.
1983 *The Hardest Drug: Heroin and Public Policy*. Chicago: University of Chicago Press.

Kassin, S.M., Ellsworth, P.C., and Smith, V.L.
1989 The "general acceptance" of psychological research on eyewitness testimony: a survey of the experts. *American Psychologist* 44:1089–98.

Katzev, R.D., and Wishart, S.S.
1985 The impact of judicial commentary concerning eyewitness identifications on jury decision making. *Journal of Criminal Law and Criminology* 76:733–45.

Kaufman, I.R.
1982 The insanity plea on trial. *New York Times Magazine*. August 8.

Kazdin, A.E.
1987 Treatment of anti-social behavior in children: current status and future directions. *Psychological Bulletin* 102:187–203.

Kellam, S.G., Adams, R.G., Brown, H.C., and Ensminger, M.E.
1982 The long term evolution of the family structure of teenage and older mothers. *Journal of Marriage and the Family* 44:539–54.

Kelling, G.L.
1974 *The Kansas City Preventive Control Experiment*. Washington, DC: The Police Foundation.

Kempf, K.L., and Austin, R.C.
1986 Older and more recent evidence on racial discrimination in sentencing. *Journal of Quantitative Criminology* 2:29–48.

Kiesler, C.A., Kiesler, S.B., and Pallak, M.S.
1967 The effect of commitment to future interaction on reactions to norm violations. *Journal of Personality* 35:585–600.

King, H., and Chambliss, J.
1982 *Harry King: A Professional Thief's Journey*. New York: Wiley.

Kirigin, K.A., Braukman, C.J., Attwater, J.D., and Wolf, M.M.
1982 An evaluation of teaching-family (Achievement Place) group homes for juvenile offenders. *Journal of Applied Behavior Analysis* 15:1–16.

Klein, M.W.
1974 Labeling, deterrence and recidivism: A study of police disposition of juvenile offenders. *Social Problems* 22:292–303.
1986 Labeling theory and delinquency policy: an experimental test. *Criminal Justice and Behavior*, 13:47–79.

Klein, M.W., and Crawford, L.F.
1967 Groups, gangs and cohesiveness. *Journal of Research in Crime and Delinquency* 4:63–75.
Klein, M.W., Teichmann, K.S., Lincoln, S.B., and Labin, S.
1977 Diversion as operationalization of labeling theory. Unpublished manuscript: University of California.
Klein, M.C., Alexander, J.F., and Parsons, B.V.
1977 Impact of family systems intervention on recidivism and sibling delinquency: a model of primary prevention and program evaluation. *Journal of Consulting and Clinical Psychology* 45:469–74.
Knapp Commission Report
1972 *Police Corruption*. New York: G. Braziller.
Knight, B.J., and West, D.J.
1975 Temporary and continuing delinquency. *British Journal of Delinquency* 15:43–50.
Knox, W.E., and Humphrey, J.A.
1981 The granting of work release. *Criminal Justice and Behavior* 8:55–78.
Koestler, A.
1940 *Darkness at Noon*. London: Jonathan Cape.
Kohlberg, L.
1964 The development of moral character. In M.C. Hoffmann, (Ed.), *Child Development*. New York: Russell Sage Foundation.
Krahn, H., Hartnagel, T.F., and Gartrell, S.W.
1986 Income inequality and homicide rates: cross-national data and criminological themes. *Criminology* 24:269–95.
Kranz, H.
1936 *Lelenschicksale Krimineller Zwillinge*. Berlin: Springer-Verlay OHG.
Krohn, M.O., Skinner, W.F., Massey, J.L., and Akers, R.L.
1983 A longitudinal examination of social learning theory as applied to adolescent cigarette smoking. Paper read to Annual meeting of the American Society of Criminology, Denver, CO, USA.
Lab, S.P., and Allen, R.B.
1984 Self-report and official measures: a further examination of the validity issue. *Journal of Criminal Justice* 12:445–55.
Lafree, G.D.
1985 Adversarial and nonadversarial justice: a comparison of guilty pleas and trials. *Criminology* 23:289–312.
Landau, S.F.
1981 Juveniles and the police. *British Journal of Criminology* 21:27–46.
Landes, W.M.
1979 An economic study of US aircraft hi-jacking, 1961–1976. In S.L. Messinger, and E. Bittner (Eds.), *Criminology Review Yearbook*, Vol. 1, pp. 111–48. Beverley Hills, CA: Sage.
Lane, R.
1980 Urban police and crime in nineteenth-century America. In N. Morris, and M. Tonry (Eds.), *Crime and Justice: An Annual Review of Research*, Vol. 2, pp. 1–44. Chicago: University of Chicago Press.
Lang, A.R., Goechner, D.J., Adesso, V.J., and Marlatt, A.G.
1975 Effects of alcohol on aggression in male social drinkers. *Journal of Abnormal Psychology* 84:508–18.

Lange, J.
1929 *Verbrechen als Schicksal*. Leipzig: Georg Thieme Verlag.
Lavrakas, P.A., and Lewis, D.A.
1980 The conceptualization and measurement of citizen's crime prevention behaviors. *Journal of Research in Crime and Delinquency* 17:254–72.
Lawrence, R.A.
1984 Police stress and personality factors: a conceptual model. *Journal of Criminal Justice* 12:247–63.
Laws, D.R.
1974 The failure of a token economy. *Federal Probation* 38:3–7.
1982 The assessment of dangerous sexual behavior. Paper read to Conference on Psychology and Law, Swansea, UK, July.
Layton-McKenzie, D., Goodstein, L.E., and Blovin, D.C.
1987 Personal control and prisoner adjustment: an empirical test of a proposed model. *Journal of Research in Crime and Delinquency* 24:49–68.
Lefkowitz, M.M., Eron, L.D., Walder, L.D., and Huesmann, L.R.
1977 *Growing Up To Be Violent: A Longitudinal Study of The Development of Aggression*. New York: Pergamon Press.
Leger, R.G.
1988 Perception of crowding, racial antagonism and aggression in a custodial prison. *Criminal Justice* 16:167–81.
Lejeune, R.
1977 The management of a mugging. *Urban Life* 6:123–48.
Lemert, E.
1972 *Human Deviance: Social Problems and Social Control*. Englewood Cliffs, NJ: Prentice-Hall.
Lemert, M.
1951 *Social Pathology*. New York: McGraw-Hill.
Lester, D.
1987 Relation of income inequality to suicide and homicide rates. *Journal of Social Psychology* 1:101–2.
Levinson, R.H.
1982 Try softer. In R. Johnson and H. Toch (Eds.), *The Pains of Imprisonment*, pp. 241–55. Beverly Hills, CA: Sage.
Lewis, D.A., and Maxfield, M.G.
1980 Fear in the neighborhoods: An investigation of the impact of crime. *Journal of Research in Crime and Delinquency* 17: 160–89.
Lewis, D.E.
1986 The general deterrent effect of longer sentences. *British Journal of Criminology* 26:47–62.
Lewis, D.O., Pincus, J.H., Bard, B., and Richardson, C.
1988 Neuropsychiatric, psychoeducational and family characteristics of 14 juveniles condemned to death in the United States. *American Journal of Psychiatry* 45:584–9.
Ley, P.
1977 Psychological studies of doctor-patient communication. In S. Rachman (Ed.), *Contributions to Medical Psychology* Vol. 1, pp. 81–102. Oxford: Pergamon Press.
Leyens, J.P., Camino, L., Parke, R.D., and Berkowitz, L.

1975 Effect of movie violence and aggression in a field setting as a function of group dominance and cohesion. *Journal of Personality and Social Psychology* 32:346–58.

Lippit, R., Polansky, N., and Rosen, R.
1952 The dynamics of power. *Human Relations* 5:37–49.

Litton, R.A.
1982 Insurance as crime prevention. Paper read to Conference on Psychology and Law, Swansea, UK, July.

Lizotte, A.J.
1985 The uniqueness of rape: reporting assaultive violence to the police. *Crime and Delinquency* 31:169–90.

Lockhart, D.L.
1983 The selection and maintenance of an effective police department. *Journal of Police Science and Administration* 11:85–9.

Lockwood, D.
1980 *Prison Sexual Violence.* New York: Elsevier.

Loeber, R., and Dishion, T.J.
1984 Boys who fight at home and school: family conditions influencing cross-setting consistency. *Journal of Consulting and Clinical Psychology* 52:759–68.
1988 Antisocial and delinquent youths: methods for their early identification. In J.D. Burchard, and S. Burchard (Eds.), *Prevention of Delinquent Behavior*. Beverly Hills, CA: Sage.

Loeber, R., Dishion, T.J., and Patterson, G.R.
1984 Multiple gating: a multistage assessment procedure for identifying youths at risk for delinquency. *Journal of Research in Crime and Delinquency* 21:7–32.

Loeber, R., and Schmalling, K.B.
1985 Empirical evidence for overt and covert patterns of antisocial conduct problems: A meta-analysis. *Journal of Abnormal Child Psychology* 13:337–53.

Loeber, R., and Stouthammer-Loeber, M.
1986 Family factors as correlates and predictors of juvenile conduct problems and delinquency. In M. Tonry, and N. Morris (Eds.), *Crime and Justice: An Annual Review of Research*, Vol. 7, pp. 29–150. Chicago: University of Chicago Press.
1987 Prediction. In H.L. Quay (Ed.), *Handbook of Juvenile Delinquency*, pp. 325–82. New York: Wiley.

Loftin, C., and McDowall, D.
1982 The police, crime and economic theory: an assessment. *American Sociological Review* 47:393–401.

Loftus, E.F.
1974 Reconstructing memory: The incredible witness. *Psychology Today* 8:116–9.
1980 Impact of expert psychological testimony on the unreliability of eyewitness identification. *Journal of Applied Psychology* 65:9–15.
1981 Eyewitness testimony: psychological research and legal thought. In M. Tonry, and N. Morris (Eds.), *Crime and justice: An Annual Review of Research*, Vol. 3, pp. 105–51. Chicago: University of Chicago Press.

Logan, C.H.
1972 Evaluation research in crime and delinquency: a reappraisal.

Journal of Research in Crime and Delinquency 63:378–87.

Lombroso, C.
1911 *Crime: Its Causes and Remedies. Boston: Little, Brown.*

London, P.
1970 The rescuers: motivational hypotheses about Christians who saved Jews from the Nazis. In J. Macaulay, and L. Berkowitz (Eds.), *Altruism and Helping Behavior*, pp. 241–250. New York, Academic Press.

Loomis, S.D.
1965 EEG abnormalities as a correlate of behavior in adolescent male delinquents. *American Journal of Psychiatry* 121:497–7.

Lundman, R.J., and Scarpitti, F.R.
1978 Delinquency prevention: recommendations for future projects. *Crime and Delinquency* 24:207–20.

Lundman, R.J., Sykes, R.E., and Clark, J.P.
1978 Police control of juveniles: a replication. *Journal of Research in Crime and Delinquency* 15:74–91.

Lynn,R., and Dziobon, J.
1980 On the intelligence of the Japanese and other Mongoloid peoples. *Personality and Individual Differences* 1:95–6.

McAllister, H.A., and Bregman, N.J.
1986 Plea bargaining by prosecutors and defense attorneys: a decision theory approach. *Journal of Applied Psychology* 71:686–90.

McCandless, B.R., Persons, W.S., II, and Roberts, A.
1972 Perceived opportunity, delinquency, race and body build among delinquent youth. *Journal of Gonsulting and Clinical Psychology* 38:281–90.

McCarthy, B.R., and Smith, B.L.
1986 The conceptualization of discrimination in the juvenile process: the impact of administrative factors and screening decisions on juvenile court dispositions. *Criminology* 24:41–64.

McCauley, R.
1982 Training parents to modify conduct problems in their children. *Journal of Child Psychology and Psychiatry* 23:335–42.

McClaughlin, T.F.
1976 A proposal for a behavioral approach to decrease shoplifting. *Corrective and Social Psychiatry* 22:12–4.

McClintock, F.H., and Gibson, E.
1961 *Robbery in London*. London: Macmillan.

McCord, J.
1978 A thirty year follow-up of treatment effects. *American Psychologist* 33:284–89.
1979 Some child rearing antecedents of criminal behavior in adult men. *Journal of Personality and Social Psychology* 37:1477–86.
1980 Myths and realities about criminal sanctions. Paper read to the American Society of Criminology Annual Meeting, San Francisco.

McDermott, J.M.
1979 *Rape Victimization in 26 American Cities*. Washington, DC: Government Printing Office.

McDonald, S.C.
1986 Does gentrification affect crime rate? In A.J. Reiss, and M. Tonry

(Eds.), *Crime and Justice: An Annual Review of Research*, Vol. 6, pp. 163–202. Chicago: University of Chicago Press.

McEachern, A.W., and Bauzer, R.
1967 Factors related to disposition in juvenile police contacts. In M.W. Klein (Ed.), *Juvenile Gangs in Context*, pp. 148–60. Englewood Cliffs, NJ: Prentice-Hall.

McFatter, R.M.
1986 Sentencing disparity: perforce or perchance? *Journal of Applied Social Psychology* 16:150–64.

McGahey, M.
1986 Economic conditions, neighborhood organization and urban crime. In A.J. Reiss, and M. Tonry (Eds.), *Crime and Justice: An Annual Review of Research*, Vo1. 8, pp. 231–70. Chicago: University of Chicago Press.

McGlothian, W.H., Anglin, M.D., and Wilson, B.D.
1977 *An Evaluation of The California Civil Addict Program*. US Department of Health, Education and Welfare. Publication No. (ADM) 78–558.

McGovern, K.B., Stewart, R.C., and LoPiccolo, J.
1975 Secondary orgasmic dysfunction. 1: Analysis and strategies for treatment. *Archives of Sexual Behavior* 4:265–74.

McGuire, W.J.
1969 The nature of attitudes and attitude change. In G. Lindzey, and E. Aronson (Eds.), *Handbook of Social Psychology*, Vol. 3, pp. 136–314. Reading, MA: Addison-Wesley.

McGuire, W.J.
1980 Communication and social influence processes. In M.P. Feldman, and J. Orford (Eds.), *Psychological Problems*, pp. 341–66. Chichester: Wiley.

McGurk, B.J., and McDougall, C.
1981 A new approach to Eysenck's theory of criminality. *Personality and Individual Differences* 2:338–40.

McGurk, B.J., and McGurk, R.
1979 Personality types among prisoners and prison officers. *British Journal of Criminology* 19:31–49.

McMichael, P.
1979 "The hen or the egg": which comes first – antisocial emotional disorders or reading ability. *British Journal of Educational Psychology* 49:226–38.

McNees, M.P., Egli, D.S., Marshall, R.S., Schnelle, J.F., and Risley, T.R.
1976 Shoplifting prevention: providing information through signs. *Journal of Applied Behavior Analysis* 9:339–405.

Maguire, M.
1980 The impact of burglary upon victims. *British Journal of Criminology* 20:261–75.

Malloy, T.E., and Mays, G.L.
1984 The police stress hypothesis: a critical evaluation. *Criminal Justice and Behavior* 11:197–224.

Marks, D.A.
1975 Retail store security in Ireland. *Top Security*, September, pp. 204–6.

Marlowe, H., Reid, J.B., Patterson, G.R., and Weinrott, M.
1986 Treating adolescent multiple offenders: a comparison and follow-up of parent training for families of chronic delinquents. Unpublished manuscript (cited by Gordon and Arbuthnot, 1987).

Marshall, W.L.
1982 Aggression in child molesters. Paper read to 8th International Conference on Law and Psychiatry. Quebec City, June.

Marshall, W.L., and Barbaree, H.E.
1984 Disorders of personality, impulse and adjustment. In S.M. Turner, and M. Hersen (Eds.), *Adult Psychopathology and Diagnosis*, pp. 406–52. New York: Wiley.
1989 Sexual violence. In K. Howells, and C.R. Hollin (Eds.), *Clinical Approaches to Violence*, pp. 205–49. London: Wiley.

Marshall, W.L. and Christie, M.M.
1981 Pedophilia and aggression. *Criminal Justice and Behavior* 8:154–8.

Martin, J.B.
1952 *My life in Crime*. New York: Harper and Row.

Martin, M., Burkholder, R., Rosenthal, T.L., Tharp, R.G., and Thorne, G.L.
1968 Programming behavior change and reintegration into school milieux of extreme adolescent deviates. *Behavior Research and Therapy* 6:371–83.

Martin, R.G., and Conger, R.D.
1980 A comparison of delinquency trends – Japan and the United States. *Journal of Criminology* 18:53–61.

Martinson, R.
1974 What works? Questions and answers about prison reform. *The Public Interest* 35:22–54.

Masters, W.H., and Johnson, V.E.
1966 *Human Sexual Response*. London: Churchill.

Matarazzo J.
1980 Behavioral health and behavioral medicine: frontiers for a new health psychology. *American Psychologist* 35:807–17.

Matza, D.
1969 *Becoming Deviant*. New York: Prentice-Hall.

Mauro, R.
1984 The constable's new clothes: effects of uniforms on perceptions and problems of police officers. *Journal of Applied Social Psychology* 14:42–56.

Mawby, R.I.
1985 Bystander responses to the victims of crime: is the Good Samaritan alive and well? *Victimology: An International Journal* 10:461–75.

Mawby, R.I., McCulloch, J.W., and Batta, I.D.
1979 Crime amongst Asian juveniles in Bradford. *International Journal of the Sociology of Law* 7:297–306.

Maxfield, M.G.
1984 *Fear of Crime in England and Wales*. London: HMSO.

Mayhew, P., and Clarke, R.V.
1982 Vandalism and its prevention. In M.P. Feldman (Ed.), *Developments in The Study of Criminal Behavior*, Vol. 2, pp. 89–110. London: Wiley.

Mays, J.B.
1963 *Crime and the Social Structure*. London: Faber.
Madnick, J.A., Gabrielli, W.F., Jr., and Hutchings, B.
1984 Genetic influences in criminal convictions: evidence from an adoption cohort. *Science* 224:891–4.
Mednick, S.A., Volavka, J., Gabrielli, W.F., Jr., and Itil, T.M.
1981 EEG as a predictor of antisocial behavior. *Criminology* 19:212–29.
Megargee, E.J.
1966 Undercontrolled and overcontrolled personality types in extreme anti-social aggression. *Psychological Monographs* 80: No. 3.
Meichenbaum, D.H., and Goodman, J.
1971 Training impulsive children to talk to themselves. *Journal of Abnormal Psychology* 77:115–24.
Mello, N.K.
1972 Behavioral studies of alcoholism. In B. Kissin, and H. Bergliefer (Eds.), *The Biology of Alcoholism*, Vol. 2. New York: Plenum Press.
Merbaum, M., and Kazaoka, K.
1967 Reports of emotional experiences by sensitizers and repressors during an interview transaction. *Journal of Abnormal Psychology* 72:101–7.
Merry, S.E.
1981 *Urban Danger: Life in a Neighborhood of Strangers*. Philadelphia: Temple University Press.
Merton, R.
1969 Social structure and anomie. In D.R. Cressey, and D.A. Ward (Eds.), *Delinquency, Crime and Social Process*, pp. 254–84. New York: Harper and Row.
Messner, S.R.
1986 Television violence and violent crime: an aggregate analysis. *Social Problems* 33:218–35.
Messner, S.F., and Tardiff, K.
1986 Economic inequality and levels of homicide: an analysis of urban neighborhoods. *Criminology* 24:297–317.
Metfessel, M., and Lovell, C.
1942 Recent literature on individual correlates of crime. *Psychological Bulletin* 39:133–64.
Michael, C.M., and Coltharp, F.C.
1962 Application of Glueck social prediction scale in the identification of potential juvenile delinquents. *American Journal of Orthopsychiatry* 32:264–5.
Michael, R.P., and Zumpe, D.
1983 Sexual violence in the United States and the role of season. *American Journal of Psychiatry* 140:883–6.
1986 An annual rhythm in the battering of women. *American Journal of Psychiatry* 143:637–40.
Mickenburg, I.
1983 Mesmerizing justice: the use of hypnotically-induced testimony in criminal trials. *Syracuse Law Review* 34:927–75.
Milavsky, J.R., Stipp, H.H., Kessler, R.C., and Rubens, W.S.
1982 *Television and Aggression: A Panel Study*. New York: Academic Press.

Milgram, S.
1974 *Obedience to Authority*. London: Tavistock.
Miller, G.R., and Boster, F.J.
1977 Three images of the trial: their implications for psychological research. In D.B. Sales (Ed.), *Psychology in The legal Process*, pp. 19–38. New York: Spectrum.
Miller, W.B.
1958 Lower-class culture as a generating milieu of gang delinquency. *Journal of Social Issues* 14:5–19.
Mills, C.M., and Walter, T.L.
1979 Reducing juvenile delinquency: employment intervention. In J.S. Stumphauzer (Ed.), *Progress in Behavior Therapy with Delinquents*. Springfield, IL: C.C. Thomas.
Minchin, L.
1982 Violence between couples. In M.P. Feldman (Ed.), *Developments in The Study of Criminal Behavior*, Vol. 2, pp. 43–66. Chichester, Wiley.
Mischel, W.
1968 *Personality and Assessment*. New York: Wiley.
Mitchell, B.
1984 The role of the public in criminal detection. *The Criminal Law Review* August:459–66
Moffit, T.E., Gabrielli, W.F., Mednick, S.A., and Schulsinger, F.
1981 Socioeconomic status, IQ and delinquency. *Journal of Abnormal Psychology* 90:152–7.
Monahan, J.
1984 The prediction of violent behavior: towards a second generation of theory and policy. *American Journal of Psychiatry* 141:10–5.
Monahan, J., and Loftus, E.F.
1982 The psychology of law. *Annual Review of Psychology* 33:441–75.
Monahan, J., and Splane, S.
1980 Psychological approaches to criminal behavior. In E. Bittner, and S. Messinger (Eds.), *Criminology Review Yearbook*, Vol. 2, pp. 17–47. Beverly Hills, CA: Sage.
Monahan, J., and Steadman, H.J.
1983 Crime and mental disorder: an epidemiological approach. In M. Tonry, and N. Morris (Eds.), *Crime and Justice: An Annual Review of Research*, Vol. 4, pp. 145–89. Chicago: University of Chicago Press.
Moore, A., Zusman, J., and Root, C.
1985 Noninstitutional treatment of sex offenders in Florida. *American Journal of Psychiatry* 142:964–6.
Moore, J.W.
1978 *Homeboys: Gangs, Drugs and Prison in the Barrios of Los Angeles*. Philadelphia: Temple University Press.
Moore, M.H.
1983 Controlling criminogenic commodities: drugs, guns and alcohol. In J.Q. Wilson (Ed.), *Crime and Public Policy*, pp. 125–44. San Francisco: ICS Press.
Moore, R.H.
1984 Shoplifting in Middle America: patterns and motivational

correlates. *International Journal of Offender Therapy and Comparative Criminology* 28:53–64.

Moran, G., and Comfort, J.C.
1986 Neither "tentative" nor "fragmentary": verdict preferences of empanelled felony jurors as a function of attitude towards capital punishment. *Journal of Applied Psychology* 71:146–55.

Morash, M.
1984 Establishment of a juvenile police record. The influence of individual and peer group characteristics. *Criminology* 22:97–111.
1986 Gender, peer group experiences and seriousness of delinquency. *Journal of Research in Crime and Delinquency* 23: 43–67.

Morgan, P.
1975 *Child Care: Sense and Fable*. London: Temple-Smith.

Moriarty, T.
1975 Crime, commitment and the responsive bystander. *Journal of Personality and Social Psychology* 31:370–6.

Morris, N.
1951 *The Habitual Criminal*. Longman Green.
1975 *The Future of Imprisonment*. Chicago: University of Chicago Press.

Morris, N., and Miller, M.
1985 Predictions of dangerousness. In M. Tonry, and N. Morris (Eds.), *Crime and Justice: An Annual Review of Research*, Vol. 6, pp. 1–50. Chicago: University of Chicago Press.

Mullen, J., and Smith, B.
1982 *American Prisons and Jails: Conditions and Costs of Confinement*. Washington, DC: Government Printing Office.

Mulvey, E.P., Blumstein, A., and Cohen, J.
1986 Reframing the research question of mental patient criminality. *International Journal of Law and Psychiatry* 9:57–65.

Murray, C.A.
1983 The physical environment and community control of crime. In J.Q. Wilson (Ed.), *Grime and Public Policy*. San Francisco: ICS.

Murray, C.A., and Cox, L.A., Jr.
1979 *Beyond Probation: Juvenile Corrections and Chronic Delinquency*. Beverly Hills, CA: Sage.

Myers, D.G., and Lamm, H.
1976 The group polarization phenomenon. *Psychological Bulletin* 83:602–27.

Nagel, I.H., and Hagan, J.
1983 Gender and crime: offense patterns and criminal court sanctions. In M. Tonry, and N. Morris (Eds.), *Crime and Justice: An Annual Review of Research*, Vol. 4, pp. 91–144. Chicago: University of Chicago Press.

National Advisory Commission on Criminal Justice
1973 *Report on Corrections Standards and Goals*. Washington, DC: Department of Justice.

National Council on Crime and Delinquency
1984 *Rethinking Juvenile Justice: National Statistical Trends*. Minneapolis: University of Minnesota.

Nelson, A.E., Grinder, R.E., and Mutterer, M.L.
1969 Sources of variance in behavioral measures of honesty in temptation situations. *Developmental Psychology* 1:265–79.

Nelson, J.D., Gelfand, D.M., and Hartmann, D.P.
1969 Children's aggression following competition and exposure to an aggressive model. *Child Development* 40:1085–97.
Newman, D.J.
1956 Pleading guilty for considerations: a study of bargain justice. *Journal of Criminal Law, Criminology and Police Science* 46:780–90.
Newman, O,
1973 *Defensible Space: Crime Prevention through Urban Design*. New York: Macmillan.
New York Times
1983 In Japan a crime wave is measured in drops. August 2, p. A2.
1988 Wall street crime. May 29, *Weekly Review*, p. 1.
1989 Felons unlimited. December 18, *Weekly Review*, p. 2.
1990 S&L's; Big money, little outcry. March 18, *Weekly Review*, pp. 2–4.
Nietzel, T.
1979 *Crime and Its Modification: A Social Learning Perspective*. New York: Pergamom Press.
Oaks, D.H., and Lehman, W.
1970 Lawyers for the poor. In A.S. Blumberg (Ed.), *The Scales of Justice*. Chicago: Aldine.
O'Dell, S.
1974 Training parents in behavior modification. *Psychological Bulletin* 81:418–33.
O'Donnell, C.R.
1980 Environmental design and the prevention of psychological problems. In M.P. Feldman, and J. Orford (Eds.), *Psychological Problems: The Social Context*, pp. 279–310. Chichester: Wiley.
O'Donnell, C.R., Chambers, E., and Ling, K.
1973 Athletics as reinforcement in a community program for academic achievement. Unpublished manuscript, Department of Psychology, University of Hawaii.
O'Donnell, C.R., and Lydgate, T.
1980 The assessment of physical resources and their relationship to crime. *Environment and Behavior* 12:320–31.
O'Donnell, C.R., Lydgate, T., and Fo, W.S.O.
1979 The buddy system; review and follow-up. *Child Behavior Therapy* 1:161–9.
O'Leary, M.R., Donovan, D.M., Freeman, C.W., and Chaney, E.F.
1976 Relationship between psychopathology, experienced control and perceived locus of control: in search of alcoholic subtypes. *Joural of Clinical Psychology* 32:899–904.
Olweus, D.
1975 Bullies and whipping boys. In J. de Wit, and W.W. Hartup (Eds.), *Determinants of Aggressive Behavior*. The Hague: Mouton.
1979 Stability of aggressive reaction patterns in males: a review. *Psychological Bulletin* 86:852–75.
Orford, J.
1982 *Excessive Appetites*. Chichester: Wiley.
Orne, M.T.
1981 Use and misuse of hypnosis in court. In M. Tonry, and N.

Morris (Eds.), *Crime and Justice: An Annual Review of Research*, Vol. 3, pp. 61–104. Chicago: University of Chicago Press.

Ortega, S.T., and Burnett, C.
1987 Age variation in female crime: in search of the new female criminal. *Journal of Crime and Justice* 10:133–69.

Osborn, S.G., and West, D.J.
1979 Conviction records of fathers and sons compared. *British Journal of Criminology* 19:120–33.

Osborne, K.
1982 Sexual violence. In M.P. Feldman (Ed.), *Developments in The Study of Criminal Behavior*, Vol. 2, pp. 67–88. Chichester: Wiley.

Osborne, R.T.
1980 *Twins: Black and White*. Athens, GA: Foundation for Human Understanding.

Osborne, R.T., and McGurk, F.C.J.
1982 *The Testing of Negro Intelligence*, Vol. 2. Athens, GA: Foundation for Human Understanding.

Ostapiuk, E.
1982 Strategies for community intervention in offender rehabilitation. In M.P. Feldman (Ed.), *Developments in The Study of Criminal Behavior*, Vol. 1, pp. 137–66. Chichester: Wiley.

Ouston, J.
1984 Delinquency, family background and educational attainment. *British Journal of Criminology* 24:2–26.

Owen, D.R.
1972 The 47, XYY male: a review. *Psychological Bulletin* 78:209–33.

Palmore, E.B., and Hammond, P.E.
1964 Interacting factors in juvenile delinquency. *American Sociological Review* 24:848–54.

Parke, R.D., Berkowitz, L., Leyens, J.P., West, S.G., and Sebastian, R.J.
1977 Some effects of violent and nonviolent movies on the behavior of juvenile delinquents. In L. Berkowitz (Ed.), *Advances in Experimental Social Psychology*, Vol. 10, pp. 135–72. New York: Academic Press.

Parker, T.
1970 *The Frying Pan: A Prison and Its Prisoners*. London: Gollancz.

Pate, T., Bowers, B.A., and Parks, R.
1976 *Three Approaches to Criminal Apprehension*. Washington, DC: The Police Foundation.

Patterson, G.R.
1980 Children who steal. In T. Hirschi and M. Gottfredsen (Eds.), *Understanding Crime: Current Theory and Research*, pp. 73–90. Beverly Hills, CA: Sage.
1986 Performance models for antisocial boys. *American Psychologist* 41:432–44.

Patterson, G.R., Chamberlain, P., and Reid, J.B.
1982 A comprehensive evaluation of a parent training program. *Behaviour Therapy* 13:638–50.

Patterson, G.R., Cobb, J.A., and Ray, R.S.
1973 A social engineering technology for retraining the families of

aggressive boys. In H.E. Adams, and I.P. Unikel (Eds.), *Issues and Trends in Behavior Therapy*. Springfield, IL: C.C. Thomas.

Patterson, G.R., DeBarsyshe, B.D., and Ramsey, E.
1989 A developmental perspective on antisocial behavior. *American Psychologist* 44:329–35.

Patterson, G.R., and Dishion, T.J.
1985 Contribution of families and peers to delinquency. *Criminology* 23:63–79.

Patterson, G.R., and Fleischman, M.J.
1979 Maintenance treatment effects: some considerations concerning family systems and follow-up data. *Behaviour Therapy* 10:168–85.

Pennel, S., Curtis, C., and Henderson, J.
1986 *Guardian Angels: An Assessment of Citizen Response to Crime. Executive Summary*. Washington, DC: National Institute of Justice.

Penrod, S.
1980 Evaluating social scientific methods of jury selection. Paper read to Mid-Western Psychological Association, St. Louis, MO.

Peoria Crime Reduction Council
1979 *Criminal Activity of Juvenile Residential Burglars*. Peoria, IL: City of Peoria.

Perkins, D.
1982 The treatment of sex offenders. In M.P. Feldman (Ed.), *Developments in the Study of Criminal Behavior*, Vol. 1, pp. 191–214. Chichester: Wiley.

Perry, K.
1984 Measuring the effectiveness of Neighborhood Crime Watch in Lakewood, Colorado. *The Police Journal* 57:221–33.

Petersen, G.I., Matousek, M., Mednick, S.A., Volavka, J., and Pollock, V.
1982 *Acta Psychiatrica Scandinavica* 65:331–8.

Petersilia, J.
1980 Criminal career research: a review of recent evidence. In N. Morris, and M. Tonry (Eds.), *Crime and Justice: An Annual Review of Research*, (Vol. 2, pp. 321–80). Chicago: University of Chicago Press.
1983 *Racial Disparities in the Criminal Justice System*. Santa Monica, CA: Rand.
1985 Racial disparities in the criminal justice system: a summary. *Crime and Delinquency* 31:15–34.

Petersilia, J., Greenwood, P.W., and Lavin, M.
1978 *Criminal Careers of Habitual Felons*. Washington, DC: US Government Printing Office.

Petersilia, J., and Turner, S.
1987 Guideline-based justice: prediction and racial minorities. In M. Tonry, and N. Morris (Eds.), *Crime and Justice: An annual Review of Research*, Vol. 9, pp. 151–201. Chicago: University of Chicago Press.

Petersilia, J., Turner, S., Kahan, J., and Peterson, J.
1985 Executive summary of Rand's study: "Grainting felons probation: public risks and alternatives." *Crime and Delinquency* 31:379–92.

Pfuhl, E.H., Jr.
1983 Police strikes and conventional crime. A look at the data. *Criminology* 21:489–503.
Phillips, D.P.
1974 The influence of suggestion on suicide. Substantive and theoretical implications of the Werther effect. *American Sociological Review* 39:340–54.
1983 . The impact of mass media violence on US, homicides. *American Sociological Review* 48:560–8.
Phillips, E.L.
1968 Achievement Place: token reinforcement procedures in a home style rehabilitation setting for "pre-delinquent" boys. *Journal of Applied Behavior Analysis* 1:213–23.
Phillips, L., and Votey, H.L., Jr.
1981 *The Economics of Crime Control*. Beverly Hills, CA: Sage.
Piaget, J.
1932 *The Moral Judgement of the Child*. London: Kegan Paul.
Pierce, C. H., and Risley, T. R.
1974 Recreations as reinforcer. *Journal of Applied Behavior Behavior Analysis* 7:403–11.
Piliavin, I.M., and Briar, S.
1964 Police encounters with juveniles. *American Journal of Sociology* 70:206–14.
Piliavin, I.M., Hardyck, J.A., and Vadum, A.C.
1969 Constraining effects of personal costs on the transgressions of juveniles. *Journal of Personality and Social Psychology* 10:227–31.
Piliavin, I.M., Thornton, C., Gartner, R., and Matsueda, R.L.
1986 Crime, deterrence and rational choice. *American Sociological Review* 51:101–19.
Piliavin, I.M., Vadum, A.L., and Hardyck, J.A.
1969 Delinquency, personal costs and parental treatment: a test of a reward-cost model. *Journal of Criminal Law, Criminology and Police Science* 60:165–72.
Pilling, D., and Pringle, M.
1978 *Controversial Issues in Child Development*. New York: Schocken Books.
Police Foundation
1981 *The Newark Foot Patrol Experiment*. Washington, DC: Police Foundation.
Polk, K.C., Alder, G., Bazemore, G., Blake, S., Cordroy, G., Coventry, J.G., and Temple, M.
1981 *An Analysis of Motivational Development from Ages 16 to 30 of a Cohort of Young Men*. Eugene, OR: Department of Sociology, University of Oregon.
Polsky, N.
1967 *Hustlers, Beats and Others*. New York: Aldine.
Powers, E., and Witmer, H.
1951 *An Experiment in The Prevention of Delinquency: The Cambridge – Somerville Youth Study*. New York: Columbia University Press.
Powell, D.A., and Creer. T.L.
1969 Interaction of developmental and environmental variables in

shock-elicited aggression. *Journal of Comparative and Physiological Psychology* 69:219–25.

President's Commission on Law Enforcement and the Administation of Justice
1967 *Task Force Report*. Washington, DC: US Government Printing Office.

Preston, M.A.
1982 Intermediate treatment: a new approach to community care. In M.P. Feldman (Ed.), *Developments in The Study of Criminal Behavior*, Vol. 1, 167–90. Chichester: Wiley.

Preston, M.A., and Carnegie, J.C.
1989 Intermediate treatment: working with juvenile offenders in the community. In C. Hollin, and K. Howells (Eds.), *Clinical Approaches to Working with Offenders*, pp. 69–77. Leicester: British Psychological Society.

Quay, H.C.
1965 Personality and delinquency. In H.C. Quay (Ed.), *Juvenile Delinquency*, pp. 139–69. Princeton, NJ: Van Nostrand.
1987a Intelligence. in H.C. Quay (Ed.), *Handbook of Juvenile Delinquency*, pp. 106–17. New York: Wiley.
1987b Patterns of delinquent behavior. In H.C. Quay (Ed.), *Handbook of Juvenile Delinquency*, pp. 118–38. New York: Wiley.
1987c Institutional treatment. In H.C. Quay (Ed.), *Handbook of Juvenile Delinquency*, pp. 244–65. New York: Wiley.

Quay, H.C., and Parsons, L.
1971 *The Differential Behavior Classification of The Juvenile Offender*. Washington, DC: US Bureau of Prisons.

Quinney, R.
1970 *The Social Reality of Crime*. Boston: Little, Brown.
1974 *Critique of Legal Order: Crime Control in Capitalist Society*. Boston: Little, Brown.

Rachman, S.J., and Wilson, G.T.
1980 *The Effects of Psychological Therapy*. Oxford: Pergamon Press.

Radeley, M.L., and Pierce, G.L.
1986 Race and prosecutorial discretion in homicide cases. *Law and Society Review*, 19:587–621.

Radzinowicz, L., and King, J.
1977 *The Growth of Crime: The International Experience*. London: Hamish Hamilton.

Rafter, N.H.
1986 Prisons for women, 1790–1980. In M. Tonry, and N. Morris (Eds.), *Crime and Justice: An Annual Review of Research*, Vol. 8, pp. 129–82. Chicago: University of Chicago Press.

Rahaim, G.L., and Brodsky, S.L.
1982 Empirical evidence versus commonsense: juror and lawyer knowledge of eyewitness accuracy. *Law and Psychology Review* 7:1–15.

Rauma, D., and Berk, R.A.
1987 Remuneration and recidivism: the long-term impact of unemployment compensation on ex-offenders. *Journal of Quantitative Criminology* 3:3–28.

Reason, J., and Lucas, D.

1984 Absent-mindedness in shops: its incidence, correlates and consequences. *British Journal of Psychology* 23:121–31.

Reckless, W.C.
1962 A noncausal explanation: containment theory. *Excerpta Criminologica* 2:131–5.

Rees, L.
1973 Constitutional factors and abnormal behavior. In H.J. Eysenck (Ed.), *Handbook of Abnormal Psychology*, 2nd Edition, pp. 487–539.

Reid, I.D.A.
1939 *The Negro Immigrant: His Background Characteristics and Social Adjustment, 1899–1937*. New York: Columbia University Press.

Reiss, A.J., Jr.
1971 *The Police and the Public*. New Haven, CT: Yale University Press.
1974 Discretionary justice in the United States. *International Journal of Criminology* 2:183–208.
1986 Why are communities important in understanding crime? In A.J. Reiss, Jr., and M. Tonry (Eds.), *Crime and Justice: An Annual Review of Research*, Vol. 8, pp. 1–35. Chicago: University of Chicago Press.
1988 Co-offending and criminal careers. In M. Tonry, and N. Norris (Eds.), *Crime and Justice: An Annual Review of Research*, Vol. 10, pp. 117–70. Chicago: University of Chicago Press.

Reiss, A.J., Jr., and Rhodes, A.L.
1963 Status deprivation and delinquency. *Sociological Quarterly* 4:135–49.

Renson, G.J., Adams, J.E. and Tinklenberg, R.
1978 Russ-Durkee assessment and validation with violent versus nonviolent chronic alcohol abusers. *Journal of Consulting and Clinical Psychology* 46:360–1.

Rettig, S.
1966 Ethical risk taking in group and individual conditions. *Journal of Personality and Social Psychology* 4:648–54.

Rettig, S., and Turoff, S.J.
1967 Exposure to group discussion and predicted ethical risk taking. *Journal of Personality and Social Psychology* 7:177–80.

Richards, P., Berk, R.A., and Forster, B.
1979 *Crime as Play: Delinquency in a Middle Class Suburb*. Cambridge, MA: Ballinger.

Richmond, M.S.
1972 Measuring the cost of correctional services. *Crime and Delinquency* 18:243–6.

Riger, S., Gordon, M.T., and Labailly, R.K.
1982 Coping with urban crime: women's use of precautionary behaviors. *American Journal of Community Psychology* 10:369–86.

Rime, B., Bonvy, H., and Rouillon, F.
1978 Psychopathy and nonverbal behavior in an interpersonal situation. *Journal of Abnormal Psychology* 87:636–43.

Robins, L.N.
1966 *Deviant Children Grow Up*. Baltimore, MD: Williams and Wilkins.

Robins, L.N., Helzer J.E., Croughan, J., and Ratcliff, K.S.
1981 National Institute of Mental Health Diagnostic Interview

Schedule. Its history, characteristics and validity. *Archives of General Psychiatry* 38:381–9.

Robins, L.N., West, P.A., and Herjanic, B.L.
1975 Arrests and delinquency in two generations: a study of black urban families and their children. *Journal of Child Psychology and Psychiatry* 16:125–40.

Roebuck, J., and Barker, T.
1974 A typology of police corruption. In R. Akers and E. Sagarin (Eds.), *Crime Prevention and Social Control*, pp. 118–27. New York: Prager.

Rogers, R.
1987 APA's position on the insanity defense: empiricism versus emotionalism. *American Psychologist* 42:840–8.

Rogosa, D.
1980 A critique of cross-lagged correlation. *Psychological Bulletin* 88:245–8.

Romig, D.A.
1978 *Justice for Our Children*. Lexington, MA: Lexington Books.

Roper Organization
1985 Opinion roundup. *Public Opinion* 5:12.

Rosanoff, A.J., Handy, L.M., and Plesset, I.R.
1941 The etiology of child behavior difficulties, juvenile delinquency and adult criminality with special reference to their occurrence in twins. *Psychiatric Monographs (California)*, No. 1. Sacramento: Department of Institutions.

Rose, G.
1967 Early identification of delinquents. *British Journal of Criminology* 7:6–18.

Rose, H.M.
1981 Black homicide and the urban environment. *Final Report to the Center for Minority Group Mental Health Programs, NIMH*. Washington, DC: US Department of Health and Human Services.

Rosenhan, D.L.
1973 On being sane in insane places. *Science* 179:250–8.

Rosenkrans, M.A., and Hartup, W.W.
1967 Imitative influences of consistent and inconsistent response consequences to a model on aggressive behavior in children. *Journal of Personality and Social Psychology* 7:429–34.

Rosenthal, D.
1971 *Genetics of Psychopathology*. New York: McGraw-Hill.

Rosenthal, R., and Jacobson, L.
1968 *Pygmalion in the Classroom*. New York: Holt, Rhinehart and Winston.

Rotter, J.B.
1966 Generalized expectancies for internal versus external control of reinforcement. *Psychological Monographs* 80:69.

Rowe, D.C.
1983 Biometrical genetic models of self-reported delinquent behavior: a twin study. *Behavior Genetics* 13:473–89.

Rubenstein, H., Murray, C.A., Motoyama, T., and Rouse, W.V.
1980 *The Link between Crime and The Built Environment: The Current State*

of Knowledge, Vol. 1. Washington, DC: US Government Printing Office.

Rushton, J.P., and Chrisjohn, R.D.
1981 Extraversion, neuroticism, psychoticism and self-reported delinquency: evidence from eight separate samples. *Personality and Individual Differences* 2:11–20.

Russell, D.E.
1982 *The Politics of Rape*. New York: Macmillan.

Rutter, M.
1978 Family, area and school influences in the genesis of conduct disorders. In L.A. Hersov, and M. Berger (Eds.), *Aggression and Anti-social Behavior in Childhood and Adolescence*,pp. 95–113. Oxford: Pergamon Press.
1981 Epidemiological–longitudinal strategies and causal research in child psychiatry. *Journal of American Academy of Child Psychiatry* 20:513–44.

Rutter, M., and Giller, H.
1984 *Juvenile Delinquency: Trends and Perspectives*. New York: Guildford Press.

Rutter, M., Maughan, B., Mortimore, P., and Ouston, J.
1979 *Fifteen Thousand Hours: Secondary Schools and their Effects on Children*. Cambridge, MA: Harvard University Press.

Sagalyn, A.C.
1971 *The Crime of Robbery in The US*. Washington, DC: National Institute of Law Enforcement and Criminal Justice.

Sameroff, A.J., and Seifer, R.
1983 Sources of continuity in parent–child relations. Paper read to meeting of the Society for Research in Child Development, Detroit, MI.

Sampson, R.J.
1985 Neighborhood and crime: the structural determinants of personal victimization. *Journal of Research in Crime and Delinquency* 22:7–40
1986 Crime in cities: the effects of formal and informal social control. In A.J. Reiss, Jr., and M. Tonry (Eds.) *Crime and Justice: An Annual Review of Reserch*, Vol. 8, pp. 271–312. Chicago: University of Chicago Press.

Sampson, R.J., and Cohen, J.
1988 Deterrent effects of the police on crime: a replication and theoretical extension. *Law and Society Review* 22: 163–89.

Sampson, R.J., and Wooldredge, J.D.
1987 Linking the micro–and macro–level dimensions of lifestyle-routine activity and opportunity models of predatory victimization. *Journal of Quantitative Criminology* 3:371–93.

Samuel, R.
1981 *East End Underworld: Chapters in The Life of Arthur Harding*. London: Routledge and Kegan Paul.

Sanday, P.R.
1981 The socio–cultural context of rape: a cross-cultural study. *Journal of Social Issues* 37: 5–27.

Sarnecki, J.
1982 *Criminality and Friend Relations: A Study of Juvenile Criminality in a*

Swedish Community. Washington, DC: National Institute of Justice, Criminal Justice Reference Service.

Scarr, H.A.
1973 *Patterns of Burglary*, 3rd Edition. Washington, DC: Government Printing Office.

Schacter, D.C.
1986 Amnesia and crime: how much do we really know. *American Psychologist* 41:286–95.

Schlesinger, S.R.
1983 Criminal procedure in the courtroom. In J.Q. Wilson (Ed.), *Crime and Public Policy*, pp. 183–206. San Francisco: ICS Press.

Schlossman, S., and Wallach, S.
1978 The crime of precocious sexuality: female juvenile delinquency in the progressive era. *Harvard Educational Review* 48:65–94.

Schneider, A.L.
1986 Restitution and recidivism rates of juvenile offenders: results from four experimental studies. *Criminology* 24:533–52.

Schneider, K.
1959 *Psychopathic Personalitis*. London: Cassell.

Schnelle, J.F., Kirchner, R.E., Casey, J.D., Uselton, P.H., and McNees, M.P.
1977 Patrol evaluation research. *Journal of Applied Behavior Analysis* 10:33–40.

Schrag, E.
1971 *Crime and Justice: American Style*. Washington, DC: US Government Printing Office.

Schuerman, L., and Kobrin, S.
1986 Community careers in crime. In A.J. Reiss, Jr., and M. Tonry (Eds.), *Crime and Justice: An Annual Review of Research*, Vol. 8, pp. 67–100. Chicago: University of Chicago Press.

Schuessler, K.F., and Cressey, D.R.
1950 Personality characteristics of criminals. *American Journal of Sociology* 5:476–84.

Schulsinger, F.
1972 Psychopathy, heredity and environment. *International Journal of Mental Health* 1:190–206.

Schwartz, R.D., and Skolnick, J.H.
1964 Two studies of legal stigma. In H.S. Becker (Ed.), *The Other Side*, pp. 103–18. New York: Free Press.

Scott, J., and Al-Thakeb, F.
1980 Perceptions of deviance cross-culturally. In G.R. Newman (Ed.), *Crime and Deviance: A Comparative Perspective*. Beverly Hills, CA: Sage.

Sechrest, L.G., and Rosenblatt, A.
1987 Research methods. In H.C. Quay (Ed.), *Handbook of Juvenile Delinquency*. New York: Wiley.

Sellin, T.
1967 *Capital Punishment*. New York: Harper and Row.

Sellin, T., and Wolfgang, M.E.
1964 *The Measurement of Delinquency*. New York: Wiley.

Severance. L.J., Greene, E., and Loftus, E.F.
1984 Toward criminal juror instructions that jurors can understand. *Journal of Criminal Law and Criminology* 75:198–233.

Shannon, L.W.
1978 Predicting adult careers from juvenile careers. Paper read to Annual Meeting of American Society of Criminology.
1980 *Assessing The Relationship of Juvenile Careers to Adult Criminal Careers*. Iowa City: University of Iowa Urban Cmmunity Research Center.
1981 *Assessing The Relationship of Adult Criminal Careers to Juvenile Careers: Final Report*. Washington, DC: National Institute of Juvenile Justice and Delinquency.
Shaw, C.R., and McKay, H.D.
1931 *Social Factors in Juvenile Delinquency*. Washington, DC: US Government Printing Office.
Shields, J.
1962 *Monozygotic Twins Brought Up Apart and Together*. Oxford: Oxford University Press.
1973 Heredity and Psychological abnormality. In H.J. Eysenck (Ed.), *Handbook of Abnormal Psychology*, 2nd Edrition, pp. 540–603. London: Pitman Medical.
Sheldon, W.H.
1942 *The Varieties of Temperament: A Psychology of Constitutional Differences*. New York: Harper.
Sheleff, L.S., and Schichor, D.
1980 Victimological aspects of bystander involvement. *Crime and Delinquency* 26:193–201.
Shelley, L.E.
1981 *Crime and Modernization: The Impact of Industrialization and Urbanization on Crime*. Carbondale, IL: SIU Press.
Sherman, L.W.
1980 Causes of police behavior: the current state of quantitative research. *Journal of Research in Crime and Delinquency* 17:69–100.
1983 Patrol strategies for police. In J.Q. Wilson (Ed.), *Crime and Public Policy*, pp. 145–65. San Francisco: ICS Press.
Shinn, M.
1978 Father absence and children's cognitive development. *Psychological Bulletin* 85:295–324.
Shoemaker, D.J., and Williams, J.S.
1987 The subculture of violence and ethnicity. *Journal of Criminal Justice* 15:461–472.
Shore, D.
1985 White House cases: psychiatric patients and the Secret Service. *American Journal of Psychiatry* 142:308–11.
Shore, M.F., and Massimo, J.L.
1979 Fifteen years after treatment: a follow-up study of comprehensive, vocationally oriented psychotherapy. *American Journal of Orthopsychiatry* 49:240–45.
Shover, N.
1983 *Age and The Changing Criminal Involvement of Ordinary Property Offenders: Final Report*. Washington, DC: National Institute of Justice.
Siddle, D.A.T., and Trasler, G.B.
1981 The psychophysiology of psychopathic behavior. In M.J.

Christie, and P.G. Mellet (Eds.), *Foundations of Psychosomatics.* Chichester: Wiley.

Siegall, R.
1978 Probability of punishment and suppression of behavior in psychopathic and nonpsychopathic offenders. *Journal of Abnormal Psychology* 87:514–22.

Sigall, H., and Ostrove, N.
1975 Beautiful but dangerous: effects of offender attractiveness and nature of the crime on juridic judgements. *Journal of Personality and Social Psychology* 31:410–4.

Silber, D.E.
1974 Controversy concerning the criminal justice system and its implications for the role of mental health workers. *American Psychologist* 29:239–44.

Silberman, C.E.
1978 *Criminal Violence, Criminal Justice.* New York: Random House.

Singer, J.L.
1971 The influence of violence portrayed in television or motion pictures upon overt aggressive behavior. In J.L. Singer (Ed.), *The Control of Aggression and Violence*, pp. 11–60. New York: Academic Press.

Singer, J.L., and Singer, D.G.
1983 Psychologists look at television: Cognitive, developmental, personality and social policy implications. *American Psychologist* 38:826–834.

Skogan, W.G.
1978 Weapon use in robbery: patterns and policy implications. Unpublished manuscript: Center for Urban Affairs, North Western University.
1979 Crime in contemporary America. In H. Graham, and T.R. Gurr (Eds.), *Violence in America.* Beverly Hills, CA: Sage.
1984 Reporting crimes to the police: The status of world research. *Journal of Research in Crime and Delinquency* 21:113–37.
1986 Fear of crime and neighborhood change. In A.J. Reiss, Jr., and M.Tonry (Eds.), *Crime and Justice: An Annual Review of Research*, Vol. 8, pp. 303–30. Chicago: University of Chicago Press.
1987 The impact of victimization on fear. *Crime and Delinquency* 33:135–54.
1988 Community organization and crime. In M.Tonry, and N. Morris (Eds.), *Crime and Justice: An Annual Review of Research*, Vol. 10, pp. 39–78. Chicago: University of Chicago Press.

Skolnick, J.H., and Bayley, J.
1988 Theme and variation in community policing. In M.Tonry, and N. Morris (Eds.), *Crime and Justice: An Annual Review of Research* Vol. 10, pp. 1–30. Chicago: University of Chicago Press.

Skolnick, J.H., and Currie, E.
1979 *Crisis in American Institutions.* Boston: Little, Brown.

Smith, D.A.
1986 The neighborhood context of police behavior. In A.J. Reiss, Jr., and M. Tonry (Eds.), *Crime and Justice: An Annual Review of Research*, Vol. 8, pp. 313–34. Chicago: University of Chicago Press.

Smith, D.A., and Visher, C.
1980 Sex and involvement in deviancy and crime: a quantitative review of the empirical literature. *American Sociological Review* 45:697–701.

Smith, D.E.
1982 Crowding and confinement. In R. Johnson, and H. Toch (Eds.), *The Pains of Imprisonment*, pp. 45–62. Beverly Hills, CA: Sage.

Smith, M.C.
1983 Hypnotic memory enhancement of witnesses: does it work? *Psychological Bulletin* 94:387–407.

Smith, M.D., and Bennett, N.
1985 Poverty, inequality and theories of forcible rape. *Crime and Delinquency* 31:295–305.

Smith, R.
1984 Grendon, the Barlinnie Special Unit and the Wormwood Scrubs Annexe: experiments in penology. *British Medical Journal* 288:472–5.

Smith, R.A.
1961 The incredible electrical conspiracy. *Fortune*, April, pp. 132–180.

Snarey, J.R.
1985 Cross-cultural universality of social moral development: a critical review of Kohlbergian research. *Psychological Bulletin* 97: 202–32.

Snyder, J., and Patterson, G.R.
1987 Family interaction and delinquent behavior. In H.C. Quay (Ed.), *Handbook of Juvenile Delinquency*, pp. 216–43. New York: Wiley.

Solzhenitsyn, A.
1970 *One Day in The Life of Ivan Denisovich*. London: Sphere Books.

Soothill, K.L., Way, C.K., and Gibbens, T.C.N.
1980 Subsequent dangerousness among compulsory hospital patients. *British Journal of Criminology* 20:289–95.

Spanier, G.B.
1980 Outsiders looking in. *The Wilson Quarterly* 4:122–35.

Sparks, R.J.
1980 A critique of Marxist criminology. In N. Morris, and M. Tonry (Eds.), *Crime and Justice: An Annual Review of Research*, Vol. 2, pp. 159–210. Chicago: University of Chicago Press.
1982 *Research on Victims of Crime*. Washington, DC: Government Printing Office.

Sparks, R.J., Genn, H.G., and Dodd, D.J.
1982 Surveying victims: a study of the measurement of criminal victimization. New York: Wiley.

Spence, S.
1982 Social skills training with young offenders. In M.P. Feldman (Ed.), *Developments in the Study of Criminal Behavior*, Vol. 1, pp. 107–34. Chichester: Wiley.

Spergel, I.
1964 *Racketville, Slumtown, Haulberg: An Exploratory Study of Delinquent Subcultures*. Chicago: University of Chicago Press.

Spitzer, R.L., and Fleiss, J.L.

1974 A re-analysis of the reliability of psychiatric diagnosis. *British Journal of Psychiatry* 125:341–7.

Spitzer, R.L., Forman, J.B.W., and Nee, J.
1979 DSM-III field trials: 1. Initial interrater diagnostic reliability. *American Journal of Psychiatry* 136:815–7.

Spivack, G., Marcus, J., and Swift, M.
1986 Early classroom behaviors and later misconduct. *Developmental Psychology* 22:124–31.

Stark, R., Doyle, D.P., and Kent, L.
1980 Rediscovering moral communities: church membership and crime. In T. Hirschi, and M. Gottfredsen (Eds.), *Understanding Crime: Curent Theory and Research*, pp. 43–52. Beverly Hills, CA: Sage.

Steadman, H.J., Coccozza, J.J., and Melick, M.E.
1978 Explaining the increased arrest role among mental patients: the changing clientele of state hospitals. *American Journal of Psychiatry* 135:816–20.

Steadman, H.J., and Felson, R.B.
1984 Self-reports of violence: ex-mental hospital patients and the general population. *Criminology* 72:321–42.

Steadman, H.J., Rosenstein, M.J., MacAskill, R.L., and Manderscheid, R.W.
1988 A profile of mentally disordered offenders admitted to inpatient psychiatric services in the United States. *Law and Human Behavior* 12:91–9.

Steblay, N.M.
1987 Helping behavior in rural and urban environments: a meta-analysis. *Psychological Bulletin* 102:346–88.

Steffensmeier, D.J.
1980a Sex differences in patterns of adult crime, 1965–77: a review and assessment. *Social Forces* 58:1081–107.
1980b Assessing the impact of the women's movement on sex-based differences in the handling of adult criminal defendants. *Crime and Delinquency* 26:344–57.
1989 Age and distribution of crime. *American Journal of Sociology* 94:803–31.

Steffensmeier, D.J., and Harer, M.D.
1987 Is the crime rate really falling? An "aging" US population and its impact on the Nation's crime rate, 1980–1984. *Journal of Research in Crime and Delinquency* 24:23–48.

Steffensmeier, D.J., Streifel, C., and Harer, M.D.
1987 Relative cohort size and youth crime in the United States, 1953–1984. *American Sociological Review* 52:702–10.

Steinberg, L.
1986 Latchkey children and susceptibility to peer pressure: an ecological analysis. *Developmental Psychology* 22:433–9.

Steinmetz, C.H.D.
1985 Bystanders of crime: some results from a national survey. *Victimology: An International Journal* 10:441–60.

Stenross, B.
1984 Police response to residential burglaries: dusting for prints as a negative rite. *Criminology* 22:389–402.

Stott, D.H.
1980 *Delinquency and Human Nature*. Baltimore, MD: University Park Press.

Stumpfl, F.
1936 *Die Ursprunge des Verbrechens am hebenslauf von Zwillingen*. Leipzig: Georg Thieme Verlag.

Stumphauzer, J.S., Aiken, T.W., and Veloz, E.V.
1977 East side story: behavioral analysis of a high juvenile crime community. *Behavioral Disorders* 2:76–84.

Suedfeld, P., Ramirez, C., Deaton, J., and Baker-Brown, G.
1982 Reactions and attributes of prisoners in solitary confinement. *Criminal Justice and Behavior* 9:303–40.

Sunday Times
1974 Cops are robbers. October 6, p. 22.

Supreme Court
1981 Rhodes versus Chapman. S. Ct. 2392 and 2400.

Sutherland, E.H.
1937 *The Professional Thief*. Chicago: Chicago University Press.
1940 White-collar criminality. *American Sociological Review* 5:1–12.

Sutherland, E.H., and Cressey, D.R.
1970 *Criminology*, 8th Edition. New Youk: Lippincott.

Sutker, P.B.
1970 Vicarious conditioning and sociopathy. *Journal of Abnormal Psychology* 76:380–6.

Suttles, D.G.
1986 *The Social Order of The Slum*. Chicago: University of Chicago Press

Sykes, G.
1966 *The Society of Captives: A Study of a Maximum Security Prison*. New York: Atheneum.

Syndulko, K.
1978 Electrocortical investigation of psychopathy. In R.D. Hare, and D. Schalling (Eds.), *Psychopathic Behavior: Approaches to Research*, pp. 145–56. Chichester: Wiley.

Tagaki, P., and Platt, T.
1978 Behind the gilded ghetto: an analysis of race, class and crime in Chinatown. *Crime and Social Justice* 9:2–25.

Taylor, P.J., and Gunn, J.
1984 Violence and psychosis: Part I. Risk of violence among psychotic men. *British Medical Journal* 288:1945–9.

Taylor, R.B., Gottfredsen, S.D., and Brower, S.
1980 The defensibility of defensible space: a critical review. In T. Hirschi, and M. Gottfredsed (Eds.), *Understanding Crime: Current Theory and Research*, pp. 53–72. Beverly Hills, CA: Sage.

Taylor, S.P., and Gammon, C.B.
1975 Effects of type and dose of alcohol on human physical aggression. *Journal of Personality and Social Psychology* 32:169–175.

Tennenbaum, D.J.
1977 Personality and criminality: a summary and implications of the literature. *Journal of Criminal Justice* 5:225–35.

Teresa, V.
1973 *My life in the Mafia*. New York: Doubleday.

Teuber, N., and Powers, E.
1953 Evaluating therapy in a delinquency prevention program. *Proceedings of the Association for Research in Nervous and Mental Diseases* 3:138–47.

Tharp, R.G., and Wetzel, R.H.
1969 *Behavior Modification in The Natural Environment*. New York: Academic Press.

Theilgard, R.
1983 Aggression and XYY personality. *International Journal of Law and Psychiatry* 6:413–21.

Thomas, A., and Chess, S.
1984 Genesis and evolution of behavioral disorders: from infancy to adult life. *American Journal Of Psychiatry* 141:1–9.

Thomas, A., Chess, S., and Birch, H.G.
1968 *Temperament and Behavior Disorders in Children*. New York: New York University Press.

Thomas, C.W.
1973 Prisonization or resocialization? A study of external factors associated with the impact of imprisonment. *Journal of Research in Crime and Delinquency* 10:13–21.

Thomas, C.W., and Sieverdes, C.M.
1975 Juvenile court intake: an analysis of discretionary decision-making. *Criminology* 12:413–32.

Thomas, D.S.
1925 *Social Aspects of The Business Cycle*. London: Routledge and Kegan Paul.

Thompson, W.C., Cowan, C.L., Ellsworth, P.C., and Harrington, J.C.
1984 Death penalty and conviction proneness: the translation of attitudes into verdicts. *Law and Human Behavior* 8:95–113.

Time.
1972 Busting public servants. April 23, p. 26.

Tittle, C.R.
1980 *Sanctions and Social Deviance. The Question of Deterrence*. New York: Praeger.

Toby, J.
1979 Delinquency in cross-cultural perspective. In L.T. Empey (Ed.), *Juvenile Justice: The Progressive Legacy and Current Reforms*, pp. 105–49. Charlottesville, VA: University Press of Virginia.
1983 Crime in the schools. In J.Q. Wilson (Ed.), *Crime and Public Policy*, pp. 69–88, San Francisco: ICS Press.

Toch, H.
1969 *Violent Men*. Chicago: Aldine.

Tonry, M.
1991 The politics and processes of sentencing commissions. *Crime and Delinquency* 37:307–29.

Trasler, G.
1973 Criminal behavior. In H.J. Eysenck (Ed.), *Handbook of Abnormal Psychology*, 2nd Edition, pp. 67–96. London: Pitman Medical.
1987 Biogenetic factors. In H.C. Quay (Ed.), *Handbook of Juvenile Delinquency*, pp. 184–215. New York: Wiley.

Trickett, P.K., and Kuczynski, L.
1986 Children's misbehaviors and parental discipline strategies in

abusive and nonabusive families. *Developmental Psychology* 22:115–23.
Turkington, C.
1986 Jury selection ruling disregards research. *Monitor*, July, p. 20.
Turner, D.H., and Tofler, D.S.
1986 Indicators of psychiatric disorder among women admitted to prison. *British Medical Journal* 292:651–3.
Ullmann, L.P., and Krasner, L.
1969 A *Psychological Approach to Abnormal Behavior*. New York: Prentice-Hall.
US Department of Justice
1984 *Annual Report to Congress on the Activities and Operations of the Public Integrity Section*. Washington, DC: US Government Printing Office.
Van Dusen, K.T., Mednick, S.A., and Gabrielli, W.F., Jr.
1983 Social class and crime in an adoption cohort. In K.T. Van Dusen, and S.A. Mednick (Eds.), *Prospective Studies of Crime and Delinquency*. Hingham, MA: Kluwer-Nijhoff.
Van Dyke
1977 *Jury Selection Procedures*. Cambridge, MA: Balinger.
Veneziano, C.A.
1986 Prison immates and consent to treatment: Problems and issues. *Law and Psychology Review* 10:129–46.
Verlade, A.J.
1978 Do delinquents really drift? *British Journal of Criminology* 18:23–39.
Vernon, W., and Ulrich, R.
1966 Classical conditioning of pain elicited aggression. *Science* 152:668–9.
Viccica, A.D.
1980 World crime trends. *International Journal of Offender Therapy and Comparative Criminology* 24:270–7.
Vinter, R.D., Downs, G., and Hall, J.
1975 *Juvenile Corrections in The States: Residential Programs and Deinsitutionalization*. Ann Arbor, MI: University of Michigan and National Assessment of Juvenile Corrections.
Vinter, R.D., Newcomb, T.M., and Kish, R. (Eds.)
1976 *Time Out: A National Study of Juvenile Correctional Programs*. Ann Arbor, MI: National Assessment of Juvenile Corrections.
Violanti, J.M.
1983 Stress patterns in police work: A longitudinal study. *Journal of Police Science and Administration* 11:211–6.
Visher, C.A.
1987 Incapacitation and crime control: does a "lock 'em up" strategy reduce crime? *Justice Quarterly* 4:513–43.
Vogel, E.
1979 *Japan as Number One: Lessons for America*. Cambridge, MA: Harvard University Press.
Voss, H.L.
1963 The predictive efficiency of the Glueck Social Prediction Scale. *Journal of Criminal Law, Criminology and Police Science* 54:421–30.

Wadsworth, M.E.J.
1975 Delinquency in a national sample of children *British Journal of Criminology* 15:167–74.

Wagenaar, W.A., and Loftus, E.F.
1990 Ten cases of eyewitness identification: logical and procedural problems. *Journal of Criminal Justice* 18:291–319.

Walker, D.B.
1983 Black police values and the black community. *Police Studies* 5:20–8

Walker, N.
1965 *Crime and Punishment in Great Britain*. Edinburgh: Edinburgh University Press.
1971 *Crimes, Courts and Figures: An Introduction to Criminal Statistics*. London: Penguin.
1983 Protecting people. In J.W. Hinton (Ed.), *Dangerousness: Problems of Assessment and Prediction*, pp. 23–8. London: Allen and Unwin.

Walker, N., Farrington, D.P., and Tucker, G.
1981 Reconviction rates of adult males after different sentences. *British Journal of Criminology* 21:357–60.

Walker, N., and McCabe, S.
1973 *Crime and Insanity in England*, Vols 1 and 2. Edinburgh: Edinburgh University Press.

Waller, I., and Okihiro, N.
1978 *Burglary: The Victim and the Public*. Toronto: University of Toronto Press.

Wallerstein, J.S., and Wyle, C.J.
1947 Our law-abiding law breakers. *Probation* 25:107–12.

Walsh, A.
1987 The sexual stratification hypothesis and sexual assault in light of the changing concepts of race. *Criminology* 25:153–73.

Walsh, D.P.
1978 *Shoplifting: Controlling a Major Crime*. London: Macmillan.
1980 *Breuk-ins: Burglary from Private Houses*. London: Constable.

Walters, R.H., and Thomas, E.L.
1963 Enhancement of punitiveness by visual and audio-visual displays. *Canadian Journal of Psychology* 17:244–55.

Walters, R.H., Thomas, E.L., and Acker, C.W.
1962 Enhancement of punitive behavior by audio-visual displays. *Science* 136:872–3.

Warr, M.
1987 Fear of victimization and sensitivity to risk. *Journal of Quantitative Criminology* 3:29–46.

Warr, M., and Stafford, M.
1984 Public goals of punishment and support for the death penalty. *Journal of Research in Crime and Delinquency* 21:95–111.

The Washington Post
1988 Life expectancy for blacks declines again. December 15.

Watson, J.B.
1919 *Psychology from the Standpoint of a Behaviorist*. Philadelphia: Lippincott.

Waters, E., and Crandall, V.J.

1964 Social class and observed maternal behavior from 1940 to 1960. *Child Development* 35:1021–32.

Waugh, E.
1928 *Decline and Fall*. London: Chapman and Hall.

Weaver, F.M., and Carroll, J.
1985 Crime perceptions in a natural setting by expert and novice shoplifters. *Social Psychology Quarterly* 48:349–59.

Weinrott, M.R., Jones, R.R., and Howard, J.R.
1982 Cost effectiveness of teaching family programs for delinquents: results of a national evaluation. *Evaluation Review* 6:173–201.

Welford, C.
1974 Crime and the dimensions of nations. *International Journal of Criminology and Penology* 2:1–10.
1975 Labelling theory and criminology: an assessment. *Social Problems* 22:332–45.

Wells, G.L., Lindsay, R.G.L., and Ferguson, T.J.
1979 Accuracy, confidence and juror perceptions in eyewitness identification. *Journal of Applied Psychology* 64:440–8.

Wells, L.E., and Rankin, J.H.
1983 Self-concept as a mediating factor in delinquency. *Social Psychology Quarterly* 46:11–22.

Werner, E.E., and Smith, R.S.
1982 *Vulnerable but Invincible: A Study of Resilient Children*. New York: McGraw-Hill.

Werner, J.S., Minkin, N., Minkin, B.L., Fixsen, D.L., Phillips, E.L., and Wolf, M.M.
1975 "Intervention package": An analysis to prepare juvenile delinquents for encounters with police officers. *Criminal Justice and Behavior* 2:22–36.

Werthman, C., and Piliavin, I.
1967 Gang members and the police. In D.L. Bordua (Ed.), *The Police: Six Sociological Essays*, pp. 56–98. New York: Wiley.

West, D.J.
1963 *The Habitual Prisoner*. London: Macmillan.
1966 *Murder Followed by Suicide*. London: Heinemann.
1982 *Delinquency: Its Roots, Careers and Prospects*. Cambridge, MA: Harvard University Press.

West, D.J., and Farrington, D.P.
1977 *The Delinquent Way of Life*. New York: Crane Russak.

Wheeler, S.
1961 Socialization in correctional communities. *American Sociological Review* 26:697–712.

Wheeler, S., Weisburd, D., and Bode, N.
1982 Sentencing the white collar offender. *American Sociological Review* 47:641–59.

Whitley, B.E., Jr., and Greenberg, M.S.
1986 The role of eyewitness confidence in juror perceptions of credibility. *Journal of Applied Psychology* 16:387–409.

Whyte, W.F.
1943 *Street Corner Society*. Chicago: University of Chicago Press.

Wiatrowski, M.D., Griswold, D.B., and Roberts, M.K.

1981 Social control and delinquency. *American Sociological Review* 46:525–41.

Wice, B.

1973 *Bail and Its Reform: A National Survey*. Washington, DC: US Department of Justice.

Widom, C.S.

1976 Interpersonal conflict and cooperation in psychopaths. *Journal of Abnormal Psychology* 85:330–4.

1978a An empirical classification of female offenders. *Criminal Justice and Behavior* 5:35–52.

1978b A methodology for studying noninstitutionalized psychopaths. In R.D. Hare, and D. Schalling (Eds.), *Psychopathic Behavior: Approaches to Research*, pp. 71–84. Chichester: Wiley.

1989 Does violence beget violence? A critical examination of the literature. *Psychological Bulletin* 106:3–28.

Wilbanks, W.

1985 Is violent crime intraracial? *Crime and Delinquency* 31:117–28.

1986 Are female felons treated more leniently by the criminal justice system? *Justice Quarterly* 3:517–29.

Williams, G.

1961 The definition of crime. In J.L. Smith, and B. Hogan (Eds.), *The Criminal Law*, 2nd Edition. London: Butterworth.

Wilson, G.D., and Cox, D.N.

1983 *The Child-lovers*. London: Owen.

Wilson, H.

1980 Parental supervision: a neglected aspect of delinquency. British Journal of Criminology 20:203–35.

Wilson, J.Q.

1968 The police and the delinquent in two cities. In S. Wheeler (Ed.), *Controlling Delinquents*, pp. 9–30. New York: Wiley.

Wilson, J.Q., and Herrenstein, R.J.

1985 *Crime and Human Nature*. New York: Simon and Schuster.

Winchester, S., and Jackson, H.

1982 *Residential Burglary: The Limits of Prevention*. Home Office Research Study No. 74. London: HMSO.

Winterdyk, R., and Roesch, R.

1982 A wilderness experiential program as an alternative for probationers: an evaluation. *Canadian Journal of Criminology* 24:39–49.

Wirtz, P.W., and Harrell, A.V.

1987 Victim and crime characteristics, coping responses and short- and long-term recovery from victimization. *Journal of Consulting and Clinical Psychology* 55:866–71.

Witkin, H.A., Mednick, S.A., Schulsinger, F., Bakkestrom, E., Christiansen, K.,O., Goodenough, D.R., Hirschhorn, K., Lundstein, C., Owen, D.R., Philip, J., Rubin, D.B., and Stocking, M.

1976 XYY and XXY men: criminality and aggression. Science 193:547–55.

Wolfe, N.T., Cullen, F.T., and Cullen, J.B.

1984 Describing the female offender: A note on the demographics of arrest. *Journal of Criminal Justice* 12:448–92.

Wolfenstein, M.

1955 Fun morality: an analysis of recent American child training literature. In M. Mead, and M. Wolfenstein (Eds.), *Childhood in Contemporary Cultures*. Chicago: University of Chicago Press.

Wolfgang, M.E.

1958 *Patterns in Criminal Homicide*. Philadelphia: University of Philadelphia Press.

1971 Why criminal statistics? In L. Radzinowicz, and M.E. Wolfgang (Eds.), *Crime and Justice:* Vol.1, *The Criminal in Society*, pp. 130–1. New York: Basic Books.

1985 *The National Survey of Crime Severity*. Washington, DC: US Department of Justice.

Wolfgang, M.E., Figlio, R.M., and Sellin, T.

1972 *Delinquency in a Birth Cohort*. Chicago: University of Chicago Press.

Wolfgang, M.E., and Tracy, P.E.

1982 The 1945 and 1958 birth cohorts: A comparison of the prevalence, incidence and severity of the delinquent behavior. Paper read to the Conference on Public Danger, Dangerous Offenders, and the Criminal Justice System, Kennedy School of Government, Harvard University.

Wootton, B.

1959 *Social Science and Social Pathology*. London: Allen and Unwin.

Worrall, A., and Pease, K.

1986 Personal crime against women: evidence from the 1982 British Crime Survey. *Howard Journal of Criminal Justice* 25:118–24.

Young, M.

1991 Women in the police: a case of structural marginality. In M. Young (Ed.), *An Inside Job: Policing and Police Culture in Britain*, pp. 191–252. Oxford: Oxford University Press.

Zatz, M.S.

1987 The changing forms of racial/ethnic bias in sentencing. *Journal of Research in Crime and Delinquency* 24:69–92.

Zeisel, H., and Diamond, S.

1978 The effect of peremptory challenge on jury and verdict: an experiment in a federal district court. *Stanford Law Review* 30:491–531.

Ziegenhan, E.A., and Brosnan, D.

1985 Victim responses to robbery and crime control policy. *Criminology* 23:675–95.

Zimring, F.E., and Hawkins, G.J.

1973 *Deterrence*. Chicago: University of Chicago Press.

Author index

Subject index